Being Elsewhere

SHELLEY BARANOWSKI AND ELLEN FURLOUGH, EDITORS

Being Elsewhere

Tourism, Consumer Culture, and
Identity in Modern Europe and
North America

Ann Arbor

THE UNIVERSITY OF MICHIGAN PRESS

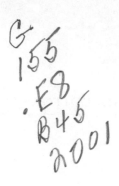
Copyright © by the University of Michigan 2001
All rights reserved
Published in the United States of America by
The University of Michigan Press
Manufactured in the United States of America
♾ Printed on acid-free paper

2004   2003   2002   2001   4   3   2   1

A CIP catalog record for this book is available from the British Library.

Library of Congress Cataloging-in-Publication Data

Being elsewhere : tourism, consumer culture, and identity in modern
    Europe and North America / Shelley Baranowski and Ellen Furlough,
    editors.
        p.   cm.
    Includes bibliographical references and index.
    ISBN 0-472-11167-1 (alk. paper)
    1. Tourism—Europe.   2. Tourism—North America.   I. Baranowski,
Shelley.   II. Furlough, Ellen, 1953–
    G155.E8 B45   2001
    338.4'7914—dc21   00-012181

Contents

Acknowledgments

The acknowledgments provide a welcome opportunity to thank those whose support has helped us to produce this volume. Our gratitude goes first to our contributors, who provided us with rich evidence and insightful analyses of the significance of tourism as a historical subject, and who have patiently accommodated our suggestions for revision. We appreciate the contributions of Nigel Morgan, Annette Pritchard, and Janet Wiita, whose essays we unfortunately could not include in the volume.

The collection as a whole has benefited enormously from the thoughtful suggestions of Alon Confino, Bonnie Smith, the anonymous first reader for the University of Michigan Press, and especially Rudy Koshar, who aided us in formulating the conceptual issues that we have developed to give this volume coherence. We are also grateful to Stephen Harp and Vanessa Schwartz, who gave close and discerning readings of an earlier draft of the introduction, challenging us to sharpen the context, scholarly and historical, for our arguments.

Finally, it is our pleasure to thank those who are responsible for transforming the manuscript into a book, especially Susan Whitlock at the University of Michigan Press, who believed in our project. Ingrid Erickson ably assumed direction of our project after Susan's departure. We are especially indebted to Jean Demaree, Kenyon College, who painstakingly typed the manuscript according to specification, juggling that undertaking with her numerous responsibilities as department secretary. Many thanks as well to Winifred George and Kym Rohrback in the history department of the University of Akron, who efficiently completed some difficult, last-minute formatting. Finally, we thank the University of Akron, Kenyon College, and the University of Kentucky for financially supporting of our individual research projects and this collection itself.

Introduction

Tourism and vacations are today among the most economically important forms of modern leisure. At the end of the twentieth century the tourist industry was the largest industry in the world, with its economic impact estimated at 3.6 trillion dollars, or 10.6 percent of the gross global product. The World Travel and Tourism Council, an industry lobby group, estimates that tourism sustains more than one in ten jobs around the world and provides work for 255 million people. Industry specialists confidently assert that tourism's economic impact will only increase in the next millennium.[1]

While the current economic importance of the tourist industry is well documented, far less is known about the history of tourism, the nature of its appeal, and the complex intersections of commerce, culture, and politics that have contributed to the maturation of tourism as a significant global industry. This volume thus focuses on the history of tourism and vacations in Europe and North America, from the early nineteenth century, when the emergent middle classes sojourned at lavish spas and seaside resorts, to the late twentieth century, when crowded beaches, charter flights, and far-flung "economy" hotel chains signaled mass tourism's appeal and its vastly expanded clientele. The book brings together new scholarship that explores tourism's historical context and geographical specificity, as well as its significance to such major historical developments as class formation, political mobilization, the tensions between nation building and regional development, and the power of consumer culture. We aim also in this collection to demonstrate the historical importance of tourism in its own right for the development of modern culture and society.

Unlike sociologists, anthropologists, geographers, and literary critics, historians have until recently not given tourism the attention it deserves. Nevertheless, the now formidable literature on related topics such as consumer culture, commercial leisure, and sites of memory is encouraging interest in a topic that in previous years might well have seemed "trivial." Indeed, the enduring stereotypes of tourists as herdlike, superficial gazers doggedly seeking amusement and guided by mass-produced guidebooks has hampered serious scholarly investigation of tourism. Such stereotypes have been difficult to dislodge and interrogate in part because they are themselves the product of long-standing, and historically specific, social and cultural anxieties in the modern industrializing and democratizing nations of Europe and North America.

One important trope that has fueled this stereotype has been the distinction between "travel" and "tourism." A long line of commentators, who have betrayed their social anxieties and based their own cultural superiority, in part, on their distance from and disdain for vulgar tourists, has invoked this distinction. Literary theorist James Buzard has traced the emergence of a notion of tourism as distinct from travel in the late eighteenth and early nineteenth centuries prior to the consolidation of a coherent tourist industry. Buzard asserts that remarks in the post-Napoleonic years on the "flood" of continental tourists were less a response to greater numbers (which remain uncertain) than a portrayal of a new travel scene. Tourists, more socially diverse than their elite predecessors on the grand tour, were frequently identified as "part of the modern 'crowd' or 'mob.' Tourists induced class anxieties, in the wake of the French Revolution, about the 'mobility' of the lower orders of society."[2] The perceived inundation by British tourists (which, significantly, did include more families and women)[3] visiting continental capitals, viewing the Alps, and touring the favored destinations of the elite grand tour, Italy, Germany and France, brought assertions by "travelers" of their cultural superiority and "authentic" (as opposed to passively received) knowledge about these sites and destinations. A distinction emerged in these years between tourists, "regarded as depending unquestioningly on the conventions that guided their tours," and the traveler, who "possessed an originality and self-sufficiency in judgement."[4]

With the onset of mass tourism in the twentieth century and working-class tourists more present and visible, claims for the cultural superiority of "travel" over tourism increased in intensity. In the 1950s, for example, the French political geographer and social critic André Siegfried criticized modern tourism as a degraded aspect of cultural and social democratization that destroyed older regimes of pleasure and substituted shallow amusements. Indicating the broader anxieties of postwar elites concerning the decline of "high" culture, he believed that the only hope for the future was with "people of refined taste, knowing how to distinguish . . . between filth and beauty."[5] Later commentators continued this characterization. Particularly influential have been the works of historian Daniel Boorstin and literary theorist Paul Fussell. Both regretted the decline of sophisticated, active, and literate travelers and the rise of the passive and amusement-seeking mass tourist. Tourism was "diluted, contrived, prefabricated," wrote Boorstin, a "pseudo-event," not the "sophisticated pleasures" enjoyed by "well-prepared men." The "traveler was active; he went strenuously in search of people, of adventure, of experience. The tourist is passive; he expects interesting things to happen to him." Fussell asserted that the final age of travel was the interwar period, after which there was only tourism. He celebrated "what it felt like to be young and clever, and literate" before the deluge of mass tourism, adding that "the resemblance between the tourist and the client of a massage parlor is closer than it would be polite to emphasize."[6] Such discourses pitting travel against tourism, coexistent with and mutually dependent on structural and social developments, have profoundly influenced the characterizations of tourism.

John Urry's more recent *The Tourist Gaze* qualifies the negative connotations associated with tourism. He celebrates its role in larger processes of democratization and dispenses with the binary opposition of travel and tourism. Nevertheless, Urry emphasizes the constructed nature of "authenticity." Borrowing from Michel Foucault's formulation of the gaze, Urry argues that the "tourist gaze" is as "socially organized and systematized as is the gaze of the medic." His work details how "the tourist gaze has changed and developed," and how "the gaze is constructed and reinforced," "who or what authorizes it," and "what its consequences are for the 'places' which are its object."[7] Tourist practices depend on distinguishing touring from the home and paid work, on the proliferation of images about the sites, and on the development of tourist professionals. Because the tourist gaze was both constructed (and inauthentic) and a product of relations of power, Urry attends to the economics of the tourist industry and the nature of work in it. The quest for "authentic" and personally meaningful touristic experiences ultimately fails, as the tourist industry and a modern visual economy of signs have already determined the meanings associated with tourism and tourist sites. Implicit in Urry's argument, then, is the assumption of touristic passivity.

However, to this assumption important challenges have arisen that implicitly and explicitly inform the concerns of this volume. The now classic work on tourism by sociologist Dean MacCannell, *The Tourist: A New Theory of the Leisure Class,* asserts that tourists are active, rather than passive, seekers of knowledge and experiences. Tourists take a voyage of discovery on which they attempt "to discover or reconstruct a cultural heritage or a social identity." A crucial element of that quest is the search for authenticity, a conviction that the sites visited are both "real" and different from everyday life.[8] In the production of tourist sites, objects, and experiences, "markers" at the tourist site itself and the "mechanical reproduction" of the site or object (prints, photographs, and so forth) enable naming and recognition, propelling "the tourist in motion on his journey to find the true object."[9] This is an important starting point for positing the potentially active and productive nature of both tourism and tourists, undermining notions of tourists as passive observers who uncritically imbibe the meanings and experiences constructed by the tourist industry. One can extend MacCannell's analysis to argue that tourists are always engaged (individually and collectively) as "sightseers" because they project their own meanings and desires on tourist sites and objects, seek new experiences, and find their own pleasure in being "elsewhere."

In an important recent essay on guidebooks and national identities, historian Rudy Koshar offers a fresh and insightful analysis that takes tourists' quest for authenticity seriously and reformulates Urry's notion of the tourist gaze.[10] Koshar argues that guidebooks in the past did not reflect the passive consumption by tourists of selected sites and destinations, but the active production of changing and historically specific social meanings. He introduces the concept of the "optics of tourism," meaning "an active search for knowledge" by tourists. His careful historical analysis of the changing contents of guidebooks in Europe and Germany focuses in particular on their representation of the nation and national identity. Both tourism and nationalism, he argues, were grounded in opposition to the everyday and represented a desire for authenticity. Because guidebooks "produced images not only of tourists but of the nations tourists consumed," both tourism and guidebooks were attempts to "visualize an authenticity that could provide meaning beyond the marketplace."[11] Koshar, then, posits a dynamic relationship among guidebooks (a major commercial institution within the tourism industry), the tourists themselves, and national identity that was neither pre- nor overdetermined.

Koshar and others who are reformulating notions of the passive gaze suggest exciting possibilities for the history of tourism and vacations. They include the "dialogue" between tourists and the people who live and work in tourist and vacation destinations, and the pleasures associated both with seeing and being seen, of being part of the crowd, as it were. Here work on the urban flaneur is instructive and suggestive of the interpretive possibilities for the engaged tourist who often was part of a crowd at tourist sites. The flaneur, who strolled the bustling streets of nineteenth-century Paris and experienced the visual and aural stimuli of the modern city, watched others as he watched himself. As Charles Baudelaire noted, the flaneur was a "passionate observer" whose "immense enjoyment" derived from the sensory stimulation of observation within the crowd.[12] Tourism and vacations can thus been seen as avenues for meaningful contact among people and with the sites visited.

These efforts to question older conceptual dichotomies of active/passive tourists having authentic/inauthentic experiences open a new and fruitful approach to the analysis of commercial tourism: situating it within the invention of the modern vacation. Sociologist Jean-Didier Urbain, for example, argues that studies of travel and tourism have not attended to the more far-reaching, and historically significant phenomenon, that of taking vacations. Urbain identifies a major cultural shift: Whereas the notion of "vacation" or "holiday" once referred to time spent away from work or from school, it has been reinvented over the past two centuries. Being on vacation has come to mean traveling to a specific destination, such as the beach, in order to stay put.[13] And yet "staying put" by no means amounts to an exercise in passivity; rather, the vacation has become a time of intense emotional engagement, involving both the care of the self and the forging of individual and collective identities.

Vacation destinations have come to represent places of metamorphosis, where individuals and families seek recuperation and liberation from the stresses of daily life, find their "true" selves, and spend their time as they wish. Urbain and others have changed the focus from tourism per se by subsuming it within the larger conceptual framework of the vacation. Thus framed, tourism has largely come to mean "excursions" undertaken from the place of vacation or, in a broader sense, something that one does on vacation.[14] Modern vacationing, in other words, has blended older notions of the vacation as "free time" liberated from work and schooling with tourism as a circular journey that ends in a return to everyday life. The vacation joined and reconstituted these understandings within new notions of time (as vacation time) and space (as vacation sites). Thus, vacationers could be tourists if they chose to do so, but tourism was not a necessary or given aspect of going on vacation.

The role of the vacation's rituals and narratives in the production of cultural meanings and social identities can also be seen in historian Cindy Aron's work, which demonstrates how middle-class Americans invented vacations for themselves after the Civil War. Aron suggests that this process was vital for forging a collective class identity that accented physical health and spiritual and emotional well-being. "Anxieties about vacations," however, spawned by the ambivalent relationship between work and leisure, "persisted even as middle-class Americans began to define themselves, in part, by their right to take vacations."[15] Vacations have historically been the site of struggles over the relationship between work and leisure, and of political and ideological contests over consumerism.[16] The vacation thereby came to be invested with, and generative of, a wide range of emotional, pleasurable, educational, and cultural issues, ranging, as we will see in this volume, from the care of the self at spas and beach resorts to visiting a national park by purposeful consumer-citizens learning of their national heritage.

These conceptual shifts in the study of tourism and vacations parallel those in the study of modern consumer cultures, and a principal contribution of this volume is to underscore the deep and mutually reinforcing relationship between modern tourism and modern consumerism. Like scholarship on tourism, earlier work on consumers and consumerism emphasized the passive nature of consumption and the manipulation of consumers by a "culture industry" that, among other things, had vanquished "authentic" or popular leisure practices outside the processes of commodification. More recent work

has underscored the agency of consumers as well as the conflictual, productive, and even subversive aspects of consumer culture. Particularly interesting
have been studies of the significant contributions of consumer cultures to the
creation of modern cultures and societies. The dynamism of modern consumerism has entailed, for example, the proliferation of new commercial
forms of leisure and entertainment for mass publics, modes of representation
and techniques linked to mechanical reproduction; heightened the mobility of
consumers and objects; and generated increasingly varied and sophisticated
techniques for arousing consumer desire.[17]

One important interpretation of the relationship between consumer culture and modernity concerns the processes and institutions of consumer capitalism. As historian Victoria de Grazia observes, the specifically modern
aspects of the development of Western consumer cultures and societies consisted in "carrying out acts of consumption within capitalist exchange networks and then in the organization of institutions, resources, and values
around ever larger flows and accumulations of commodities."[18] Along with
the growth and maturation of other consumer institutions, profit-making
institutions were established to facilitate tourism and to serve its clients, the
tourists, during the course of the nineteenth century. These institutions,
which included tour operators, hotels, the Baedeker, guidebooks, seaside
resorts, specialized tourist destinations, and later travel agencies, operated as
commercial enterprises that administered or promoted leisure travel through
increasingly bureaucratic and rationalized means. Tourists became, in
essence, consumers of the places, experiences, and souvenirs sold and promoted by the enabling elements of the growing tourist business, although as
we shall see in this volume, the tourists and vacationers themselves often used
the products of the tourism industry for their own ends. At the same time,
tourism also came increasingly to rely upon the institutions of the broader
consumer culture, for example advertising and later market research, to promote tourist destinations.

As a consumer good, however, tourism and vacations differed, and continue to differ, from other commodities. Particularly after the middle to late
nineteenth century, the "product" being purchased was a pastiche of heterogeneous elements amalgamated by advertising and marketing, the emergent
tourism industry, and later the mass media, rather than a tangible commodity
such as such as soap, clothing, or an automobile. Those elements have
included services (accommodations, dining, transportation, recreation), culture (national heritage, monuments, expositions, festivals), and a rich mixture
of anticipated pleasures and experiences.[19] Indeed, the perceived "experience"
of tourism and vacations increasingly became the "product" being purchased,
which in turn shaped the tourist industry's formation and its articulation of
cultural values that tourism sites represented. Another difference between

tourism and other consumer goods has resided in the process of circulation within the market; the tourist-consumer traveled to the "good" rather than the other way around.[20]

What, then, can an historical analysis offer to the study of tourism and vacations? First, as this anthology testifies, historians can by training assess the long-term development and impact of tourism and vacations and their relationship to broad social, political, economic, and cultural changes. Although uneven in its chronological and geographical focus, an emerging body of scholarship demonstrates that tourism and vacations provide fresh insights into the most significant historical developments of the past two centuries. The essays in the collection are particularly focused upon the ways in which tourism and vacations have been constitutive of class, social status, and collective identities and have served as increasingly important aspects of regional development, mass political mobilization, and nation building and national identity. These essays also demonstrate vital contributions by tourism and vacations to the evolution of modern cultures and societies.

Second, historical investigations of tourism complicate the "class to mass" trajectory that earlier studies of tourism have suggested. To be sure, we emphasize the mutually constructive relationships among tourism, vacationing, and middle-class identities from the early nineteenth century and the gradual access to tourism and vacations by working-class people in the twentieth century. On the other hand, historical case studies reveal the ways earlier developments anticipated later ones. John Walton's essay in this volume, for example, shows how the English seaside resort of Blackpool became the "mecca of the English (and increasingly Welsh and Scottish) working class" from the mid–nineteenth century, and Suzanne Kaufman describes the popular, socially diverse nature of the touristic, and increasingly commercialized, pilgrimages to the French Catholic shrine at Lourdes during the same period. Historical analysis thus complicates a purely linear interpretation of social access; it reveals not only the relations of class embedded within the development of tourism and vacations, but their important roles in enacting and representing a range of subtle social distinctions and (re)producing social hierarchies and inequalities. In this way the histories within this volume reveal the uneven entry of different social groups into the cultures and practices of tourism and vacations and the contributions of heterogeneous tourists and vacationers to the myriad uses and cultural meanings of this form of leisure.

Third, a historical perspective deepens our understanding of the complex interplay of politics and ideologies that have shaped tourism and vacations and the larger societies and cultures of which they were a part. We trace in this collection the increasing salience of patriotism and nationalism for the growth of tourism, as nation-states in the late nineteenth century began to recognize its potential as an engine of national and regional economic development and as a means of enhancing national loyalty. By the mid–twentieth century, nation-states came to see tourism and vacations as essential to the creation of con-sumer-citizens. Various state, regional, and civic endeavors recognized the value of tourism for the authoritative representation of "ourselves," "our land-scape," and "our cultural ways and traditions" and in the process forged inti-mate associations between commerce, community, and collective identities.[21] During the twentieth century, as several of the essays in this volume argue, new ideological and political agendas were also advanced through tourism and vacations. In the interwar period National Socialists in Germany, social demo-crats in Sweden, and New Dealers in the United States all embraced tourism and paid vacations as a venue for advancing political concerns and demon-strating different understandings of the benefits of citizenship.

Fourth, the history of tourism and vacations reveals new perspectives on the historical development of modernity. Certainly the conventions that industrialization spawned, the standardization of movement, the bureaucrati-zation of travel and sight-seeing infrastructures, and the mechanical produc-tion of images, as well as the creation of leisure time and the commodification of experience, provided the conditions for the development of tourism and vacations. The industrializing regions and nation-states of the North Atlantic economy first created the material conditions that made mass tourism possi-ble, and for these reasons, the geographical focus of this volume is limited to Europe and North America.[22] Industrial capitalism, with its urbanization, its generation of wealth, its rapid means of transportation, communication, and advertising, and its production of goods that defined class and status, com-posed the raw materials of a tourism industry.[23] Its (albeit ambivalent) sanc-tioning of speculation encouraged the search for profit not only from tangible property, but also from intangible assets such as values, fantasies, and aspira-tions to acquire experiences that differed from daily routine, the very stuff of tourist sites.[24] The extension of leisure time and paid vacations as respites from work, an offspring of the social tensions within industrial capitalism, helped to transform tourism and vacations from the practice of leisured elites to a mass endeavor by the middle of the twentieth century.

Tourism's contributions to modernity can also be seen in three addi-tional themes highlighted in this volume: movement, visuality, and landscapes of consumption. While tourism and vacations by the late nineteenth century became laced with appeals to "know your country," they also depended upon displacement, being "someplace else." Orvar Löfgren notes in his contribution to this volume that even the effort to have citizens view their landscapes and tourist sites through a national lens depended upon an international frame-work of comparison.

More explicitly, the physical mobility of tourism, as well as the learned recognitions of visual icons through domestic and international travel and vacationing, shaped the cultural cosmopolitanism of increasingly socially diverse tourist-consumers. From Thomas Cook's first foray by rail into organized holiday tours in the early 1840s, to automobile travel for tourism and family vacations in the early twentieth century, to the advent of tourist-class jet air travel in the late 1950s, middle-class and later working-class tourists gained access to older sites of elite leisure and high culture.

Modern technology forged both the modes of mobility and the shaping of visual expectations. As John Urry has observed, "It is not the pedestrian *flâneur* who is emblematic of modernity but rather the train passenger, car driver, and jet plane passenger."[25] Urry's comment points to the vital link between tourism's modernity and new forms of transportation. Yet there is a larger point to be made about visuality and narration. As Wolfgang Shivelbusch brilliantly illustrates in *The Railway Journey: The Industrialization of Time and Space in the Nineteenth Century,* new forms of transportation profoundly affected older notions of time and distance, as well as visuality and perception.[26] Both train and automobile travel contributed important new aspects to the experience of tourism, from the sensations of rapid bodily movement through space and distance, to the framing of sites through the passenger window. This "framing" was then extended visually to the technologically produced images of tourist sites and in descriptive, written portrayals in guidebook and site markers.

The dense web of signification embedded in tourist sites and vacation destinations, from paintings, postcards, posters, and the press in the nineteenth century, to film, mass advertising, and television in the twentieth,[27] enabled the pleasure of recognizing and experiencing the reality of "being there" for tourists and vacationers. The combination of experiencing and visualizing tourist sites and destinations also became synonymous with "knowing" them, of acquiring the cultural capital of cosmopolitan modernity. Historian Vanessa Schwartz has observed for another context that "the visual representation of reality . . . created a common culture and sense of shared experience through which people might begin to imagine themselves as participating in a metropolitan culture because they had visual evidence that such a shared world, of which they were a part, existed."[28] Tourism created new forms of knowledge, defining what "ought" to be seen, a valorization that engaged both visual and written texts concerning tourist sites themselves. One can also argue that the mobility of tourists reinvented aspects of *flânerie* in a different context. The mobile gaze and sensory engagement of the strolling flaneur increased in velocity as railroads, automobiles, or airplanes whisked tourists to their destinations. The jarring dislocation involved in modern modes of transport's shrinking of time, space, and distance may have increased the appeal of tourist sites that were perceived as stable and unchanging, such as medieval cathedrals or folk museums. Hence, both the heightened mobility of tourists themselves and the mobilization by tourist institutions of their visual and experiential expectations contributed to the creation of modern life, of vision and experience "in motion," as it were.[29]

Rapid mobility and new forms of transportation, together with the proliferation and circulation of place images, also gave rise over the nineteenth and twentieth centuries to the "spatialization" of consumer capitalism in the form of new landscapes of consumption associated with tourism and vacations. We see the invention of new landscapes and the reinvention of older ones in the essays herein by John Walton, by Ellen Furlough and Rosemary Wakeman on seaside resorts, by Catherine Cocks on urban tourism, and by Bertram Gordon on cultural tourism.[30] In the development of the seaside resort, for example, a historical perspective allows us to see both continuities and changes associated with the evolution of new rituals and practices of modernity. The therapeutic association between sea bathing and physical health has persisted, although newer meanings and motives associated with vacations have resulted in a shift "from therapeutic aims to hedonistic ones."[31] Here we can learn much about the pleasures and anxieties of modernity, from the "promiscuous mixing" of male and female bathers and the sexual titillations of form-clinging bathing costumes on nineteenth-century beaches, to twentieth-century notions of desire and bodily pleasures associated with beaches where "sea, sun, sand, and sex" reigned, as distinct from more sedate "family beaches."

This volume, therefore, acknowledges the broad historical outlines of the widening social access to tourism and vacations that developments in transportation, increased leisure time, and rising incomes made possible. Yet it substantially broadens the analysis to examine tourism's social, cultural, political, and symbolic dimensions. We highlight the specific contexts for the invention, reinvention, and ebbing of a range of tourist practices and expectations, as well as their meanings and representations. As such, the essays illuminate both continuity and change in the social, political, and cultural dimensions of tourism and vacations, which have contained the potential for transforming the self, encountering the sacred, however defined, and shaping collective identities.

The central paradox suggested by these essays is that while tourism and vacations were increasingly enmeshed within cultures of consumption, mechanically produced images, and various political and economic agendas, tourism and vacations have enabled a persistent quest for experiences of the self and its pleasures, and for education and knowledge. If these essays look closely at the use of tourism by its promoters, whether public agencies or private entrepreneurs, they also demonstrate that people impose their own meanings on tourist sites, often in ways that may or may not correspond to the intentions of organizers.[32] Going on vacation and engaging in tourism have historically been perceived as an expression of collective and individual identities and values, and as a time of relief from the exigencies and alienations of everyday life. These perspectives have represented a quest by commercialized means for experiences and values not necessarily market-based—experiences of the "authentic" and liberated self, engagement with other cultures or with one's "own" culture, sociability and group belonging, and patriotism. While all of these assumptions can be critically interrogated, they do provide insight into the appeal and pleasures associated with tourism and vacations, and they question analytical frameworks that presume travelers are manipulated and passive.

With these historical, conceptual, and thematic concerns in mind, the organization of *Tourism, Commercial Leisure, and National Identities* delineates three distinct, if partially overlapping, historical phases in the dynamic and mutually constitutive relationships between tourism and vacations and modern class identities, consumer cultures, and national, regional, and local identities. Part 1, "Tourism, Bourgeois Identity, and the Politics of Nation Building," opens with the resumption of peace after the Napoleonic wars and closes with the outbreak of World War I. This section investigates tourism's contributions to a bourgeois culture of consumption, as well as its significance for the regional and national politics that bourgeois notables increasingly defined. During the nineteenth century, vacations and tourism became an integral part of the rhythm of modern life and key elements in the construction of social status as they shaped and signified the cultural expectations and (often ambivalent) leisure ethic of the emergent middle classes.

Leisure travel prior to the late eighteenth and early nineteenth centuries was primarily the prerogative of aristocrats and other wealthy elites. Aristocratic and elite young men participated in the embodiment of elite leisure travel, the grand tour, which supplemented their cultural education, health, and pleasure and provided "a socially acceptable form of escape, a way of sowing wild oats."[33] The grand tour also signaled and represented elite (and generally, although not exclusively, male) status. During the nineteenth century, however, a version of the grand tour came to signify and construct middle-class identity as well, and aspects of the tour changed as a result. Tourism for the middle classes, for one thing, entailed shorter durations, as the work ethic did not tend to allow for the extended leisurely travel of wealthy landed elites. Spas, resorts, travel agencies, and guidebooks, moreover, articulated middle-class values of self-improvement, time discipline, privacy, and predictability, modifying the hedonistic pleasure-seeking that the bourgeoisie attributed to the aristocracy. Guidebooks became more utilitarian and less exclusively focused upon commentaries on art and descriptions of life in the urban destinations. The Murray and Baedeker "handbooks" provided more practical advice on transportation timetables, for example, and included in their books shorter itineraries for middle-class tourists. Spas in nineteenth-century

France, as Douglas Mackaman's essay details, changed from being sites for an aristocratic sociability to centerpieces of "medicalized leisure" that helped shape and express emergent middle-class sensibilities. Given the middle-class ambivalence toward leisure in general and emphasis on the values of work, industry, and self-discipline, Mackaman argues, spas themselves became enmeshed within middle-class concepts of rationality, respectability, privacy, gender segregation, and the social authority of science—in short, an important milieu for enacting a middle-class worldview within the realm of leisure.

Other essays in this collection further develop an analysis of tourism and vacations as purchasable experiences that were vital elements for creating collective identities and the social and cultural exclusions and hierarchies that accompanied their creation. As the upper bourgeoisie in particular challenged the aristocracy for dominance, visits to historic sites, natural wonders, concert halls, museums, and palaces became a means of demonstrating "taste" and effacing the socially questionable—that is, commercial—sources of bourgeois wealth.[34] Even in the United States, which lacked a titled nobility, newly monied entrepreneurs flocked to Europe, especially to France, to signify their cultural attainment and wrest status from the older American landed and mercantile elite.[35]

Yet tourism did not remain the preserve of the well-to-do bourgeoisie, nor did it stay rooted in an ethic of explicit self-denial. The proliferation of middle-class occupations—professionals, civil servants, managers, shopkeepers, and salaried employees—during the nineteenth century created a broader audience for leisure travel. Savvy tourism entrepreneurs, beginning with the most famous of them, Thomas Cook, structured their enterprises in response to intraclass segmentation. Moving beyond modest beginnings in transporting religious Nonconformists to temperance meetings and organizing low-cost tours for working people, Cook's package tours, scaled according to income, catered to the growing market for continental leisure travel and for an increasingly diverse middle class.[36] By the second half of the nineteenth century, the rapidly growing tourism apparatus of guidebooks, hotels, restaurants, and transportation differentiated the middle classes according to their ability to project material display within an increasingly common desire for the pursuit of pleasure and recreation. Comfort, relaxation away from everyday stresses, and the minimizing of risk in unfamiliar environments coexisted uneasily with self-improvement and self-discipline.[37] Tourism became emblematic of the tension within capitalism itself between the valorization of production on the one hand and the capacity for unrestrained excess on the other, especially because the increasing presence of women among the tourists reinforced the tendency to feminize the presumed irrationality of consumption.[38]

In addition to providing a means of social distinction, tourism contributed significantly to grander bourgeois projects. Once the lubricant of dynastic politics and international relations,[39] it facilitated capitalist development and nation building. Local boosters and citizens' groups revivified older itineraries while creating new touristic landscapes that combined pride in regional assets with the desire for profit. In turn, promoters of middle-class tourism marketed regional assets as evidence of the values of the nation writ small so as to reconcile the quintessentially modern tension between national and local loyalty.[40] Driven by faster and more efficient modes of transportation, such as the railroad and steamship, and the new culture of consumption and leisure, nineteenth-century tourism featured a seemingly paradoxical amalgam of destinations that invited tourists simultaneously to consume and to transcend consumption. Drawing sustenance from romanticism's valorization of nature and history, which the proliferation of seaside resorts, "sublime" landscapes, and historical preservation projects evidenced, tourism spoke as much to the misgivings regarding urbanization and the desire for continuity with the past as it did to the desire for health, relaxation, and a cultural education.[41] Yet as is clear in Catherine Cocks's essay, middle-class notables were eager to market the attractions of the cities in which they lived, not only as venues of culture, but also as places of excitement and modernity. Even seaside resorts, as John Walton's contribution suggests, joined apparent opposites, the appreciation of nature and the appropriation of urban amusements.[42]

Although eclectic in its choice of sites, the messages of bourgeois tourism, progress, and national unity betrayed a wariness toward challenges to the middle-class ascendancy. The very improvements in transportation that facilitated tourism in the first place enabled the mobility of millions and the popularization of leisure travel, even if only for a day or two. That placed additional pressure on the wealthiest bourgeois especially to elevate themselves not only above older elites and the middling sort, but also the working classes. While it is important to underscore the presence of different social groups at these new leisure sites, zoning restrictions and the topographical peculiarities of seaside resorts, as well as the careful selection of appropriate seasons for travel, provided the tools of social differentiation and segregation. These strategies competed with the potential of leisure sites to modify rigid social boundaries and undermine moral conventions.[43] As Douglas Mackaman's and John Walton's essays in this volume note, spas and seaside resorts frequently reproduced class divisions in their social policies and spatial layouts. Supporting a concept of citizenship that placed bourgeois notables at the top by virtue of talent and achievement, bourgeois tourism promoters organized festivals that maximized profit through entertainment, according to Catherine Cocks, while limiting popular access to political power and cultural capital. Discursive strategies were equally important to reinforcing separation, however. The attempt to divide "purposeful," reverent, and self-improving travel from the vulgar and profane tourism of the "masses," first emerged in response to the need for distinction in an era of increasing mobility.

Regardless, those efforts could not prevent others besides the bourgeois from appropriating tourism for their own purposes, not just the working class but also institutions that developed an interest in the practice. In France, for example, pillars of the ancien régime such as the Catholic Church revitalized older forms of religious devotion, notably the pilgrimage, in their campaign against secularism and republicanism. Suzanne Kaufman's essay reveals that despite Catholic leaders' deep ambivalence toward the apparent conflation of sacred and profane in modernized rituals, shrines such as Lourdes fused the mass production and commercialization of religious relics with the mobilization of lower-middle-class and working-class pilgrims. This troubled bourgeois republican sensibilities, as pilgrimages raised the specter of unrestrained consumption and popular participation, not to mention religious obscurantism and political "reaction" that threatened the ideological underpinnings of republican citizenship. The very fact that Lourdes resulted from a young peasant girl's vision of the Virgin Mary, a testament to the "feminization" of religious practice in nineteenth-century Europe, no doubt reinforced the tendency to use female attributes to describe the excesses of consumerism and religious emotion both.[44] Yet the lingering institutions of the ancien régime were not the only challengers. The fissiparous tendencies of modern nationalism and ethnic self-assertion intruded as well. As Jill Steward's essay demonstrates, the utility of tourism in forging the bourgeois "nation" proved especially problematic in multinational states such as the Austro-Hungarian Empire, where by 1914 it had done more to foster ethnic division than cohesion among the Habsburg dynasty's territories. The attempts of German-speaking tourist clubs specifically to promote tourism privileged the Austrian alpine lands, for not only were the Alpine regions already popular with German tourists, they were also less tainted by association with "oriental" otherness. They thus appeared more attractive to British tourists than other parts of the Habsburg realm.

If Catholic shrines and ethnic tensions in part 1 underscore tourism's appeal to diverse constituencies, part 2, "Tourism, Mass Mobilization, and the Nation-State," explores the intervention of central governments in democratizing access to leisure travel from the late nineteenth century to World War II. The increasing political activism of the lower middle and working classes, as the extension of the franchise and the development of mass parties attest, undermined the politics of notables and pressured governments into assuming responsibilities well beyond their traditional obligations of policing, law, and defense. Along with extending public education, regulating public health, monitoring household consumption, and introducing social welfare measures, governments used tourism to compensate for the social limits of private tourism organizations, hoping thereby to solidify the "nation" against social fragmentation. National parks, "grand tours" to the nation's scenic wonders, and the tourist-oriented refurbishing of historical sites designated as part of the national patrimony came to signify the unique and unchanging "essence" of the nation.[45] Although sites of technology and modernity were not ignored, tourism as nation building usually championed "pristine" wildernesses and a simpler way of life before industrialization complicated the social order. Using tourism as an instrument to forge national identity became crucial to such a far-flung nation as the United States, where it encouraged Americans to claim the West as a geographical and imaginative construction.[46] After World War I, Marguerite Shaffer's essay explains, the newly created National Park Service championed a conservative, even primeval, version of the American nation, opting for a rhetoric of organic nationalism at the expense of its competition, that of democratic citizenship. The National Parks Service discouraged the visits of the ethnic working classes and African Americans. Yet tourism as nation building was not limited to larger states, as Orvar Löfgren's essay on Sweden makes clear. The marketing of "authentic" folklore and customs was intended to incorporate—indeed domesticate—regional peculiarities within a mythic national whole. States expected that the extension of paid vacations and the promotion of mass tourism would dissipate class tensions, a major reason governments and private agencies promoted tourism so energetically during the depression. Michael Berkowitz's detailed account of American mass tourism's emergence in the 1930s locates a similar desire to utilize tourism as an antidote to the social tensions and economic hardships of capitalism's worst crisis. By the time of America's entry in World War II, the tourism industry equaled automobile manufacture, petroleum, and lumber in the size of its workforce and capital investment.[47]

The economic benefits of tourism as well presented themselves to national leaderships, who competed with those of other nations to attract foreign tourists. By the early twentieth century, many states established central agencies for promoting the nation as tourist destination, collaborating with business and private tourism associations to market attractive and salable images. This often forced the hosts to market conflicting conceptions of themselves in conformity with commercialized inventions of their national "character." Löfgren's essay notes that the image that proved most popular with foreign visitors to Sweden was that of a premodern, peasant nation set in a "romantic" wilderness, a vision that defied the intent of tourism promoters to sell Sweden's modernity and technological sophistication. Most advanced nations, however, sought to exploit tourism's potential for improving the balance of payments and developing regional economies within nation-states, the putative benefits of which would contribute to social stability. The use of tourism to generate economic growth became entwined with patriotic duty, especially in the aftermath of World War I, when personal loss and collective memory required the healing of touristic pilgrimage. The French tire manufacturer Michelin combined patriotism with the imperatives of corporate profitability as well-heeled tourists toting their Michelin guides motored to Verdun or to the Somme in autos outfitted with the maker's product.[48]

Because the interwar period, and especially the 1930s, was a time of extraordinary political and economic tensions, tourism and vacations became a site for competing cultural policies and heightened efforts toward political mobilization. Tourism and vacations in this era were even more intensely politicized and ideologically inflected, and as cultural practices they showed striking similarities across political divides. During this era, for example, European governments—both fascist and democratic—for the first time legislated paid vacations as a right of citizenship. Paid vacations were also significantly expanded during the 1930s in the United States, although they continued to be linked to employment contracts rather than national legislation.[49] The close examinations of tourism and vacation policies by Baranowski for Germany and Berkowitz for the United States reveal a remarkably similar emphasis on tourism and vacations as a means toward social and national harmony, as well as their potential to mitigate conflict and promote the "democratization of leisure" through expanded access to leisure practices connoting social prestige. In both Germany and the United States, the benefits of tourism and vacation were touted for workers' health, hygiene, and, ultimately, productivity once back on the job.

Nonetheless, the broad political and ideological goals differed significantly. We see the political and ideological shading of interwar tourism in Baranowski's essay describing the interweaving of racism and anti-Semitism in the programs of the Nazi leisure-time and tourism organization, Strength through Joy, as well as Strength through Joy's use of leisure to enhance Germany's warmaking capacity. By contrast, Löfgren's work suggests that the bicycle tourism of Swedish youth fostered the aims of a democratic welfare state and individual emancipation. And despite the instrumentalism implicit in the aims of federal tourism agencies, oil companies, railroads, bus companies, local chambers of commerce, and auto clubs that Berkowitz describes, the "New Deal" for leisure suitably testified to the rise of a populist democratic national coalition that significantly modified the conservatism of national park tourism that Shaffer observes for the twenties. Without minimizing the racist and imperial messages in American tourism generally,[50] or the conformity implicit in the Swedish attempt to build citizenship,[51] one may distinguish them from a Nazi tourism that promoted the outright militarization of the "national community" toward a racial reconstruction of the European continent, an enterprise that envisioned not only the rigid enforcement of colonial hierarchies, but also the total extermination of the Jews.

With the exception of the United States, the effort to extend tourism to wider social constituencies met with limited success until after World War II. Despite a growing working-class tourist contingent, constrained finances and priorities that favored improving the workplace took precedence over the promotion of leisure-time activities. Swedish bicyclists remained predominantly middle class, and arguably the most "worker-friendly" government in Western Europe, the Popular Front in France, did not survive long enough to see the two-week paid vacations it legislated for workers used for extensive leisure travel.[52] In addition, state efforts to negotiate the balance of power between the nation and its constituent regions, defuse political conflicts, and forge a genuine national community through tourism could just as easily backfire as succeed. Ostensibly "totalitarian" attempts to create national integration, such as those of Fascist Italy, ran afoul of local preferences, less regimented and more cosmopolitan touristic practices, the practical virtues of cultural eclecticism, and the partial incompatibility of Fascist and middle-class goals.[53] Finally, the intentions and experiences of tourists themselves failed to meet the lofty goals of public and private tourism promoters. Political and national sentiments could certainly motivate tourists, at least subliminally. Yet, self-fulfillment, relaxation, and the quest for pleasurable experiences competed with the yearning for national belonging, even in the most politicized of touristic projects such as Strength through Joy, as Baranowski notes. Nevertheless, the state's increased advocacy of paid vacations and its promotion of mass tourism illustrate the degree to which the political entry of the "masses" redefined the commitments of governments.

Part 3, "Global Mass Tourism and the Representation of Place," centers on the "golden age" of prosperity after World War II,[54] when welfare states, the politics of growth, and full employment firmly established the goal of material well-being as a birthright for all.[55] Propelled now by the automobile and jet plane, tourism signified the "good life" of consumerism and leisure that has characterized Western Europe and North America, a purchasable commodity that rendered the West superior to the Soviet bloc in securing a decent standard of living.[56] The bitter social conflicts that defined politics between the wars dissipated into the ostensibly one-class character of consumer citizenship, while tourism's ability to articulate and satisfy individual desires testified to the "freedom" guaranteed by welfare capitalist democracies. During the interwar period, the Left had pioneered in providing travel and tourism opportunities for its members, fostering recreation, solidarity, and ideological fortification. In the West, however, such "social" tourism, that is, tourism organized around the principle of collective solidarity and entitlement rather than individual desire, fell well behind the commercial tourism that by the onset of the sixties created a full-throttle global industry.[57] The fear of want, indeed the actual experience of it, that had once spawned popular political mobilization gave way to broad-based consumer confidence, which encouraged the pursuit of individual fulfillment through commodified leisure and promoted the cultivation of the body beautiful.

Yet if postwar tourism bears little resemblance to the (self-described) edifying journeys of the early-nineteenth-century bourgeoisie, it nonetheless defies reduction to pleasure seeking or the meaningless consumption of images, places, and artifacts.[58] It has retained the capacity for the representation of collective values, not least because the fragmentation characteristic of postmodern identity politics has brought forth numerous tourisms of collective identity, be they cultural tourism, ecotourism, or heritage tourism.[59] The explosion in Holocaust tourism, especially after the disintegration of the Soviet bloc permitted greater access to extermination sites, represents the pronouncement of ethnic and religious survival, as well as remembrance, after an appalling cataclysm.[60] Sites of battle and wartime victimization, Oradour-sur-Glane, Compiègne, Omaha Beach, and the Vélodrome d'Hiver, as Bertram Gordon's essay makes clear, speak to the complex attempts to sanctify the French nation, even if they have provoked more disagreement than consensus as to what the nation embodies. Although especially fractured because of the legacy of Vichy, the French experience with war commemoration is by no means unique. The sacralization of sites of war and the "lessons" they are presumed to convey have generally intensified the contestation of memories because understandings of the past embrace competing visions of the nation.[61]

Even in the latter twentieth century, when using tourism for mass political mobilization has waned considerably, the nation remains a prominent touristic subject despite, and even because of, the tourism's transnationalism. Nation-states and national tourist interests continue to authoritatively represent and market the nation to their own citizens and to foreign tourists, prepare touristic infrastructures, upgrade the training of tourism professionals, secure public cooperation, identify appropriate attractions that purportedly capture the nation's essence, and regulate tourist flows. As postwar consumer economies have expanded, states have looked to their tourist sites as economic engines for the revival of "underdeveloped" regions, even though their initiatives often fail to yield the intended results. As Ellen Furlough and Rosemary Wakeman indicate in their study of the French seaside resort of La Grand Motte, this project begun in the sixties as the quintessential exercise in Gaullist modernization and a centralized assault on provincial "backwardness" came to express vernacularisms in its architecture and serve a local clientele. Moreover, as James Buzard's and Karen Dubinsky's essays on Britain and Canada reveal, the determination of states to encapsulate their "uniqueness" in a series of images and places for touristic consumption has often reflected a vulnerability to external domination. For Canada, that vulnerability has appeared in the claim to Canadians that their efforts to welcome American tourists reaffirms their own citizenship. For Britain, it has expressed itself in the trope of Romantic nationalism, which contains an archaic vision of itself for touristic consumption. Attractions such as English "stately homes," once the signifiers of aristocratic privilege, have been represented as the embodiment of "British" values that are in turn distributed to a mass tourism market.[62]

This collection does not claim to exhaust tourism's potential as a lively and important topic for historians, and much work remains to be done. We would like to highlight four avenues for further research here. First, questions remain concerning the putative separation between everyday life and tourism-vacations. Too often, analyses of tourism and vacations reproduce the tourism industry's description of them as "time in parentheses" apart from the everyday; indeed selling tourism and vacations as a consumer good has depended upon invoking antinomies between work time and leisure time. This in turn has obscured the imbrication of tourism and vacations within the culture and social imagination of everyday life, as well as the labor involved in producing, sustaining, and paying for those times of leisure. The very bourgeois tendency to reproduce in their vacations values associated with work suggests the porous boundaries between work and leisure. Furthermore, the historically rapid growth of people working within the tourism industry suggests the need to rethink conceptual categories that assert the separation of work and leisure as characteristic of Fordist modernity in particular.[63] Further work might also interrogate the relationship between, on one hand, the representation of tourism and vacations as a time apart, conducive to trying out new personal behaviors, marking social distinctions, "knowing one's country," and (re)discovering the self, and, on the other, the forging of consumerism's culture of distraction, fantasy, desire, and "lifestyles." Was this representation historically compensatory, further binding the middle classes and workers to capitalism in order to consume? Or do we need to take seriously what Frederic Jameson called "the problem of pleasure," which challenges scholars to take seriously the pleasurable appeal of consumer culture rather than dismiss commodified manifestations of mass consumption as "mere diversion"?[64]

Second, because tourism is not only a formidable industry, but also an appeal to the imagination, the interactions among tourists, vacationers, and promoters also merits further investigation. The recent suggestion of Christoph Hennig that tourism should receive consideration similar to that given to other symbolic products such as art, ritual, and play is a promising way to explore its cultural meanings, as well as its commercial operations.[65] The stereotypes of tourists should continue to be critically examined, particularly since, as we have noted, the historical development of tourism and vacations suggests the ways they become a search for family togetherness, collective identities, historical rootedness, and fantasy and the satisfaction of individual desires. For example, further work on the topic could build upon the recent acknowledgment that tourism promoters have frequently demonstrated a precocious sensitivity to the possibilities of potential tourist sites when little recommended them other than the most subtle changes in values and needs.[66] Additional case studies might analyze also how tourists and vacationers perceive their own experiences,[67] and thus question older models of transmission and reception between tourists and tourist promoters.

Third, despite our attention to tourism as a mechanism for state intervention and nation building in Europe and North America, there is little that speaks to the historical function and meaning of tourism in the Soviet Union and Eastern Europe, or in their post-Communist successor states.[68] Yet tourism, at least in the form of vacation trips for productive workers, could well have boosted domestic support for Stalinism. Given the emphasis in recent Soviet scholarship on the sources of consent for Stalinism, tourism could emerge as another means of demonstrating the weakness of explanations for the regime's survival that stress the terror.[69] Furthermore, we should interrogate tourism's role in the Soviet bloc's post-Stalinist sensitivity to "quality of life" issues, increasing the standard of living, and providing a better material existence.[70] Despite the self-defeating preference for large military budgets and antiquated forms of heavy industry among the Warsaw Pact nations, the Soviet bloc's collective preoccupation with its "backwardness" relative to the West yielded manifold, if fitful, attempts to prove the ability of "socialism" to best market economies in generating consumer prosperity. Ironically, tourism played a significant role in the Soviet bloc's disintegration, despite the heavy travel restrictions on ordinary citizens. In the spring of 1989, East Germans made effective use of their only opportunity for international travel, tourism to other "socialist" nations, to escape through Hungary's recently opened border with Austria. The competition between East and West was more than just an arms race. It amounted to a contest over which side could provide its citizens with "the good life." In the end, mass tourism's original spawning ground won out.

Finally, there is as well relatively little work that analyzes the role of tourism in the representation, acquisition, extension, and relinquishment of empire, despite the burgeoning interest in the culture of imperialism and travel writing in recent years.[71] Close attention to the historical relationships between tourism and empire could also illuminate their complex effects on individual and collective identities, as well as patterns of economic development, within the "contact zones."[72] Representations of empire promoted the urge to see other cultures. This took place within the metropole through vectors of consumer culture, including posters, advertising, cinema, comic strips, wax museums, zoos, and particularly in the tourist-oriented colonial expositions.[73] These modes of representation and experience within imperializing countries required contact with colonial subjects and cultures first by bringing them "home," and then by encouraging travel to the colonies themselves.[74]

The history of Thomas Cook and Sons further suggests tourism's relevance to the erection of the infrastructures of empire, the racial and class hierarchies upon which imperialism was based, and the forging of metropolitan and colonial identities both.[75] Cook began to organize tours to Egypt once Egypt could no longer resist British penetration, and, in fact, the Cook agency became the largest employer of Egyptian labor. Thomas's son, John Mason Cook, played a crucial role in rescuing General Gordon from Khartoum in 1884 because of his experience in navigating the Nile, and he also took charge of transporting Kitchener's army to the Sudan five years later. Yet if Cook's wealthy tourists came to the "East" because of its so-called exoticism, thus implicating themselves in the tourism industry's manifold influences on, and hierarchical representations of, local cultures, they insulated themselves from the "natives" in their posh hotels and first-class transport, except for the servants whose labor they relied upon for services. Postcolonial tourism has in most instances differed little in this regard. As the French tourist organization Club Méditerranée illustrates, postcolonial tourism has striven to recapture and commodify the nostalgia associated with colonialism, while deploying notions of the "primitive" to reproduce racial hierarchies. Such hierarchies are operative in the employment practices of the tourism industry itself. They not only give us further reason to question tourism's development along a simple trajectory from "class to mass," they also suggest the limits of tourism's democratization, especially since World War II.[76] Tourism remains primarily the preserve of the guests from the wealthy nations of western Europe and North America, even if the "hosts" in the former colonies are not without resources to negotiate their participation in the global tourism industry.

The essays in this collection thus suggest that tourism and vacations can be interpreted as laboratories of modern life in the industrialized world. While the relative newness of tourism as a historical topic has necessarily limited the scope of this volume, these essays make two major points. First, a historical analysis of tourism and vacation expands our optic into the grand narratives of modern history: class formation, nation building, economic development, and the emergence of consumer cultures. Second, explorations into the history of tourism and vacations reveal their salience for constructing modern cultural meanings of experience, desire, visuality, mobility, and the care of the self, as well as for representing the "good life" and the benefits of consumer culture.

NOTES

1. "Dream Factories," *Economist,* January 10, 1998, 3. For statistical information on tourism, see also Donald E. Lundberg and Carolyn B. Lundberg, *International Travel and Tourism,* 2d ed. (New York: Wiley, 1993); periodic publications of the World Tourism Organization; and the *Travel Industry World Yearbook: The Big Picture,* published annually by the American Society of Travel Agents in New York.

2. James Buzard, *The Beaten Track: European Tourism, Literature, and the Ways to Culture, 1800–1918* (Oxford: Clarendon Press, 1993), 82. It is instructive that the word *tourist* entered into the French language *(touriste)* in 1816. Jean-Didier Urbain, *L'Idiot du voyage: Histoires de touristes* (Paris: Plon, 1991), 28.

3. The history of women and tourism remains understudied, although work on women and travel (primarily by literary scholars) has recently accelerated. See J. A. Mains, "British Travellers in Switzerland, with Special Reference to Some Women Travellers between 1750 and 1850," Ph.D. diss., University of Edinburgh, 1966; P. J. B. Meyer, "No Land Too Remote: Women Travelers in the Georgian Age," Ph.D. diss., University of Massachusetts, 1978; Mary Russell, *The Blessings of a Good Thick Skirt: Women Travellers and Their World* (London: Collins, 1986); Dea Birkett, *Spinsters Abroad: Victorian Lady Travellers* (Oxford: Blackwell, 1989); Sara Mills, *Discourses of Difference: An Analysis of Women's Travel Writing and Colonialism* (London: Routledge, 1991), Billie Melman, *Women's Orients: English Women and the Middle East, 1718–1918* (Ann Arbor: University of Michigan Press, 1992); and Susan Morgan, *Place Matters: Gendered Geography in Victorian Women's Travel Books about Southeast Asia* (New Brunswick, N.J.: Rutgers University Press, 1996). Useful introductions to contemporary tourism and gender are V. Kinnaird and D. Hall, eds., *Tourism: A Gender Analysis* (Chichester: Wiley, 1994); and M. Swain, "Gender in Tourism," *Annals of Tourism Research* 22 (1995): 247–66.

4. Among others, Buzard cites Wordsworth's lament that "instead of travelers proceeding, with leisure to observe and feel," one would find tourists "carried along in their carriages, not a few of them perhaps discussing the merits of the last new Novel, or poring over their Guide-books, or fast asleep" (*The Beaten Track,* 27–29).

5. André Siegfried, *Aspects du XXe siècle* (Paris: Hachette, 1955), 107, 123–25, and 148.

6. Daniel J. Boorstin, *The Image: A Guide to Pseudo-Events in America* (1961; New York: Atheneum, 1987), 77–117; and Paul Fussell, *Abroad: British Literary Travelling between the Wars* (New York: Oxford University Press, 1980), vii and 42. Fussell has reiterated many of these themes in his recent essay "Travel, Tourism, and International Understanding," in *Thank God for the Atom Bomb and Other Essays* (New York: Ballantine Books, 1990), 124–46. Critics from the left have been equally derogative of tourism. Guy Debord, for example, decried tourism's tendency toward pure spectacle and its proliferation of stereotypical images. As he put it, "Tourism is the chance to go and see what has been made banal." *La Société du spectacle* (Paris: Buchet/Chastel, 1967), 120. Translation: *The Society of the Spectacle* (New York: Zone Books, 1994).

7. John Urry, *The Tourist Gaze: Leisure and Travel in Contemporary Societies* (London: Sage, 1990), 1.

8. Dean MacCannell, *The Tourist: A New Theory of the Leisure Class* (1976; New York: Schocken, 1989), 13–14. MacCannell also emphasizes the ways tourists' search for authenticity is frequently frustrated by the "staged" nature of tourism's purportedly "authentic" sites (91–107). The issue of "authenticity" as it relates to tourism is partic-

ularly vexed. See Erik Cohen, "Authenticity and Commoditization in Tourism" *Annals of Tourism Research* 15 (1988): 371–86.

9. MacCannell, *The Tourist,* 45.

10. Rudy Koshar, "'What Ought to Be Seen': Tourists' Guidebooks and National Identities in Modern Germany and Europe," *Journal of Contemporary History* 33, no. 3 (1998): 323–40.

11. Koshar, "What Ought to Be Seen," 339.

12. Quoted in Alan Swingewood, *Cultural Theory and the Problem of Modernity* (New York: St. Martin's Press, 1998), 141. On the flâneur, note Keith Tester, *The Flâneur* (London: Routledge, 1994); and Janet Wolff, "The Invisible *Flâneuse:* Women and the Literature of Modernity," in *Feminine Sentences* (Berkeley and Los Angeles: University of California Press, 1990).

13. Jean-Didier Urbain, *Sur la plage: Moeurs et coutumes balnéaires* (Paris: Payot, 1994). Urbain's work also suggests exciting possibilities for reinterpreting *flânerie* in the context of the beach vacations that emerged in the nineteenth century. Here the sensual pleasures of spectatorship, of observing and being observed resurface in the ebb and flow of bodies along the shoreline. See further evidence of this conceptual shift from travel/tourism to vacations in Ellen Furlough, "Making Mass Vacations: Tourism and Consumer Culture in France, 1930s–1970s," *Comparative Studies in Society and History* 10, no. 3 (1998): 247–86; and the recent book by Orvar Löfgren, *On Holiday: A History of Vacationing* (Berkeley and Los Angeles: University of California Press, 1999).

14. Urbain, *Sur la plage,* 15–16.

15. Cindy Aron, *Working at Play: A History of Vacations in the United States* (New York: Oxford University Press, 1999), 9. The intense personal and familial engagement associated with vacations can be seen in Aron's introduction, which evokes her memories of family summers at the beach.

16. Gary Cross, *Time and Money: The Making of Consumer Culture* (London: Routledge, 1993), especially 95–98, 114–27, and 176–83.

17. For examples of this literature, see Ellen Furlough, "Gender and Consumption in Historical Perspective: A Selective Bibliography," 389–409, as well the other essays collected in *The Sex of Things: Gender and Consumption in Historical Perspective,* ed. Victoria de Grazia with Ellen Furlough (Berkeley and Los Angeles: University of California Press, 1996).

18. Victoria de Grazia, introduction to *The Sex of Things,* 4.

19. See Furlough, "Making Mass Vacations," for further elaboration on this point.

20. József Böröcz, "Travel Capitalism: The Structure of Europe and the Advent of the Tourist," *Comparative Studies in Society and History,* 32, no. 4 (1992): 709. Note also Celia Lury's analysis of the social and cultural movement of tourist objects, "The Objects of Travel," in *Touring Cultures: Transformations of Travel and Theory,* ed. Chris Rojek and John Urry (London: Routledge, 1997), 75–95.

21. The project of knowing and representing "our culture" has been advanced through the notion of "heritage" and its blending with tourism. Key texts on heritage include David Lowenthal, *Possessed by the Past: The Heritage Crusade and the Spoils of History* (New York: Cambridge University Press, 1996); Robert Hewison, *The Heritage Industry: Britain in a Climate of Decline* (London: Methuen, 1987); and Raphael Samuel, *Theatres of Memory,* vol. 1, *Past and Present in Contemporary Culture* (London: Verso, 1994). On heritage and tourism, see Barbara Kirshenblatt-Gimblett, *Destination Culture: Tourism, Museums, and Heritage* (Berkeley and Los Angeles: University

of California Press, 1998); Priscilla Boniface and Peter J. Fowler, *Heritage and Tourism in "The Global Village"* (London: Routledge, 1993); and John Urry, "Gazing on History," in *The Tourist Gaze,* 104–34.

22. While these trends emerged earliest in Europe and North America, the historical trajectories within this region were not uniform, and we were unable due to the constraints of space and the unevenness of the historical research to represent examples of the full variety of histories even within this geographical range. For historical studies of geographical areas not covered in this volume, see Paul Bernard, *Rush to the Alps: The Evolution of Vacationing in Switzerland* (Boulder, CO: East European Quarterly; New York: distributed by Columbia University Press, 1978); John Pemble, *The Mediterranean Passion: Victorians and Edwardians in the South* (Oxford: Clarendon Press, 1987); R. Eisner, *Travellers to an Antique Land: The History and Literature of Travel to Greece* (Ann Arbor: University of Michigan Press, 1991); and Robert Shannan Peckham, "The Exoticism of the Familiar and the Familiarity of the Exotic: *Fin-de-Siècle* Travellers to Greece," in *Writes of Passage: Reading Travel Writing,* ed. James Duncan and Derek Gregory (London: Routledge, 1999), 164–84.

23. The economic weight of international tourism remains overwhelmingly located in Europe and North America. In 1991, the top ten tourist destinations, in order were France, United States, Spain, Italy, Hungary, Austria, United Kingdom, Mexico, Germany, and Canada. The citizens from the following countries, in order, spent the most money when traveling abroad: United States, Germany, Japan, United Kingdom, Italy, France, Canada, Netherlands, Austria, Switzerland (Lundburg and Lundberg, *International Travel and Tourism,* 7 and 11).

24. The relationship between speculation and the creation of touristic images arises as a prominent theme in Eric Purchase's new study, *Out of Nowhere: Disaster and Tourism in the White Mountains* (Baltimore: Johns Hopkins University Press, 1999), especially 76–84.

25. John Urry, "Tourism, Travel, and the Modern Subject," in *Consuming Places* (London: Routledge, 1995), 141.

26. Wolfgang Schivelbusch, *The Railway Journey: The Industrialization of Time and Space in the Nineteenth Century* (1977; rpt., Berkeley: University of California Press, 1986). See also Stephen Kern, *The Culture of Time and Space, 1880–1918* (Cambridge, Mass.: Harvard University Press, 1983).

27. For examples, see Orvar Löfgren, "Wish Your Were Here! Holiday Images and Picture Postcards," *Ethnologia Scandinavica* 15 (1985): 90–107; Malcolm Andrews, *The Search for the Picturesque: Landscape Aesthetics and Tourism in Britain, 1760–1800* (Stanford, Calif.: Stanford University Press, 1989); Alain Corbin, *Le Territoire du Vide: l'Occident et la désir du rivage, 1750–1840* (Paris: Aubier, 1988), trans. as *The Lure of the Sea: The Discovery of the Seaside in the Western World, 1750–1840,* trans. Jocelyn Phelps (Berkeley and Los Angeles: University of California Press, 1994); Robert Herbert, *Monet on the Normandy Coast* (New Haven: Yale University Press, 1994); Tom Selwyn, ed., *The Tourist Image: Myths and Myth-Making in Tourism* (Chichester: Wiley, 1996); and Carol Crawshaw and John Urry, "Tourism and the Photographic Eye," in Rojek and Urry, *Touring Cultures,* 176–95.

28. Vanessa R. Schwartz, *Spectacular Realities: Early Mass Culture in Fin-de-Siècle Paris* (Berkeley and Los Angeles: University of California Press, 1998), 6.

29. For the interpretive similarities between our comments here on tourism and the modernity of film, see Leo Charney and Vanessa R. Schwartz, introduction to *Cinema and the Invention of Modern Life* (Berkeley: University of California Press, 1995), 1–12.

30. Particularly relevant is Sharon Zukin's definition of landscape to denote not only "the usual geographical meaning of 'physical surroundings,'" but also "an ensemble of material and social practices and their symbolic representation." *Landscapes of Power: From Detroit to Disney World* (Berkeley and Los Angeles: University of California Press, 1991), 16.

31. Corbin, *Lure of the Sea,* 272.

32. This occurs even in the most manipulative of tourist settings, such as Sea World in San Diego, a site that its corporate sponsor, Budweiser, has carefully crafted to meet its commercial objectives. See Susan G. Davis, *Spectacular Nature: Corporate Culture and the Sea World Experience* (Berkeley and Los Angeles: University of California Press, 1997), 117–51. Note as well the desire of tourists to Disney World to reaffirm the nuclear family, which corresponds with Disney's intention; see The Project on Disney's *Inside the Mouse: Work and Play at Disney World* (Durham, N.C.: Duke University Press, 1995), 34–53. Anthropologist Daniel Miller's observations regarding consumption can be equally applied to tourism: "Consumption is simply a process of objectification—that is, a use of goods and services in which the object or activity becomes simultaneously a practice in the world and a form in which we construct our understandings of ourselves in the world. . . . I would continue to maintain that consumption is much more autonomous of business intentions and manipulations of the symbolic potential of commodities than was previously thought." *Acknowledging Consumption: A Review of New Studies,* ed. Daniel Miller (London: Routledge, 1995), 30. See also Koshar, "What Ought to Be Seen."

33. Lynn Withey, *Grand Tours and Cook's Tours: A History of Leisure Travel, 1750–1915* (New York: Aurum, 1997), 3.

34. See, for example, Douglas P. Mackaman, *Leisure Settings: Bourgeois Culture, Medicine, and the Spa in Modern France* (Chicago: University of Chicago Press, 1998); and Ian Ousby, *The Englishman's England: Taste, Travel, and the Rise of Tourism* (Cambridge: Cambridge University Press, 1990).

35. Harvey Levenstein, *Seductive Journey: American Tourists in France from Jefferson to the Jazz Age* (Chicago: University of Chicago Press, 1998), especially 13–81.

36. On the emergence and development of the Cook firm, see Buzard, *The Beaten Track,* 47–65; Withey, *Grand Tours,* 135–66; P. Brendon, *Thomas Cook: 150 Years of Popular Tourism* (London: Secker and Warburg, 1991); and Edmund Swinglehurst, *Cook's Tours: The Story of Popular Travel* (London: Pool and Dorset, 1982).

37. For the evolution of bourgeois tourism, consult Withey, *Grand Tours,* 167–219; Levenstein, *Seductive Journey,* 125–213; and Jon R. Sterngass, "Cities of Play: Saratoga Springs, Newport, and Coney Island in the Nineteenth Century," Ph.D. diss., City University of New York, 1998, for their discussions of American leisure travel; and Mackaman, *Leisure Settings,* especially 85–154, for the French.

38. Consult Victoria de Grazia's thoughtful introductory remarks in de Grazia with Furlough, *Sex of Things,* 11–24. For the beginnings of leisured travel among women, see the recent dissertation of Helen Mary Lowry, "'Reisen, Sollte Ich Reisen! England Sehen!' A Study of Eighteenth-Century Travel Accounts: Sophie von La Roche, Johanna Schopenhauer, and Others," Ph.D. diss., Queen's University, 1999.

39. This is the observation of John K. Walton, "Taking the History of Tourism Seriously," *European History Quarterly* 27, no. 4 (1997): 564. For an analysis of the relationship between tourism and the Marshall Plan, see the work of Brian Angus McKenzie, "Deep Impact: The Cultural Policy of the United States in France, 1948–1952," Ph.D. diss., State University of New York at Stony Brook, 1999. Note as well Chris

Endy's essay concerning the relationship between American travelers in Europe and U.S. foreign affairs, "Travel and World Power: Americans in Europe, 1890–1917," *Diplomatic History* 22, no. 4 (1998): 565–95.

40. There is an array of recent work that offers rich suggestions as to the economic, cultural, and national significance of the local and regional. They include for Germany, Celia Applegate, *A Nation of Provincials: The German Idea of Heimat* (Berkeley and Los Angeles: University of California Press, 1990); Alon Confino, *The Nation as a Local Metaphor: Württemberg, Imperial Germany, and National Memory, 1871–1918* (Chapel Hill: University of North Carolina Press, 1997); Rudy Koshar, *Preservation and National Memory in the Twentieth Century* (Chapel Hill: University of North Carolina Press, 1998), especially 17–73; and Charlotte Tacke, *Denkmal im sozialen Raum. Nationale Symbole in Deutschland und Frankreich im 19. Jahrhundert* (Göttingen: Vandenhoeck and Ruprecht, 1995); for the United States, Dona Brown, *Inventing New England: Regional Tourism in the Nineteenth Century* (Washington, D.C.: Smithsonian Institution Press, 1995); Purchase, *Out of Nowhere;* and John F. Sears, *Sacred Places: American Tourist Attractions in the Nineteenth Century* (Amherst: University of Massachusetts Press, 1998).

41. On the impact of romanticism especially, see Corbin, *Lure of the Sea*, 1–96; and Jonas Frykman and Orvar Löfgren, *Culture Builders: A Historical Anthropology of Middle-Class Life,* trans. Alan Crozier (New Brunswick, N.J.: Rutgers University Press, 1987), 42–87.

42. The celebration of urbanism and technology in tourist sites was especially evident in the United States. See William R. Taylor, ed., *Inventing Times Square: Commerce and Culture at the Crossroads of the World* (New York: Russell Sage Foundation, 1991); and the evolution of Niagara Falls to a both natural wonder and technological marvel in William Irwin, *The New Niagara: Tourism, Technology, and the Landscape of Niagara Falls, 1776–1917* (University Park: Pennsylvania State University Press, 1996). Yet the amalgamation of nature and urban, bourgeois values in the creation of tourist sites was prominent in England as well. See Donald Ingram Ulin, "The Making of the English Countryside: Tourism and Literary Representation in Nineteenth-Century England," Ph.D. diss., Indiana University, 1998. On contemporary urban tourism, see Christopher M. Law, ed., *Tourism in Major Cities* (London: Routledge, 1996).

43. For the relationship between bourgeois privacy and the segregation of the poor in French spas, see Mackaman, *Leisure Settings,* 67–84. The tension between the accessibility of seaside resorts and the desire of the wealthy to maintain social distance is an especially prominent theme in John K. Walton's *The English Seaside Resort: A Social History, 1750–1914* (New York: Leicester University Press and St. Martin's Press, 1983). For additional literature on resorts, see J. Walvin, *Beside the Seaside: A Social History of the Popular Seaside Holiday* (London: Allen Lane, 1978); J. D. Marshall and J. K. Walton, *The Lake Counties from 1830 to the Mid Twentieth Century* (Manchester: Manchester University Press, 1981); Mary Blume, *Côte d'Azur: Inventing the French Riviera* (London: Thames and Hudson, 1992); J. V. N. Soane, *Fashionable Resort Regions: Their Evolution and Transformation* (Wallingford: CAB Publications, 1993); R. Balzani, "The Concept of the Seaside Resort as a Vacation for the Masses along the Romagna Coast," *Risorgimento* 45 (1993): 155–66; John Towner and M. T. Newton, eds., *Tourism in Spain: Critical Issues* (Wallingford: CAB Publications, 1996); Lena Lenek and Gideon Bosker, *The Beach: The History of Paradise on Earth* (New York: Viking, 1998); as well as Sterngass, "Cities of Play."

44. The growing scholarship on nineteenth-century popular religiosity, particularly

among Catholics, indicates that historians have in recent years come to appreciate the significance of religious practice in a putatively "secular" age. See especially David Blackbourn, *Marpingen: Apparitions of the Virgin Mary in Bismarckian Germany* (New York: Vintage, 1995); Thomas Kselman, *Miracles and Prophecies in Nineteenth-Century France* (New Brunswick, N.J.: Rutgers University Press, 1983); and Ruth Harris, *Lourdes: Body and Spirit in the Secular Age* (New York: Viking Press, 1999).

45. On the relationship between national memory and nature especially, see Simon Schama's evocative work *Landscape and Memory* (New York: Knopf, 1995).

46. The scholarship on tourism to the American West has grown formidable. See Anne Farrar Hyde, *An American Vision: Far Western Landscape and National Culture, 1820–1920* (New York: New York University Press, 1990); Drake Hokanson, *The Lincoln Highway: Main Street across America* (Iowa City: University of Iowa Press, 1988); John A. Jakle, *The Tourist: Travel in Twentieth-Century North America* (Lincoln: University of Nebraska Press, 1985); Kerwin L. Klein, "Frontier Products: Tourism, Consumerism, and the Southwestern Public Lands, 1890–1990," *Pacific Historical Review* 62, no. 1 (1993): 39–71; Earl Pomeroy, *In Search of the Golden West: The Tourist in Western America* (New York: Knopf, 1957); Hal Rothman, *Devil's Bargains: Tourism in the Twentieth Century American West* (Lawrence: University Press of Kansas, 1998); Marguerite S. Shaffer, "'See America First': Re-Envisioning Nation and Region through Western Tourism," *Pacific Historical Review* 65, no. 4 (1996): 559–81, and her *See America First: Tourism and National Identity, 1880–1940* (Washington, D.C.: Smithsonian Institution Press, 1999) and "Yosemite and Ansel Adams: Art, Commerce, and Western Tourism," *Pacific Historical Review* 65, no. 4 (November 1996): 615–39.

47. Berkowitz's essay complements the recent findings of Aron, *Working at Play*, 237–57, who argues that the depression did not mean the termination of vacations, only the form that they took, a return to the nineteenth-century practice of stressing leisure for the purposes of self-improvement.

48. See David W. Lloyd, *Battlefield Tourism: Pilgrimage and the Commemoration of the Great War in Britain, Australia, and Canada, 1919–1939* (Oxford: Berg, 1998); and Elizabeth Diller and Ricardo Scofidio, eds., *Back to the Front: Tourism of War* (New York: Princeton Architectural Press, 1994). On Michelin, see Stephen L. Harp, *Marketing Michelin: Advertising and National Culture in Twentieth-Century France* (Baltimore: Johns Hopkins University Press, forthcoming). For the Great War and memory more generally, see Thomas W. Laqueur, "Memory and Naming in the Great War," in *Commemorations: The Politics of National Identity*, ed. John R. Gillis (Princeton, N.J.: Princeton University Press, 1994), 150–67; Antoine Prost, "Monuments to the Dead," *Realms of Memory: The Construction of the French Past*, ed. Pierre Nora, trans. Arthur Goldhammer, vol. 2, *Traditions* (New York: Columbia University Press, 1997), 307–30; Jay Winter, *Sites of Memory, Sites of Mourning: The Great War in European Cultural History* (Cambridge: Cambridge University Press, 1995); and especially Daniel J. Sherman, "Objects of Memory: History and Narratives in French War Museums," *French Historical Studies* 19, no. 1 (1995): 49–74.

49. See the report of the International Labour Office, Studies and Reports, Series G (Housing and Welfare), no. 5, *Facilities for the Use of Workers' Leisure During Holidays* (Geneva, 1939).

50. For examples, see the excellent essay of Annie Gilbert Coleman, "The Unbearable Whiteness of Skiing," *Pacific Historical Review* 65, no. 4 (1996): 583–614, a piece of her Ph.D. diss., "The Unbearable Whiteness of Skiing," University of Colorado, 1996; as well as the use of tourism by the white elites of Charleston in Stephanie Eileen Yuhl's

"High Culture in the Low Country: Arts, Identity, and Tourism in Charleston, South Carolina, 1920–1940," Ph.D. diss., Duke University, 1998; and New Orleans, in Monique Guillory's "Some Enchanted Evening on the Auction Block: The Cultural Legacy of New Orleans Quadroon Balls," Ph.D. diss., New York University, 1999.

51. See Orvar Löfgren, "Being a Good Swede: National Identity as a Cultural Battleground," in *Articulating Hidden Histories: Exploring the Influence of Eric R. Wolf*, ed. Jane Schneider and Rayna Rapp (Berkeley and Los Angeles: University of California Press, 1995), 268–70.

52. See Furlough, "Making Mass Vacations," especially 252–60; Gary Cross, "Vacations for All: The Leisure Question in the Era of the Popular Front," *Journal of Contemporary History* 24 (1989): 599–621; Julian Jackson, *The Popular Front in France: Defending Democracy, 1934–38* (Cambridge: Cambridge University Press, 1988). For a discussion of paid vacations more broadly, note Jean-Claude Richez and Léon Strauss, "Un Temps nouveau pour les ouvriers: Les congés payés," in *L'Avènement des loisirs, 1850–1960*, ed. Alain Corbin (Paris: Aubier, 1995), 376–412.

53. For Germany, Christine Keitz, *Reisen also Leitbild: Die Entstehung des modernen Massentourismus in Deutschland* (Munich: Deutscher Taschenbuch Verlag, 1997), 234–54; as well as Hasso Spode, "'Der deutsche Arbeiter reist.' Massentourismus im Dritten Reich," in *Sozialgeschichte der Freizeit: Untersuchungen zum Wandel der Alltagskultur in Deutschland*, ed. Gerhard Huck (Wuppertal: Peter Hammer Verlag, 1980), 281–306, and "Arbeiterurlaub im Dritten Reich," in *Angst, Belohnung, Zucht, und Ordnung: Herrshaftsmechanismen im Nationalsozialismus*, ed. Carola Sachse et al. (Opladen: Westdeutscher Verlag, 1982), 275–328. For Italy, R. J. B. Bosworth, "Tourist Planning in Fascist Italy and the Limits of a Totalitarian Culture," *Contemporary European History* 6, no. 1 (1997): 1–25, and "The Touring Club Italiano and the Nationalization of the Italian Bourgeoisie," *European History Quarterly* 27, no. 3 (1997): 371–410; as well as Marla Susan Stone, *The Patron State: Culture and Politics in Fascist Italy* (Princeton, N.J.: Princeton University Press, 1998), 32–43, 196–216, on the Venice Biennale under Fascism. The best work on the broader topic of leisure in Fascist Italy belongs to Victoria de Grazia, *The Culture of Consent: Mass Organization of Leisure in Fascist Italy* (Cambridge: Cambridge University Press, 1981).

54. So referred to by Eric Hobsbawm in his *The Age of Extremes: A History of the World, 1914–1991* (New York: Pantheon Books, 1994), 223.

55. Essay collections that represent the state of the scholarship on consumerism include de Grazia with Furlough, *The Sex of Things*; and Susan Strasser, Charles McGovern, and Matthias Judt, eds., *Getting and Spending: European and American Consumer Societies in the Twentieth Century* (Cambridge: Cambridge University Press, 1998).

56. The political subtext of consumerism was relentless in West Germany, considered to have been on the "front line" of the Cold War. See Erica Carter, *How German Is She? Postwar West German Reconstruction and the Consuming Woman* (Ann Arbor: University of Michigan Press, 1997).

57. Furlough, "Making Mass Vacations," 265–73; Keitz, *Reisen als Leitbild*, 272–85.

58. Even tourist sites most open to ridicule, such as Elvis Presley's home, Graceland, prompt rituals of remembrance that carry deep meaning for the visitors. See Karal Ann Marlin, *Graceland: Going Home with Elvis* (Cambridge: Harvard University Press, 1996), especially 198–213.

59. For tourism, race, and ethnicity, see Owen Thomas, "Cultural Tourism, Commemorative Plaques, and African-Canadian Historiography: Challenging Historical

Marginality," *Histoire Sociale—Social History* 29, no. 58 (1996): 431–39; and Judy Tzu-Chun Wu, "'Loveliest Daughter of Our Ancient Cathay!' Representations of Ethnic and Gender Identity in the Miss Chinatown U.S.A. Beauty Pageant," *Journal of Social History* 31, no. 1 (1997): 5–31.

60. Jack Kugelmann, "Why We Go to Poland: Holocaust Tourism as Secular Ritual," in *The Art of Memory: Holocaust Memorials in History,* ed. James E. Young (New York: Prestel, 1994), 175–85, and "The Rites of the Tribe: The Meaning of Poland for American Jewish Tourists," *Yivo Annual* 21 (1993): 395–453.

61. See for example, Edward Tabor Linenthal, *Sacred Ground: Americans and Their Battlefields* (Urbana: University of Illinois Press, 1991).

62. Ironically titled owners seeking to offset the costs of maintaining stately homes have often acquired enough business expertise to update their image; to wit, the shrewd efforts of Earl Spencer, the brother of Princess Diana, to exploit the commercial possibilities of Diana's grave at Althorp while simultaneously preserving the site's touristic sacredness. On the evolution of aristocratic country houses into emblems of "heritage," see Peter Mandler, *The Fall and Rise of the Stately Home* (New Haven: Yale University Press, 1997), 355–401; and Adrian Tinniswood, *The Polite Tourist: Four Centuries of Country House Visiting* (New York: National Trust and Harry N. Abrams, 1999).

63. David Harvey has argued that the separation of work as leisure was part of the modern rationalization and separation of spheres that helped define Fordist modernity from the early twentieth century to around the mid-1970s. Yet, as we have noted, tourism and vacations involve work, and their cultural images and material artifacts were part of, and extended, everyday life. See Harvey's *The Condition of Postmodernity: An Enquiry into the Origins of Cultural Change* (Cambridge, Mass.: Blackwell, 1989, 1990), especially chapter 8, "Fordism," and part 3, "The Experience of Space and Time."

64. Frederic Jameson, "Pleasure: A Political Issue," in *Formations of Pleasure* (London: Routledge, 1983), 1–14. See also Richard Butsch, "Leisure and Hegemony in America," in *For Fun and Profit: The Transformation of Leisure into Consumption,* ed. Richard Butsch (Philadelphia: Temple University Press, 1990).

65. Christoph Hennig, *Reiselust: Touristen, Tourismus, und Urlaubskultur* (Frankfurt am Main: Insel Verlag, 1997).

66. Namely from Purchase, *Out of Nowhere.*

67. An excellent model for this kind of analysis is Levinstein, *Seductive Journey.*

68. For an earlier period in Russian history, see Christopher Ely, "The Search for a Russian Picturesque: Monasteries and Travel Writing, 1820 to 1850," in *Architectures of Russian Identity, 1500 to the Present,* ed. James Cracraft and Daniel Rowland (Bloomington, IN: Slavica, forthcoming). Two examples from the post-Communist successor states are Vladimír Baláž, "Tourism and Regional Development in the Slovak Republic," *European Urban and Regional Studies* 1, no. 2 (1994): 171–77; and Jean Poncet, "Le Développement du tourisme en Bulgarie," *Annales de Géographie* 85 (1976): 155–77.

69. A good example being Sheila Fitzpatrick, *Everyday Stalinism: Ordinary Life in Extraordinary Times, Soviet Russia in the 1930s* (New York: Oxford University Press, 1999).

70. Hasso Spode has suggested for East Germany that the vacation and holiday offerings of the Free German Trade Union Federation to arrange holidays for workers and their families exceeded those of Strength through Joy in the thirties. See his edited volume, *Goldstrand und Teutonengrill: Kultur-und Sozialgeschichte des Tourismus in*

Deutschland (Berlin: Werner Moser, Verlag für universitäre Kommunikation, 1996). It is notable, however, that aside from one essay on Berlin, only three of twelve contributions deals with tourism in the GDR.

71. For tourism and imperialism, see the essays in Carol A. Breckenridge, ed., *Consuming Modernity: Public Culture in a South Asian World* (Minneapolis: University of Minnesota Press, 1995); Rosalie Schwartz, *Pleasure Island: Tourism and Temptation in Cuba* (Lincoln: University of Nebraska Press, 1997); Janice Lee Jayes, "'Strangers to Each Other': The American Encounter with Mexico, 1877–1910," Ph.D. diss., American University, 1999, and "The Fighting Man as Tourist: The Politics of Tourist Culture in Hawaii during World War II," *Pacific Historical Review* 65, no. 4 (1996): 641–60. See also Patrick Young, "'Dépaysé sans Être Abandonné': Tourism in French North Africa, 1900–1914," in "The Consumer as National Subject: Bourgeois Tourism in Third Republic France, 1871–1914," Ph.D. diss., Columbia University, 1999; and Barbara N. Ramusack, "Tourism and Icons: The Packaging of the Princely States of Rajasthan" in *Perceptions of South Asia's Visual Past,* ed. Catherine B. Asher and Thomas R. Metcalf (New Delhi: American Institute of Indian Studies, 1994), 235–55. For outstanding recent studies on the cultural and commercial impact of imperialism, see Anne McClintock, *Imperial Leather: Race, Gender, and Sexuality in the Colonial Contest* (New York: Routledge, 1995); Thomas Richards, *The Commodity Culture of Victorian England: Advertising and Spectacle, 1851–1914* (Stanford, Calif.: Stanford University Press, 1990); and Kristin Ross, *Fast Cars, Clean Bodies: Decolonization and the Reordering of French Culture* (Cambridge: MIT Press, 1995). For Germany, see Susanne Zantop, *Colonial Fantasies: Conquest, Family, and Nation in Precolonial Germany, 1770–1870* (Durham, N.C.: Duke University Press, 1997); and Sara Friedrichsmeyer, Sara Lennox, and Susanne Zantop, *The Imperialist Imagination: German Colonialism and Its Legacy* (Ann Arbor: University of Michigan Press, 1998). The best studies on colonial travel writing are Mary Louise Pratt, *Imperial Eyes: Travel Writing and Transculturation* (London: Routledge, 1992); and Inderpal Grewal, *Home and Harem: Nation, Gender, Empire, and the Cultures of Travel* (Durham, N.C.: Duke University Press, 1996).

72. As Mary Louise Pratt puts it, "contact zone" refers to "the space of colonial encounters, the space in which peoples geographically and historically separated come into contact with each other and establish ongoing relations, usually involving conditions of coercion, radical inequality, and intractable conflict. . . . A 'contact perspective' emphasizes how subjects are constituted in and by their relations to each other. It treats the relations among colonizers and colonized . . . not in terms of separateness or apartheid, but in terms of copresence, interaction, interlocking understandings and practices, often within radically asymmetrical relations of power" (*Imperial Eyes,* 6–7).

73. See John M. MacKenzie, ed., *Imperialism and Popular Culture* (Manchester: Manchester University Press, 1986); and Nicolas Bancel et al., eds., *Images et colonies: Iconographie et propagande coloniale sur l'Afrique française de 1880 à 1962* (Paris: ACHAC: Syros/Alternatives, 1993).

74. Our thanks to Vanessa Schwartz for this observation. See Ellen Furlough, "A Lesson of Things: Tourism, Empire, and the Nation to Interwar France." *French Historical Studies,* forthcoming.

75. On the role of travel in the complicity of colonial subjects in colonial systems, in this case Australians and the British empire, see Angela Woollacott, "'All This Is the Empire I Told Myself': Australian Women's Voyages 'Home' and the Articulation of Colonial Whiteness," *American Historical Review* 102 no. 4 (1997): 1003–29). Note as

well Tzvetan Todorov's discussion of travel, tourism, and exoticism in *On Human Diversity: Nationalism, Racism, and Exoticism in French Thought* (Cambridge, Mass.: Harvard University Press, 1993), esp. 300–352.

76. Ellen Furlough, "Packaging Pleasures: Club Méditerranée and French Consumer Culture, 1950–1968," *French Historical Studies* 18, no. 1 (1993): 65–81. On the labor force of skiing locales, see Coleman, "Unbearable Whiteness," 607.

PART 1

Tourism, Bourgeois Identity, and the Politics of Nation Building

The Tactics of Retreat

Spa Vacations and Bourgeois Identity in
Nineteenth-Century France

Under the pretext of bathing in warm water and drinking sulfur, I have
everyday a new, unexpected and marvelous spectacle.
                                              —Victor Hugo, 1843

Although beaches, casinos, resort towns, and so forth have all recently found
scholarly interest, historians of French holiday making have not always done
enough to "denaturalize" our familiarity with the cultural practices, social settings, and landscapes that have combined to stand as France's spatial and
human expressions of ideas about leisure and tourism.[1] Similarly, scholars of
French travel and vacationing have produced various kinds of histories—
institutional, local, and discursive being among the more important—without
seeking to explore where and when social and national identities were at least
partly formulated through the rise of modern modes of tourism and vacationing.[2] How national identities were framed and contested through the practice
of tourism, both in the nineteenth and the twentieth centuries, is an enormous
question that some of the essays of this volume seek at least partly to address.[3]
But the matter of social identity and its rapport with travel and holidays presents a more discrete and manageable subject, in that a particular segment of
French society can be assessed for the degree to which its modes of tourism
and vacationing served to construct class identity.[4]

In disentangling the threads of linkage between the processes of class formation and the rise of just one sort of leisure and touristic experience—the
spa vacation of the nineteenth century—this study will explore how and why
the bourgeoisie rhythmed its holidays to produce the distinctly medical and
"productive" beat that was the modern spa vacation.[5] Focusing on the period
1820–60, which was both the great era of spa medicalization and the epoch
when France's bourgeoisie saw its social, political, economic, and cultural
ascension, what I seek to reveal is how spas helped France's bourgeoisie to cre-

ate and refine an acceptable and "disciplined" practice of leisure on vacation. Enmeshed with overarching concepts like rationality, respectability, and the social authority of science, which, together, stood for something like an emerging bourgeois worldview, medicalization was an effective and appealing mode of order at the spas precisely because vacationers knew it in other guises, understood it, and welcomed it. Thus it is my largest argument that spas— because they architecturally, administratively, and medically produced leisured versions of privacy, decency, "time discipline," and other features of an embourgeoisement—constituted an important milieu where the emerging bourgeoisie would first move collectively to the peculiar rhythms of its rest.

Taking the waters at a French spa became an immensely popular practice over the course of the nineteenth century. With nearly one million annual visitors at the fin de siècle, French watering places had changed in a hundred year's time from outposts of aristocratic sociability and doctoring to become center-pieces of the modern vacation industry. Vichy, for example, which had had a summer population of only nine hundred persons in 1831, welcomed a total of sixteen thousand visitors in 1861, whereas by 1905 its summer population would swell to more than seventy thousand persons.[6] Comprising networks of transportation, the business of hospitality, health care administration, and excursion tourism, the spa milieu expanded over the century to become wildly profitable on local, regional, and national levels. Indeed, as an industry that employed many thousands of service personnel and builders—who saw to the maintenance and general operation of more than three hundred bathing establishments and the municipal facilities that webbed around the spas—this vital branch of the tourist economy created capital and jobs in mammoth proportions by the century's end.[7]

That spas would become so popular was hardly obvious to the entrepreneurs and doctors who first began to promote and develop them in the latter years of the First Empire.[8] On the contrary, these early experts in the fledgling tourist trade had to contend with the fact that the French Revolution had not only left most bathing establishments in ruins but had also scattered the mainstay of the spas' summer population—the nobility—all across the continent and to England. Yet if it took some imagination for local doctors to look at their neglected spas and see much reason for optimism, the vast expenses for improvement projects began to seem bearable enough when it became clear that many of the spas' aristocratic guests would return and be joined by the ranks of the French bourgeoisie.[9] Weekly visitor lists to the spas showed, already in the first years of the Restoration, the steadily rising presence of lawyers, architects, functionaries, entrepreneurs, and other guests who gave themselves a bourgeois designation.[10] And spa doctors, together with other administrators and local developers, immediately set to the business of understanding this emerging "market" and how it might best be captured.[11]

First and foremost on this agenda were projects that would transform the bathing places of France and their surrounding towns so as to accord with rising ideas about privacy and respectability. The mixing of rich and poor people in a spa locale or within a thermal establishment, which had been relatively common under the old regime as well as during the revolutionary and imperial eras, was everywhere decried in the era of the Restoration, 1815–30.[12] Spa developers more or less suddenly began issuing warnings that the "public order and tranquility" of their municipalities was threatened by the presence of indigent visitors.[13] And wealthy visitors, who could register their complaints at most bathing places in a series of books reserved for that purpose, now felt that poor bathers tended to be unruly and disturb the "silence so essential when taking the waters."[14] Local authorities in spa towns across France worried that their city's paths were "not guarded as they should be with gates and closures."[15] In reporting to the prefect of Allier in 1827, for example, municipal leaders of Bourbon l'Archambault sought to stress that their spa's new pavilion would feature such security measures as a fence, gates, and surveillance posts.[16] A show of order of this sort, or so one developer hoped, would insure that the "greatest possible propriety could be secured in the center of the village and on its public promenades."[17]

If the presence of poor bathers caused concern in spa municipalities during the Restoration and after, anxieties within French bathing establishments proper were infinitely higher. As the mayor of one spa town saw the situation, more discretion between the classes was an important demand of his market: "The persons of premier distinction who frequent our baths today wish to see adequate and separate facilities established for the less well-off patients."[18] And in a succinct corroboration of the mayor, a local spa doctor reported that "delicate people of the easy classes, and of course all children, find it upsetting to share the same water with disreputable persons."[19] With these desires so apparently strong among French spa-goers, it was probably inevitable that spa developers should recognize the "utility of having baths that would be uniquely the destination of the poor."[20] Vichy was first in the hospitalization movement, beginning work on a civil hospital for the poor in 1819 and completing the project over the next decade.[21] By the middle of the 1830s, most major thermal establishments in France had built not only separate bathing facilities for indigents but also hospitals in which they could be securely lodged for the duration of their stay.[22]

The rise of spa hospitals after 1830 did much to address the important issue of privacy at the spas, just as it seemed to articulate in a leisure locale the very anxieties that Louis Chevallier and others historians have analyzed for urban France in the period.[23] But privacy and discretion, as these concepts were understood in the thermal milieu and other bourgeois circles of the nineteenth century, were by no means solely matters of class. Even before the separation of indigent and elite bathers had been begun, it was already clear to spa developers that their thermal establishments had somehow become places—even when the question of the poor was not raised—that made people feel uncomfortable.[24] More than anything else, what troubled travelers and developers alike was the often reported "indecency" and "primitive distribution" of France's bathing establishments.[25] Collective bathing, which had already fallen into disfavor with many spa-goers of the later eighteenth century, had become by the 1820s entirely unacceptable to most visitors. Yet within virtually all of the major spas of France, bathing space continued to be collectively organized through the 1820s and into the 1830s. With large but shallow basins at their center, spas like Néris, Bagnères-de-Bigorre, and Aix-les-Bains prominently featured a recognizable version of the traditional group bath even after bathers had increasingly come to demand the "comfort and privacy" afforded by individual bath cabinets and their enclosed zinc bathtubs.[26]

In fact, wherever such comfortable and private facilities existed, their popularity all but rendered the old interior basin obsolete.[27] Where bath cabinets were not yet found, or where the capacity of only a few such rooms was insufficient to meet visitor demand, guests were frequently displeased. As one spa developer related in 1822, "People often complain upon their arrival, because it is impossible to find a proper bath in the bathing establishment."[28] These dissatisfied visitors, to the consternation of the doctors who were eager to treat them, frequently rented a bathtub in their rooming houses and paid a team of porters to deliver water from the spa's source.[29] The rise of such treatments, and the fact that they were scarcely profitable to a bathing institution, provided an abundantly clear example to spa developers of exactly how valued private facilities had become. Developers learned and acted upon this lesson with haste, and the 1820s and 1830s witnessed a revolution in the design of France's spa interiors.[30]

The alterations planned for Vichy's thermal facility in these years were typical of the new movement in spa design. Out of an establishment that had formerly been little more than a collection of open pools, there emerged a veritable monument to private bathing.[31] The new bath was built as a quadrangle, with each segment organized around an ornamental basin. There were twenty-three individual baths surrounding each basin, amounting to forty-six bathrooms on either side of the main hallway. Each bathroom was made sufficiently large so that its occupant could undress within, ending the old practice of having to change into one's bathing costume before arriving to take the waters. In the opinion of one doctor who had seen the plans for Vichy's new spa, the most important and novel feature of the establishment-in-progress was that "all the cabinets [were] completely isolated, each with its own commodious and spacious domestic style bath, the one from the other."[32] The high level of individual privacy was further guaranteed by an overarching organizational scheme whose function was to segregate the bathing cohort by gender. According to Vichy's developers and their counterparts at other French spas, women in particular were strong advocates of gender-specific bathing facilities. Male bathers, themselves so apparently immodest that bathing costumes had to be made a matter of regulation at Aix-les-Bains in 1832, typically conducted themselves in a manner that, according to one disgusted doctor, "regularly elicit[ed] strong complaints from foreign women."[33] Women, in their advocacy of separate baths, may well have specified exactly why common bathing had for them become "the cause of such embarrassment."[34] But when that advocacy was echoed by the developers of France's spas, as they complained of facilities that were "impossible" or able to "provide only the crudest services thinkable," the need for gendered baths was not justified in the specific and painful terms that contemporary women might have employed.[35] Rather, as one physician explained to the speculative group from which his spa drew the capital for its improvement project, "The service of men, conducted in perfect isolation from that of women, is mandated by morality, public decency and religion." The doctor further expounded that all such measures were "applauded by the majority of women."[36] Beginning with the completion of Vichy's establishment, which served men and women on opposite sides of its main corridor, gendered facilities proliferated throughout the spas of France, until such ordered interiors became a matter of state law.[37]

Beyond the spa milieu, of course, privacy assumed gendered and class-specific terms in many of the bourgeoisie's social arenas. Writ large on a city like Paris, for example, there emerged an expression of gendered or "separate" spheres that contemporaries and historians alike would notice and interrogate just as domestic interiors, perhaps more quickly and completely than the exteriors which bounded them, were mapped in the era of the spa's "reformation" according to gendered principles of privacy. While boulevards, parks, smoking rooms, libraries, and studies were cast as male space, so were drawing rooms, parlors, and museums made over into respectable havens for women. What the bourgeois applied to itself with respect to gendered spatializations of privacy, however, it did with the zeal of a people who liked the logic of privacy and its capacity to order social settings. Thus public works projects from this era, oriented toward the popular classes, reveal that bathhouses, hospitals, asylums and so forth all had come in fifty years time to enshrine the quest for modesty, decency, and respectability that spas of the nineteenth century would use gendered and classed space to achieve.

Certainly the built environment of the reformed spa went a long way toward tracing the contours that the bourgeois vacation would assume. But administrative practices, design principles, and the rise of private baths did not in and of themselves construct the cultural practices of spa-going in this period. Neither did these several features of the new spa contribute directly to the creation of a bourgeois conception of leisure. Indeed, the diverse practices that would comprise social behavior at the spas by midcentury and after were, during the Restoration and early years of the July Monarchy, almost entirely unscripted. Spas had attracted bathers for many centuries, but those earlier travelers had not gone to their vacations as bourgeois. Accordingly, the repertoire of practices that had been current at the old regime spa provided nineteenth-century tourists with only outdated examples of how, practically speaking, to conduct one's leisure in the thermal milieu.

Moreover, the very place of leisure in upper-class life had seen a drastic transformation since the latter years of the eighteenth century. Productivity had become an individual and collective attribute with which the bourgeoisie in its various social configurations liked to identify. For, as one historian of French society in the nineteenth century has written, "The first fact of life as a bourgeois was work."[38] Particularly during the Restoration and the 1830s, the endless work of a family firm or business was an exhausting burden that husbands and wives shared.[39] Diaries from the 1830s recount that spouses "would work long hours, often until midnight, in their . . . business."[40] Again and again, contemporaries of this period stressed that "everyone [involved in commerce] worked from 6 A.M. till 8 P.M. and went right to bed after dinner."[41] One historian of bourgeois families and commerce has noted that "few among [these people] did not deliberately spend most of their lives acquiring capital. Most boasted that they were the hardest workers in their factories or other enterprises—the first to arrive in the morning, the last to leave at night."[42] For these ambitious producers, therefore, neither the slothful excess of the working classes nor the decadence of aristocrats at play could stand as a means for understanding or organizing leisure.

Similarly, in the category of style of life, where affluent bourgeois could boast a quantity of leisure that probably approximated what aristocrats of the old regime had known, idleness and excesses of the flesh were everywhere supplanted in bourgeois sensibilities by a more constructive and purposeful pursuit of pleasure. But if gardening, social circles, novel reading, the collecting of natural specimens, and board games gave meaning and order to bourgeois leisure of the everyday, it was medicine generally—and the science of hydrotherapy more specifically—that would establish how one was to "do" a spa vacation and what the vacation's larger meanings would be to the French bourgeoisie.

The relationship between time and ideas of productivity was of keen importance to the bourgeoisie of the early nineteenth century. Not wishing to "waste" time or miss opportunities for learning, betterment, or the prosecution of work, commercial bourgeois and their counterparts in the professions were uneager to simply lay about as they made use of their leisure. For many of the same reasons that had seen factories and other "productive" sites adopt principles of time-discipline, spas, too pinned their order of operations to the dictates of a clock.[43] Efficiency was probably first among the concerns that prompted administrators in the thermal milieu to deploy their medicine in time-specific quantities. After all, the period of the Restoration saw a significant increase in the annual number of bathers at most spas. Vichy and other establishments began keeping their curative centers open around the clock, while at Aix-les-Bains and elsewhere, bathers had to take great care to be on time for their cures. Reserved in advance by as much as a week, cure sessions were supposed to begin promptly according to a well-posted schedule. At tightly scheduled spas, tardiness was treated as a serious offense. First-time delinquents were warned at these establishments not to be late for curing a second time, for subsequent tardiness was punished by the patients having to "forfeit medical examinations and all rights to the diverse medical cleansing services of the day."[44]

But desires on the part of medical authorities to make hydrotherapy seem more rational and credible undoubtedly outweighed the issue of efficiency in the thinking of France's bath administrators. Spa doctors in this period and later found themselves constantly having to defend their favored mode of treatment. Clearly, the temporal reorganization of bathing served some of the same representational purposes as individuated bathing cabinets, gendered interiors, and carefully calibrated systems of surveillance. Like these spatial characteristics of the new spas, time-discipline subjected the experience of bathing to a rationalizing process of compartmentalization and incrementalization. Thus practitioners, who still found it necessary in the 1850s to declare that "mineral waters are a serious remedy that cure maladies by themselves and solely as a function of their chemical properties,"[45] often used references to time-discipline as a subtle commentary on the seriousness of hydrotherapeutic medicine. In one such defense of spa medicine, a doctor warned his readers that "all newly arrived bathers had to know one thing related to the amount of time that should be spent in bathing." Too many bathers, this doctor stressed, wrongly believed "that the value of mineral water is increased by prolonging a bath." On the contrary, this practitioner and his medical colleagues sought to stress, successful bathing depended on careful medical administration of mineral water. And baths, which spa physicians warned had to be "taken at precisely the temperature prescribed by the patient's doctor," were not to be wallowed in as though their waters were merely warm and pleasing.[46] In this way, the increasingly strict incrementalization of thermal medical practice, which cast the water cure and its practitioners in a serious and scientific light, was itself an indirect form of spa promotion.

Bathing establishments proper were the seat of medical authority in the thermal milieu, and it was within these facilities that the medicalization of free time was most fully realized.[47] At larger or thoroughly renovated spas, for instance, bells were often installed to mark the passage of medical time. This way, if warm waters had somehow lulled a patient into such a state of repose as to forget a doctor's prescriptions, institutional reminders were always at hand. But bells hardly replaced the presence of administrators in a spa's corridors or attendants within the bathing cabinets themselves. For these staff members, as personnel rules from the period never failed to stress, were ultimately responsible for the timely circulation of patients through an establishment's facilities.

Regardless of how time-discipline was made systematic at the spas, there was little variation as to the seriousness with which doctors and other administrators applied its principles. Spas routinely issued medical and administrative guidelines stipulating specific instructions for the duration of cures. And such rules left decidedly little room for misinterpretation on the part of bathers. Baths, for example, which were considered to be the most gentle type of cure at most establishments, seldom continued beyond one hour and fifteen minutes. While more extreme forms of hydrotherapy, such as the high-pressure *douche massage,* virtually never continued beyond twenty minutes.

By the Revolution of 1830 or very shortly thereafter, French bathing places began to seem like medical institutions to a degree that they never had before.[48] Doctors took control of the thermal milieu to such an extent that spas all across France made it virtually illegal for anyone to bathe without having first consulted with an accredited physician.[49] As the posted rules at one establishment summarized, "All persons who wish to use the waters, showers, or vapors are required to obtain a medical certificate."[50] More than the padding of French doctors' pockets, required consultations went a long way toward enrolling healthy tourists in a highly regimented course of medical treatment. For, as one spa physician wrote in 1841, "a single case has not [fallen] under my observation in which careful examination could not detect a deranged state in the [body's] functions."[51]

Doctors agreed that the effectiveness of mineral water cures depended upon little more than the patient's willingness to "suspend all affairs" in favor of a "sane and regular regime."[52] That regularity, more than anything else, was based on an intensely close relationship between doctor and patient. Dr. Victor Noyer of Vichy stated the importance of this relationship clearly enough as he expressed, too, the extent to which physicians were to have authority over the lives of their patients: "In order to gain all the advantages promised by the waters . . . the patient, when on vacation, must follow exactly whatever advice he is given by his doctor."[53] Indeed most spa-goers began each of their twenty-one days on vacation with at least a brief medical consultation. In virtually all cases, spa doctors attempted to establish a medical perimeter in which curists were to conduct themselves during their holidays. Part of the hydrotherapeutic regimen, for example, sought to monitor the level of mental activity in which patients engaged. A noted practitioner at Aix-les-Bains who wrote extensively on this issue, Dr. Auguste Forestier, advised spa-goers to "leave all thoughts of weighty matters at the door of the thermal establishment."[54] Worries about one's profession or business, these doctors warned, would necessarily interfere with the success of the cure. Even artists and poets were told to ignore their muses, for "passions of the soul" had to be limited too in order for hydrotherapy to achieve its potential.[55] In the same spirit, doctors routinely advised their patients to maintain a low level of social contact and fight "the great temptation . . . to join the social circle."[56] The "risk" of too much sociability and mental activity, doctors lamented, was simply "not worth the consequences which it entailed."[57] Or, as one especially curmudgeonly practitioner stated the situation, "I should strongly advise invalids to frequent the salon as little as possible in the evenings."[58]

Prescriptions concerning eating and drinking were part of the hydrotherapeutic regimen, too.[59] Spa hotels typically boasted bountiful tables, but doctors warned their patients to avoid indulging excessively. Most doctors offered only general prescriptions in this context, usually counseling patients to "eat only light meals at regular intervals."[60] Indeed, a "well researched and healthy diet," while not easily maintained in the face of an "appetite that [could be] overactivated by the change of air," was, in the studied opinion of the spas' medical experts, "a necessary foundation for any successful course of hydrotherapy."[61] As one practitioner stated the matter, "the importance of establishing and carrying out a suitable diet, or of initiating desirable changes in dietary habits, in connection with a course of mineral waters, cannot be over-estimated."[62] The fact that doctors could create a dietary regimen for their patients and, at least in part, oversee patient compliance was, in the opinion of spa practitioners, "one of the great advantages attending this method of treatment."[63]

Beyond the medicalization of these several components of spa life, doctors sought to create for patients a comprehensive regimen—a daily rhythm that organized in full nearly every hour of a patient's leisure according to the dictates of hydrotherapeutic medicine. Doctors went so far as to establish, both in their guidebooks and among the patients on whom they practiced, a daily schedule that assigned specific times for waking, eating, exercising, thermal curing, resting, walking, and going to bed.[64] Thus, as one doctor at Vichy wrote regarding his patients' mornings, "early hours are the rule here."[65] By this, the doctor meant that "at six o'clock [in the morning], drinking and bathing commence[d] seriously."[66] Those whose prescriptions called for the drinking of mineral water were encouraged to "drink water gradually [while] chatting and promenading."[67] Then, after their baths, they were told to allow for "a half and hour or an hour of absolute repose."[68]

Upon completing one's cure, spa afternoons offered a generous share of amusements and distractions. Bands and orchestras played at regular intervals throughout the day, and doctors' only advice to their patients was to not enjoy these pleasures at the expense of their prescribed walks. Rather, doctors counseled patients to promenade while they listened to such performances. This combination, doctors stressed, was the most healthful and safe way to "fill-up . . . the afternoons until the evening meal at five or six."[69]

Evening, by contrast, was not thought to be a medically "safe" time of day by most physicians. Prescriptions concerning mental exercise, sociability, and diet clearly cast spa doctors as the opponents of the thermal milieu's after-dark pleasures. Casinos, balls, theatrical productions, and orchestral concerts were featured at least weekly during the summer season at most larger spas. And there can be little doubt that these distractions were frequented by many if not most patients. For these patients, after all, were, in large numbers, not in any way the desperate invalids that their daily regimens suggested. Regardless of this fact, doctors did all that they could to frighten their patients into at least a measured and moderate pursuit of evening pleasures. For, as one doctor summarized the opinion of many of his professional associates with respect to the evening pleasures at spa, "in these [amusements], with their attendant evils, invalids do join, and from them they suffer."[70]

Above all else, doctors warned, "it was always advisable to be under cover at, and for an hour or two after, sundown when the temperature falls considerably."[71] But being indoors, especially in a ballroom or a casino, was thought by doctors to be almost as dangerous as the chilled outdoors. As one doctor wrote, such facilities tended to have "poor ventilation" that was only exacerbated by "overcrowding." This "injurious atmosphere," doctors recognized, was a "consequence of the population of seasonal visitors who [knew] each other" and their understandable desire for "social entertainments, balls, dinners and theatrical . . . events."[72]

The nineteenth century saw hydrotherapy emerge as an increasingly well defined science with highly differentiated medical applications. Accordingly, spa doctors had an ever-expanding arsenal of diagnostic, prescriptive, and therapeutic principles in which to ground their rising authority over the practice of thermal leisure. But even as the perimeter of spa medicine grew to include a host of new curative techniques, there emerged within French baths something like a standard or routine course of treatment. Virtually every spa-goer received from her or his doctor a prescription to bathe in and drink mineral water.[73] The former of these treatments was a perennial favorite among French spa-goers and had been for centuries. By the middle 1840s, for instance, when a large spa like Aix-les-Bains was seeing around twenty-five hundred visitors each year, the bathing establishment was issuing more than eighty-five hundred tickets to its private bathtubs.[74] More detailed accounting of bathing at Bourbon l'Archambault, from records kept in the 1820s, reveals that of 111 spa visitors in the summer, only 15 did not have at least an immersion in a bathtub. The 96 persons who bathed at Bourbon in this period took a total of 1,438 baths, for an average of around fourteen baths per person. Indeed, fully one-third of those who bathed at all took at least a one bath per day.[75] Doctors wished for their patients to recognize that bathing, though it might feel pleasing to the body, was an entirely medical procedure. "It [was] only the doctor," wrote one physician, "who [could] appreciate the need for a bath and determine the duration for bathing as well as make decisions regarding temperature."[76] No longer anything like the crude science of the old regime, hydrotherapeutic bathing had to be practiced with great precision, "because," as doctors recognized, "a bath taken at a slightly elevated or lowered temperature [could] alter completely the intended results."[77]

In addition to offering specific prescriptions as to how long a patient was to bathe, spa doctors medicalized the very practice of bathing. Thus, as one doctor described, patients were to enter a bath cabinet only when they were calm and collected. For, as this doctor stressed, "it [was] dangerous to bathe when heated or perspiring." To insure medical effectiveness, doctors warned that "persons taking a whole bath should immerse themselves into the water only by slow degrees, up to the neck, having previously sponged the chest and abdomen with the bath water." After this cautious introduction of the body to the water, patients were instructed to lie calm and still. At predetermined intervals in the bathing hour, however, this repose was interrupted by the reappearance of bath attendants whose task it was to "use friction, by means of a brush or sponge," to stimulate the patient's skin. Patients were told not to relax too much when bathing, just as they were counseled to avoid sleeping immediately after curing. For fatigue, either during or after bathing, tended to "spoil the appetite, weaken the patient and put him out of humor all day."[78]

This relatively passive and pleasant form of therapy, however, were little more than a curist's introduction to the medical arts of the spa. Indeed, hydrotherapy routinely became a punishing and even painful tonic for many bathers, especially those whose health was solid enough to weather a more extreme form of therapeutics. Cold-water cures enjoyed a great vogue among the hydrotherapeutic medical community after their apparent success in French asylums and at the seaside watering places of France and England.[79] Less popular by far at spas than simple baths, cold cures were, nevertheless, routinely prescribed by spa doctors from the 1830s onward.[80] One form of this therapy, known as the "wet sheet treatment," was employed at many of France's Alpine spas. The wet sheet bath required that a wide sheet be left in frigid water for a period of several hours. At a predetermined hour, the frosty cloth was removed from its tub and immediately wrapped around an awaiting patient. Proper technique called for many woolen blankets to then be dumped on the sheeted curist and, finally, for the entire wrap to be secured at the patient's feet and throat. Left, in one survivor's account, "bound head and foot in a state of utter helplessness," the cold curist was liberated only after beginning to feel warm again.[81] The wet sheet bath usually lasted no longer than an hour, but its critics certainly felt that amount of time was plenty to endure. Writing about his experience under the wet sheet, one patient recounted, "I could scarcely refrain from screaming out; indeed it is quite possible that I did scream."[82]

More commonly administered than the wet sheet treatment, cold-water showers and baths required just as much strength and stamina to endure. Usually reserved for women whose "profuse menstruation of the constitutional origin" had rendered them uncomfortable or infertile, cold-water immersions were nothing if not punishing and disciplining experiences.[83] Patients unlucky enough to get this prescription, called the Scotch Shower at most spas, after the Scottish reputation for enjoying constitutions of the cold and wet sort, usually had to take up to fifteen minutes or more of a freezing cold bath or shower. Showering was by far the more common mode of treatment—Aix-les-Bains administered nearly four thousand of these treatments each year of the 1820s to a bathing population of less than twenty-five hundred—and many spas installed handhold bars and other special facilities to accommodate the therapy.[84] Because the freezing water of these showers was routinely propelled from a height of fifteen feet or more, it reached the curists in a relentless blast that patients described as being "a liquid needle as thick as a man's arm."[85] One such curist recalled how in the wake of her shower that "the whole surface of my body, even my hands and face, became very sensitive to the touch of cold water." Further, she recounted that her "nerves [had been] laid bare [and that she was] left with a perfect horror of cold water, a kind of hydrophobia."[86]

Another form of French hydrotherapy introduced patients to a combination of hot and extraordinarily pressurized water. Usually administered in a small stall underneath a bathing establishment's principal facilities—where intense humidity and the stench of sulphur or alkaline vapors made it difficult for patients to breathe—these cures were both officially and popularly known as "the showers of hell."[87] While not as commonly prescribed as many other forms of hydrotherapy, these cures were hardly unknown. At Aix-les-Bains through the 1840s, each summer nearly two thousand of these treatments were performed—on a bathing population that was less than three thousand persons.[88] Especially suited to combat skin diseases and rashes of many sorts, hot showers required great caution on the doctor's part. For too much exposure to the curative properties of the hot shower, doctors warned, could have truly painful side effects. Particularly among patients with a sensitive constitution, such scalding waters tended to blister the skin and cause it to fall off. Like the bathing cells used for cold-water showering, the chambers used in these cures were equipped with handhold bars to help besieged patients steady themselves.

Mud baths offered some of the same sensations that patients experienced in the hot shower. But in the mud bath, a patient's movements were almost entirely constrained. Buried beneath many pounds of mud—typically heated to a temperature of more than 120 degrees and then quickly dumped upon the curist—patients were instructed to lie as still as possible.[89] The deeply heated mud invariably caused the patient an intense burning sensation. But, doctors stressed, this sense of burning disappeared quickly if the patient agreed to remain motionless. Doctors warned that "when, however, a limb is moved, and therefore the relative position of the mud to the skin changes, the intense heat is again felt.[90] The mud used in these operations was not just any mud. Carefully collected from earthen pools that were richly penetrated by thermal waters, therapeutic mud was scientifically quantified and prescribed accordingly. Thus, depending on whether a patient's complaint was gouty or rheumatic in origin, doctors favored certain muds and avoided others.

Extreme confinement and steamed heat were other unpleasant characteristics of certain medical procedures at the spas of this period. The vapor-box bath was among the more widely prescribed and torturous of all hydrotherapeutic techniques. These baths were conducted in miniature wooden cells whose dimensions were only slightly greater than a patient's body. As one guide described it, the vapor bath was conducted within "a curious wooden box with a round hole in its moveable lid." The hole allowed the patient's neck and head to remain at liberty from the box bath. The balance of the patient's body was assaulted with a steam-curing whose extreme heat regularly surpassed 150 degrees Fahrenheit and caused an increase in body temperature of three to four degrees.[91]

Even in the writing of spa promoters, box bathing was not gently or charitably described. In one doctor's testimony, the typical vapor bath began painlessly enough:

> After undressing, he steps into the wooden box and finds that he is shut in all except the head, the round hole being occupied by his neck. Immediately a valve on the level of the floor is opened, the hot vapor rises about him and he soon begins to perspire freely.

DOUCHE BERTHOLET.

Par force, ou par bonne volonté !!!

» Parlez-moi d'une invention comme celle-là, si le
» malade est méchant, le Doucheur est à l'abri! »

"By force or by a good choking." The tortuous extremes of vapor box bathing, according to a caricaturist of the Second Empire. (Reprinted from Nicole Pagotto, *Le Thermalisme à Aix-les-Bains au dix-neuvième siècle* [Chambéry: Institut d'Études Savoisiennes, 1975].)

But, as the doctor went on to describe, the bather was not cooled by "the perspiration, running now from his brow and trickling down his face." The heavy sweating was instead a ticklishly hot irritant that the patient, whose arms and hands were confined within the bathing case, could do little to relieve. Meanwhile, within the vapor box, the patient—as "he feels the steam flowing down his sides and legs"—had to endure "an extreme feeling of oppression and debility."[92] As another spa doctor described it, patients inevitably had a "subjective sense of burning in the skin" in the moments before their cure was completed.[93]

But if doctors were candid as to the unpleasantness of vapor bathing, they were by no means willing to let this form of hydrotherapeutics—or any other for that matter—fall victim to an entirely negative set of representations. For spa doctors, hygiene—just as it had informed the spatial and representational goals that spa physicians had sought to achieve in the interiors of their new buildings—had to be clearly established throughout their therapeutic realm. As this doctor and guidebook author stated plainly enough, "floors, walls and all the apparatus used should always be kept perfectly clean." Notwithstanding the medical motives behind such hygienic impulses, however, the doctor stressed that it was what hygiene represented that made its value in the spas so great:

> Not only should they be clean, but, for the sake of the impression on the patient's mind, they should always look clean. It must be owned that the sight of box vapor baths, the seats used for rectal douches and other apparatus, is often anything but pleasant; although they may in reality be clean, yet owing to discoloration and want of repair, they often look dirty.[94]

In other words, vapor boxes and other highly medicalized examples of the new hydrotherapeutics required a certain level of maintenance with respect to patients' sensibilities. The medically justifiable discomfort associated with such cures could be borne by patients only if the entire treatment scenario was conducted within a scientific context. And that context was both easily and dramatically achieved through the representational virtues of hygiene.

Of all active hydrotherapeutic procedures developed and prescribed by spa doctors of this era—which is to exclude water drinking, simple bathing, and swimming cures—none was experienced by more patients than the so-called douche or shower massager. Out of an annual total of bathing operations that approached twenty thousand at larger spas already in the 1820s, shower massages accounted for nearly three-fourths of that number.[95] This ratio changed very little throughout the period of the July Monarchy and after. In the 1840s at Aix-les-Bains, for instance, a curist population of approximately twenty-five hundred to three thousand persons was administered nearly seventeen thousand courses of the shower massage—compared with fewer than five thousand swimming or bathtub cures.[96] Of the 111 visitors to Bourbon l'Archambault in one period of 1824, for example, fully 50 persons took eighteen or more courses of a shower treatment.[97] Unlike cold-water cures and vapor bathing, which curists experienced only occasionally during a spa holiday, the scalding water of the shower bath was a regular part of their

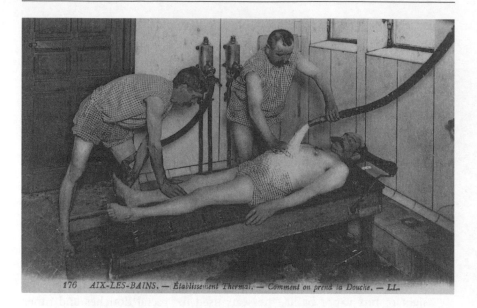

176   AIX-LES-BAINS. — Établissement Thermal. — Comment on prend la Douche. — LL.

A full-body douche massage in progress. (Reprinted from Jean-Pierre
Leguay, *Histoire d'Aix-les-Bains et sa région: Une grand station thermale*
[Aix: Avenir, 1988].)

lives—such cures were typically conducted every second or third day of a
patient's stay at a spa.[98]

The spa shower was a form of hydrotherapy that derived its purported
curative force from a careful combination of mineral waters and massage.
Most commonly given to patients with rheumatic symptoms, shower massages were administered in a special chair that allowed for both sitting and
reclining. The typical cure, as one doctor described it later in the century,
involved an "attendant pour[ing] water over the body from a hose, while, at
the same time, [another] attendant shampoo[ed], knead[ed] and rub[bed]
according to the directions given by the physician."[99] There was hardly a medical complaint imaginable for which doctors were not willing to prescribe a
steady course of the shower massage, provided that the patient in question was
healthy enough to bear such treatment.

Perhaps no hydrotherapeutic system relied more on complicated technology and scientific administration than did these showers. Such cures
depended upon a complex array of hoses and water gauges to insure that
patients received the thermal product at the correct temperature and volume.
The perfect calibration of these various mechanisms, all doctors stressed,
determined the degree to which the cure either succeeded or failed. In this
technology, even proponents of strictly differentiated therapeutics could take

solace, because the infinite gradations and combinations of temperature, types of mineral water, and force created a curative system that differed vastly according to medical conditions.[100]

No amount of properly deployed technology, however, could compensate for the fact that the shower massage was often an uncomfortable and even painful form of medicine. As one doctor recounted, having visited a number of French spas to study the development of hydrotherapeutics and follow a course of therapy at Aix-les-Bains, this technique stopped just short of being brutal in some of its side effects. "I myself," the doctor wrote, "experienced an extraordinarily unpleasant sensation during my first shower and immediately after it." This sensation, he hastened to add, was not present in the "initial ten or twelve minutes of the shower," during which his feet, legs, and shoulders were "masterfully" and "vigorously" rubbed.[101] By the session's end, however, the temperature and force of the shower's water had been recalibrated to an extreme degree. Simultaneously, the strong hands of his technicians had kneaded his upper and lower body to the point of an excruciating exhaustion. As a result, the doctor left his treatment breathless and in the throes of a pounding pulse and headache.

Yet his greatest discomfort still awaited the beleaguered doctor, for once he was placed within his bath chair, whose porters immediately began carrying him toward his hotel, the doctor "experienced an overwhelming sense of suffocation and an unprecedented rush of blood to the head." Feeling "flushed and powerfully oppressed," he "demanded" to be let out of his bath chair. Only when he could breath "fresh air" and gulp "several glasses of cool water" did the doctor's painful reaction to the massage begin to subside.[102] Because of his own authority as a doctor, this patient's subsequent experiences with the douche were vastly different. The doctor merely assigned himself a kinder course of therapy: he had, after all, enjoyed his first moments in the bath technicians' hands.

From the first years of the 1850s, spa administrations all over France had begun to count their seasonal population in two separate categories. The first of these, which had been the sole figure of great interest authorities since the Restoration, was the number of persons who purchased admission cards to a bathing facility and followed a course of hydrotherapeutic treatment. The new statistic, however, measured the number of people who visited a spa municipality without registering to cure. More than the unpleasant fact that both numbers now needed counting, what horrified spa doctors everywhere by the middle of the 1860s was that the number of noncurists had begun to surpass at most spas the number of actual curists.[103]

The gradual and partial migration away from the spas' treatment centers obviously did not bode well for the profitability of French thermal establishments, and spa practitioners mobilized as best they could to fight it. The way they chose to compete for disinclined curists was to soften as best they could the harsher medical regimes of hydrotherapy. The government of the Second Empire and the French Academy of Medicine both helped in this regard, by formally stipulating in 1860 that no spa could require its patients to consult with a doctor before taking the waters.[104] Individual spa doctors and publicists did more by way of relinquishing a measure of medical control over the spa experience.[105] Aix-les-Bains' Dr. Berthet, for example, in his medical and topographical guide of 1862, cautiously denounced important aspects of the hydrotherapeutic regimen he and his colleagues had but recently established. Regarding food and drink, for instance, Berthet promised that "taking the waters imposed no dietary restrictions of any kind . . . people [could] and should follow their own inclinations and habits."[106]

Moreover, Berthet addressed the issue of medicalized leisure, explaining that the hydrotherapeutic system was little more than a harmless form of role-playing. Berthet wrote that new curists should not be surprised "to see, from time to time, the 'sad' figure of some patient, carefully enveloped in a closed chaise a porteur." But this "spectacle," Berthet noted, was illusory rather than real. For, as the doctor explained, "the young and pretty people who pass in this manner, imprisoned in toweling that shrouds a delicate body whose expiration seems imminent, should not sadden anyone." On the contrary, Berthet wrote, "these people, these immobile and mute invalids who leave the bathing establishment carried like cadavers, having grimaced and suffered through their treatments—these are the same people who appear in the evening, elegantly dressed and with fresh, happy, and healthy faces, dancing at the ball."[107]

The miraculous transformations Berthet described would continue to the century's end and beyond to be signatures of the spa experience for many visitors, either through personal resurrections or the witnessing of such events. Yet the gradual ebbing of medicalized leisure, against which Berthet and other doctors mobilized, would continue throughout the latter decades of the century. Accounting for the slow but steady diminishment of medicalized leisure after 1850 is not easy, yet three visions of the shifting terms of the bourgeois vacation seem to be worth some consideration. First, it has to be understood that the statistics around bathing and vacationing are just as difficult to use as are tallies of other kinds. Thus, because all bathers were no longer required to see doctors after 1850, it is at least possible that the medically driven logic for accurate counting was lost and that more people cured than the spas ever counted in the later period. Secondly, the apparent decline of medicalized leisure coincided with the beginnings of tourism and curism for the French middle classes, which is say that middle segment of the bourgeoisie whose economic and political prominence would be generally revealed only in the latter decades of the century. Prefiguring this rise to social importance of the middling bourgeoisie were the successful efforts of railroad marketers and travel promoters, the combined efforts of which packaged vacationing such that these lesser bourgeois were enticed to travel in significant numbers in the years after midcentury. If many of these new visitors would try hydrotherapy and even follow its dictatorial and disciplining terms, which would account for the fact that the number of medical curist increased at every major spa in the latter decades of the nineteenth century, then it is also clear that most new-comers to spas went on holidays in this period that would include little or no medicine.[108]

The most fulfilling explanation for the weakening of hydrotherapy's hold over bourgeois vacationing seems to be that a critical mass of the bourgeoisie, by the middle decades of the century, had acquired extensive experience in the arts of leisure practice. Although still respecting of medical authority and doctors, spa-goers no longer needed doctors or medical principles to give order and purposefulness to the time of their vacations. Instead of seeking a medicalized mode of leisure that implanted productivity where uncertainty might otherwise have taken root, many bourgeois vacationers went to spas in the latter half of the nineteenth century confident of who they were. The complex processes of identity formation, which spa medicine had bolstered and would continue to gird—if with less urgency—through the rest of the century, had reached by the 1850s a point where those "things" that the bourgeoisie had come to recognize as the cornerstones of a lifestyle—taste and comfort—would start to transform leisure according to a fashion whose terms were not those of the clinic.

NOTES

1. Several important studies on the French vacation include Patrice Boussel, *Histoire des vacances* (Paris: Éditions Berger-Levrault, 1961); Gaston Féneyrou, *La Vie des eaux thermo-minérales* (Toulouse: Editions Erés, 1989); Paul Gerbod, "Les Fièvres thermales en France au 19e siècle," *Revue Historique* 562 (April 1987); Institut Français d'Architecture, *Villes d'eaux en France* (Paris: Hazan, 1985); more recent and synthetic histories include Alain Corbin, ed. *L'Avènement des loisirs, 1850–1960* (Paris: Aubier, 1995); and André Rauch, *Vancaes en France: De 1830 à nos jours* (Paris: Hachette, 1996).

2. Important institutional and local histories of French leisure locales include James Haug, *Leisure and Urbanism in Nineteenth-Century Nice* (Lawrence: Regents Press of Kansas, 1982); Jean Aubert, *En Auvergne: Les villes d'eaux autrefois* (Lyon: Horvath, 1993); P. Bouloumie, *Histoire de Vittel* (Paris: Maloine, 1925); Jean-Pierre Bousquet, *Enghien-les-Bains en 1900: L'histoire du lac et des bains d'Enghien vue en cartes postales* (Paris: Cofimag, 1983); G. Frieh, *Le Grand Cercle d'Aix-les-Bains: Histoire d'un casino* (Aix: Musumeci Éditeur, 1984); Christian Jamot, *Thermalisme et les villes thermales en France* (Clermont-Ferrand: Institut d'Études du Massif Central, 1988); Dominique Jarrasse, *Les Thermes romantiques: Bains et villégiatures en France de 1800 à 1850* (Clermont-Ferrand: Institut d'Études du Massif Central, 1992); studies of vaca-

tioning with a discursive orientation include most notably Alain Corbin, *Le Territoire du vide: l'Occident et le désir du rivage* (1750–1840), (Paris: Aubier, 1988); also see Barbara Benedict, "The Printed Resort: Erotic Consumption and the Gender of Leisure in Eighteenth-Century Spa Literature," typescript, available from the author.

3. For a tentative beginning to what I intend to produce by way of a synthetic study of tourism and national identity in France, see my essay "The Lost Provinces Revisited: Touristic Framings of Frenchness in Alsace-Lorraine, 1870–1919," available upon request from the author.

4. For challenging interpretations on the relationship between leisure and class, especially on the moralizing aspects of leisure reform in nineteenth-century England, see P. Bailey, *Leisure and Class and Victorian England: Rational Recreation and the Contest for Control, 1830–1885* (London: Routledge, 1987); Hugh Cunningham, *Leisure in the Industrial Revolution, 1780–1880* (New York: St. Martin's Press, 1980); and Anthony Hern, *The Seaside Holiday: The History of the English Seaside Resort* (New York: Hilary House, 1967).

5. It is problematical to designate any set of cultural attributes as being "bourgeois," for the nineteenth century or for any other epoch. Yet commonalities in political, social, economic, and gender organizations of class experience surely did give at least some semblance of class order to what contemporaries called the bourgeoisie. For recent assessments of bourgeois sensibilities, which follow the methodology of the "new cultural history," see Catherine Kudlick, *Cholera in Post-revolutionary Paris: A Cultural History* (Berkeley and Los Angeles: University of California Press, 1996); Philippe Perrot, *Fashioning the Bourgeoisie: A History of Clothing in the Nineteenth Century*, trans. Richard Bienvenu (Princeton, N.J.: Princeton University Press, 1994); Whitney Walton, *France at the Crystal Palace: Bourgeois Taste and Artisan Manufacture in the Nineteenth Century* (Berkeley and Los Angeles: University of California Press, 1992); Leora Auslander, *Taste and Power: Furnishing Modern France* (Berkeley and Los Angeles: University of California Press, 1996).

6. Aix-les-Bains saw a similar pattern of growth, although its statistics were less impressive. From a bathing population of twenty-three hundred in 1830, Aix more than doubled its total summer population by 1861. And within thirty more years, the municipality could boast a summer population that approached thirty thousand tourists. Douglas P. Mackaman, *Leisure Settings: Bourgeois Culture, Medicine, and the Spa in Modern France* (Chicago: University of Chicago Press, 1998), 65.

7. In the larger spa cities, it was common to find more than two-thirds of the active population working in the thermal industry. In all of France, the thermal industry employed at least half a million persons by 1900. In the same year, the industry generated more than three hundred million francs (Mackaman, *Leisure Settings,* 66).

8. It was standard practice at every thermal establishment in France for the resident medical inspector, who was the head practitioner of a given spa, to file a formal and exhaustive report with the Royal Academy of Medicine for each thermal season. The reports considered equally medical, administrative, surveillance and fiscal affairs. This procedure, adopted at Aix-les-Bains under the French occupation, was followed there even after the Sardinian monarchy regained control of the Savoy and Aix's spa in the Restoration. For an interesting secondary account of the French medical inspectorate and its decline in the nineteenth century, see George Weisz, "Water Cures and Science: The French Academy of Medicine and Mineral Waters in the Nineteenth-Century," *Bulletin of the History of Medicine* 64, no. 3 (1990): 393–416. The estimate of France's spa population comes from Anne Martin-Fugier, *La Vie élégante ou la formation du Tout-Paris, 1815–1848* (Paris: Fayard, 1990), 120.

9. Indeed, upper-class bathers began to embrace spa-going in the early nineteenth century in far greater numbers than ever during the old regime. At Aix-les-Bains in Savoy, for example, more than twice as many voyagers were counted in each year of the decade after 1810 than the five hundred or so annual visitors in the 1780s. "Rapport du médecin inspecteur des bains d'Aix-en-Savoie sur l'exercise de l'année 1818," Archives Departementales de la Savoie: 1FS 2803 (hereafter cited as AD Savoie). By 1820, Aix and many other spas were welcoming three times the number of visitors they had typically seen in the later years of the old regime. Scattered throughout more than two dozen notable spa towns, a visiting population of more than thirty-one thousand persons went on vacation in each year of the 1820s. In annual reports that dutifully noted the name, domicile, local addresses, and bathing activity of every summer visitor, administrators verified that their affluent visitors were indeed no longer almost exclusively noble in origin. Archives municipales d'Aix-les-Bains: I 120.

10. The spas all began keeping and publishing weekly "lists of visitors" during the early 1820s, a practice that would continue throughout the century. These lists showed that the bourgeoisie was emerging in the 1820s and 1830s as a major group among spa visitors. One such list, for example, compiled by the municipal authorities of Aix-les-Bains for the first week of July 1820, noted the arrival of 126 individuals or families. This was not the sum total of Aix's summer population at the time, of course, because arrivals from at least the preceding two weeks were probably still in residence. After declaring their names and cities of origin, nearly half of these visitors chose to add information with respect to the source of their livelihood. Of the fifty-eight heads of families who identified the source of their livelihood, thirty-one labeled themselves as proprietors or landowners. There were seven lawyers, three government employees, one book merchant, one architect, one entrepreneur, one merchant, and three priests. Only two persons on the list had noble titles; one was a count and the other was a countess. Lists from other thermal establishments suggest the same trends in the 1820s (AD Savoie: 1FS 2804). At Bourbon l'Archambault, for example, of 111 bathers registered during the 1824 season, only 18 appear to have been of the nobility. Archives Departementales d'Allier, Series X (cited hereafter as AD Allier). Similar lists from the 1830s and 1840s showed the continued presence of bourgeois spa-goers clearly enough. Between June 25 and 30, 1834, for example, ninety-five individuals or familial groups arrived in Aix-les-Bains. In these five days, no fewer than fifteen members of the bourgeois professions, eleven of whom were lawyers, went to the spa—as compared to only three persons with noble titles.

11. Ibid. The spa had became even more apparently bourgeois by the 1840s. On June 8, 9, and 10, 1842, forty heads of families arrived in the city of Aix-les-Bains. Only six from this group failed to provide biographical information regarding the source of their wealth. Of the thirty-four who did list such information, thirteen described themselves as property owners, six were lawyers, six were doctors, four were priests, three were employees of the state, and two were manufacturers. Only two nobles appeared on this list; one was a count and the other was a baron. Not even counting those who listed themselves as being owners of property, nearly half of the arrivals appear to have been bourgeois.

12. As a local historian of Plombières noted in 1748, basins were public and social places that made no allowances for modesty. For in these baths, the historian described, people "bathe[d] indiscriminately, men, women, children, priests, monks, nuns all in the same pool and almost naked." Dom Calmet, *Traité historique des eaux et des bains de Plombières* (1748), cited in Institut Français d'Architecture, *Villes d'eaux en France* (Paris: Hazan, 1985), 336. In certain locales, such as at Aix-les-Bains, spa

basins hardly even separated their human users from the lame or otherwise sick horses and cattle who sought the benefits of a mineral water cure. It was not only at French watering places, however, that communal bathing and sociability characterized the experience of being at a spa. At England's famous Bath, which was by far and away the most frequented watering place in all of eighteenth-century Europe, bathing was conducted in a basin that was strikingly similar to those at Plombières, Néris, or Aix-les-Bains. For a fascinating description and contemporary defense of this watering place and its curative techniques, see Joseph Spry, *A Practical Treatise on the Bath Waters* (London: Longman, 1822); a less rich but more culturally and socially concerned study of the facility and its important place in eighteenth-century society can be found in A. Barbeau, *Life and Letters at Bath in the Eighteenth Century* (London: Heinemann, 1904); a nineteenth-century moralist and medical critique of the open bath can be found in A. B. Granville, *The Spas of England and Principal Sea-Bathing Places* (Bath, 1841). For a discussion of spa design and the spatiality of curing at the baths of the old regime, see Mackaman, *Leisure Settings.*

13. This complaint was so worded in sundry reports made by spa doctors of this period to their speculative, administrative, and governmental colleagues. The specific citation comes from AD Savoie: 1FS 2803. Next to the aristocracy in the old regime, destitute invalids comprised the greatest cohort among the spa's summer population. People who could prove their poverty and medical necessity to the authorities of their village or region were often granted a modest sum of money with which to pay for travel to a spa. Allowances to the poor were sometimes made as well by a parish priest, but the amount of money in either case was never great. Paternalism from other sources saw to it that wounded soldiers, aging veterans, clerical authorities, and members of religious orders could obtain enough charity to travel to a spa. And at the spas too, an enduring paternalism—dating in many cases from the Middle Ages—allowed these travelers to make free and unlimited use of a town's mineral waters and medical services. For a concise history of spa paternalism with respect to indigence, see E. Guitard, "Le Prestige passe des eaux minérales," *Societé historique de la pharmacie* (1931), 59.

14. AD Savoie: 1FS 2803.

15. Ibid. Specific use of this phrase comes from "Rapport historico-médical sur la saison d'Aix-en-Savoie, 1819," AD Savoie: 1FS 2803.

16. Report to the prefect of Allier, August 8, 1827, AD Allier, Series X.

17. "Rapport historico-médical sur la saison."

18. Letter of July 25, 1822, from J. Degaillon, mayor of Aix-les-Bains, AD Savoie: 1FS 2804.

19. "Rapport médical sur les bains d'Aix-en-Savoie pour l'année 1829," AD Savoie: 1FS 2803.

20. "Extrait des régistre des déliberations de la commission administrative des bains d'Aix, 4 mars 1824," AD Savoie: 1FS 2804.

21. P. P. Barthes, *Guide pratiques des malades aux eaux de Vichy* (Paris: Ballière, 1851), 30.

22. To the mayors, pharmacists, doctors, and others involved in the development of French thermalism in the nineteenth century, it was common knowledge that upper-class bathers were more likely to frequent a spa where the presence of the poor had been securely confined. To those who questioned the wisdom of investing dear capital in such an apparently profitless place as a hospital for the poor, one needed to look only at the phenomenal success of Aix-les-Bains in the years immediately follow-

ing the highly publicized completion of its hospital. In 1830, the first summer after Aix's Haldimand Hospital was built, one thousand more persons visited the thermal establishment than had come the previous year, even as revolution engulfed Paris, Brussels and other important cities from which the spa's clientele was traditionally drawn (Archives municipales d'Aix-les-Bains: I 120).

23. These facilities collected lower-class and indigent bathers, who might otherwise have lodged and sought treatment at the same places frequented by upper-class bathers, and subjected them to a combination of spatial and administrative sequestration. While there can be little doubt that needy bathers received better and more rationalized medical care in spa hospitals than they had before, the humanitarian potential of these institutions was never more than a partial justification for their presence in a spa town. The solution spa developers found in hospitalization would remain fundamentally unaltered—although segregating the poor was occasionally a politically contested practice when it was taken to mean that access to the medicinal virtues of mineral water had in fact been limited—well into the twentieth century. Particularly in the wake of the Revolution of 1848, radical and certain liberal critics denounced the fact that French indigents had so little access to the medical benefits of the country's spas. In 1849, for example, a rare government official spoke out on behalf of increased indigent access to the spas. One Jules Francois, engineer and chief of mines for the department of the Vosges, in a published report of that year, contended that thermal spas should be completely open—in all of their facilities—especially to poor persons needing cures. For his passionate plea on this issue, see Archives Nationales: f14 8278.

24. The source of this unease was not merely the fact that most bathing establishments, by 1816, were regularly serving more people than they ever had before. In fact, crowding was not even among the main complaints that bathers lodged with their water doctors.

25. This description of spa interiors, authored by a doctor, referred to thermal establishments in Europe generally ("Rapport médical sur saison").

26. This description of private bath cabinets is taken from the "Prospectus pour l'établissement d'une société d'actionnaires pour l'ameliorations des bains d'Aix-en-Savoie," July 23, 1822, AD Savoie: 1FS 2801.

27. The *médecins d'eaux* of Aix-les-Bains reported that their basin was no longer used with any frequency by the middle 1820s. "Rapport de la commission administrative des bains d'Aix," 1824, AD Savoie: 1FS 2803.

28. "Prospectus pour l'établissement." Too-frequent bathing in this period was taken as a sign of invalidism. Daily baths often meant that one's health was fragile or even failing. Just to prepare a bath at home was a major endeavor, requiring the assistance of several domestics. For an interesting cultural, social, and medical history of domestic bathing in this period, see Jacques Léonard, *Archives du corps: La santé aux XIXe siècle* (Paris: Ouest-France, 1986).

29. In 1823 the doctors of Aix-les-Bains estimated that some three thousand baths were administered to curists at their hotels. "Séance de la commission administrative des bains d'Aix, 26 April 1824," Archives des thermes nationaux: L26. This type of bathing was a variation on a standard practice in many French urban centers of the period. In Paris and other major cities in the 1820s, bathtubs and the water for them were rented when needed. One of some one thousand contractors, individuals, or companies whose business it was to lease collapsible tubs and warm water would be contracted for the specific date on which the rare bath was to be taken. As late as July 1852, the council on hygiene for the city of Nantes could note: "Simple baths are more

an object of luxury than necessity; the vast majority of men and women have never taken a bath, and one can see that they are not at all worse for this lack" (Léonard, *Archives du corps,* 119).

30. It is interesting that this period saw some prefigured "Victorianism" emerge in French bath design, at precisely a time when English spas were neglecting to make any significant architectural concessions to bourgeois modesty. Bath's visiting population declined markedly in the decades preceding its eventual creation of an entirely new bathing establishment, which would not occur until around the middle of the nineteenth century. German spas, by contrast—such as Baden-Baden—were already featuring privacy and individuated bathrooms by the time Vichy and other spas would complete their "modernization."

31. For a brief discussion of the genesis of spa architecture in France, see Institut Français d'Architecture, *Villes d'eaux en France,* 68–73. Because the new spas at Vichy and Luchon, completed in the first two decades of the nineteenth century, both featured central basins surrounded by private baths, the authors of *Villes d'eaux en France* argue that these establishments were more traditional than they were modern in their design. I have argued elsewhere that the basins at these spas, which were never used for bathing, were strictly ornamental. Thus private bathing, not its collective and traditional counterpart, was the point of the Vichy and Luchon design. The architects of these spas, even as they paid homage to certain conventional features in spa interior design, were clearly creating spaces that departed from tradition.

32. "Rapport médical sur la saison."

33. Ibid.

34. Ibid.

35. Report of June 27, 1818, AD Allier, Series X.

36. "Rapport médical sur la saison."

37. Promulgated on July 14, the law in question was concerned with "Des conditions d'ordre et de salubrité dans les établissements d'eaux minérales naturelles." In effect, this legislation offered legal grounding to principles of spa design and administration that had been in place at many establishments for a quarter of a century. The state made it a matter of law that every bathing establishment in France had to conform to strict standards regarding privacy, medical administration, and hygiene. In summarizing the law, the state's reporter emphasized most of all the importance that had become attached to private and gendered interiors within the spas: "In each thermal establishment, distinct locales must be set aside, to the extent that it is possible, so that the two sexes can be treated separately." Projet de decret sur l'exploitation, le service medicale, et la police des etablissements d'eaux minerales naturelles, article 14, title 3 of article 19 of the law of 14 July 1856, Archives Nationales: f14 8279.

38. Bonnie Smith, *Ladies of the Leisure Class: The Bourgeoises of Northern France in the Nineteenth Century* (Princeton, N.J.: Princeton University Press, 1981), 35.

39. Sharing of work was especially common with husbands and wives of smaller enterprises. Adeline Daumard, *Les Bourgeois et la bourgeoisie en France depuis 1815* (Paris: Flammarion, 1991), 214.

40. Smith, *Ladies of the Leisure Class,* 37.

41. Elinor Barber, *The Bourgeoisie in Eighteenth-Century France* (Princeton, N.J.: Princeton University Press, 1955), 82.

42. Smith, *Ladies of the Leisure Class,* 21.

43. For a thoughtful analysis of time discipline in nineteenth-century French industry, see Michelle Perrot, "The Three Ages of Industrial Discipline," in *Conscious-*

ness and Class Experience in Nineteenth-Century Europe, ed. John Merriman (New York: Holmes and Meier, 1979). A seminal work on factory discipline is still E. P. Thompson, "Time, Work-Discipline, and Industrial Capitalism," Past and Present 38 (December 1967): 56–97. A good general account of discipline in the industrial revolution is still S. Pollard, "Factory Discipline in the Industrial Revolution," Economic History Review 16, no. 2 (1963): 254–71.

44. Armand Wallon, La Vie quotidiènne dans les villes d'eaux (Paris: Hachette, 1986), 191.

45. Dr. Auguste Forestier, Le Conseil du baigneur (Chambéry: Gouvernement, 1857), 62.

46. Ibid., 85.

47. Corbin has shown that this was the case too with respect to seaside resorts (89).

48. And this was, of course, a matter of degree. Doctors had long been entrenched at the spas of France, and many of them had labored throughout the eighteenth century in particular to codify and further rationalize their curative systems and techniques. For more extended arguments about medicalization at spas in the seventeenth and eighteenth centuries, see Laurence Brockliss, "The Development of the Spa in Seventeenth-Century France," in The Medical History of Waters and Spas, ed. Roy Porter, Medical History, supplement no. 10 (London: Wellcome Institute for the History of Medicine, 1990), 23–47; and also Laurence Brockliss's The Medical World of Early Modern France (Oxford: Oxford University Press, 1997).

49. This trend, however vast, was never organized at the state level or under the auspices of the French Academy of Medicine. Rather, individual spas and their medical corps instituted such policies more or less on their own (Weisz, "Water Cures and Science," 401). Although less rigidly enforced at the seaside watering places of this period, medical consultations were certainly encouraged in conjunction with sea bathing both in France and in England. For a discussion of this, see Corbin, Le Territoire du vide, 82, 84, and 89.

50. Section 2, article 9, Regalement et Taif de l'établissement thermal d'Aix-les-Bains (Chambéry: Imprimerie de Deletraz, 1834), 10.

51. James Clark, The Sanative Influence of Climate: With an Account of the Best Places of Resort in England, the South of Europe, etc. (Philadelphia: Waldie, 1841), 27.

52. Dr. Chasseloup, Guide pittoresque aux eaux d'Aix-en-Savoie (1834), 13.

53. Dr. Victor Noyer, Lettres topographiques et médicals sur Vichy (1833), 191.

54. Forestier, Le Conseil du baigneur, 81.

55. Ibid.

56. Dr. Edward Sparks, The Riviera (London: Churchill, 1879), 158.

57. Ibid.

58. Ibid.

59. Corbin's discussion of medical regimens at the seaside watering places of France and England suggests that sea bathing, rather than being a therapeutic strategy that was to work in conjunction with a host of other prescriptions concerning diet, et cetera, was the sole prescriptive element in the seaside cure. In fact, Corbin notes, sea bathing was supposed to help one rediscover one's appetite (Corbin, Le Territoire du vide, 76).

60. Chasseloup, Guide pittoresque, 26.

61. Ibid.

62. Dr. Issac Yeo, Health Resorts and Their Uses (London: Chapman and Hall, 1882), 49. There were multiple printings of this text from the 1850s through the 1880s.

63. Ibid.

64. While doctors at the spas' seaside counterparts clearly had impulses in the direction of a regimented day, they, according to Corbin, typically allowed patients to make major decisions concerning what to do when not curing (*Le Territoire du vide*, 82).

65. Yeo, *Health Resorts*, 367.

66. Ibid.

67. Dr. Herman Weber, *Climatotherapy and Balneotherapy* (London: Smith and Elden, n.d.), 364.

68. Yeo, *Health Resorts*, 367.

69. Sparks, *The Riviera*, 158.

70. Ibid.

71. Ibid., 159.

72. Ibid., 158.

73. If bathing at a spa had become a private and medical experience during the Restoration, such cures had hardly ceased to be pleasurable. Even spa doctors seldom failed to note that curists felt "an agreeable sense of warmth" upon entering their baths. Dr. James Johnson, *Pilgrimage to the Spas* (London: Highler, 1841), 52. In the words of another practitioner, the "euphoria" of the patient "must never be inconvenienced in the bath by the least unpleasant impression." Victor Scheuer, *Guide pratique du baigneur* (Paris, 1854), 69, 70.

74. For the bathing patterns of Aix-les-Bains in this period, see any of the published *Bulletin des eaux d'Aix-en-Savoie* that were written by the spa's medical directors. For the particular statistics cited in the text, see Dr. Vidal, *Notice historique et médicale sur l'hospice d'Aix en Savoie* (1853), 36, AD Savoie: C51.

75. AD Allier, Series X.

76. Barthes, *Guide pratiques*, 238.

77. Ibid.

78. Johnson, *Pilgrimage to the Spas*, 60.

79. On the use of cold-water hydrotherapy in public hospitals and asylums in France, see Paul Vidart, *De la cure d'eau froide à l'institut hydrothérapique de Divonne* (Paris: Chebruliez, 1852); and by the same author, *Etudes pratiques sur l'hydrothérapie, ou traitement des maladies par l'eau froide* (Paris, 1855); for a discussion of cold-water plunging at the seaside watering places of France and England, see Corbin, *Le Territoire du vide*, 89–96.

80. Following the exact instructions of the German doctor Vincent Priessnitz, whose reputation as the father of cold-water bathing was widespread and respected all over Europe, French doctors brought the agonies of cold-water bathing to a generations of curists whose medical complaints ranged from bronchial disorders to obesity. The greatest influence of Priessnitz in France can be found in Bigel, *Manuel d'hydrosupathie, ou traitement des maladies par l'eau froide suivant la méthode de V. Priessnitz à Graefenberg* (Paris: Ballière, 1840); a second important work on cold-water hydrotherapy is Baldou, *L'hydrothérapie, méthode rationelle du traitement par l'eau froide, le régime et l'exercise* (Paris, 1841); perhaps the most widely read French specialist in hydrotherapy, Constantin James, was also a great champion of cold-water cures. His notable work on the subject was *Etudes sur l'hydrothérapie, ou traitement par l'eau froide* (Paris: Dusillion, 1846).

81. Henry C. Wright, *Six Months at Graefenberg* (London, 1845), 44. For a more sympathetic account of this and other cold-water cures by a French champion of this

treatment, see L. Rul, *Quatre ans à Graefenberg* (Paris, 1858). Corbin has shown that some of this disempowerment figured into the practice of sea bathing at the watering places of France and England, where bath technicians decided exactly when bathers were to be subjected to a "brutal immersion" in freezing cold sea water (*Le Territoire du vide*, 89).

82. Wright, *Six Months at Graefenberg*, 45.

83. Dr. Herman Weber, *Climatotherapy and Balneotherapy* (London: Smith and Elden, 1898), 311. For the standard medical texts on the hydrotherapeutic treatment of women's health, see L. Allain, *Etudes cliniques sur l'hydrothérapie* (Paris, 1856); also J. Pigeaire, *Des avantages de l'hydrothérapie appliques aux maladies chroniques et aux affections nerveuses* (Paris: Ballière, 1847); E. Duvivier, *De l'hypocondrie et de la melancolie* (Paris, 1853); and J. Brachet, *Traité complet de l'hypochondrie* (Paris: Ballière, 1847). As Corbin has rightly argued, cold-water bathing at the seaside was a punishing experience too. Bathers in this context experienced a strong sense of suffocation from the shock of their icy plunges (*Le Territoire du vide*, 89, 90).

84. "Rapport médical sur la saison."

85. Wright, *Six Months at Graefenberg*, 119.

86. Ibid., 119, 120.

87. Aix-les-Bains even had its *division d'énfer*, with separate bathing cells for men and women.

88. Dr. Louis Bertier, *Compte-rendu des eaux thermales sulfureuses d'Aix en Savoie pendant la saison de 1857 suivi de considérations pratiques sur leur action curative* (Chambéry: Puthod fils, 1858), 17.

89. For a detailed description of mud baths at the spas of the 1830s and 1840s, see Dr. Constant Despine, *Manuel topographique et médical de l'étranger* (Annecy: Burdet, 1834), 177–81.

90. Weber, *Climatotherapy and Balneotherapy*, 337.

91. Yeo, *Health Resorts*, 58.

92. Ibid.

93. Chasseloup, *Guide pittoresque*, 68.

94. Weber, *Climatotherapy and Balneotherapy*, 305.

95. "Rapport médical sur la saison."

96. Statement of bath receipts for the period 1840–50, AD Savoie: 1FS 2805.

97. AD Allier, Series X.

98. The frequency of the shower massage obviously varied, but many guides noted that a variety of different ailments were best combated by a dozen or more showers per vacation. Thus the average number of bathing operations per summer at the spas was far higher than the average number of summer visitors. At Aix-les-Bains in 1833, for example, 28,303 treatments were administered to only 2,913 people (Archives municipales d'Aix-les-Bains: I 120). At more than two times the price of any other form of the spa cure—a standard shower in the 1840s cost two francs, while a private bath cost one franc and a piscine cure was sixty-five centimes—patients, by the time they quit their spa, had invested not only a significant portion of their time but also a great deal of money following their shower cures (AD Savoie: 1FS 2803).

99. Dr. Thomas Linn, *The Health Resorts of Europe* (New York, 1893), 90, 91.

100. To show the degree of the cure's differentiation and medicalization, guides from this period often included illustrations of bath technology. In one such illustration from the 1830s, for example, a guidebook's author depicted forty-four different features of the complicated water delivery system of the hot shower (Despine, *Manuel topographique et médical*).

101. Dr. H. C. Lombard, *Une cure aux bains d'Aix-en-Savoie* (Geneva: Fick, 1853), 16.

102. Ibid.

103. One Albert Constant, in a 1856 report to the ministry of commerce entitled "Des eaux minerales dans leurs rapports avec l'economie publique," estimated that only two of every five persons on holiday actually took a medical cure. (Constant's report is cited in A. Veyrat, *Compte rendu de la saison des eaux thermales pendant l'année 1856* [Chambéry: Impremerie nationale, 1857], 26.) At Aix-les-Bains, for example, only 3,940 persons of an annual total of 7,617 made use of the thermal establishment in 1861. For contemporary comment on this statistic, see J. Bonjean, *Guide de l'étranger aux eaux d'Aix-en-Savoie, Chambéry et leurs environs* (Chambery, 1862), 19–20.

104. Weisz, "Water Cures and Science," 401.

105. Extremely ambitious spa doctors, like Louis Berthet of Aix-les-Bains, argued that spas should begin administering cures throughout the year, rather than just in the summer months. Another common idea among doctors was to try to lengthen the average curist's stay at a spa. See Berthet, *Aix-les-Bains et ses thermes* (Chambéry, 1862).

106. Ibid., 216.

107. Ibid, 12.

108. Which is not to suggest that middle-class vacations went to the spas in hungry pursuit of pleasure. For an assessment of their didactic and socially strategic uses of spa vacationing, see Douglas P. Mackaman, "The Landscape of the Ville d'eau: Public Space and Social Practice at the Spas of France, 1850–1890," *Proceedings of the 1992 Meeting of the Western Society for French History* (Las Cruces, NM: New Mexico State University Press, 1992) and *Leisure Settings*, chap. 5.

Selling Lourdes

Pilgrimage, Tourism, and the Mass-Marketing of the Sacred in Nineteenth-Century France

What is the relationship between the religious act of pilgrimage and the development of secular tourism? This question has been the source of much debate for scholars interested in the development of tourism in Europe and North America. Debate has focused on whether modern mass tourism in the twentieth century is a departure from the traditional act of pilgrimage or its logical extension, a new spiritual search for a sacred center in the modern age. The first position has been effectively argued by scholars like Daniel Boorstin and Paul Fussell. They have characterized the medieval pilgrimage of the Christian world as a form of "serious travel." Like the ancient traveler who searched for new knowledge or the modern literary traveler who followed the grand tour, the medieval pilgrim made a serious journey in search of spiritual truth and divine union. The development of modern tourism, Boorstin and Fussell maintain, put an end to this older form of sophisticated and thoughtful travel. The modern tourist no longer journeys in search of knowledge or truth. Instead, the tourist embarks on a vacation, traveling in comfort and pursuing mindless forms of pleasure.[1]

In response to this interpretation of the decline of the intelligent traveler, a diverse group of sociologists, anthropologists, and historians interested in the study of mass culture have maintained that modern tourism is indeed a serious undertaking. Dean MacCannell, one of the first scholars to argue that tourism was itself a new kind of pilgrimage, set the terms for this revisionist position. He argued that the tourist vacation, as a form of ritualized travel that is set apart from daily life, is also a journey of self-renewal and a search for "authentic" experience. Even while tourists engage in frivolous pleasures and distractions, they are at a deeper level attempting to break with their humdrum daily lives in order to find a more genuine and satisfying encounter with the world. MacCannell concluded that while tourists might not be aware of their deeper search, they are in fact engaged in a pilgrimage quest to re-create a sacred center.[2]

While these two schools of thought present opposing views of tourism in the modern age, their arguments are predicated on an almost identical understanding of Christian pilgrimage as an unchanging and uniform activity. This essay seeks to add another dimension to the discussion of pilgrimage and tourism by examining the historical practices and meanings of modern Catholic pilgrimage. It looks specifically at the development of the Lourdes pilgrimage in late-nineteenth-century France in order to explore how secular and religious forms of travel mutually developed and defined each other in the modern era. Tourism scholars in both camps have constructed a highly idealized image of religious travel that not only oversimplifies the role of traditional pilgrimage in premodern societies, but also overlooks the ways in which pilgrimage itself has changed over time. Boorstin and Fussell make this simplification in order to lament the demise of serious travel. Revisionist scholars, relying on the ideas of Victor Turner, paint a subtler picture of Christian pilgrimage as a liminal event whereby the faithful enter a world of communitas or antistructure through the ritual celebration of the divine. This liminal quality is said to be a key component of modern secular travel, from visiting sites of historical significance to vacationing in Disneyland. While the notion of liminality has enriched new studies on tourism, it has unintentionally perpetuated an ahistorical view of pilgrimage.[3]

I contend that Catholic pilgrimage in western Europe was altered by the very developments that created modern tourism during the second half of the nineteenth century: the advancement of railway technology, modern advertising techniques, the mass press, and the manufacturing of mass-produced consumer goods. In short, the emergence of a consumer-oriented society in the late nineteenth century not only paved the way for modern tourism in Europe, as many have argued, but also created new forms and practices of Catholic pilgrimage. Using Lourdes as a case study, I argue that the rise of consumer culture during this period transformed the act of pilgrimage into an early form of tourism characterized by inexpensive church-organized voyages and the buying and selling of mass-produced sacred goods.[4]

Furthermore, this new type of pilgrimage experience had a profound and unsettling impact on modern French society. As the act of pilgrimage was connected to the practices of mass consumption, the Lourdes shrine became a site of conflict over the relationship between religion and commercialized tourism. Church officials, faithful Catholics, and even anticlerical observers all feared the social effects of large-scale pilgrimages and the mechanical reproduction of religious goods, even as they fought over the precise meanings of these new activities. For the devout, the critical questions were these: What type of religious value did mass-produced sacred goods have, and what constituted appropriate behavior for a pilgrimage that merged penance with secular amusements? On the other hand, anticlerical critics of Lourdes wondered if the progressive nature of capitalism could be destroyed by the blending of religion and commerce. Both sides wanted to determine the difference between religion and commerce, pilgrimage and tourism, and ultimately the sacred and the secular. These tensions now defined not only the modern pilgrimage experience but broader social debates as well.[5]

The Development of a Modern Pilgrimage Site

The sacred grotto of Lourdes in the French Pyrenees was the most popular healing shrine in late-nineteenth-century France and much of the Western world. It is still the best-known site of Christian pilgrimage in the world today, with the possible exceptions of Jerusalem and Rome. Each year almost six million pilgrims visit the sanctuary. The history of this most celebrated pilgrimage began with the visions of Bernadette Soubirous. On February 11, 1858, this fourteen-year-old peasant girl saw her first vision of the Virgin Mary in a grotto called Massabieille. Bernadette saw the Virgin seventeen more times before thousands of witnesses during the next five months. In the course of these continuing visions, Bernadette discovered a spring of water and revealed that the lady in the apparition called herself the Immaculate Conception. Immediately, local inhabitants sought out the spring for its curative powers and made Lourdes a site of local pilgrimage. News of the visions and proclaimed miracles soon spread throughout France, and by the summer of 1858 Lourdes was attracting faithful pilgrims and curious onlookers from as far away as Paris.[6]

This display of popular religiosity was not extraordinary for the period. Throughout the nineteenth century women and children claimed to have visions of the Virgin Mary. Popular cults quickly developed around these seers, and the places of their supernatural experiences became sites of pilgrimage.[7] What was extraordinary at Lourdes was the church's quick approval of the Marian visions and the rapid development of the local pilgrimage site. The local bishop, Monsignor Bertrand-Sévère Laurence of Tarbes, astutely recognized the staying power of the Lourdes piety and called for an episcopal commission in July 1858 (five months after Bernadette's first visions) to investigate the apparitions and the miraculous cures being claimed at the grotto. The resolve to investigate Bernadette's visions was followed by another decision to discredit other visionaries who were also claiming to have seen the Virgin Mary at Lourdes or in nearby villages. Bernadette's fame had unleashed a rash of visions by other young women and children who tried to claim some of the sacred authority that Bernadette had gained among the local populace. The church investigated these incidents but quickly silenced most of the visionaries and effectively suppressed the spread of these other apparitions. Under these circumstances, the bishop felt assured of his control over the emerging sacred site. Thus in 1862, just four years after the initial visions, the bishop proclaimed that the Virgin Mary had truly appeared to Bernadette. He also recognized seven cures as miraculous.[8]

After authorizing the new cult of the grotto of Lourdes, the bishop acted swiftly to transform the site into an official Catholic pilgrimage shrine. He gathered church resources to buy the territory of the grotto and build a chapel on the site.[9] In 1866 Bishop Laurence dispatched a full-time missionary order to run the shrine. The Missionaries of the Immaculate Conception, known simply as the Grotto fathers, soon gained ecclesiastic jurisdiction over all matters at the site. They initially organized regional pilgrimages and were quick to use various technologies like the railway to bring large crowds to the shrine. One of their first acts in 1866 was the transportation of sixty thousand pilgrims to Lourdes for the celebration of the inauguration of the crypt of the future basilica. The construction of a trunk railway line connecting Lourdes to the departmental capital of Tarbes in the 1860s was a critical ingredient to developing mass pilgrimages to the grotto.[10]

The Augustinian Fathers of the Assumption were later given full responsibility for the organization of the pilgrimages to Lourdes. They too used the railway in innovative ways as they sought to augment the number of pilgrims coming to the sacred site. They coordinated special trains for pilgrimages, designed compartments to transport sick and disabled pilgrims, and secured reductions in prices of 20 to 30 percent for third-class tickets. Their most important innovation was the creation of a three-day annual pilgrimage known as the National Pilgrimage to Lourdes.[11] Launched in 1873, the first National Pilgrimage met with only marginal success, drawing fewer than a thousand pilgrims. However, the Augustinian Fathers (commonly called the Assumptionists) soon learned to use the mass press, especially their daily *La Croix* and the weekly journal *Le Pèlerin,* to publicize the event to a national audience. Within ten years an estimated twenty thousand French men and women were participating each year in the National Pilgrimage to Lourdes.[12]

While the Assumptionists used their energies to attract and organize thousands of faithful Catholics from all over France, the Grotto fathers concentrated on transforming the actual site of the grotto into a well-run, modern pilgrimage shrine. The grotto administration seized on every opportunity to renovate the town of Lourdes and develop commercial activities during the 1870s and 1880s. The administration actively worked with municipal authorities to rebuild older neighborhoods and construct new city streets. Joint projects included the installation of electricity at Lourdes, the construction of hotels along the new Boulevard de la Grotte, and the building of tramways and a funicular. The most important of these projects was the construction of a new boulevard connecting national Route 21 directly to the shrine without detours through the town of Lourdes. Citing issues of public safety, both municipal leaders and church authorities sought to minimize the congestion within the town due to the constant flow of pilgrims descending to the grotto via narrow and often steep older roads.[13]

The grotto administration also took up the project so it could create a better view of the shrine for the throng of arriving pilgrims. A government report in 1899 noted the complaints made by the Grotto fathers about the old road to the shrine: "The visitor, upon arriving, would not be struck by a single glimpse of the religious monuments as a whole; the picturesque tableau that nature has made of these monuments was not put to good use." The report added: "The general perspective, in short, left much to be desired: For the grotto administration needs the imagination of the pilgrim to be sparked at first glance by the spectacle before his eyes." The construction of the new boulevard created an impressive vista whereby the basilica and the complex of buildings could be seen almost immediately upon entering the town.[14]

The grotto administration also developed its own commercial establishments that sold religious goods to the public. Among the most successful enterprises was the sanctuary's candle boutique. One skeptical government official noted with dismay the huge profits being made from the candle shop and discussed the church's business tactics in some detail. Located next to the grotto, the shop was legally leased to a Lourdes resident, one Monsieur Berger. However, according to the government report of commissioner-administrator Monsourat, "Everyone in Lourdes is convinced that Berger is only a front man." Monsourat concluded that "the taper business is very important: the resulting benefits are certainly considerable and I am convinced that the holy fathers themselves are profiting from this store through the intermediary of Berger." Monsourat reasoned that by pretending to rent this business for a sum of four thousand francs to Berger, the fathers avoided paying sales taxes. If one accepts Monsourat's argument, the profits made from the sale of candles were indeed considerable. The commissioner-administrator estimated revenues at one hundred thousand francs for the year 1899.[15]

However, it was the sale of sacred Lourdes water that became the most profitable marketing venture for the shrine. Although the Grotto fathers did not charge for the water itself, they did impose a price to cover the cost of the bottles, corks, carpentry, labor, and transport. Monsourat calculated that the Grotto fathers made a profit of approximately sixty to eight-five centimes on each bottle shipped. He concluded that "the fathers, according to accounts received, shipped around one hundred thousand bottles per year." Thus the Lourdes sanctuary earned at least sixty thousand francs from the sale of its sacred water in the year 1899. Monsourat confidently concluded that "the

Advertising for the distiller Sabatier-Lavigne (1887). The Grotto Fathers threatened to sue the distilling company Maison Victor Sabatier in 1887 for printing the phrase "se vend au profit des oeuvres de la grotte." The company eliminated the phrase from its advertising materials. (AG, 6PI, Publicité commerciale, commercialization de l'eau.)

returns realized by the fathers of Lourdes are considerable; establishing above all that the fathers do not neglect a single resource in their power to add to the revenues of the shrine."[16]

The success of the Lourdes shrine was due largely to the church's use of modern-day advertising techniques. At the height of the pilgrimages to Lourdes, in the late 1890s and early 1900s, the religious authorities began advertising the sanctuary on a whole new scale. The church produced specialized guidebooks and manuals for the Lourdes shrine that promoted not just the pilgrimage but the hundreds of attractions and events going on in the town. These guidebooks were a mix of spiritual meditation about the meaning of the pilgrimage and secular concerns for touring the region and seeing the town's many attractions. Capitalizing on the creation of new leisure activities and tourism for the middle class, the church also promoted Lourdes as an ideal vacation spot. Yet these guidebooks were careful to list restaurants, lodgings, and special outings that even the most humble pilgrim could afford. All the faithful, rich and poor alike, were expected to participate in the activities of Lourdes.

A guidebook from 1893 written by Abbé Martin typified this advertising genre. A religious manual intended to instruct pilgrims on proper behavior at Lourdes, it provided needed details about Bernadette's apparitions and the creation of the shrine. This same handbook also suggested daily outings and sight-seeing. The guide listed day trips to the Pyrenees and longer visits to other thermal resorts. The guide also promoted such tourist attractions as a diorama that showed the grotto "at the moment of the first apparition, with such exactitude of detail that one might believe oneself present at the marvelous scene of the Blessed Virgin speaking to Bernadette." Another diorama portrayed the death of Bernadette at the convent of Saint-Gildard in Nevers. The tableau presented the Virgin, surrounded by angels, descending from heaven to give Bernadette a crown. Not only could one see these dioramas for fifty centimes each, but the guidebook also boasted of a more elaborate panorama that represented the seventeenth apparition of the Virgin in which the flame of Bernadette's candle touched her own hand without burning it. The guide remarked that "this scene is reproduced by the artists with such an accent of truth that one is defenseless against the emotions it produces."[17]

Not unlike the dioramas and attractions displayed during the same period at the Paris Expositions or the wax exhibits at the Musée Grévin, these expositions reproduced the shrine and various religious moments from the past for a mass audience—anyone who could pay the small fee of fifty centimes or a franc. Thus pilgrims could actively participate in present-day religious processions at the shrine and simultaneously indulge their fantasies of being part of a sacred past. By claiming that visitors could "authentically" experience re-created moments from the Lourdes sacred past, these guides encouraged pilgrims to venerate commercialized attractions as holy sites. Thus Lourdes guide books not only educated visitors to be good pilgrims, but also taught them to be good consumers of the shrine.[18]

The successful selling of Lourdes was manifested in a steady flow of pilgrims, estimated at two hundred thousand per year into the first decade of the twentieth century. The high point for these pilgrimages came in 1908, when over one million pilgrims went to Lourdes to celebrate the fiftieth anniversary of Bernadette's apparitions.[19] This constant flow of visitors transformed both the town of Lourdes and the entire region of the Pyrenees. What was once a sleepy village of little consequence to the region became a key center of commerce and leisure activity. One measure of the town's accelerated economic importance was its tenfold increase in communal revenues from land clearance, construction, rents, and the sale of drinking water during the period 1860 to 1906. Its communal budget also increased tenfold during this same period. Furthermore, important financial institutions like the Banque de France, Crédit Lyonnais, and Société Générale had investments in the small city of Lourdes. Older thermal stations in the Pyrenees like Gavarnie and Cauterets, once thriving centers of recreation and rehabilitation for the upper classes, were indebted to the sanctuary for bringing new customers to its spas; about half of the clientele who went to thermal resorts in the Pyrenees were also on a pilgrimage to Lourdes. According to one government report written in 1908, the sacred shrine had by this time become a commercial center "that has incontestable economic repercussions . . . not only on the town of Lourdes, but also on the region and even the entire country."[20]

The economic development of the shrine thus transformed the pilgrimage itself into a mass-produced religious experience. Through the shrine's marketing of sacred water as well as the commercial production of religious souvenirs, Lourdes was able to reach even those individuals unable to make the journey. One advertisement for the *Pastilles de Lourdes,* lozenges made with Lourdes water and sugar, proudly trumpeted its ability to make the sacred source available to all who needed it: "Not everyone can come to the waters of the Fountain and respond to the inclination of their heart . . . but the waters of the fountain can go to everyone." The advertisement promised that its goods would "allow parents and friends remaining at home to be supplied with perfectly authentic souvenirs of a pilgrimage that the privileged alone can carry out." The commercialization of the site would aid in bringing needed religious comfort to the world.[21]

Not only were pilgrims able to bring back a piece of the sacred in the form of souvenirs, bottled water, and inexpensive religious trinkets, they were also able to experience life in a thriving commercial center. The grotto administration and private entrepreneurs used innovative advertising techniques to capture a mass audience and capitalized on forms of entertainment found

La Rue de la Grotte (Avenue of the Grotto), 1912. (Photograph collection,
Musée Pyrénéen, château fort, Lourdes.)

mainly in large cities to and edify these pious visitors. While Lourdes was no
Paris, it was an important town where early forms of mass consumption and
cross-class leisure activities were developed for a largely rural populace. Marcel Jouhandeau wrote in his memoirs that his grandmother discovered a larger
universe by going to Lourdes, the first and only voyage she made outside the
region where she was born: "She discovered there the world around her, never
having suspected its scope and almost having departed the world without
knowing it."[22]

A Pilgrimage Transformed: Interpreting the Lourdes Sanctuary

The church worked hard to make Lourdes a national shrine that attracted
thousands of Catholics on an annual basis. For the Grotto fathers and the
Assumptionists, the success of the National Pilgrimage to Lourdes was a sign
of the re-Christianization of France. It was a valuable weapon in the fight
against the anticlerical laws of the Third Republic.[23] Yet the very success of the
National Pilgrimage forced the church to confront a deep ambivalence about

its own commercial activities and the appropriate relationship between commerce and piety. While the church encouraged secular amusements, tourist excursions, and religious panoramas, it also consciously warned against making the Lourdes pilgrimage into a tourist holiday. Religious guidebooks and manuals of the 1890s attempted to separate religious worship from mere tourism. By the turn of the century the church began to emphasize proper pilgrimage behavior and orthodox Catholic ritual. An 1899 Lourdes manual cautioned that "a pilgrimage is not a journey of pleasure but of expiation." Another manual from the Archdiocese of Auch made the same point: "A pilgrimage is not an ordinary journey, much less . . . one of pleasure. It is a religious act. Praying, doing penance, giving thanks to God and Mary . . . such are the goals of pilgrimage." An 1898 guidebook, *Lourdes, guide pratique à l'usage des pèlerins,* began by asserting that "this guide is not made for tourists, but for pilgrims." It also stated that the grotto "is the center and entire reason for the pilgrimages to Lourdes." Despite its reassertion of proper religious values over crass tourism, the guidebook still focused attention on "promenades" and "excursions" in the Pyrenees as well as practical information for taking advantage of the town's many attractions.[24]

The commercial life at Lourdes also engendered ambivalent feelings for pious Catholics. For while the devout had long merged religious and commercial activities at pilgrimage sites, the appearance of sacred merchandising at Lourdes prompted a new concern that such behavior was now inappropriate. The sanctuary received numerous letters from worried and sometimes displeased pilgrims, voicing their dismay over the excesses of commercialized religion. In 1888 a pilgrim from Toulouse wrote to the head of the Grotto fathers to express his outrage over the selling of the newfangled *Pastille de Lourdes:* "During my last pilgrimage to Notre-Dame de Lourdes, I was struck by the existence of a steam-works that manufactures, people say, lozenges from *Lourdes water*. My reaction was sorrow and pain." Clarifying his outrage, he explained that "the thought came to me that this so-called factory had no other purpose than realizing great profits . . . from a blessed and sacred thing." The very idea that businessmen or the church should be making money from sacred worship was intolerable for some Catholics. This particular pilgrim ended his letter by asking the director why he was not doing all he could to stop this "desecration."[25]

Another pressing matter for believing Catholics was the spread of fraudulent vendors selling counterfeit sacred goods throughout the countryside. Itinerant peddling of religious articles, once a valuable means of providing access to sacred artifacts and *objets de piété,* now began to seem suspect in an age of mass consumption. The Lourdes sanctuary received numerous letters complaining that such dealers were selling forged or overpriced religious goods and relics from Lourdes. Maire Rataboul, a woman from the town of Lauzerte in the department of Tarn-et-Garonne, wrote to the director of the sanctuary about two individuals who passed through her town selling "objects having belonged to Bernadette." She was concerned because "they were selling these objects at highly inflated prices." The two peddlers insisted that the money would be used to celebrate masses at the grotto. One of the peddlers stated, moreover, that he had been cured from a long-suffering illness with the aid of Lourdes water. The woman's letter ended with a plea to know if these two men were legitimate vendors of relics: "As we live in a century where swindlers are everywhere, I beseech you, Director, to tell me if all these things are truthful and if not, to put a halt to these individuals who would so exploit the faith of worthy people."[26] The source of Maire Rataboul's anxiety lay in the threat of being cheated by smooth-talking swindlers. As she so aptly stated, living in the modern world meant living in an age of con men and charlatans. Her fears of being taken by such crooks betray an even profounder anxiety that the authentic nature of the sacred, embodied in sacred relics, was being compromised by the ability to mechanically reproduce such objects.[27]

Not only were peddlers selling sacred relics from Lourdes, but they were also selling all sorts of mass-produced statuettes, medals, and other religious merchandise. A man expressed his outrage over traveling peddlers who "have the audacity . . . to promise healing by means of plastic medallions." He ended his letter to the sanctuary by urging that the grotto "put a stop to this state of things and punish these brutes who mock the faithful." That mass-produced plastic goods were being sold as sacred items with healing powers seemed to undermine the notion of the religious relic. Jules Robert wrote: "Be so kind as to tell us if it is really true that these men are sent by you . . . and if they are charged with selling rosaries, statuettes, medals, and other religious objects."[28] If plastic religious objects had the same sacred power as "genuine" sacred relics from Lourdes, what did the sacred signify in the modern age? Confronted by scores of itinerant peddlers selling a variety of homemade and mass-produced religious goods, believing Catholics wanted to be reassured of the authentic nature of the miraculous.

Interestingly, most of the believing Catholics who wrote to the sanctuary had already bought the goods in question. They clearly wanted to believe in the authentic character of the objects and had already endowed them with some religious meaning. Yet the nature of the commercial transactions coupled with the mass-produced quality of some of the goods generated fears that these *objets de piété* might not be the "real things." The church was finally compelled to take action against fraudulent peddlers as a way to calm the worries of the faithful and reclaim its position as the true arbitrator of the sacred. The bishop

of Tarbes issued a mandate to the Catholic populace and the clergy condemning the commercial exploitation of the Lourdes shrine and particularly
denouncing crooked peddlers. The mandate began with a general declaration
of prevailing abuses connected to the Lourdes sanctuary: "The bishop of Tarbes
is compelled to point out and stigmatize certain abuses that are being committed, in various places, with the name, water, sacred objects, and (souvenirs) of
Notre-Dame de Lourdes." The bishop specified three types of abuses: "There is,
first, industrial exploitation that hides behind the appearance of religion (and
that can fool the credulous)," and second, "the odious hoaxes of the peddlers,
who, with their sacred objects, sell pretended *relics of the grotto.*" The third
threat came from "those swindlers who demand several sous for the sanctuary
to cover the fees of saying a mass celebrated at Lourdes."[29]

To prohibit inappropriate forms of commercialism, the church had to
label and distinguish proper and improper commercial transactions in the
domain of religion. The bishop's mandate did this by advising the faithful to
be "warned to regard as false all those individuals who do not carry the signature and the seal of arms of the bishop of Tarbes in an authentic manner."[30]
Thus the church did not actually condemn the buying and selling of mass-
produced *objets de piété.* Rather, it maintained that the faithful must procure
such goods from the church alone. The selling of religious objects was not
wrong in itself if conducted by the Catholic Church. The bishop's mandate, in
many ways, usurped the power of these commercial practices and made them
part of the official worship of the church. The solution, however, ignored the
very fact that many of the peddlers had forged papers claiming they were
authorized by the sanctuary to sell their wares. Thus while the mandate
intended to make the church the final judge over religious commerce, it in fact
granted a certain degree of decision-making power to the faithful, who ultimately had to determine whether the peddlers and the goods they sold were
genuine. In an age of large-scale pilgrimages and mass-marketing of religious
goods, it was impossible for the church to have complete control over the religious commerce associated with Lourdes. Increasingly, the faithful had to
decide which goods were authentic and incorporate them into their worship
as they saw fit.

Many prominent Catholics were unhappy with the church's stance
toward the burgeoning religious commerce at Lourdes. Some believed that the
church had compromised itself and desecrated the Catholic religion by con-
doning the business activities that grew up around mass pilgrimages to Lourdes. One Catholic intellectual who vociferously condemned the new religious
practices of mass pilgrimage was Joris Karl Huysmans. By the early twentieth
century, the famed decadent writer had become a devout Catholic, visiting the
Lourdes sanctuary on more than one occasion. While Huysmans was inspired
by the sacred aura of the grotto, he was offended by the crowds of Catholics

who overran the site every year. They were too easily caught up in the buying
of goods and seeing the attractions around the town. For Huysmans, these pilgrims not only misunderstood the religious significance of Lourdes, but they
were instrumental in corrupting it. In a letter to a friend, Huysmans lamented
that the inhabitants of Lourdes had "given up work to sell sausages and
rosaries and bleed the pilgrims dry."[31]

Huysmans soon made public his criticisms of the Lourdes sanctuary.
Published in 1906, his last novel, *Les Foules de Lourdes (The Crowds of
Lourdes)*, ridiculed this commercialization of the shrine. Huysmans had
already in 1884 in his novel *A Rebours (Against the Grain)* attacked the church
for allowing modern market practices to contaminate the Catholic religion.[32]
In the last years of his life, he turned his full attention to Lourdes itself, focusing his disgust on this most popular shrine in France. Huysmans lamented that
the irresistible trade in religious goods was destroying the sacred aura of the
grotto. With caustic humor and hyperbole, his final novel created an image of
an ever-increasing supply of sacred kitsch that engulfed the touring pilgrims:

> Not a single shop is without its medals and candles and rosaries and
> scapulars and pamphlets full of miracles; both old and new Lourdes are
> crammed with them; even the hotels have them on sale; and that goes on
> in street after street for miles, starting from old Lourdes with the poor
> woman who hawks little rosaries with steel chains and crosses and huge
> characteristic Lourdes rosaries of chocolate-coloured wood . . . and
> harshly tinted chromos of Bernadette kneeling taper in hand at the Vir-
> gin's feet, and Lilliputian statues and medals . . . and all these things grow
> better and bigger and larger as you get nearer the new town; the statues
> swarm increasingly and end by becoming, not less ugly, but enormous.

For Huysmans, this never-ending wave of goods seemed to overwhelm the pilgrims. As the crowds became swept up in their desires for sacred merchandise,
they lost all rational control: "And then begins a frantic competition; you are
hooked in at every step by the shops all over the town; and you go to and from
and turn this way and that amidst the tumult."[33]

Huysmans's critique of Lourdes was grounded in a type of antimodernist
elitism. He saw the commerce at Lourdes as an entirely new and unpleasant
phenomenon associated with the rise of the masses and new forms of capitalist development. For Huysmans, the development of mass pilgrimages to the
site had created an elaborate commercial life that reduced the shrine to a place
of vulgar trafficking in goods and irrational spending by naive pilgrims. Huysmans's novel not only revealed his anxiety over the state of modern religious
worship but also betrayed his fears over the democratizing impulse of mass
consumption. Now that the ordinary person could come to Lourdes, the reli-

gious site had become spoiled, and its aura was lost. The economic benefits to be made from mass pilgrimage would ultimately destroy the sacred value of the shrine. Huysmans feared that religious life was becoming commodified as it became available to a mass audience.[34]

Elite Catholic intellectuals were not the only critics of Lourdes to use this line of reasoning. Anticlerical republicans also condemned the merchandising of religious goods and the selling of Lourdes as a vacation spot. As the government of the Third Republic waged its battle with the Catholic Church, Lourdes played an increasingly public and polemical role in the republican debates about the reactionary nature of the church. Like Huysmans, republicans felt threatened by the huge numbers of people visiting the shrine. While Huysmans bemoaned the impact the new shrine was having on religious worship, republicans feared that Lourdes threatened the health of the Third Republic. These sentiments were vividly expressed in the republican press, which made the Lourdes sanctuary a favorite topic of ridicule and criticism in the late nineteenth century.[35]

An article of 1893 in the radical republican newspaper *La Lanterne* captured the mocking yet fearful tone of much of this anti-Lourdes rhetoric. Titled "The Virgin for Sale: Scapularies, Cookies, Candies, and Benedictions," it began with ironic praise for the French clergy's ability to make money for the church: "The clerics, who invented indulgences . . . and direct tickets to heaven (round-trip), are savvy salesmen; we must give them their due." Turning its full attention to Lourdes, the article noted the latest entrepreneural efforts of the church: "The businesses at Lourdes no longer operate as before, now they have put into action the Blessed Virgin of this country to incorporate a limited company with variable capital from the products of Lourdes." Listing the diverse products sold at the sanctuary from typical objects of piety to rather bizarre sacred foodstuffs, the article enlisted common sense to criticize the selling of such absurd goods: "To begin with, there are the scapularies, the rosaries, the medals, etc., then come the Béarnaise waffles, the Saint Mary vanilla cookies, the Lourdes lozenges, the Virgins, Christs, saints covered in chocolate or barley sugar. All this will be blessed." In the final paragraph of the tirade, the author revealed his utter contempt for the devout populace itself who too readily bought this sacred kitsch and thus helped to enrich a debased clergy: "We are not inventing this; our information is authentic. What fate is in store for this kind of enterprise? We will ignore it. But there are so many imbeciles on earth that it is quite possible that it will do a thriving business."[36]

Republican attacks upon the commerce at Lourdes often focused on the problem of authenticity. Republicans seemed as concerned as Catholics that the religious goods could be fraudulent. However, they feared that naive pilgrims were being duped not by peddlers or businessmen but by the church itself. Journalists often presented their concerns as honest journalistic investigations into the unfair selling practices of religious authorities. An article in *Le XIXe Siècle* claimed to have uncovered the unscrupulous practices of one religious shop. The shop in question charged two francs per liter for Lourdes water which, the journalist proclaimed, was outright exploitation. Not only were the clerics who ran the business making a huge profit from such sales, but one could not even be sure if the water was authentic. Another article in a republican daily, *La Dépêche,* presented an investigation into the printing of phony miracle stories in the religious press. After examining two such stories, the article concluded that "if all of the miracles at Lourdes recounted by *L'Univers* and other exploiters of public credulity resemble these two, we are in a fine mess."[37]

In attacking the commerce at Lourdes, the republican press was expressing its own discomfort with the blending of religion and commerce. While this blending made Catholics fear that they had lost an authentic sacred experience, republicans worried that it compromised the true nature of capitalism, which was progressive and forward-looking. The fact that a religious institution, the supposed embodiment of reactionary politics, could be caught up in modern commercial activity produced profound anxieties over the meaning of such commercialism and capitalist enterprise in the first place. Even while the republicans were engaged in a war with the church for being obscurantist and antimodern, they assailed and feared the church's use of modern technology and newfangled merchandising techniques. Ironically, the republican press condemned the church for *not* remaining outside of modern economic developments even while it called the church a bastion of reactionary superstition. This desire to keep religion separate from modern commercial life was an attempt to maintain the distinctions between secular-minded republicans and reactionary Catholics in an age when those distinctions were no longer clear.

An article in *Le Journal* expressed these tensions as it attacked a church brochure, *Lourdes: Autrefois, aujourd'hui et demain,* for its crass selling of the sanctuary as a vacation spot. Maligning the religious order that published it, the article claimed, "This order begins to manage Lourdes as others might run a seaside resort or a spa." The pamphlet "resembles, almost to perfection, those exquisitely illustrated brochures prepared by the railroad companies to excite the tourist." The author was dismayed that the church was resorting to tourist schemes to attract the faithful into making this pilgrimage: "It is curious to see the church . . . using new procedures for calling to its sanctuaries the crowds." For secular-minded Parisians, religion became even more dangerous when it was mixed up in these commercial ventures. If the church promoted Lourdes like any other tourist site, then secular-minded citizens might be attracted to the shrine.[38] Republicans feared that the selling of Lourdes could entice the masses into the hands of the church and Catholic superstition.

The republican daily *Le Siècle* warned that "once again, we must put the faithful on guard against certain advertising in which the commercial spirit allies itself with a sacrilegious abuse of piety." Rather than condemn the Catholic religion altogether, the newspaper criticized the mixing of business with religion. Religious worship was legitimate if it remained in its proper sphere, which was outside of modern economic life. *Le Siècle* was outraged that various businesses were advertising their goods as "therapeutic" because they were made with Lourdes water. The article asserted:

> Sometime ago, we reported the manufacture of unleavened bread supposedly prepared with the water from the Lourdes grotto. Today, it is the syrup of Notre-Dame de Lourdes, the miraculous elixir of Notre-Dame de Lourdes . . . the miraculous liqueur of Notre-Dame de Lourdes. . . . Suffice it to say that we disapprove of such practices and we pray that the faithful will look upon them as unworthy of the Christian spirit.

Such comments reveal a profound unease with the conditions of modern religious life. These remarks even betray a certain nostalgic yearning for a traditional faith untainted by commercialism.[39]

Another republican critic of Lourdes was the writer Émile Zola. At the time of his first visit to the sacred city in 1891, he declared that "there was material here for just the sort of novel that I like to write—a novel in which great masses of men can be shown in motion." He returned the next year to participate in the three-day National Pilgrimage and recorded each moment of the event in his exacting naturalist style. At the time of his visit, Zola was already a national celebrity and a known republican. His visit and the eventual publication of the book *Lourdes* in 1894 was a major publicity event in itself, as the religious and secular press commented upon the actual voyage as well as the novel. Zola thus helped to bring Lourdes into the public spotlight in the 1890s. The radical republican daily *La Lanterne* criticized the church for its attempt to profit from Zola's novel. In an article titled "Pious Begging," a journalist censured the Grotto fathers for their vulgar commercialism and concluded that the success of Zola's novel unwittingly "has suggested to the clergy the idea of profiting from the publicity created by the author of the Rougon-Macquart series for the grotto of Bernadette Soubirous in order to start up, itself, a little business."[40]

Zola's novel was not an outright attack upon Lourdes. Rather, it was a depiction of the role religion still played in the lives of those who suffered, those without hope. While the novel did parody the church, passages looked sympathetically at poor and sick individuals who turned to religion. In seven hundred sweeping pages, filled with nearly a hundred characters, the

novel traced the journey of pilgrims, priests, doctors, and other curious visitors who came to Lourdes for a National Pilgrimage. Zola depicted the
train ride, the processions, the grotto pools, and the people in the street. He
detailed the bustling commerce at the site and described the thousands of
shops that lined the boulevards around the sanctuary. The religious commerce of Lourdes was an essential part of the pilgrimage experience that
Zola was determined to capture. These shops "formed a regular bazaar of
open stalls, encroaching on the pavements so as to tempt people to stop as
they passed along. For more than three hundred yards no other trade was
plied: a river of chaplets, medals, and statuettes streamed without end
behind the windows."[41]

Zola was intent on capturing the spectacular nature of Lourdes. He had
already written about crowds when he composed Germinal (published in 1885)
and had devoted serious attention to the development of mass consumption
as embodied in the new, exotic department stores of Paris in his Au Bonheur
des Dames (The Ladies' Paradise), published in 1884.[42] Now he turned his
attention to Lourdes, where his interest in the crowd and modern consumption collided. Indeed, the crowd and the religious goods themselves dominated large sections of the novel. Capturing not only the bustling commerce at
Lourdes, Zola's novel also showed the frenzied collecting of sacred objects by
hordes of pilgrims at the end of their three-day stay:

> The thousands of pilgrims of the national pilgrimage streamed along the
> thoroughfares and besieged the shops in a final scramble. You would
> have taken the cries, the jostling, and the sudden rushes for those at some
> fair just breaking up amidst a ceaseless roll of vehicles. Many, providing
> themselves with provisions for the journey, cleared the open-air stalls
> where bread and slices of sausages and ham were sold. . . . But what the
> crowd more particularly purchased were religious articles, and those
> hawkers whose barrows were loaded with statuettes and sacred engrav-
> ings were reaping golden gains.

While Zola did not blatantly condemn this religious commerce as republican
journalists did, his description nonetheless betrayed a sense of anxiety at the
unrestrained desires to buy at Lourdes:

> And the fever of dealing, the pleasure of spending one's money, of
> returning home with one's pockets crammed with photographs and
> medals, lit up all the faces with a holiday expression, transforming the
> radiant gathering into a fair-field crowd with appetites either beyond
> control or satisfied.[43]

As Zola described the frenzied commercial transactions of the pilgrims, he tried to convince his readers that Lourdes was no longer a traditional religious shrine. It was now a fairground or holiday getaway. This transformation disturbed Zola because it made the religious site unduly alluring to a French populace eager for inexpensive forms of recreation. For Zola, Lourdes came to symbolize a new kind of religious experience, one that used marketing ploys and advertising techniques to renovate the Catholic faith and keep superstition alive. He, like other anticlerical republicans, tried to undermine the appeal of mass pilgrimage by depicting it as frenzied, irrational, and contrary to traditional religious worship. In many ways, republicans sounded like their Catholic adversaries when they talked about the problem of religious commerce and mass pilgrimage. By condemning the Lourdes shrine, they tried to distinguish between legitimate and illegitimate forms of worship. In the end, republican critics were instrumental in defining Catholic pilgrimage as a traditional, premodern act even while it was undergoing changes that made it a part of modern mass society.

The development of the Lourdes shrine and the debates over religious commerce in late-nineteenth-century France suggest new directions for the study of pilgrimage and tourism. Firstly, scholars of tourism need to move beyond an idealized view of Christian pilgrimage that depicts it as a premodern act immune to change. In fact, this definition of pilgrimage is itself a nineteenth-century creation. It emerged at the exact moment when pilgrimage and tourism were becoming indistinguishable. As pilgrimage was transformed into a mass cultural event that entailed the mechanical reproduction of sacred objects and the promotion of inexpensive amusements, both faithful Catholics and secular observers sought to differentiate the sacred from the secular. While Catholics needed reassurance that pilgrimage was still connected to divine power, critics of the church wanted to distance religious worship from emerging forms of secular entertainment and progressive capitalist development. Thus both sides sought to reconstruct pilgrimage and tourism as antithetic activities. Yet the inability to maintain this distinction between pilgrimage and tourism was a clear reminder of the impossibility of the task.

In this way, Lourdes was prototypical of a pilgrimage experience that became normative in the twentieth century. Today, the Catholic Church, its faithful followers, and its critics are still struggling to sort out legitimate and illegitimate religious commerce and trying to designate appropriate behavior for pilgrims. At Lourdes, debates among the faithful over the value of plastic Madonnas and other sacred trinkets continue. Furthermore, the church now claims that even secular tourists can be touched by the spiritual message of the shrine.[44] The case of Lourdes thus turns around the question commonly asked by scholars of tourism: Is modern tourism informed by religious pilgrimage?

Such a question accepts the nineteenth-century discourse that produced the two activities as binary oppositions. Instead, one might ask how pilgrimage and tourism have mutually influenced each other and what is at stake in viewing them as essentially different activities. Once we understand that pilgrimage and tourism have always been unstable constructs with a long history of convergence, we might in turn ask these same questions about the construction of the sacred and the secular in the modern era.

NOTES

Research and writing for this essay have been generously supported by a Bourse Chateaubriand and a grant from the National Endowment for the Humanities. I wish to thank Joan Scott, Bonnie Smith, William Sites, and the editors of this volume for their comments and suggestions.

1. See Daniel J. Boorstin, *The Image: A Guide to Pseudo-Events in America* (New York: Atheneum, 1987), 77–117; and Paul Fussell, *Abroad: British Literary Traveling between the Wars* (New York: Oxford University Press, 1980). See also Louis Turner and John Ash, *The Golden Hordes: International Tourism and the Pleasure Periphery* (London, 1975).

2. Dean MacCannell, *The Tourist: A New Theory of the Leisure Class* (New York: Schocken, 1976). For interpretations that have further elaborated the tourist-as-modern-pilgrim thesis, see J. B. Allcock, "Tourism as a Sacred Journey," *Loisir et Société* 11, no. 1 (1988): 33–48; Nelson H. Graburn, "Tourism: The Sacred Journey," in *Hosts and Guests: The Anthropology of Tourism,* ed. Valene L. Smith (Philadelphia: University of Pennsylvania Press, 1989), 21–36; Alexander Moore, "Walt Disney World: Bounded Ritual Space and the Playful Pilgrimage Center," *Anthropological Quarterly* 53, no. 4 (1980): 207–18; Bryan Pfaffenberger, "Serious Pilgrims and Frivolous Tourists," *Annals of Tourism Research* 19 (1983): 57–74; Jean-Didier Urbain, *L'Idiot du voyage: Histoires de touristes* (Paris: Plon, 1991).

3. On Turner's idea of pilgrimage as a liminal experience, see Victor Turner and Edith Turner, *Image and Pilgrimage in Christian Culture: Anthropological Perspectives* (New York, 1978), 1–39, 243–55. Central to their argument is the belief that the liminal experience of the pilgrimage brings about a leveling of social hierarchies and creates a moment of common humanity that lasts throughout the pilgrimage. Some anthropologists and sociologists of tourism have begun to question this concept of pilgrimage. In a 1992 special issue of *Annals of Tourism Research,* devoted to examining the relationship between pilgrimage and tourism, several scholars criticized Turner's use of liminality because it posited (rather than interrogated) an opposition between the sacred and the secular elements of the pilgrimage journey. Three of the articles in this issue have helped to shape my own argument; see John Eade, "Pilgrimage and Tourism at Lourdes, France," *Annals of Tourism Research* 19 (1992): 18–32; Erik Cohen, "Pilgrimage Centers: Concentric and Exocentric," *Annals of Tourism Research* 19 (1992): 33–50; Boris Vukonic, "Medjugorje's Religion and Pilgrimage Connection," *Annals of Tourism Research* 19 (1992): 79–91. See also Erik Cohen, "Pilgrimage and Tourism: Convergence and Divergence," in *Sacred Journeys: The Anthropology of Pilgrimage,* ed. E. Alan Morinis (Westport, Conn.: Greenwood Press, 1992), 47–61; and

Boris Vukonic, *Tourism and Religion* (New York: Pergamon, 1996), especially chaps. 8, 9, and 14.

4. I am not arguing that the twinning of commerce and religion was a new phenomenon. Indeed, since at least the early medieval period, major sacred sites all over western Europe have sold religious goods. Medieval shrine tenders and special guilds specialized in the selling of medals, badges, and printed broadsheets as well as trading sacred relics. Itinerant peddlers also hawked religious and secular goods around the holy site. When pilgrims went to religious shrines, they wanted and expected to buy these religious souvenirs. Such commercial exchanges not only satisfied the desires of pilgrims but also served to spread the word of the holy site and thus acted as a form of early religious publicity. Furthermore, these medieval and early-modern pilgrimages often coincided with seasonal fairs and festivals that created an atmosphere of both the popular marketplace and the carnival. Thus commerce and piety have been deeply interconnected activities for the devout who went on pilgrimage. Yet I do want to argue that the scale and scope of using capitalist market practices in the nineteenth century not only transformed the act of pilgrimage into a mass-produced experience but now confronted a mass public with conflicts over the appropriate relationship between commerce and faith. For a discussion of the commerce around medieval and early modern religious shrines and pilgrimage sites, see Jean Chélini and Henry Branthomme, *Les Chemins de Dieu: Histoire des pèlerinages chrétiens des origines à nos jours* (Paris: Hachette, 1982); William A. Christian, Jr., *Apparitions in Late Medieval and Renaissance Spain* (Princeton: Princeton University Press, 1981), and *Local Religion in Sixteenth-Century Spain* (Princeton: Princeton University Press, 1981); Alphonse Dupront, *Du sacré: Croisades et pèlerinages, images et langages* (Paris: Gallimard, 1987); Ronald C. Finucane, *Miracles and Pilgrims: Popular Beliefs in Medieval England* (Totowa, NY: Rowman and Littlefield, 1977), especially chaps. 2 and 3; Pierre André Sigal, *Les Marcheurs de Dieu: Pèlerinages et pèlerins au Moyen Age* (Paris: A. Colin, 1974).

5. It is surprising how little attention historians of religion have paid to the commercialization of religious life in nineteenth-century France. Despite a wealth of new scholarship that examines the relationship between religious practice and the political, social and cultural life of modern France, much of this literature has either ignored or slighted the role of commerce in the lives of religious believers. This is not to say that historians have denied the Church's innovative use of new technologies and modern market practices in cultivating worship. Indeed, work on nineteenth-century Catholic pilgrimage has established that the railway and mass press enabled large numbers of pilgrims to reach hitherto-remote sacred sites. Historians have also noted that new commercial practices brought great wealth to certain religious orders and specific pilgrimage towns. Yet few scholars of modern pilgrimage have sought to explore how commercialization has shaped the devotional practices and beliefs of ordinary lay Catholics. By this I mean that the emergence of new forms of commercial activity actually altered, in fundamental ways, how modern Catholics intereacted with the sacred. The important new study of Lourdes by Ruth Harris (cited below), for example, provides no analysis of the commercialization of religious practices at the shrine. For seminal historical work that examines French Catholic pilgrimage in the nineteenth century, see Philippe Boutry and Michel Cinquin, *Deux Pèlerinages au XIXe Siècle: Ars et Paray-le-Monial* (Paris: Beauchesne, 1980); Gérard Cholvy and Yves Marie Hilaire, *Histoire religieuse de la France contemporaine, 1800–1880*, 2 vols. (Toulouse: Privat, 1985–86); Judith Devlin, *The Superstitious Mind: French Peasants and the Supernatural*

in the Nineteenth Century (New Haven: Yale University Press, 1987); Ralph Gibson, *A Social History of French Catholicism, 1789–1914* (London: Routledge, 1989); Ruth Harris, *Lourdes: Body and Spirit in the Secular Age* (New York: Viking, 1999); Raymond A. Jonas, "Restoring a Sacred Center: Pilgrimage, Politics, and the Sacré-Coeur," *Historical Reflections/Réflexions Historiques* 20, no. 1 (winter 1994): 95–123; Thomas A. Kselman, *Miracles and Prophecies in Nineteenth-Century France* (New Brunswick, NJ: Rutgers University Press, 1983); Michael R. Marrus, "Cultures on the Move: Pilgrims and Pilgrimages in Nineteenth-Century France," *Stanford French Review* 1 (1977): 205–20; Barbara Corrado Pope, "Immaculate and Powerful: The Marian Revival in the Nineteenth Century," in *Immaculate and Powerful: The Female in Sacred Image and Social Reality,* ed. Clarissa W. Atkinson, Constance H. Buchanan, and Margaret R. Miles (Boston: Beacon Press, 1985), 173–200; Bonnie G. Smith, *Ladies of the Leisure Class: The Bourgeoises of Northern France in the Nineteenth Century* (Princeton: Princeton University Press, 1981). Also see David Blackbourn, *Marpingen: Apparitions of the Virgin Mary in Nineteenth-Century Germany* (New York: Knopf, 1994) for an important analysis of Catholic pilgrimage in Germany.

6. For a more comprehensive analysis of the apparitions of Bernadette Soubirous, see Harris, *Lourdes,* chapters 1–3. Also see the seven-volume compilation of documents concerning the apparitions and later development of the pilgrimage site, edited and annotated by René Laurentin and Bernard Billet: *Lourdes: Dossier des documents authentiques,* 7 vols. (Paris: P. Lethielleax, 1957–62). As priests and the church-authorized chroniclers of the Lourdes apparitions, Laurentin and Billet promote an uncritical view of the supernatural events at the grotto. See also Kselman, *Miracles and Prophesies,* for an analysis of Lourdes in the context of nineteenth-century religiosity.

7. This manifestation of popular faith has been interpreted by many historians as part of a larger process of feminization of Catholic practice. Not only were the seers women and children but the faithful who flocked to these new places of pilgrimage were also predominantly women. Lourdes was no exception to this phenomenon. During the five months of Bernadette's visionary experience women outnumbered men as pious witnesses at the site. They continued to outnumber men as pilgrims throughout the nineteenth century. For works that address the predominance of women in Catholic worship and analyze the meaning of this feminization of religious experience, see Boutry and Cinquin, *Deux pèlerinages;* Cholvy and Hilaire, *Histoire religieuse;* Gibson, *Social History;* Olwen Hufton, "The Reconstruction of a Church, 1796–1801," in *Beyond the Terror: Essays in French Regional and Social History, 1794–1815,* ed. Gwynne Lewis and Colin Lucas (Cambridge: Cambridge University Press, 1983), 21–52; Kselman, *Miracles and Prophecies;* Claude Langlois, *Le Catholicisme au féminin: Les congrégations françaises à supérieure générale au XIXe siècle* (Paris: Cerf, 1984); Pope, "Immaculate and Powerful," 173–200; Smith, *Ladies of Leisure Class;* Sandra L. Zimdars-Swartz, *Encountering Mary from La Salette to Medjugorje* (Princeton: Princeton University Press, 1991). For a summary of this material with an attempt to locate the causes and ramifications of this feminization, see Ralph Gibson, "Le Catholicisme et les femmes en France au XIXe siècle," *Revue d'Histoire de l'Eglise de France* 79 (1993): 63–93. Historians who have looked at the feminization of religious experience in different national and religious contexts include Blackbourn, *Marpingen;* Ann Douglas, *The Feminization of American Culture* (New York: Knopf, 1977); and Nancy F. Cott, *The Bonds of Womanhood: "Woman's Sphere" in New England, 1780–1835* (New Haven: Yale University Press, 1977).

8. Of the hundreds of proclaimed apparitions in nineteenth-century France, the

church recognized only three others as authentic. They were the visions of Catherine Labouré in Paris (1830), of Mélanie Calvat and Maximin Giraud at La Salette (1846), and of five peasant children in Pontmain (1871). The church was reluctant to accept popular visionary experience because it threatened the hierarchy and doctrine of the male-dominated faith. However, once the church investigated the situation and acknowledged the staying power of such displays of popular piety, it successfully incorporated them into mainstream Catholic thought. Lourdes was typical of this pattern of behavior by the church. When religious authorities took control of the grotto at Lourdes, they consciously tried to limit any further activity by Bernadette. In 1860, the local curé arranged for Bernadette to be a boarder at the hospice school of the Sisters of Charity in Lourdes. In 1866 Bernadette was accepted into the order of the Sisters of Charity and moved to the town of Nevers, where she spent the rest of her short life in the convent of Saint-Gildard. She died on April 16, 1879. For the church's attitude toward the Marian piety of the nineteenth century, see Blackbourn, *Marpingen*, chap. 1; Kselman, *Miracles and Prophesies*, chap. 1; Pope, "Immaculate and Powerful"; Zimdars-Swartz, *Encountering Mary*, 25–92, 165–90. For the church's attitude toward Bernadette and her life after the apparitions, see Harris, *Lourdes*, chapters 3–5.

9. He bought the grotto of Massabieille in 1861 for a mere 971 francs and continued to acquire substantial amounts of property around the site and in the city of Lourdes until 1882. Information about these financial transactions comes from an 1899 government report appraising the economic worth of the Lourdes shrine. The government administrator, M. Monsourat, divided the bishop's acquisitions into two distinct periods: acquisitions from 1861 through 1874 comprising the buying of the grotto property and the surrounding territory needed for the goal "of enlarging the domain of the Grotto administration" and a second period from 1875 through 1882 that included the buying of land in the city of Lourdes "in order to permit the widening of the Boulevard de la grotte." See Archives Nationales (hereafter AN) BB18 1589, Affaires criminelles, "Administration de la mense épiscopale de Tarbes: Rapport de M. Monsourat, Commissaire-Administrateur," December 27, 1899, 63–85. For a discussion of the church's decision to buy the property of the grotto, see Kselman, *Miracles and Prophesies*, 156–57.

10. Kselman, *Miracles and Prophesies*, 160–66, 172–79; Laurentin and Billet, *Lourdes*, 7:11; Marrus, "Cultures on the Move," 213–20. Marrus argues convincingly that local village pilgrimages to older sacred sites died out in the late nineteenth century and were replaced by church-run national pilgrimages to newer sites like Lourdes. The church's use of the railway and the mass press to promote Lourdes played a key role in this shift.

11. Founded in 1843 by Father Emmanuel d'Alzon, the Augustinian Fathers of the Assumption (the Assumptionists) were a nationwide missionary order dedicated to fighting against "the de-Christianization of the nation" by promoting a more sentimental and popular form of Catholicism. The impact of the Assumptionists on French Catholicism cannot be overestimated. The ultramontane religious order came to prominence immediately after France's defeat in the Franco-Prussian War. Many Frenchmen and women, shocked by France's loss in the war and even more shocked by Thiers's violent suppression of the Commune, looked to religious explanations to make sense of these events. During the thirty years from 1871 to 1901, the Assumptionists exploited this sense of horror and guilt over 1871 and promoted various forms of public prayer and ritual. The National Pilgrimage to Lourdes was one of the most successful of these public rituals dedicated to a renewal of faith among the masses in

France. René Rémond, in analyzing the period after the Franco-Prussian War, has concluded that the Assumptionists were largely responsible for shaping the religious revival of the 1870s and 1880s. See René Rémond, *The Right Wing in France from 1815 to De Gaulle*, trans. James M. Laux (Philadelphia: University of Pennsylvania Press, 1966), 184–88. Also see Cholvy and Hilaire, *Histoire religieuse*, 1:166–67, 194–95. For a discussion of the personal motivations of key members of the Assumptionists and how these motivations shaped the public behavior and political activities of the order, see Harris, *Lourdes*, chapter 7.

12. Kselman, *Miracles and Prophesies*, 163; Marrus, "Culture on the Move," 216–18; Pope, "Immaculate and Powerful," 185–87. These sources differ slightly on the number of pilgrims going to Lourdes on national pilgrimages. I cite the most conservative estimates.

13. While the plan to build the national route was approved by the central government in August 1875, the protests of Lourdes inhabitants stalled construction until 1880. Many townspeople feared a loss of revenue to their shops if pilgrims were rerouted away from the inner city and went directly to the sanctuary below. The dispute was finally settled when the municipality of Lourdes agreed that the new route be linked to the city by two adjoining streets (AN BB18 1589, "Administration de la mense," 76–78). For the joint projects of the 1880s, see Archives de l'Oeuvre de la Grotte (hereafter AG) A16, Rapports avec la Mairie de Lourdes/police de la grotte, carton I, dossier 4, Lettre de Père Sempé au maire de Lourdes, Lourdes, March 23, 1881; AG 1E1, Etat comparatif des avantages procurés à la ville de Lourdes par la movement des pèlerinages (1860–1906).

14. AN BB18 1589, "Administration de la mense," 76.

15. AN BB18 1589, "Administration de la mense," 14, 43.

16. AN BB18 1589, "Administration de la mense," 40–45, 87.

17. Abbé Martin, *Guide de Lourdes et ses environs à l'usage des pèlerins* (Saumur: C. Charier, 1893), 37. See pages 8–18 for discussions of the proper religious behavior of pilgrims and for the presentation of the history of Bernadette and the shrine, pages 47–55 for practical information for making the pilgrimage, and 25–46 for suggestions for excursions into the countryside and other sight-seeing activities. For other typical guidebooks of the period see G. Marès, *Lourdes et ses environs* (Bordeaux: Impr. de G. Gounouilhou, 1894); Bernard Dauberive, *Lourdes et ses environs, Guide du Pèlerin et du Touriste* (Poitiers: G. Bonamy, 1896); J. Couret, *Guide-Almanach de Notre-Dame de Lourdes 1900* (Bordeaux, 1900).

18. For an examination of the Paris Exposition of 1900 and its relationship to the emerging consumer culture of France at the turn of the century, see Rosalind H. Williams, *Dream Worlds: Mass Consumption in Late Nineteenth-Century France* (Berkeley: University of California Press, 1982), chap. 3. For an analysis of the Musée Grévin's wax exhibits and the dioramas of Paris as new forms of commercial entertainment for a mass audience, see Vanessa R. Schwartz, *Spectacular Realities: Early Mass Culture in Fin-de Siècle Paris* (Berkeley: University of California Press, 1999), chaps. 3 and 4. By the 1890s, the Lourdes sanctuary was capitalizing on these same forms of commercial entertainment innovated by Parisian entrepreneurs.

19. For church and government statistics on the numbers of pilgrims and visitors to the shrine, see AG 18E3, Listes des pèlerinages, Journal des chapelains, 1903–1909, statistique envoyée à M. le Chanoine Berengers; AN F7 12734, Rapport du préfet des Hautes-Pyrénées au ministère de l'Intérieur, Tarbes, November 15, 1908, 1–5. By the early twentieth century pilgrims from every region of France went to Lourdes on orga-

nized church pilgrimages. The majority of these organized pilgrims came by train on either diocesan pilgrimages or national pilgrimages. Yet despite the increase in the number of pilgrims and the growth in regional diversity, the profile of the average pilgrim remained remarkably similar to the early followers of Bernadette. Church records reveal that women outnumbered men as participants in organized pilgrimage until the outbreak of World War I. The records show that at least twice as many women as men were bathed in the sacred waters of the grotto pools during the period 1893 to 1913. See AG 18E4, Statistiques généralités (1893–1977), Statistiques fournies par l'hospitalité. Furthermore, organized pilgrimages from the southwest of France far outweighed the number of organized pilgrimages from other regions of France. The dioceses around Brittany and the north were a close second and third. There were virtually no pilgrimages from the east of France and few from Paris. During the period 1866 to 1887 there were only six diocesan pilgrimages from Paris, sending an estimated twenty-five hundred pilgrims. See AG 12E2, Liste des localités venues en pèlerinage à Lourdes (1868–87). The social and economic positions of these pilgrims are much harder to determine. According to early government reports, the initial followers of Bernadette came from both the lower and upper classes of village society. Church authorities also noted the class differences during the early regional pilgrimages of the 1860s. See AN F19 2374 for the series of letters from Commissaire Jacomet to Préfet Massy, February–June 1858 and AG 1HD1, Processions, guérisons et pèlerinages divers (1866–1950), Journal du Sanctuaire de Notre-Dame de Lourdes, especially years 1867–68. Yet these distinctions were recorded less often once the church developed the National Pilgrimage in the 1870s and used a more inclusive language of nationalism to describe the processions. However, given the prosperity of entrepreneurs who ran restaurants and hotels for people of varying economic levels, I suspect that a cross-class dimension remained a pronounced part of the Lourdes pilgrimage experience.

20. For exact figures on the growth of the Lourdes communal revenues and budget, see AG 1E1, Etat comparatif des avantages procurés à la ville de Lourdes, sections 2 and 3; see section 13 for information on thermal spas in the region. For information on the investments of various financial institutions, see AN F7 12734, Rapport du préfet des Hautes-Pyrénées au ministère de l'Intérieur, Tarbes, November 15, 1908, 6–8, 9–13. It is interesting to note that the population of Lourdes did not increase as dramatically as its revenues did. During the same period (1861–1906) the population almost doubled from 4,510 to 8,708 permanent inhabitants; see AG 1E1, Etat comparatif, section 1. However, this figure does not include the hundreds of laborers who came to Lourdes for seasonal employment during the pilgrimage months (May through September). By the early twentieth century, Lourdes functioned like a modern tourist city. A small permanent population catered to a mass influx of visitors, dramatically increasing the wealth of the town and the entire region.

21. See AG 7P3, Affaire vente d'eau de la grotte (1879–88), Advertising brochure for Pastilles à l'Eau de Lourdes, F. Valette & Co., 1888.

22. Marcel Jouhandeau, Mémorial, vol. 2 (Paris, 1951), 51. This reference comes from Eugen Weber, France: Fin de Siècle (Cambridge, Mass., 1986), 189–90.

23. With the founding of the Third Republic in 1870, republican politicians tried to limit the institutional power of the Catholic Church. Embracing Enlightenment ideals of scientific progress and secularism, they saw the church as an antiliberal force to be contained. By 1879 the republicans had defeated their enemies and were in a position to enact their anticlerical program, which pushed the church out of educational, military, and civic spheres of French society. The laic laws of the 1880s created tax-sup-

ported public primary education, reducing Catholic influence over schooling. All ecclesiastical members were removed from the high council of education, while lay teachers replaced priests and nuns in public primary schools. Further anticlerical legislation passed in the 1890s sought to regulate all religious orders and outlawed nonauthorized ones. This legislation culminated in the separation of church and state in 1905. For a brief history of anticlericalism in this period, see Paul A. Gagnon, *France since 1789* (New York, 1964), 198–238. For a more detailed account of the Third Republic's anticlerical campaigns of the 1890s, see Pierre Sorlin, *Waldeck-Rousseau* (Paris: A. Colin, 1966); and Malcolm O. Partin, *Waldeck-Rousseau, Combes, and the Church: The Politics of Anti-Clericalism, 1899–1905* (Durham, N.C.: Duke University Press, 1969). For an analysis of the impact of these antliclerical laws on one region in France, see Caroline Ford, *Creating the Nation in Provincial France: Religion and Political Identity in Brittany* (Princeton: Princeton University Press, 1993), especially chaps. 5 and 6.

24. *Manuel du Pèlerinage Lorrain à Notre-Dame de Lourdes*, 12th ed. (Saint-Dié: Imp. de Humbert, 1899), 8; *Manuel des Pèlerins de l'Archidiocèse d'Auch à Notre-Dame de Lourdes* (Arras (Pas de Calais): Imprimerie de la Presse Populaire, 1911), 16; *Lourdes, guide pratique à l'usage des pèlerins* (Paris and Poitiers: H. Oudin, 1898), 3, 5–8, 10–13.

25. AG 7P3, Affaire vente d'eau de la grotte (1879–88), dossier 1, Lettre de Louis Baron au Père Sempé, Toulouse, April 12, 1888.

26. AG 7P3, Affaire vente d'eau de la grotte (1879–88), dossier 2, Lettre de Maire Rataboul au Directeur du sanctuaire de Lourdes, Lauzerte (Tarn-et-Garonne), n.d.

27. My analysis here is shaped by the work of Walter Benjamin. In "The Work of Art in the Age of Mechanical Reproduction," Benjamin noted that with the mechanical reproduction of art (especially photography and later film), art lost its "aura," its uniqueness and authenticity: "The technique of reproduction detaches the reproduced object from the domain of tradition. By making many reproductions it substitutes a plurality of copies for a unique existence." (*Illuminations*, ed. Hannah Arendt, trans. Harry Zohn [New York: Harcourt, Brace & World, 1968], 221). Benjamin's analysis of art lends itself to an analysis of the religious experience at Lourdes in the late nineteenth century. A traditional Christian pilgrimage site and its sacred objects are endowed with both a sense of sacred aura and miraculous power by their association with a unique divine power: Jesus, Mary, or a saint. This sacred aura and miraculous power was thrown into question at Lourdes by the mass-marketing of the shrine and its goods.

28. AG 7P3, Affaire vente d'eau de la grotte (1879–88), dossier 2, Lettre anonyme au Directeur du sanctuaire de Lourdes, January 4, 1888; Lettre de Jules Robert au Supérieur des missionnaires de Notre-Dame de Lourdes, January 9, 1888. There are numerous letters in AG, 7P3 that discuss other cases of fraud committed against the Lourdes sanctuary and the family of Bernadette.

29. AG 7P3, Affaire vente d'eau de la grotte (1879–88), dossier 1, Mandat de l'évêque de Tarbes, Tarbes, May 2, 1888.

30. AG 7P3, Mandat de l'évêque de Tarbes, Tarbes, May 2, 1888.

31. Letter from Joris Karl Huysmans to Henry Céard, Lourdes, March 19, 1903, in *The Road From Decadence: From Brothel to Cloister, Selected Letters of J.-K. Huysmans*, ed. Barbara Beaumont (London: Athlone, 1989), 219.

32. Rosalind Williams provides an interesting analysis of Huysmans's *A Rebours* in *Dream Worlds*, 126–50. Williams looks at Huysmans's attack on the emerging mass consumption in French society, which included a critique of the church's acceptance of modern market practices and values.

33. Joris Karl Huysmans, *The Crowds of Lourdes,* trans. W. H. Mitchell (New York: Benziger Brothers, 1925), 27–28.

34. Huysmans was not alone in his views. His ideas fit into a larger elite response to mass consumption in the late nineteenth century. See Williams, *Dream Worlds,* chaps. 4–8, for an analysis of both elite and democratic responses to the rise of mass consumer culture.

35. In her analysis of the debates around the consumer revolution in the late nineteenth century (*Dream Worlds,* chaps. 4–8), Williams found that republicans expressed great anxiety around the issue of the democratization of luxury. These same fears were voiced over religious matters when republicans discussed the commercialization of the Lourdes shrine at the turn of the century.

36. AN F19 2376, Coupures de presse, "La Vierge en Actions: Scapulaires, biscuits, bonbons, et bénédictions," *La Lanterne,* May 29, 1893.

37. AN F19 2376, Coupures de presse, "Pharmacie Cléricale chez Le Marchand d'Eau de Lourdes," *Le XIXe Siècle,* September 24, 1890; AN F19 2374, Cultes, "Jonglerie Charlatanisme," *La Dépêche,* September 25, 1881.

38. AN F19 2376, Coupures de presse, "Une réclame bien faite," *Le Journal,* July 27, 1893.

39. AN F19 2376, Coupures de presse, "La Concurrence à Lourdes," *Le Siècle,* January 20, 1904.

40. Ernest A. Vizetelly, preface to Émile Zola, *The Three Cities: Lourdes,* trans. Ernest A. Vizetelly, 2 vols. (New York: Macmillan, 1899), 1:v; AN F19 2374, Coupures de presse, "Pieuse Mendicité," *La Lanterne,* May 5, 1894. Zola's extended visit to Lourdes in 1892 also received serious attention in the left- and right-wing press; see "Le Pèlerinage de Lourdes," *Le Gaulois,* August 19, 1892; "Encore M. Zola à Lourdes," *Le Monde,* August 28, 1892; "M. Zola et le pèlerinage de Lourdes," *Le Temps,* August 26, 1892.

41. Zola, *The Three Cities,* 2:281.

42. For a historical analysis of Zola's interest in the crowd as it was depicted in *Germinal,* see Susanna Barrows, *Distorting Mirrors: Visions of the Crowd in Late Nineteenth-Century France* (New Haven: Yale University Press, 1981). For a discussion of Zola's interest in consumer culture and the department store, see Williams, *Dream Worlds,* 67–68, 198–99, 315–16; and the introduction by Kristin Ross of Émile Zola, *The Ladies' Paradise* (Berkeley: University of California Press, 1992).

43. Zola, *The Three Cities,* 2:279–80.

44. See Eade, "Pilgrimage and Tourism," 27–29.

The Chamber of Commerce's Carnival

City Festivals and Urban Tourism in the United States, 1890–1915

Nineteenth-century urban Americans were fond of parades and processions. Military troops and brass bands, carriages full of public officials, smartly marching schoolboys, and various fraternal and benevolent associations poured into the streets to celebrate the Fourth of July and other holidays. Working men constructed floats to demonstrate their trades and manufacturers to advertise their products. Yet, although these events were grand spectacles drawing huge crowds, they were not primarily tourist attractions. The loosely organized network of elected and other civic leaders who planned such events made little reference to, and few arrangements for, out-of-town visitors. Civic ceremonies composed of the various corporate bodies into which urban citizens organized themselves, these events enacted in the most public fashion possible the city's social order.[1]

But in 1899 the editor of the *Chicago Tribune* complained, "Long ranks of troops all in the same low-toned uniforms, Knights of Pythias, letter carriers, citizens in carriages, civic bodies, etc., are well enough in their way, but they furnish no spectacle for the eye and speedily they grow monotonous." In asserting that "What our processions need is life, diversity, picturesqueness, and rich color effects . . . ," he merely affirmed a change already well under way in celebratory practices. From the 1890s on, city festivals largely organized by urban business associations displaced the enactment of civic order in favor of grand historical and carnival spectacles. A San Francisco parade celebrating the city's Spanish origins included floats representing historical sites, such as the Mission Dolores, as well as some bearing Chinese sages, Japanese samurai, Philip of Macedon, and the intrepid tea-hurlers of 1773, among others.[2]

Such events offered onlookers a lavish public party whose meaning lay more in the capacity of fun to soothe the stresses of industrial life than in the expression of the city's social organization. The change in emphasis corresponded with businessmen's growing interest in attracting tourists. Once

89

undreamed of, urban tourism was on the rise at the turn of the century, and a plethora of local, state, and national centennials provided convenient occasions for encouraging the practice.[3] The organizers' desire to appeal to tourists steadily eroded the events' civic content. Placing rationalized leisure at the center of public life, the chamber of commerce's carnival encouraged residents to behave like tourists, to be consumers of entertainment rather than members of a civic order.

Although the wish to bring in visitors displaced the once central representations of work and civic bonds, it did not eliminate them. The newly popular historical parades presented a heroic narrative of American progress and ethnic assimilation that could and did represent a city to itself in a way analogous to the institutional model of earlier parades. Thousands of city dwellers participated in the construction of floats, performed as Founding Fathers, Miss Columbia, or Montezuma, and marched in parade delegations. But even as this participation continued the older custom of representing the city's social groups, it now foregrounded ethnic origins. Urbanites' cultures, rather than their civic roles, were on display.[4]

Business leaders saw no conflict between fostering urban harmony and attracting free-spending tourists. Along with their commercial potential, historical and carnival parades promised to address the vexed question of how to represent the city's contending social groups fairly. Like many middle-class reformers, the members of business associations in cities as diverse as New York, Chicago, Washington, D.C., and San Francisco had long been concerned about the deep rifts of class and ethnicity that divided urbanites in these years. They hoped that grand civic events would "have the effect of promoting a more brotherly spirit among the citizens themselves." Heroic history and brightly-colored whimsy offered a renovated sense of nationality and civic spirit through rational leisure: "Chicago forgot itself yesterday, and for the first time the fall festival became a carnival in reality. . . . Buying and selling were forgotten."[5] Such events, their sponsors hoped, would at once disarm conflicts over work and politics and marshal the support of city dwellers behind the providers of the fun—increasingly, business organizations.

Officially free to all comers and accessible to all who could walk in the streets, the festivals were ideal occasions to encourage civic unity. As an orderly, undifferentiated "great human mass" enjoying a spectacle they did not create, the citizens of Chicago who walked through the Court of Honor marked the Autumn Festival's democratic success. The sale of goods and services such as railroad tickets, hotel rooms, restaurant meals, and souvenirs to tourists funded the events, making them a perfect reconciliation of civic and commercial aims. In the view of organized businessmen, the tourist trade would simultaneously provide the money needed to grease the city's often cranky social machinery, occasions for cooperation and pride among urban residents, and a model for ideal urban citizenship.[6]

The ability of organized businessmen to adapt existing celebratory traditions to their commercial and civic purposes in the 1890s derived from several interwoven factors: the "improvement" of the physical and cultural infrastructure of major cities; a quarter-century's worth of experience with national and international industrial expositions; the growth of a tourist industry; changing attitudes toward public, commercial leisure; and the cultivation of a heroic narrative of an American past that included an influential model of class and racial hierarchy.[7] The chamber of commerce's carnival forged strong links among national history, civic spirit, and the aestheticization and commodification of cultural differences.

Beginning in the late nineteenth century, municipalities and wealthy urbanites devoted large sums to building everything from sewer systems and electric streetcar lines to libraries, museums, and opera houses. Large, carefully landscaped public parks and broad, smoothly paved boulevards embellished urban peripheries and contributed to the development of expensive residence districts. Sky-scraping office buildings with beautifully adorned lobbies decorated the business districts, as sprawling department stores, hotels, and theaters did the retail areas. By the turn of the century, many large cities were cleaner and healthier than they had been for much of the nineteenth century and boasted strikingly modern architecture.[8]

On their own, however, such improvements could not make American cities attractive to tourists. The emergence of new attitudes toward urban leisure endowed urban physical improvements with the cultural resonance that had long lured pleasure travelers to European cities. Throughout much of the preceding century, the conventional view of American cities had been that their relentless commercialism made them cold, utilitarian places. The ugly functionality of business houses and the gaudy excess of millionaires' mansions were the architectural expression of this materialism. Real estate development cannibalized what few traces of the brief past that might linger in urban built environments, and anyway Americans hardly had any past to celebrate. Thoroughly modern monuments to commerce, American cities possessed little to attract the nineteenth-century tourist.[9]

The physical improvements of the turn of the century, combined with the growing respectability of commercial leisure that they stimulated, meant that the nation's cities no longer seemed unsuitable for tourists. Their parks, theaters, opera houses, museums, and lavish retail districts attracted growing numbers of Americans whose chief aim was to see the sights, do a little shopping, dine at a first-class restaurant, and perhaps take in a show. Even as American cities remained the great symbols of the nation's commercial and

industrial might, the buildings and institutions that symbolized these achievements now also represented—rather than being at odds with—urban leisure
and beauty. The possibility of urban tourism exemplified the reconciliation of
commerce with culture characteristic of the period.[10]

But urban tourism was not simply the unintended consequence of
broader cultural changes. The organized businessmen of many cities took the
lead promoting their hometowns as tourist attractions and in general fostering
the respectability of commercialized leisure. For many, their initial experience
joining more traditional boosterism with the promotion of tourism came in
holding a national or international exposition. The expositions held on American soil between 1876 and 1915 modeled both the pragmatic and the philosophical means of reconciling commerce and culture through profitable
leisure. At the most obvious level, all of the great world's fairs were urban
events sponsored by local business elites who expected them to benefit their
city economically. The products and methods of large-scale, capitalist industry
were the raison d'être of expositions. Moreover, in the United States the events
were largely funded by private capital and managed by businessmen rather
than public officials. Consequently, they provided a model for the business-
organized and business-centered celebration of events of public importance.[11]

The expositions also encouraged the integration of American cities into
existing tourist itineraries, which until the late nineteenth century had been
oriented almost exclusively toward rural scenery and country resorts. In competing for exposition visitors and at the instigation of fair organizers, hotel
managers and other firms catering to travelers expanded old services and
developed new ones. The commissioners of the Centennial Exposition in
Philadelphia (1876) seem to have made no effort to regulate hotel rates or
assist visitors in obtaining housing. The rapacity of landlords and the overcrowding of the city's hotels and boardinghouses became a staple of satirical
commentary on the exposition. The directors of San Francisco's Panama-
Pacific International Exposition (1915), in contrast, made a serious and quite
rancorous effort to cap hotel rates and to provide visitors with housing information. By the turn of the century, no big-city festival was without its official
hotel information bureau.[12]

At the same time, established tour companies expanded their enterprises,
and new ones sprang up to serve and to encourage the people who wanted to
visit regional, national, and international fairs and festivals. The best known of
the early organized tour agencies, Britain's Thomas Cook and Son, dominated
travel between Europe and the United States from the 1870s, but a significant
number of American firms had entered the field by the early 1880s. A decade
later, the railroads' general passenger departments were more actively court-
ing pleasure travelers as well. Travel information bureaus proliferated, usually
as adjuncts to newspapers, magazines, guidebook publishers, and organiza-

tions of resort owners. New England, New York, and the San Francisco Bay Area supported organizations dedicated to promoting urban and regional tourism in the early twentieth century. By 1912, the tourist business had become big enough to support its own trade show, a "Travel and Vacation Exhibition," in New York City. The tourist industry had come of age.[13]

Although rural and resort tourism remained dominant, major cities received a growing amount of publicity as tourist sites during these years. City presses had a long tradition of producing local handbooks, urban sketches, and directories that offered "points of interest" along with useful information about city officials, the water system, the fire department, and the public schools. By the early twentieth century, chambers of commerce adapted this tradition to their newfound interest in tourism, producing both cheap and glossy, limited-edition city guides. Following the lead of Chicago's Rand, McNally, regional and national firms specializing in guidebooks also began to produce a large number of city-specific guidebooks in the 1890s. Catering specifically to pleasure travelers, these guidebooks emphasized information about hotels, train stations, and sight-seeing itineraries rather than civic infrastructure.[14]

Once in existence, tourist enterprises had strong commercial reasons for wanting to broaden the range of both destinations and clientele for their services. More importantly, they promoted the vision of self-fulfillment and social harmony by means of commercialized leisure that was central to the cultural significance of department stores, world's fairs—and business-organized urban festivals. "All sensible people recognize the fact," one tour company publication asserted in 1892, "that by taking a rational amount of rest and recreation, a man not only obtains more pleasure and satisfaction in life, but is enabled to accomplish more and better work."[15] Essential to the health of the individual, properly organized leisure was also a necessary lubricant for an industrial society, a necessary complement to the work ethic. In selling pleasure travel, tourist enterprises situated commerce at the core of genteel leisure. Businessmen endorsed this revaluation of recreation in sponsoring festivals with the twin aims of social reconciliation and making money off tourists.

Without a moneyed clientele, the efforts of tourist agencies and organized business to recast commercialized leisure as the means to the good life would have had little effect. Despite chronic, severe recessions and inflationary pressures, a rising number of middle-class Americans earned enough to consider a summer vacation trip by the turn of the century. Still, their newly gained disposable income did not permit the months' long luxury tours costing hundreds of dollars that dominated tour agency offerings. Responding to and soliciting such well-to-do but not wealthy potential customers, agencies began by the 1890s to market relatively inexpensive three-day city tours as well as transcontinental, European, and round-the-world journeys.[16]

Noting the addition of "a numerous array of low-priced tours" to its repertoire in 1890, Raymond and Whitcomb, the premiere American tour company, explained that "They have been arranged with a view to meeting the wishes of large number of our patrons who find it inconvenient to absent themselves from home or business ties for the time required in the longer excursions. . . ." Such tours constituted an affordable, efficient holiday for the busy professional man and middle-class housewife. By the 1890s Thomas Cook and Son also offered three-day tours from East Coast cities to Washington, D.C., for between $9 and $13.25. As with all its other tours, members of these parties enjoyed the best rail and hotel accommodations. Paying the higher price bought a carriage drive and a steamboat ride up the Potomac to Mt. Vernon. Such a tour was within the reach of comfortably middle-class people earning between fifteen hundred and thirty-five hundred dollars a year.[17]

The national capital was the chief beneficiary of such tours. It had attracted pleasure travelers since its official opening in 1800, for its fine public buildings and the absence of large-scale commerce or industry made it unlike most other American cities. But tourist firms and urban business organizations in more commercial and industrial metropolises were not slow to promote their own attractions. The vacationer, they insisted with growing vigor, might want urban hustle and excitement as much as a pastoral, restful encounter with nature. One Illinois Central Railroad folder sighed, "Thoughts of Rest and Recreation now begin to call up mental pictures of delightful and cool summer resorts of lakes, mountains and seashore" and, it added, "of the attractions of the large and interesting cities. . . . Why not visit Chicago[?]. . . . It is a city everyone desires to see."[18]

Particularly for cities like Washington, D.C., which had never had significant commerce or industry, and San Francisco, whose dominance of West Coast commerce was declining relative to Los Angeles, Portland, and Seattle by the 1890s, the promotion of tourism promised to improve or bolster the local economy. In 1898, the annual report of Washington's board of trade acknowledged frankly, "Much of Washington's strength, like that of a woman, is in its beauty; its face is its fortune. Among the Board's most important committees, therefore, are those which labor to increase the city's material prosperity by developing its external attractiveness." But even major industrial and manufacturing centers felt the need to attract well-heeled visitors. The Publicity Bureau of the Merchants Association of New York pointed out in 1914 that "no city is too large to profit by having its name constantly before the outside public."[19]

In addition to stimulating the tourist trade and advancing the rationalization of commerce and culture, expositions helped to make urban tourism an attractive option in other ways. Between 1876 and 1915, the fairs and a growing number of historical celebrations drew many people to cities and put them on display. The positive vision of the possibilities of urban life that the world's fairs embodied encouraged the integration of American cities into tourist itineraries no less than the provision of services for the fair's visitors. Occupying many large and architecturally grand buildings set in carefully landscaped parks outside the heavily settled areas of the city, the fairgrounds eliminated the chaos, dirt, and danger that typified American urban areas in the late nineteenth century. People visiting the exposition grounds entered into a world of genteel leisure in which stately art and architecture obscured the utilitarianism and uncertain social relations that made possible the commercial abundance that the fair celebrated. Visions of the ideal city, successful expositions seemed to prove that tourism could underwrite both urban prosperity and harmony.[20]

Contemporary commentators readily perceived the spatial, architectural, and social lessons the expositions expressed. Visiting the unfinished grounds of the World's Columbian Exposition in 1892, Julian Hawthorne rhapsodized to his sister that "the Fair is a world. . . . in which ugliness and useless[ness] have been extirpated, and the beautiful and useful alone admitted." Such a world would be at its best "when the vast grounds and illimitable floors are thronged with the countless thousands of well-dressed people" instead of the "Micks and Dagos and the scattered and dazed sightseers who now mottle the barren spaces . . ."[21] Hawthorne's socially and architecturally knowledgeable fairgoers were the essential counterpart to the ideal urban landscape. Neither workers nor "ethnics," their presence and their sensitivity to its high-cultural meanings represented the fair's—and a city's—financial and social success. Their rationalized leisure underwrote an imagined urban harmony. Expositions exemplified the combination of pecuniary and cultural aims that shaped the chamber of commerce's carnival.

In the eyes of turn-of-the-century chamber of commerce members, beautifying and publicizing a city to attract well-to-do visitors was part and parcel of improving the city's economic and social relations. Exemplifying this rationale was the organizations' frequent endorsements of City Beautiful plans to reform the urban landscape. By means of magnificent public architecture, carefully designed roadways, and the best in allegorical and historical statuary, the "city beautiful" was intended to provide an architectural mold for urban harmony. Advocates argued that a properly designed city environment would inculcate residents with republican virtues and inspire their loyalty to nation and community, overcoming any doubts about the political and economic status quo.[22]

Of course, if this beautiful city was to exercise its uplifting power, people had to exercise themselves. Architect and City Beautiful advocate Henry Rutgers Marshall pointed out that "in order that a person may gain a sense of beauty from these works, he must move from spot to spot . . ." Underscoring his point, Marshall urged his listeners to consider "the vast throngs who were instructed in merely walking through the magnificent 'Court of Honor,'" the central plaza at the World's Columbian Exposition. When citizens walked or rode through the City Beautiful, they would enact the leisured harmony of exposition visitors or tourists, for "in these stately squares and monumental public buildings life takes on a festal aspect even for the poorest." In the view of Marshall and his fellow reformers, the aesthetic aims and leisured transience characteristic of tourism would also uplift a city's poor residents and unify urbanites in appreciation of republican architecture and, by extension, the political institutions it housed.[23]

City Beautiful advocates argued vigorously that lovely landscapes would attract tourists whose deep pockets would fund the ambitious plans and whose mere presence would signal the city's aesthetic success. Unfortunately, none of the nation's largest cities succeeded in implementing City Beautiful plans. The planners' ambitious, utopian desire to restructure entire cities around monumental civic buildings and high-cultural aesthetic principles was neither commercially viable nor politically palatable to property owners and taxpayers in most big cities.[24] Unable or unwilling to translate the grandest exposition architecture into reality, organized businessmen instead deployed the fairs' commercial extravagance and carefully ordered racial and ethnic diversity. These were the fairs' most popular and profitable aspects, if not their most edifying. They played an important role in transforming civic parades into business-controlled carnivals.

The historical festivals funded and managed by business associations retained many elements typical of nineteenth-century parades: soldiers, schoolboys, and public officials remained integral elements. But by the 1890s, historical and allegorical floats and costumed ethnic delegations were displacing the dully garbed troops, "Knights of Pythias, letter carriers, citizens in carriages, civic bodies, etc." that made the editor of the *Chicago Tribune* yawn in 1899. The new-style processions included a wide range of participants and offered immigrant communities an opportunity to assert both their pride in their homeland and their loyalty to their new country. Yet they also enabled well-to-do sightseers to perceive the marchers as picturesque ethnics more than fellow citizens, a perspective particularly amenable to the growing number of well-to-do tourists.[25]

The development of a heroic narrative of an American past that contained a model for class and racial relations in the present was crucial to the blend of commerce and culture in these festivals. The expositions again played an important role in developing and staging this narrative. American fairs frequently celebrated national anniversaries at the same time that they showcased the nation's productive prowess and commercial abundance. Industrial fairs marked the national centennial in 1876, the Columbus quadricentennial in 1893 (a year late), and the one hundredth anniversary of the Louisiana Purchase in 1904. Historical festivals linked commercial abundance and national progress in a similar way, as when New York celebrated the achievements of explorer Henry Hudson and steamboat inventor Robert Fulton in 1909. Publicity materials and other accounts constantly compared "then" and "now," implying that love of country necessarily entailed approving of the economic order: "'It Has Been a Wonderful Century in New York,' Said Father Knickerbocker, as He Stepped Aside to Avoid an Automobile."[26]

For Anglo-Americans, a heroic narrative focusing on the colonial and revolutionary past endowed urban built environments with a significance beyond the usual perception that they were simply real estate markets and places of toil. A growing vogue for historical commemoration and preservation encouraged well-to-do Americans, including a growing number of tourists, to view cities as places deeply resonant with their own heroic heritage and colorfully embellished with ethnic flourishes. The proliferating tour brochures, city guidebooks, and festival programs packaged both urban landscapes and urban dwellers as sights to be seen rather than the often conflicting elements making up a built and social environment.[27]

The organization of expositions and historical festivals publicly enacted this heroic narrative. Even as organizers encouraged most of a city's many nationalities to participate, the arrangement of the floats situated the foreign born as picturesque sidekicks in an epic that was not theirs. New York's Hudson-Fulton Celebration in 1909 is a good example. Predictably asserting that the celebration was "educational, not commercial," organizer Edward Hagaman Hall noted that its chief goal was "to promote the assimilation of our adopted population. Knowledge of the history of a city . . . serves to bind a people together, make it more homogeneous and give it stability. . . ." In service to this aim, "the people of every nationality were invited to take part in the parades and festivals." Thus Irish, Italian, Bohemian, Hungarian, and other "ethnic" honor guards flanked the historical floats marking the Indian, Dutch, English, and American periods of New York's history.[28]

This organization was not unlike the corporate composition of processions typical of nineteenth-century parades. Yet the emphasis on history and ethnicity rather than the public function of the various groups meant that this parade enacted the city as a collection of racial groups. The growing similarity between some parade floats and midway exhibits underscored the change and suggests its meaning for onlookers. At the expositions, the "midway" or entertainment zone contained "ethnic" exhibits and sideshows that were the commercial, slightly risqué counterpart of the architectural and industrial edification provided in the main buildings. In the latter areas, national products were on display; on the midway, people and pastimes were the attraction.[29]

Both parade floats and midway concessions packaged cultural and social differences in discrete, conventionalized forms. They separated onlookers from their objects while making the latter highly visible, condensed symbols of racial difference. The spatial organization of midway concessions and floats in the chronological historical parades embodied contemporary notions of racial hierarchy and evolution, with the most ancient or "primitive" always giving way to the most modern or "civilized": The Indians before the Dutch before the English before the Americans. The emphasis on a particular historical and ethnic hierarchy stretched across time obscured class and racial antagonisms, helping to define and stabilize social relations in the present in a way that recast cities as safe, exciting places for well-to-do Americans.[30]

The importance of racial packaging in assuring a safe spectacle made an externally imposed "authenticity" essential. The Hudson-Fulton Celebration Commission contracted with one F. E. Moore to provide "125 Indians for use in the official ceremonies." The parties "agreed that the Indians aforesaid shall be real New York State Indians [i.e., Iroquois], not halfbreeds. . . ." Moore was to provide the Indians with appropriate costumes and accessories and to ensure that they "perform such games, dances, or other motions as may be necessary for the proper rendition of the scenes in which they take part."[31] Camping in city parks, Indians staged dances, games, and battles for white spectators during many festivals. Without the proper accoutrements and stylized activities, onlookers might have to encounter the Indians as fellow citizens rather than living souvenirs of a dying, primitive, and alien race. The requirement that the Indians perform their culture as a series of entertainments reduced irreconcilable conflicts to sideshows.

This emphasis on "authenticity" marked the distance between the new carnivals and earlier civic festivals, which had enacted city dwellers' roles as citizens, workers, and public officials. By the turn of the century, ethnic and racial minorities were required to enact themselves as definitively, culturally "other," unassimilable to American modernity—but also no threat to it when properly contained. Yet, at the same time, their performances dramatized their integration into an increasingly rationalized economy whose public face was commercialized leisure. The packaging of ethnic differences in historical pageantry readily lent itself to the economic aims of festival organizers and to the desires of tourists. It had mixed effects for ethnic minorities and for civic society.

The selection by the organizers of San Francisco's Portolá festival of one Nicholas A. Covarrubias to play the part of the first governor of the state, Don Gaspar de Portolá, illustrates the way that this packaging both enabled and carefully limited the participation of ethnic minorities in a city's public life. Unlike Moore's hired Iroquois, Covarrubias did not need to be coached to play the part correctly; "He will reign over the revels of the Portolá Festival fortified by many years' experience as a fiesta king."[32] An "authentic" Californio, or member of the Mexican elite that dominated the area prior to the

American takeover, Covarrubias was also an experienced performer whose only authority lay in his ethnic identity. Like the Native Americans, he incorporated himself into the urban, industrial order by staging his history and culture for the entertainment of Anglo-Americans. Though severely limited by ethnic stereotypes, such performances did give ethnic minorities a visible place in the civic community.

But in the early twentieth century, historical anniversaries receded in importance, and with them faded the imperative to invite the participation of all of the city's ethnic and racial groups. The more commercial the festival became, the less important it was for the communities making up the city to represent themselves. Carnival fun rather than civic or historical symbolism became the key to attracting tourists. The arguments in favor of San Francisco's Carnival of the Pacific illustrate the trend. One partisan insisted that even though the city lacked a native festival tradition, it had plenty of colorful ethnic cultures to draw on. "There are the islands in the Pacific Ocean, and the lands beyond, which could be represented by maskers in strange dress, with novel equipment, giving brilliance, color, and interest to the event."[33] In attempting to cash in on San Francisco's proximity to the mysterious East in white Americans' imagination, promoters abandoned the assimilationist goals espoused by the organizers of commemorative events. In the Carnival of the Pacific, Asian and Oceanic dress and artifacts would be used as revelers' masks rather than representing the native traditions, however ersatz, of a distinct community within the city.

Despite the organizers' decreasing interest in literally representing the city, the new festivals continued to offer an opportunity to claim membership in the city's social order. Like ethnic minorities elsewhere, San Francisco's Chinese residents continued to march and build lavish floats for city parades, taking great pride in representing both of their homelands. But the growing emphasis on carnival meant that the participation of ordinary people in their role as citizens and ethnic groups became less important. San Francisco's proposed carnival was not intended to represent the city to itself but to be "the 'big show' of the year, a recurring custom of the City, attracting visitors from all the Pacific Coast states . . . to enjoy a pleasant vacation and do their yearly shopping at the same time."[34]

As the presence of thousands of tourists became increasingly important in evaluating the success of city festivals, an emphasis on rationalized, commercial leisure displaced the rhetoric of city unity and immigrant assimilation. Play itself promised profit and social peace. As one writer put it, the carnival "made the cold realities of business and trade seem themselves but fanciful and left mirth and dazzle and revelry to be the common state of life." Organized businessmen continued to insist that their festivals promoted civic unity, but now they did so by rationalizing the "spontaneous" pleasures of city dwellers. Writing in favor of the Carnival of the Pacific, one San Franciscan argued that the "carnival spirit rises spontaneously in San Francisco at New Year's. It should have artistic and effective expression, instead of merely venting itself in a tolerable sort of rowdyism and license." Another writer agreed: "All it needs is a little intelligent direction and management to grow into a civic institution of importance and value."[35]

After the festival took place, the anonymous voice of the city's Merchants' Association approved: "the unmistakable carnival spirit was abroad. . . . The bands, automobiles, electric floats and other features provided by the committee in charge served their purpose and gave the crowds something to talk about." This was no "mere outpouring of crowds into the streets" but an orderly jubilee in which people enjoyed "such restricted reveling as could keep itself within the bounds of due propriety." Best of all, the local businesses who funded the mobile and stationary floats with their bands and maskers made lots of money. The rationalization of leisure was intended to be even more marked during New York's Hudson-Fulton Celebration, where the subjects of "King Carnival" "will not be allowed to run riot in the streets. All throwing of confetti has been prohibited. . . , and any carnival high jinks will be confined solely to the marching army's maneuvers."[36]

It is difficult to discover what local residents or visitors thought of the rationalization of customary celebrations. Clearly enough San Franciscans enjoyed the floats, music, and dancing to please the sponsors of the new New Year's festival. Newspaper editors routinely praised the size, good nature, and enthusiasm of festival crowds and asserted each event's unifying power. Contradicting their editors, reporters noted the deployment of extra police during festivals and some officers' tendency to club overeager spectators on the head. And, echoing the complaints of host communities everywhere, New Yorkers reportedly "grew peevish" when jostled by crowds of tourists along Fifth Avenue.[37]

The most serious challenge to the chamber of commerce's carnival occurred in New York in 1909. The sale of bleacher seats along the Hudson-Fulton parade route prompted scandalous price-gouging, seat stealing, and a lawsuit against the city. The plaintiff argued that the streets and squares were public spaces, and the sale of seats meant that "only those who have the price of a seat can view the festivities." One reporter estimated that fewer than 10 percent of residents and visitors would be able to see the parade because of the erection of the bleachers. The lawsuit on behalf of the "sons of toil" apparently represented "popular murmurings of discontent" at the prices of the seats: five dollars was the legal cap, but prices ranged up to fifteen dollars, nearly a week's wages for some workingmen. But a judge ruled that the city did have the right to sell permits for privately owned bleachers in public areas, and the speculation went on.[38] The decision underscored the extent to which businessmen's (and the municipality's) commercial motives made a mockery of the parade's civic and assimilationist aims. If only the well-to-do could see it, the parade had no justification save profit. Its attractiveness to the well-heeled, including tourists, mattered more than its civic benefits.

By 1915, business-sponsored festivals united commerce and community around leisure in a new way, one that valued the pleasures of tourists above the roles of citizens. "[L]et it not be supposed," Hudson-Fulton Celebration publicist Hall wrote with a nod to the usual civic and assimilationist aims of civic festivals, "that this [unity] is the only end to be attained; such brilliant spectacles are a good in themselves" because "the poorest and the richest will share equally in the enjoyment of the various splendid and artistic spectacles." With the aim of achieving this equality in pleasure, he urged Americans to "abandon themselves . . . to a rational festival."[39] By acting like tourists and by serving tourists, urbanites would contribute to the city's commercial success and form a community united in the pursuit of profit. That was the aim of the chamber of commerce's carnival.

NOTES

1. This essay is based chiefly on the journals, promotional brochures, annual reports, and event programs that businessmen's associations in these four cities published, along with a survey of the *San Francisco Chronicle*, the *Chicago Tribune*, and the *New York Herald* around the time of major festivals and expositions. For a fuller discussion of the rise of urban tourism, see Cocks, *A Nice Place to Visit: The Rise of Urban Tourism in the United States, 1850–1915* (forthcoming, University of California Press), chap. 4. On nineteenth-century parades, see Susan Davis, *Parades and Power: Street Theatre in Nineteenth-Century Philadelphia* (Berkeley and Los Angeles: University of California Press, 1986); Mary Ryan, *Women in Public: Between Banners and Ballots, 1825–1880* (Baltimore: Johns Hopkins University Press, 1990); Roy Rosenzweig, *Eight Hours for What We Will: Workers and Leisure in an Industrial City, 1870–1920* (Cambridge: Cambridge University Press, 1983); also *City of San Francisco. Celebration of the Eighty-Eighth Anniversary of the National Independence of the United States, July 4th, 1864* (San Francisco: Painter and Co., 1864); *Celebration of Washington's Birthday at New-York, On the 22d of February, 1851* (New York: Van Norden and Amerman, 1851); "The Inauguration of the Jackson Monument," *Frank Leslie's Illustrated Newspaper*, March 1, 1856, 178. Boys from public and private schools and colleges regularly marched in military-style units in city parades, while girls presented flowers to dignitaries, sang songs, and sat on floats. Parades were gender-segregated, as Ryan notes.

2. "The Chinese Pageant," *Chicago Tribune*, October 11, 1899, 12. The editor was praising the Chinese community's efforts in the recent autumn festival; "History Is Repeated in Brilliant Floats," *San Francisco Chronicle*, October 22, 1909, 2. See also "San Francisco's Festival," *San Francisco Chronicle*, October 24, 1909, 32.

3. Neil Harris, "Urban Tourism and the Commercial City," in *Inventing Times Square: Commerce and Culture at the Crossroads of the World*, ed. William R. Taylor (New York: Russell Sage, 1991), 66–82; Cocks, *Nice Place to Visit*, chaps. 4–5.

4. Davis, *Parades and Power,* and Ryan, *Women in Public,* both note changes in the composition of parades and the rising importance of ethnicity. "Hibernian" and other nationally designated groups had marched throughout the nineteenth century, but as representatives of benevolent, fraternal, or political associations also found among Anglo-Americans. By the turn of the century, marchers often represented their ethnic backgrounds absent any contemporary social organization. See David Glassberg, *American Historical Pageantry: The Uses of Tradition in the Early Twentieth Century* (Chapel Hill: University of North Carolina Press, 1990). Philip Ethington, *The Public City: The Political Construction of Urban Life in San Francisco, 1850–1900* (New York: Cambridge University Press, 1994), argues that ethnicity only became politically significant at the turn of the century. On residents' participation, see "History Is Repeated," 2; picture captioned "Mrs. Charles Brown, Who Will Personate Columbia," *San Francisco Chronicle,* January 24, 1898, 10; "School Children Portray the City's History," *New York Herald,* September 30, 1909, 6; "Great Pageant of Light to Form Climax of Fetes," *New York Herald,* September 23, 1909, 6; "Parade of Many Nations," *Chicago Tribune,* October 6, 1899, 3. The *Tribune* seemed to be more interested in counting lightbulbs and dollars than people.

5. The first quotation is from A. S. Baldwin in "Carnival Is City's Crowning Success," *San Francisco Chronicle,* October 24, 1909, 29; the second, "All Nations in Night Pageant," *Chicago Tribune,* October 10, 1899, 1. Cocks, *Nice Place to Visit,* chap. 4; Glassberg, *American Historical Pageantry.* On the growing importance of rational leisure, see Richard Wightman Fox, "The Discipline of Amusement," in Taylor, *Inventing Times Square,* 83–98; David Nasaw, *Going Out: The Rise and Fall of Public Amusements in America* (New York: Basic Books, 1993). Amy Kaplan, *The Social Construction of American Realism* (Chicago: University of Chicago Press, 1988), analyzes the struggle of realist novelists to represent and thus redress the antagonism between social classes; I use *representation* in the same strong sense here.

6. The quotation is from "The Parade of All Chicago," *Chicago Tribune,* October 7, 1899, 12; Glassberg, *American Historical Pageantry,* notes that the decision not to hold historical pageants in indoor arenas and charge admission was a deliberate, "democratic" abandonment of the British precedent. Providing a "free" event making the purchases of goods and services necessary also corresponds with the growing vogue for advertising and public relations pioneered by department stores and other firms; see William Leach, *Land of Desire: Merchants, Power, and the Rise of a New American Culture* (New York: Vintage, 1994; also, "Centennial Celebration Plans," *Chicago Tribune,* September 20, 1903, 47; "City's Crowning Success," 29.

7. See Cocks, *Nice Place to Visit,* chaps. 4, 6; on expositions, Robert Rydell, *All the World's a Fair: Visions of Empire at American International Expositions, 1876–1916* (Chicago: University of Chicago Press, 1984); Alan Trachtenberg, "White City," in *The Incorporation of America: Culture and Society in the Gilded Age* (New York: Hill and Wang, 1982), 208–34; on the uses of history, Michael Kammen, *Mystic Chords of Memory: The Transformation of Tradition in American Culture* (New York: Basic Books, 1991); and Glassberg, *American Historical Pageantry.* On racial hierarchies and American culture, see Rydell, *All the World's a Fair;* T. J. Jackson Lears, *No Place of Grace: Antimodernism and the Transformation of American Culture, 1880–1920* (New York: Pantheon, 1981), 107–16; and Gail Bederman, *Manliness and Civilization: A Cultural History of Gender and Race in the United States, 1880–1917* (Chicago: University of Chicago Press, 1995).

8. Daniel Bluestone, *Constructing Chicago* (New Haven: Yale University Press,

1991); Helen Lefkowitz Horowitz, *Culture and the City: Cultural Philanthropy in Chicago from the 1880s to 1917* (Lexington: University Press of Kentucky, 1976); Judd Kahn, *Imperial San Francisco: Politics and Planning in an American City, 1897–1906* (Lincoln: University of Nebraska Press, 1979); Michele Bogart, *Public Sculpture and the Civic Ideal in New York City, 1890–1930* (Chicago: University of Chicago Press, 1989); William Wilson, *The City Beautiful Movement* (Baltimore: Johns Hopkins University Press, 1989); Harris, "Urban Tourism"; Alan Lessoff, *The Nation and Its City: Politics, "Corruption," and Progress in Washington, D.C., 1861–1902* (Baltimore: Johns Hopkins University Press, 1994); Howard Gillette Jr., *Between Justice and Beauty: Race, Planning, and the Failure of Urban Policy in Washington, D.C.* (Baltimore: Johns Hopkins University Press, 1995).

9. For examples of the conventional wisdom, see "Customs of the Country," *Frank Leslie's Illustrated Newspaper*, April 28, 1877, 130–31; Mrs. E. H. Blashfield, "How to Make New York a Beautiful City," address to the Nineteenth Century Club, March 12, 1895, 31, pamphlet at the New York Public Library; Hutchins Hapgood, *Types from the City Streets* (New York: Funk and Wagnalls, 1910), 120 and passim. On the literary and aesthetic preferences of nineteenth-century tourists, see John Sears, *Sacred Places: American Tourist Attractions in the Nineteenth Century* (Oxford: Oxford University Press, 1989); Dona Brown, *Inventing New England: Regional Tourism in the Nineteenth Century* (Washington, D.C.: Smithsonian Institution Press, 1995); and Harvey Levenstein, *Seductive Journey: American Tourists in France from Jefferson to the Jazz Age* (Chicago: University of Chicago Press, 1998). American parades seemed equally pragmatic and dull to some; see "San Francisco's Festival," 32.

10. See Cocks, *Nice Place to Visit*, chaps. 2, 3, and 4; also Harris, "Urban Tourism"; William Taylor, *In Pursuit of Gotham: Culture and Commerce in New York* (New York: Oxford University Press, 1992); Nasaw, *Going Out*; Leach, *Land of Desire*; Richard Ohmann, *Selling Culture: Magazines, Markets, and Class at the Turn of the Century* (New York: Verso, 1996).

11. Many scholars have examined the significance and organization of the world's fairs; see the works cited in note 7; also Nasaw, *Going Out*, chap. 6; James Gilbert, *Perfect Cities: Chicago's Utopias of 1893* (Chicago: University of Chicago Press, 1991), chaps. 3, 4; Robert Rydell, "The Literature of International Expositions," introduction to *The Books of the Fairs: Materials about World's Fairs, 1834–1916, in the Smithsonian Institution Libraries* (Chicago: American Library Association, 1992), 1–62.

12. On the Centennial Exposition, see *Visitors' Guide to the Centennial Exposition and Philadelphia* (Philadelphia: J. B. Lippincott, 1876); and *Going to the Centennial and a Guy to the Exhibition, by Bricktop* (New York: Collin and Small, 1876); on the Panama-Pacific International Exposition, see carton 9, folder 1–35.10, "Tour Companies," carton 15, folder 1–51.50, "Hotel Bureau," and carton 38, folder "Requests for Information re Tours," Panama-Pacific International Exposition Papers, Bancroft Library. The hotel information bureaus usually kept a registry of subscribing hotels and boardinghouses and provided information to applicants free of charge.

13. On the development of tour agencies, see Cocks, *Nice Place to Visit*, chap. 4, and Hugh DeSantis, "The Democratization of Travel: The Travel Agent in American History," *Journal of American Culture* 1 (spring 1978): 1–17. The *Brooklyn Eagle, Town and Country, New York Journal,* and other metropolitan dailies and periodicals had travel information bureaus and ran excursions. American Express launched its travelers' checks for travelers to Europe in 1891 but did not enter the organized tour business until the twentieth century; see Peter Z. Grossman, *American Express: The Unofficial*

History of the People Who Built the Great Financial Empire (New York: Crown, 1987), chap. 3. On rural and resort tourism in the United States, see Sears, *Sacred Places;* and Brown, *Inventing New England.* For the trade show, see "Travel and Vacation Exhibition, 2nd Annual," brochure and application form in the Warshaw Collection of Business Americana, Tours, box 4, in the Archives Center, National Museum of American History, Smithsonian Institution.

14. Cocks, *Nice Place to Visit,* chaps. 4, 5; Rand, McNally, the Standard Guide Co., and Rider's were among the leading national publishers; the major railroads, especially the New York Central, Pennsylvania Central, Atchison, Topeka, and Santa Fe, and the Southern Pacific also produced guidebooks to the cities along their routes. The first Baedeker's for the United States appeared in 1893; see [J. F. Muirhead], *The United States, with an Excursion into Mexico: A Hand-Book for Travelers, 1893* (New York and Leipzig, 1893; facsimile ed., New York: Da Capo Press, 1971). George W. Englehardt, *New York the Metropolis: The Book of Its Merchants' Association and Co-operating Public Bodies* (New York: George W. Englehardt, 1902); *A Guide to the City of Chicago* (Chicago: Chicago Association of Commerce, 1909); Frank Morton Todd, *San Francisco* (San Francisco: Chamber of Commerce, 1915).

15. *Cook's Excursionist and Home and Foreign Advertiser,* August 1892, 10; this periodical was the advertising organ of Cook and Son. Businessmen were not alone, of course; the period is noted for the growing acceptance of recreation as a social need; see Fox, "The Discipline of Amusement."

16. Cocks, *Nice Place to Visit,* chap. 4; see also Hal Rothman, *Devil's Bargains: Tourism in the Twentieth Century American West* (Lawrence: University Press of Kansas, 1998); and Cindy Aron, *Working at Play: A History of Vacations in the United States* (New York: Oxford University Press, 1999).

17. *Raymond's Vacation Excursions, Thirty Summer Tours!* (1890), 6. Founded in the late 1880s, the Boston-based Raymond and Whitcomb epitomized luxury organized travel in the United States in this era; see DeSantis, "The Democraticization of Travel." Note the delicate avoidance of any mention of cost or class. See *Cook's Excursionist,* April 1892, 30, for the rates; see the January 1892 issue for the initial announcement. See also "Tours," *Travelers' Condensed Guide,* Raymond and Whitcomb Tours, January 1904, 63; "Royal Blue Three-Day Tours from New York, Philadelphia and Intermediate Points to Washington," *The Book of the Royal Blue,* January 1900, inside back cover; "Specimen Tours and Tickets/Popular Three-Day Tours to Washington, D.C.," *The Tourist's Monthly Magazine,* January 1908, 30. The railroads also provided excursion fares for working people: "Great Exodus for Three Day Outing . . . Thousands Will Spend Labor Day in Country," *New York Herald,* September 4, 1909, 7. On income, see Nell Irvin Painter, *Standing at Armageddon: The United States, 1877–1919* (New York: W. W. Norton), xxiii–xxiv.

18. "When Planning the Summer Outing," Illinois Central Railroad folder, 1917, Warshaw Collection, Tours, box 4, Archives Center, National Museum of American History; urban businessmen's organizations made similar claims in the guidebooks and promotional circulars they published; see Cocks, *Nice Place to Visit,* chap. 4.

19. The first quotation is from the Washington Board of Trade, *Eighth Annual Report* (Washington, D.C., 1898), 8; Kahn, *Imperial San Francisco,* chap. 1; Constance McLaughlin Green, *Washington: A History of the Capital, 1800–1950,* vol. 2 (Princeton, N.J.: Princeton University Press, 1962), chaps. 2, 9. The second quotation is from the Report of the Publicity Bureau, Merchants' Association of New York, *Yearbook* (n.p., 1914), 31; on the Publicity and Convention bureaus of this organization, see 16–18,

49–52. For Chicago, see "Merchants' Meetings" and "National Conventions," *Commerce* [Chicago], June 15, 1906, 1, September 21, 1906, 2, report of the Convention Bureau.

20. Trachtenberg, "White City"; Russell Lewis, "Everything under One Roof: World's Fairs and Department Stores in Paris and Chicago," *Chicago History* 12, no. 3 (1983): 28–47; Gilbert, *Perfect Cities*, chap. 4; Cocks, *Nice Place to Visit*, chaps. 4, 5.

21. Julian Hawthorne, letter to his sister entitled "A Description of the Inexpressible" (Chicago Historical Society, 1892), 2. While expositions were open, the people who had built them—often "Micks" and "Dagos"—were conspicuously absent. Few working-class Americans could afford the carfare to the parks, much less the fifty-cent admission fee. Some fairs closed on Sunday, the only day working people could attend.

22. Wilson, *The City Beautiful Movement*, pts. 2 and 3; also Kahn, *Imperial San Francisco;* Bluestone, *Constructing Chicago;* and John Reps, *Monumental Washington: The Planning and Development of the Capital Center* (Princeton, N.J.: Princeton University Press, 1967); Gillette, *Between Justice and Beauty.* Republicanism has a long historiography; I use it here much as the city beautiful advocates did, as a term broadly equated with an endorsement of the American governmental system and a simultaneous respect for private property and the formal political equality of white men.

23. The first two quotations are from Marshall, "How to Make New York a Beautiful City," address before the Nineteenth Century Club, New York, March 12, 1895, 9–10, pamphlet at the New York Public Library; the third, Blashfield, "How to Make," 40.

24. Joseph D. Redding, "The Practical Benefits of Municipal Adornment," address before the San Francisco Downtown Association, April 19, 1911, 10–11, pamphlet at the Bancroft Library; D. H. Burnham, "The Commercial Value of Beauty," *Park Improvement Papers* no. 11 (Washington, D.C.: Government Printing Office, 1903); and the Chicago Association of Commerce's journal *Commerce,* November 2, 1906, 1–2. A few midsized cities, notably Washington, D.C., did succeed in instituting such plans; the popularity of the ideal among many Americans strengthened the connections between commerce, community, and tourism that the expositions had established. Washington's early-twentieth-century rebuilding was possible in large part because the city was controlled by Congress; its disenfranchised citizens did not have the political means to block it, as their counterparts in other cities did. See Wilson, *The City Beautiful Movement,* chap. 4, on other successful rebuildings.

25. "The Chinese Pageant," *Chicago Tribune,* October 11, 1899, 12; Cocks, *Nice Place to Visit,* chaps. 4, 6; see also Glassberg, *American Historical Pageantry;* Kammen, *Mystic Chords of Memory;* Ryan, *Women in Public.*

26. The quotation is the caption for a picture illustrating "City's Century of Magical Change," *New York Herald,* September 26, 1909, 2; see also the diary of Mary Fargo Antisdel, Chicago Historical Society, 1893; Cocks, *Nice Place to Visit,* chaps. 4, 6; Rydell, *All the World's a Fair;* Glassberg, *American Historical Pageantry.*

27. Kammen, *Mystic Chords of Memory;* Glassberg, *American Historical Pageantry;* Cocks, *Nice Place to Visit,* chap. 6.

28. The quotations are from Edward Hagaman Hall, introduction to *The Hudson-Fulton Celebration, 1909: The Fourth Annual Report of the Hudson-Fulton Celebration Commission to the Legislature of the State of New York* (Albany: J. B. Lyon Co., 1910), 5, 7; on the honor guards, see *Hudson-Fulton Celebration Souvenir Program* (New York: Board of Aldermen, 1909). Glassberg, *American Historical Pageantry,* 114–15, points out that the only group routinely excluded from such events were African Americans,

unless the organizers needed them to portray Native Americans, who were often in short supply. That was not the case in New York; see below. Marianna Torgovnick, *Gone Primitive: Savage Intellects, Modern Lives* (Chicago: University of Chicago Press, 1990), addresses the uses of the "primitive" by "modern" Europeans and Americans.

29. Rydell, *All the World's a Fair;* see also Nasaw, *Going Out,* chap. 6.

30. Cocks, *Nice Place to Visit,* chap. 6; also Rydell, *All the World's a Fair,* on the racial ideology that shaped the midway exhibits; and Curtis M. Hinsley, "The World as Marketplace: Commodification of the Exotic at the World's Columbian Exposition, Chicago, 1893," in *Exhibiting Cultures: The Poetics and Politics of Museum Display,* ed. Ivan Karp and Steven D. Levine (Washington, D.C.: Smithsonian Institution Press, 1991), 344–65.

31. Contract between the Hudson-Fulton Celebration Commission and F. E. Moore, August 15, 1909, in the Hudson-Fulton Celebration Commission Papers, New-York Historical Society, 1; see also "Golden Days Come Again," *San Francisco Chronicle,* January 21, 1898, 5; "Indians Invade City at Dawn," *Chicago Tribune,* September 27, 1903, 2; "The Lighter Side of Big Celebration," *New York Herald,* September 28, 1909, 5. L. G. Moses, *Wild West Shows and the Images of American Indians, 1883–1933* (Albuquerque: University of New Mexico Press, 1996), explores what the shows meant to the Indians who participated.

32. *Portolá Festival, Official Souvenir Program,* San Francisco, October 19–23, 1909, 55, Bancroft Library. The festival queen, on the other hand, was the young, Anglo-American winner of a beauty contest. For another example, see Maria Sermolino's memoir of growing up in her father's Italian restaurant in turn of the century New York City: *Papa's Table d'Hôte* (Philadelphia: J. B. Lippincott, 1952).

33. "A Carnival of the Pacific," *Merchants' Association Review,* November 1908, 12. See also Leach, *Land of Desire,* on parades and pageants sponsored by department stores.

34. The quotation is from "Carnival of the Pacific," 12. Thomas W. Chinn, *Bridging the Pacific: San Francisco Chinatown and Its People* (San Francisco: Chinese Historical Society of America, 1989), 15–19; see also "San Francisco's Chinese Dragon for the Parade of All Nations," *Chicago Tribune,* October 2, 1899, 4.

35. The first quotation appears in Walter Gifford Smith, "Dominating Note of Fete Is Laughter," *San Francisco Chronicle,* October 22, 1909, 1; the second in "Carnival of the Pacific," 12; the third in "Give Us a Greater and Finer Carnival," *Merchants' Association Review,* February 1907, 12. For a description of the New Year's celebration before the Merchants' Association took an interest, see "Noisy New Year's Eve on Downtown Streets," *San Francisco Chronicle,* January 1, 1898, 3. New Orleans's Mardi Gras was the envy of other cities' elites and their model. Mardi Gras itself was increasingly commercialized and oriented toward tourists from the 1880s; see James Gill, *The Lords of Misrule: Mardi Gras and the Politics of Race in New Orleans* (Jackson: University of Mississippi Press, 1997).

36. "San Francisco Carnival to Become an Annual Event," *Merchants' Association Review,* February 1909, 6; for "such restricted reveling" see "A Carnival of the Pacific," 12. I have used pieces encouraging the staging of the festival as well as those reporting on it; both indicate the goals of the organizers. On the Hudson-Fulton Celebration: "Great Pageant of Light to Form Climax of Fetes," *New York Herald,* September 23, 1909, 6.

37. "Order Amid Revelry," *San Francisco Chronicle,* October 23, 1909, 6; "Parade Crowd Good-Natured," *San Francisco Chronicle,* October 22, 1909, 4; "Parade of All

Chicago," 12. Police were "compelled to use their clubs to drive back those who fought for positions of vantage," in "History Is Repeated in Brilliant Floats," *San Francisco Chronicle,* October 22, 1909, 2; "Police Will Clear Streets," *Chicago Tribune,* October 9, 1899, 2; "Welcome Dewey at the Capital . . . Police Charge Crowd," *Chicago Tribune,* October 3, 1899, 1; "Excellent Work of the Police," *New York Herald,* September 30, 1909, 10; "6,000 Police Will Guard Big Parade," *New York Herald,* September 28, 1909, 5, in which was noted, "To minimize the danger of some policeman losing his temper and damaging the man responsible for it, it has been expressly ordered that nightsticks shall be left in the station house." On the peevish locals, see "Dripping Crowds Crane Their Necks," *New York Herald,* September 28, 1909, 6. See Brown, *Inventing New England,* and Rothman, *Devil's Bargains,* on the effects of tourism on host communities.

38. The first two quotations are from "Delays Decision on Parade Stands," *New York Herald,* September 29, 1909, 6, internal quotations from Louis Epstein, the plaintiff bringing the case; the third quotation is from "Calls on Mayor to Take Stands Off the Streets," *New York Herald,* September 24, 1909, 5. The second article refers to a similar case brought by a Mr. Leary that later disappeared from news accounts, replaced by Epstein's. The 10 percent estimate appears in "Decide Fight for Free Seats To-Day," *New York Herald,* September 28, 1909, 6. The verdict appears in "Park Stands May Stay, Says Court," *New York Herald,* September 30, 1909, 6.

39. For the first quotation, see Edward Hagaman Hall, *Hudson and Fulton: A Brief History of Henry Hudson and Robert Fulton with Suggestions Designed to Aid the Holding of General Commemorative Exercises* (New York: Hudson-Fulton Celebration Commission, 1909), 316; for the third, Hall, *Hudson-Fulton Celebration,* 12.

Tourism in Late Imperial Austria

The Development of Tourist Cultures and Their Associated Images of Place

Today the tourist industry is central to the Austrian economy. During the interwar period mass tourism emerged as one of the country's most important industries when, no longer imperial and much reduced in size, Austria struggled to reestablish itself industrially and commercially. Even before the First World War, however, parts of imperial Austria were becoming dependent on the presence of tourists to the extent that they displayed signs of the kind of tourist culture that flourished in neighboring Switzerland and Bavaria. The most popular tourist areas, particularly the alpine and subalpine lands, soon felt the need to maintain a regular flow of visitors and responded to their expectations by providing them with suitable services and facilities.

In the early twentieth century the increasing competitiveness of the tourist industry encouraged the different regions and localities to emphasize the different features of their environment and culture that they felt to be most distinctive, a process that helped to reinforce awareness within Austria of internal regional and cultural differences. Their existence was unsurprising in a country that encompassed not just the alpine and subalpine regions of the Tyrol and Lower and Upper Austria, but also Polish Galicia and Bukowina, parts of northern Italy, the crown lands of Bohemia and Moravia, and the southern Slavic lands of Slovenia and Croatia. Furthermore, at the end of the nineteenth century cultural identity was a controversial and contested issue in many of these regions as the growth of nationalism led the different ethnic groups to advance claims to their own distinctive histories and cultural identities.[1] A study of the early growth of tourism, particularly in the German-speaking lands of Austria, suggests that its nascent tourist cultures played a role in the forging of these identities while, at the same time, contributing to the forces of fragmentation that threatened the Habsburg Empire.

Even before the days of systematic marketing and image promotion, touristic images of places were instrumental in attracting visitors.[2] In the third quarter of the nineteenth century Austria, unlike Switzerland, France, and Italy, was not generally regarded as a tourist destination. Most western tourists still thought of it as part of the Habsburg Monarchy and therefore geographically and culturally remote.[3] By the early twentieth century the contribution of foreign tourists to the economies of the alpine regions and Vienna was sufficiently important to spur the industry and its associated organizations to make efforts to increase their share of the market. Generalized touristic images of Austria began to circulate in the commercialized public spaces of foreign trade exhibitions and the travel agencies. Literature aimed at tourists depicted Austria as a land of alpine scenery, picturesque urban landscapes, royal glamour, and cozy *(gemütlich)* charm: images that were at odds with other ways in which the empire was often seen abroad. The attempts of the travel industry to select the aspects of Austria that would appeal to foreigners found a parallel in the attempts of the ruling Habsburg dynasty to generate support for itself and its self-imposed "mission." This it attempted to do by presenting itself as the center of a united "family of nations," an image that was constantly invoked in a vain attempt to suppress general awareness of the growing conflicts caused by the demands for cultural and political autonomy made by the different ethnic groups.[4]

THE EARLY DAYS OF AUSTRIAN TOURISM AND THE GROWTH OF TOURIST CULTURES

The building of the central European railway systems in the 1840s made it possible for people to travel in relative comfort for purposes that included leisure and entertainment. By facilitating the rapid growth of the region's economic infrastructure, the railways accelerated social changes and supported newly developing patterns of culture and leisure among the middle classes. It was these that gave rise to the major expansion of tourism in the 1880s when it began to develop rapidly, a process of growth that continued steadily until the First World War.[5]

During this early period Austria's resorts drew their guests mainly from the domestic tourist system. Like their German neighbors, of whom it was remarked that "an excuse to visit a watering place the summer is essential to life," most Austrians who could afford it paid a summer visit to some kind of spa, and the continued popularity of this habit helped to lay the foundations of the subsequent expansion of leisure tourism.[6] Initially this was most apparent in rural areas relatively close to Vienna (a major tourist host in its own right), and to the industrializing regions of Bohemia and Moravia. Such foreign visitors as there were came mostly from Germany, many from industrial Saxony, with much smaller numbers from Russia, France, and Britain.[7] In the early twentieth century continued growth meant that the major tourist centers of Vienna, the Bohemian spas, the Tyrol and the Voralberg, the eastern Alps and the Salzkammergut, Styria and the Dolomites, the Tatra Mountains, and the Istrian coast had developed many of the features associated with modern tourist culture. The number of foreign visitors also began to rise.[8]

Austria's link with the modern tourist industry began with the International Exhibition of 1873 staged in Vienna. The British travel agent Thomas Cook used the opportunity to make package trips to the exhibition into one of his earliest big foreign ventures, as well as incorporating the German and Austrian railways into his travel system.[9] However Vienna's difficulties in accommodating visitors to the exhibition showed that the city's infrastructure was not yet geared up to handling large numbers of tourists. The lack of facilities and the extortionate prices charged by greedy hoteliers, curbed only by the intervention of the magistrates, gave rise to much bad foreign publicity. An outbreak of cholera and the collapse of the stock exchange helped to turn the event into a financial disaster.[10] Nevertheless, the size and scale of the exhibition was a source of wonder to its visitors and helped to stimulate the tourist industry to the extent that, by the 1880s, Vienna had become the main center of tourism in Austria. The numerous hotels and restaurants that began to appear near the railway stations, between the inner Ring and the outer ring of the Gürtel, along the Ringstrasse, and in the inner city clearly marked particular areas out as tourist zones.

The same phenomena were evident in many of the leading watering places and resorts elsewhere in Austria as new hotels and villas sprang up to accommodate the wealthy and leisured middle classes as they tried to emulate the lifestyle of the social elites. The latter had traditionally spent their summers at spas or in the summer residences that ringed the leading towns and cities of the Monarchy. Now the advent of the railways made it easy to travel to resorts farther afield, particularly to the new spa and health resort colonies like on Semmering in the eastern Alps or the Wörtersee in Carinthia.[11] Forms of tourist culture began to develop in the regions most affected by the influx of tourists, the Salzkammergut, west Bohemia, the Tyrol, parts of Styria and Carinthia, the Tatra and Vienna, a consequence of improvements in the communication networks, the development of economic infrastructures capable of dealing with tourists, and entrepreneurial attitudes among the local inhabitants. In the Tyrol the arrival of the summer holiday-makers (*Sommerfrischler*) helped the old roadside towns along the routes to the Brenner Pass and the Inn Valley to recover from the effects of the collapse of the mines and the disappearance of the transalpine travelers and freighters of former times, now superseded by the railways. Some entrepreneurs bought up dilapidated old castles let out as flats or used as *Pensionen*.[12] In the Tatra Mountains, around the health resort of Zakopane, holiday chalets were built for the growing number of visitors from industrial Poland attracted by the scenery and pure air.

As the main centers of tourism developed, they were differentiated from each other by the different kinds of services and facilities they offered and the social and ethnic profile of their clientele, who were also distinguished by their place of origin and particular tastes. These features also influenced the tourist cultures of individual resorts. Destinations in the Tyrol, a region popular with all social classes, were differentiated from each other by the social class of their guests and the kind of recreational activities in which they engaged. In some places hotels opened up segregated facilities for humbler travelers and the many casual walkers *(Pässebummler)*, who, as the market widened, were distinguished from the summer holiday-makers and the serious mountain climbers *(Hochtouristen)*.[13] Other establishments, catering for the upper end of the market and increasingly sensitive to the expectations of foreign visitors and the standards of hygiene to which they were now accustomed, installed "English plumbing." In the health resorts the local authorities and health commissions encouraged entrepreneurs and joint-stock companies to invest in new buildings and facilities such as sanatoriums, music pavilions, and theaters. Sometimes local conservatism and the clash of interests delayed developments such as the proposed new *Kurhaus* in the suburbs of Meran.[14] Daily rituals of status display had been part of the elite life in the Monarchy since the end of the seventeenth century. Two centuries later these continued to play a role in the social lives of the upper classes who visited the burgeoning health and spa resorts catering for the new leisure tourism.[15] Along with urban-style *flânerie* and the importance of exercise in many cure regimes (even if this amounted to no more than gentle walks), this required the provision and beautification of the appropriate forms of public space such as shady gardens and promenades, paid for out of the taxes imposed on visitors. As sport became popular, facilities for golf and tennis were also provided.

In some resorts the guests changed with the seasons. Mountain and lakeside resorts that were particularly noted for the beneficial effects of their air and climate were sometimes visited by invalids in the winter when rates were cheap. In some places the elite passion for winter sports also extended the season. Visitors from the more remote and isolated parts of the empire valued the urban pleasures of the larger resorts or the sophisticated distractions of Vienna. The latter benefited from its long-standing reputation for culture, gaiety, and social life. The quality of the latter was an important factor in the appeal of the elegant and Bohemian spas of Karlsbad and Marienbad, whose relatively highly developed facilities and smart aristocratic clientele attracted wealthy and important visitors from all over Europe. Meran and Cortina were favored by the British and Americans for their sunny climate and nearness to Italy.

Although middle-class patronage stimulated the growth of many resorts, it also encouraged attempts by the elite classes to maintain the exclusiveness of their holiday retreats by avoiding their imitators. One strategy was to congregate in small and exclusive resorts in southern Austria or the Adriatic; another was to travel abroad to North Africa or the Middle East. Spas associated with royalty like Bad Ischl and Marienbad also attracted a certain kind of fashionable clientele. This phenomenon repelled other visitors who preferred somewhere quieter or more select. Mme de Laszowska wrote of Bad Ischl in 1896, "It is a lovely place but rather too fashionable for my taste and the Emperor spends the summer here which of course brings [shoals] of grandees in his train as well as that odious class—rich Jews who always run after the court like moths round a candle and who manage to infuse irritation and discomfort wherever they are—however the place suits my husband very well . . . music, reading novels and flat shady walks."[16]

The growth in tourist numbers was particularly marked in the leading spa towns. While touring Austrian spas in the mid–nineteenth century Dr. A. B. Granville had written of Marienbad that it was "not a Spa of pleasures. It is a lovely and enchanting retreat for invalids."[17] In 1837, the spa's visitors had numbered around eleven hundred. By 1905, when King Edward VII paid the first of his regular visits to Marienbad, the number had grown to around twenty-three thousand. Two years later it had risen to around thirty thousand. The British politician Campbell-Bannerman, a patron of Marienbad from its quiet days in the 1870s, commented on "the extra-ordinary number of 'tainted ladies' present in the American and English contingents." A short car ride away, Karlsbad also benefited from the royal presence as its numbers rose from fifty thousand visitors in 1905 to around sixty-two thousand in 1907.[18] Visitors included a growing number of English tourists, diplomats, journalists, and members of the continental demimonde. The rise in the number of visitors to the Tyrol, attracted there by the desire to escape the Swiss crowds, meant that others began to find its tourist culture too highly developed, preferring the solitude of the Tatra Mountains of the east or the Dolomites to the south.[19]

A striking feature of the Austrian tourist industry was the complementary relationship that existed between health tourism and the expansion in recreational tourism. The modern tourist continued to value places as much for their benefits to health as for their other amenities, with the result that health resorts sprang up wherever mineral springs could support them. In Vienna this trend was evident in the growth of health settlements around the city. Kaltenleutgeben boasted two hydropathic establishments, including one that was founded by a disciple of the cold-water cure, Victor Priessnitz, and that was frequented by aristocrats and artists as well as Mark Twain's wife.[20] Medically licensed spas and small watering places developed various kinds of leisure facilities, developing rapidly into holiday resorts as they attracted an ever-widening section of the tourist market. Ordinary leisure resorts marketed themselves as forms of health resort by emphasizing the quality of their air and targeting urban dwellers wishing to cultivate their bodies and fearful of the degenerative effects of urban life. The general preoccupation with health was evident as more and more people made "day trips," bicycling out into the "fresh air" of the surrounding countryside at weekends and visiting bathing places.[21]

It was not just the well-to-do who hoped for cures and wished for health. Throughout Catholic Europe the culture of the "cure" was strongly rooted and was bound up with pilgrimage traditions. As in neighboring Bavaria this was a major factor in generating a tourist culture in which many different sectors of society participated,[22] so that when, in the early twentieth century, as more workers received the right to fixed holidays and regular hours, the foundations were laid for their participation in the culture of leisure and entertainment associated with tourism. This phenomenon was visible in major pilgrimage towns such as Mariazell and villages like Weissenstein in the Tyrol where local families provided lodgings for pilgrims. One tourist on a walking holiday recalls the *Gasthaus,* "crammed with pilgrims, who had come from near and far to celebrate St. Michael's day and it was impossible to procure a bed in either the inn or village." Directed to the "clean, if comfortless, monastery," he ate his meals at the *Gasthaus* "among a noisy, unwashed crowd, most of whom were provided with their own food, but drank the wine and beer of the inn, where they spent the night singing and drinking and passed the night together packed in bedrooms, or sleeping on benches in the public rooms."[23] Tiny bathing establishments with basic accommodation, such as Ratzes in the Southern Tyrol, also a pilgrimage center, catered for "the humbler classes." Here seventy beds accommodated small tradesmen from Botzen and their families and peasant farmers from neighboring villages.[24]

Pilgrimage travel and "cures" were not the only way in which the Austrian tourist industry was indebted to the persistence of preexisting "cultures of travel." Journeymen, students, businessmen, civil servants, and artists had their own established travel practices and related forms of consumption.[25] As more social groups experienced prosperity in the late nineteenth and early twentieth centuries, these older patterns of travel were adapted to incorporate the new commercialized forms of leisure and entertainment associated with modern tourism. This was particularly noticeable in Vienna, which, because of its position as the administrative and symbolic center of the Monarchy and the home of its ruling dynasty, attracted many visitors from within the Habsburg territories. As economic modernization gradually spread across the Monarchy, travel to Vienna for commercial and business purposes increased.[26] Some visitors to the city went there because of its reputation as a medical and educational center, while many others visited family and friends.

An important element in the city's attractiveness was its long-standing reputation as a cultural center. Mark Twain, the American writer and one of the city's better-known visitors, visited Vienna to further his daughter's musical education. Other foreign tourists included the city on their itinerary because of personal contacts, or because of the city's traditional relationship with the grand tour and the persistence of its associated practices and discourses among the German bourgeoisie.[27] The architectural monuments of the newly constructed Ringstrasse, built in the appropriate historical styles, the Kunsthistorisches Museum, the Opera House, and the Burgtheater, contributed to the city's image as the home of Mozart and Beethoven and an aristocratic way of life in which the cultivation of art and music was central.[28] Other attractions included the city's famous social life, luxury shopping, and entertainment facilities including its many dance halls, theaters, and concerts. Particularly popular with tourists were the wine gardens *(Heurigen)* of the Vienna Woods (Wienerwald) and the open spaces of the Prater, easily accessible by the city's new urban transport system with its urban railway and electric trams.[29] The numerous cinemas gave a distinctively modern feel to Vienna's attractions.

The main support for the development of the tourist industry came from the various organizations founded for this purpose, particularly the various alpine associations formed in the second half of the nineteenth century. The initial aim of the latter was to promote the love of the mountains, but they soon became important vehicles for the development of tourism. Founded in 1862, the Austrian Alpine Association (Österreichishe Alpenverein), joined with its Munich-based counterpart in 1869 and seven years later it became part of the powerful German Austrian alpine Association (Deutsche Österreichische Alpenverein) in 1876. By 1913 it had around one hundred thousand members, while the Austrian Tourist Club (Österreichischen Touristen-Klub) was somewhat smaller. The functions that these tourist associations performed for their members included the building and marking of mountain paths, erecting protective huts, the organizing of alpine rescues, and the provision of mountain guides. Similar associations were established for the Tatra mountains.[30] By the turn of the century all towns and villages with summer visitors had their own associations for beautifying the landscape *(Verschönerungs-vereine)*, identifying viewing points, repairing dangerous paths, and putting up signposts.

In Styria, the Association for the Promotion of Tourism in Styria (Verein zur Forderungen des Fremdenverkehrs in der Steiermark), founded in 1881, operated as the tourist association for the region. Its activities included improving the accessibility of its historic towns, monuments, museums, and collections; setting up an accommodation agency; and helping the police with the management of tourist statistics.[31] This particular organization, which became a model for numerous others, worked to improve the quality of tourist services through such measures as the introduction of price lists intended to restrain the greed of hoteliers and restaurateurs. Tourist guides helped visitors to organize their routes, and special newspapers listed sights of interest and events put on to keep visitors amused, particularly during periods of bad weather. In the larger resorts, such as Meran, these included carnival balls, the corso promenade, battles of flowers, confetti fights, and beauty competitions. Local conservatism and the clash of interests, however, delayed much-needed developments such as the proposed new *Kurhaus* in the suburbs.[32] In Vienna the Association for the Promotion of Tourism (Verein der Hebung des Fremdenvehrkehrs), founded in 1882, provided support for congresses, balls, and exhibitions as well as organized spectacles such as the flower *corso*.

In the early days of the industry the state gave little direct financial support, although the industry continued to look for ways of making its views known to the government. This included events such as a meeting held in Graz in 1884 to discuss the development of tourism in the alpine lands: the representatives of the state railways and post and trade associations participated, and the Ministry of Trade (Handelsminsterium) was represented. The Viennese Association for the Promotion of Tourism received a subsidy from the municipal council of three hundred florins in 1884, a sum that rose to six hundred florins, supplemented by contributions from public and private sources. Outside Vienna such financial support as there was came from the district and regional authorities and the railway companies that, recognizing the economic potential of tourism, began to cooperate with the tourist associations, included organizing cut-price deals for their members. The privately owned Südbahn railway opened hotels in the resorts adjacent to its routes to the south, on the Semmering for example, and at Abbazia, where it initiated the transformation of a villa colony into a fashionable seaside resort. Initially the only direct state support for tourism came from the Railways Ministry. Founded in 1896, its responsibility for overseeing the development of tourism took the form of dealing with general publicity and timetables. Collaborating with the Ministry of the Interior, the Foreign Office, and the Trade Ministry, it attempted to inform and attract tourists by setting up information and travel bureaus in centers of tourism in Vienna, Innsbruck, and Graz. It reinforced these efforts through newspaper articles, magic lantern shows and lectures, exhibitions, and posters. By the turn of the century the government was sufficiently aware of the relationship between tourism and the balance of trade for the Ministry for Railways to open a travel bureau in London in 1902, aimed at the British upper classes, followed by others in New York, Paris, and Berlin.

As the dynamic of industrial development gradually shifted away from Vienna and the alpine regions toward Bohemia, they became increasingly aware of tourism as a significant source of income and a stimulant to the production and consumption of local arts and crafts. The continuous growth in the Tyrol's popularity with both domestic and foreign tourists was indicated by the numerous editions of *Baedeker's Eastern Alps,* published by 1911, and its prominence in other continental tourist guides.[33] Lying on the old pilgrim route through the Alps along which German Catholics had traveled to Rome, the area's economy was inextricably linked to that of the whole alpine region. The influx of domestic tourists to the Tyrol and the neighboring Vorarlberg reinforced the economic relationship of these areas with the rest of Austria (their popularity with German tourists shown by the names of the mountain huts throughout the area) and helped to maintain their traditional economic and cultural links with southern Germany.[34] In tourist regions that also attracted visitors from over the imperial borders like the Croatian and the Slovenian resorts of the southern Austria and the Tatra Mountains in the east, similar effects were discernible as internal tourist traffic expanded within areas bound together by long-standing economic ties and cultural affinities.

THE INFLUENCE OF TOURISM ON THE CONSTRUCTION OF CULTURAL IDENTITY

As Austria became more urbanized, peasant life became a subject of interest to tourists and specimens of their handicrafts sought after as desirable souvenirs. Some of the cultural consequences of this kind of attention were clearly evident in the Tyrol, an area with a strong sense of its own historical and cultural identity. This was most clearly expressed in the devotion of its inhabitants to Andreas Hofer, a patriot famous for his loyalty to Austria, who was commemorated in various monuments and relics all over the region.[35] An annual dramatization of Hofer's life was included in the hero plays of Meran. Initiated in 1884, these were financed by local organizations and were performed by the peasants. They were popular with both local people and foreign tourists, and the scale of the 1909 centenary celebrations revealed not just Hofer's role as a tourist attraction but also the political and cultural significance attached to his figure with the region. The pervasiveness of the Hofer cult was merely one example of the ways in which the region becoming orientated to tourists. Going about their daily business, Tyrolean peasants found themselves the subject of much curiosity among visitors used to different social customs and ideas. Like their Swiss and Bavarian neighbors, they soon became aware of the distinctive elements of their particular culture as well as the commercial opportunities those could generate. As competition for tourists became stronger, there were additional incentives for the inhabitants of the Tyrol and the Vorarlberg to emphasize the unique aspects of their history and culture since these also differentiated them from their foreign rivals.[36] At the same time commercialization of the Tyrolean versions of the alpine yodel and *Schuhplattler* folk dance, performed by professional companies of dancers who traveled through the region,[37] and the promotion of Hofer monuments as tourist sites facilitated their use as symbols of regional and cultural identity within a wider commercial and political arena.[38]

Much the same was true of Salzburg and its relationship with Munich and Vienna.[39] Only fully incorporated into the Habsburg crownlands in 1861, this city had a long tradition as a tourist host. Lying on one of the traditional routes from Germany to Italy and the Holy Land, it was well placed to benefit from the growth of tourism.[40] The city's relationship with Austria was complicated by the strength of its economic, social, and cultural connections with southern Germany, so that its efforts to encourage tourism were also bound up with its attempt to construct and maintain a distinctive identity for itself. Salzburg's two main tourist attractions were its baroque architecture and its relationship with Mozart. It was this fortunate connection that became the central element in Salzburg's career as a major site of cultural tourism. A monument dedicated to the composer in 1842 initiated a flurry of commercial activity that led to a Mozart centenary in 1856. The Mozarteum, the force behind the musical life of Salzburg, generated an irregular series of Mozart festivals beginning in 1877 that were modeled on the Wagner festival held the previous year at Bayreuth.[41] The invention of the chocolate *Mozartkugel* in 1890 rapidly proved to be the ultimate form of tourist souvenir-cum-advertisement.[42]

 One of the more distinctive features of Viennese culture as it was depicted for tourists was the pleasure-loving behavior of its inhabitants. This included both the social life of its elites and the popular culture of the working people. It had long been customary for the latter to make weekend and evening outings to the public houses and wine taverns *(Heurigen)* of the old wine-growing villages on the edge of the Vienna Woods. This habit persisted even when the arrival of the railways made it possible to make day trips to nearby resorts such as Baden and Mödling. By the end of the century, however, the larger *Heurigen* establishments were increasingly oriented toward the tourist market, while many of the entertainments put on in the Prater, the other main center of amusements, were directed toward tourists.[43] Part of the Prater was also one of the main centers of Vienna's extensive prostitution industry.

In the early twentieth century the numbers of foreign tourists continued to grow, but the competition became fiercer. The German bourgeoisie still constituted an expanding market, but the influence of nationalism led many Germans to holiday at home in the Black Forest or Bavaria.[44] The availability of relatively comfortable package trips to destinations further afield to North Africa and the Near East made them popular with the fashionable elites, especially after the German kaiser's trip to Palestine in 1898. As more and more Austrians looked to tourism as a source of income, the strength of the competition became a matter of concern to the industry, particularly in Vienna, still Austria's main tourist destination. Tourists also constituted an important part of the market for the city's luxury goods so that it was not surprising that it was both concerned and chagrined by its failure to attract more foreign visitors. However, despite the steady growth in its size and the number of its visitors, Vienna could not begin to compete with Paris, long acknowledged as the tourist capital of the world, nor with Berlin and Munich. In 1890 Vienna received a total of 200,000 visitors, while 334,000 visited Berlin. By 1913 the number of foreign visitors had risen to over 100,000, but this still compared unfavorably with the 400,000 who visited Paris.[45] The Vienna correspondent of the *Times* of London, Henry Wickham Steed, wrote that "for forty years the Viennese have been studying how to draw a stream of foreign visitors to their city and for forty years have been astounded at their failure."[46]

There were several reasons for this of which the most obvious was the city's remoteness from Europe's most industrially advanced regions and its position to the east of the main tourist routes that ran from the north to the south. From the west, Vienna seemed remote in a different way. In 1837 Frances Trollope had written that "there is no country in Europe so little known, and so little understood." This was still true in the early twentieth century as the rise of nationalism made the cultural identity of the multiethnic empire and its components appear increasingly problematic to foreigners.[47] Commenting on the diversity of the peoples who composed the empire, Steed remarked, "There is, in reality, no Austrian, Hungarian or Austro-Hungarian 'people.' There are the peoples that inhabit the Monarchy, Hapsburg peoples, but no Hapsburg people."[48] One of the great attractions of Switzerland, the Riviera, and Italy for western visitors was their sense of its "familiarity," stemming from their well-established position as tourist destinations and the reassuring presence of compatriots.[49] By contrast, imperial Austria appeared deeply unfamiliar, the streets of its principal towns and streets cities revealing the ethnic, religious, and linguistic diversity of its peoples. Even in Innsbruck, in the familiar territory of the western Alps, foreigners were struck by the ethnic diversity of the Austrian visitors and even more so in Vienna, where the distinctiveness of its cuisine and its social, political, and cultural political life reflected the fact that, according to the 1890 census, 65.5 percent of its inhabitants had been born elsewhere in the empire.[50]

A persistent and related element in the empire's traditional image was its position on the cultural borderland between Western Christendom and the Muslim East. A visitor to the 1873 exhibition had written of its "cosmopolite nature, a mingling of the modern and the medieval, the East and the West." Both the Muslims of the Balkans and the extensive Jewish populations found throughout the empire were often referred to by Western visitors as "Orientals." Reflecting on his experiences, Wickham Steed wrote that "what is incomprehensible to every non-Austrian, nay the eternally unintelligible about Austria is the Asiatic in Austria."[51] On the streets of Vienna visitors were struck by the conspicuously exotic and outlandish eastern Jews (Ostjuden) from Galicia marked out by their strange black clothing and speech. In Marienbad, Sir Arthur Ponsonby, equerry to Edward VII, was struck by the "bearded and ringletted Polish Jews, who wore a curious old-fashioned coat and long boots."[52] An additional factor that colored Austria's traditional image for European Protestants was its association with the culture of Catholicism. In this respect, Vienna, the home of the Habsburgs, traditional defenders of the Catholic faith, was almost as problematic as Rome. Its theatrically Baroque churches exhibited the same qualities of operatic passion and excess that many still associated with the seductive and dangerous aspects of the Latin culture of the Italians, as well as the Slavic, Magyar, and Gypsy peoples of the empire.[53] In 1868 the non-Conformist Thomas Cook had informed readers of the *Excursionist* that Viennese Sundays were "a carnival of folly and vice" while reassuring prospective customers that suitable religious facilities were also available.[54] The implication of these associations, mediated through the literary culture of "Bohemia," was made explicit in the behavior of the French poet Gérard de Nerval, who, on his way to "the Orient" (Egypt) had passed through Munich, where he studied the monuments and works of art, while in Vienna he chased women.[55] Perhaps more importantly, many liberally inclined Western observers like Cook found Austria's political regime deeply unattractive. By the early twentieth century the country was formally held together only by its relationship to the Habsburg dynasty and an increasingly bureaucratic administrative system. The rise of nationalism and overseas colonialism made the polyglot, multiethnic empire appear increasingly marginal and politically decrepit. Austria's refusal to cede Venetia to Italy in the 1850s and 1860s aroused considerable indignation and much anti-Austrian feeling in the West that persisted. This attitude subsequently gave rise to sympathy for the Hungarians and a small but growing interest in the Czechs.[56] Even Vienna's reputation as a "city of pleasure," the foundations of which were laid at the Congress of Vienna in 1814, was capable of evoking political distrust. An observer at the time remarked that "that gaiety, that brilliancy, and those pleasures, were contrived more for political ends, than for the apparent purpose of rendering Vienna, for the time, the most attractive and agreeable capital in Europe."[57] Foreigners continued to comment on the way that the authorities appeared to use the pleasure-loving disposition of the people to maintain their compliance.[58]

The Western view of imperial Austria was at odds with that embodied in official Habsburg "mythology," which justified the empire to its inhabitants by identifying the emperor, Francis Joseph, as a kind of folk hero and the empire as a "family of nations." In Vienna the "myth" received specific expression in various tourist "sights" linked to the Habsburgs such as the emperor's summer palace at Schönbrunn. Further afield, the royal family were constantly out and about in the empire unveiling plaques and monuments to themselves. The jubilee celebrations that punctuated the emperor's reign were tourist attractions in their own right, constructing an image of the Austrian half of the Monarchy as a peacefully coexisting, heterogeneously picturesque collection of ethnic groups, bound together by the benevolent rule of the emperor. Unfortunately, it was now increasingly unclear what it meant to be an "Austrian" in a country where the only clear and uncontested image of its cultural identity stemmed from its identification with the Habsburg dynasty.[59] Public spectacles such as the jubilee pageants simply masked the growing problem posed by the conflicting claims to national and cultural identity of different ethnic groups, claims that conflicted with the imperial philosophy of the "family of nations."[60]

In the regions where there was the greatest potential for division, these concerns were supported by the growth of tourist cultures that reinforced, not only awareness of the distinctive nature of regional cultural identities, but also their political significance. In the eastern provinces by the 1880s the spa resort of Zakopane in the Tatra Mountains had become a major site of pilgrimage for Polish artists and intellectuals from Kraków who regarded the vernacular peasant architecture of the region as the epitome of true "Polishness" and the "Zakopianskí style" as synonymous with the national style of Poland. A few years later organizations in Kraków involved with the conservation of the city's Polish architectural and cultural monuments drew on established patterns of travel by encouraging Poles to visit them as pilgrimage sites.[61] In Bohemia, by now the economic heartland of the empire, the increasingly self-assertive Czechs continued to resent German dominance in educational and cultural matters. German-speaking citizens in the region felt that they had more in common with the new empire in the north than their Czech neighbors and the other Slavic nationalities that were also demanding greater cultural autonomy. As a consequence, cultural monuments such as the Bohemian Museum (1885–90) and the Czecho-Slavonic Ethnographical Museum, both in Prague, became important tourist attractions within the region that helped to instill in the Czech community an awareness of its own cultural heritage. The founder of the Bohemian Industrial Museum, the Czech patriot Vojta Náprstek, firmly believed in the role that travel and visits to significant places could play in the cultivation of a historic sense.[62] Visiting Vienna, these Czechs viewed its monuments to German culture, such as the statue of Goethe, in a very different way than the Bohemian Gemans who identified with the German language and erected numerous monuments to Joseph II as a symbols of their allegiance.[63]

By the early twentieth century national feelings increasingly influenced

Postcard c. 1910. Polish peasant women in their distinctive costume for touristic consumption. (Author's collection.)

the way in which Austrians and Germans selected and viewed their holiday
destinations. The Vienna edition of Cook's *Welt-Reise-Zeitung* ran a series of
articles in 1908 covering all the main regions of Austria. However, the emphasis it placed on the most highly developed tourist regions of western Austria
was in tune with the "mental geography" of the great bulk of its market, the
German-speaking Austrians, mainly from Bohemia, Vienna, and Lower Austria, who wished to distance themselves from their troublesome Slavic neighbors and who were coming to identify with the part of Austria where they

spent most of their holidays.[64] The prosperous Bohemian Czechs, whose lands were the most industrially developed part of the empire and who formed a large part of Austria's domestic tourist market, increasingly preferred to holiday in the Slavic lands of the Adriatic coast rather than the alpine areas favored by their German-speaking neighbors, while Poles and Moravians sought out their own numerous spas. National feeling and political events reinforced the inclination of the Hungarian Magyars to patronize resorts in Hungary.

TOURISM AND THE "IMAGING" OF AUSTRIA

Perhaps, because of the popularity of the alpine lands, the diversity of Austria's different regions and the lack of a clear image of the empire itself, an image of Austria began to circulate abroad that identified it culturally with a generalized image of the western alpine lands rather than the relatively undeveloped south or the eastern provinces. One of the most important sources of "touristic" Austria were the verbal and visual images of the promotional literature put out by the travel industry and the different kinds of travel writing aimed at an increasingly differentiated reading publics. In the second half of the nineteenth century visual images were important elements in travel and tourist literature: their presence supported by the emergence of a visual culture manifested in the popularity of dioramas, panoramas, stereographs, and, subsequently, postcards.[65] Images of the Alps and their inhabitants were popular subjects and helped to shape the expectations that visitors brought to their experiences.

An influx of visitors into any region where tourism was relatively undeveloped meant that its landscapes and their inhabitants acquired a new commercial significance as professional and amateur painters and photographers began to represent them in a way that matched touristic tastes.[66] Apart from the usual scenes of mountains and genre paintings of peasant life in the style of Friedrich Wäldmüller, a feature of the Tyrol that appealed to artists was its romantic past expressed in the work of landscape artists such as Eduard Zetsche, who specialized in ruined castles and Albion Egger-Lienz, who painted numerous pictures relating to Hofer. By 1900 many of these images were reproduced for the postcard trade.[67] These developments were replicated in the other tourist regions. Images aimed at tourists invariably featured the kind of urban and rural landscapes that appealed to the modern sense of the "picturesque," a word that liberally splattered any accompanying text. By the early twentieth century this usually meant scenes that were in tune with the general reaction against the unpleasant aspects of modern urban life and that were expressive of a nostalgic interest in, and a regret, for ways of life that were fast disappearing as the waves of tourists swept further up the valleys. In rural resorts this impulse was evident in the touristic desire to witness scenes of authentic, picturesque peasant culture, now under threat, and a preference for old-style vernacular buildings rather than their more practical but less aesthetically pleasing replacements. To secularized urban visitors the traditional signs of rural Catholicism, with its wayside shrines and pilgrimages, stood for quaint country customs and a threatened way of life.[68] Images of peasant life like those of the Czech painters Jöza Urbrika and Emil Orlik, viewed out of context, ceased to be explorations of cultural identity and became simply picturesque evocations of rural jollity.[69]

In Vienna, where the new suburbs were fast swallowing up the old villages and former summer resort areas, the pressures of overcrowding and the threat to the Vienna Woods generated many images of the landscape around in and around the city well suited to the tourist market.[70] The popularity of pictures of Beethoven's home in Heilingenstadt, a version of the old wooden *Pawlatschenhaus* that was a form of vernacular architecture now only found in the suburbs, allied culture to picturesque "old Vienna." The geography of Vienna made it relatively easy to view the city in this way since the heart of the principal tourist zone was its compact, old, aristocratic core. By 1900 its picturesque old streets and squares, undeveloped apart from luxury shops and hotels, were insulated from the aesthetic and social ugliness of modern life by the parks and monuments of the Ringstrasse.[71] Events such as the daily social display of the Kärtner *corso* and the now commercialized *Fiaker* Ball of the carnival season, were evocative of a pleasanter social world. The extreme poverty of Vienna's urban poor, many of them recent immigrants from the eastern part of the empire, remained hidden away in the industrial suburbs of Birgittenau and Ottakring, and they were alluded to only as picturesque additions to the urban scene.[72]

Guidebooks played a particularly important role in determining a visitor's sense of a place and its significant features, while travel books with literary pretensions often directed visitors to places they might otherwise have overlooked. The town of St. Ulrich in the Gröden valley in the Tyrol received many more English visitors after Amelia B. Edward's account of "Toyland," while other writers praised the beauties of Dalmatia and the Dolomites.[73] The appearance of guidebooks addressing different kinds of publics and pockets indicated the broadening of the tourist market, with the popular ones usually the most generously illustrated. The *Wiener Cicerone* and Bermann's *Illustrated Guide to Vienna*, both published in Vienna and aimed at German-speaking visitors, marked out the sights, verbally and visually, so that there could be no mistakes of recognition.[74] Some of the illustrations in the *Wiener Cicerone*, originating as postcards, were photographs of actors posing as Viennese types, superimposed on other photographs of places on the tourist route, placing them as if in a stage set, turning the city into an extension of its own theatrical space. Images of this kind contributed to the commodification of the city as its inhabitants were encouraged to "perform" for the now ubiquitous Kodak according to the established stereotypes. Of Salzburg, one visitor remarked that "as a general rule the market folk are good models both for artists and amateur photographers, though some of the younger women coquettishly pretend that they object to be photographed, whilst all the while they are desperately anxious to come into the picture."[75]

Invented in Austria in 1869, produced and retailed by many of the publishing houses, postcards were sold everywhere: a tiny shop in an alpine village could sell up to five thousand cards in a summer. By identifying and dramatizing local activities and customs as well as the seasonal festivals and rituals of *Corpus Christi*, Easter, and Christmas, postcard images divorced them from their everyday context and assisted their absorption into the developing tourist culture. At the same time, circulated and collected throughout Europe, they helped to create an image of Austria's gemütlich charm, a kind of mental coziness. In Vienna *Gemütlichkeit* was the quality that the local press ascribed to the "true" Viennese as opposed to "foreigners," thereby evoking a time before the building of the Ringstrasse, an era of wine gardens, cafés, and villages and "characters" in beer houses, now overtaken by the new suburbs with their ethnically diverse populations.[76] In a similar vein, the *Wiener Cicerone* identified Viennese "types," lamenting that they were no longer as common as they used to be.[77]

MARKETING "AUSTRIA" AS A TOURIST DESTINATION

This system of verbal and visual representation made a substantial contribution to the way in which the regions of Austria represented themselves in foreign exhibitions. By the turn of the century exhibitions of various kinds had come to be important vehicles for displaying a country's progress and for promoting trade and tourism. Although Austria had participated in the big international exhibitions in Chicago (1893), Paris (1900), and St. Louis (1904), the Government had no clear exhibitions policy, nor did the imperial "family of nations" myth fit comfortably into the format of this type of exhibition, which was increasingly used to justify a modernizing overseas colonialism. The situation was aggravated by the restiveness of the non-German nationalities, especially the Czechs, the Serbs, and the other Slavic groups.[78] It was not surprising, therefore, that the Austrian trade and tourist associations responded enthusiastically to the suggestion that they should participate in the staging of a large trade exhibition in London in 1906 at Earl's Court.[79]

Encouraged by the emperor, the Government gave official support but kept to its usual policy by which the bulk of the considerable cost was paid by the exhibiting organizations. The exhibition was divided into sections that included a large photographic journey through southern Austria, while the main feature was a reconstruction of a Tyrolean village.[80] The latter, an Austrian version an established genre, drew on aspects of alpine tourism popular with British tourists. Set on a picturesque mountainside, the village square was a "meeting place" where "inhabitants" engaged in rural crafts and their visitors enjoyed the inevitable *Schuhplattler* dance. The homely rural values evoked by the vernacular format and the choice of the Tyrolean peasant as the representative of Austria's diverse ethnic groups firmly aligned the country with the alpine "playgrounds" of the West rather than the "uncivilized" borderlands of the East.[81] By contrast, Vienna was represented as a cosmopolitan city of culture, elegance, and high-class shopping facilities: an image supported by the numerous trade exhibits of luxury goods and arts and crafts, and the presence of its major art organizations, including the Secession.[82] In honor of the exhibition the London art journal *The Studio* published a special issue with illustrations supporting the exhibition's general theme.[83] The whirl of high-profile social events accompanying the exhibition reinforced the British image of pleasure-loving Austria and its peoples. The political troubles that beset the empire could not be left behind. The handbook that accompanied the Bohemian section of the exhibition, put on under the auspices of the City of Prague and organized by the Czech patriot Count Franz Lützow, made it clear that the relationship with Austria was not a happy one and clearly set out Bohemia's claims to a separate historical and cultural identity. It also expressed frustration with the traditional image of Bohemia that it associated with the "uncivilized" Slavonian tribes from the east.[84] The authors made much of the region's links with the Protestant Hussites, evidently hoping that the presence of sympathetic Protestant tourists might be politically advantageous.

Despite the favorable publicity attracted by the exhibition, the traditional image of the empire still persisted in Britain. This was evident in the picture published, just after the exhibition closed, in the *Illustrated London News*. This was a tableau of the peoples of the empire in an alpine setting, in which three discreetly placed "Civilized Gypsies" symbolized the sophisticated and modern city of Vienna.[85] The caption ran, "A Hard Family to govern: the Emperor Franz Josef's Motley Empire—The extraordinary diversity of nationalities composing the Austrian-Hungarian empire," indicating that the empire's political problems and stereotypes of its more "uncivilized" and unruly inhabitants still influenced the way it was viewed abroad. In Vienna itself the same kind of contradiction was apparent in the discrepancy between the image of the empire, as it was constructed for the 1908 jubilee pageant, and the way in which the different ethnic and national groups now saw themselves. An elaborately theatrical spectacle, the jubilee was a tribute to the "family of nations"

Gruß vom Kaiser-Jubiläums-Huldigungs-Festzug, Wien 1908

Franz-Joseph's jubilee procession, Vienna, 1908. (Author's collection.)

that encompassed all parts of the Monarchy, every epoch of Habsburg history, and every single ethnic group. The London edition of Cook's *Travellers Gazette* overlooked the jubilee, but its feature on the "City of Pleasure" reproduced all the standard clichés. "It is the art of enjoying life that gives Vienna the air of a City of Pleasure, but of pleasure upon which the Muses have never ceased to smile."[86] By the end of the month Austria's annexation of Bosnia and Herzegovina provoked the Western press into denunciations of the uncivilized and anachronistic nature of the Monarchy. The *London Illustrated News* illustrated the leading players in the affair together with pictures of wild-looking scenery and brigand-like peasants.[87]

The increased efforts of the authorities in the main tourist centers to attract visitors indicated the important role that tourism was beginning to play in the economy. In the jubilee year the Austrian government had founded the Ministry for Public Works with a budget of five hundred thousand kroner for the promotion of tourism. The ineffectiveness of this arrangement was such that, by the end of the prewar period, the budget was nearly cut while the Railways Ministry retained all its former responsibilities. The failure of Austria's balance-of-trade figures to improve made tourism even more valuable, especially in Vienna, where the increase in guests could not keep up with the supply of beds.[88] A civic visit to Vienna by the lord mayor of London generated a lengthy feature in the *Illustrated London News*. Calculated to appeal to the modern tourist, it emphasized the city's modern amenities, healthiness, and proximity to winter sports facilities with their fashionable clientele. A Eucharistic Congress attracted many foreign visitors, and the following year, copying the rival city's of Munich and Salzburg, the city capitalized on its reputation as a musical center by introducing a music festival, while the Austrian railways followed the Bavarians and introduced American-style observation cars on selected routes.

Promotional activity of this kind, supported by a growing flood of tourist literature praising the beauties of the Tyrol, Dalmatia, and the Dolomites, particularly in Britain, helped to circulate generalized images of Austria as a place of unspoiled mountain scenery, frivolous gaiety, royal glamour, and picturesque peasants. Identifying Austria with its alpine and subalpine regions, they isolated the latter from its troublesome eastern neighbors and formed a counterpoint to the more negative associations still evoked abroad by the idea of the Monarchy, serving to divert the attention of tourists from the serious nature of Austria's social and political problems just as these were becoming more pressing.[89] For domestic tourists the historical and cultural identities promoted within the individual regions like the Tyrol, Galicia, Moravia, and the Slovenian and Croatian territories helped to give some focus to the notion of ethnic identity that grew stronger as that of the Monarchy grew weaker.[90] Paradoxically, however, the Habsburg dynasty was turned into one of Austria's greatest tourist assets, although by identifying the regime with scenes of nostalgic picturesqueness it also reinforced the prevailing sense of its anachronistic nature. The popular success of Franz Lehár's operetta *The Merry Widow* (1905) and Anthony Hope's novel *The Prisoner of Zenda* (1909) contributed to the strength of this image, which survived the First World War and the difficult years of "Red Vienna."[91]

By then, no longer imperial, Austrian territory was reduced to the German-speaking region around Vienna and the alpine lands of the west. This meant that it was relatively easy for the Austrian tourist industry to reconstruct an image of Austria from well-established and familiar ingredients together with newer themes of climate and happy families. This paralleled official attempts to construct a cultural identity for a country in which, despite the demise of the old empire, regional differences persisted and where cultural identity continued to be uncertain.[92] After the Second World War the nature of Austria's cultural identity continued to be problematic, a situation compounded by the country's location on the boundary between East and West. Following the end of the Cold War the situation has become even more complicated with the highly controversial issue of Austria's conceptual location within the "imaginative geography" of Europe as yet unresolved and with the nature of Austrian cultural identity still an issue. Nevertheless, for the outside world the country's strongest images continue to be those promoted by the tourist board and the cultural industries, of "Habsburg Vienna," picturesque Salzburg, and beautiful alpine scenery.

NOTES

1. For a survey of recent literature on the topic, see William D. Bowman, "Regional History and the Austrian Nation," *Journal of Modern History* 67 (December 1995): 873–97; also Ritchie Robertson and Edward Timms, eds., *The Habsburg Legacy: National Identity in Historical Perspective*, Austrian Studies 5 (Edinburgh: Edinburgh University Press, 1994).

2. Tourist place-images have usually been discussed in relation to the promotional activities of contemporary tourism rather than in the context of tourism history. See, for example, Tom Selwyn, ed., *The Tourist Image* (Chichester: Wiley, 1996); Gerry Kearns and Chris Philo, eds., *Selling the City: The City as Cultural Capital, Past and Present* (Oxford: Pergamon, 1993); John R. Gold and Stephen Ward, eds., *Place Promotion: The Use of Advertising and Marketing to Sell Towns and Regions* (Chichester: Wiley, 1994). For a review of tourism history see John Towner, "Tourism History: Past, Present, and Future," in *Tourism: The State of the Art*, ed. A. V. Seaton (Chichester: John Wiley, 1994), 721–28.

3. After 1867 Austria and Hungary formed the two main parts of the Habsburg Empire with the status of quasi states within the framework of an imperial monetary and customs union.

4. James Shedel, "Emperor, Church, and People; Religion and Dynastic Loyalty during the Golden Jubilee of Franz-Joseph," *Catholic History Review* 6 (1990): 71–93; Andrew Wheatcroft, *The Habsburgs: Embodying Empire* (London: Viking, 1995), 279–84.

5. Jozsef Böröcz, *Leisure Migration: A Sociological Study on Tourism* (Oxford: Pergamon, 1996), 33–52. For the economic development of the regions see David F. Good, *The Economic Rise of the Habsburg Empire* (Berkeley and Los Angeles: University of California Press, 1984); and for an overview of discussions of the Austrian economy during this period, Max-Stephan Schulze, "Article Economic Development in the Nineteenth-Century Habsburg Empire," *Austrian History Yearbook* 28 (1997): 1–27.

6. John Murray, *A Handbook for Travellers on the Continent* (London: John Murray, 1840), 217. See also Jill Steward, "The Spa Towns of the Austro-Hungarian Empire and the Growth of Tourist Culture," in *European Urban Culture in the Mirror of Art, Health, and Medicine*, ed. Peter Borsay, Gunther Hirschfelder, and Ruth Mohrmann (Munster and New York: Waxmann, 2000).

7. Peter Jordan, "Die Entwicklung der Fremdensverkehrsströme in Mitteleuropa (1910–1990) als Ausdruck Politischer und Wirtschaftlicher Veränderungen," in *Mitteilungen der österreichishen geographischen Gesellschaft* (Vienna) 132 (1990): 144–71, for a discussion of the problems of dealing with the tourist statistics. Also Böröcz, *Leisure Migration*, 62–81.

8. For the concept of tourist culture see John Urry, *Consuming Places* (London: Routledge, 1995), 164. See also Franz Baltzarek, "Fremdenverkehr und Sport," in Schloss Grafenegg, *Das Zeitalter Kaiser Franz Josephs- Glanz und Elend 1880–1916*, vol. 2 (Vienna: Amt des NÖ Landesmuseums, 1985), 167.

9. *Cook's Excursionist and International Tourist Advertiser* (London), April 1873, 3–4, May 1873, 4–5. I am indebted to the Thomas Cook Archive, London, for this information.

10. *Excursionist*, May 1873, 4–5, August 1873, 3–4. For the exhibition see the *Art Journal*, July 1873; and Karl Roschitz, *Wiener Weltausstellung 1873* (Vienna: Böhlau, 1989).

11. In 1898 70 percent of the visitors to the Semmering came from Vienna; only 7 percent came from Budapest. See Wolfgang Kos, ed., *Die Eroberung der Landschaft: Semmering, Rax, Schneeberg; Katalog zur niederösterreichische Landesaustellung Schloss Gloggnitz* (Vienna: Falter, 1992), 260.

12. W. A. Bailie Grohman, *The Land in the Mountains: Being an Account of the Past and Present of Tyrol, Its People and Its Castles* (London: Simpkin, Marshall, Hamilton, Kent, 1907), 70–71; W. D. McCrackan, *The Tyrol* (London: Duckworth, 1885).

13. See also J. Matzettner, "Alpinismus and Tourismus (Fremdenverkehr)," in *Alpinism and Tourism and Other Problems of the Geography of Tourism: Proceedings of the IGU Working Group: Geography of Tourism and Recreation* (Frankfurt am Main: Institut für Wirtschafts- und Sozialgeograpie der Johann Wolfgang Goethe-Universität, 1982).

14. Frederick Wolcott Stoddard, *Tramps through the Tyrol*, 2d ed. (London: Mills and Boon, 1912), 209, 228–29. Paul Bernecker, "Die Entwicklung des Fremdenverkehrs in Österreich," in *Österreich—50 Jahre Republik 1968–1981*, ed. Institut für Österreichkunde (Vienna: Ferdinand Hirt, 1968), 236.

15. See Dr. A. B. Granville, *The Spas of Germany*, vol. 2 (London: Henry Colburn, 1837). For a discussion of the spectacular culture of Vienna see Donald D. Olsen, *The City as a Work of Art: London, Paris, and Vienna* (New Haven: Yale University Press, 1986), 235–50.

16. 1896, Blackwoods Archive, MS 4647, 271, National Library of Scotland.

17. Granville, *The Spas of Germany*, 68.

18. Figures from Karl Baedeker, *Austria-Hungary*, 10th ed. (Leipzig, 1905), *Österreich-Ungarn*, 17th ed. (Leipzig: Karl Baedeker, 1907), but see J. Mikoletsky, "Zur Sozialgeschichte des österreichischen Kurorts im 19. Jahrhundert: Kurlisten and Kurtaxordnungen als sozialhistorische Quelle," *Mitteilungen des Instituts für österreiche Geschichtsforschung* 99, no. 3 (1991): 393–433, for an analysis of visitor numbers. Arthur Ponsonby, *Recollections of Three Reigns* (London: Eyre and Spottiswood, 1975), 28. See also Gordon Brook-Shepherd, *Uncle of Europe: The Social and Diplomatic Life of Edward VII* (London: Collins, 1975), 210–15.

19. James Bryce, "The Tátra," in *Memories of Travel* (London: Macmillan, 1923), 44–140

20. Carl Dolmetsch, *Our Famous Guest: Mark Twain in Vienna* (Athens: University of Georgia Press, 1992), 221–23. On attitudes to health and body cultivation see for example, Carmen Feuchtner, "Rekord kostet Anmut, meine Damen! Zur Körper-Kultur der Frau im Bürgertum Wiens (1880–1930)," *Tel Aviver Jahrbuch für deutsche Geschichte* 21 (1992): 127–51.

21. Ernst Gerhard Eder, *Bade- und Schwimmenkulture in Wien: Sozialhistorische und kulturanthropologische Untersuchen* (Vienna: Böhlau, 1995).

22. For Bavaria, see Helen Waddy Lepowitz, "Gateway to the Mountains: Tourism and Positive Deindustrialization in the Bavarian Alps," *German History* 7 (1989): 293–318, and "Pilgrims, Painters, and Patients," in *Historical Reflexions* 8, no. 1 (1992): 121–45.

23. Stoddard, *Tramps through the Tyrol*, 63–64.

24. Amelia B. Edwards, *Untrodden Peaks and Unfrequented Valleys: A Midsummer Ramble in the Dolomites* (London: Longmans and Green, 1873), 381–82.

25. Judith Adler, "Youth on the Road: Reflections on the History of Tramping,"

Annals of Tourism Research 12 (1985): 335–54; Nigel Thrift and Paul Glennie, "Historical Geographies of Urban Life and Modern Consumption," in Kearns and Philo, *Selling the City*, 33–48.

26. See Françoise Knopper, "Berlin et Vienne dans les relations de voyage 1900–1930," *Cahiers d"études Germaniques* 24 (1993): 253–66.

27. See Gottfried Korff, "Museumreisen," in *Reisekultur: Von der Pilgerfahrt zum modernen Tourismus*, ed. Herman Bausinger, Klaus Beyerer, and Gottfried Korff (Munich: Beck, 1998), 311–19. Vienna was a lesser center on the British grand tour routes: see John Towner, "The Grand Tour: A Key Phase in the History of Tourism," *Annals of Tourism Research* 12 (1985): 315. Wolfgang Kaschuba, "German Bürgerlichkeit after 1800: Culture as a Symbolic Practice," in *Bourgeois Society in Nineteenth-Century Europe*, ed. Jürgen Kocka and Allan Mitchell (Oxford: Berg, 1993).

28. See Carl E. Schorske, *Fin-de-Siècle Vienna: Politics and Culture* (New York: Knopf, 1980).

29. Robert Rotenberg, "Viennese Wine Gardens and Their Magic," *East European Quarterly* 4 (1984): 447–60; Baedeker, *Austria-Hungary*, 65.

30. Bryce, "The Tátra," 82; Baedeker, *Öesterreich-Ungarn*, 435–36.

31. *Styria, Austria: An Illustrated Guide* (Graz: Official Tourist Office of Styria, 1914). The cult of monuments in the late nineteenth century led to considerable controversy about the respective merits of preservation or conservation. See Margaret Olin, "Alois Riegl and the Crisis of Representation in Art Theory," Ph.D. diss., University of Chicago, 1984, 195.

32. Stoddard, *Tramps through the Tyrol*, 209, 228–29; Bernecker, "Die Entwicklung des Fremdenverkehrs," 326.

33. Of the editions of Baedeker, only twelve were English, while thirty-four were German. The 1911 edition could be cut into sections for mountaineers and pedestrians wishing to travel light and were suitable for walking tours popular with members of the Alpine associations. For an analysis of the changing emphasis given to specific regions in Baedeker see Böröcz, *Leisure Migration*, 54–60. Examples of other guides with a strong emphasis on Austrian resorts are the souvenirs published by the shipping companies such as the North-German Lloyd Company's *Guide through Central-Europe and Italy etc* (Berlin: Reichmann, 1896), and the Hamburg-American Line's *Guide through Europe* (Berlin: Herz, 1901). Spa guides such as Thomas Linn's *Health Resorts of Europe*, 10th ed. (London: Reynold-Ball, 1910) also gave paid them plenty of attention.

34. Jordan, "Die Entwicklung der Fremdensverkehrsstrome," 150.

35. Stoddard, *Tramps through the Tyrol*, 33–37, 215; "The Andreas Hofer and Liberty War Centenary in Tyrol," *Cook's Traveller's Gazette*, April 17, 1909, 16; Clive Holland, *The Tyrol and Its People* (London: Mills and Boon, 1909), 198–99.

36. "Das kleine walsertal—das Land der "freyen" Walser!" *Cook's Welt-Reise-Zeitung* (Vienna), July 1912, 3–12; Bowman, "Regional History," 878–79.

37. Franz Rainer, a peasant from the Zillertal valley, took his company abroad and was so successful that he was able to return, buy a large old castle, and turn it into a guesthouse (Stoddard, *Tramps through the Tyrol*, 43).

38. The importance these acquired can be seen in the prohibition by the Italians in the interwar period of picture of Andreas Hofer and other heroes associated with the Austrian Tyrol. C. H. Herford, trans. and ed., *The Case of German South Tyrol against Italy* (London: George Allen and Unwin, 1927), 70–71.

39. For Munich see Robin Lenman, *Artists and Society in Germany, 1850–1914* (Manchester: Manchester University Press, 1997).

40. Georg Stadler, *Von der Kavalierstour zum Sozialtourismus; Kulturgeschichte des Salzburger Fremdenverkehrs* (Salzburg: Universitatsverlag Anton Pustet, 1975); G. Müller, "Salzburg als Fremdenverkehrsland," *Österrreich in Geschichte und Literatur* 28, no. 1 (1984): 29–39; Ernst Hanisch and Ulrike Fleischer, *Im Schatten berühmter Zeiten: Salzburg in den Jahren Georg Trakls (1887–1914)* (Salzburg: Otto Müller Verlag, 1986).

41. Michael Steinberg, *The Meaning of the Salzburg Festival: Austria as Theater and Ideology, 1890–1938* (Ithaca, N.Y.: Cornell University Press, 1990).

42. Ulrike Kammerhafer-Aggermann, "The Mozartkugel: From a Local Specialty to Austria's 'National Symbol,'" *Finnish Studies in Ethnology* 21 (1993): 46–53.

43. J. G. Kohl, *Austria: Vienna, Prague, Hungary, Bohemia, and the Danube; Galicia, Styria, Moravia, Bukovina and the Military Frontier* (London: Chapman and Hall, 1843), 156–57. For an example of the Prater's attractions see Norbert Rubey and Peter Schoenwald, eds., *Venedig in Wien; Theater- und Vergnüngsstadt der Jahrhundertwende* (Vienna: Ueberreuter, 1996).

44. Northern Germany was served by the Hamburg edition of Cook's *Welt-Reise Zeitung,* in which references to Austria became increasingly infrequent after 1900 apart from the occasional reference to Karlsbad.

45. Baltzarek, "Fremdenverkehr und Sport," 167.

46. Wickham Steed, *The Hapsburg Monarchy,* 4th ed. (London: Constable and Constable, 1919), 206.

47. Frances Trollope, *Vienna and the Austrians; with some account of a journey through Swabia, Bavaria, the Tyrol, and the Salzburg* (London, Richard Bentley, 1838), 138.

48. Steed, *The Hapsburg Monarchy,* 120.

49. For the role of Switzerland in British tourism see Lynne Withey, *Grand Tours and Cook's Tours: A History of Leisure Travel, 1750–1915* (London: Aurum, 1998).

50. Eda Sagarra, "Vienna and Its Population in the Late Nineteenth Century: Social and Demographic Change, 1870–1910," in *Fin-de-Siècle Vienna,* ed. Gilbert J. Carr and Eda Sagarra (Dublin: Trinity College, 1985), 187–203. For a French view see Victor Tissot, *Vienne et la viennoise* (Paris, 1878).

51. Steed, *The Hapsburg Monarchy,* xix.

52. Ponsonby, *Recollections of Three Reigns,* 228.

53. See Chloe Chard, "Nakedness and Tourism: Classical Sculpture and the Imaginative Geography of the Grand Tour," *Oxford Art Journal* 18, no. 1 (1995): 14–28.

54. *The Excursionist* (London), August 15, 1868, 15. Piers Brendon remarks that similar depreciating remarks about Paris seemed to add to its attraction. See his *Thomas Cook: 150 Years of Popular Travel* (London: Secker and Warburg, 1986).

55. Gérald de Nerval, *Voyage en Orient,* in *Les oeuvres complètes,* vol. 2 (Paris: François Bernouard, 1867), 77: "Hier au soir, me trouvant desoeuvré dans ce théâtre, et presque seul entre les prétendus civilisés, le reste se composant de Hongrois, de Bohèmes, de Grecs, de Turcs, de Tyroliens de Roumains et de Transylvaniens, j'ai songé à recommencer ce role de Casanova, déjà assez bien entame l'avant-veille." For the relationship with the literary imaging of "Bohemia" see Meryl Tyers, "Beyond Words: In Search of Bohemia," *Romance Studies* 25 (1995): 85–97.

56. From 1849 to 1866 Austria maintained a garrison in Venice, to the distaste and

inconvenience of western tourists. See John Pemble, *Venice Rediscovered* (Oxford: Oxford University Press, 1996), 22–25.

57. *Austria and the Austrians,* vol. 2 (London: Henry Colburn, 1837).

58. Virginio Gayda, *Modern Austria; Her Social and Racial Problems, Italia Irridentia, 1913,* trans. Z. M. Gibson and C. A. Miles (London: T. Fisher Unwin, 1915), 295–96.

59. Claudio Magris, *Der Habsburgische Mythos in der österreichischen Literatur* (Salzburg: Muller, 1966).

60. One of the most notable was the emperor's silver wedding pageant in 1878, which involved ten thousand or so participants dressed in the costumes of Habsburg Flanders designed and orchestrated by the history painter, Hans Makart. It revolved around the theme of the benign effects of the reign of the Habsburgs on art and industry. Werner Telesko, "Die Wiener historischen Festzüge von 1879 und 1908: Zum Problem der dynastischen Identitätsfindung des Hauses Österreich," *Wiener Geschichtsblätter* 51, no. 3 (1996): 133–46.

61. See Stephan Muthesius, *Art, Architecture, and Design in Poland, 966–1990: An Introduction* (Konigstein im Taunus: Verlag Langewiesche Nachfolger, 1994), 79; David Crowley, "Castles, Cabarets, and Cartoons: Claims on Polishness in Kraców around 1905," in *The City in Central Europe: Culture and Society,* ed. Malcolm Gee, Tim Kirk, and Jill Steward (London: Ashgate, 1999), 101–17.

62. Will S. Monroe, *Bohemia and the Czechs; The History of the People, Institutions, and the Geography of the Kingdom, together with Accounts of Moravia and Silesia* (London: G. Bell, 1910). Also Milan Hlavačka František Kolár, "Tschechen, Deutsche und die Jubiläumsaustellung 1891," *Bohemia* 32, no. 2 (1991) 380–411. For an account of the relationships among museums, language, and nationalism see Benedict Anderson, *Imagined Communities: Reflections on the Origins and Spread of Nationalism,* 2d ed. (London: Verso, 1983).

63. For the political implications of cultural monuments see Russell Berman, *Modern Culture and Critical Theory: Art, Politics, and the Legacy of the Frankfurt School* (Madison: University of Wisconsin Press, 1989), 165. Nancy Meriwether Wingfield, "Conflicting Constructions of Memory: Attacks on Statues of Joseph II in the Bohemian Lands after the Great War," *Austrian History Yearbook* 28 (1997): 151–53.

64. Cook's *Welt-Reise Zeitung* (Vienna), May 5, 1908, and October 10, 1908, 3–9. This trend was also visible in the London edition, which contained articles such as "The Mountain Resorts of the Tyrol," August 13, 1908, and "The Beautiful Salzkammergut District," June 11, 1908. For a discussion of the relationship between Vienna and the rest of Austria see Bowman, "Regional History," 894–97.

65. Richard D. Altick, *The Shows of London* (Cambridge: Harvard University Press, 1978); Anne Friedberg, *Window Shopping: Cinema and the Postmodern* (Berkeley and Los Angeles: University of California Press, 1993).

66. Robin Lenman, "Art and Tourism in Southern Germany, 1850–1930," in *Art, Literature, and Society,* ed. Arthur Marwick (London: Routledge, 1990), 163–79. For a discussion of Austrian landscape painting of an earlier period see Walter Koschatzky, *Viennese Watercolors of the Nineteenth Century* (New York: Harry Abrams, 1987).

67. Eduard Zetsche, *Bilder aus der Ostmark: Ein Wiener Wanderbuch geschrieben and gezeichnet von Eduard Zetsche* (Innsbruck: R. Edlinger, 1902); *Neuestes Monumental Album von Wien* (Vienna: Halm und Goldmann, 1908).

68. For example, Friedrich Zschokke, *Aus goldenen Tagen: Wanderungen in Österreich* (Zurich, 1916).

69. See, for example, the illustrations accompanying Ludvig Hevesi, "Modern

Painting in Austria," in *The Art Revival in Austria*, special summer issue, ed. Charles Holmes (London: Studio, 1906), xi–xvi.

70. See *Wiener Landschaften* (Vienna: Historischen Museums der Stadt Wien, 1993–94); and Robert Rotenberg, *Landscape and Power in Vienna* (Baltimore: John Hopkins University Press, 1995).

71. Peter Payer, "'Das Stadtbild von Wien ist traurig verändert': Michael Freiherr von Pidolls kritik des beginnenden Automobilzeitalters," in *Wiener Geschichtsblätter* 53, no. 4 (1998): 221–32.

72. Roger Paulin, "The Beidermeier Anomaly: Cultural Conservatism and Technological Progress," in *The Enlightenment and its Aftermath*, Austrian Studies 2 (Edinburgh: Edinburgh University Press, 1991), 88–89. See Koschatzky, *Viennese Watercolors* on the Viennese *veduta* tradition and for the work of Franz Witt and Ernst Graner in Schloss Grafenegg, *Das Zeitalter Kaiser Franz Josephs*, vol. 2, cat. nos. 1.11.3, 26.1.4.

73. Edwards, *Untrodden Peaks*, 361–67; Julius Meurer, *Illustrierter Führer durch die Dolomiten* (Vienna, 1890). Hartleben's *Illustrierter Führer durch Dalmatien* (1912) advertises a German translation of Maude Holbach, *Dalmatien: Das Land wo Ost und West sich Begnegnen* (Vienna, 1908).

74. Examples include Dr. Hermann Klencke, *Das Taschenbuch für Badereisende und Kürgaste* (Leipzig: Eduard Rummer, 1875); Julius Meurer, *Kleiner illustrierter Führer durch die Hochalpen Österreichs* (Vienna, 1885–87), and *Kleiner illustrierter Führer durch Salzburg und das Berchtesgadener Land: Mit Illustrationen* (Vienna, 1889); for a typically English view, Holland, *Tyrol and Its People*, 311–16. Moritz Bermann, *Illustrierter Führer durch Wien und Umgebungen* (Vienna: A. Hartleben, 1908); Eugen Guglia, *Führer durch die Stadt Wien und Umgebung* (Vienna: Gerlach und Wiedling, c. 1900); F. Hollrigl, *Wiener Cicerone. Illustrierter Fremden-Führer durch Vienna und Umgebung*, *14th ed.* (Vienna: Alexander Dorn, 1907); Julius Meurer, *A Handy Illustrated Guide to Vienna and Its Environs* (Vienna: A. Hartleben, 1906), and *Illustrierter Führer durch Österreich, mit Anschluss von Galizien under Bukowina* (Vienna, 1888).

75. Holland, *The Tyrol*, 191.

76. Ilsa Barea, *Vienna: Legend and Reality* (London: Pimlico, 1992), 318–23. Not all Viennese shared these sentiments. The critic Karl Kraus attacked this view of Vienna as vitriolically as he attacked its press in his journal *Die Faekel*.

77. Hollrigl, *Wiener Cicerone*, 9–15.

78. See Paul Greenhalgh, "Ephemeral Vistas: The Expositions Universelles, Great Exhibitions, and World Fairs, 1851–1939," in *Studies in Imperialism* (Manchester: Manchester University Press, 1988), 73–74.

79. Harold Hartley, *Eighty-five Not Out: A Record of Happy Memories* (London: Frederich Muller, 1939); *Berichts über die österreische Austellung, London, 1906* (Vienna: Staatsdruckerei, 1907).

80. An earlier version had been successfully tried out at the Chicago World Fair of 1893.

81. For the British relationship with the Alps see A. Bürstmuller, "Der Anteil britischer Bergsteiger an der Erschliessung der Ostalpen," in *Österreich und die angelsächsische Welt; Kulturbegnungen- und Vergleiche*, ed. Otto Hietsch (Vienna: Wilhelm Braumüller, 1968).

82. Catalog of the *Imperial Royal Austrian Exhibition* (Vienna, 1906).

83. Holmes, *Art Revival in Austria*.

84. *Bohemian Section at the Austrian Exhibition; Earl's Court, London: A Guide to the Bohemian Section and the Kingdom of Bohemia: A Memento* (Prague: Alois Wiesner,

1906); Franz Lützow, *The Story of Prague* (London: J. M. Dent, 1902); J. V. Polisensky, *Britain and Czechoslovakia* (Prague: Orbis, 1968), 64–65.

85. *Illustrated London News,* December 15, 1906, 895.

86. Cook's *Traveller's Gazette* (London), August 8, 1908, 9.

87. For a discussion of attitudes to Austria, see Frank R. Bridge, *Great Britain and Austria-Hungary, 1906–1914: A Diplomatic History* (London: Weidenfeld and Nicolson, 1972).

88. Karl Pauschenwein, "Die Entwicklung des Fremdenverkehrs in Wien und Niederdonau," Phil. diss., Hochschule für Welthandel Wien, August 1941, National-bibliothek, 67.

89. See, for example, Harry De Windt, *Through Savage Europe* (London: Collins, c. 1907). For a discussion of perceptions of the eastern empire in British literature in the late nineteenth and early twentieth centuries see Stephen Arata, "The Occidental Tourist: Dracula and the Anxiety of Reverse Colonialization," Victorian Studies 33, no. 4 (1990): 621–45.

90. The spa town of Luhatschowitz, for example, was redeveloped into a resort frequented by Moravian intellectuals and writers.

91. Moritz Czáky, *Ideologie der Operette und Wiener Modern: Ein Kulturhistorischer Essay zur österreichischen Identität* (Vienna: Böhlau, 1996).

92. I am indebted to Corinna Peniston-Bird (Lancaster) for information on the way that parallel themes were present in official attempts of the period to construct an image of Austrian national identity. See also Berman, *Modern Culture,* 169.

PART 2

Tourism, Mass Mobilization, and the Nation-State

Know Your Country

A Comparative Perspective on Tourism and Nation Building in Sweden

See America First! Discover Japan! Know Your Country! At various times the rallying cry for domestic tourism has been heard, for different reasons. There could be ideas about national integration: a nation under canvas united around the campfires all over the country; a meeting of classes down at the beach; citizens on pilgrimages to national shrines, learning to share a common heritage. The push for domestic tourism can also be an attempt to keep tourists from squandering currency abroad and instead using it at home.[1]

Campaigns for tourism at home are a recurrent theme in the history of holiday making, and such campaigns are forced to explore what is special about the attractions found within the boundaries of the nation. This process of selecting, framing, and presenting a national heritage with specific sceneries and sights has usually been accomplished through a rather standardized international framework. In the following essay I look at the interplay between national culture-building and the development of domestic tourism from two perspectives. The first part of the paper views the production of national tourist sights and attractions, mainly during the nineteenth century. Here the perspective is comparative, profiling the Swedish experience against examples from North America and northern Europe. How were ideas about a unique cultural heritage and national sceneries developed in constant comparison and competition with other nations? The second part of the paper looks at the ways in which this national tourist landscape was explored and transformed through the development of mass-based domestic tourism in twentieth-century Sweden. Finally, I briefly discuss how national mindscapes and actual vacationscapes are confronted in the tourist experience.[2]

THE STANDARIZATION OF CULTURAL DIFFERENCE

"But they don't have much culture here you know," a tourist in Malta complained to an anthropologist in the early 1990s, adding, "like crafts and things."[3] When a Swedish tour company guarantees that their Mediterranean holiday resorts are surrounded by "rich local culture," they are thinking in terms of the standard guidebook taxonomy of local culture, with chapters like "customs, fiestas, arts and crafts, historical buildings and monuments."[4] In Malta, a new, more flamboyant kind of folklore dancing was developed during the last decades to meet the expectations of those tourists who had been to Spain or Greece.

The idea of a colorful folk dance tradition as a local attraction is one of the examples of the production of standardized inventories of national culture. This specific item has a complex history of globalization. It was, for example, furthered by Joseph Stalin's early insistence that each Soviet ethnic group or nation should demonstrate its unique culture through an official folk dance troupe—a concept that spread from Eastern Europe over the globe during the twentieth century. Gradually folk dance became part of an official cultural heritage, but also something tourists expected to find wherever they traveled.[5]

In order to understand such standardizations of cultural difference, we have to move back in time and start with the emergence of modern nationalism. This is the ideological site for the development of "national landscapes" of tourism.

The interesting paradox in the emergence of modern nationalism from the end of the eighteenth century onward is that it was a highly international ideology imported for national ends. In this perspective we may view the ideology of nationalism as a gigantic do-it-yourself kit. Gradually a more and more detailed list of ideas was developed as to what elements make up a proper nation. Fixed conceptions emerged in the nineteenth century about how a cultural heritage should be shaped, how a national anthem should sound, and when the flag should be waved. National galleries were founded; national mentalities discovered; national cuisines elaborated. In this parallel work of nation-building, cultural matrices were freely borrowed across national frontiers. For example, national museums of folk culture were built in Europe, following the pioneer model in Berlin, and areas of native beauty were selected for transformation—after an American idea—into national parks.

Sweden exported the idea of "Skansen" from 1892, the open-air museum as a miniaturization of the nation.[6] The Skansen park was built in the middle of Stockholm and rapidly became a tourist success. Here the bourgeoisie of Stockholm went to discover their rural roots, and visitors from various corners of the nation and from abroad could get a condensed vision of "the essential Sweden." Walking along authentic buildings moved from all over the country with caretakers in national costumes and viewing a selection of the Swedish fauna, from sheep to wolves, you learned to see Sweden as a harmonious and well-integrated mosaic of regional parts. The imagined community of the nation, in Benedict Anderson's term,[7] was materialized in very concrete ways.

The important point here is the manner in which national projects were made transnational, imported and transformed into new, unique national settings. During the nineteenth century nations started to construct their heritage and tourist attractions in contrast and comparison with others. This production of cultural difference also led to increased competition: which nation could be best, oldest, biggest, have the most interesting or colorful heritage or the most beautiful sceneries? At the first international exhibition in London in 1851 it was already obvious that an arena had been created where nations could be compared and ranked in a great variety of ways: who produced the most modern technology or the best beer, who could show off the most imposing pavilion or the most beautiful folk costumes?

One field of competition was cultural heritage. The possession of a national folk culture became an important resource, and not least in the Scandinavian countries, artists and historians were busy discussing how this symbolic capital could be shaped. They looked back into history, eagerly searching for epochs and expressions that could form the raw material for this production of cultural distinctiveness. The sense of belonging to a backward periphery in nineteenth-century Europe meant that many of the Nordic countries initially thought that they should show themselves off as progressive, modern, technologically minded nations rather than exhibiting old folk culture. Peasant culture symbolized stagnation; looking backward merely revealed that one had not climbed far enough up the cultural ladder of modernity or civilization. To the surprise of the exhibitors, however, it turned out that it was precisely this exotic folk culture that attracted the visitors' interest and won gold medals.[8]

The great exhibitions were not just showcases for the world, but also patriotic illustrations for a domestic audience.[9] The model of the world exhibition was used for national as well as regional exhibitions, and there was a strong educational ambition to present and synthesize the nation for visitors. The exhibitions were thus great tourist attractions in themselves as well as laboratories for developing national or regional profiles of tourism. Allan Pred has analyzed the way this national enthusiasm was stage-managed at the Stockholm exhibitions of 1897 and 1930, which attracted big tourist crowds. He has also shown how this educational ambition could fail: the retouched microcosm of the nation displayed was not a landscape that everyone could feel at home in.[10]

Nations had to develop different strategies in this international competition. If one could not be biggest, best, or most modern, one could at least have the most beautiful scenery, the finest domestic crafts, the oldest cultural heritage, or the most exotic folk culture. The strategy in Sweden and other Nordic countries was to concentrate on the peasant heritage and the romance of the wild. This production of a national inventory of tourist attractions occurred in a constant dialectic between nation building and attempts to promote visits from international tourists.

When the first Scandinavian travel agency was opened in the Norwegian capital in 1850 by a private firm, it was primarily an answer to the new British interest in the Norwegian mountains and salmon rivers. Folklore, however, soon became another important ingredient for the nascent tourism industry. Living in an enforced union with Sweden since 1814, Norwegian intellectuals were busy creating a distinct national culture, emphasizing the cultural differences both to the former rulers (the Danes) and the present ones. In this process the celebration of a Norwegian folk heritage became important. It is no coincidence that these early nationalists located the authentic Norwegian peasant in the remote mountain valleys of Telemark. The mountainscapes were the focus not only of British alpinists but also of patriotic writers and artists; here, their argument ran, one found both the free Norwegian spirit (the alpine landscape was in this romantic era seen as a symbol of freedom and independence) as well as a traditional and uncontaminated Norwegian peasant life.[11] The authentic Swedish peasant culture was located in Dalecarlia, while true Finnish folk culture survived in the forests of Karelia—again in contrast both to the old Swedish nation and to the new Russian rulers. The truly national peasant culture had first of all to be distinct and different from that of the neighbors.[12] For Hungary Tamás Hofer has analyzed a similar process of stereotyping. The colorful Hungarian peasant of the plains was created as a national contrast to the Austrian mountain peasant.[13]

Examples like these illustrate the ways in which folk culture becomes nationalized (and also sacralized). A correct, authorized and timeless version of folk life is produced through the processes of selection, categorization, relocation and "freezing." One of the most interesting parts of this process is what is left out, disregarded (more or less unconsciously) or ignored as not being worthy of entering the showcases of the new national museums, the pages of the folklore heritage publications or the guidebooks.

The cultural grammar of developing a national folk culture also became the model for promoting local or regional heritages for touristic purposes. Local regions profiled themselves with the help of the inventories of national culture: they were all supposed to have a regional cuisine, regional landscapes, regional mentalities, and icons of identity. The inventories and rules of symmetry used in producing difference here were the same as in the packaging of "national" tourist profiles. This kind of "regional otherness" was an appetizing one. It was not supposed to threaten the national project, unlike the cases of regional separatism.[14]

The world exhibition thus started a process that has come to shape much of modern tourism. A standardization of cultural difference is developed, ways in which the unique, the exotic, the sublime has to be packaged and presented in appealing and recognizable forms in order for it to compete on the tourist market. As the project of producing cultural contrast turns into comparison ("How are we doing?") and then into competition, the paradox is enhanced: competition meant increased standardization of the tracks and the rules of the game. In other words, with their attempts to become more different, more special, nations at the same time become more and more structurally alike. This competitive self-representation has been carried on through cultural festivals and tourism fairs among developing countries in the period after the Second World War. Here you encounter the same ambivalence as among the nineteenth-century Scandinavian nations. Developing countries want to appear modern and dynamic while staging a unique and timeless cultural heritage for the tourist market.[15]

The cultural inventories of nation building have thus been employed for a number of tourist purposes but have also been important in emotionalizing local sights and attractions. This is especially striking in the making of national landscapes and sceneries. In the cultural nation-building of the nineteenth century, many of the northern nations, from the Scandinavian countries to the United States and later Canada, focused on nature. These were countries with an inferiority complex that saw themselves as marginal to the grand narrative of Western civilization. They thus developed an alternative focus, a strong tendency to nationalize nature and especially the wilderness. This reevaluation of the landscape was for many reasons perhaps most striking in the United States. John Sears has attributed the making of "sacred places" in early American tourism to both a strong religious tradition and a postrevolutionary nationalism.[16] Others have pointed to the marked inferiority complex of nineteenth-century American intellectuals, the constant harping on the lack of culture and history in the new nation, which Richard Hofstadter has summarized: "No monuments, no ruins, no Eton, no Oxford, no Epsom, no Ascot, no antiquity, no legends, no society in the received sense of the word—the grievance runs from Hawthorne to Henry James."[17]

The idea that America was "an under-aged nation" lacking in culture directed the focus onto the wilderness.[18] When John Ruskin wrote, "I could not even for a couple of months live in a country so miserable not to possess castles,"[19] this struck a note among American travelers who deplored the lack of picturesque ruins. But couldn't the rugged mountains and the craggy rocks, the strange and twisted trees of the primeval forests compensate for this lack? A new language of "organic ruins" developed in American tourism, and, in the tradition of the sublime, there was a marked religious element in this new celebration of the truly American wilderness, the awesome panoramas and the mighty mountain cathedrals.[20]

In this production of new national monuments, sceneries, and sublime sights, artists and writers played an important role, as did natural scientists and other academics who tended to dominate the early wilderness movement of the mountaineering clubs, which were founded all over the Western world during the latter part of the nineteenth century. The early and intense focus on the sublime American wilderness resulted in an American contribution to the lists of institutions "every serious nation must have," namely national parks, an idea that was rapidly transplanted to many countries. (Yellowstone, established in 1872, was the first.)

The establishment of national parks in Sweden was proposed in 1909. Other terms such as "nature park" had been suggested, but the important thing about the ideas for the new parks was their patriotic dimension. In 1899 the Swedish natural historian Gustaf Kolthoff wrote, "Few countries are richer or more glorious in nature than our own. The knowledge and love of this nature must greatly assist in increasing the love of our native land—one of the noblest of feelings."[21] In Sweden at the turn of the century there was a strong belief in nature and its appreciation as an educational tool. The proposed law on nature conservation of 1909 pointed out how important it was that the new national parks should be "visual material for teaching patriotism."[22]

The link between nature tourism and national identity had been developed at the beginning of the nineteenth century. In 1808 the Dane Laurits Engeltoft wrote in his "Thoughts on National Education" of the importance of educating citizens to give them a feeling for the nation's language, geography, and history, and the same message was expressed by the Swedish educationalist Carl Eric Broocman in his speech of 1810, "On Teaching Patriotism." He pointed out that hiking ought to be an important medium for learning the geography of the homeland; in this way people could learn to love its nature.[23] Another enthusiastic propagandist for these patriotic walks was the author Carl Jonas Love Almqvist. By wandering in their mother's bosom, people could "drink health and true nourishment in every breath; by roving in Sweden's landscape, among Svea's people, become Swedish."[24]

If walking was one way to become Swedish, another was learning to view the landscape through national lenses. During the latter part of the nineteenth century, Scandinavian artists returned from Switzerland, Germany, Italy, and Paris to capture the essence of the Nordic landscape. The Danish art historian Høyen appealed in 1844 to the newly founded Scandinavian Society in Rome in a famous proclamation, "On the Conditions for the Development of a National Scandinavian Art," in which he urged his fellow artists to devote themselves less to trips to Italy and more to voyages of discovery in their unknown native countries. "Paint Swedish" was a slogan later launched by the influential painter Richard Bergh.[25] The making of national landscapes transformed everyday natural scenes into "homelands," charged with history and national symbolism. There was a heightening of the sublime, a sacralization, in this process that we find on both sides of the Atlantic.

The tourism pioneers of the early mountaineering clubs also saw their task as a patriotic one. Bringing wilderness tourism to their fellow citizens was a way of producing a deeper and more emotional attachment to the nation. The Swedish Tourist Association, started in 1885, was first dominated by mountaineers. It was, however, not only a mountaineering club, but an organization that also wanted to promote domestic tourism. The founders choose as their motto "Know Your Country!" just as the newly started national museum of folk culture in Stockholm carried the motto "Know Yourself!"

But the wilderness was only one arena for this nationalization of the landscape. Drawing on the old established structure of the grand tour to southern Europe, "national tours" were established in many countries during the nineteenth century. The grand American tour, which developed during the first half of the nineteenth century with visits to the Hudson River, the Catskills, Niagara, and Yosemite, is one example.

These tourist pilgrimage routes combined visits to striking natural sceneries, sites of historic or symbolic importance, as well as rural and "folksy" settings. Over the years the routes and compositions of such "national tours" were transformed, reflecting changing foci in domestic tourism.

These pilgrimages also introduced a new element in tourism. National sceneries and sites could best be appreciated by the nation's own citizens. In their unique Americanness or Swedishness these landscapes were, so to speak, taken out of the tourist competition, since one supposedly had to be a true American or a true Swede to understand and to take in their greatness. Thus the nationalization of the sublime added a new dimension of the sacred: the feeling that in certain landscapes the citizen was in communion not only with nature but with the spirit of the nation itself. The linking of landscape and heritage made for a very powerful experience:

> The English landscape at its finest—such as I saw it this morning—possesses a quality that the landscapes of other nations, however more superficially dramatic, inevitably fails to possess. It is, I believe, a quality that will mark out the English landscape to any objective observer, as the most deeply satisfying in the world.[26]

These are thoughts of the old butler, the main character in Kazuo Ishiguro's novel *The Remains of the Day*, as he reflects on the day's sight-seeing. He is touring the countryside and feels strongly moved by the sceneries of "Deepest England": the rural landscapes of the South, with thatched cottages, rolling fields, green hills, and winding country lanes. These had already been defined as the essence of England,[27] the kind of landscape evoked in patriotic appeals in pictures, songs, and poems to the soldiers of the First and Second World Wars, of whom the overwhelming majority came from towns and cities:

> There'll always be an England
> While there's a country lane,
> Wherever there's a cottage small
> Beside a field of grain.

The ruralization of England was the making of a mindscape loaded with powerful emotions, as in Stanley Baldwin's classic statement from 1924: "To me England is the country, and the country is England. And when I ask myself what I mean by England when I am abroad, England comes to me through my various senses—through the ear, through the eye, and through certain imperishable scents."[28]

On the Move: Democratic Tourism, Nature, and Nostalgia

Nineteenth- and early-twentieth-century patriotism produced a national tourist landscape, of routes and destinations, of sights and attractions, through a constant transnational dialogue. Certain sceneries and settings were emotionalized in this process and became objects of tourist pilgrimages, but during most of the nineteenth century such travel remained the pastime of a small elite in most Western nations. What happens when domestic tourism is turned into a mass movement and people start to experience the nation not only as images and mindscapes but as actual holiday experiences? In the following I discuss this transformation during the era of mass travel in late-nineteenth- and twentieth-century Sweden.

In Sweden, as in most other nations, cheap steamboat and railway travel was the first prerequisite for large-scale domestic tourism. For the old tourist elite this invasion, which started in the latter part of the nineteenth century, was viewed with mixed feelings. In 1892 W. W. Thomas Jr., envoy extraordinary and minister plenipotentiary of the United States to Sweden, found himself crowded out by a large party of miners and their families during a summer steamboat excursion out of Stockholm: "For the moment any number of individuals become demoralized into an excursion, they develop a fatal facility of appropriating all the accommodations, eating all the food, filling all the cars and boats, and crowding and hustling the politeness and patience out of everybody else."[29]

The early success of the Swedish Tourist Association had to do with the construction of new railroads. It was founded in 1886, one year after the first rail connection between Stockholm and the northern alpine regions. During the 1897 Stockholm exhibition the organizers produced excursion packages with cheap rail fares, to ensure that great numbers of working-class visitors from all over the country could visit this manifestation of Swedish national pride.[30]

The new railways also made the region of Dalecarlia—the site of "true Swedish peasant life"—easily accessible from Stockholm. This region rapidly developed into a favorite tourist destination toward the end of the nineteenth century. Going to Dalecarlia was making a pilgrimage to Sweden's spiritual home, or as one visitor put it in 1899: "Nowhere else you feel so happy and proud of being Swedish as here."[31] For the rising urban bourgeoisie in Stockholm the proud and independent peasants still found here represented the kind of heritage they could identify with. Dalecarlia was in many ways an atypical peasant region, populated by smallholders who clung to a colorful peasant past, still wearing the folk costumes that had been discarded elsewhere. Their traditional lifestyle was seen as democratic and egalitarian, which fitted nicely with the new liberal ideologies. Many of the tourists from Stockholm bought old farmhouses or built new ones in "traditional style." Others were guests in new boardinghouses where they were served by young women in folk costumes. The tourist invasion revitalized (and thus transformed) this lifestyle. In Stockholm department stores you could buy Dalecarlian costumes, and the one from Rättvik became a kind of middle-class national dress. Meanwhile many locals were busy distancing themselves from their peasant past. A Dalecarlian author put it this way in a 1906 novel: "This is a strange exchange. In the city the bourgeoisie wander about dressed in folk costume; out in the country the peasants walk in urban attire."[32] Like any area turned into a national shrine, there was a pressure on both the landscape and its inhabitants to conform to tourist expectations.

Domestic tourism transformed the national sceneries one had learned to identify in schoolbooks, museum exhibits, and the pictures decorating urban homes into a personal experience. In Sweden as in many other nations the school field trip became a central institution for these kinds of pilgrimages, strongly promoted by the Swedish Tourist Association, which published yearly reports of the rising popularity of such excursions during the first half of the twentieth century. Schoolchildren learned to save money and organize bazaars for the great event at the end of the school year. The most popular destination was the national capital, and during the early decades of the twentieth century the Stockholm visit turned into a stable institution with a fixed program. One had to visit the Royal Palace and the changing of the guards, as well as the open-air museum of Skansen, but in the reminiscences of schoolchildren it was often the more mundane details that stood out in memory. The train journey itself could be a sensation, as well as the window-shopping in the big department stores or the taste of the pancakes in a cafeteria. Reading the essays children wrote after the trip, one cannot but notice that the lessons children learned through such a journey were not always the lessons planned by the organizers.

The development of the school field trip into a mass movement depended first on cheap train fares and later on the bus coach. Motoring opened up new "national tours." This occurred quite early in the United States, with the development of automobile camping and trailer life in the 1920s and 1930s. In Sweden as in most other European countries driving remained an elite occupation until the 1950s and 1960s; here the democratization of holiday making was based upon a different kind of technology and infrastructure.

In 1935 the Swedish Tourist Association celebrated its first half-century. In a contribution to the yearbook one of its staff, Gösta Lundquist, reflected on the changes in domestic tourism during this period. He mused over the old-fashioned attitude to tourism of the early pioneers in their pilgrimages to Dalecarlia and pointed out that the slogan "Know your country" focused too much on the unique and picturesque. There was a museum-like atmosphere surrounding the early selections of national sights and sceneries. In 1935 the slogan was given a new content. "All of our country is worth knowing," Lundquist asserted, not only the peculiar or special. Any region was worthy of tourist attention, evidence of a new democratic spirit permeating modern tourism. "Know your country" was now a rallying call that should embrace the whole nation, not just the old traveling elites.[33]

Lundquist was himself writing this in a midst of such a democratic journey, on a biking tour with six teenagers who had won the top prizes in a jubilee competition by describing their experiences as tourists at home. They were pedaling through Sweden using the new network of youth hostels that the association started to develop in 1933 and that two years later counted almost two hundred stopovers offering inexpensive lodgings with self-catering. The idea was imported from the continent and given the Swedish name *vandrarhem* (hiking homes), though it was not hikers but cyclists who made up the most of the guests.

In the early 1930s only one Swede in sixty had a car, but one in six owned a bicycle, and the biking holiday became the new form of domestic mass tourism. The biking holiday was a child of the new welfare state that emerged as the Social Democrats came to power in the Nordic countries during the interwar years. In the making of a truly democratic society tourism and leisure had an important position. As a tourist one should be prepared to meet fellow citizens from other walks of life, learn about their living conditions, and thus help to integrate the nation further. Gösta Lundquist described in enthusiastic terms the new patterns of contact. In the youth hostels young workers and farmers as well as students met "under the most favorable auspices," and, bik-

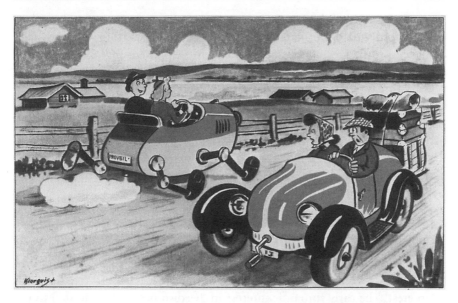

Postcard, 1920s. Auto campers were still a novelty in the Swedish tourist landscape and a popular theme for postcard artists. (Author's collection.)

ing through the landscape, the urban youth encountered ordinary people in their daily toil. "Out of this something must grow," he stated, but despite his enthusiasm it was still the middle-class youth that dominated this modern tourism.

The holiday infrastructure of biking, camping, and youth hostels needed one more element to open up tourism for working-class participation. In 1938 the Social Democrats passed legislation that guaranteed all workers a two-week vacation with full pay. Some middle-class observers were worried about such new freedoms. Would the workers really be able to use their vacation for good and healthy purposes, instead of just wasting time doing nothing? The Swedish Tourist Association produced a small handbook with hints on how to spend a vacation.

There was a strong sense of freedom that came with the first statutory holidays: the mind-boggling thought of having two whole weeks at one's own disposal. "Biking holidays as utopia," Magnus Wikdahl has called this first conquest of leisure time in a study of working-class leisure of the 1930s. The possibility of being able to pack a tent and equipment on the bicycles and set off into the landscape remains a powerful memory for this working-class generation.[34] It was an intoxicating sense of freedom, as if the world had suddenly opened and their horizons had widened.

What did this new generation of campers have in common with nineteenth-century nature tourists? Descriptions of domestic tourism in Sweden often tend to underline continuity, seeing development mainly in terms of opening up an established tourist landscape to new groups. The nineteenth-century romantic worship of nature was passed on to twentieth-century hikers and campers. The traditional nostalgia for an authentic folk culture materialized as a summer cottage culture in later generations, as more than a quarter of the Swedish population spent their holidays in a country cottage by the 1980s.[35] If, however, we compare the nineteenth-century visions of a national heritage and the mass tourism of the twentieth century, we notice striking transformations.

In 1985 an international survey asked persons between the ages of eighteen and twenty-four what they were most proud of in their countries. Unlike most of the others, young people in Sweden put nature at the top of the list.[36] This harmonizes well with the description of Sweden as "a nation of naturelovers," but this label obscures differences over time in the structure of such an interest. The early romantic interest in Swedish nature was limited to the rising liberal bourgeoisie, but toward the end of the nineteenth century the love of nature was given a new content. This was a period of strong political confrontations in Sweden. For the ruling conservatives the image of the wilderness as a national shrine met the need for an arena "above class strife"; for the liberals it represented a less bombastic patriotism. Everybody should learn to love Swedish nature, and in this didactic ambition of reforming or educating the masses there was an idea that neither the peasants nor the new workers really knew how to experience nature in the correct way. It is no coincidence that this was the era that saw the import of the national park concept.

During the interwar years the love of nature was given new ideological connotations. For the Social Democrats, who came into power in 1932, leisure became a laboratory of modernity. Biking through Sweden, camping in the woods, or mingling on the beach should foster a new and classless breed of modern citizens with healthy tanned bodies, in overalls and sandals. There was a focus on mobility in all kinds of forms: physical and mental. The new welfare state had to be a nation on the move, discarding antiquated routines and habits of the past, a nation forging a new unity by doing things together: communal gymnastics, sports, singing, traveling. The tourist became a progressive symbol.

Similar ambitions could be heard in other settings of the 1930s, from Roosevelt's New Deal and the French Popular Front to the totalitarian settings of Italy and Germany. Despite striking similarities in the rhetorics of this modern mass tourism, however, differences are revealed by the ways various political regimes put the campaigns for domestic tourism into practice. Some of the statements of the ideologues in the Scandinavian Social Democratic

FRISKSPORTARE

Postcard from the 1940s. Hiking became a Swedish mass movement in the 1930s and a favorite topic of cartoonists as well.
(Author's collection.)

movements of the 1930s have a totalitarian ring to them. For example, the
manifesto for the first Swedish exhibition of leisure and tourism in 1936 stated:

Leisure time should certainly be *free* time without any burdensome
obligations and wearisome restrictions on the individual, yet on the other
hand it should not be *dead* time frittered away on idle amusement which
can only lead to dissipation, or listless loafing which breeds boredom and

dissatisfaction. If the people are unable to fill up their leisure hours in such a way that they derive health and pleasure from it, then it is for the community to help them by advice and action, give them the possibility of spending their leisure time in a richer, finer and more profitable manner. The leisure time in this way becomes a concern of the community with an importance as great as that of working time.[37]

"Community" was a metaphor for the state in this 1930s setting, but as Jonas Frykman has pointed out in his studies of Swedish leisure and body politics during the interwar period, we must be wary of focusing too much on the ideological discourse here. If one looks at the cultural practices emerging out of the new holiday activities, he argues, the picture is different. Here we may see how the programmatic ambitions were transformed by the actual holiday experiences. People experienced a new liberation, exploring new aspects of themselves and their relations both to the landscape and to other holiday makers. Mass tourism no doubt was part of the making of a new welfare state nationalism, but it was also a democratizing and emancipatory movement. It was not a disciplined mass movement but an arena of individual experimentation, requiring an analysis of the complex relations between rhetoric and practice.[38]

A historical comparison thus illustrates that the label "nature-lovers" obscures very different tourist modes of viewing and handling nature. The idea of Swedes as born nature-lovers, who all harbor the secret holiday dream of a little red cottage in the country, gradually became a standard item of national self-definition during the later part of the twentieth century. During the last decades we have seen that this identity also can turn into a critique of those who do not really belong out in Swedish nature: tourists from abroad as well as the new immigrants. As the number of German holiday-makers expanded during the 1960s and 1970s, irritation grew over the newcomers' purported abuse of the generous rights of public access to the landscape. A new folklore emerged, with stories about the ways in which non-Swedes, including immigrants, were not showing proper care of the national wild. The love of nature had become a national virtue, but also a weapon against outsiders.

Two central metaphors in Swedish domestic tourism of the last centuries are discovery and travel through history, but again these metaphors have had a changing content. What is it that you are supposed to discover? In late-nineteenth-century Sweden knowing yourself and knowing your country were directly linked. Exploring the nation was a journey in both time and space. The eighteenth-century quest for the picturesque and the sublime had developed the tourist skill of historical daydreaming. By visiting certain sceneries one had the chance of going back in time, finding one's national roots. It was the powerful linking of landscape and history that made such daydreaming easy: Here, where we are standing now, our forefathers walked before us. This is the magic place to get in touch with a national past.

The emergence of the metaphor of the nation as a home in the nineteenth century influenced the routes of domestic tourism. Where was this national home located, how could it be experienced? From the Swedish experience we may learn that it does not always have a stable location, and the way in which new national pilgrimages develop tells us something about the constantly changing national discourse.

In the travels to discover one's own country, the theme of loss was often marked. Tourism at home was not only about locating the national home, but also traveling back to the land of childhood called summer holidays. The nostalgia of homecoming, with or without a melancholy streak, is a strong element in many of these quests.[39]

In the same manner the idea of looking for "the folk" or a national heritage of folk culture came to take on very different forms. For the eighteenth-century tourist pioneers traveling in search of the picturesque the addition of a representative of "the simple people" could enrich the scenery. The folk was mostly represented by a single individual, a rugged shepherd, a peasant resting in the shadow, or a fisherman by the brook. The picturesque folk were thus more of a silent prop in the landscape, rather like the hermit in the romantic garden. On the whole the common people did not fit into the landscape of the picturesque or sublime. In the nineteenth-century romantic search for a folk culture, embodying the wellspring of the nation, there was, as we have seen, a wish to locate "the real folk"—untarnished by the contemporary ills of urbanization and industrialization. These new pilgrimages, often to isolated or marginal parts of the country, created new tourist destinations and a folklorization of such settings during the later part of the century. This was time travel to more "natural" and simple folkways, to villages "where time stood still." With the making of twentieth-century welfare nationalism and the idea of a democratic fellowship of modern citizens, the old folk gave way to new forms for discovering the national: experiencing everyday life in all nooks and corners of your country. Still, the metaphors of discovery were firmly rooted in a middle-class ideology: the benign interest in the life of all those "others."

Another strong middle-class theme was the search for serenity and simplicity, and hence pilgrimages to places that could serve as antidotes to a stressful urban life. This was domestic tourism as an escape, or a getaway from certain problems of the everyday. The quest for stillness and sacred space also meant that the presence of pleasure-seeking urban crowds, whether working-class outings with harmonica and singsongs in the 1880s or inner-city kids with ghetto blasters in the 1980s, was a disturbing element. In these explorations we thus find a constant exclusion of settings, situations, and people that do not belong, that are not part of the national landscape.

MINDSCAPES AND VACATIONSCAPES

Over a period of two centuries domestic tourism in search of "the national" has created strange cultural clashes, as very different segments of society have been brought into interaction. There have been fights about rights of definition: who owns this setting, this scenery, not only in terms of property laws but in terms of spiritual ownership? Do these sceneries belong to that diffuse entity called "the nation," to the visiting pilgrims, to the locals? Different groups may have felt displaced by the presence of others. People moved in the same landscape, but in different mindscapes. Some experienced the double exposures of walking not only in the present but also in a landscape of childhood memories or nostalgic images. "My landscape" did not have to be yours.

These are not conflicts that can be narrowed down to an opposition between locals and middle-class tourists. A much more complex social landscape is involved, especially as the social spectrum of tourism widens during the twentieth century. Behind the label of "the locals" we also find very different interests and positions.[40]

My historical examples illustrate that the nationalization of the tourist landscape can be seen as a process of crystallization: "typically Swedish sceneries" have gradually been demarcated and concentrated to symbolic spaces. This selection and stereotyping has taken place through a number of different media, through the consumption of music, texts, and pictures in every conceivable form, ranging from geography books to oil paintings in museums to the prints found in the home—from oleographs to picture postcards. These scenes have been emotionalized as archetypically Swedish: "the quintessential Sweden," representing a certain "very Swedish mood." Together these images of Sweden form a shared symbolic estate (and a collection of tourist clichés), redolent of Swedishness. The way we react to a piece of landscape today is often the result of a long process of institutionalization, a development that has condensed a scene into a cultural matrix. It is this powerful condensation that means that perhaps only a detail, the merest hint, is needed for us to paint a landscape of the mind; the image of a single fir tree on a picture postcard rack can fill us with patriotic ardor or profound homesickness. It is striking that this national iconography shows a marked continuity: the favorite landscapes are very much the same today as in 1900.

Domestic tourism merged these mindscapes with actual travel experiences. The spring meadow with wildflowers became not only a postcard or a schoolbook illustration, but carried sensual memories, tastes and smells of childhood excursions and picnics to precisely such settings. But travel also personalized these national images and clichés, coloring them through individual experience and memories.

The process of framing and institutionalization also allows for the classic processes of mental wear and tear in tourism. Some sights become trivial; some classic sacred national sceneries may be experienced as tacky or even comical. The mass-mediated preconceptions can also turn expectations into frustrations, as tourists are confronted with "the real thing": is this all? On the surface the inventory of national sights and attractions may seem the same, but the continuity is misleading. Every new generation redefines the cultural heritage, and its tourist experiences are never identical.

NOTES

1. Michael Kammen discusses the "See America First" campaign in *Mystic Chords of Memory: The Transformation of Tradition in American Culture* (New York: Knopf, 1991), 338ff. See also Marguerite S. Schaffer's contribution in this volume. "Discover Japan" is discussed by Marilyn Ivy, *Discourses of the Vanishing: Modernity, Phantasm, Japan* (Chicago: University of Chicago Press, 1995), 29ff.

2. For a discussion of the relation between "mental" and "physical" landscapes see Orvar Löfgren, *On Holiday: A History of Vacationing* (Berkeley and Los Angeles: University of California Press, 1999).

3. Annabel Black, "Negotiating the Tourist Gaze: The Example of Malta," in *Coping with Tourists: European Reactions to Mass Tourism*, ed. Jeremy Boissevain (Providence: Berghahn, 1996), 113.

4. Ibid.

5. See the discussion in Orvar Löfgren, "Materializing the Nation in Sweden and America," *Ethnos* 58, nos. 3–4 (1993): 163.

6. See Orvar Löfgren, "The Nationalization of Culture," *Ethnologia Europea* 19, no. 1 (1989): 5ff.

7. Benedict Anderson, *Imagined Communities: Reflections on the Origins and Spread of Nationalism* (London: Verso, 1983).

8. See the discussion in Billy Ehn, Jonas Frykman, and Orvar Löfgren, *Försvenskningen av Sverige: Det nationellas förvandlingar* (Stockholm: Natur och Kultur, 1993), 36ff.

9. See Burton Benedict, ed., *The Anthropology of World's Fairs: San Francisco's Panama Pacific International Exposition of 1915* (Berkeley: Scholar Press, 1983); Robert W. Rydell, *All the World's a Fair: Visions of Empire at American International Expositions, 1876–1916* (Chicago: University of Chicago Press, 1984).

10. Allan Pred, *Recognizing European Identities: A Montage of the Present* (London: Routledge, 1995).

11. See the discussion in Löfgren, *On Holiday.*

12. See the discussion on the nationalization of Dalecarlia in Göran Rosander, "The 'Nationalization' of Dalecarlia: How a Special Province Became a National Symbol for Sweden," *Arv* 42 (1986): 93–142. For Norway see Brit Berggreen, *Da Kulturen kom til Norge* (Oslo: Aschehoug, 1989). For a general discussion of Scandinavia, see Lauri Honko, ed., *Folklore och nationsbyggande I Norden* (Åbo: Publications of the Nordic Folklore Institute, 1980).

13. Tamás Hofer, "Construction of the Folk Cultural Heritage," *Ethnologia Europea* 21, no. 2 (1991): 145–70.

14. See Löfgren, "The Nationalization of Culture."

15. Brian Wallis, "Selling Nations," *Art in America,* September 1991, 85–91.

16. John F. Sears, *Sacred Places: American Tourist Attractions in the Nineteenth Century* (New York: Oxford University Press, 1989).

17. Richard Hofstadter, *Anti-intellectualism in American Life* (New York: Vintage, 1963), 405.

18. Leah Greenfield, *Nationalism: Five Roads to Modernity* (Cambridge: Harvard University Press), 442.

19. Quoted after Paul Shepard, *Man in the Landscape: A Historic View of the Aesthetics of Nature* (New York: Knopf, 1967), 186.

20. See the discussion in Sears, *Sacred Places;* Peter J. Schmitt, *Back to Nature: The Arcadian Myth in Urban America* (Baltimore: John Hopkins University Press 1990); Shepard, *Man in the Landscape;* Roland Van Zandt, *The Catskill Mountain House* (New Brunswick, N.J.: Rutgers University Press, 1966).

21. Désirée Haraldsson, *Skydda vår natur! Svenska Naturskyddsföreningens framväxt och tidiga utveckling,* Bibliotheca Historica Lundensis, 63 (Lund: Lund University Press, 1987), 71.

22. Sverker Sörlin, *Framtidslandet: Debatten om Norrland och naturresurserna under det industriella genombrottet* (Stockholm: Carlsson, 1988), 82.

23. Bo Grandien, "Landskap och människa: Om den litterära och konstnärliga fotvandringen under 1800-talet," in *Historiens vingslag: Konst historia och ornitologi,* ed. Hedvig Brander Jonsson et al. (Stockholm: Atlantis, 1988), 37.

24. Quoted in Grandien, "Landskap och människa," 38. For a discussion of the revival of walking as a tourist movement in Britain see the discussion in Anne D. Wallace, *Walking, Literature, and English Culture: The Origins and Uses of Peripatetic in the Nineteenth Century* (Oxford: Oxford University Press, 1993).

25. See Orvar Löfgren, "Landscapes and Mindscapes," *Folk* 31 (1990): 183–208.

26. Kazuo Ishiguro, *The Remains of the Day* (London: Faber and Faber, 1989), 28.

27. See Alan Howkins, "The Discovery of Rural England," in *Englishness: Politics and Culture, 1880–1920,* ed. Robert Colls and Philip Dodds (Beckenham: Croom Helm, 1986), 62–88; Patrick Wright, *On Living in an Old Country: The National Past in Contemporary Britain* (London: Verso, 1985).

28. Quoted after Howkins, "Discovery of Rural England," 82.

29. William Widgery Thomas, *Sweden and the Swedes* (Chicago: Rand McNally, 1892), 505.

30. See the discussion in Pred, *Recognizing European Identities.*

31. Quoted in Rosander, "The Nationalization of Dalecarlia," 93.

32. Rosander, "The Nationalization of Dalecarlia," 96.

33. Gösta Lundquist, "Tvåhundra vandrarhem," *Svenska Turistförenings årsskrift* (1936), 246–72.

34. See Magnus Wikdahl, *Varvets tid* (Stockholm: Gidlunds, 1992).

35. See Löfgren, *On Holiday.*

36. Reported in *Sydsvenska Dagbladet,* March 8, 1985.

37. Quoted in Jonas Frykman and Orvar Löfgren, *Culture Builders: A Historical Anthropology of Middle Class Life* (New Brunswick, N.J.: Rutgers University Press, 1987), 40.

38. Jonas Frykman, "Becoming the Perfect Swede: Modernity, Body Politics, and National Processes in Twentieth-Century Sweden," *Ethnos* 58, nos. 3–4 (1993): 259–74.

39. See also the analysis of nostalgia in Ivy, *Discourses of the Vanishing.*

40. Orvar Löfgren, "Learning to Be a Tourist," *Ethnologia Scandinavica* 24 (1994): 102–25.

Seeing the Nature of America

The National Parks as National Assets, 1914–1929

In his report to the secretary of the department of interior in 1915, Mark Daniels, the general superintendent and landscape engineer of the national parks, noted, "We, as a people, have been accused of lacking in that love of country which our neighbors in Europe are so plentifully blessed." Advocating the development of a tourist infrastructure in the parks and the creation of a centralized national park bureau, Daniels commented, "To love a thing one must know it. . . . [O]urs is a great country, stretching from sea to sea, and a knowledge of all its glories is given to but few. What more noble purpose could our national parks serve than to become the instrument by which the people shall be lured into the far corners of their land that they may learn to love it?" Daniels believed that one of the central functions the parks served was to stimulate national patriotism. "For one who will encompass the circuit of our parks," he explained, "passing over the great mesas of Colorado, crossing the painted desert, threading the sparkling Sierra Nevada, and viewing the glaciers and snow-capped peaks of the great Northwest will surely return with a burning determination to love and work for, and if necessary to fight for and die for the glorious land which is his."[1] Daniels was not alone in linking the development of tourism in the national parks to a national consciousness.

The years surrounding World War I marked a pivotal moment for the development of tourism in the United States, specifically in the national parks. In August 1914 the outbreak of war stranded 150,000 Americans in Europe.[2] The war effectively closed European resorts and attractions to American tourists. Simultaneously, it intensified the discourse of patriotism and loyalty in the United States. Tourist promoters who had begun at the turn of the century to champion the slogan See America First, which advocated scenery as an economic asset, seized the moment to promote a national tourism.[3] The railroads, which for many years had been the sole proponents of domestic tourism in the United States, expanded their promotional campaigns.[4] Good-roads advocates and automobile enthusiasts such as the Lincoln Highway Association celebrated the expanding opportunities for touring via automobile.[5] Promoters and exhibitors at the Panama-Pacific International Exposition, which opened in San Francisco in 1915, defined a grand tour of western America with the exposition as the grand finale.[6] In this context, touring in the United States took on the patriotic and commercial connotations of "Buy American."[7] Amid this fervor, the parks were transformed into America's preeminent tourist attractions, and touring the parks was presented as a ritual of citizenship. Park administrators worked to define a national tourism centered around the established system of national parks and monuments, and in doing so they participated in the larger process of nation building by defining and promoting an ideal of America as "nature's nation."[8] To borrow Ernest Gellner's words, they worked to inscribe the nation into "the *nature* of things."[9]

Throughout their history, Americans have been engaged in the cultural invention of the United States as a unified nation. In the early years of the republic, political and cultural nationalism were tied to the Revolutionary principles and practices of democracy. However, as the nation-state began to expand, national consciousness and the concept of the nation became more complicated. Shifting territorial boundaries, an influx of diverse immigrants seeking citizenship, a growing commercial infrastructure, and the development of a more centralized federal government added new dimensions to the idea of the nation and the ideologies of nationalism. The political notion of the United States as a nation formed and sustained by democratic contract became intertwined with a more romantic ideal of the nation grounded on the traditions and mythologies of a unified culture rooted in common traditions and a bounded territory.[10]

During the late eighteenth and nineteenth centuries a shared set of national symbols, myths, traditions, and rituals began to emerge, reinforcing the ideological construct that bound the country together as a nation. Business and civic leaders, alone and in collaboration with the local, state, and national governments, sponsored national holidays, commemorative acts, nationalistic pilgrimages, world's fairs, and political rituals; hereditary, historical, and patriotic organizations were formed; and the landscape was marked and shaped with national structures, symbols, and images; all of which served to reinforce the development of a nation-state.[11]After the Civil War the infrastructure of the nation-state—a strong and active national government, an established national territory, a national transportation and communication network, and a national market—solidified. An official nationalism, "emanating from the state, and serving the interests of the state first and foremost," developed in tandem with the emergence of the nation-state during the late nineteenth and early twentieth centuries.[12] This official nationalism was manifested not only by increasing government regulation of the commercial sphere, but also by a more active imperialist policy and the increasing symbolic power of the presidency. However, the emergence of this official nationalism did not assure a homogeneous and monolithic national consciousness throughout the United States. Rather, the development of the nation-state and the magnification of official nationalism sparked a heated discourse concerning national identity in which various constituencies attempted to secure their ideal of America as the official ideal of the nation.[13]

As the country struggled to come to terms with its role as a world power and as a modern nation during the early decades of the twentieth century, nationalism emerged as a critical issue. On the world stage, the United States had begun the century by establishing itself as an imperialistic power with the Spanish-American War, maturing into an international mediator and economic power in the aftermath of World War I. At home, expanding corporate power, massive immigration, and increased urbanization prompted many Americans to reexamine their conception of individuality and citizenship, as well as nationality and nation. While affluent elites reaffirmed their identity as "pure" Americans as the nation embarked on its imperial crusade—subduing and enlightening "inferior" races—others turned their interest to American folklore and literature, historical organizations and clubs, as well as nativist organizations and Americanization programs. Intellectuals such as Van Wyck Brooks, Lewis Mumford, and Constance Rourke worked to define a "usable past," and established American aristocrats such as Henry Adams struggled to preserve their status in American society. Similarly, the white middle classes championed 100 percent Americanism, supported the Red Scare, and embraced the rebirth of the Ku Klux Klan. In the commercial sphere, consumption replaced politics as a rite of citizenship.[14]

In this atmosphere, tourism emerged as a popular means of giving form and substance to the physical character and identity of the nation. In consciously constructed and marketing tourist sites, highlighting certain meanings and myths and deliberately selecting and arranging historical events, places, anecdotes, and views into a coherent whole, tourist industries engaged in the cultural production of national identity.[15] Building on the established tradition of scenic nationalism that looked to America's dramatic natural landscapes to legitimize American culture, advocates of domestic tourism worked to construct a robust image of America that celebrated the natural richness and beauty of the American landscape and America's unique history and culture.[16] Promoters argued that in seeing the nation's sacred landscapes firsthand, tourists enacted a patriotic rite that allowed them to embrace their true identity as Americans. In this context, the national parks emerged as the preeminent tourist attractions of the nation.

In the period between 1914 and 1929, the nascent Park Service transformed the national parks from a collection of independent scenic wonders managed by various private railroad corporations into a system of nationalized tourist attractions overseen by an official, independent government bureau. As the larger political culture debated traditional notions of liberalism, the power of the federal government, the process of reform, and the issue of nationalism, park administrators participated by negotiating between private corporations and the federal government in an effort to define and promote the parks as a unified national system. For the first time the state became actively involved in the promotion of national tourism. Building on the broad structural changes that transformed America into a modern, urban-industrial nation-state—the construction of a national transportation network, the solidification of a national market, the development of a national print media, and the emergence of an economy of leisure—a small branch of the federal bureaucracy tentatively embraced tourism as a means of evoking a popular national consciousness that could "rally the citizenry in a collective ritual of nation building and national unification" and thus reinforce the emerging nation-state.[17] Tourism embodied a unique and symbolically powerful double-edged sword: it represented a form of consumption that depended on and supported the growing infrastructure of the nation-state, and it offered a means of generating patriotism, thus reinforcing the democratic ideal of the nation and fostering a shared national consciousness. In mediating between the market and the nation, it became a kind of virtuous consumption. In effect, the Park Service, in defining and promoting the parks as national tourist attractions, tried to reconcile the democratic ideal of the nation with an organic ideal of the nation in an attempt to come to terms with the emerging nation-state.

Promoting the Parks

In the fall of 1914, as plans for the Panama-Pacific International Exposition began to solidify, Secretary of the Interior Franklin K. Lane initiated a "parks preparedness" campaign to develop and publicize the national parks, especially Yosemite, so that they might be ready for the crowds that would arrive in San Francisco for the exposition.[18] Lane turned to a former University of California classmate and Chicago borax millionaire, Stephen Tyng Mather, to launch this new publicity and development campaign.[19] In January 1915, Mather was sworn in as assistant secretary of the interior. Secretary Lane charged him with the task of establishing "a business administration" to manage the fourteen existing national parks and the eighteen existing national monuments.[20]

Building on the See America First idea, Mather began by organizing an extensive publicity campaign that sought to capture a diverse audience that might respond to and benefit from the development of the parks. Although he was primarily concerned with establishing the parks on a "business basis" and securing the congressional appropriations necessary to maintain and develop them, Mather also hoped to tap into the growing interest in outdoor recreation and nature preservation to establish a core constituency for the parks. He actively courted sympathetic and influential politicians such as Congressman Frederick H. Gillett, ranking Republican on the Appropriations Committee, as well as tourist promoters such as Ernest O. McCormick, vice president of the Southern Pacific Railroad, and nature enthusiasts such as Henry Fairfield Osborn, president of the American Museum of Natural History, among others.[21] Ideally, he hoped to link the increase in patriotic fervor with the growing enthusiasm for popular nature pursuits such as camping, hiking, and automobile touring to generate widespread acclaim for the national parks.[22]

The Third Annual National Parks Conference held at the University of California in Berkeley during the Panama-Pacific International Exposition initiated this national parks publicity campaign. In his introductory speech, Mather articulated his ideas about the necessity for park publicity. "The parks," he said, "must be, of course, much better known that [sic] they are today if they are going to be the true playgrounds of the people that we want them to be. There is much that can be done in making them better known. There are many ways in which they can be brought home to the great mass of eastern people." Those at the conference agreed that "the policy of the present Administration to exploit the move to 'See America First' is a step in the right direction, and should be commended by the American public to the extent that they will make it their duty as well as their pleasure to assist in this patriotic movement."[23]

Mather hired Robert Sterling Yard "to work up a nationwide publicity campaign" to "get the people behind the parks."[24] Yard, an authority on publishing who had worked with Mather on the *New York Sun* and later edited the *Century Magazine* and the Sunday edition of the *New York Herald,* was hired as the national parks publicity chief.[25] Although Yard was a self-admitted "tenderfoot" when it came to western wilderness, he proceeded to organize a park publicity bureau.[26] He began gathering information about travel to foreign countries and the promotion of tourists sights and then set out to tour the parks, gathering "information about our own scenic resources." On his return he established a national parks news service and began writing articles for magazines, issuing press bulletins, and "encourag[ing] the preparation of publicity material by everybody in and out of government who had talents to be exploited."[27]

Yard's research and travels in 1915 culminated in two important publications that promoted the parks: the *National Parks Portfolio,* an expensive picture book published in 1916, and a less expensive pamphlet, *Glimpses of Our National Parks.*[28] The portfolio was composed of a series of pamphlets describing Yellowstone, Yosemite, Sequoia, Mount Rainier, Crater Lake, Mesa Verde, Glacier, and Rocky Mountain, the most prominent national parks, in addition to one on the Grand Canyon National Monument. Each park description was illustrated by a number of dramatic photographs, interspersed with brief tables providing an overview of all the parks, and bound together in an expensive cloth folder.[29] The book came out in the midst of the congressional debate over the National Park Service Bill, and every member of Congress received a copy. In total, 275,000 copies were distributed by the United States government free of charge to a select list of recipients considered as potential park supporters. Similarly, *Glimpses of Our National Parks* was a short illustrated booklet providing general information about the existing national parks to the tourist.[30]

Both the *National Parks Portfolio* and *Glimpses of Our National Parks* were meant to educate the American people about the "wonders" of their own country, to instill a scenic patriotism that would unite the touring public in support of the national parks. In his preface to the portfolio Mather drew on an established See America First argument. "This Nation is richer in natural scenery of the first order than any other nation," he wrote, "but it does not know it. . . . In its national parks it has neglected, because it has quite overlooked, an economic asset of incalculable value." He went on to explain that "the main object of this portfolio, therefore is to present to the people of this country a panorama of our principle national parks." Mather noted that this was the first "representative presentation of American scenery of grandeur" to be published, and he dedicated it to the American people. "It is my great hope," he concluded, "that it will serve to turn the busy eyes of the Nation upon its national parks long enough to bring some realization of what these pleasure gardens ought to mean, of what so easily they may be made to mean, to this people."[31]

The National Parks Portfolio functioned as a catalog of the parks, displaying, codifying, and enumerating the dramatic natural landscapes that the government had set aside as "playgrounds for the people." The colorful descriptions of the eight major western parks and the Grand Canyon, combined with over two hundred photographs of mountain views, lakes and water falls, glaciers, wild animals, and rustic hotels, stated that the national parks embodied a physical experience that promised "thrills . . . never before experienced," "fairyland and the awe of infinity," "romantic Indian legend," along with health and peacefulness. Each section detailed the spectacles of one park, providing information on scenic character, the geological formations, wildlife, the Indians if applicable, and park accommodations. The purpose of the portfolio was to establish the parks as national assets, making them valuable national property rather than simply land set aside by the national government and thus designated as "unusable." It accomplished this by presenting the parks as ceremonial landscapes, icons of the nation.[32] Written descriptions celebrated the "sublimity" of the park landscapes, suggesting that they had the ability to inspire and uplift. The many photographs captured scenic views from their most alluring perspective, transforming the natural landscape into pristine iconographic images. In a number of the photographs solitary viewers or groups of sightseers were pictured surveying the landscape, in effect worshipping the natural icons that embodied the nation. In each section the text reasserted that not only did the parks promise an "unrivaled" experience, but also that they had value for their natural formations that allowed for the first-hand study of nature. As Secretary Lane wrote, they were "the public laboratories of nature study for the Nation."[33] As landscapes administered by the United States government, they embodied the democratic imperative of the nation. At the end of each descriptive section readers were reminded that the national parks belonged to them. However, it was clear that the imagined tourists, as evidenced by the photographs depicting well-dressed and elaborately outfitted sightseers, were white upper- and middle-class Americans who could afford to travel by train or automobile and spend a week or more vacationing in the parks. In promoting the national parks, the portfolio gave official government sanction to the preservation of scenery. The justification for preservation was based not so much on the aesthetic or intrinsic value of nature, but on the educational and the national value of scenic landscapes.

Like the *National Parks Portfolio, Glimpses of Our National Parks* sought to establish the value of national parks as national assets. "The national parks, unlike the national forests, are not properties in a commercial sense, but natural preserves for the rest, recreation, and education of the people. They remain under nature's own chosen conditions. They alone maintain 'the forest primeval,'" wrote Yard. In separating the parks from the realm of commerce, *Glimpses of Our National Parks* defined their value in other terms, most notably through their potential to educate. Yard encouraged tourists to explore the national parks: to go "hunting . . . with a camera in Yellowstone," to study the formation of glaciers in Mount Rainier, to ponder the development of prehistoric civilizations in Mesa Verde, or to consider Major John Wesley Powell's "perilous passage" in the Grand Canyon. The dramatic land formations, the ancient Indian ruins, the giant trees, and the volcanic and glacial phenomena all revealed nature in its "pristine" form, untouched by man. In stating that the value of the parks rested on their "extraordinary scenic beauty," and "remarkable phenomenon," Yard set up an implicit opposition between "nature" as represented in the parks and the ordinary built and natural environment. His celebration of the educational value of dramatic landscapes of the parks and his promotion of nature study raised the national parks to a level above the crass concerns of commercialism and the cheap amusements of common tourist attractions. "Every person living in the United States," Yard wrote, "ought to know about these eight national parks and ought to visit them when possible, for, considered together, they contain more features of conspicuous grandeur than are readily accessible in all the rest of the world."[34] Building on a long-established national mythology that identified America as "nature's nation," Yard essentially argued that the landscapes embodied in the national parks evinced America's greatness.

Mather supplemented and further spread Yard's publicity work through a series of highly publicized park tours, speaking to chambers of commerce, wilderness groups, automobile associations, and other interested organizations to disseminate his ideas about developing the parks and making them more accessible to the American people.[35] He met with railroad representatives to negotiate reduced rates, suggesting that they issue "park tour tickets which [would] enable tourists to buy tickets at the starting point for a definite tour of national parks, all accommodations paid for and arranged in advance." In addition, he asked the roads to include information about the parks in their tourist brochures.[36] He also supported the formation of a national park-to-park highway. In addition, Mather cultivated valuable working relationships with both Gilbert Grosvenor, editor of the *National Geographic* magazine, and George Horace Lorimer, editor of the *Saturday Evening Post*.[37] These connections assured a constant flow of park publicity that helped to solidify a wide constituency of park supporters that included established nature enthusiasts and preservationists as well as railroad and automobile representatives, tourists advocates, and armchair travelers. Although noted preservationist John Muir had likened the tourist hordes in Yosemite to locustlike sheep, few if any early on in the parks promotional campaign expressed concern that the commercial and technological underpinnings of tourism would threaten the ideals of nature preservation or the sanctity of park environments.

In 1918 the administrative policy for the newly established National Park Service was outlined in an official letter from the secretary of the interior to Mather. In defining the criteria for the creation of new national parks, the letter stated that the Park Service should seek out "scenery of supreme and distinctive quality or some natural feature so extraordinary or unique as to be of national interest or importance." The role of the Park Service, according to Lane, was to promote three broad principles: preservation, use, and national interest. Not only did these guidelines set the criteria for the establishment of new parks, but they also defined the value of preestablished parks. The national park system, according to the 1918 annual report of the secretary of the interior, "constituted one of America's greatest national assets."[38] This celebration of the dramatic natural scenery of the West, the remains of ancient civilizations, and pristine wilderness—the landscapes embraced by the parks—moved beyond the rhetoric of economic nationalism to express an ideal of nationhood. By focusing on wilderness, scenery, and ruins, park publicity glorified not the commercial and industrial developments that were catapulting the United States to world power and solidifying the nation-state, but the natural landscapes and ancient ruins that were symbolic of America's origins. The essence of American identity, according to the narrative of nationalism constructed by the Park Service, rested primarily in western wilderness, landscapes once inhabited by more primitive civilizations, left untouched by man, yet still symbolizing the bounty of American nature. In this way the American landscape was infused with an ancient past and a divine promise. These "unique" landscapes embodied the "untouched" wilderness of the North American continent that had helped to forge a distinct American nation.[39]

The growing wave of reactionary patriotism that swept across the nation with the outbreak of World War I brought added value to the national character of the parks. With Europe closed to American tourists, the economic argument associated with See America First, which had previously been used to promote tourism in the United States, lost its intensity and its edge. The interest in the Pacific expositions and the dramatic increase in park visitors proved that American tourists attractions could hold the interest of American tourists. Touring America became a fashionable patriotic pastime. As various groups struggled to define the character of the nation, those interested in promoting the parks began to argue that not only were the parks valuable because of the commercial possibilities of tourism, but they also had patriotic value. As the Chicago *Tribune* editorialized:

> There is a higher and stronger reason for our effort to encourage better acquaintance with and greater use of the resources of natural beauty on this continent. It is a measure of Americanism. The nation needs a tonic knowledge of the physical thing called America, a love of the body of Columbia, an inspiring sense of the nobility and splendor, the epic sweep and the intimate beauty of the land to whom our forebearers gave their devotion and we ourselves claim home. . . . An acquaintance with the mere physical quality of the country west of the Alleghenies would notably assist a deeper understanding of the American Spirit. The east should go west as the west goes east. There would be less colonialism there if that could be brought about.[40]

Yard developed and expanded on this idea in his various park publications and in the process began to define the parks in terms of an organic definition of nationalism. In other words, he presented the parks as representative of a distinctly American homeland. Now the parks were more than just economic assets; they were also natural laboratories and quintessentially American landscapes. Mark Daniels elaborated on this idea, explaining that there are three great functions of the national parks: "1. The stimulation of National Patriotism; 2. The furthering of knowledge and health; 3. The retention of tourist travel within the United States."[41] The connection between national parks and national consciousness had come to define their central value.

Clearly, this publicity campaign had laid the symbolic ground work for the transformation of the parks into a system of national assets. Despite this flurry of publicity, the nascent Park Service still faced the issue of laying claim to the parks as national landscapes controlled by the federal government. Specifically, this meant separating individual parks from the independent railroad corporations that had developed them, popularizing the parks as public landscapes, and making them more accessible to the American people. And this task meant constructing an official image of the parks as a system of national landscapes, linking the experience of touring the parks with a national consciousness, and lifting the experience of touring the parks above the crass commercialism of tourism to a more virtuous or patriotic level. The mobilization effort for World War I and the eventual entry of the United States into the war provided the impetus for this transformation.

NATIONALIZING THE PARKS

In December 1917, President Wilson placed the railroads under the control of the United States Railroad Administration, where they remained until 1920. The Railroad Administration nationalized the railroads in an effort to speed and streamline the transportation of supplies and men to the war front, and all unnecessary expenditures on the part of the railroads were forbidden. In January 1918, Secretary Lane conferred with the head of the U.S. Railroad Administration concerning wartime travel, and it was agreed that the national parks would remain open and that visitors to the national parks would be accommodated on regular trains.[42] The administration nominally restricted railroad travel and limited luxury train service but continued to allow for and promote travel to the parks. In April 1918, Mather proposed the creation of a western tourist bureau, the purpose being to make up for the decrease in individual railroads' publicity efforts resulting from the demands of the war. The Western Roads Bureau of Service was established as part of the U.S. Railroad Administration in the spring of 1918 to fill the gap. In essence, the bureau was to represent all railroads associated with the national parks. More specifically, as Howard Hays, director of the bureau, explained, "The Bureau shall take over from general passenger departments of railroads the correspondence relative to National Parks."[43]

Previously, transcontinental railroad lines had adopted extensive public relations strategies that allied them with individual parks. Many of these independent lines had spent as much as one hundred thousand dollars on advertising budgets for booklets and printed matter, newspaper and magazine advertisements, as well as billboards and lectures. Because the Railroad Administration forbade the expenditure of unnecessary funds for promotional materials during the war, railroads cut their advertising budgets and curtailed their extensive promotional campaigns. The Western Roads Bureau of Service was not only meant to make up for this dramatic loss in advertising, but also to streamline the promotion of western attractions. This cooperative publicity effort on the part of railroads and the national government served to effectively nationalize the national parks, presenting them as a set of national attractions rather than as separate sights accessible only by separate roads. As Hays explained, "We see no reason why National Parks, as government properties, supported by national taxation, should not receive complete representation in every part of the United States. . . . Let us lift the principal National Parks and Monuments onto a higher level so that ticket agents throughout the United States will be converted to, and prepared for the great National Park idea which we must drive home to the American people when competition with European resorts is re-established."[44] By overseeing lectures, slide presentations, films, and photographs, by circulating pamphlets and booklets, by distributing newspaper and magazine advertising, by deploying bureau clerks nationwide to answer questions and supply information, and by regulating tourist tariffs, the bureau of service presented itself as the official tourist bureau of the nation.[45]

During its first summer under existence, the bureau walked a fine line between serving the war effort and promoting the parks. It hoped to quell rumors about the closing of the parks during the war while simultaneously understating park publicity in consideration of the wartime emergency. It used its official status to provide the appropriate character for its wartime promotional efforts. As the director explained in his first report, "[Railroad] Administration rulings against the encouragement of travel have compelled the Bureau to proceed cautiously."[46] However, even before the November armistice was reached, Howard Hays had already been considering the activities of the bureau after the war.[47] In the fall of 1918, Hays proposed that a series of booklets advertising the national parks be put together to overview available tourist possibilities. He requested the services of Robert Sterling Yard, chief of the Educational Division of the National Park Service to assist in preparing the material.[48] By February 1919, the Railroad Administration had approved the publication of eighteen booklets promoting the principal national parks and monuments along with various other prominent tourist destinations.[49]

In the spring of 1919, the Railroad Administration dropped all barriers to a full-scale parks publicity campaign announcing the removal of all restrictions on railroad travel. A circular letter sent out to railroad ticket agents explained, "One year ago, under the pressure of war necessities, the public was requested to refrain from all unnecessary travel, and, under the stress of war conditions, the public was necessarily subjected to a great deal of inconvenience when it did have to travel. Now the war necessity is passed and it is the settled policy of the Railroad Administration to do everything reasonably within its power to facilitate passenger travel and to make it more attractive."[50] In addition to issuing the national parks booklets, the bureau also planned to spend almost a half a million dollars on a national newspaper and magazine advertising campaign to promote the parks.[51] During the first six months of 1919, the bureau distributed approximately 1.7 million booklets and descriptive folders to railroads, ticket offices, tourist agencies, and travel bureaus.[52] This extensive effort amounted to the first full-scale nationalized tourist campaign in the United States.

In some ways the national crisis brought on by American involvement in the war and the demands of mobilization served to solidify the nationalization of the national parks. For a very brief period in 1919 the ideals, the demands, the desires of those who had long called for the government to promote an American tourist industry were achieved. Thus, the bureau of service as it existed under government control might best be seen as the culmination of the See America First publicity campaign begun by Lane and Mather in the early days of 1915.[53] Although the bureau did not remain as a permanent government-sponsored organization, it did help to shift the parks from separate and independent attractions into a system of national assets. In transferring the burden of publicity from independent railroad corporations to the parks service and then on to the bureau of service, the parks became truly "national" parks, meaning they were no longer simply separate and unique scenic wonders connected with the nation through ideals of monumentalism.[54] Rather, through the official sanction of the Department of the Interior beginning in 1915, the creation of a special park bureau in 1916, and the nationalization of the publicity effort by the bureau of service between 1918 and 1919, the parks were defined as more than just scenic wonders. They became quintessentially American landscapes that objectified the American character and embodied the essence of the American nation, and in the tradition of democracy, they belonged to the people ever available for their benefit and pleasure.

After the war, the Park Service expanded on this connection between the parks and the nation. Despite the fact that after the war the Park Service publicity efforts were restricted due to funding cutbacks, the Park Service returned to collaborating with various organizations, individuals, and corporations interested in promoting the parks in an effort to compete effectively with the resurgence of European touring possibilities.[55] Building on previous publicity that had touted the parks as playgrounds of the people and linked seeing the parks with patriotic duty, the Park Service worked with park enthusiasts to capitalize on the rising postwar fervor for Americanization. In an article overviewing the various resources scattered throughout the United States that showcased dramatic photographs of the national parks, Franklin K. Lane championed the cause of Americanization. "I find in dealing with this problem of making the foreign-born understand what Americanization is," explained Lane, "is that the first great difficulty is to make the American-born realize fully and be conscious of America in all its various senses and moods and spirits. And one of the things that I should like to conduct, if I were free to do so and had the means, would be a real geography class." What followed in the article was an attempt to do just that, and the national parks played a prominent role in his overview of the wonders and benefits of America. He concluded, "To know America is to love it. . . . Out of its wealth in things of the earth and its greater wealth in things of the spirit it is making a new society, different from any that is or that has been."[56] Building on this fervor over Americanization, Park Service administrators helped to forward the ideal that seeing the parks was akin to assisting in the postwar reconstruction effort. The parks were promoted as natural sanctuaries where war-worn soldiers could recuperate. "We know," Mather asserted, "that recreation, or rather, re-creation, will be needed more than ever [after the war]; that our men coming back from the front will want to have a place where they can go for recuperation."[57]

A number of individuals and organizations interested in the promotion of domestic travel worked in conjunction with the Park Service to link the parks with the larger campaign for Americanization. In 1920 the Far Western Traveler's Association, an organization of traveling salesmen, took up the national park cause and initiated a publicity program in association with the Park Service. In his address before the annual banquet, John B. Patton, president of the organization, asserted that "every Far Western Traveler will become a salesman for the Parks." He explained that the association had "determined to take a vigorous part in the carrying out the government's reconstruction program. The association believes that Americanization is the most important plank in the reconstruction platform and that seeing America first is one of the most important courses of instruction through which Americanization will be attained." Not only would the annual banquet be devoted to celebrating park landscapes, but a yearbook was to be distributed at the banquet, with articles by Mather, Yard, and other park enthusiasts, illustrated with "color and halftone reproductions portraying the chief points of scenic interests," and edited by Sewell Haggard, formerly associated with *McClure's* and *Cosmopolitan*.[58] Park service administrators willingly assisted in the compilation of the booklet.[59]

At the annual banquet in 1920, members of the association agreed on a program to promote the See America First idea and the national parks. It was decided that the organization would sponsor a trip for twenty Boy Scouts to the national parks.[60] As President Patton explained, "We want them to see America because it will help them to grow up better Americans."[61] Building on the touted educational value of the parks, the organization believed that seeing the parks would inculcate a sense of patriotic duty in city-bound boys, and they encouraged other organizations to join with them in forwarding the cause of Americanization in connection with promoting the parks. "If we can set on fire the spirit of romance that burns in the heart of each youth of this city and other cities with the inspiration that comes from mountains and the great drama of the pioneers who built the West, we can lay a foundation for the future of our nation that will make it eternal."[62] Parks administrators reinforced this ideal, exclaiming in the annual yearbook, "Scenic assets of the highest importance, they will continue to play an ever-increasing part in the upbuilding of American manhood and womanhood and, through them, of national efficiency and contentment."[63]

During the 1920s, park enthusiasts worked in conjunction with the Park Service to develop the tourist infrastructure and expand on the idea of the parks as a unified system. Projects like the national park-to-park highway were promoted in an effort to actualize the ideals developed in earlier Park Service publicity. Before the war, administrators focused primarily on publicity, but also on organizing management, defining a concessionaire policy, and standardizing the relationship between superintendents, the Washington office, and the various concessionaires.[64] Once the management policy was settled, the Park Service could move from general publicity about the parks and the various sites to see and begin to promote a specific tourist program that encouraged a process of seeing the parks. The park-to-park highway was central to facilitating a national tourist experience. The Park Service encouraged tourists to see more than one park, presenting the parks as a canon of American tourist attractions. The park-to-park tour became the equivalent of the modern-day grand tour in America.

The freedom of automobile touring, made possible by publicly owned and accessible roads, provided the necessary infrastructure to promote and develop park-to-park touring, and the park-to-park highway championed by the Park Service provided the means of promoting this type of touring. As early as 1916, at a meeting of western commercial club members in Yellowstone, Mather suggested the development of an automobile highway connecting all the parks. In the aftermath of the meeting the Yellowstone Highway Association was formed in an effort to develop a road between Yellowstone and Glacier National Parks that was then extended to include Yosemite, the Grand Canyon, Mesa Verde, and Rocky Mountain National Park as well as a number of noted scenic attractions in between.[65]

The absence of a federal highway policy and funding system hindered the development of the national park-to-park highway, and the war effort curtailed private fund-raising efforts. However, after the war, with the return of railroads to private control, the effort to promote a park-to-park highway was revived. Automobile touring not only seemed to be the wave of the future, but it also promised to facilitate a touring program that furthered the newly emerging nationalized image of the parks. In the spring of 1919, Secretary Lane announced a plan to develop "an automobile line from Denver, Colorado to and through Rocky Mountain, Yellowstone, and Glacier National Parks." A fleet of touring cars managed by H. W. Child and Row Emory, who held the transportation concessions in Yellowstone and Glacier respectively, was to run between the three parks, facilitating the process of interpark travel and forwarding the process of postwar reconstruction. As the secretary's press release explained, "It is Secretary Lane's belief that the Federal Government ought to actively encourage travel to American health and recreation resorts. . . . He believes that the National Park Service, which is in more than one sense the travel bureau of the Federal Government, ought to perform the same service for the American public that the Swiss, French, and other foreign government travel bureaus accomplish for European resorts."[66] In an effort to publicize this new touring service, the National Park Service dedicated the so-called Geysers to Glaciers Motor Trail by escorting a select group of the *Brooklyn Daily Eagle* touring party on an inaugural run from Yellowstone to Glacier.[67] The publicity surrounding this official opening of the road linking Yellowstone and Glacier National Parks rekindled local interest in the development of a park-to-park highway, and in 1920 the Yellowstone Highway Association reformed as the National Park-to-Park Highway Association. The association adopted the slogan You Sing "America"—Why Not See It? and envisioned a master scenic highway connecting all the western parks and centered on Salt Lake City, where a series of highways radiating like spokes would connect the points of the circle.[68]

Extending from his support of automobile touring and his focus on park-to-park touring, Mather had begun by the midtwenties to articulate and promote an ideal of the park touring experience that connected the possibilities of automobile touring with an ideal of national consciousness. Touring the national parks helped to "break down sectional prejudice through the bringing together of tourists from all sections of the country," Mather explained. He noted, "In the national parks there is one thing that the motorists are doing, and that is making them a great melting pot for the American people. . . . This will go far in developing a love and pride in our own country and a realization of what a wonderful place it is. There is no way to bring it home to them in a better way than by going from park to park, through the medium of an automobile, and camping out in the open. . . . It is just by trips of that kind that people learn what America is."[69]

The Parks as National Assets

As the parks became more popular and their scenic attractions became more accessible, administrators at the Park Service increasingly underscored the educational value of the parks to reaffirm their status as national assets. After the war, the Park Service had worked to promote the educational use of the parks. A nature guide service had been set up in Yosemite and Glacier by 1922. In 1923, Arno B. Cammerer, acting director of the National Parks Service, sent out letters to 134 universities and colleges throughout the United States in an effort to have them initiate some form of summer travel in the parks, calling on each school to form a "National Parks Travel Committee."[70] In a reformulation of national park policy in 1925, Secretary of Interior Hubert Work restated the three broad principles that Mather and Lane had laid out in 1918. In general, Work adhered to the principles of preservation, use, and national interest as the three central concerns of the Park Service. However, Work reformulated the second principle, which originally stated that the parks had been "set apart for the use, observation, health and pleasure of the people," substituting "education" for "observation."[71] Work's restatement of the Park Service mission reflected the growing interest in the educational value of the parks that began to emerge after World War I. Thus, by 1925 the tourist program envisioned by the Park Service involved more than just seeing the parks and enjoying dramatic scenery: it meant learning about history, geology, botany, archeology, and biology; in essence it meant learning about the character and spirit of the nation. This emphasis on the educational value of the parks emerged early in the twenties as a means of further defining the national value of the national park system.

The formation of the National Parks Association and Robert Sterling Yard's work in promoting the parks also began to focus attention on this issue of education. Yard called the parks "museums of native America" or "national museums." In summarizing park concerns for the National Parks Association in 1923, Acting Director of the Park Service Cammerer noted, "Particular attention is given to the development of the educational side of Park work,—the establishment of museums and nature guide service, which is going forward in leaps and bounds. The interest shown by universities in what the Parks have to offer in this regard is most gratifying, and a few more years will see this detail of service to the public developed to a high standard."[72] Cammerer explained in one promotional essay overviewing the parks, "To the observant visitor . . . soon comes the realization that aside from the recreational values, the national parks are from an educational standpoint,—biologic, historic, geologic, and botanic,—really outdoor classrooms of the country; that in fact, the future may see in them no less great educational centers of learning than a means to health and pleasure." Cammerer concluded, "It is, therefore, obviously not an exaggeration to say that the National Parks are truly Nature's outdoor classrooms, and that whatever their enormous value at this time as the great national play and recreation grounds, as Civilization crowds westwardly and the great open spaces are taken up bit by bit, the parks in their refreshing natural state, will constitute the Nation's great exhibition spaces where still the native flora, the wild life with its geologic and historic setting, are found untouched as in the days when this country was young."[73] Whether revealing the workings of volcanic action, glaciation, or erosion, or harboring native flora and fauna, or simply providing an escape from urban scurry and workaday routines, the parks offered an array of benefits to American tourists. This newly defined educational value of the parks assigned the parks the same role as the a national museum or public school system—to inculcate the spirit of patriotism and teach the values and meanings of citizenship.

This emphasis on education revealed not only the association made between the parks and the growing concern for Americanization, but also reflected the increasingly pervasive theories of progressive educators that stressed learning through experience. This combination resulted in a theory of nationalism that grounded citizenship not simply in the ideal of a democratic political contract, but also in relationship to territory or homeland. Building on the romantic notion of organic nationalism, the nation became a unique geographical entity. The feeling of American-ness was integrally connected to the physical territory of the nation. Natural wonders and dramatic scenery came to symbolize not just the promise of tourist revenues and congressional appropriations, but more importantly an ideal of homeland. Specifically, the American nation became an extension of wilderness as represented by the dramatic natural landscapes of the national parks.

During the 1920s, the Park Service in cooperation with a number of outside businesses and organizations, most prominently the National Parks Association, continued to publicize the parks widely, establishing them as the nation's preeminent tourist attractions. In the process, the notion of the national parks as national assets was further embellished and the ideal of the nation connected with the parks further solidified. Building on the educational value of the parks, promotional material defined the parks as the nation's natural laboratories and the nation's museum, or alternatively "the museums of native America."[74] In a promotional speech to the Travel Club of America, Mather explained, "The National Parks are national museums. Their purpose is to preserve forever, in their original untouched condition, certain few, widely-separated examples of the American Wilderness of the pioneer and the frontiersman, of the works and process of Nature unblemished by man's hand; of our native wild animals living natural lives in the natural homes of their ancestors. We can pass on to posterity no other pleasure-giving and profit giving quality, combined with unique usefulness to history and science as the Museums of Native America."[75] Thus, the parks became more than just the "playgrounds of the people," they became the equivalent of a recreational public school system where through the act of tourism Americans could not only learn about the history and historical geology of their country and become familiar with the native flora and fauna of the nation, but also imbibe the spirit or essence of America and rekindle their sense of patriotism.

Anthropologist Richard Handler has argued that the museum is "the temple of authenticity" for a nation or a culture in that it allows people to come in contact with "authentic pieces of culture," thus enabling them to "appropriate their authenticity, incorporating that magical proof of existence into what we call our personal experience." He explains that authenticity is a cultural construct that is key to "the modern Western world."[76] Related to the emergence of individualism, the concept of authenticity allows the modern individual to define him- or herself in opposition to the rest of the world. Handler goes on to note that this notion of authenticity is also applicable to individual cultures defining themselves as unique entities. Drawing on the work of historian T. J. Jackson Lears, Handler argues that in a society anxious about the "unreality" of modern life, this fascination with authenticity reflects an "anxiety over the credibility of existence."[77] This, in turn, can be linked to nationalist anxieties of the nation-state struggling for recognition. From this perspective, Handler argues, "The existence of a national collectivity depends upon the 'possession' of an authentic culture."[78] In other words, a shared national consciousness depends upon the collection, preservation, and display of this culture. In this way the metaphor of the parks as national museums or public classrooms served to sanctify an ideal of the nation.

In 1922 and 1923 a barrage of material promoting and defining the parks expanded on their image as a unified system of national landscapes. Increasingly during the twenties, as the parks suffered a series of attacks against their protected status, the Park Service began to emphasize the notion of controlled development in the context of wilderness preservation. Emphasizing education allowed the Park Service to lift tourism to the level of highbrow culture. In this way tourism in the parks could be disassociated from commercialism and consumption and the parks could maintain their status as sacred national landscapes. During the 1920s a number of events coalesced to bring about a shift in the Park Service's promotional techniques. The attempts to allow some commercial use of the parks during the war threatened to weaken the protective status of the parks during the 1920s. Water power and irrigation interests, specifically the Federal Water Power Act, which gave the power to lease public waters including those in the national parks for power generation, and the Fall River Basin bill, which proposed the damming of Yellowstone basin for irrigation purposes, threatened the integrity of national parks. In addition, the increasing popularity of parks as tourist attractions, resulting not only from extensive advertising, but also from increased automobile use, was threatening to transform the parks into amusement parks. "So rapid is the increase of travel to the parks," noted Robert Sterling Yard, "that it is none too early to anticipate the time when their popularity shall threaten their primary purpose.... While we are fighting for the protection of the national parks system from its enemies, we may also have to protect it from its friends."[79]

Responding to these commercializing threats, the Park Service and park advocates worked to redefine the value of the parks as above and beyond commercial interest. Park Superintendent Roger Toll explained that the parks were established "to set aside for the enjoyment of this and future generations, certain areas that are typical of our finest scenery. They are to be held free from commercial exploitation. The standing forests will prove more valuable than the lumber they would produce, the graceful waterfall will prove more precious than the power it would yield, the unscarred beauty of the mountain is worth more than the mineral wealth that may be buried in its heart." To preserve these representative natural landscapes while also making them publicly accessible, Toll recommended a multitiered plan for park development. He argued that some parts of each park should remain accessible by automobile; in other parts of the parks horse trails and hiking trails should encourage a more intimate experience of nature. "The development of a park will, therefore, not be uniform throughout. Some portions will be fully developed, others partly developed, and still others will be left in their natural, wild condition." Toll asserted, "The parks should be popular, but never commonplace. They should accommodate crowds if necessary, but without over-crowding. Animals should be protected in their natural surroundings rather than caged in a zoo. Outdoor recreation should supplant cheap amusements. Museums and nature study should be offered to stimulate interest along educational and beneficial lines rather than to accentuate sight seeing of an unintelligent order."[80] In this way the parks could be maintained as sacred national landscapes. They existed as sublime nature—God's creations—removed from the base concerns of commerce, and as such they were meant to remind Americans of their roots and rekindle an ideal of virtuous citizenship.

Other park supporters reiterated these themes throughout the 1920s. As executive secretary of the National Parks Association, Robert Sterling Yard became a vociferous advocate for the national value of the parks. In an attempt to fend off the commercial encroachment, Yard went so far as to argue that the parks had become "the shining badge of the nation's glory, sharing somewhat even of the sacredness of the flag.... They have become a part of the general popular conception of the greatness of America."[81] Their national greatness rested in the fact that they existed beyond the concerns of commerce and industry: "That they embodied in actual reality, and in splendor, the American-born ideal of nature conservation, creating and protecting by law a mighty system of national museums of the primitive American wilderness, was an inspiring offset to the sordid commercialism and much advertised political rottenness of the times." As "national museums" the parks preserved not just wilderness and wildlife, but "the geologic sequence of America's making." As such the parks benefited the "national mind" in a variety of ways, education being the most prominent. But Yard also argued that the parks promoted democracy:

> Nowhere else do people from all the states mingle in quite the same spirit as they do in their national parks. One sits at dinner, say, between a Missouri farmer and an Idaho miner, and at supper between a New York artist and an Oregon shop-keeper. One stages it with people from Florida, Minnesota and Utah, climbs mountains with a chance crowd from Vermont, Louisiana and Texas, and sits around the evening camp fire with a California grape grower, a locomotive engineer from Massachusetts, and a banker from Michigan. Here the social distances so insisted on at home just don't exist. Perhaps for the first time one realizes the common America—and loves it. . . . It is the enforced democracy and the sense of common ownership in these parks that works this magic. They have rediscovered to us the American people. Elsewhere travelers divide among resorts and hotels according to their ability to pay, and maintain their home attitudes. In the national parks all are just Americans.

Highlighting a cross-section of the expanding American middle class from across the country, clearly, Yard's understanding of democracy focused more on geography than race or class. "[T]he great body of national park visitors," according to Yard, included "politicians, merchants, statesmen, legislators, artists of every variety, bankers, judges, millionaires and the merely fashionable," as well as "business and professional men and their families, teachers, lawyers, brokers, manufacturers of everything on earth, writers, publishers, advertising men—the well-to-do of all sorts and degrees."[82] Implying a nostalgia for the republican ideal of a nation of free laborers, Yard's enumeration of park tourists celebrated a geographically diverse group of productive citizens ranging from farmers and miners to bankers and businessmen.[83] The rising numbers of unskilled laborers were left unsung, as were other minority groups. What Yard did not mention was that the Park Service consciously discouraged African Americans in the parks. As Yard stated in a section of the minutes at the annual parks conference in 1922 entitled "Accommodations for Colored People," "Individual cases can be handled, although even this is awkward, but organized parties could not be taken care of. . . . While we cannot openly discriminate against them, they should be told that the parks have no facilities for taking care of them."[84] Thus, the ideals of democracy, the nation, and the citizen defined by park advocates and the Park Service were embodied by a newly emerging dominant class, which was becoming a predominantly white, middle- and upper-class constituency in the twentieth century.[85]

John Wesley Hill, park supporter and chancellor of Lincoln Memorial University, perhaps best expressed the ideal of the parks as national assets that had emerged after the war in his speech marking the annual opening of Yellowstone in 1923. Hill began by linking the creation of Yellowstone with the civilizing of the wilderness by the pioneer and forging of a unified nation by the railroads, noting that "the railroads came, and here we are in this wonderland of today, breathing its pure atmosphere, and exulting in our national estate because the railroads pioneered the way, because men of brain and faith and courage laughed deserts and mountains and hardship and poverty and opposition to scorn." Hill went on to note that now people come by railroad and automobile from all sections of the country to mingle together in the national parks, "forming a higher, broader type of citizenship." But for Hill, the parks offered more than just the opportunity to view nature's wonders and overcome provincialism. In places like Yellowstone, according to Hill, "the soul of man hearing the voice of God in a wilderness of burning bushes, steps into the Presence Chamber of the Infinite and bows before the granite alter of God's vast Gothic cathedral." Thus according to Hill, the national parks embodied a combination of knowledge, democracy, and the sublime, and in doing so, they objectified the spirit of the nation and instilled a sense of national pride. "What is it that inspires love of the flag, that tunes the ear of America to sing, 'My country 'tis of thee?'" Hill asked.

> Is it superficial area, industrial efficiency, irrigation statistics or trade output? Is it our marvels of mining shown in the hideous ore dumps of the sordid mining camp? Is it the grim power house in which is harnessed the power of Niagara? Is it the blackened waste that follows the devastation of much of our forest wealth? Is it the smoking factory of the grimy mill town, the malodorous wharves along navigable rivers? Is it the mutilating bill boards plastered with spread eagle advertisements that disfigure the broken landscapes along our line of travel? Is it even the lofty Metropolitan sky scraper that shuts out the sun and throws its dismal shadow over all below?

Hill argued it was none of these things. Rather, he stated, "Our devotion to the flag is inspired by love of country. Patriotism is the religion of the soil . . . [and] National Parks are our richest patrimony. They constitute a heritage which must be preserved inviolate by the American people." Hill asserted that commercialism posed the biggest threat to the national park system and as such to the ideal of the nation. He likened those who would invade the parks for commercial ends to "money changers" in the temple. Hill queried, "The subjugation and utilization of the forces and products of nature by man is the foundation of successful economic existence and development, but is nature untouched unnecessary or undesired in our complicated scheme of living? Are not reserved places of rare natural beauty as important in daily life as those utilized areas that supply our physical needs?" The march of progress continued: "Gradually the open spaces are being settled. . . . Are we to relinquish even one square mile of the choicest exhibits of our great national recreation areas without considering their inestimable value to the countless generations yet to come?"[86] For the sake of the future of the nation, Hill argued, the people needed to rise up and demand that the parks remain unscathed by commercial development.

This eloquent celebration of the national parks and dramatic plea for preservation revealed the value of the parks as sacred national landscapes. As sanctuaries of nature—the last vestiges of "virgin" land—that existed beyond the corrupting forces of corporate capitalism, the parks manifested an ideal of the nation grounded in a nostalgic republican tradition that linked pristine nature or free land with an ideal of civic virtue.[87] Ironically, in a capitalist society wedded to an ideology of progress reliant on private property and extensive natural resources, preserved nature, existing beyond the reach of commerce and industry, came to embody the ideal of the nation. And tourism, defined as a patriotic act, became a ritual of citizenship that transformed consumption into civic duty. These ironies reveal the fraught process of nation building.

Through a multistaged process—beginning with a publicity campaign that redefined the parks in national terms, moving through a process of nationalization whereby the state officially sanctioned the parks as national tourist attractions, and culminating in a crusade for preservation that transformed the parks into sacred national landscapes—the parks were infused with national value. They came to represent the essence of the nation, and the act of touring allowed the individual to experience and possess these sacred national landscapes, actualizing his or her membership in the nation. In effect, the cultural production of the parks as national assets sought to officially confirm the nation as a God-given entity embodied in the unique natural landscapes scattered across the continental United States. Defined as "primeval" wilderness, these landscapes suggested that it was not democracy or progress alone that begot the nation. The nation was not a product of the forces of history. Rather, it was preordained, innate, divine. By thus "inscribing the nation into the nature of things," the parks were a means to disregard the process of incorporation, subjugation, and exclusion that marked the transformation of the United States into a modern nation-state. This totalizing process could mask the social, political, and cultural conflict with a universal ideal of a cohesive nation. Just at the moment when the mechanisms of incorporation—the emergence of a national market, the completion of a national media and transportation network, and the development of a strong national state—bound American society more closely together, solidifying the infrastructure of the modern nation-state, state officials became actively involved in the production of a shared national consciousness that depended upon and ignored those very forces of incorporation. Tourism as consumption depended upon the commercial and technological infrastructure that underlay the nation-state. Tourism as civic duty promised to revive the sentiment of patriotism that rested on an ideal of America as "nature's nation." In this way, the symbolism of the parks as national tourist attractions, defining an organic ideal of the nation, mediated the tensions between the national myth that celebrated democracy, individualism, and liberty and the nation-state that depended on incorporation, hierarchy, and hegemony.

NOTES

1. U.S. Department of the Interior, *Report of the General Superintendent and Landscape Engineer of National Parks to the Secretary of the Interior, 1915* (Washington, D.C.: Government Printing Office, 1915), 6.

2. John A. Jakle, *The Tourist: Travel in Twentieth-Century North America* (Lincoln: University of Nebraska Press, 1985), 102.

3. For a history of the See America First idea see Marguerite S. Shaffer, "See America First: Tourism and National Identity, 1905–1930," Ph.D. diss., Harvard University, 1994, "'See America First': Re-envisioning Nation and Region through Western Tourism," *Pacific Historical Review* 65 (November 1996): 559–81, and "Negotiating National Identity: Western Tourism and 'See America First,'" in *The Second Opening of the American West,* ed. Hal K. Rothman (Tucson: University of Arizona Press, 1998).

4. For a history of the relationship between railroads and the development of tourism see J. Valerie Fifer, *American Progress: The Growth of Transport, Tourist, and Information Industries in the Nineteenth-Century West* (Chester, Conn.: Pequot Press, 1988); Alfred Runte, "Pragmatic Alliance: Western Railroads and the National Parks," *National Parks and Conservation,* April 1974, 14–21, *Trains of Discovery: Western Railroads and the National Parks* (Self-published, 1984), and "Promoting Wonderland: Western Railroads and the Evolution of National Park Advertising," *Journal of the West* 31 (January 1992): 43–48; and Carlos Schwantes, "Tourists in Wonderland: Early Railroad Tourism in the Pacific Northwest," *Columbia* 7 (1993–94): 22–30, and "Landscapes of Opportunity: Phases of Railroad Promotion of the Pacific Northwest, " *Montana* 43 (spring 1993): 38–51.

5. Shaffer, "See America First," 199–253. For the history of the good-roads movement see Peter J. Hugill, "Good Roads and the Automobile in the United States, 1880–1929," *Geography Review* 72, no. 3 (1982): 327–49; and Philip Parker Mason, "The League of American Wheelmen and the Good Roads Movement, 1880–1905," Ph.D. diss., University of Michigan, 1957. For a history of the Lincoln Highway Association

see Drake Hokanson, *The Lincoln Highway: Main Street across America* (Iowa City: University of Iowa Press, 1988).

6. Shaffer, "See America First," 168–77.

7. In the fall of 1914, following the outbreak of World War I, *Collier's* ran a series of editorials advocating commercial patriotism, and domestic tourism was promoted as a means of supporting the American economy. See "Free Trade for Americans—with Americans," October 3, 1914, n.p.; "A Billion Dollar Sentiment," October 10, 1914, n.p.; "Giving the American Label Its Due," October 17, 1914, n.p.; "Patriotism That Pays," October 24, 1914, n.p.; "See America First," October 31, 1914, n.p.; "U.S. Spells US," November 7, 1914, n.p.

8. For a discussion of the ideal of "nature's nation" see Perry Miller, "The Romantic Dilemma in American Nationalism and the Concept of Nature," in *Nature's Nation* (Cambridge: Belknap Press of Harvard University Press, 1967), 196–207. See also Hans Huth, *Nature and the American: Three Centuries of Changing Attitudes*, rev. ed. (Lincoln: University of Nebraska Press, 1990), 30–53; Roderick Nash, *Wilderness and the American Mind*, 3d ed. (New Haven: Yale University Press, 1982), 67–83; Alfred Runte, *National Parks: The American Experience*, 2d ed. (Lincoln: University of Nebraska Press, 1987), 11–32; Barbara Novak, *Nature and Culture: American Landscape and Painting, 1825–1875* (New York: Oxford University Press, 1980); and David Lowenthal, "The Place of the Past in the American Landscape," in *Geographies of the Mind*, ed. David Lowenthal and Martyn J. Bow (New York: Oxford University Press, 1976), 89–117.

9. Ernest Gellner, *Nations and Nationalism* (Ithaca, N.Y.: Cornell University Press, 1983), 48–49; emphasis added.

10. For surveys of American nationalism see Merle Curti, *The Roots of American Loyalty* (New York: Columbia University Press, 1946); Michael Kammen, *Mystic Chords of Memory: The Transformation of Tradition in American Culture* (New York: Vintage, 1993); and Hans Kohn, *American Nationalism: An Interpretive Essay* (New York: Macmillan, 1957).

11. Wilbur Zelinsky, *Nation into State: The Shifting Symbolic Foundations of American Nationalism* (Chapel Hill: University of North Carolina Press, 1988); and Kammen, *Mystic Chords of Memory*.

12. Benedict Anderson, *Imagined Communities: Reflections on the Origin and Spread of Nationalism* rev. ed. (London: Verso, 1991), 159.

13. For a discussion of the cultural repercussions of this transformation see Alan Trachtenberg, *The Incorporation of America: Culture and Society in the Gilded Age* (New York: Hill and Wang, 1982).

14. For discussion of American nationalism during World War I see John Higham, *Strangers in the Land: Patterns of American Nativism, 1860–1925* (New York: Atheneum, 1985), 194–233; Philip Gleason, "American Identity and Americanization," in *Concepts of Ethnicity* (Cambridge: Belknap Press of Harvard University Press, 1982), 80–109; and David M. Kennedy, *Over Here: The First World War and American Society* (New York: Oxford University Press, 1980). See also Michael E. McGerr, *The Decline of Popular Politics: The American North, 1865–1928* (New York: Oxford University Press, 1986); Charles McGovern, "Consumption and Citizenship in the United States, 1900–1940," in *Getting and Spending: European and American Consumer Societies in the Twentieth Century*, ed. Susan Strasser, Charles McGovern, and Matthias Judt (Cambridge: Cambridge University Press, 1998); and Charles F. McGovern, "Sold American: Inventing the Consumer, 1890–1940," Ph.D. diss., Harvard University, 1993.

15. Wai-Teng Leong, "Culture and the State: Manufacturing Traditions for

Tourism," *Critical Studies in Mass Communication* 6 (December 1989): 355–75. For a broader discussion of the construction of national identity see Anderson, *Imagined Communities;* Gellner, *Nations and Nationalism;* Richard Handler, "Authenticity, " *Anthropology Today* 2 (February 1986): 2–4, and "On Having a Culture: Nationalism and the Preservation of Quebec's 'Patrimonie,'" in *Objects and Others: Essays on Museums and Material Culture,* ed. George W. Stocking Jr. (Madison: University of Wisconsin Press, 1985), 192–217.

16. For the history of scenic nationalism see Runte, *National Parks,* 11–32. Huth, *Nature and the American,* 30–53; Nash, *Wilderness,* 67–83; Earl Pomeroy, *In Search of the Golden West: The Tourist in Western America* (rpt., Lincoln: University of Nebraska Press, 1990), 31–72; Miller, "Romantic Dilemma"; Lowenthal, "Place of the Past"; Joni Kinsey, *Thomas Moran and the Surveying of the American West* (Washington, D.C.: Smithsonian Institution Press, 1992); and Novak, *Nature and Culture,* all address this issue of the America's natural legacy.

17. Leong, "Culture and the State," 357.

18. Robert Sterling Yard, "Historical Basis of National Parks Standards," *National Parks Bulletin,* November 1929, 3, Stephen Tyng Mather Papers, Bancroft Library, University of California, Berkeley; hereafter cited as Mather MSS. Note that a version of this material examining the park service publicity campaign developed between 1914 and 1918 has been published in an essay examining the history of the "See America First" slogan. See Shaffer, "Negotiating National Identity."

19. Robert Shankland, *Steve Mather of the National Parks,* 3d ed. (New York: Knopf, 1970), provides a comprehensive overview of Mather's career as director of the national parks. In addition, Donald C. Swain, *Wilderness Defender: Horace M. Albright and Conservation* (Chicago: University of Chicago Press, 1970); Horace M. Albright and Robert Cahn, *The Birth of the National Park Service: The Founding Years, 1913–33* (Chicago: Howe Brothers, 1985); John Ise, *Our National Park Policy: A Critical History* (Baltimore: Johns Hopkins University Press, 1961); and Hal Rothman, *Preserving Different Pasts: The American National Monuments* (Chicago: University of Illinois Press, 1989), 89–118, also provide information on Mather's work for the Park Service. I am also indebted to Peter J. Blodgett for sharing his unpublished history of national park publicity during the Mather/Albright era, "Selling Scenery: Advertising and the National Parks, 1916–1933," Huntington Library, 1996. A small collection of Mather's papers, most notably scrapbooks covering his career and obituaries overviewing his life, are held by the Bancroft Library, University of California, Berkeley. A few of Mather's papers are scattered throughout the National Park Service Records, Record Group (hereafter RG) 79, at the United States National Archives, College Park, Md. (hereafter NA). However, the Park Service Records contain no organized collection of his papers.

20. Stephen Tyng Mather, "The National Parks on a Business Basis," *American Review of Reviews* (April 1915): 429.

21. See Shankland, *Steve Mather,* 68–73; Swain, *Wilderness Defender,* 46–52; and Albright and Cahn, *Birth,* 24–26.

22. For an overview of the growing popularity of outdoor recreation and nature pursuits see Huth, *Nature and the American;* Nash, *Wilderness;* and Peter J. Schmitt, *Back to Nature: The Arcadian Myth in Urban America* (rpt., Baltimore: Johns Hopkins University Press, 1990).

23. *Proceedings of the National Parks Conference, Berkeley, California, March 11, 12, and 13, 1915* (Washington, D.C.: Government Printing Office, 1915), 11, 79; "Heads of

National Parks Are to Meet," *San Francisco Examiner,* February 15, 1915; "To Make the Parks People's Own," *Los Angeles Times,* March 8, 1915; "National Park Chief Opens Sessions To-Day," "Steps Taken to Make U.S. Parks More Accessible," *Christian Science Monitor,* March 18, 1915. Scrapbooks, vol. 4, Clippings Re Public Official Career, 1915–1916, Mather MSS.

24. Robert Sterling Yard, "Historical Basis of National Parks Standards," 3, U.S. National Park Service, carton 1, Mather MSS.

25. See Robert Sterling Yard, *The Publisher* (Boston: Houghton Mifflin, 1913). Yard was hired at a salary of thirty dollars per month by the U.S. Geological Survey and given a small office in the Bureau of Mines. Mather supplemented his salary by five thousand dollars per year (Shankland, *Steve Mather,* 59).

26. *Proceedings of Conference,* 151.

27. Horace M. Albright, "Making the Parks Known to the People," *The Living Wilderness,* December 1945, 6, S. T. Mather Clippings, carton 1; "World Will Be Told of State's Wonder," *Rocky Mountain News,* September 3, 1915, Scrapbooks, vol. 9, Personal Clippings, 1915–1929, Mather MSS.

28. United States Department of the Interior, *The National Parks Portfolio* (New York: Scribners, 1916); and *Glimpses of Our National Parks* (Washington, D.C.: Government Printing Office, 1916).

29. Mather donated five thousand dollars to finance the publishing of the book and secured the additional forty-three thousand from seventeen Western railroads. Yard arranged to have *Scribners* put out the first edition. See Ise, *Our National Park Policy,* 196; Shankland, *Steve Mather,* 97–98; and Swain, *Wilderness Defender,* 57–58.

30. Albright, "Making Parks Known"; Ise, *Our National Park Policy,* 196; Shankland, *Steve Mather,* 97–98; Swain, *Wilderness Defender,* 57–58. A second edition of the *National Parks Portfolio* was issued by the Government Printing Office in 1917. For more information on later editions see RG 79, Central Classified Files, Entry 7, Portfolio of the National Parks, NA.

31. Quotations from *The National Parks Portfolio,* n.p.

32. Kenneth A. Erickson, "Ceremonial Landscapes of the American West," *Landscape* 22 (autumn 1977): 39–41, provides an interesting discussion of "ceremonial landscapes." Also see John F. Sears, *Sacred Places: American Tourist Attractions in the Nineteenth Century* (New York: Oxford University Press, 1989), 5, suggests that nineteenth-century American tourist attractions were depicted as "ceremonial landscapes," arguing that they "assumed some of the functions of sacred places in traditional societies."

33. *The National Parks Portfolio,* n.p.

34. *Glimpses of Our National Parks.* Quotations may be found on pp. 3, 7–8, and 45.

35. See clippings in Scrapbooks, vols. 4–7, Mather MSS.

36. "Colorado—a Game Sanctuary," *Rocky Mountain News,* March 26, 1915; and "Trying to Turn Travel to Wonderlands of the U.S.," Scrapbooks, vol. 4, Clippings Re Public Official Career, 1915–1916, Mather MSS.

37. In the spring of 1916, when the National Park Service bill was being debated in Congress, Grosvenor devoted the April issue of *National Geographic* to American scenery. He wrote the only feature article, "Land of the Best," which was illustrated with over one hundred photographs of American sites and scenery. Lorimer also actively supported the parks not only by printing editorials discussing park issues, but also by constantly featuring articles on the parks by such writers and park enthusiasts as Emerson Hough, Herbert Quick, Hal Evarts, and Mary Roberts Rinehart. The

national park articles produced by these various writers for the *Saturday Evening Post* covered a wide array of topics ranging from descriptions of specific parks to wildlife and nature study to tourism to park administrative issues. For an overview of the park publicity provided by the *Saturday Evening Post* see Scrapbooks, vols. 4–7, especially vol. 5, Clippings Re Public Official Career, 1916–1919, Mather MSS. See also Shankland, *Steve Mather*, 85–92. Note that correspondence between Hal Evarts and Mather reveals that Mather kept Evarts abreast of park issues, provided him with information, and included him in park events. In 1920 when President Harding traveled to Yosemite, Mather invited Evarts to join the party. See Hal G. Evarts/Stephen Tyng Mather correspondence, Hal G. Evarts Papers, 1919–1951, University of Oregon, Eugene. Both Shankland and Swain suggest that Herbert Quick and Emerson Hough were also in close contact with the Park Service. See Shankland, *Steve Mather;* and Swain, *Wilderness Defender.*

38. United States Department of the Interior, *Annual Report of the Secretary of the Interior, 1918*, 119, 122. Note that John Ise suggests that Mather probably drafted the letter for Secretary Lane (*Our National Park Policy*, 195).

39. For a discussion of the ways in which western landscapes were represented as quintessential American landscapes see Anne Farrar Hyde, *An American Vision: Far Western Landscape and National Culture, 1820–1920* (New York: New York University Press, 1990).

40. Clipping, "Development of the National Parks," *Chicago Tribune*, January 18, 1916, Scrapbooks, vol. 4, Clippings Re Public Official Career, 1915–1916, Mather MSS.

41. Mark Daniels, "Scenic Resources in the United States," *California Forestry* 1 (May 1917): 12.

42. Stephen T. Mather to P. C. Spencer, April 15, 1918, RG 79, Central Classified Files, Entry 6, General, Tours: Miscellaneous, April 10, 1917, to November 10, 1919, NA.

43. Howard H. Hayes to P. S. Eustis, May 29, 1918, in RG 79, Entry 6, General, Western Lines Bureau of Service, part 1, April 30, 1918, to November 11, 1918, NA.

44. Ibid.

45. For the various publicity strategies used by the bureau of service see Howard H. Hays to Stephen T. Mather, June 25, 1918; Stephen T. Mather to Howard H. Hays, June 27, 1918; "Statement on Handling Correspondence about National Parks and Monuments Originating from Inquiries Received by Western Lines," n.d.; Howard H. Hays to Stephen T. Mather, July 17, 1918; Memorandum, September 17, 1918, in RG 79, Entry 6, General, Western Lines Bureau of Service, part 1, April 30, 1918, to November 11, 1918, NA.

46. For an overview of the promotional activities undertaken by the Bureau of Service see Howard H. Hays, "Bureau of Service Resume, June 1 to September 30, 1918," in RG 79, Entry 6, General, Western Lines Bureau of Service, part 1, April 30, 1918, to November 11, 1918, NA.

47. Ibid.; and Howard H. Hays to Stephen T. Mather, November 15, 1918, in RG 79, Entry 6, General, Western Lines Bureau of Service, part 2, November 14, 1918, to April 14, 1919, NA.

48. Howard H. Hays to Horace M. Albright, December 17, 1918, and Horace M. Albright to Howard H. Hays, December 20, 1918, in RG 79, Entry 6, General, Western Lines Bureau of Service, part 2, November 14, 1918, to April 14, 1919, NA.

49. Howard H. Hayes to Stephen T. Mather, February 1, 1919, in RG 79, Entry 6, General, Western Lines Bureau of Service, part 2, November 14, 1918, to April 14, 1919, NA.

50. Walter P. Hines to The Ticket Agent, May 15, 1919, in RG 79, Entry 6, General, Western Lines Bureau of Service, Loose Papers, NA.

51. Circular No. 86, "Promotive Advertising of National Parks and Principal Western Resort Regions," May 10, 1919, in RG 79, Entry 6, General, Western Bureau of Service, NA.

52. "Bureau of Service Resume, January 1st to September 30, 1919," in RG 79, Entry 6, General, Western Bureau of Service Lines, part 4, NA.

53. See Shaffer, "See America First," 144–98.

54. For a discussion of the ideal of scenic monumentalism see Runte, *National Parks*, 11–47.

55. For post–World War I restrictions on park service publicity see Stephen T. Mather to H. H. Hunkins, April 5, 1920, in RG 79, Entry 6, General, Western Bureau of Service Lines, part 4, NA.

56. Franklin K. Lane, "A Mind's Eye Map of America," *National Geographic*, June 1920, 479 and 510.

57. Stephen T. Mather, "National Parks in War Time," *Bulletin of the American Game Protective Association*, April 1918, in Scrapbooks, vol. 5, Clippings Re Public Official Career, 1916–1919, Mather MSS.

58. John B. Patton, "National Parks Banquet," in RG 79, Entry 6, General, Publicity: Far Western Travelers Association, June 23, 1919, to April 3, 1920, NA.

59. A. B. Cammerer to C. R. Richards, September 16, 1919, in RG 79, Entry 6, General, Publicity: Far Western Travelers Association, June 23, 1919, to April 3, 1920. Cammerer notes that he is sending a copy of the article on national parks for the forthcoming yearbook. See also, attached, "The National Parks, Our Scenic Wonderlands," in RG 79, Entry 6, General, Publicity: Far Western Travelers Association, June 23, 1919, to April 3, 1920, NA.

60. Huston Thompson, "Our National Parks," ["Address of Hon. Houston A. Thompson Vice Chairman of the Federal Trade Commission Formerly Assistant Attorney General of the United States, Before the Far Western Traveler's Association at Hotel Plaza, New York City, February 7, 1920] in RG 79, Entry 6, General, Publicity: Far Western Travelers Association, June 23, 1919, to April 3, 1920, NA.

61. Press release, "Why the Far Western Travelers are Sending a Party of Boy Scouts to the West, " April 3, 1920, in RG 79, Entry 6, General, Publicity: Far Western Travelers Association, June 23, 1919, to April 3, 1920, NA.

62. Thompson, "Our National Parks," 4.

63. "The National Parks, Our Scenic Wonderlands," 5, in RG 79, Entry 6, General, Publicity: Far Western Travelers Association, June 23, 1919, to April 3, 1920, NA.

64. See Peter J. Blodgett, "Striking a Balance; Managing Concessions in the National Parks, 1916–1933," *Forest and Conservation History* 34 (April 1990): 60–68.

65. Clipping, "National Park-to-Park Highway Association," Scrapbooks, vol. 4, Clippings Re Public Official Career, 1915–1916, Mather MSS.

66. "Memorandum of the Press," May 16, 1919, in RG 79, Entry 6, General, Tours: Brooklyn Daily Eagle Tour, part 1, NA.

67. The ideal of an inaugural run was specifically suggested by H. V. Kaltenborn, assistant managing editor and tour director of the *Brooklyn Daily Eagle*. See copy of letter, H. V. Kaltenborn to Chauncey, May 20, 1919, in RG 79, Entry 6, General, Tours: Brooklyn Daily Eagle Tour, part 1. For the details of promoting and organizing the tour see Stephen T. Mather to Mr. H. W. Child, May 24, 1919; Horace M. Albright to Howard H. Hays, May 27, 1919; Horace M. Albright to H. H. Hunkins, May 27, 1919;

Horace M. Albright to H. W. Child, June 4, 1919. For the naming of the road see Horace M. Albright to M. Max Goodsill, May 28, 1919, in RG 79, Entry 6, General, Tours: Brooklyn Daily Eagle Tour, part 1, NA.

68. Gus Holmes to Librarian, Bureau of Public Roads, December 22, 1921, and attached pamphlet, "The National Park to Park Highway National Park to Park Highway," Vertical files, U.S. Department of Transportation Library, Washington, D.C.; and clipping, "Road Sponsors Close Sessions," *Salt Lake Tribune,* July 18, 1921, in RG 79, Entry 6, General, Maps: Second Annual Convention, National Park to Park Highway Association, Salt Lake City, Utah, June 16–17, 1921, NA.

69. Clipping, "State Parks: For the Beauty of America," *National Republican,* March 22, 1924, Scrapbooks, vol. 9, Personal Clippings, 1915–1929, Mather MSS.

70. Arno B. Cammerer to Abbott Lowell, February 23, 1923; see also letters to colleges and universities making the same request in RG 79, General, Tours: Universities and Colleges, part 1, February 23, to June 12, 1923, NA.

71. Franklin K. Lane to Stephen T. Mather, May 13, 1918, in RG 79, Entry 6, General, Manual, Loose Papers; and Hubert Work, "Statement of National Park Policy," March 11, 1925, in RG 79, Central Classified Files, Entry 7, General Administration and Personnel Policy, NA.

72. Arno B. Cammerer, "Memorandum for Mr. Yard," May 2, 1923, in RG 79, Entry 6, General, National Parks Association, NA.

73. Arno B. Cammerer, "The National Parks, Our Out-of-Door Classrooms," 2, in RG 79, Entry 6, General, Publicity: Far Western Travelers Association, part 2, April 8, 1920, to December 30, 1922, NA.

74. Executive Committee to the Members of the National Parks Association, November 24, 1920, in RG 79, Entry 6, General, National Parks Association, NA.

75. Announcement, "Annual Dinner of the Travel Club of America," January 21, 1922, in RG 79, Entry 6, General, Exhibits: part 1, September 21, 1920, to March 30, 1922. Note that Robert Sterling Yard reiterated these comments verbatim in promotional material for the National Parks Association, "Essential Facts Concerning the War on the National Parks," n.d., in RG 79, Entry 6, General, National Parks Association, NA.

76. Richard Handler, "Authenticity," 2, 4. For an examination of the fascination with authenticity in American culture see Kammen, *Mystic Chords of Memory;* and Miles Orvell, *The Real Thing: Imitation and Authenticity in American Culture, 1880–1940* (Chapel Hill: University of North Carolina Press, 1989).

77. Lionel Trilling, *Sincerity and Authenticity* (Cambridge: Harvard University Press, 1971), 93, quoted in Handler, "Authenticity," 3.

78. Handler, "Authenticity," 4.

79. Robert S. Yard, "Economic Aspects of Our National Parks Policy," *Scientific Monthly,* April 1923, 387.

80. Roger W. Toll, "National Park Development Without Over-Development," n.p. in RG 79, Entry 6, General, Minutes, Sixth National Parks Conference, 1922, NA.

81. Robert Sterling Yard, "The People and the National Parks," *Survey Graphic* 1 (August 1922): 547. Note that Yard develops and reiterates this argument in "Economic Aspects," 385.

82. Yard, "People and National Parks," 547–48, 550, 583, and 552.

83. For an overview of republican notions of free labor see J. G. A. Pocock, *The Machiavellian Moment: Florentine Political Thought and the Atlantic Republican Tradition* (Princeton: Princeton University Press, 1975). See also Eric Foner, *Free Soil, Free Labor, Free Men: The Ideology of the Republican Party Before the Civil War* (New York:

Oxford University Press, 1970); James Livingston, *Pragmatism and the Political Economy of Cultural Revolution, 1850–1940* (Chapel Hill: University of North Carolina Press, 1994), 24–83; and Dorothy Ross, "The Liberal Tradition Revisited and the Republican Tradition Addressed," in *New Directions in American Intellectual History*, ed. John Higham and Paul Conkin (Baltimore: Johns Hopkins University Press, 1977).

84. "Accommodations for Colored People," in RG 79, Entry 6, General, Minutes, Sixth National Parks Conference, 1922, NA.

85. Although the Park Service rhetoric still relied on traditional republican notions of free labor and virtuous citizenship to characterize this increasingly exclusive notion of citizenship and nation, in effect American consumer culture empowered the emerging professional managerial class. For an overview of the emergence of this professional managerial class see Richard M. Ohmann, *Selling Culture: Magazines, Markets, and Class at the Turn of the Century* (London: Verso, 1996). For a discussion of the increasing whiteness of that class see George Lipsitz, "The Possessive Investment in Whiteness: Racialized Social Democracy and the White Problem in American Studies," *American Quarterly* 47 (September 1995): 369–87; and Lisabeth Cohen, "From Town Center to Shopping Center: The Reconfiguration of Community Marketplaces in Postwar America," *American Historical Review* 101 (October 1996): 1050–81.

86. John Wesley Hill, "Extract from a speech delivered at the Opening of Yellowstone National Park, June 20, 1923," 3, in RG 79, Entry 6, General, Dr. John Wesley Hill, part 1, May 26, 1923, to September 20, 1923, NA, 3, 6, 8, 9–11, and 14.

87. Henry Nash Smith, *Virgin Land: The American West as Symbol and Myth* (New York: Vintage, 1957). For further discussion of the republican ideal of the American nation see J. G. A. Pocock, *The Machiavellian Moment: Floretine Political Thought and the Atlantic Republican Tradition* (Princeton, N.J.: Princeton University Press, 1975); and Dorothy Ross, "The Liberal Tradition Revisited and the Republican Tradition Addressed," in *New Directions in American Intellectual History*, ed. John Higham and Paul Conkin (Baltimore: Johns Hopkins University Press, 1977), 116–31.

A "New Deal" for Leisure

Making Mass Tourism during the
Great Depression

Dorothea Lange's photograph *Toward Los Angeles,* taken for the Farm Security Administration in 1937, exposes one of the most significant anomalies of
the Great Depression. Her ironic image of poor migrants, walking along a
highway toward Los Angeles, juxtaposed with a billboard promoting leisurely
travel by rail, raises the question: why did a period of drastically declining
national income and the profound need to create work coincide with the
development of new leisure practices, especially that of mass tourism?[1]

That same year, the research of an economist, Julius Weinberger, writing
in the *Harvard Business Review* confirmed this paradox. Examining consumer
spending on recreation from 1909 to 1935, Weinberger discovered that vacation expenditures as a percentage of national income not only rose steadily
during the boom years of the 1920s but also increased consistently over the
first six years of the depression. Even more surprisingly, his study revealed that
tourism appeared more integral to the economy of the 1930s than it had been
during the previous decade of reputedly unparalleled economic activity.
While tourist spending in relation to national income averaged 2.96 percent
during the twenties, it averaged 3.94 percent during the ensuing years of economic decline, reaching as much as 4.37 percent in 1935.[2]

Notwithstanding Lange's and Weinberger's observations, academic and
popular commentators have, over the ensuing decades, been slow to address
the issue of depression-era tourism expansion. In a preface to a collection of
depression-era documents published a quarter century ago, the cultural historian Warren Susman noted that most of those who had commented on the
remarkable mobility of the Great Depression had stressed the movement of
"Okies" out of the Dust Bowl or the circulation of unemployed vagrants and
tramps throughout the nation. Yet an increasing number of Americans other
than the Okies and the unemployed were also on the move—not for the purposes of finding work or better places to live, but for the purposes of leisure and

Dorothea Lange, *Toward Los Angeles*, 1937. (Library of Congress Farm Security Administration collection.)

tourism. Unfortunately, Susman never completed his analysis of the relationship between mobility and leisure during the depression. While he did point out that the 1930s were as much the era of the automobile, the streamlined train, the Greyhound bus, and the motor court as they were the decade of the hobo, the breadline, and the migrant labor camp, Susman never (nor has anyone else) explained the depression's role in the making of mass tourism.[3]

The making of mass tourism was a complex process. It was the result of the accretion and confluence of decades-long developments, the most significant of which intensified and came to fruition during the 1930s due to the exigencies of the depression. This essay examines the two most important of these developments—the expansion of paid vacations and the maturation of an aggressive and sophisticated promotional apparatus for tourism. This latter consisted of both an array of local, state, and regional promotional associations, referred to at the time as "community advertising organizations," and the tourism-related agencies of the federal government, most notably the National Park Service, the United States Forest Service, and especially during the late 1930s, the United States Travel Bureau.[4]

The movement for paid vacations first emerged around the turn of the century. The initial efforts by railroads and resorts to encourage recreational travel dated back to at least the mid-1800s. It was not, however, until the decade after World War I that paid vacations were finally extended to a majority of salaried workers, and that local business leaders and government officials began to establish a network of professional tourism promotional associations. By this time, employers had come to accept the idea put forth by progressive management experts and social commentators that vacations renewed the spirit, energy, and efficiency of the salaried middle class. Community businessmen and government officials, for their part, observing the rise of paid vacations and improvements in transportation, began viewing tourism as a potential strategy of economic development and created local promotional associations to help develop the tourist trade. As a result, by the late 1920s tourism had developed into a favored middle-class cultural practice and had contributed significantly to the decade's economic boom.[5]

The crisis of the depression was ultimately responsible for completing the transformation of tourism into a mass phenomenon. As the 1930s progressed, management's desire to secure industrial peace and labor's increasing militancy and consumerist ideology brought about a frenzied expansion of paid vacations to a majority of wage earners. At the same time, the New Deal–era interest in promoting social harmony and in encouraging new consumption practices to revitalize the economy compelled business leaders and government officials on both the local and national levels to intensify their tourism promotional activities and spread vacationing beyond its formerly middle- and upper-class base. As a result, by the end of the New Deal era, over twenty-five million workers received vacations with pay, and sixty million Americans were taking at least a week's vacation away from home. Indeed, by the eve of World War II, advocates of paid vacation and tourism promoters had not only made tourism into a mass phenomenon, they had also helped fashion the view that the mass consumption of leisure, especially in the form of vacations and tourism, was a necessity for the social, cultural, and economic health of the nation.

THE RISE OF PAID VACATIONS

Prior to the late 1930s, the majority of American workers had neither the money nor the time to take vacations. In fact, until the 1920s, the very idea of a vacation rarely occurred to most Americans, whether from the middle or working classes. One respondent to the 1920s *Middletown* survey, in commenting on the status of vacationing in previous decades, had sardonically proclaimed: "Vacations in the 1890s? Why, the word wasn't in the dictionary."[6] By and large, during the late nineteenth century, extended time for leisure was the prerogative of the very wealthy. Most employers, imbued with the ideology of the work ethic, saw little need to give either white-collar personnel or manual workers paid vacations. Wage earners, for their part, were uninterested in extended periods of time off that, for them, generally meant unemployment, not vacation. Instead, they put their energy into obtaining an eight-hour day, a five-day work week, and higher wages. And for those third of Americans who worked on their own or others' farms, the rhythms of agricultural life did not permit them to enjoy extended periods of leisure away from home. Accordingly, at the turn of the century, the majority of those in the nation's workforce who received vacations with pay were high-level executives and managers, a group that comprised no more than 10 percent of all salaried workers.[7]

During the first decades of the twentieth century, management experts and social commentators interested in the question of leisure and vacations promulgated the idea that all salaried employees, from executives down to clerical workers, should receive some form of extended time off with pay. Believing that white-collar labor in modern business enterprises undermined the vitality, productivity, and health of those who worked with their "brains," they asserted that middle-class workers needed to find ways to reinvigorate their character. Champions of the cult of "strenuous life"—most famously Theodore Roosevelt—pointed to leisurely pursuits such as rowing, boxing, and hunting. Others were not so insistent on the need of such vigorous experiences. A mere vacation from work would do. "Americans should be taught to play; to realize that a vacation is a necessity," declared one vacation advocate in testimony in front of Congress, "that to commune with nature better fits one for the strenuous business life. A vacation is a builder of health, mind, body, and soul. . . . I believe that it [taking a vacation] is as vitally necessary as their diet or their morning daily dozen."[8]

Thus, yearly vacations with pay would provide white-collar workers with the opportunity to recuperate from their demanding mental tasks while enhancing the productivity of American business and industry. Most importantly, vacations would ultimately improve the "social health" of the entire middle class. With this line of thinking becoming increasingly popular, paid vacations spread beyond the most elite segments of the workforce. Studies undertaken by the Bureau of Labor Statistics indicated that nearly 40 percent of all white-collar workers received annual vacations with pay by 1920. A decade later, the percentage had more than doubled to 80 percent.[9]

Although by the 1920s employers and managers considered their salaried personnel to be deserving of paid vacations, they did not regard their wage-earning employees as meriting equal treatment. During the early twentieth century, employers and management experts distinguished between mental labor and manual labor, by and large regarding physical labor as less demanding. Consequently, those who worked with their hands were considered to be less deserving of vacation time. As one *Nation* editorialist sarcastically opined:

> Behind this corporate and community practice in granting vacations is a vaguely defined philosophy. Men and women who work with their brains are sensitive, fine-strung, in constant need of replenishing burned-out energy; men and women who work primarily with their hands are stolid, ox-like, in need of thick beefsteak and a sound sleep to prepare them adequately for the next day's work.

Thus, not surprisingly, by 1920 company vacation plans covered no more than 5 percent of wage earners.[10]

From the late nineteenth century, rank-and-file workers and organized labor had taken the lead in the struggle for the eight-hour day and the five-day work week. Nevertheless, until the 1930s, American workers, unlike their European counterparts, rarely requested paid vacations, infrequently had vacation benefits written into their bargaining agreements, and never went on strike to obtain paid time off from work. Instead, self-identified progressive management organizations and business groups, most notably the National Industrial Conference Board (an organization consisting of eleven of the nation's most significant trade associations), the Rockefeller-funded Industrial Relations Counselors, the Metropolitan Life Insurance Company, and management-oriented magazines such as *Factory* and *System* pioneered the paid-vacation movement for wage earners. As early as 1920, these organizations and periodicals began issuing studies and articles that promoted the idea that vacations were a necessity for all workers. As was the case with salaried workers, these advocates of paid vacations for wage earners argued that extended time off with pay would increase the productivity, efficiency, and health of workers. In addition, as with other company-sponsored benefit programs, they contended that vacations would enhance the loyalty of workers, decrease labor turnover, diminish workplace conflict, and undermine workers' desire to organize unions. The comments of one manager succinctly reflected the Taylorist sensibility that characterized much of management thinking on the questions of paid vacations: "Few employees can do their best without a periodical rest. The company benefits in the way of production in receiving the employees' renewed energy upon their return from vacation." A 1925 management textbook was even more explicit in providing the rationale behind the need for vacation policies:

The grind of fifty-two weeks of work a year may be necessary for the factory, but the consensus of liberal opinion certainly favors a vacation of at least two weeks every year for each worker. When a period of idleness is converted into a healthful vacation, the expenditure brings physical and psychological values which probably result in added efficiency when the wage-earner returns. Even if the benefit to production did not entirely justify it on business grounds, it is necessary for social reasons.[11]

Despite this growing interest in paid vacations for wage earners during a period of a booming economy, by the late 1920s few companies actually provided vacation benefits to hourly workers. And those that did were hardly liberal in what they provided. In almost all cases, vacation eligibility was linked to extremely long service requirements. At General Electric, for instance, one-week vacations with pay were granted to wage-earning personnel who had worked continuously at the company for ten years. Vacations of two weeks' duration were granted only after working continuously for twenty-five years. By 1930, less than 10 percent of manual laborers received vacation benefits from their employers.[12]

Although the crisis of the depression ultimately sparked a tremendous increase in the number of wage earners receiving vacations with pay, the economic downturn did initially influence many companies to reevaluate the efficacy of their existing vacation plans. According to a study conducted by the NICB, nearly half of all vacation plans for wage earners that had been adopted previous to the depression were abandoned between 1929 and 1935. For many firms, the need to lay off workers made it unnecessary to maintain vacations as a strategy of attracting or maintaining a steady supply of labor. Moreover, with profits declining, many companies could no longer justify the expense of their vacation plans.

The NICB study revealed, however, that all was not ominous for the paid-vacation movement. One-half of all companies surveyed had in fact maintained their vacation plans through the early years of the depression. A quarter of the plans that had been abandoned had been reinstated. And at least another half of those that had been dropped were expected to be reinstated after 1935. The Conference Board survey also indicated, as did studies conducted by the Princeton University Industrial Relations Section and the Bureau of Labor Statistics, that a substantial number of companies initiated wage-earner vacation plans between 1929 and 1935. As a result, by the mid-1930s, the percentage of wage earners who received vacations with pay actually exceeded predepression levels. As the Conference Board study remarked, the fact that so many plans had been maintained, reestablished, and even initiated during the depths of the depression was "the best evidence that vacation policies have become firmly established in management policy." A 1935 *Forbes* article summarizing the results of the Princeton study added: "The [vacation] movement is coming back, perhaps stronger than ever."[13]

During the remaining years of the depression, the paid vacation did, as *Forbes* had presciently suggested, become an institutionalized feature of American labor relations. Whereas in 1935, a little more than 10 percent of wage earners received vacations with pay, by the end of 1937, the percentage of wage earners covered by vacation plans rose tremendously: close to 40 percent had obtained them. Moreover, by the eve of World War II, paid-vacation coverage had been extended to a majority of all wage earners—a development that represented a major change in American life.[14]

At first glance, it appears that the depression was an unlikely moment for such a dramatic expansion in the number of workers receiving vacations with pay. Vast unemployment, troublesome business conditions, and increasing labor-management tensions, on the face of it, did not seem to be prime conditions for such a significant transformation in the prevailing system of industrial relations. Nevertheless, the practice of granting paid vacations to wage earners did expand dramatically during the latter years of the depression, and moreover, it was largely because of, and not in spite of, the depression that such a development took place.

During the New Deal era, employers were faced with rank-and-file labor unrest, organizing drives by unions, and after the passage of the National Industrial Recovery Act (NIRA) and later the Wagner Act, a federal government seemingly partial to these organizing efforts. Desperately interested in preventing unionization while simultaneously hoping to better relations with their workers, companies throughout the nation began to institute or liberalize already existing paid-vacation plans in an attempt to purchase employees' loyalty and subvert their interest in joining unions. One notable effort of this sort occurred in the steel industry, where, prior to the midthirties, companies, which had displayed little interest in providing their wage-earning employees with vacations with pay, did so en masse. In 1936, confronted by an aggressive industry-wide unionization drive by the Steel Workers Organizing Committee (SWOC), the nation's major steel companies, among them United States Steel, Bethlehem Steel, and Republic Steel, granted paid vacations to over two hundred thousand wage earners, a strategy that in the long run failed to convince employees to side with management rather than organized labor. By World War II, the entire steel industry had been successfully unionized by the SWOC, and vacations for steelworkers, instead of being bestowed as a result of the prerogative of management, were provided as a result of the collective bargaining process.[15]

Although prior to the depression, wage earners had never expressed much interest in the idea of paid vacations, by the midthirties, at the time that employers were trying to purchase their loyalty by offering them such benefits, workers, in turn, had begun to develop a new attitude toward vacations with pay. Increasingly, they made the attainment, and in the cases where they already existed, the liberalization, of paid-vacation plans, if not a priority, at least an important demand. "[E]mployee representatives under works council plans have usually included among their first demands the extension of the vacation privilege to the wage-earning group," noted the NICB. It continued, "In the present drive for unionization, organized labor also has . . . endeavored to force the inclusion of a vacations-with-pay provision in agreements that it has negotiated."[16]

What explains wage earners' newfound interest in paid vacations? To a large extent, it was the result of the decades worth of intensive travel promotion (discussed later in this essay) as well as of paid-vacation advocacy by progressive management experts, both of which placed new leisure practices at the heart of American economic and cultural life. In fact, throughout the late thirties, the language of and reasoning behind worker requests for liberalization of or the institution of paid vacations borrowed as much from the discourse of the era's tourism promotional apparatus and management-sponsored paid-vacation movement and as it did from that of depression-era labor militancy. For example, a 1935 request of a works council at a Du Pont plant to extend the length of vacation from one week to two contended that

> the payroll employe is just as much entitled to two weeks vacations as a salaried employe, that the health of the employes would be improved, that the morale of the employes has shown a marked improvement since the one week vacation plan has been in effect and would be further improved with an additional week, that an extension of the plan would be equally as profitable to the DuPont company as to the employe, that other companies had extended two weeks of vacation to payroll employes, and that DuPont earnings were evidence that the DuPont Company could afford to pay the cost of vacation extension.[17]

In another instance in 1937, the Executive Council of the American Federation of Labor declared itself fully in favor of vacations with pay, explaining that

> in this day of automobiles, well paved roads, trailers, inexpensive bus tours to national parks and places of interest, a vacation of one or two weeks has more to offer than ever before. A working man and his family may step out of their daily routine into a life full of new interest, mentally stimulating with a chance to learn something of the world outside the shop and home. Such an opportunity is of immense value to wage earners; it gives perspective and sends a man back to his work with a new outlook.[18]

In effect, after years of being subjected to advertising and propaganda campaigns that repeatedly confirmed the value of the leisure class's definitions of the "good life," the working class, like the middle class of the teens and twenties before them, had come to accept the idea that vacationing should be a central component of their standard of living. As Pete Seeger's song of 1941, "Talking Union," indicated, the idea of "Vacations with pay, / Take your kids to the seashore" had become a working-class aspiration.[19]

To a large extent, the wage-earner desire for paid vacations did represent a growing *embourgeoisement* of the working class. At the same time, however, their newfound interest in demanding what had only recently become a middle-class birthright provided workers with a new issue to contest the power of their employers, thereby enhancing their militance and, at times, their class solidarity. From 1940 through 1941, for example, railway workers' dissatisfaction with management over the failure to provide paid vacations led to a massive disruption in the stability of labor relations and ultimately to the intervention of Franklin Roosevelt. During the spring of 1940, fourteen railway brotherhoods representing 750,000 wage earners demanded vacations with pay from the rail carriers. After several months of negotiation in which no agreement was reached, the membership of the fourteen brotherhoods voted to strike if their demands were not met. Before they could walk off the job, Roosevelt appointed an emergency board under the terms of the Railway Labor Act and barred any strike activity pending the recommendations of the board. After hearing the testimony of both the brotherhoods and the carriers in the fall of 1941, the emergency board recommended that each employee receive at least six consecutive workdays off a year after a year of continuous service. Another round of negotiations and strike threats ensued, but by December 1941, the brotherhoods and the carriers agreed to a plan that provided three-quarters of a million workers vacations with pay for the first time. After this, railway workers as well as the more than 50 percent of wage earners and 95 percent of salaried workers could now take their kids to the seashore as well as to the variety of other tourist destinations that were being aggressively promoted.[20]

COMMUNITY TOURISM PROMOTION AS
ECONOMIC DEVELOPMENT

As a result of the expanding pervasiveness of paid vacations as well as the development of improved roads and inexpensive automobiles, Americans increasingly possessed the time and the means to take at least a weeklong vacation away from home. Nevertheless, the desire to travel to a seashore, a national park, a historic site, a cosmopolitan city, or a world's fair was neither a natural nor an inevitable outcome of the mere existence of paid vacations and improved transportation methods. Notwithstanding the conventional wisdom of the era that explained that the upsurge in tourism resulted from humanity's innate wanderlust and natural inclination to travel, there were many other activities that Americans, both salaried and waged, could pursue with their newly gained time and money. For example, they could use the vacations to moonlight for another employer or search for another job. They could work around the home, performing maintenance or, as was the case with many working-class families, use the time and money provided by paid vacations to build their own homes. And, if they did travel away from home, it might be to visit family members and friends. The most common fear among employers was that their employees would do nothing, thereby squandering the opportunity for rejuvenation that would make them more efficient workers. As one manager of a small New York company explained: "We do not believe that a vacation benefits a factory worker unless he actually goes away somewhere. . . . If they just use their vacation time to hang around the corners, they had much better be at work."[21] Consequently, many business executives, management experts, civic leaders, and government officials believed that the desire to "go on vacation" needed to be actively facilitated and promoted. As Don Thomas, the executive director of the nation's foremost tourism promotional organization, remarked, "The travel habit was not born with most Americans. It's an acquired taste and one which must be religiously and patiently cultivated by the seller."[22]

During the interwar period, and particularly during the depression, this task of cultivating the "travel habit" was assumed by a diffuse yet aggressive network of tourism promotion organizations that emerged coincident with the effort to provide American workers with paid vacations. Among the most active institutions in this network were community-advertising organizations and the United States government. In promoting the idea that all working Americans should use their newly obtained vacation time to travel away from home, these institutions pioneered a new ethic of leisure—one that fundamentally shaped the cultural life of New Deal America while simultaneously helping to create a commercialized, profit-driven industry of enormous economic power.[23]

Community advertisers were the most aggressive and self-conscious promoters of the "travel habit" during the interwar period and particularly during the depression. Dating from 1919 when the first community-advertising association expressly dedicated to the promotion of tourism was established in San Diego, these organizations developed and deployed a comprehensive mechanism for selling travel that marketed the psychological benefits of vacationing to prospective tourists while simultaneously promoting the economic benefits of the tourist trade to local businessmen, government officials, and fellow residents.

Although it is impossible to measure the extent to which the sophisticated marketing strategies employed by community advertisers were actually responsible for changing the habits and transforming the consciousness of the American people, those who worked in the tourist trade assigned the community-advertising movement a large degree of responsibility for the making of mass tourism during the twenties and thirties. "The automobile and extensive highway systems gave us the opportunity to travel," noted Don Thomas in 1940 in a speech addressing the growth of tourism over the previous two decades. But, he concluded, it was a "new force [that] provide[d] our residents with the urge to travel, widening their viewpoint and stimulating a real curiosity about the rest of America. This force was and is community promotion."[24]

The origins of the community-advertising movement, nonetheless, had little to do with tourism promotion. In fact, as a term of art, community advertising was to a large extent a voguish name used to describe one set of promotional activities performed by the chambers of commerce and cooperative-marketing associations that had first appeared during the late nineteenth century. Recognizing that it was often more efficacious to cooperate than to compete, especially in attempting to capture national markets and investment, businessmen and civic leaders in communities across the United States had established such organizations to promote the economic growth of their respective regions through the encouragement of manufacturing, agriculture, and immigration. These promotional activities most often involved the advertising of a region's agricultural and manufactured commodities, the richness of its resources, and its favorable business conditions in a variety of national agricultural, industrial, and business publications, in self-published pamphlets and booklets, and in exhibits at regional and national fairs and expositions. Funds for these efforts were usually raised by company donations, but financing was also at times secured through government appropriations.[25]

During the years 1910–19, many of those associated with the chamber of commerce movement as well as those in the rapidly developing advertising industry—newspaper and magazine publishers, members of the advertising trade press, as well as advertising executives—began to call for a firmer understanding of how "scientific" advertising and "professional" publicity techniques could further the cause of community promotion. In addition, they saw a need to develop closer cooperation between the variety of organizations that worked in the field. Increasingly, advertising trade journals such as *Printer's Ink* and *Western Advertising and Business* used the phrase *community advertising* to describe this closer cooperation between professional advertising people and community development interests.[26]

Immediately after World War I, the community-advertising movement blossomed: businessmen and civic leaders in communities throughout the nation established centralized cooperative-advertising organizations to promote the economic interests of their communities. As was the case with the chambers of commerce of the previous decades, the majority of these new organizations promoted manufacturing, immigration, and, at times, agriculture. A few of these organizations, however, most notably the All-Year Club of Southern California and Californians Inc. (representing the San Francisco Bay area), had the express purpose of marketing the tourist assets of their respective communities. Their guiding assumption, one that was to be repeated constantly throughout the interwar period, was that tourists were economically beneficial because they brought "new money"—that is, income generated elsewhere—into a region. Crucial to economic growth, new money circulated through many levels of the local economy, leading to greater consumer demand for manufactured and agricultural products, thereby creating new businesses, new jobs, and new investment opportunities that would ultimately attract new immigrants. As Don Thomas explained: "It is the continuous stream of money from outside sources which energizes local trade. No community increases its wealth by having the residents merely swap dollars."[27]

By the late 1920s, both tourism promotion and recreational travel had grown dramatically. Approximately seventy communities throughout the United States had established tourism promotional associations, whereas in 1921, no more than fifteen communities had done so. The most prolific community advertiser, the All-Year Club of Southern California, spent over three million dollars during the course of the decade. Advertisements appearing in the *Saturday Evening Post, Literary Digest,* and *Cosmopolitan* as well as in major metropolitan newspapers promoted Los Angeles and its environs as an all-in-one vacation destination. Headlines called on tourists to "Visit Southern California and See the World," and to take "A Trip Abroad in Your Own United States." In effect, the marketing program represented a variation on the then popular "See America First" idea: this time, however, promoting Southern California as a vacation destination preferable to other American as well as to European ones. And throughout the 1920s, the All-Year Club marketing appears to have successfully generated new money for the region. In spite of Southern California's great distance from the population centers of the nation, the number of tourists it attracted increased from 248,000 in 1921 to 858,0000 in 1929, and tourist expenditures rose from one hundred million to three hundred million dollars. Californians Inc. had similar success in promoting the San Francisco Bay Area. Advertising San Francisco as the cosmopolitan center of a "vacation land" that included the redwood forests, the Sierra Nevada, and Yosemite, the organization attracted more than 585,000 tourists to the region in 1929, a sixfold increase over the course of the decade.[28]

Despite the apparent success of community tourism promotion in generating tourists and new money, many businessmen and government officials in communities throughout the nation considered tourism a trivial leisure pursuit rather than the foundation upon which to build a regional economy. During the twenties and through much of the depression, many of those who lived, worked, and invested in areas that are now considered the nation's premier tourist destinations—cities such as Los Angeles and San Francisco and regions such as the Southwest and New England—did not immediately identify tourism as a vehicle for economic stability and growth. In their understanding of the economic world, productive practices such as manufacturing and perhaps financial services such as banking stimulated the economy. Consumption, especially leisure practices such as tourism, would in their estimation—foreshadowing contemporary concerns in the Third World and in the deindustrializing sections of the First World—only lead to burdensome taxes, increased traffic congestion, and unwanted social changes. Thus, in communities across the United States, residents required substantial and convincing proof of tourism's benefits before they justified spending the funds necessary to develop and promote the tourist resources of their region. In fact, Don Thomas regularly informed his colleagues in the community-advertising movement that tourism promotion meant more than convincing people from afar that they should take a trip to one's region. It also meant having to "sell the home folks," that is, members of the host community, on the economic benefits of developing and promoting tourism. "Unless a community sells the campaign to the people at home as aggressively as it endeavors to advertise away from home," he announced, "the campaign cannot live, even though its basic set-up be as right as right can be."[29]

Ultimately, the crisis of the depression provided the opportunity for community tourism promoters to intensify their selling of tourism to both the "home folks" and the residents of distant communities. The depression forced businessmen and government officials to reevaluate their assumptions as to how best to promote economic development and stability. Immediately working to increase manufacturing or agricultural capacity seemed pointless given that the depression appeared to be a crisis of overproduction. Moreover, promoting immigration was no longer seen as economically beneficial because it would only increase unemployment. Local tourism promoters, however, reminded businessmen, government officials, and other civic-minded residents in their communities that tourists could bring in new money, stimulate the economy, and lower the tax burden, all without depleting resources. Moreover, they noted that other municipalities, states, and regions had begun to seize upon tourism as a strategy of economic development and were either increasing their own advertising budgets or creating their own promotional agencies in an effort to gain their share of the tourist trade. Their warnings were severe: if communities failed to promote their tourist assets, they were in danger of losing the gains that they had made during the boom years of twenties. In many towns, cities, regions, and states across the nation such a combination of scare tactics and salesmanship paid off. By 1941, more than 250 communities, including forty-two states, had established promotional associations, which were spending a total of over 6.5 million dollars on extensive marketing campaigns in the nation's mass media.

These depression-era community promotional campaigns employed a number of strategies. First and foremost, advertisements and guidebooks promoted the particular attributes of the community being marketed—for, example the majesty of Mt. Rainier, the beauty of Miami's beaches, the excitement of New York City's urban landscape, or as in the case of Southern California, the fact that it was an all-in-one vacation destination. At the same time, however, two other depression-era marketing strategies stood out: first, the promotion of the idea that vacationing could be easy and inexpensive, and, second, the promotion of the idea that vacationing was relaxing and restorative. Both of these strategies were employed and ultimately resonated with potential tourists because ads promising "Amazing Vacation Bargains in New England," or calling on potential vacationers to "Take Two Weeks Out of Life—for Really Living," responded to the deep psychological and economic concerns that Americans faced during the 1930s.[30]

Campaigns promoting the idea that vacationing could be easy and inexpensive represented a response and a cultivation of the incipient one- and two-week vacation market. By the early depression, it had become increasingly clear to community advertisers that making these recent recipients of paid vacations into tourists was a necessity if a community was going to reap the benefits of the tourist trade. Although attracting elite tourists remained important because they generated a great deal of revenue per visit, communities had to attract the increasing number of one- and two-week vacationers, especially in the face of growing competition from other regions of the country. As an All-Year Club newsletter reported, "Valuable as this class [that of wealthy tourists] is they do not comprise the group whose expenditures aggregate the great total spent by Americans for travel. . . . The lion's share of the total expenditures for pleasure travel, and most everything else, is by persons of average means."[31]

In order to attract a broader class of vacationers, community tourism promotion during the depression was often quite didactic, providing vacationers with prices, timetables, distances, and step-by-step itineraries within ads and in guidebooks. These marketing campaigns operated under an interesting assumption, which in hindsight appears quite perceptive: even if previous promotional efforts had sparked the interest of the middle class or the better-off working class, many of these would-be tourists would have little idea how to take a vacation. Although it had become easier and cheaper to travel with improved roads and less expensive rail fares, most one- or two-week vacationers were neophytes. They had no idea how to plan, budget, or take a pleasure trip. And although some could and did turn to their local auto club or to oil company travel bureaus for help in planning a vacation, many community-advertising executives believed that this new pool of vacationers had to be taught how to take a vacation trip. "We can't expect people to travel of their own volition," noted Don Thomas in a letter to the director of the National Park Service, Horace Albright; "its [sic] too easy for them to stay anchored in their arm chairs. We not only have to paint the lure of travel but we have to follow through to show them how to save enough money to make the trip and how worthwhile it will be, tell them exactly what to see and do when they get here."[32] In effect, the in-depth information on travel methods, costs, timetables, affordable accommodations, and touring possibilities that community advertisers began to provide operated as a do-it-yourself bargain-rate version of the packaged tour. Now middle-class and wage-earning Americans who were increasingly becoming consumers of mass-produced goods could also purchase vacations that would be, in the words of one community advertiser, "packaged, price-tagged and merchandised like any other commodity."[33]

The second predominant marketing strategy of the depression years, suggesting that vacations were an antidote to problems confronted on the job and a way to ensure one's productivity upon the return to work, was a message borrowed directly from the pages of the paid-vacation movement: in this era of tension brought about by problems in the world of production, the world of consumption—in the form of a vacation—could bring individuals as well as the nation out of the depths of the economic and psychological depression into which they had plunged. In these campaigns, potential tourists were informed that vacations could, in the words of one jointly sponsored Pacific Coast advertisement, "fit you for the work ahead." Another early 1930s advertising campaign, was particularly explicit in promoting vacationing as the solution to the worries of the depression. Showing a group of relaxed vacationers, it counseled, "Bake out your troubles. . . . Work . . . worry . . . taut nerves . . . fear of the future. . . . Forget for a while . . . and have some *fun*." A decade later, with war jitters on the horizon, the ad was recycled. The headline asked, "Have You Been Snapping at People?" It then advised that "in these days of stress . . . [a] vacation [is] not only a necessary relaxation, but a sound investment." Indeed, according to these ads, the taking of a vacation was not merely relaxing, it was a personal Keynesian stimulus—an investment that made one a more productive member of the economy and the nation.[34]

In conducting these campaigns, community advertisers became the most prolific and skilled advertisers in the tourist trade. In using state-of-the-art marketing surveys, professional advertising techniques, and a pioneering understanding of the importance of market segmentation, they had created a promotional apparatus that had regularly issued billions of advertisements in "class" and mass-circulation magazines as well as in major metropolitan newspapers. They also had distributed millions of posters, brochures, and guidebooks in railway offices and travel bureaus throughout the nation. Thus, wherever a literate person turned during the 1930s, he or she was bombarded with professionally designed images and copy promoting the advantages of two-week vacation opportunities, vacation bargains, and all-in-one destinations. Although no one image or cleverly phrased slogan brought a tourist to a particular region, the aggregate effect of such advertising had created a cultural climate in which tourism could become increasingly accepted as a psychic necessity. More than advertising a particular product, community tourism promotion had advertised a particular way of life.[35]

THE FEDERAL GOVERNMENT, TOURISM PROMOTION, AND THE UNITED STATES TRAVEL BUREAU

Prior to the 1930s, the federal government's engagement in the realm of tourism had largely been limited to its establishment and management of national parks and monuments, to that point largely sites for upper-middle-class travel. And although the establishment of the National Park Service in 1916 had provided an institutional foundation for tourism promotion within the American state apparatus, throughout its first decade and a half, Congress failed to appropriate sufficient funds to enable the service to conduct promotional campaigns without extragovernmental aid. As a result, during his twelve-year tenure, the Park Service's first director, Stephen Mather, a wealthy borax tycoon and former journalist turned preservationist, had to continue the preservationist movement's pragmatic reliance on private sector support and funding for national park promotion. Mather, with the aid of his lieutenant, Horace Albright, courted wealthy benefactors such as John D. Rockefeller Jr. He encouraged his former colleagues in the newspaper and magazine business to publish editorials and articles promoting travel to the parks. He developed friendships with painters of wilderness scenes and found sponsors to exhibit their works. He opened the parks to photographers and moviemakers. He worked with women's clubs, regional promotional associations, travel agencies, highway associations, and automobile clubs. Most significantly, he maintained the national parks' relationship with the railroad industry, which, unable to foresee that most visitors to the parks would soon be coming in automobiles, expanded its role in promoting travel to the national parks. In support of the establishment of the Park Service, for example, seventeen railroads contributed tens of thousands of dollars to fund the first edition of the *National Parks Portfolio,* a booklet of pictures prepared by Mather's friend, the former Sunday editor of the *New York Herald,* Robert Sterling Yard. A tremendous success—272,000 copies were distributed in 1916—the booklet was updated and reissued each year over the next two decades as a government publication. Throughout the teens and twenties, the railroads also continued special publicity campaigns, introduced excursion rates, improved park accommodations, and provided direct subsidies to Park Service projects. As a result, by the year of Mather's retirement, 1929, park attendance had increased to over 2.75 million from 356,000 in 1916.[36]

After Mather's retirement, Horace Albright continued his predecessor's promotional work. Even after the onset of the depression, he as able to increase government appropriations and private sector support for Park Service tourism-related projects. Still, what the Park Service accomplished from 1929 to 1933 was nothing compared to what it achieved in the years after the change in the administrations. The New Deal brought new energy to and opportunities for the Service, enabling it to extend its constituency beyond its formerly elite and upper-middle-class base. During the Hundred Days, Franklin Roosevelt, a longtime supporter of national parks, ordered his secretary of the interior, Harold Ickes, to expand the Park Service's authority over the management of most federally owned tourist attractions—the battlefields, parks, monuments, and buildings that had been formerly managed by the War and Agriculture Departments. Later that year, the federal government, at Ickes instigation, initiated an intensive promotional campaign, under the slogan "1934—A National Parks Year." The Department of the Interior encouraged the railroads to commission a series of posters promoting travel to different parks. The Park Service sponsored radio programs and lectures on national park topics; and the United States Post Office issued stamps depicting what are now familiar views of America's parks. Even FDR played the role of mass tourism promoter, taking his family on visits to Hawaii National Park and Glacier National Park. In a nationally broadcast radio address from Glacier, he suggested that "every year ought to be a National Parks Year." And sounding like an advertising spokesman for a mass-marketed good, he declared to his audience,

> I express to you that hope that each and every one of you who can possibly find the means and opportunity for so doing will visit our national parks and use them as they are intended to be used. They are not for the rich alone. Camping is free, the sanitation is excellent. . . . You will find glorious scenery of every character; you will find every climate; you will perform the double function of enjoying and learning much.[37]

But for all their enthusiasm for mass travel to national parks, FDR, Ickes, and Park Service officials had yet to imagine a new role for the government in travel promotion. For over a decade, the number of Americans traveling for recreational purposes had increased dramatically as more workers received paid vacations, better roads were constructed, and less expensive forms of transportation such as automobiles and buses became more readily available. Still, during the early years of the New Deal, roughly 1933 through 1936, the federal government was primarily concerned with promoting tourism within the national park system. And outside of the special national park stamp issue (which ultimately paid for itself), the early New Deal provided no new funds for advertising and promotion. In fact, the number of Park Service employees responsible for publicity and information services remained at 1920's levels. (Funds for the development of new trails and camps as well as road maintenance were, however, forthcoming from the Civilian Conservation Corps' and Public Works Administration's budgets). Park Service promotion, therefore, as in years past, had to rely on the private sector for organizational support and funding. Without the aid of the railroads, community advertisers, automobile associations, newspapers, magazines, radio stations, and park concessionaires, a promotional venture such as National Parks Year could not have even been attempted.[38]

Change, however, was in the air. As early as the late 1920s, travel industry officials, regional tourism promoters, and political leaders from states with large or potentially significant tourist industries had begun clamoring for the government to assume a more active role in tourism promotion, not only to national parks, but to tourist attractions nationwide. Of primary concern was the fact that the governments of several European nations along with Canada, Japan, and a few Caribbean countries were aggressively promoting tourism in American mass circulation magazines and major metropolitan newspapers. In fact, by 1929 over forty and by 1935 close to sixty foreign governments had established official travel bureaus in New York City. As a result, throughout the 1930s, advocates of aggressive government tourism promotion repeatedly introduced legislation in Congress calling for the creation of a national tourism agency either within the Department of Commerce or the Department of the Interior. According to Representative Leonidas Dyer of Missouri, a primary sponsor of one of the travel bills, America needed to "take steps similar to those which have been taken by most of the nations of the world in assisting and in coordinating travel, recognizing . . . that travel is a great industry . . . worthy of the consideration . . . of the Congress." Conservatives in both the Republican and Democratic parties, however, opposed the creation of a new government bureaucracy as well as the apparent fiscal impropriety of increasing the budget to encourage more leisure at a time when the lack of work seemed more the issue. As one congressional opponent of tourism legislation put it, "I think it is almost ridiculous to assume that the government was organized for such a purpose at all, or that it comes within either the letter or spirit of the constitution."[39]

By the late 1930s, however, conservative opposition to state intervention in the tourist trade began to give way to an emerging consensus that recognized the importance of government-sponsored tourism promotion and coordination. In 1937, for example, the federal government through the Federal Writers' Project of the Works Progress Administration embarked on one of its most notable contributions to mass tourism, the *American Guide Series*. These extensively researched guidebooks to each of the forty-eight states, numerous cities, counties, and regions, and major automobile routes such as the Ocean Highway and Route 1 not only provided federal support for struggling writers and researchers, but indicated that the American state would no longer refrain from intervening in the nongovernmental tourist arena, even if it meant competing with privately sponsored initiatives.[40]

The creation of a national tourist agency, the United States Travel Bureau (USTB), was the federal government's most significant contribution to the field of tourism promotion and coordination. Established in February 1937 by Interior Secretary Harold Ickes with funding and staff from the CCC and the WPA, Congress gave the USTB official authorization and an independent appropriation in 1940. Though shut down after the first months of World War II, the bureau during its brief tenure reshaped the federal government's role in tourism promotion. Imitating its foreign competitors, the travel bureau assumed the role of a national clearinghouse of valuable tourist-related information, issuing a series of newsletters, bulletins, events calendars, research reports, and promotional aids to travel agencies, transportation companies, tour operators, and members of the hospitality industry. It facilitated relations between the constituent parts of the nation's rapidly growing yet inchoate tourist industry by creating a National Travel Advisory Board consisting of executives and officials from transportation and travel-related businesses and organizations. It directly assisted tourists, establishing local offices in New York City, San Francisco, and Washington, where it held lectures, screened travel-related motion pictures, staged exhibits, and distributed travel literature for government as well as nongovernment tourist attractions. The bureau also sponsored a series of radio programs throughout the nation as well as created and coordinated special promotional campaigns such as the Travel America Year campaign proclaimed by FDR for 1940 and the See the Old West campaign organized by eleven western states for 1941. In addition, special travel bureau posters, promoting travel in general and not just to the national parks, were produced by the WPA, a significant departure in government promotional practice. Perhaps the bureau's most novel project was its attempt to serve previously neglected populations who were in the process of becoming tourists for the first time. For example, it created a Division of Negro Activities that produced guides such as a handbook listing hotels and motels suitable for "Negro" travelers.[41]

After two decades of slow and piecemeal movement on the travel promotion front, why did the American state finally assume such an aggressive and central role? Three factors particular to the crisis of depression generated this development. First, with the fear of internal social division, radical revolution, and right-wing reaction, and subsequently of foreign aggression, intensifying during the 1930s, a sufficient number of congressmen and administration officials increasingly accepted the idea that recreational travel could make Americans into better citizens. In their estimation, touring the nation's historic shrines, scenic wonders, and cultural and commercial centers would enable people to transcend the regional, class, and other social differences that too often divided them, ultimately making the nation more prepared to confront threats from both within and outside its borders. As one weekly radio program endorsing Travel America Year advised: "In view of what is happening in the rest of the world, it is the timely duty of all Americans to know their country first, to understand and appreciate it, to become America-conscious, to obtain first-hand knowledge of the history, beauty, resources and power of the 48 sovereign States of their great country." The 1941 slogan of the USTB expressed this notion even more succinctly: "Travel Strengthens America. It promotes the nation's health, wealth, and unity."[42]

Second, with unemployment reaching unparalleled levels, with consumer and business confidence reaching all-time lows, and, after the recession of 1937, with increasing fear that a full recovery was in fact impossible, many New Dealers, like the community advertisers who favored travel promotion, began to view the promotion of leisure practices such as tourism as a potential solution to the problems of economic instability. In their estimation, tourism could bring vast economic benefits. In the stagnant economies that characterized the depressed regions of the country, tourism would aid the cause of regional development, redistributing and circulating new income, thereby stimulating business activity and creating jobs. And on the national level, tourism would help the sluggish economy by stimulating demand for commodities such as gasoline, oil, automobiles, rubber, and other products of heavy industry.[43]

Lastly, most government, business, and civic leaders interested in promoting the social and economic benefits of tourism came to a New Deal–inspired conclusion as the decade advanced: that tourism promotion could be successful only with the active participation of the federal government. Although the network of travel-related businesses and organizations had developed substantially since World War I, the tourist industry as a whole remained rather disparate, unorganized, and undercapitalized. As a result, the loose web of community promotional associations, automobile clubs, oil company travel bureaus, hotels, motels, and transportation companies desperately needed the guidance and aid that a government-sponsored travel bureau could provide. As Ruth Bryan Rhode, the daughter of William Jennings Bryan and herself a travel promoter of some note, offered:

> Without the properly implemented action of a Federal travel bureau, it is difficult to see how promotion and educational travel activities could be carried out effectively even within one country. . . . [P]rivate [organizations] are not equipped to place before the entire public a complete picture of the varied educational and recreational facilities which lie within our borders. A Government travel bureau has innumerable avenues for its dissemination.[44]

Not surprisingly, Secretary of the Interior Ickes wholeheartedly agreed. Upon obtaining congressional authorization for the U.S. Travel Bureau, he proclaimed:

> There has long been a need for a governmental agency to co-ordinate travel activities within the United States. . . . [M]ore than a major economic enterprise that offers a livelihood to hundreds of thousands of people, [tourism serves] the tremendously important function of bringing men together, of broadening horizons and of narrowing prejudices . . . [and] should be, one of the important activities of any government, particularly of a democratic government.[45]

To a large extent, Ickes's rhetorical flourish represented the highpoint in the ideological conception of the role of a government-sponsored travel bureau. And, indeed, the USTB's promotion and coordination efforts did represent a significant departure from the American state's pre-depression role in travel promotion—a role that helped make mass tourism during the depression.

A "NEW DEAL" FOR LEISURE

The aggressive promotional efforts of community advertisers, federal government tourism agencies, paid-vacation advocates as well as by local auto clubs and the American Automobile Association, oil companies, the railroads, and bus companies made a substantial mark on American economic life. In 1915, those few tourists fortunate to have the time and money for a vacation had spent approximately 500 million dollars on domestic travel-related activity. By the eve of World War II, tourism ranked as one of the largest industries in the nation—as large as the automobile, petroleum, and lumber industries combined and 50 percent larger than iron and steel production. More than five million Americans gained their livelihood from the tourist trade. Capital investment in the travel industry had reached nearly thirty billion dollars, one of the nation's largest industrial investments. Travel accounted for close to 8 percent of national purchasing power, representing an expenditure of over six billion dollars a year. More than two hundred municipalities and forty-two states had established community-advertising organizations that spent over 6.5 million dollars promoting their beaches, mountains, beaches, historic sites, and urban landscapes as vacation attractions. The federal government operated twenty-six national parks, eighty-two national monuments, and fifty-one national historic and military areas that drew over twenty million visits in 1941, a more than fiftyfold increase over attendance in 1916, the year the National Park Service was created. As Don Thomas noted in a speech at the first National Travel Congress in November 1941, it was "plain that travel has vitally changed during the previous two decades. Not so very long ago, travel was a luxury enjoyed by the limited few. Now it is regarded as a necessity purchased by 60 million Americans."[46]

The growth of paid vacations and the development of tourism promotion also reshaped American social and cultural life, providing Americans of varying classes and social groups the opportunity to participate more fully in the nation's midcentury mass consumer culture, albeit on their own terms. In this era before the tourist industry became dominated by corporate chains in the lodging, resort, and entertainment business, vacationing was not the monolithic mass cultural experience that much of the historical and sociological literature assumes mass cultural practices to be. Rather, as Pierre Bourdieu has shown with leisure practices in France, American tourists could in their vacation choices reaffirm their class-based, ethnic, and even generational identities while simultaneously taking part in the growing and expansive mass national consumption culture that surrounded them. At the same time, with the annual vacation away from home no longer the prerogative of a few but becoming an accepted, even expected, part of the lifestyles of a large and growing number of people, vacations could merely provide those who needed it a degree of freedom and release from the routine of their daily lives. Going on vacation meant not having to deal with contentious managers, bosses, and fellow workers. It sometimes meant escaping one's children, parents, and spouse or conversely meant having the opportunity to engage more fully with one's family. Most significantly for them, going on vacation meant not working— relaxing at a mountain getaway or beach resort or being stimulated by hiking in a national park or by consuming in an urban center. Such activities were for most Americans certainly preferable to working.[47]

Thus, by the eve of World War II, the depression-era intensification of the decades worth of paid-vacation advocacy and aggressive tourism promotion had created a cultural climate in which Americans had come to view vacationing as more than a trivial diversion. Americans, whether wage earners in the steel mills or executives in major corporations, considered tourism essential to their personal pursuit of happiness as well as to the proper functioning of the American economy and workplace. Indeed, with the majority of the nation finally possessing the time, money, and inclination to take at least a week's vacation away from home, mass tourism had not only helped bolster the American social and economic system at a moment when it had been at its most fragile, it had also become one of the defining features of the midcentury American way of life, a development that truly represented a "new deal" for leisure.

NOTES

1. Dorothea Lange, *Toward Los Angeles* (1937), Farm Security Administration Collection, Library of Congress.

2. Julius Weinberger, "Economic Aspects of Recreation," *Harvard Business Review* 15 (summer 1937): 448–63.

3. Warren Susman, "The New Landscape," in *Culture and Commitment, 1929–1945* (New York: Braziller, 1973), 46–56. For histories of American tourism, see Earl Pomeroy, *In Search of the Golden West: The Tourist in Western America* (New York: Knopf, 1957); John Jakle, *The Tourist: Travel in Twentieth Century America* (Lincoln: University of Nebraska Press, 1985); and Hal Rothman, *Devil's Bargains: Tourism in the Twentieth Century American West* (Lawrence: University of Kansas Press, 1998).

4. Other important developments in the making of mass tourism during the first half of the twentieth century were related to transportation: the building of better roads, the organization of an interstate highway system, the production of inexpensive, durable automobiles, the establishment of roadside tourist camps and other forms of low-cost lodging, the reduction in rail costs, and the establishment of long-distance bus service. See James J. Flink, *The Automobile Age* (Cambridge: MIT Press, 1990); and Warren Belasco, *Americans on the Road: From Autocamp to Motel, 1910–1945* (Cambridge: MIT Press, 1979).

5. For data on paid vacations for white-collar worker at the turn of the century, see Jurgen Kocka, *White Collar Workers in America, 1890–1940* (London: Sages, 1980). For examples of tourism promotion during the nineteenth century, see Dona Brown, *Inventing New England: Regional Tourism in the Nineteenth Century* (Washington, D.C.: Smithsonian Institution Press, 1995); and William Irwin, *The New Niagara: Tourism, Technology, and the Landscape of Niagara Falls, 1776–1917* (University Park: Pennsylvania State University Press, 1996).

6. Robert Lynd and Helen Merrell Lynd, *Middletown: A Study in Modern American Culture* (New York: Harcourt, Brace, and Jovanovich, 1929), 261.

7. "Vacations with Pay," *Monthly Labor Review*, August 1938, 272; David Roediger and Philip Foner, *Our Own Time: A History of American Labor and the Working Day* (New York: Verso, 1989); Benjamin Hunnicutt, *Work without End: Abandoning Shorter Hours for the Right to Work* (Philadelphia: Temple University Press, 1988); and Alexan-

der Keyssar, *Out of Work: The First Century of Unemployment in Massachusetts* (New York: Cambridge, 1986). Throughout this essay, I will use the terms *salaried, white collar,* and *middle class* interchangeably unless specifically indicated otherwise. I will use *wage earning, blue collar, manual, hourly,* and *working class* interchangeably as well. This latter group does not include agricultural workers or those in domestic service.

8. Charles Hatfield quoted in House Committee on Interstate and Foreign Commerce, *Bureau of Foreign and Domestic Commerce Travel Division,* 71st Cong., 3d Sess., January 23, 1931, 35, 36. For more on the "strenuous life," see Theodore Roosevelt, "The Strenuous Life," in *The Works of Theodore Roosevelt,* vol. 15 (New York: Scribners, 1926), 267–81; Peter Schmitt, *Back to Nature: The Arcadian Myth in Urban America* (rpt., Baltimore: Johns Hopkins University Press, 1990), 11–14; and Roderick Nash, *Wilderness and the American Mind* (New Haven: Yale University Press, 1982), 150–51.

9. For further examples of this line of thought, see the abundant personnel management literature of the period, including Lee K. Frankel and Alexander Fleisher, *The Human Factor in History* (New York: Macmillan, 1920), 131; Ordway Tead and Henry C. Metcalf, *Personnel Administration: Its Principles and Practice* (New York: McGraw Hill, 1920), 76–77; and Daniel Bloomfield, *Vacation Principles and Practices for Persons of Responsibility: An Appraisal of Policy* (New York: American Management Association, 1926). The Bureau of Labor Statistics also indicated that 95 percent of salaried workers received vacations with pay by 1937 ("Vacations with Pay," 272).

10. *Nation,* September 5, 1928, 215. In an extensive survey, Charles Mills found that only eighty-three companies nationwide provided vacations with pay to their hourly workers. See his *Vacations for Industrial Workers* (New York: Ronald Press, 1927), 272. Also see "Vacations with Pay," 271–73. Some of the data on paid vacations is derived from information gathered by Donna Allen in *Fringe Benefits: Wages or Social Obligations?* (Ithaca, N.Y.: Cornell University Press, 1964), 66. Before 1920, a significant number of wage earners covered by paid vacation plans were women, many of whom worked in the retail and textile trades—a testimony to the gendered assumption of the period that women needed protection from overwork.

11. Herman Feldman, *The Regularization of Employment* (New York: Harper and Bros., 1925), 245; Mills, *Vacations for Industrial Workers,* 269. Examples of these articles and studies include "Factory Vacations That Help Instead of Hinder," *Factory, the Magazine of Management* 32 (1924): 829–30; F. I. Charles, "Can a Business Shut Down for Vacation?" *System* 43 (1923): 593; Meyer Bloomfield and Daniel Bloomfield, *Employee Vacation Plans* (Boston: Bloomfield's Labor Digest, 1923); Metropolitan Life Insurance Company, *Vacations for Industrial Workers* (New York, 1930); and National Industrial Conference Board, *Service Letter on Industrial Relations,* January 5, 1929.

12. General Electric Company, *Manual for Employees* (1926), 23; "Vacations with Pay," 271–73.

13. National Industrial Conference Board, *Vacations with Pay for Wage Earners* (1935), 3, 10–11; Eleanor Davis, *Recent Trends in Vacation Policies for Wage Earners* (Princeton, N.J.: Industrial Relations Section, Princeton University, 1935); "Vacations with Pay," 269–74; "Vacation Policies," *Forbes,* May 15, 1935, 20.

14. "Vacations with Pay," 269; Charles E. Payne, "Trends in Company Vacation Policy," *Studies in Personnel Policy* 21 (April 1940): 3; Bureau of Labor Statistics, *Vacation and Holiday Provisions in Union Agreements, January 1943,* bulletin no. 743 (Washington, D.C.: GPO), 1; and Albert K. Dawson, "Vacation Market Is Made Up of 30 Million Wage Earners," *Domestic Commerce,* August 1946, 57.

15. In the face of unionization efforts by the Steel Workers Organizing Committee, Inland Steel offered paid vacations to its 10,326 wage-earning personnel in 1935. See Inland Steel, *Annual Report,* 1936, 5; "Vacations with Pay Offered to 200,000," *Steel,* May 18, 1936, 16; "Weirton Employee Vacation Plan," *Iron Age,* June 4, 1936, 78; "Vacations with Pay for Employees," *Bethlehem Review,* July 3,1936, 4; "Lukens Optional Vacation Plan," July 30, 1936, Lukens Steel Company Records, box 2037, Hagley Museum and Library, Wilmington, Del. For more on the SWOC campaign and the steel industry's response, see Irving Bernstein, *The Turbulent Years* (Boston: Houghton, Mifflin, 1969), 432–98; and for collective bargaining in the steel industry over paid vacations, "Vacations with Pay in Union Agreements," *Monthly Labor Review,* November 1940, 1070–71.

16. National Industrial Conference Board, "Vacations-with-Pay Plans for Wage Earners," *Conference Board Information Services,* Domestic Affairs Series Memorandum no. 56 (New York: National Industrial Conference Board, 1937), 1.

17. "Excerpt from Dye Works Council Meeting February 19, 1936," Records of E. I. du Pont de Nemours and Co., series 2, part 2, box 22, file 9, Hagley Museum and Library.

18. American Federation of Labor, "Vacations," in *History, Encyclopedia, and Reference Book,* vol. 3, part 3 (rpt., Westport, Conn.: Greenwood Press, 1977), 2477.

19. Millard Lampell, Lee Hays, and Pete Seeger, "Talking Union" (1941).

20. United States Emergency Board, *Report to the President by the Emergency Board,* November 5, 1941, 4–7, 79; "Non-Ops Settle Labor Controversy," *Railway Age,* December 20, 1941, 1055; Payne, "Trends in Personnel Policy," *Studies,* 3; Bureau of Labor Statistics, *Vacation and Holiday Provisions in Union Agreements,* 1; Dawson, "Vacations Are Up," 57. For other examples of working-class consumer ideology and its relationship to the making of mass cultural norms, see Lizabeth Cohen, *Making a New Deal: Industrial Workers in Chicago, 1919–1939* (New York: Cambridge, 1990), especially chap. 4, and Lawrence B. Glickman, *A Living Wage: American Workers and the Making of Consumer Society* (Ithaca, N.Y.: Cornell University Press, 1997).

21. The quotation is from Mills, *Vacations for Industrial Workers,* 67. Another writer, William S. Hobbes, commented, "True, the workingman may abuse his privilege in the use he puts of his vacation." He, however, believed those times to be rare. In fact, he suggested that it was the lack of leisure for the workingman that was the cause of labor unrest ("Employees' Vacation as an Asset," *Power,* August 14, 1928, 270). The idea that the desire to travel was an inherent characteristic of humanity was a consistent theme in the explanations for the rise of tourism, appearing in popular articles, academic analyses, congressional reports, and the like. See Don Francisco, "Why People Leave Home," *Nation's Business,* May 1929, 66; and Joe H. Thompson, *Tourism— as an Industry* (Denver: Conoco Travel Bureau, 1938), 16. For a discussion of working-class interest in owning and building their own homes, see Olivier Zunz, *The Changing Face of Inequality: Urbanization, Industrial Development, and Immigrants in Detroit, 1880–1920* (Chicago: University of Chicago Press, 1982), 171–76.

22. Don Thomas, "What a Visitor Means to Southern California," 1930, box 38, file 9, Greater Los Angeles Visitors and Convention Bureau Collection, Urban Archive Center, California State University, Northridge, Northridge, Calif. (hereafter referred to as GLAVCB Collection).

23. Other important members of the maturing tourism promotional network at this time were the auto-related travel institutions, the American Automobile Association and oil company travel bureaus. Railroads continued to spend a great deal of

money on advertising during the interwar period, but as a mode of recreational transportation, it was rapidly losing favor.

24. "Travel—Builder of International Goodwill," 1940, box 45, file 7, GLAVCB Collection.

25. For examples of pamphlets and exhibits produced for fairs and expositions, see Delancey M. Ellis, *New York at the Louisiana Purchase Exposition* (Albany: J. B. Lyon, 1907); and T. G. Daniells, *California: Its Products, Resources, Industries, and Attractions: What It Offers the Immigrant, Homeseeker, Investor, and Tourist* (Sacramento: Louisiana Purchase Exposition Commission, 1904).

26. Don E. Mowry, *Community Advertising: How to Advertise the Community Where You Live* (Madison: Cantwell Press, 1924); Alderson Wroe, *Advertising for Community Promotion* (Washington, D.C.: GPO, 1928).

27. Quotation is from "How Tourists 'Cushioned' Shock of 1930 Business Depression," January 1931, box 1, file 2, GLAVCB Collection; "Why Advertise Southern California," 1921, box 31, file 12, GLAVCB Collection; "All-Year Club History," box 58, file 15, GLAVCB Collection; Californians, Inc., *What's Ahead for San Francisco,* in James Duvall Phelan Papers, carton 20, file "Californians, Inc.," Bancroft Library, University of California, Berkeley.

28. "That's Our Story—and We Stick to It!" *Western Advertising,* April 1933, 26; Don Thomas, "In Competition for American Tourists and Capital," *California Journal of Development,* April 1930, 10–11, 28–29; Californians, Inc., *What's Ahead for San Francisco.* For a discussion of the "See America First" idea and the movement surrounding it, Marguerite S. Shaffer, "See America First: Tourism and National Identity, 1905–1930," Ph.D. diss., Harvard University, 1994.

29. Thomas's comments appear in Douglas G. McPhee, "Needed: Depression Insurance," *Western Advertising,* October 1, 1931, 66. See Thomas, "You've Got to Have the Figures," *Western Advertising,* September 5, 1929, 70; "Smoke Stacks Rather Than Tourists," *Printers' Ink,* February 17, 1927, 144; and "Survey Reveals New Community Facts," *Western Advertising and Business,* September 5, 1929, 60, 127. For critiques of tourism as a tool of economic development, see G. Young, *Tourism: Blessing or Blight* (Harmondsworth: Penguin, 1973); and E. de Kadt, *Tourism: Passport to Development?* (New York: Oxford University Press, 1979).

30. "Take a Drive through Scenic New York State," *Selling New York State to the Nation,* 1939, advertising portfolio in the New York State Archives; Ross Kearney, "Stories of Steeptown: The Campaigns of Californians, Inc.," *San Francisco News Letter and Wasp,* July 30, 1937; All-Year Club, "Fun Map," *Saturday Evening Post,* February 20, 1937, 57; Californians, Inc., "Take Two Weeks Out of Life—for Really Living," *Saturday Evening Post,* March 7, 1931, 100; Kay Winn, "How and Why States Advertise," *Advertising and Selling,* September 24, 1936, 25–26, 32, 34.

31. Thomas, "In Competition," 10–11, 28–29. Quotation is from "A New 'Package' to Sell a Rich New Market!" April 1930, box 1 file, 2, GLAVCB Collection.

32. Don Thomas to Horace Albright, June 7, 1932, Record Group 79, Central Classified Files, 1907–1949, General Files, box 176, file "All-Year Club," National Park Service Records, National Archives and Records Administration, College Park, Md. By the late thirties, entire guidebooks geared to budget travelers, teaching them how to take inexpensive vacations, were being offered by publishers. see for example, Horace Coon, *101 Vacations Costing from $25 to $250: A Budgeted Guide for Holiday Spending* (New York: Doubleday, Doran, 1940); and Robert Spiers Benjamin, *How to Travel on Little Money* (Reader Mail, Inc., 1939).

33. All-Year Club, *New Money*, 31. At the time, packaged tours were mostly available only to wealthier tourists.

34. "Let a Thrilling Pacific Coast Vacation Fit You for the Work Ahead," *Saturday Evening Post*, March 21, 1931, 79–82; "Bake Out Your Troubles," *Saturday Evening Post*, December 17, 1932, 53; "Have You Been Snapping at People?" *Saturday Evening Post*, January 18, 1941, 69.

35. Michael Schudson, "Advertising as Capitalist Realism," in *Advertising, the Uneasy Persuasion* (New York: Basic Books, 1984), chap. 7.

36. For more on the history of conservation, preservation, national parks, and railroads see Samuel P. Hays, *Conservation and the Gospel of Efficiency: The Progressive Conservation Movement, 1890–1920* (Cambridge: Harvard University Press, 1959); Nash, *Wilderness and American Mind*; Donald C. Swain, *Wilderness Defender: Horace M. Albright and Conservation* (Chicago: University of Chicago Press, 1969); Alfred Runte, *National Parks: The American Experience*, 2d ed. (Lincoln: University of Nebraska Press, 1987); Hal Rothman, *America's National Monuments: The Politics of Preservation* (Lawrence: University Press of Kansas Press, 1989); and Richard West Sellars, *Preserving Nature in the National Parks* (New Haven: Yale University Press, 1997). Also see the *Report of the Director of the National Parks Service* for the years 1917 to 1920. National park data is from Bureau of the Census, *Historical Statistics of the United States, Colonial Times to 1970* (Washington, D.C.: GPO, 1976), 396.

37. Franklin Delano Roosevelt, "Speech at Two Medicine Chalet, Glacier National Park, August 5, 1934," reprinted in Edgar B. Nixon, *Franklin D. Roosevelt and Conservation, 1911–1945*, vol. 1 (Hyde Park, N.Y.: General Services Administration, National Archives and Records Service, Franklin D. Roosevelt Library, 1957), 333. For more on "National Parks Year," see Arno B. Cammerer, "National Park Service," in *Report of the Secretary of the Interior, 1935* (Washington, D.C.: GPO, 1935), 179–80. For the reorganization of the National Park Service, see Swain, "The National Park Service and the New Deal, 1933–1940," *Pacific Historical Review* 4 (August 1972): 312–32; and Swain, "Harold Ickes, Horace Albright, and the Hundred Days," *Pacific Historical Review* 34 (1965): 455–65.

38. See the sections on promotion and publicity in the *Reports of the Director of the National Park Service* for the 1930s; Swain, "National Park Service," 312–32.

39. Leonidas Dyer in House Committee on Interstate and Foreign Commerce, *Bureau of Foreign and Domestic Commerce Travel Division*, 71st Cong., 3d Sess., January 23, 1931, 2, and Olger Burtness on p. 41. Other congressional hearings on travel promotion include House Committee on Interstate and Foreign Commerce, *Bureau of Foreign and Domestic Commerce Travel Division*, 71st Cong., 3d Sess., January 23, 1931; Senate Committee on Commerce, *United States Travel Commission*, 74th Cong., 1st Sess., May 13, 1935; House Subcommittee on Interstate and Foreign Commerce, *Tourist Travel Division*, 74th Cong., 1st Sess., June 14, 1935; House Subcommittee on Interstate and Foreign Commerce, *National Travel Board*, 76th Cong., 1st Sess., March 28, 1939. Data on foreign travel bureaus appears in "Travel Promotion Potentialities," *Advertising and Selling*, December 19, 1935, 44.

40. For a history of the *American Guide Series*, see Monty Noam Penkower, *The Federal Writers' Project: A Study in Government Patronage of the Arts* (Urbana: University of Illinois Press, 1977). Katharine Kellock, the editor of the touring section of the *American Guide Series*, also wrote radio scripts for the United States Travel Bureau promoting the use of the guides as an aid for recreational travel. Katharine A. Kellock to Oscar Chapman, July 15, 1939, RG 48, Department of Interior Records, series 768, box 34, file "Travel Bureau," NARA.

41. See Department of Interior Records, series 749, box 3789, file "United States Travel Bureau—Correspondence," NARA. Examples of materials published by the U.S. Travel Bureau include *Directory of Travel Agencies in the United States* (Washington, D.C., 1938); *A Directory of Negro Hotels and Guest Houses* (Washington, D.C.: Department of Interior, 1941; as well as the monthlies *Calendar of Events, Official Bulletin, Travel West, Eastern Travel Today,* and *Travel Newsletter.*

42. Michael Young, "The March of the States," box 13, file "Tourist Bureau," Department of Interior Records, NARA; W. Bruce MacNamee, "Travel Looks Ahead to Another Big Year," *New York Times,* December 19, 1940.

43. "American Express Official Sees Travel Boom," *United States Travel Bureau Official Bulletin,* December 25, 1939, 3.

44. Ruth Bryan Rhode, "Why a Federal Travel Bureau?" *Travel and Recreation News Letter,* December 5, 1939, 3.

45. United States Travel Bureau, *Official Bulletin,* July–August 1940, 1.

46. The data on the amount spent by tourists during the 1920s and 1930s is unreliable, but most analysts asserted that domestic tourism was in the two- to four-billion-dollar range in 1929 and in the five- to six-billion-dollar range in 1941. The lowest figures were reported by Julius Weinberger in "Economic Aspects of Recreation," 448–62, and the highest by the United States Travel Bureau. Also see Charles Frederick Carter, "Three Billion Dollars Go Touring," *Nation's Business,* June 1929, 45–47; "American Tourism Heads for Top," *Business Week,* May 18, 1940, 20, 22–24; "Travel's Vital New Job during and after the War," October 14, 1941, box 39, file 3, GLAVCB Collection; "National Parks, Monuments, and Allied Areas—Number, Area, and Visits: 1850–1970," in Bureau of the Census, *Historical Statistics of the United States,* 396; "Bird's Eye View of Community Activity," *Western Advertising,* November 5, 1941, 32; "This Is 'Travel America Year,'—Billions of Miles, Millions of Dollars," *National Petroleum News,* June 19, 1940, 19–31; "Six Billion Dollar Travel Budget Creates Unique Marketing Program," *Sales Management,* June 15, 1940, 42–54; California State Chamber of Commerce, Research Department, *Tourist Visitors and Their Expenditures in California, 1928–1952,* Economic Survey Series, no. 12 (1953–54); "Florida Having Its Greatest Tourist Season," *United States Travel Bureau Official Bulletin,* March–April 1941, 5; Don Thomas quotation appears in "Travel's Vital New Job," GLAVCB Collection.

47. For a more detailed analysis of the social reproduction of distinction in the context of France, see Pierre Bourdieu, *Distinction: A Social Critique of the Judgement of Taste,* trans. Richard Nice (Cambridge: Harvard University Press, 1984). For works that treat pre–World War II consumer and mass culture as homogeneous, see Stuart Ewen, *Captains of Consciousness: Advertising and the Social Roots of Consumer Culture* (New York: McGraw-Hill, 1976); and William Leach, *Land of Desire: Merchants, Power, and the Rise of a New American Culture* (New York: Pantheon, 1993). For a discussion and critique of the utopian elements of mass culture, see Frederic Jameson, "Reification and Utopia in Mass Culture," *Social Text* 1 (1979): 130–48.

Strength through Joy

Tourism and National Integration in the Third Reich

"Now you can travel too!" exclaims a poster from the Nazi leisure-time and tourism agency, Strength through Joy (Kraft durch Freude, or KdF). Using the familiar form of "you" *(du)*, the poster depicts handsome, informally but presentably dressed figures, gazing serenely ahead as their cruise ship glides through the Norwegian fjords. Some of them sport workingmen's caps. The passengers seem relaxed, content in the knowledge that the Third Reich has presented them a once-unimaginable opportunity. No longer would travel to distant shores be the privilege of the well-to-do, the poster claims, for Strength through Joy was now extending the luxury of tourism to the working masses. To be sure, the "Nordic" features of the poster's subjects and setting claim our attention: They exemplify the regime's politicization of all manner of cultural practices toward its foremost aim, the creation of an enlarged, racially purified "national community" (*Volksgemeinschaft*). Nonetheless, the KdF advertisement reveals the Third Reich's equally pronounced obsession with ending regional, religious, and especially class conflict. In the Nazi "national community," the social boundaries that internally divided Germany would dissolve, and tourism would serve as a vehicle for achieving that goal.[1]

Attempting to integrate those whom the regime perceived as being the most alienated from the social order, namely manual wage laborers, Strength through Joy's recreational and vacation programs became the Third Reich's most ingenious means of realizing the national community. The Nazi leadership proposed to give workers at least the semblance of well-being and status enhancement by expanding their leisure-time activities to middle- and upper-class practices. The regime understood that repression alone, however effective in destroying the organizations of the Left, would not secure the plebiscitary consent that the regime unceasingly demanded. Paradoxically, however, the regime could ill afford to give free rein to a market-based sphere of leisure and consumption as a means of social integration, nor could it afford wage

"Now you can travel too!" A Strength through Joy poster
shows workers on their vacation cruise. (Bundesarchiv
Koblenz, poster number 3/18/29. Reproduced with the
archive's permission.)

increases sufficient to allow workers to participate in such a sphere. Although
some consumer and leisure-time products industries, notably radio manufacture, expanded before the outbreak of war in 1939, rearmament distorted the
Reich's economy.[2] Nevertheless, the task of revitalizing the nation could not
rely solely on appeals to discipline, obedience, and sacrifice. The Third Reich
also had to convince its less privileged citizens that it would meet their expec-

tations of a better life, an obligation that coexisted uneasily with the regime's admonitions of austerity.

Implicit in Strength through Joy's recreational offerings was the determination to soften the contradiction between entitlement and sacrifice, present expectations and delayed gratification. By providing low-cost travel, recreation, and entertainment as a substitute for higher wages and impermissible levels of consumption, the functionaries of Strength through Joy and its parent organization, the German Labor Front (Deutsche Arbeitsfront, or DAF), hoped that workers would achieve an improved standard of "living" (Lebensstandard) without wage increases. According to the Labor Front's leader, Robert Ley, the affordability of leisure-time activities, package tours, and cultural events would break the endless demand for higher wages while opening the door to hitherto inaccessible pleasures.[3] Moreover, Strength through Joy insisted on the compatibility of a higher standard of living and rearmament. Bettering the lives of workers, especially those in war-related industries, would engender support for undoing the Treaty of Versailles and acquiring "living space" (Lebensraum). Strength through Joy's leaders expected that their recreational activities and vacation packages would bring workers physical and psychological regeneration away from the numbing routine of the factory, and that renewal would raise productivity after workers returned to the job. Finally, territorial expansion would produce the empire of the future; one that would not only subordinate or eliminate racial "undesirables," but also permanently guarantee the well-being of Germans upon which domestic harmony depended. Although Strength through Joy appears tangential to the Nazi regime's racism and expansionism, it became intertwined with the imperatives of empire, both as a mechanism for nationalizing the masses and as the exemplar of rewards for racially acceptable Germans that the greater German Reich would permanently secure.[4]

FROM CLASS TO NATIONAL COMMUNITY: STRENGTH THROUGH JOY AND SOCIAL ENTITLEMENT

The German Labor Front launched "The National Socialist Community Strength through Joy" in November 1933, six months after the destruction of the Left and the "synchronization" (Gleichschaltung) of its numerous cultural and leisure-time clubs. The name of the new agency conveyed Ley's attempt to improve upon the model suggested by the Italian Fascist "After Work" (Dopolavoro) organization. Instead of a conglomeration of occupational units that perpetuated social fragmentation and limited its activities to the hours following quitting time, Strength through Joy's "community" proposed to heal divisions and encompass the entirety of one's "creative life" (Schaf-

fensleben).[5] Strength through Joy meant to expand the opportunities for relaxation and cultural enrichment available to workers during both working hours and leisure time. With the intermittent financial support of business, it secured blocks of concert, museum, and theater tickets and extended instruction in a variety of activities, including sports such as horseback riding, sailing, and tennis that ordinarily only the wealthy could afford. Moreover, it sponsored adult education programs, once the preserve of the Left,[6] while subsidizing day outings, weekend excursions, ski trips, and most spectacularly, cruises. In 1937, the German Labor Front assumed the financing of the Volkswagen project, which raised Ley's prestige against that of his rivals in the Nazi party hierarchy and demonstrated the regime's tentative but genuine flirtation with consumerism as a means of social pacification. The head of Strength through Joy's Office for Travel, Hiking, and Vacations, Dr. Bodo Lafferentz, became the Labor Front's representative on the Volkswagen board. The "KdF-Wagen," the brainchild of Ferdinand Porsche, aimed to use the mass-production techniques of Ford and General Motors to mass produce an affordable automobile that would give the worker the possibility of experiencing nature, the countryside, and humanity.[7] Against the opinion of the German automobile industry, Hitler insisted that the purchase price of the Volkswagen should not exceed 990 RM, a sum that implicitly testified to the project's domestic political purposes.[8]

Defining itself as the "socialism of deed" against the sham version of the Left, the Nazi regime sought to lure the working class away from Marxist doctrines of proletarian internationalism and class struggle. In addition to building support for the regime, Nazi leaders believed that they could ease class tensions by making paid vacations the norm for workers, extending the duration of paid vacations already in place, and organizing leisure-time activities, including tourism.[9] Those practices would guarantee a quality of life that transcended the daily struggle for subsistence. Moreover, the distinctive working-class culture that the Left did much to sustain would disintegrate when wage earners obtained goods and services once solely accessible to the classes above them. Indeed Strength through Joy's programs, especially its vacation trips, proved attractive. By 1938, fifty-four million Germans, a number not much less than the nation's total population, had availed themselves of Strength through Joy's offerings. With a staff of nearly 140,000 that in the last prewar year mobilized 8.5 million tourists, Strength through Joy grew into the largest travel agency in Germany. Its international reputation became such that the German Labor Front earned several trophies from the International Olympic Committee in recognition of its efforts in fostering organized recreation.[10] To be sure, the coming of war forced the suspension of Strength through Joy's outings and vacation trips, for the Wehrmacht quickly appropriated the trains, ships, and busses once used to transport tourists. Yet sponsored recre-

ational and entertainment programs during the war in the apparently successful attempt to maintain morale among troops and civilians alike.[11]

Organized at the *Gau* (district) level, Strength through Joy offered packages ranging from one-day and weekend outings to sites of historical and cultural significance close to home, to vacation tours that lasted up to three
weeks. Negotiations with the German Railroad and, to an increasing extent,
with bus lines produced cut-rate fares that allowed Strength through Joy to
move "participants" between destinations below the actual cost of the service
provided.[12] In addition to its excursions to such well-known destinations as
the Rhine, the Black Forest, and the Bavarian Alps, Strength through Joy
encouraged travel to less-sought-out places, particularly in Germany's impov-
erished border regions, for it intended to promote economic development
while deepening the patriotism of tourists and local residents both. Strength
through Joy's district leaders never tired of emphasizing that such trips would
provide opportunities for their citizens, who were notorious for their local
and regional loyalties, to "get acquainted with" the beauty and conviviality of
other parts of the Reich. Its proponents championed Strength through Joy's
ability to combine the best traditions of working-class sociability, the richness
of experience arising from seeing the countryside, and the efficiency of modern tourism.[13] In the last year and a half before the war, Strength through Joy
offered travel packages to the newly annexed territories of Austria and the
Sudetenland, eager to capitalize on the regime's expansionism.

Domestic tourism, however, proved less of a showpiece than Strength
through Joy's abroad to Norway, Greece, Italy, Yugoslavia, and Portugal,
especially the Portuguese island of Madeira, a vacation spot long associated
with the British leisured classes. As floating advertisements for the regime's
alleged democratization of tourism, Strength through Joy's ships partially
eliminated the class stratification of commercial luxury liners by removing the
physical barriers between decks and transforming some staterooms into quarters that could accommodate more persons. Because Portugal and Italy in particular maintained friendly relations with the Reich, German tourists disembarked to performances of fascist solidarity from welcoming compatriots and
partied on board with invited foreign guests, who presumably stood in awe of
the scale and generosity of the Third Reich's social policy. The cruises served
yet another important function, that of reconnecting Germans living in
"colonies" abroad with their homeland. Expatriates frequently served as tour
guides in Strength through Joy's ports of call, and they took part in the festivities staged for Strength through Joy "participants."[14] By spring 1939, Strength
through Joy managed twelve cruise ships, ten of them chartered or purchased
from private shipping firms. The two others, the *Wilhelm Gustloff* and the
Robert Ley, were built especially for Strength through Joy, for constructing
"classless" cruise ships from scratch proved more cost-effective than over-

hauling older ships that, despite their refitting, retained signs of their former segmentation. In interviews with the press, Ley projected a fleet of twenty ships, as well as an enlarged harbor at Bremen complete with a sizable hotel and an entertainment center for tourists waiting to disembark. Strength through Joy's public relations blitz that accompanied the maiden voyage of the *Robert Ley* not only included press releases with photos of the führer socializing pleasantly with the ship's passengers, but also brochures describing such appointments as a two-story theater, five thousand square meters of deck space, a gymnasium, and comfortable cabins. Like the venerable luxury liner that catered to the wealthy, the *Robert Ley* emerged as the *Bremen* of the working class, now available to "Volk comrades" of modest means.[15] In fact, the cruises brought Strength through Joy considerable international attention, for by comparison with attempts to organize leisure in other nations, Strength through Joy's tourism appeared to be the most ambitious state-sponsored attempt yet to make that practice available to the lower orders.[16]

To add to its investment in cruises, Strength through Joy strove to capitalize on the lure of beaches as places of relaxation, health, and spatial removal from daily routine by making seaside vacations accessible to workers. In 1936, it commissioned the construction of a twenty-thousand-bed resort at Prora between Sassnitz and Binz on Rügen, an island off the Pomeranian coast. A complex that combined the megalomania typical of Nazi architecture with the imperatives of mass tourism, Prora was merely the first of five such projects planned for the Baltic and North seacoasts. Although Strength through Joy continued the practice that under the Weimar Republic had been the preserve of the Left, establishing working-class vacation hostels, Prora vastly exceeded such residences in scale and appointments in its effort to reproduce the amenities of upper-class spas. Scheduled to open in spring 1940, the Rügen complex incorporated a mammoth entertainment center, cafes, cinemas, billiard rooms, bowling alleys, parking garages for the Volkswagens of vacationers, and a restaurant atop an eighty-five-meter-high structure that dwarfed the Berlin radio tower. Moreover, it included an enclosed, heated swimming pool that would allow the resort to stay open from spring until late fall. Measuring forty by one hundred meters, it came fitted with a wave-making machine. Descriptions of the guest quarters at the resort exposed the paradox of Nazi leisure-time policy; the simultaneous evocation of sacrifice and abundance. Described as "simple but modern," each room would have such creature comforts as hot and cold running water, central heating, closets, and some upholstered furniture. Every room in the five-kilometer complex would have a view of the sea. For a mere twenty marks, claimed Ley, working-class families could enjoy a week's vacation at the beach.[17] Prora not only typified Strength through Joy's determination to lift workers above the narrow class-based horizons of neighborhood and shop floor, it also testified to the regime's ongoing project of eliminating the attractions of "Marxism."

In fact, Strength through Joy's bureaucracy penetrated the workplace itself, restructuring the workplace not only to defuse it as a site of class conflict, but also to overcome the divide between work and leisure. Its office, Beauty of Work (Schönheit der Arbeit), originally under Albert Speer's direction, stressed the development of a healthier and more agreeable work environment. Although managers often resisted assuming the costs associated with plant improvements, Beauty of Work pushed for structural modifications, such as good lighting, better sanitation, ventilation, and windows, along with aesthetic melioration, such as the planting of lawns and flowers, and the construction of recreation rooms and sport facilities. Its agenda soon extended to nutrition programs for employees. In 1938, Beauty through Work launched a campaign on behalf of hot midday meals that promoted the benefits of good digestion and lunchtime camaraderie. The salubrious effect of such improvements on workers accorded with the Nazi vision of German families sustained by male breadwinners and devoted housewives, however much that ideal did not correspond to reality.[18] Beauty of Work reforms would carry over from the shop floor to the home, "for a man who [was] accustomed to an attractive workplace [would] only feel comfortable in a clean, attractive abode."[19] In addition, Strength through Joy sponsored cultural events for the workplace, including concerts and exhibits featuring the works of contemporary German artists that it arranged in partnership with the Reich Chamber of the Visual Arts. Its adult education courses, also promoted and organized through the workplace, afforded the chance to learn a foreign language, play a musical instrument, take painting lessons, and enjoy museums, as well as absorb Nazi theories of race and geopolitics. Strength through Joy programs intended not merely to render manual labor a less alienating and degrading experience, they also strove to inculcate an appreciation for, and pride in, Germany's cultural and racial superiority. The enjoyment of the nation's "cultural heritage" *(kulturelle Güter)* would no longer be restricted to the rich.[20]

The name *Strength through Joy* corresponded to the Third Reich's broadest objectives. However disparate its programs, Strength through Joy signified the interpenetration of foreign and domestic policy, social pacification and racially grounded expansionism. To raise productivity ("strength"), Strength through Joy combined Taylorist management theory and industrial psychology so as to reward individual achievement as a substitute for collective bargaining and industry-wide wage agreements. Strength through Joy services often became rewards, either for good performance or for the self-discipline that it took to save for a vacation.[21] Moreover, the aims of Strength through

Joy as a leisure-time organization broadly conformed to those arising from a discussion that occurred continuously throughout the industrialized world, including the Soviet Union, during the twenties and thirties: How should social policy break the monotony of factory work, the inevitable consequence of industrial rationalization, without sacrificing work discipline or encouraging idleness? Social engineers conceived of vacations as a reward for work and as an opportunity for purchasing consumer goods, including vacation packages themselves. Most important, vacations as discrete periods of leisure became a way to pacify working people while resisting the attempts of the Left to secure a shorter workday.[22]

For the Nazis, however, Strength through Joy was to serve a more lethal end: the racial reorganization and domination of the continent. Enhanced productivity and technocratic efficiency, after all, merged with preparations for aggressive warfare. Brief periods of regeneration for industrial workers were a small price to pay given the scale of the Nazi task, and the regime prodded industry to extend paid vacations, especially to workers under the age of eighteen, to the point where Germany led other industrialized countries in that deceptively progressive practice.[23] Strength through Joy's brochures and monthly programs emphasized the productivist and expansionist purposes behind the regime's vacation policy. Its cruises conveniently crossed paths with German battleships and strategic redoubts such as Helgoland and Gibraltar, thus allowing their passengers to gaze at the Reich's military power close up.[24] Its ships frequently docked at ports of call together. In Italy, Portugal, and Greece, nations that could not compete with Germany economically, tourists disembarked en masse both to advertise the regime's "enlightened" and "democratic" social policy and to dominate the foreign environment.[25] Strength through Joy tours with their repeated calls for discipline and subordination to tour leaders, not to mention the swastika-draped ceremonies that opened each morning on the cruise ships, accorded smoothly with the regimented, self-sacrificing image of the *Volksgemeinschaft*. Words from the führer championed the refreshment afforded by leisure time and tourism, for both would strengthen the backbone of the *Volk*. And only a *Volk* with fortified nerves would be up to the tasks facing the nation.[26]

Nevertheless, satisfying the material and status needs of the working class ("joy") was necessary to alleviate the antagonism among classes, for in the Nazi view, social conflict had "prevented" victory in World War I, undermined the Hohenzollern empire, and expedited the spread of "Marxism." Leisure time and recreation programs comprised but a part of the larger consumerist and cultural agenda that Strength through Joy envisioned for the future. Strength through Joy's planning embraced affordable single-family homes in suburban settings, enhanced social insurance benefits, as well as the Volkswagen—the fusion of German engineering and Fordism that would propel workers into the arms of the system.[27] The Third Reich was prescient enough to recognize that relocation and mobility, combined with the elimination of want, could dissolve the working-class neighborhoods that bred class identity, and during the war Ley frequently proclaimed the superiority of Nazi social programs over those of Germany's enemies. The Beveridge Report that would lay foundations for the British welfare state deserved admiration, admitted Ley in 1942. Yet because Beveridge's blueprint provided cushions for the unemployed, rather than envisioning the elimination of unemployment altogether, Ley claimed, it could not rival the Reich's progressive social agenda. The New Deal in America, in his view, was but a sham, for it elevated the power of Jewish industrialists and bankers while leaving poverty untouched. Thus it produced only an oxymoron, "a planned economy without real planning."[28]

Strength through Joy infused its rewards for enhanced productivity with racial significance. Taken together, Strength through Joy's diverse attempts to incorporate the working class in the *Volksgemeinschaft* comprised badges of distinction that would separate workers from the growing number of racial "inferiors," who toiled so that Germans could expect a future of spiritual and material comfort. The regime's designated *Untermenschen* remained backward, unclean, diseased, and devastated from overwork, while Nazism presented an image of German workers, who were clean, efficient, modern, and refreshed by periodic respites. Beauty of Work functionaries insisted that good china and silverware should be used at midday meals in the workplace so that workers would learn the virtues of good table manners and civilized conversation with their colleagues.[29] Regenerating body and soul through recreation, cultural outings, travel, and a sanitized workplace clashed sharply with the primitive, filthy, and brutal working conditions—not to mention elimination—that would become the lot of the conquered peoples, particularly from Eastern Europe and the Soviet Union.[30]

Strength through Joy's emphasis on regeneration was hardly novel. Personal health as the key to a healthy nation figured prominently in the organized recreation of the Weimar period. What was new was Strength through Joy's marriage of health, both personal and collective, to the Nazi regime's vicious, racialist expansionism. The Volkswagen was to be large enough to accommodate "child-rich" families, a stimulus to the population growth that the regime believed would enable racial domination. Tourism, with its potential for magnifying cultural difference and reinforcing feelings of national solidarity and racial superiority, served a similar purpose for the Third Reich, as intelligence reports and Strength through Joy's vacation brochures consistently noted. Announcements of trips to East Prussia rarely missed an opportunity to trumpet that region's significance to the German "civilizing" of the Slavic lands during the Middle Ages or to the invalidity of Germany's postwar eastern boundaries that separated East Prussia from the Reich.[31] Yet even tours to the friendly nations of Italy and Portugal encouraged German travelers to pity the poverty and squalor that they found in Naples, Palermo, and Lisbon and praise the higher standard of living that the Third Reich instituted at home. As Ley himself envisioned, workers would come to appreciate "racial" differences only if they observed them firsthand.[32]

Strength through Joy did not simply exclude racially "unworthy" workers from its material promises. Rather, consonant with the regime that spawned it, Strength through Joy surmised that a permanent improvement in the lifestyles of workers, or more precisely, the elevation of working-class lives to mimic those of the middle classes, would occur only through the creation of an autarkic continental empire that provided raw materials, "living space," and labor to support the Reich's racially defined millennial paradise. The obvious economic conflict between "guns" and "butter" that intruded even before war broke out,[33] the tension between demanding sacrifice and freezing wages while promising an improvement in the standard of living, would ultimately dissolve in successful conquest. "The source of all our social misery," claimed Ley, "lies above all in the fact that we have too little space. We are a Volk without space."[34] Peaceful competition in the international market place was no option, a conclusion that the Nazi leadership drew from witnessing the crisis-ridden global economy of the twenties. Although deserving criticism for his reduction of Nazism to modernization[35]—*modernization* hardly captures the uniquely racist dynamism of the Third Reich—Rainer Zitelmann convincingly shows how deeply Hitler's own conception of America influenced his thinking. If consumption in America depended far less on state intervention than the Nazis planned, America nonetheless represented a self-sufficient economic powerhouse ensconced between two oceans; one with a vast internal market, rich natural resources, and workers pacified with mass-produced commodities such as the automobile, all of which resulted from the westward expansion of Europeans at the expense of indigenous peoples.[36] What Weimar rationalization could not accomplish within the constraints of Versailles and a collapsing international economy, the Third Reich *would* achieve, especially through dirigism, invasion, and the racial reconfiguration of the East. The subjugation of Poles, Russians, and particularly the Jews would underwrite Germany's harmonious "national community."

Because Strength through Joy defined itself root and branch against the Left, its programs and publications served as vehicles for the circulation of Nazism's lethal fusion of antisocialism and anti-Semitism. In Nazi ideology, the Jew served as a symbol of the pernicious aspects of international capitalism, but the Jew as "Marxist" emerged as the most powerful impulse behind the Third Reich's anti-Jewish measures before 1939 and the Final Solution afterward.[37] "Marxist" internationalism and dialectical materialism grounded in the theory of class struggle directly challenged the Nazi vision of a harmonious *Volksgemeinschaft*. Strength through Joy's monthly programs and annual reports added something more to the Jewish-Marxist equation, namely the claim that Marxism could not provide social entitlements and status improvement for workers, however much it claimed to advance their class interests. As the offspring of "an alien race," Marxism presupposed the permanent segregation, inferiority, and impoverishment of the working class. Moreover, the Jew inverted the virtues of cleanliness and order that KdF imparted to German workers as signifiers of their racial distinction. Strength through Joy's frequent references to workers as *die Schaffende* (creators) was no accident, for "creative" labor undertaken for the good of the "national community" contrasted with that which was parasitic, exploitative, and therefore Jewish.[38] In short, the Jew personified social and cultural disintegration, the subordination of Germany internationally, the material and biological collapse of Germany, and the destruction of living standards that Strength through Joy attributed to Bolshevism. As an ongoing demonstration of the Nazi regime's commitment to giving workers a better life, Strength through Joy would end the class divisions that "Jewish Marxism" implicitly championed.

THE NATIONAL COMMUNITY AND SELF-FULFILLMENT:
STRENGTH THROUGH JOY AND POPULAR CONSENT IN
THE THIRD REICH

In reality, Strength through Joy could not but fall short of its ambitious goal, a tautly synchronized *Volksgemeinschaft* brought to fruition by delivering leisure and culture to the masses. Security Service (Sicherheitsdienst, or SD) informers frequently acknowledged regionally based tensions among tourists, as well as between tour groups and their hosts. Heavily Catholic regions, in particular, appeared less than hospitable to Strength through Joy tours because of the unpopularity of the Nazi regime's attempts to undermine the social and cultural influence of the church. Such tensions became especially evident on the cruises, in which long days at sea magnified conflicts between groups of passengers already balkanized by the central mechanism of Strength through Joy travel, organization by district.[39] Moreover, Strength through Joy tourism attracted few "participants" from the countryside, despite the sensation its advertisements created, for vacations and leisured travel conformed little to the seasonal rhythms and cultural practices of agrarian life.[40]

More intractable still were the obstacles facing workers that precluded their purchase of such luxuries as travel, for well before the war lengthened workdays and exacted its privations, scarcity characterized working-class lives. To be sure, Strength through Joy *did* mobilize more workers than the work-

ing-class travel agencies that emerged during the Weimar Republic, thus lend-
ing substance to the Nazis' claim that they could improve workers' lives better
than the Left. On balance, however, the Nazi regime's promise to square the
circle of low wages and expanded social entitlements remained just that.[41]
When the average gross weekly wage hovered slightly above twenty-five
marks, many workers could not afford to buy Strength through Joy's vacation
trips despite their low cost compared to commercial offerings. Rather, they
confined themselves to the cheapest weekend or overnight excursions, or to
the entertainment evenings, such as plays, concerts, and variety shows. The
most talked about of the Strength through Joy programs, the cruises,
remained financially beyond the grasp for all but the highly skilled, best-paid,
and generally single, workers, or workers whose employers chartered space on
Strength through Joy's liners for company-sponsored outings. Gender distinctions and cultural inhibitions intervened as well: Because women workers
received less paid vacation than working-class men, their participation in
Strength through Joy trips correspondingly suffered. Moreover, even male
workers put more stock in improving the quality of their working lives than in
claiming "entitlements" such as vacation travel.[42]

Instead, urban salaried employees, whose numbers included many
young, single women, easily comprised the largest contingent of Strength
through Joy tourists, continuing a trend that began during the Weimar
period, when white-collar workers availed themselves of package tours in
appreciable numbers.[43] Local Strength through Joy functionaries relaxed the
income limits set on participating in its trips, opening loopholes that strained
the agency's original intentions.[44] In fact, the plans for the Baltic resorts
responded to nagging criticisms regarding the inaccessibility of Strength
through Joy vacations to wage earners. Apart from the necessity of proving the
sincerity of the regime's democratic pretensions, vacation packages that
remained financially beyond the reach of working-class families conflicted
with a racially grounded population policy that privileged healthy, harmonious, child-rich marriages.[45] Despite Labor Front subsidies yielded from
mandatory dues and the confiscated assets of the trade unions, as well as periodic corporate subventions, individuals assumed the burden of saving for
their trips through weekly deposits. An improved quality of life required
delayed gratification and, above all, sufficient income to put aside for a long-
term goal. Not surprisingly, worker participation in the Volkswagen savings
program was negligible.[46]

The persistence of class distinctions among German tourists emerges as a
prominent theme not only in the situation reports of the Social Democratic
Party in Exile (Sopade), but also in the surveillance of the SD and in Strength
through Joy's own literature. Middle- and upper-class vacationers complained about the invasion of their accustomed watering holes by shabbily

dressed tourists. The Sopade accounts recorded the distaste of tourists, who resented the herdlike organization, oppressive regimentation, and eavesdropping that tour guides, outing leaders, and SD agents in "disguise" imposed on them. For those workers who participated, the condescension often accorded to mass tourism belied the regime's professed valorization of manual labor. Second-class treatment by innkeepers and restaurateurs, who insisted that Strength through Joy tourists had no right to expect first-class accommodations, de facto segregation by class on board ship, in which workers retreated to the security of their skat games away from the public rooms where the better-off congregated, the discomfort of modestly paid passengers, who were crammed into the least desirable sleeping quarters, exhausting transport in third-class train compartments to destinations, and the relegation of workers to the cheapest seats at the theater and opera testify eloquently to the tension between the dream of the "national community" and the intractability of class barriers. The Rügen project, although radically reconfiguring a coastline that had epitomized seaside vacations for the privileged since the nineteenth century, once again accommodated the reality of social distinctions. Instead of delivering workers to established resorts, Strength through Joy would entice them to a safe working-class preserve constructed in an architectural style that allegedly conformed to the tastes of its prospective guests.[47]

Nevertheless, measuring Strength through Joy's impact solely against its utopian aims is to miss its significance. Its popularity alone, although likely exaggerated for public consumption, suggests that Strength through Joy reinforced the destruction of class-based politics, despite the incompleteness of its hyperpoliticized nation-building and its capitulation to the class divisions that it claimed to have eliminated.[48] Massive repression was the essential precondition for Nazi social policy because it eliminated rival political parties and cultural institutions, particularly those of the Left. The Nazi party attracted large numbers of workers on its road to power, yet workers whom the dense network of Social Democratic and Communist organizations had integrated proved most resistant to the Hitler movement.[49] Filling the space that emergency decrees and concentration camps provided, the regime constructed a vision of a future, disseminated through images of invigorated alpine skiers and smiling, relaxed cruise passengers, that combined personal fulfillment and freedom from want, while condemning Marxism for wallowing in the inevitability of scarcity. Vacation packages, hikes, and evenings of entertainment offered detachment from "normal" activities, including politics, and they provided diversions that complemented the depoliticizing of the workplace through increased rationalization.[50] Although determined to circumvent market-based leisure and consumption, Strength through Joy might still have encouraged claims to individual well-being of the sort that characterize market-driven consumer cultures; claims that have historically undermined the legitimacy and efficacy of politics grounded in representing the interests of specific classes.[51]

Much of the evidence regarding Strength through Joy's popular reception suggests an individualist search for pleasure and self-fulfillment that took advantage of the regime's attempts to build national solidarity through leisure and tourism, even as it resisted Strength through Joy's most heavy-handed attempts at indoctrination. Cruise passengers shunned newspapers, refused to use the "German greeting," tuned out speeches and propaganda broadcasts, and frequently chafed at Strength through Joy's demands for conformity and military-like discipline. Tourists drank to excess, danced, played games, flirted, and made love in the lifeboats after the sun went down. They rode atop camels and bargained in bazaars in North Africa, and they listened closely to guides who explained the history and architecture of St. Mark's Piazza in Venice, the ruins at Delphi, or the Acropolis in Athens. SD agents shuddered at the "shameless" behavior of young German women, who while on shore availed themselves of the company of handsome Mediterranean men. Complained one report, five women tourists disappeared into the woods with their Italian escorts immediately after arriving on Ischia, an island off of Italy's west coast: "One is forced to assume," it coyly remarked, "that most of the women joined the Italian trip for erotic purposes.[52] Other German tourists, especially those visiting border regions, violated regulations with scant regard for the regime's security concerns and critically low reserves of foreign exchange. Crossing borders to mail a postcard with a foreign stamp on it, look up a relative, or pose with a Czech or Swiss customs official happened regularly despite the (equally regular) remonstrances of tour guides.[53]

Ironically, Strength through Joy's own literature reinforced such tendencies so as to attract consumers for its products. Given Strength through Joy's mission, its travel brochures hardly avoided endowing tourist sites with political significance, good examples being Munich, where National Socialism began, as well as the triumphantly annexed lands of Austria and the Sudetenland. Nevertheless, they increasingly resorted to the strategies of commercial tourism, relying less on detailed textual descriptions of destinations and more on photographic images, captivating readers with majestic or soothing panoramas. Strength through Joy–sponsored competitions encouraged tourists to submit snapshots from their trips depicting quaint subjects and scenic views.[54] Moreover, such publications merged subtle images of physical and racial perfection with the explicit catering to a fun-loving audience that belied the regime's admonitions of self-sacrifice and discipline. Well-proportioned, youthful, and tanned models romping in the surf or sunbathing projected the promise of rejuvenation. Despite misogynist complaints in surveillance reports about flirtatious women, Strength through Joy brochures displayed young, attractive, and obviously single female models embarking on their vacations.[55] Only stories of vacationers finding true love during their travels that appeared often in KdF monthly programs confirmed the regime's advocacy of marriage. It may well be that a highly politicized, state-directed program such as Strength through Joy had little appeal for Germans, at least in the Federal Republic, once commercial tourism and consumption expanded in the late fifties and early sixties. Yet along with propagandizing the goal of national solidarity, Strength through Joy's advertising eerily anticipated later consumerist messages geared to a mass culture. Those messages cultivated a yearning for upward mobility and material well-being, while suggesting that communism could provide neither.[56]

In addition to its contributions to the erosion of class-based politics, Strength through Joy could also have enhanced the Nazi regime's legitimacy by encouraging its participants to excuse Nazi brutality as they experienced the pleasures of travel. According to some passengers, who participated in a cruise to southern Italy, the poverty of Naples and Palermo contrasted sharply with German "cleanliness." Complainers, they opined, should be forced to live for a while in such abject conditions, which nonetheless would be better than spending a year in a concentration camp.[57] The exposure to German military prowess on cruises occasioned contempt for Germany's enemies, as the snide remark of one vacationer reveals: To the glee of his fellow passengers on a cruise to Norway less than a month before the outbreak of war, the jokester quipped that the Polish liner *Piłsudski,* seen off in the distance, would soon be German.[58] Such evidence conforms to the findings of recent scholarship on popular opinion that has clarified the extent to which the Third Reich enjoyed substantial support despite intermittent discontent and a declining receptivity to ideological mobilization. Although that scholarship reveals a strikingly differentiated mosaic of strategies and attitudes that complicates the exercise of identifying fixed ideological positions either for or against Nazism,[59] it nonetheless reminds us that the Third Reich could not have pursued its hideous goals without the willingness of Germany's population to condone, or at minimum turn aside from, the regime's horrors. Even many workers, once assumed to have remained immune from Nazi racism, anti-Semitism, and hypernationalism, admired the regime's "accomplishments," including full employment and the restoration of German prestige abroad. And if shop-floor conditions in many cases did not replicate the accomplishments that Beauty of Work claimed for itself, workers took pride in the way the regime "honored" labor, recognizing their own experience and their achievements as producers of quality goods in the symbolism that the regime deployed.[60] Many bruited their "superiority" over the legions of fungible "alien" workers from the East, notwithstanding occasional expressions of sympathy for the regime's captives.[61] It is easy to dismiss the rapturous testimonies in Strength through Joy periodicals regarding the *Gemeinschaft*-inducing properties of the cruises, not to mention the ritualistic expressions of gratitude to the führer for making travel possible.[62] Yet the insidious expressions of contempt by German tourists for dark-skinned foreigners that conjoined with pleasure seeking and curiosity remind us not only that pleasure seeking could have a subtle political content, even when tourists used their vacations to escape daily routine, but also that Nazi tourism could reinforce and exploit deep-seated prejudices.

The diary of a judicial employee, Otto Kühn, from Stettin about his cruise to Portugal and Madeira encourages such an interpretation. Kühn admitted his unfavorable impressions of the curious Portuguese, who greeted his ship in Lisbon, noting the raggedly clothed children who begged for handouts from tourists, as well as the racial composition of the audience. White harbor workers composed the majority, he observed, "but mixed in were halfbreeds (Bastarden) and a few Negroes." On the second day of his sojourn, Lisbon's inhabitants actually won him over, for he saw well-dressed people on a tour through the city's better neighborhoods, whose purposefulness disqualified them as examples of "southern nonchalance (Lässigkeit)." Kühn closed his meticulously prepared diary, complete with well-composed snapshots, with an expression of appreciation for all that he had learned about Portugal. Yet he had to confess that the voyage deepened his patriotism. Some may claim the attractions of Portugal, he said, but "our great northern Heimat with its mountains and valleys, plains, lakes, and seacoasts is nevertheless far more beautiful."[63] Those sentiments are, to be sure, not uncommon among tourists visiting an alien culture. Yet in the context of the Third Reich, such "mundane" racism as reflected in Kühn's diary carried disturbing implications, for it meant that few roadblocks existed to stop the implementation of the obsessive and apocalyptic variety of Nazi ideologues. Throughout the fifties, the public memory of National Socialism remained overwhelmingly positive because, for most Germans, the regime had improved living conditions, restored "order," and eradicated the worst hardships of the depression, at least until the military reverses at Stalingrad during the winter of 1942–43. The experience of the occupation compared unfavorably with popular perceptions of the Third Reich.[64]

The ruins of Strength through Joy's resort at Prora that remain to this day serve as a metaphor for KdF's unfulfilled promises. The war not only meant the suspension of tourism, but also the postponement of the Levittown-like housing projects and the production of Volkswagens, the vehicles of social integration through consumerism. Hitler's totalistic vision of a prosperous economy that promoted mass consumption for the racially purified and prosperous "master race" (Herrenvolk) required the consolidation of an empire that would not materialize. Nevertheless until its defeat, the Nazi regime sought to assuage the austerity of the present with assurances of a better life to come, for, always sensitive to the popular mood, the regime could not get away with delivering unalloyed hardship, even as the realities of war increasingly hit home. The Labor Front pressed for longer vacations to curb working-class dissatisfaction with wage freezes and increased hours on the job, while Strength through Joy–sponsored entertainment substituted for the cessation of travel.[65] As the regime's on-again, off-again rationing demonstrates, the fear that material deprivation would lead to social conditions similar to those that undermined the imperial government during World War I never lay far from the surface.[66] Until the paper shortages forced their termination, Strength through Joy monthly programs reassured their readers that their sacrifices would be but temporary, and advertisements for the Volkswagen surrounded the auto with the personification of promise, members of the Hitler Youth. The caption of one read, "The building block to a beautiful future. Build for you and yours!"[67] Glossy brochures, complete with color photographs, continued to appear featuring contented vacationers seduced by the beauty of Madeira. As such, they served as keepsakes of happier times and as an incentive for imagining a bright future after the war.[68] On the cover of one, the image of a grimy, dark-skinned Portuguese boy sitting in a tree wordlessly testified to the essentials of Strength through Joy's mission, the creation of solidarity through entitlements and the magnification of racial difference.

NOTES

1. In reacting against Marxist approaches that stress the class bases of Nazi rule, recent scholarship emphasizes the centrality of Nazi racism. For a good example of this trend, see Michael Burleigh and Wolfgang Wippermann, *The Racial State: Germany, 1933–1945* (Cambridge: Cambridge University Press, 1991).

2. Karl-Heinz Weissmann, *Der Weg in den Abgrund. Deutschland unter Hitler 1933 bis 1945* (Berlin: Propyläen Verlag, 1995), 178–81. See as well Hartmut Berghoff, "Konsumgüterindustrie im Nationalsozialismus: Marketing im Spannungsfeld von Profit- und Regimeinteressen," *Archiv für Sozialgeschichte* 36 (1996): 293–322; and especially Inge Marssolek and Adelheid von Saldern, eds., *Zuhören und Gehörtwerden I: Radio im Nationalsozialismus Zwischen Lenkung und Ablenkung* (Tübingen: Edition Diskord, 1998). Rearmament constantly interfered with major Nazi domestic projects, even those, such as the autobahn, that were rumored to have a military purpose. See Erhard Schütz and Eckhard Gruber, *Mythos Reichsautobahn: Bau und Inszenierung der "Straßen des Führers" 1933–1941* (Berlin: Christoph Links Verlag 1996).

3. See Robert Ley, *Soldaten der Arbeit* (Munich: Franz Eher Verlag, 1942), 77–78. Because of the simultaneous need to squeeze wages and promote a nonmaterialistic alternative to "Marxism," KdF leaders defined "standard of living" as accessibility to the cultural and recreational pastimes of the wealthy. A good example is Gerhard Starcke, "Kraft durch Freude hebt den Lebensstandard unseres Volkes: Der sozialpolitische Sinn der KdF-Gemeinschaft," *Arbeitertum*, February 15, 1936, 3–4. Although Tim Mason's argument that a "domestic crisis" pushed the regime into war prematurely has found few supporters, Mason's seminal work, *Sozialpolitik im Dritten Reich:*

Arbeiterklasse und Volksgemeinschaft (Opladen: Westdeutscher Verlag, 1977), identified the tension between "guns" and "butter" in the Nazi regime's social policy. His book has since been translated with a new introduction and epilogue as *Social Policy in the Third Reich: The Working Class and the "National Community,"* trans. John Broadwin and ed. Jane Caplan (Oxford: Berg, 1993).

4. Although rich in detail, Wolfhard Buchholz's "Die Nationalsozialistische Gemeinschaft 'Kraft durch Freude': Freizeitgestaltung und Arbeiterschaft im Dritten Reich," Ph.D diss., University of Munich, 1976, 3, 57–58, asserts that little connection existed between KdF and the Nazi regime's racial and foreign policy. This work remains the most comprehensive and most widely cited study of KdF to date. The earlier dissertation of Laurence Van Zandt Moyer, "The Kraft durch Freude Movement in Germany, 1933–1939," Northwestern University, 1967, is more aware of the compatibility between the regime's repression and its leisure-time policies. Still, the apparent dissonance between KdF and the regime's horrors helps to explain why no work yet exists on Strength through Joy that compares to Victoria de Grazia's work on the analogous organization in Italy, *Dopolavoro: The Culture of Consent: Mass Organization of Leisure in Fascist Italy* (Cambridge: Cambridge University Press, 1981).

5. Kraft durch Freude Kundgebung, Bundesarchiv, Abteilung Potsdam (hereinafter cited as BAP) R43II/557, 4–5; Unterlagen betr. MinRat A.D. Horst Dressler-Andress, 1932–75. Protokoll des Gesprächs mit Herrn Dressler-Andress am Juli 1964 in Berlin-Karlshorst, Archiv, Institut für Zeitgeschichte (hereinafter cited as IfZ); Munich, F104, 1.

6. See Dieter Langewiesche, "Freizeit und Massenbildung. Zur Ideologie und Praxis der Volksbildung in der Weimarer Republik," in *Sozialgeschichte der Freizeit: Untersuchungen zum Wandel der Alltagskultur in Deutschland,* ed. Gerhard Huck (Wupperthal: Hammer, 1980), 223–47.

7. Die Reichsorganisationsleiter der NSDAP, *Organisationsbuch der NSDAP* (Munich: Franz Eher Verlag, 1943), 210.

8. Consult Erhard Forndran, *Die Stadt-und Industriegründungen Wolfsburg und Salzgitter: Entscheidungsprozesse im nationalsozialistische Herrschaftssytem* (Frankfurt am Main: Campus Verlag, 1984); and Marie-Luise Recker, *Die Großstadt als Wohn-und Lebensbereich im Nationalsozialismus: Zur Gründung der "Stadt des KdF-Wagens"* (Frankfurt am Main: Campus Verlag, 1984), for the Volkswagen's beginnings, as well as the construction of Wolfsburg. The most comprehensive study of the Volkswagen project is Hans Mommsen and Manfred Grieger, *Das Volkswagenwerk und seine Arbeiter im Dritten Reich* (Düsseldorf: Econ Verlag, 1996). See especially 92–202.

9. See Hasso Spode, "Arbeiterurlaub im Dritten Reich," in *Angst, Belohnung, Zucht, und Ordnung: Herrschaftsmechanismen im Nationalsozialismus,* ed. Carola Sachse (Opladen: Westdeutscher Verlag, 1983), 277–79. During the 1920s almost all workers who were incorporated by collective bargaining agreements received paid vacations. Yet a significant number of workers were not covered by such agreements. Moreover, over 50 percent of workers with paid vacations received fewer than four days per year.

10. "Die Deutsche Arbeitsfront erhielt den Olympischen Pokal," *Braunschweiger Neueste Nachrichten,* May 5, 1938, Niedersächsisches Hauptstaatsarchiv, Hannover (hereinafter cited as NHH), VVP 17, no. 2455. For the statistics, see Peter Reichel, *Der schöne Schein des Dritten Reiches: Faszination und Gewalt des Faschismus* (Frankfurt am Main: Fischer Verlag, 1993), 245–46; and Ronald Smelser, *Robert Ley: Hitler's Labor Front Leader* (Oxford: Berg, 1988), 211–12.

11. For its fifth anniversary, KdF released a lavish "coffee table" book, *Unter dem Sonnenrad: Ein Buch von Kraft durch Freude,* ed. Reichsamtsleitung Kraft durch Freude (Berlin: Verlag der Deutschen Arbeitsfront, 1938), describing its growth and popularity. For the war years, see Alan E. Steinweis, *Art, Ideology, and Economics in Nazi Germany: The Reich Chambers of Music, Theater, and the Visual Arts* (Chapel Hill: University of North Carolina Press,1993), 147, 152–53; and Heinz Boberach, ed., *Meldungen aus dem Reich: Die geheimen Lageberichte des Sicherheitsdients der SS 1938–1945* (Herrsching: Pawlak, 1984), vol. 4, no. 69 (March 27, 1940), 918–20; vol. 4, no. 77 (April 15, 1940), 998–99; vol. 6, no. 146 (December 2, 1940), 1824–27; and vol. 6, no. 147 (December 5, 1940), 1836–39.

12. See Christine Keitz, *Reisen als Leitbild: Die Entstehung des modernen Massentourismus in Deutschland* (Munich: DTV, 1997), 224–33; and Alfred C. Mierzejewski, "The German National Railway between the World Wars: Modernization or Participation for War?" *Journal of Transport History* 11 (1990): 53–54. It bears exploration as to whether the 23 percent increase in railroad passengers alone that Mierzejewski cites could have resulted, at least in part, from KdF tourism.

13. Werner Kahl, *Der deutsche Arbeiter reist!* (Berlin: Verlag der Deutschen Arbeitsfront, 1940), 60–63.

14. German Legation in Lisbon to Foreign Ministry, Berlin, June 14, 1938, Auswärtiges Amt Politisches Archiv (Bonn), (hereafter cited as AA-PA) R49245. At times, foreign governments raised objections to the use of ethnic Germans as tour guides, as was the case in Latvia. Central Office, National Socialist Community Strength through Joy to German Legation in Riga, June 21, 1939, AA-PA, No. 473, s. 7 (Deutsche Gesandtschaft, Riga).

15. "Der Führer fuhr mit uns," NSG Kraft durch Freude, Gau Köln-Aachen, *Kraft durch Freude 1939,* vol. 4, no. 5 (May 1939), 4–6; Die Deutsche Arbeitsfront, NS-Gemeinschaft "Kraft durch Freude," Reichsamt Reisen, Wandern und Urlaub, "KdF-Schiff Robert Ley" (Berlin: Verlag der Deutschen Arbeitsfront, 1939); "Unterredung mit Dr. Ley," *Hannoverscher Anzeiger,* March 27, 1938, NHH, VVP, no. 2456. For detailed discussions of KdF vacations, see Spode, "Arbeiterurlaub im Dritten Reich," and "'Der deutsche Arbeiter reist': Massentourismus im Dritten Reich," in Huck, *Sozialgeschichte der Freizeit,* 281–306. A description of the Bremen project can be found in the M.A. thesis of Bruno Frommann, "Reisen mit 'Kraft durch Freude': Eine Darstellung der KdF-Reisen unter besonderer Berücksichtigung der Auslandsfahrten," Karlsruhe, 1977, 193–99.

16. Although relations between the German Labor Front and the International Labour Office were far from harmonious, the ILO nonetheless recognized that the KdF cruises represented "the most extensive official experiment" in providing travel excursions. See International Labour Office, Studies and Reports, Series G (Housing and Welfare), no. 5, *Facilities for the Use of Workers' Leisure during Holidays* (Geneva: International Labour Office, 1939), 44.

17. For the development of seaside resorts, see Alain Corbin, *The Lure of the Sea: The Discovery of the Seaside, 1750–1840* (London: Penguin, 1994); Thomas Richards, *The Commodity Culture of Victorian England: Advertising and Spectacle, 1851–1914* (Stanford, Calif.: Stanford University Press, 1990); and John Urry, *The Tourist Gaze: Leisure and Travel in Contemporary Societies* (London: Sage, 1996), 16–33. The best discussions of the Rügen project are Jürgen Rostock and Franz Zadniček, *Paradiesruinen: Das KdF-Seebad der Zwanzigtausend auf Rügen* (Berlin: Christoph Links Verlag, 1995) and Hasso Spode, "Ein Seebad für zwanzigtausend Volksgenossen: zur Grammatik

und Geschichte des fordistischen Urlaubs," in *Reisekultur in Deutschland: Von der Weimarer Republik zum Dritten Reich*. ed. Peter J. Brenner (Tübingen: Max Niemeyer Verlag, 1997), 7–47. Contemporary descriptions are in Kahl, *Der Deutsche Arbeiter reist!* 60–63, and in "KdF-Bad auf Rügen wird Wirklichkeit: Ferien-Eldorado der 20,000—Fernheizwerk und 'Wolkan-Restaurant,'" September 22, 1937, NHH, VVP 17, no. 2456. Unfortunately, the name of the newspaper in which this article appeared is indecipherable.

18. In fact, the regime could not reduce women's participation in the labor force, despite its rhetoric about confining them to the home. For a recent summary of the scholarship on women in the Third Reich, see Mary Nolan, "Work, Gender, and Everyday Life: Reflections of Continuity, Normality, and Agency in Twentieth-Century Germany," in *Stalinism and Nazism: Dictatorships in Comparison*, ed. Ian Kershaw and Moshe Lewin (Cambridge: Cambridge University Press, 1997), 311–42, especially 329–37. See also Anson G. Rabinbach, "The Aesthetics of Production in the Third Reich," in *International Fascism: New Thoughts and New Approaches*, ed. George L. Mosse (London and Beverly Hills: Sage Publications, 1979), 189–222, for an excellent assessment of the Beauty of Work.

19. Robert Ley, *Deutschland ist schöner geworden* (Munich: Franz Eher Verlag, 1942), 92.

20. "5 Jahre Nationalsozialistische Freizeitorganisation!" Nationalsozialistische Gemeinschaft "Kraft durch Freude," Gau Köln-Aachen, *Kraft durch Freude 1939*, vol. 4, no. 1 (January 1939): 5–7. See Matthias Frese, *Betriebspolitik im "Dritten Reich": Deutsche Arbeitsfront, Unternehmer und Staatsbürokratie in der westdeutsche Großindustrie, 1933–1939* (Paderborn: Schöningh, 1991), 383–95.

21. Mary Nolan's *Visions of Modernity: American Business and the Modernization of Industry* (Oxford: Oxford University Press, 1994), and Tilla Siegel's *Leistung und Lohn in der nationalsozialistische "Ordnung der Arbeit"* (Opladen: Westdeutscher Verlag, 1989), are indispensable to understanding industrial relations in interwar Germany.

22. For this argument, see Gary Cross, *Time and Money: The Making of Consumer Culture* (London: Routledge, 1993).

23. Spode, "Arbeiterurlaub im Dritten Reich," 284–87. The DAF did not approach Ley's stated goal of a three- to four-week vacation for all workers. Nevertheless, paid vacations had become the rule by the outbreak of war.

24. There were negotiations to this end between Ley and the German navy. "Bilanz über 1. Jahr. 'Kraft durch Freude' 1934," Bundesarchiv Berlin-Lichtenberg, NS 22/781, 6. The itinerary of the cruise ship *Wilhelm Gustloff* included crossing paths with the training ship *Brummer* and a view of Helgoland: "Auf Wiedersehen im Salzkammergut. Eine unvergessliche Nordsee-Fahrt für 1000 österreicher KdF-Fahren," *Niedersächsische Tageszeitung*, March 26–27, 1938, NHH, VVP 17, no. 2456. Similarly, the steamer *Oceana* came across the destroyer *Deutschland* and four torpedo boats while rounding Gibraltar. Bericht des SS.-Hauptsturmführer Wossagk, BAP R58, no. 950, 81.

25. By contrast, passengers could not go ashore in Norway. Local hostility reinforced this policy. Betr.: KdF-Fahrt nach Norwegen v. 9.–14.1939, BAP R58, no. 948, 125.

26. Hitler's words were set opposite a photograph of the führer overlooking the mountains in the pamphlet *Urlaubsreisen 1937*, put out by Kraft durch Freude, Gau Berlin. Following breakfast, the cruise ships staged a morning parade complete with flags, the singing of German lieder, and commemorations appropriate to the day.

27. For Ley's ambitions alone, see Smelser, *Robert Ley*, 98–99, 149–217.

28. Ley, *Grosse Stunde: Das Deutsche Volk im Totalen Kriegseinsatz* (Munich: Franz Eher Verlag, 1943), 38–43; and *Roosevelt verrät Amerika!* (Berlin: Verlag der Deutschen Arbeitsfront, 1942).

29. "Essen und Essen ist Zweierlei," *Schönheit der Arbeit*, vol. 2, no. 11 (March 1938), 446–50.

30. Kristin Ross's suggestion for postwar France in *Fast Cars, Clean Bodies: Decolonization and the Reordering of French Culture* (Cambridge: MIT Press, 1995), 71–122, could easily be applied to the Third Reich. The Nazis built upon the bourgeois obsession with cleanliness and health. See especially Jonas Frykman and Orvar Löfgren, *Culture Builders: A Historical Anthropology of Middle-Class Life* (New Brunswick, N.J.: Rutgers University Press, 1987), 157–263; and Anne McClintock, *Imperial Leather: Race, Gender, and Sexuality in the Colonial Conquest* (London: Routledge, 1995), 152–55 and 207–31.

31. Such as the brochure *Jahresfahrtenbuch 1939*, 7, put out by Kraft durch Freude, Gau Halle-Merseburg. See James Buzard, *Off the Beaten Track: European Tourism, Literature, and the Ways to Culture, 1800–1918* (Oxford: Clarendon, 1993), 321–24, for the connections between tourism, the military, and imperialism.

32. See Eric J. Leed, *The Mind of the Traveler: From Gilgamesh to Global Tourism* (New York: Basic Books, 1991), especially 291. For the distinctiveness of Nazi leisure-time policy, consult Carola Sachse, "Freizeit zwischen Betrieb und Volksgemeinschaft. Betriebliche Freizeitpolitik im Nationalsozialismus," *Archiv für Sozialgeschichte* 33 (1993): 305–28. For the relationship between KdF tourism, especially its cruises, and the regime's expansionism, see Daniela Liebscher, "Mit KdF 'die Welt erschließen': Der Beitrag der KdF-Reisen zur Außenpolitik der Deutschen Arbeitsfront 1934–1939," *Zeitschrift für Sozialgeschichte des 20. und 21. Jahrhunderts* 14, no. 1 (1999): 42–72. According to one SD agent, passengers returning from Madeira made frequent comparisons between the living standards of Germany and Portugal. He claimed that the workers aboard asserted "that they would not change places with the Portuguese." Bericht über die Reise des K.d.F.-Schiffes "Der Deutsche" nach Madeira vom. 21.4.38–7.5.38, BAP, R58, no. 950, 241–42. Such comments appeared frequently in SD surveillance reports. See also Ley, *Schmiede des Schwertes: Der deutsche Arbeiter im Großdeutschen Freiheitskampf* (Munich: Franz Eher Verlag, 1942), 145.

33. To wit, the defensiveness of Strength through Joy functionaries regarding complaints that arose from the last-minute cancellation of cruises to Norway because KdF ships were being used to transport the Condor legion home from Spain: "Ein Wort an alle KdF-Urlauber. Antwort auf viele Fragen, die uns erreichen," Nationalsozialistische Gemeinschaft Kraft durch Freude, Gau Köln-Aachen, *Kraft durch Freude*, vol. 4, no. 7 (July 1939), 4–5.

34. Ley, *Soldaten der Arbeit*, 221.

35. See Hans Mommsen, "Noch einmal: Nationalsozialismus und Modernisierung," *Geschichte und Gesellschaft* 21, no. 3 (1995): 391–402.

36. Rainer Zitelmann, *Hitler: Selbstverständnis eines Revolutionäres*, 2d ed. (Stuttgart: Klett-Cotta, 1987), 349–78, especially 355–58.

37. Although criticized for downplaying anti-Semitism in the Third Reich, Arno Mayer's *"Why Did the Heavens Not Darken?" The Final Solution in History* (New York: Pantheon, 1988), demonstrates the centrality of anti-Bolshevism in Nazi ideology and practice.

38. This becomes clear in the contrasting images that KdF employed to advocate clean and efficient workplaces. "Ein jüdischer 'Musterbetrieb,'" Nationalsozialistische

Gemeinschaft Kraft durch Freude, Gau Sachsen, *Monatsprogramm*, March 1936, 25–27, accused an ostensibly Jewish-owned metallurgy plant in Dresden of tolerating an unhealthy work environment and exploiting German workers. For the connection between Marxism and Jews, see Ley, *Die deutsche Arbeitsfront: Ihr Werden und Ihre Aufgaben* (Munich: Franz Eher Verlag, 1934).

39. A good example of the reactions of Catholic communities is in the Auswertungsnotiz aus beim Gestapa vorhandenen FMR-Berichten über KdF-Reisen. Zeit Frühjahr 1937 bis 10.10.1937, BAP R58, no. 943, 120. The Dienstbericht des Reisebegleiters über die KdF-Urlaubsfahrt mit Dampfer "Stuttgart" nach Italien vom 13.–25. November 1938, BAP R58, no. 950, 356 reports the increasingly bitter divide between Rhinelanders and Silesians. The rift became so great that the two groups refused to eat their meals together.

40. See the memoir of Christian Graf von Krockow on rural life in Pomerania, *Die Reise nach Pommern: Bericht aus einem verschwiegenen Land* (Stuttgart: Deutsche Verlagsanstalt, 1985), 84. Theresia Bauer's account of Bavarian peasant life in the Third Reich, *Nationalsozialistische Agrarpolitik und bäuerliches Verhalten im Zweiten Weltkrieg: Eine Regionalstudie zur ländlichen Gesellschaft in Bayern* (Frankfurt am Main: Peter Lang, 1996), 113–14, 143–44, and 194, makes the case that peasants remained relatively untouched by the regime's social programs, especially vacations and tourism. Church holidays continued to define what leisure time they were able to extract.

41. Keitz, *Reisen als Leitbild*, 252.

42. Mommsen and Grieger, *Das Volkswagenwerk und seine Arbeiter*, 201. A Norwegian cruise originating from Gau Swabia cost RM 61.50, more than twice an average worker's weekly wage: NSG Kraft durch Freude, Gau Schwaben, *Jahres-Urlaubsprogramm 1935* (Berlin, 1935). See also the comments of the Social Democratic underground in *Deutschland-Berichte der Sopade* (Frankfurt am Main: Verlag Nettlebeck, 1980), September–October 1934, 523–27; July 1935; 175–78 and 845–51; as well as Spode, "Arbeiterurlaub im Dritten Reich," 304–5; and Frese, *Betriebspolitik im Dritten Reich*, 382–83. My own assessment of the social composition of the cruises, drawn from the Sicherheitsdienst reports (BAP R58, nos. 943–50), agrees with Spode that workers were underrepresented relative to their numbers in the population. Consult also the more recent discussion by Christine Keitz, *Reisen als Leitbild*, 248–54, who, in addition to describing the economic and cultural barriers to working-class tourism, provides a breakdown by gender. For the memories of hardship during the interwar period, see Michael Wildt, *Vom kleinen Wohlstand: Eine Konsumgeschichte der fünfziger Jahre* (Hamburg: Fischer Verlag, 1994), 14–30.

43. Despite the differences between the commercial tourism of postwar West Germany and the state-directed variety of Kraft durch Freude, the salaried contingent of Strength through Joy tourism even anticipated that of West German tourists in the sixties. See Axel Schildt, *Moderne Zeiten: Freizeit, Massenmedien und "Zeitgeist" in der Bundesrepublik der 50er Jahre* (Hamburg: Christians Verlag, 1995), 189. See also Keitz, "Die Anfänge des modernen Massentourismus in der Weimarer Republik," *Archiv für Sozialgeschichte* 22 (1993): 179–209.

44. Sponsoring a trip for a low-income person was one way to elude the RM 250 per month income limit. Reich and Prussian Minister of the Interior to Oberpräsident Provinz Hannover, August 14, 1937, NHH, Hann. 122a, VIII, no. 577, 227. Constraints on high earners, such as a large family or a serious illness, could also mean a waiver.

45. For remarks about family vacations, see Kahl, *Der deutsche Arbeiter reist!* 34–36, 63.

46. Mommsen and Grieger, *Das Volkswagenwerk und seine Arbeiter,* 201.

47. Sopade's attention to KdF was extensive, reflecting its concern that the regime was winning over German workers. See *Deutschland-Berichte,* September–October 1934, 523–27; February 1935, 175–78; July 1935, 845–51; December 1935, 1455–62; July 1936, 879–87; February 1938, 149–75; and April 1939, 463–90. Even Ley, *Deutschland ist schöner geworden,* 72, became defensive over the snobbishness directed toward KdF tourists. For the modernist architecture of the Rügen project, see Rostock and Zadniček, *Paradiesruinen,* 63, and Spade, "Seebad," 34–37.

48. The numbers KdF often produced did not specify repeated trips by individuals.

49. The recent argument that the Nazi *Volkspartei* transcended entrenched milieus receives this important qualification from Claus-Christian Szejnmann, *Nazism in Central Germany: the Brownshirts in "Red" Saxony* (New York and Oxford: Berghahn, 1999), esp. 92–141.

50. Tilla Siegel, "Whatever Was the Attitude of German Workers? Reflections on Recent Interpretations," in *Fascist Italy and Nazi Germany: Comparisons and Contrasts,* ed. Richard Bessel (Cambridge: Cambridge University Press, 1996), 61–77, esp. 74.

51. See *The Sex of Things: Gender and Consumption in Historical Perspective,* ed. Victoria de Grazia with Ellen Furlough (Berkeley and Los Angeles: University of California Press, 1996), 280.

52. Bericht über die KdF-Reise Dalmatien-Griechenland mit der Reichsbahn und dem Dampfer "Oceana" vom 2.3. 1939 bis 15.3.1939, BAP R58, no. 950, 626; Bericht über die Rund um Italienfahrt v. 1.–12.1938 der KdF mit dem Schiff "Oceana," BAP R58, no. 950, 447.

53. The DAF asked the Reich Main Security Office to monitor the tours, fearing that tourists would either bump into leftist exiles or would cross borders on unauthorized excursions. BAP R58, no. 943 contains the correspondence authorizing surveillance, as well as reports of incidents.

54. NSG Kraft durch Freude, Gau Sachsen, *Monatsprogramm,* December 1938, 2–6. This contest received five thousand photos from eight hundred contestants. The 1939 brochure for Gau Saxony, NSG Kraft durch Freude, Gau Sachsen, *Mit Kraft durch Freude in Deutschlands Gaue. Die Urlaubsfahrten der Gauen Sachsen 1939,* emphasizes trips to the newly acquired territories, providing detailed maps for readers, who presumably knew little of their geography.

55. For example, "Dein Urlaub 1939 mit Kraft durch Freude," published by Kraft durch Freude, Gau Oberdonau (Berlin, 1938?), presents a full-page photo of a worker on the job, followed by an equally large photo of a blond, handsome, and tanned young couple sunning themselves on the beach.

56. See Schildt, *Moderne Zeiten,* 180–202; and Michael Wildt, *Am Beginn der Konsumgesellschaft: Mangelerfahrung, Lebenshaltung, Wohlstandshoffnung in Westdeutschland in den fünfziger Jahren* (Hamburg: Ergebnisse Verlag, 1994), 264–65. For the anti-Communist implications of the "Social Market Economy," see Erica Carter, *How German Is She? Postwar West German Reconstruction and the Consuming Woman* (Ann Arbor: University of Michigan Press, 1997); and A. J. Nicholls, *Freedom with Responsibility: The Social Market Economy in Germany, 1918–1963* (Oxford: Oxford University Press, 1994). William Brustein's *The Logic of Evil: The Social Origins of the Nazi Party, 1925–1933* (New Haven: Yale University Press, 1996), 120–60, argues that rising expectations characterized many workers, which is why the Nazi party rivaled the SPD and KDP for working-class support.

57. Bericht des SS Oberscharführers Otto-Wilhelm Wandesleben über die vom 6. November 1938 stattgefundene KdF-Reise nach Italien, BAP R58, no. 950, 384. The connection between delight in the exercise of power that characterized imperialism and the refusal of imperialists to recognize the violence they perpetuated has been noted. See Edward Said, *Culture and Imperialism* (New York: Vintage, 1993), 131. Such an observation can apply to Nazism.

58. Norwegenfahrt der NS-Gemeinschaft "Kraft durch Freude," Gau Mgd./Anh. Mit dem KdF-Dampfer "Der Deutsche" vom 2.–8.39, BAP R58, no. 948, 127–29.

59. See Detlev J. K. Peukert, *Inside Nazi Germany: Conformity, Opposition, and Racism in Everyday Life,* trans. Richard Deveson (New Haven: Yale University Press, 1987).

60. Alf Lüdtke's "'Ehre der Arbeit': Industriearbeiter und Macht der Symbole. Zur Reichweite symbolischer Orientierung im Nationalsozialismus," in *Arbeiter im 20. Jahrhundert,* ed. Klaus Tenfelde (Stuttgart: Klett-Cotta, 1991) describes how the regime attracted workers by exploiting the symbolic systems of skilled labor.

61. See Ulrich Herbert, "Apartheid nebenan: Erinnerungen an die Fremdarbeiter im Ruhrgebiet," in *"Die Jahre weiß man nicht, wo man die heute hinsetzen soll": Faschismuserfahrungen im Ruhrgebiet 1930 bis 1960,* vol. 1, ed. Lutz Niethammer (Berlin: J. H. W. Dietz, 1983), 233–66.

62. Upon hearing that the kaiser once sailed the Norwegian fjords, one miner, who was himself enjoying his Norwegian cruise, was reported to have said, "Under Adolf Hitler we are now all kaisers." Bericht über die KdF-Fahrt vom 2.–10.8.1938 auf dem Dampfer "Sierra Cordoba," BAP R58, no. 948, 60–61.

63. Otto Kühn, "Mit 'Kraft durch Freude' nach Madeira 1936," IfZ, Munich, MS 127.

64. Ian Kershaw's *The Hitler Myth: Image and Reality in the Third Reich* (Oxford: Clarendon, 1987), 210–11, suggests such a conclusion, as does Schildt, *Moderne Zeit,* 306–23. For the attitudes of German women, see Robert G. Moeller, *Protecting Motherhood: Women and the Family in the Politics of Postwar West Germany* (Berkeley and Los Angeles: University of California Press, 1993), 8–37.

65. Frese, *Betriebspolitik im Dritten Reich,* 376; Nolan, *Visions of Modernity,* 232–35; Smelser, *Robert Ley,* 171–73, 199–200; and Spode, "Arbeiterurlaub im Dritten Reich," 309. Had war not come, the VW project still would have been undercapitalized and lacking in essential raw materials. See Mommsen and Grieger, *Das Volkswagenwerk und seine Arbeiter,* 226.

66. See Martin Kitchen, *Nazi Germany at War* (London: Longman, 1995), 79–84.

67. Kraft durch Freude, Gau Steiermark, *Monatsprogramm,* July 1940, 16.

68. "Nach den Glücklichen Inseln: Mit dem KdF-Flagschiff 'Robert Ley' nach der farbenprächtigen Welt von Madeira und Teneriffa," ed. Karl Busch with introduction by Bodo Lafferenz (Berlin, 1940), Landeshauptarchiv Koblenz, Bestand 714, no. 3838.

PART 3

Global Mass Tourism and the Representation of Place

French Cultural Tourism and the Vichy Problem

CULTURAL TOURISM, THE VICHY PROBLEM, AND SITES OF MEMORY

The growth of world tourism in the second half of the twentieth century, by one estimate four billion trips in a year, makes its role increasingly significant in the construction of social identities and the formation of political values and beliefs.[1] Students of tourism have long known that its history could be studied "for the light which the knowledge of tourism can throw on other aspects of life."[2] This chapter focuses on tourism as it relates to the social construction of memory by means of the construction and designation of war memorials and battlefield sites, their role in contested memory, the relationship of pilgrimage with what has sometimes been called "cultural tourism," and the problem of the preservation of monuments that often necessitates the kind of intervention that can call into question their authenticity. The focus is World War II France, itself a point of controversy, extending from the wartime years through the present, in shorthand termed the "Vichy problem."

Despite the fact that France, by any standard of measurement, is one of the world's most popular tourist areas, the role of tourism in informing the ways in which the war was remembered has been neglected by most historians.[3] The configuration and reconfiguration of war-related tourist sites in France, however, has formed a continual process of "revisionism," subject to contested political interpretation, reflecting the continually shifting retrospective views of the war itself.[4] Although distinctions have been made between cultural tourism, defined as the specific orientation toward interest in history and "tradition," including the picturesque and "local color," on the one hand, and pilgrimages, on the other, it is not always easy to separate the presumably sincere religious "pilgrim" from the more casual "tourist," whether among those participating in medieval religious treks to Canterbury and Santiago de Compostella or the more recent shrines depicted in the film *Schindler's List*.[5]

These sites are "marked," or designated, as Dean MacCannell suggested, and often acquire a sacred quality, forming part of a pilgrimage route, sometimes called "heritage," which David Lowenthal defined as "the chief focus of patriotism and a prime lure of tourism."[6] Chris Rojek and John Urry have noted that "how people come to know and experience 'their culture' is an obviously huge and daunting issue."[7] The reasons for visiting wartime monuments may range from religious sentiments of devotion to "morbid curiosity."[8] Undoubtedly visitors often tour such monuments with a shifting mixture of sentiments; a group of tourists ascending from the French Maginot Line fortifications was seen by the author of this chapter to be more solemn than the same people earlier entering the site.

The connection between the establishment of World War II memorials and tourism in France was articulated as early as June 1945 in an issue of *For You*, a monthly tourist guide published in English for British, American, and Canadian troops in France. English-speaking service personnel then in France were urged to join the French in visiting the ruined town of Oradour-sur-Glane, site of an SS massacre of civilians thirteen months earlier.[9] An explicit function of the 1965 *Blue Guide* for Normandy was to help make the battlefields and historic monuments of World War II accessible to the tourist.[10] More recently in France, Jean-Pierre Bady emphasized tourism as one of the most important reasons for the designation of historical monuments. The point of creating monuments was that they might be visited, and Bady urged that the French monuments be as accessible as possible to tourists.[11] Many of the kinds of physical mementos, such as books, reproductions, maps, and artwork, that, in the words of Jennifer Craik, help "translate" or give meaning to a site, were made available at places such as the Maginot Line forts.

Despite the awareness in France of the political importance of cultural tourism, its relationship to war and the recollection of war has barely been studied. Consequently there is little literature that addresses the reactions of tourists to the wartime monuments. The recent discussion of Vichy has developed in the context of a literary vogue oriented to "sites" and "memory," in the fashion of the seven-volume *Les Lieux de mémoire* (The sites of memory), edited by Pierre Nora from 1984 through 1992 in France.[12] Nora's "sites of memory" may relate metaphorically to "places" within our memories rather than to specific itineraries on a Michelin road map. He and his colleagues emphasized, however, the role of physical locations, often war memorials or related monuments, in shaping memory and constructing political identity. Debates in France over the erection of tourist sites with regard to World War II have often taken place in the context of disputes over the meaning of and control over France's patrimony *(patrimoine)*.[13] Since World War II, groups contesting the significance of France's patrimony and attempting to build competing configurations of identity through the use of sites of memory have included Vichyites, Pétainists, pro-German collaborators of varying political tendencies,

Gaullist and Communist Resistance veterans, and Jewish and other victims of Nazi and Vichy persecution in France. In 1996, for example, the president of the Bas-Rhin (Alsace) General Council moved to block the publication of a tourist guidebook that covered, among other areas, the northern portion of Alsace. He complained that the book, financed by three regional tourism offices and assigned for publication to a German firm, said nothing of the war years, never even mentioning Hitler. The guidebook was described as transmitting to the public an "unconscious revisionism," referring to the rewriting the history of the war to eradicate the memory of German crimes.[14]

The shifting tourist iconicity regarding wartime France is best illustrated by the town of Vichy itself. A tourist spa before the war, Vichy became the site of the Marshal Philippe Pétain's French government, which collaborated with Nazi Germany during the Occupation years. After the war, local leaders struggled in Vichy with the stigma of the association of their city with pro-Nazi collaboration, while other persons visited to tour the sites associated with the Pétain government. The Maginot Line, erected in the 1930s as a defensive fortification against German invasion, was toured by victorious Germans after their defeat of France in 1940 and became an object of tourist attention in the postwar period. The Seine River bridges in Paris, already invested with tourist significance, acquired new interest among tourists interested in seeing the sites were street fighting took place during the liberation of Paris in 1944. Plaques mark the spots where Resistance fighters were killed in action.

Even before the war, extensions of leisure and travel by the 1936 Popular Front government raised questions of tourism and political identity. The 1940 defeat continued this discussion, despite the privations of wartime and Occupation restrictions in France. After the 1944 Liberation, war-related sites were given Resistance signification as succeeding governments, following the suggestion of General Charles de Gaulle, portrayed a France united in resistance to the Nazis. By the mid-1950s, a restored European prosperity, the rise of a peaceful Federal Republic of Germany, and the easing of immediate postwar passions began to lend more historical distance to the sites connected with the war.[15] From then on, tourist meaning continued to be contested among the different French political groups. The Resistance narrative of General de Gaulle was joined by other versions of the wartime experience. Sites related to the Jewish Holocaust assumed increased visibility with the Barbie, Touvier, and Papon trials of the 1980s and 1990s.[16]

CULTURAL TOURISM AND POLITICAL ICONS IN INTERWAR AND WARTIME FRANCE

Governmental leaders in France have long shown an awareness of cultural tourism and its potential for shaping notions of national identity and social cohesion. They established sites of memory long before Nora's popularization of the term. In 1935, the French government established a Tourism Commissariat (Commissariat au Tourisme) to help promote tourism in France. The Popular Front administration of 1936 introduced two-week paid vacations, which together with the developing youth hostel movement emphasized touring in, and becoming acquainted with, the various regions of one's own country. This political use of tourism paralleled the contemporary Soviet Intourist, the Fascist Italian Dopolavoro, and the Nazi German Kraft durch Freude. The tourism encouraged by the French Popular Front, notes Julian Jackson, "was not only a distraction it was also a discovery of France and French history."[17] Christian Faure has shown that this agenda was continued in the regional and national folklore emphasis of Vichy's cultural politics and the related tourism promoted by the Pétain government.[18]

War in 1939 and defeat and occupation in 1940 brought severe restrictions in interwar patterns of touristic activity in France but introduced new tourists among the thousands of German military and civilian personnel given tours in Paris and other parts of occupied France.[19] In the brief transfer of political power that followed the defeat of 1940, France witnessed the development of new cultural sites and the revision of older ones. Within the first weeks of the new Vichy government's existence, these sets of symbols bifurcated along the split between the Free French Resistance on the one side and Vichy on the other. The cross of Lorraine and the Strasbourg cathedral acquired new signification in the culture of the Free French, whereas the town of Vichy acquired new meaning for the Vichy government. All became highly charged code words in French political discourse, as did Joan of Arc, whose sites and images were used by both sides, and the entire city of Paris itself, declared an open city to spare it in June 1940 and the site of high political drama in 1944.

Advocacy of the economic potential of cultural tourism did not stop with defeat and occupation in 1940. Gaston Mortier, the president of a French hotel trade organization, welcomed the "very modern" phenomenon of "intellectual tourism."[20] Reflecting the values of Vichy's National Revolution, *Lyon-Touriste*, published by Lyon's Regional Tourism Bureau, wrote that foreigners would be invited to see the "French soul," meaning rural France, rather than the France of luxury, by implication the case before the war.[21] The *Hôtelier Alpin*, a regional hotel trade publication, encouraged the discovery of lesser-known French regions when it asserted in March 1943 that whereas foreigners came to France to visit Paris, the Riviera, and the Basque coast, they should be encouraged to visit all of France. Tourism, unlike agricultural and industrial products, it argued, was an inexhaustible resource.[22]

The tourist spa town of Vichy, selected as the provisional capital in part because of its spacious hotels, could be used to accommodate government agencies. During the Occupation years, the Vichy region increased in population from 30,000 to 130,000, reflecting an influx of government functionaries into the provisional capital. Although Georges Mathiot, vice president of the Lorraine-Vosges-Alsace chamber of commerce, saw these new arrivals as destructive of tourism, they also spurred tourist activity in the spas and restaurants of the town.[23] As a term, *Vichy* came into disrepute early in both French and English. An Escoffier cookbook published in English in 1941 changed the name of vichyssoise to *crème Gauloise,* and in 1943 a New York restaurant listed it as *de Gaullesoise* [*sic*].[24] Another case of tourist symbols turned around by Occupation politics saw Paris authorities threatening to close the "American bars" because of their name. An issue of *L'Hôtelier Français,* ironically, one day before the Normandy invasion, reminded its readers and the authorities that these bars were "clearly French and Parisian" and that they had no connection with the United States.[25]

The small northeastern city of Compiègne, new on the tourist circuit as the site of the armistice ending hostilities with a defeated Germany in 1918, became another tourist site transformed by the events of 1940. The November 11, 1918 armistice had been signed in a railway car in the Rethondes clearing near Compiègne. During the interwar years the French government had returned the railway car to the Rethondes clearing and had turned the site into a shrine. In June 1940, the meaning of the site changed dramatically, entering the tourist itineraries of the victorious Germans after Hitler selected the identical spot and the same railway car in which to dictate his armistice terms to the defeated French.[26] As a tourist site, Strasbourg's meaning shifted with the changing military fortunes in 1940 and 1944. The capital of Alsace, acquired by Louis XIV in 1681, Strasbourg was lost to the Germans in 1871, regained in 1918, and lost again in 1940. Heinrich Hoffmann, Hitler's personal photographer, published a photo album of the 1940 victory in the west, intended for popular consumption in Germany, showing Hitler crossing the Rhine bridge at Kehl to enter "German Straßburg" and then touring the cathedral there.[27] On the French side, General Philippe Leclerc (Philippe Leclerc de Hauteclocque), the Free French military commander of equatorial Africa, vowed "to stop [fighting] only when the French flag again flies over Metz and Strasbourg," an oath he redeemed on November 23, 1944, when he led Free French forces into Strasbourg.[28]

With the German victory in 1940, the Maginot Line changed in meaning almost overnight from an expensive state-of-the-art network of defensive fortifications to a site of touristic curiosity on the part of the victorious Germans.[29] Said to be "all the rage" as a destination among the Germans in June 1940, the freshly captured fortifications were visited first by Hitler, then by German officers and journalists, who were given guided tours. According to one account, visiting Luftwaffe officers were so deeply impressed by the strength of the fortifications that they wept openly after seeing how little damage their bombs had inflicted.[30] "Maginot mentality" came to symbolize both in France and elsewhere a state of mind in which one retreated behind a supposedly impregnable and highly expensive wall, which failed, however, to keep out disaster.[31]

Its chief site of memory, Paris in its entirety was and remains France's premier tourist site. The centrality of Paris had been evoked by Hitler, who claimed to have spared the city during the fighting of 1940.[32] On the morning of June 23, 1940, Hitler was among the first Germans to tour defeated Paris. His tour was filmed by Hoffmann, with clips that have since become famous showing Hitler with tourist sites as backdrops.[33] For the French, the tourist iconicity of Paris was expressed by General de Gaulle from the balcony of the city hall (hôtel de ville) at the time of the Liberation: "Paris brisée, Paris martyrisée, mais Paris libérée" [Paris broken, Paris martyred, but Paris liberated].[34] Paris was also recalled in the literature and films describing the capital's escaping destruction by the Germans during its liberation in August 1944. The story of Hitler's order for the destruction of Paris, the pleading for the city by Pierre Taittinger, who headed its municipal council, and the ultimate refusal by the local German commander General Dietrich von Choltitz to obey Hitler's order, has been told many times, notably by Larry Collins and Dominique Lapierre. Paris, according to the initiator of the insurrection, Henri Tanguy, known also as Colonel Rol, was worth two hundred thousand dead.[35] The different perspectives of Rol, a Communist insurrectionist, and Taittinger, Vichy's appointed municipal leader, converged on the centrality of Paris, which did not figure at all in the thinking of General Dwight Eisenhower, who had been prepared to bypass it en route to Germany. Taittinger's words to von Choltitz, while they stood together on a balcony of the German command post in the Hôtel Meurice, overlooking the Louvre and the Place de la Concorde, are emblematic:

> Often [Taittinger said] it is given to a general to destroy, rarely to preserve. Imagine that one day it may be given to you to stand on this balcony again, as a tourist, to look once more on these monuments to our joys, our sufferings, and to be able to say, "One day I could have destroyed all this, and I preserved it as a gift for humanity." General, is not that worth all a conqueror's glory?[36]

TOURISM AND THE BATTLE FOR MEMORY
FOLLOWING THE LIBERATION

The Liberation of France in 1944 brought another turnaround in the meaning of war-related sites. Symbolic places such as Strasbourg and Paris informed the cultural perspectives of the Resistance even during the Occupation, but it remained for the 1944 Liberation, followed by the end of the war and the subsequent increases in tourism, to more extensively develop Resistance perspectives. These became embroiled in what has been called "battles for memory."[37] Established in the immediate aftermath of the war, before the reconciliation with the new Federal Republic of Germany, these sites were often celebrated with admonitions against future German aggression. The construction of sites of memory and their related tourist itineraries after the Liberation reflected what historian Henry Rousso called the Gaullist effort to create a unified "resistancialist" (résistancialiste) memory of the war, according to which virtually all France had resisted the German invaders. As an example, Rousso cites a monument, located near Fontainebleau, to Georges Mandel, the Third Republic minister assassinated by Vichy's militia (milice) in July 1944. As Rousso noted, the inscription states that Mandel had been "murdered by the enemies of France." These enemies, Rousso continued, were unidentified and "might have been not miliciens but Germans, and in the mind of today's casual tourist they probably are."[38] Efforts to perpetuate a unified Resistance image through the sanctification of places of memory as tourist sites began within months of the Liberation. Because governmental approval was needed to erect public monuments in France, all such proposals, even if they were supported by private funding, required state sanction. One proposal, in mid-1945, was to erect a monument at the Place Saint-Michel in the heart of the city, recalling those who had died during the August 1944 fighting to liberate Paris.[39]

Tourist literature about Paris often evoked the August 1944 insurrection against the Germans that broke out shortly before the arrival of General Leclerc's liberation forces. In 1945, the Committee for Paris Tourism (Comité de Tourisme de Paris) published an illustrated English-language account of the liberation of the city, informed by the Gaullist Resistance narrative of the events and at the same time specifically addressing the role of tourism in the liberation of the city. Alexandre Parodi, a key figure in the August 1944 Parisian insurrection, wrote the introduction.[40] On August 26, Parodi joined General de Gaulle in the march down the Champs-Élysées that had celebrated the liberation of Paris. As the Germans fled eastward, Parodi wrote that "the lorries of the Wehrmacht reawakened the interest of the onlooker and made him forget his cares, made him an interested spectator, an adversary. The main thing was to be in the street, to enjoy the spectacle, to discuss it. . . . As the week advanced, Paris counted more passers-by; soon they did not pass but stayed, living in the streets, the women with folding stools and knitting." Paris, he continued, "liberated, welcomed the Allied soldiers, old companions in arms, whose approach had made possible, but not accomplished its liberation."[41] Of twenty-nine identifiable sites photographed for the book, four showed the city hall; three each the Latin Quarter; the police prefecture headquarters, where the insurrection had begun; and the Place de la Concorde. There were two photos each of the Notre Dame cathedral, where General de Gaulle had celebrated a mass amid shots ringing out shortly after the liberation; the Opéra; and the Arc de Triomphe.

Similarly evoking the liberation of Paris, the English-language guidebook *For You* featured the Arc de Triomphe on its cover and reminded its readers that "Paris, the most beautiful city in the world, [had] emerged from the battle intact."[42] Ossip Pernikoff, the head of a tour company prior to the war and technical attaché for tourism and transportation for the 1937 Paris World's Fair, found the city to be "decapitated" by the loss of many of its bronze statues, routinely melted down by the Germans for their war needs during the Occupation. With American support, Pernikoff assembled a group of volunteer supporters to restore the Paris statues, cautiously making certain, however, to use only materials that had no potential value to any future invader.[43] The expressions by personalities as different in French political life as Taittinger, Rol Tanguy, Parodi, and Pernikoff all spoke to the continuing centrality of Paris in French life. French and foreign tourists were expected to feel the weight of "eternal France" in their visits to her capital.

Parodi's account of the liberation of Paris, which expressed the Gaullist view, contrasted with the Communists' version in the construction of Resistance tourist circuits. French Communists paid special attention to the sites marking the August 1944 insurrection that had accompanied the liberation of Paris, whereas the Gaullists focused on the Arc de Triomphe and the renewal of the celebration of the November 11 World War I armistice in 1945.[44] Debate over the memory of the war erupted in the deliberations as to the kind of memorial to erect at Mont Valérien, the site near Paris used by the Germans for reprisals against Resistance fighters. After the June 1941 German invasion of Soviet Russia, many of the Mont Valérien victims had been Communists. The number of those shot remains in dispute with estimates running as high as forty-five hundred. Gaullists and Communists, however, disputed the significance of the site, the former wishing to celebrate annually the anniversary of General de Gaulle's call to resistance of June 18, 1940, the latter focusing on the clearing where the victims had been shot and which they called the "Golgotha of Paris." A private initiative, in 1947, sought to construct a via dolorosa linking the Tomb of the Unknown Soldier under the Arc de Triomphe to Mont Valérien, a stretch of more than four kilometers. Steles, with the inscribed names of some ten thousand victims, were proposed for the route. This proposal, as well as many others, was blocked by the government, which argued that a Mont Valérien monument should be a public rather than a private venture.[45]

Problems also arose when efforts to retain what were considered proper aesthetic standards for public monuments came into conflict with the interests of the tourist trade. In one compromise, to meet the advertising needs of local tourist interests, the Ministry of Education, under whose jurisdiction the erection of commemorative monuments fell, in 1948 proposed a law authorizing local prefects to allow tourist advertisements to be posted at classified sites. Commercial signs indicating the directions to various tourist attractions could thereby be displayed at the monuments.[46] Local groups were also active in the promotion of war-related tourist sites. Verdun, the site of the sanguinary 1916 World War I battle, was also the scene of a summary execution of sixteen prisoners by fleeing Gestapo troops during the German retreat from France in late 1944. The remains were discovered in the Tavannes forest, near a fort that had been part of the Verdun defense network during World War I. In 1948 a local committee sponsored the erection of a memorial to the sixteen victims that was also to serve as a monument to the August 31, 1944, liberation of Verdun. In the words of R. Panau, the Departmental Delegate for French Remembrance:

> A hundred meters from there [the site of the memorial] in August 1916, as we said previously, the last assault wave of the great Germany was broken in a supreme attempt to approach the Fort of Tavannes.
>
> Thus, twice, with an interval of twenty-eight years, this same Tavannes ravine had been the theater of the last act of impotent rage of the Germans, to whom Verdun was unattainable.
>
> 1916–1944. Tavannes is well deserving of the title "historic site" *(lieu historique).*[47]

In addition to the plaques, steles, and monuments that serve as tourist sites commemorating the war, museums also play key roles in the touristic memory circuit. Specific sites by their own historicity have become museums, such as the relics of the martyred town of Oradour-sur-Glane and the fortifications of the Maginot Line. Compiègne, already on the memory circuit as the site of the 1918 and 1940 armistices, acquired renewed meaning after September 1, 1944, when American forces liberated the armistice clearing. By the following November 11, the anniversary of the World War I armistice, German prisoners of war had restored the clearing. A ceremony took place that day in the presence of General Pierre Koenig, commander in chief of the French Forces of the Interior (Forces Françaises de l'Intérieur), French and American soldiers, and veterans of World War I. Scouts lit fires on braziers, and the area was set afire. All that was left standing was the statue of Marshal Ferdinand Foch that Hitler had also spared in 1940—according to one subsequent French account, to allow Foch to survey the destruction of his work rather than out of respect for him.[48] The "shame of June 1940" was extinguished by fire four years later. With Foch's railway car having been destroyed, a similar one was found in Romania and refitted exactly as the original. Otherwise, the clearing was restored as it had been on November 11, 1918. By 1946 the site had become a sacralized place of pilgrimage, but, according to *Le Monde* at the time, this was due in part to the tourists arriving from reasons of curiosity or commerce.[49]

Compiègne had also been the location of a prison camp at Royal-Lieu, where thousands of resisters had been interned during the Occupation. In addition, it had witnessed the first contingents of the so-called *Relève*, a scheme by which Pierre Laval, Pétain's de facto prime minister, in 1942 had arranged to have one French prisoner of war in Germany released for every three skilled French workers sent there to work.[50] In 1948, war veterans and groups of former prisoners of war, under the patronage of President Vincent Auriol and Veterans and War Victims Minister François Mitterrand, requested the creation of a monument at Compiègne to commemorate those who had fallen for the liberation of France.[51] The touristic focus in Compiègne, however, continued to be the restored armistice clearing. In 1950, the conservator of the Carrefour de l'Armistice (Armistice Crossroads) defined the purpose of the site:

> More than ten years have passed since Hitler's profanation of a site surrounded by the respect of all the French.
>
> At the Armistice clearing the outrage is effaced. A new force is born in the remembrance of November 11, 1918, and comes to sustain our hopes across the clouds that might again rise over the world.[52]

As with Compiègne and other tourist sites, the symbolism of Strasbourg changed over time. The heritage of both German and French cultures in Strasbourg, together with the history of conflict, led to the consideration of Strasbourg as an international center of reconciliation and peace. In 1949 the city was chosen as the seat for the Council of Europe, a supranational organization to promote human rights and improve cultural and social life in Europe, independently of the European Union (EU).[53] In stark contrast to the message of international reconciliation in Strasbourg is Oradour-sur-Glane, the martyred village in the Haute Vienne. Whereas the French government promoted dramatic change in the touristic symbolism of Strasbourg after the war, it tried to preserve inviolate the ruins of Oradour as they were following the massacre of June 10, 1944.

On June 7, 1944, the Second SS Panzer Division, "Das Reich," began a move northward from southern France to engage the Allies, who had landed in Normandy the previous day. Three days later, after an officer of the division had been captured by Resistance forces, the commander of the first battalion, a friend of the missing man, arrived in Oradour with the elite "Der Führer" regiment's third company. Acting on a tip that the missing officer was in Oradour, SS troops assembled the inhabitants in the town square. Women, children, and elderly were forced into the town's church, while the men were taken into other buildings. On command, the soldiers began shooting their captives. Afterward, they set fire to the church and buildings, killing nearly everyone. In all, the Germans killed 643 men, women, and children.[54] With the Liberation, the ruins of the town were turned into a shrine. Historian Sarah Bennett Farmer describes the site as a "topography" of memory created to make the site available to "pilgrims," "visitors," and "tourists," situating the pilgrims in a tradition of Christian visitors to holy sites.[55]

If Oradour, Strasbourg, and Paris represented starkly different touristic images of the war—Oradour, a brutal Nazi legacy to be preserved forever; Strasbourg, transformed into a place of European reconciliation, a France redeemed; and Paris, eternal France, bloodied but unbowed—the sites connected with the Maginot Line were more ambiguous. After the war, the Maginot fortifications remained in the hands of the French military. Many of the forts along the line had suffered little damage in the 1940 fighting; others were more severely damaged by American shelling in 1944. The French military attempted to modernize the forts to adopt them to missile warfare for NATO. They suspended these efforts in the face of higher-priority needs for the war in Algeria after 1955. The tourist development of the Maginot Line would come after 1964.

With the end of the Occupation, local leaders in Vichy found it impossible to separate the image of their town from that of the Pétain government. In September 1944, Vichy's municipal council requested that any allusion to the "Vichy" government be stricken from the French language.[56] The first issue of the *Michelin Guide* to appear after the Liberation, compiled in October 1944 and published in the spring of 1945, made no mention of the Occupation in its section on Vichy. Its silence contrasted with the years after World War I, when the Michelin company had published a series of extensive guides to the battlefields of France. The only reference to Marshal Pétain in the 1945 *Michelin Guide* was an indication of the Rue Maréchal Pétain (Marshal Pétain Street) on a map of the town.[57] Even local Resistance leaders had difficulties in restoring the good name of the town. In November 1944, the municipal council protested again, this time against what it called the undeserved opprobrium associated with the term *Vichy government*.[58]

While Vichy's leaders struggled with the stigma attached to their town, those who were nostalgic for the Pétain government developed their own tourist circuits. Given the centrality of Pétain's role as head of the Vichy state, and his earlier leadership in winning the World War I battle of Verdun in 1916 and in suppressing the military mutinies of 1917, sites associated with him continued to arouse touristic interest and controversy. Convicted of treason in his postwar trial at age eighty-eight, Pétain ended his days a prisoner on the Île d'Yeu, off the Atlantic coast of France, where he died at age ninety-five on July 23, 1951. In a move designed to thwart tourism to the grave site, the marshal was buried at Port-Joinville, on the relatively inaccessible island. Nonetheless, the interment proceedings brought out General Maxime Weygand and several other prominent personalities, themselves the objects of considerable curiosity from the small number of tourists taking summer holidays on the tiny island.[59]

Tourism and the Battle for Memory through the Mitterrand Era

By the early 1950s, following the death of Pétain, the Gaullist narrative of the war was securely in place. An example was the account of the 1944 liberation of France, which itself assumed touristic iconicity and highlighted Normandy on the tourist map. A three-day touring itinerary, entitled the "Liberation Circuit," organized in 1953 by the French Tourism Company (Compagnie Française de Tourisme), focused on the Allied landing beaches. The illustration for the Liberation Circuit included a cross of Lorraine, a soldier, and the inscription *Jour "J"* (D-Day). En route from Paris to Normandy, one visited Alençon, "liberated August 12, 1944, by the tanks of the glorious Leclerc Division" (in reference to General Leclerc's Free French forces). Battlefield sites upon arrival in Normandy on Day One included a thicket near Mortain, where a panzer division had been annihilated while trying to cut off the Americans. On the second day, visitors saw more battlefields and bombed towns, as well as the Utah and Omaha landing beaches. On the third day, the tour visited Arromanches, site of a British-built artificial port, and Courseulles, liberated by Canadian tanks. Courseulles was followed by a "pilgrimage" to Bény-Riviers, where more than two thousand Canadian soldiers lay buried. Caen, described as a "martyred city," had suffered seventy days of nearly uninterrupted bombing, during which three-quarters of the city had been destroyed, some eight thousand of ten thousand buildings demolished. Finally, on the return to Paris, there was a visit to Evreux, whose town center had been "devastated in 1940 by German artillery" and where on August 30, 1944, General de Gaulle's provisional government had installed its first Republican Regional Commission, a local government agency.[60] Another of the French Tourism Company Normandy itineraries featured the artificial port at Arromanches.[61]

In addition to the Gaullist tourist circuit, Jewish sites were built. In 1953, the first stone was placed for what was then called the Tomb of the Unknown Martyred Jew at 17, rue Geoffroy l'Asnier in Paris, the location of the Center for Contemporary Jewish Documentation (Centre de Documentation Juive

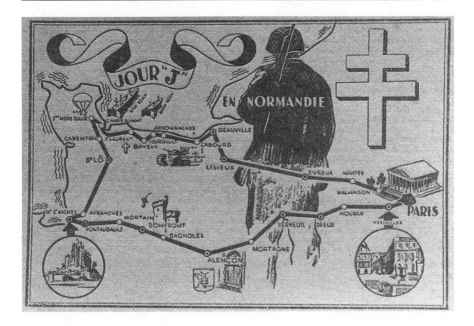

Tour itinerary, the "liberation circuit." (Reprinted from *Horizons de France et d'Europe* [Paris: Compagnie Française de Tourisme, 1953].)

Contemporaine).[62] Although Gaullist and Jewish perspectives remained strong, the passage of time began to effect subtle changes. The easing of the immediate postwar passions together with restored prosperity and increased tourism, in short a return to what might be called "normalcy," shifted the struggle over memory and tourism as the passage of time by the mid-1950s brought new perspectives to bear on the war.

Tensions between commemorative and tourist considerations were exemplified in the fate of a statue of Léon Gambetta, one of the founders of the Third Republic in the 1870s. Prior to the war, the statue had stood in the Cour Napoléon, a courtyard in the Louvre in Paris. During the Occupation, however, the Germans had melted down its bronze decorations. A sound and light show was planned for the 1954 tourist season at the Cour Napoléon, but the Gambetta statue stood in the way. In the name of "urban planning," which meant, among other things, the development of tourism in Paris, French authorities removed the statue. A patriot of the 1870 Franco-Prussian War, Gambetta, who at least in statue form had survived the German occupation of 1940–44, fell to the postwar tourist trade.[63]

Contested memory of the war became more apparent in the 1950s with the efforts of the Association to Defend the Memory of Marshal Pétain (Association pour Défendre la Mémoire du Maréchal Pétain, also known by its initials as ADMP) to convert locales associated with his life into tourist sites of pilgrimage. The ADMP attempted to turn Marshal Pétain's wartime apartment in Vichy's Hôtel du Parc, which had since been converted to private residences, into a museum. To honor Pétain, a plaque was affixed to the building. It was removed by the local Resistance veterans organization, which also harassed all attempts to set up the museum. In addition, Resistance veterans accosted those who visited the site ritually each November 11 to lay wreaths there in honor of Pétain.[64] In 1959, the ADMP magazine, Le Maréchal, added the house where Pétain was born, in Cauchy-la-Tour, Pas de Calais, to the list of tourist sites to be visited by way of honoring Pétain.[65] The next issue of Le Maréchal included another tourist reference, a war museum (the Musée de la Guerre Berrichon), ten kilometers from Châteauroux in the Indre, which contained artifacts from the wars of 1870, 1914, and 1939 and devoted an entire room to Pétain.[66] By 1959, Le Maréchal had identified a cluster of buildings on the Île d'Yeu as a pilgrimage shrine to Pétain's memory, including the Port-Joinville house in which he died, the local church, and the "provisional tomb," where his remains awaited the anticipated transfer to Douaumont, one of the 1916 Verdun forts where Pétain had requested to be buried. As the period around July 23, the anniversary of Pétain's death, was overcrowded, the magazine advised visitors to schedule trips at times other than the summer months and to write to the guardian of the tomb for help in finding accommodations on the small island.[67] During the annual Joan of Arc Day pilgrimage to the shrine of Verdelais in 1959, the Bordeaux section of the Fraternité de Notre-Dame de la Merci identified Pétain and Vichy with Joan and called upon pilgrims to remember the "the victims of the 1944 Revolution and especially Marshal Pétain."[68]

Meanwhile, disagreements between Gaullist and Communist Resistance veterans and their supporters had stymied action on a Mont Valérien memorial since the late 1940s. With the return to power of General de Gaulle in 1958, a compromise was reached in the design of the memorial and the crypt, featuring both the cross of Lorraine and the clearing in which the victims had been shot. The monument was dedicated in two stages, in 1960 and in 1962.[69] General de Gaulle also used his personal prestige to promote the Gaullist version of the war. In April 1959, newly installed as president of the Fifth Republic, he visited Vichy, which he called the "queen of spas." Emphasizing that the French were "one people," de Gaulle stated that the divisions of the past should be laid to rest. He ended his address with a cry of "Vive Vichy!"[70]

Commercial factors also shaped the development of tourist sites of remembrance, as seen in the proposal of a local committee to erect a monument to the Resistance in Le Havre, on the English Channel, in 1961. A private committee cited Le Havre's popularity with both French and foreign tourists and argued that the proposed monument would attract visitors drawn to the other tourist spots in the city. At the same time, it suggested, a memorial would bring in new tourists who would also visit the other local sites.[71] Requests for government funding to replace statues destroyed by the Germans appeared in France as late as 1962.[72] Although most of these requests went unheeded, there were many memorials to greet the tourist throughout France. In the words of one guidebook to the Resistance sites in Brittany, the tourist could expect to find plaques, steles, and monuments in every village.[73]

Anniversaries also played a part in the development of war-related tourism, as exemplified in the case of the Normandy invasion sites. A guidebook to these sites, prepared for the twentieth anniversary of the invasion in 1964, contained a preface by General Koenig. The guidebook, the first of its kind to Koenig's knowledge, was intended for veterans of the war, families coming to pay respects to their dead, and, "naturally, tourists traveling these regions heavy with history."[74] In addition to a brief history of the events leading up to the Normandy invasion, the guidebook listed seven touring itineraries, one relating to the British parachute troops' landings, another devoted to the events from the battle of Cherbourg to that of Caen, plus five other tours, each focusing on one of the landing beaches: Sword, Juno, Gold, Omaha, and Utah. The book concluded with a chronology and a bibliography.

The year 1964 also marked two very different types of tourist commemorations of the war: the reinterment of the remains of Resistance hero Jean Moulin in the Panthéon, which houses the remains of French heroes in Paris, and the beginning of the conversion of some of the Maginot forts into primarily tourist sites. In contrast to Mont Valérien, the Gaullist-Communist divisions were not found in the case of Jean Moulin, who had unified the Resistance in France before being captured, tortured, and killed by the Germans in 1943. The transfer of his remains to the Panthéon in 1964 became the apotheosis of one of the relatively few images that reflected a nearly unified memory of the war.[75] In contrast, in 1964, the French government, no longer feeling threatened by Germany and now more interested in its nuclear weapons program, ceased maintaining the Maginot Line fortifications. A sequence of television programs in 1965 brought the Maginot Line's new status to the attention of the French public. From 1964 through 1970 French military engineers used several of the fortifications for study. The army maintained the Simserhof fortifications and established a museum there in 1966 with an extensive collection of artillery, shells, and related military materiel.[76]

The resignation of General de Gaulle in 1969 and his death the next year contributed to the turning of a page in postwar French history in which non-Gaullist representations of the wartime past, while hardly new, acquired greater currency than at any time since 1944. In 1970, the government began selling some of the Maginot fortifications. The release in 1971 of Marcel

Ophuls's film *The Sorrow and the Pity (Le Chagrin et la pitié)*, which dealt with the war as experienced in the city of Clermont-Ferrand and questioned the vision of a united France resisting the Nazis, showed footage of soldiers bunkered down in the Maginot fortresses in 1939 and 1940. In 1972, the Commune of Marckolsheim acquired its local fortification, restored it, and opened it to the public. A series of histories of the line in the 1970s by Roger Bruge, starting with his *Blow Up the Maginot Line (Faites sauter la Ligne Maginot)* in 1973, contributed to a reawakening of public interest in the sites.[77] On July 9, 1973, searchers found the last seventeen French defenders who had been suffocated during a German attack on La Ferté, one of the Maginot fortifications. Plaques placed on the site by the French government and the veterans of the German unit that had fought against them honored these last soldiers to be discovered. Several of the soldiers were buried in a small military cemetery opposite the road from the bunker in which they had been entombed. A memorial ceremony is held each year for them on the Sunday closest to May 19, the day they died in 1940. In the early 1970s the fort was bought by the Committee to Remember the Defenders of Villy-La Ferté (Comité du Souvenir des Défenseurs de Villy-La Ferté), who opened it to tourists.[78] In the mid-1970s, additional forts along the line, abandoned except for scavengers who removed copper from them, were purchased by private associations, sometimes in conjunction with the local municipalities, and opened to the public.

The Sorrow and the Pity also helped put the Hohenzollern castle at Sigmaringen in Germany on the Vichy tourist circuit. The large and dour castle, where many of the Vichy leaders and collaborators found refuge during the nine months from the Liberation of France to the defeat of Germany in May 1945, was the location of an interview in the film with Christian de la Mazière, a French volunteer in the Waffen-SS. In 1973 the movement to sacralize Pétain may have crested with the kidnapping of his remains by supporters who removed them from the Île d'Yeu and tried to transfer them to Douaumont. Police patrols along the roads to Verdun led to the arrest of the body snatchers, who refused to divulge the location of Pétain's remains without a promise of reburial at the Invalides church in Paris. Ultimately the police located the remains and returned them to the Île d'Yeu for reburial.[79] In 1974, the Tomb of the Unknown Martyred Jew, dedicated in 1953 in Paris, was reconsecrated as the Memorial of the Unknown Martyred Jew. Public commemorations are held there annually on the anniversaries of the Warsaw ghetto uprising and the July 16, 1942, Vélodrome d'Hiver (a bicycle racing arena) roundup of Jews for ultimate deportation to the extermination camps.[80]

Despite the attention paid to maintaining Oradour as a site of memory, the martyred town was not entirely successful in fulfilling its role in the years after the war. A 1976 guidebook to French pilgrimage sites failed to mention it.

This guidebook, of more than two hundred pages, listed only one place related to World War II, Saint-Martin-de-Vercors, the site of a pilgrimage route created to honor the Resistance martyrs of Vercors in 1948.[81] In contrast to the attempt to make time stand still at Oradour, the symbolism of Strasbourg continued to change in the postwar years. Already the seat of the Council of Europe since 1949, the city emerged in the late 1950s as one of Europe's "capitals," subsequently the home of the European Parliament (of the European Community, now the European Union). The Palais d'Europe, opened in 1977 in Strasbourg, became the seat of the regular plenary sessions of the European Parliament and the unrelated Council of Europe. With its surrounding buildings, the Palais d'Europe became the center of the city's "European quarter," buttressing Strasbourg's claim to be a "capital of Europe."[82] The 1970s tourist circuit, with sites as different as Oradour and Strasbourg, continued to include Vichy, still unable to overcome its association with Pétain. Having failed to establish their museum in the Hôtel du Parc, the Pétainists moved their commemorative activities to the celebration of a mass at Vichy's Saint-Louis Church on each succeeding anniversary of the marshal's death. Though church authorities pleaded that the Pétainists be allowed to have their mass, confrontations ensued, and in 1978 units of the CRS (Compagnies Républicaines de Sécurité), a special police force, were called in. The bishop stopped the celebrations.[83]

Public interest in the Maginot Line continued to develop in the 1970s with private organizations raising funds and, often in conjunction with the military authorities, restoring many of the forts. Hackenberg, the largest of the Maginot fortifications, near Metz, was the subject of a 1976 guidebook, published in both French and German. Hackenberg, it noted, had taken five and one-half years to build, reached ten kilometers in length, and at its deepest point extended ninety-six meters into the earth.[84] Published with the aid of the Association Amifort, a private group that administered the site, the guidebook described an extensive tour that included a ride on the fortification's underground railway and a climb to ground level, from which the surrounding countryside could be observed. The private Association de l'Ouvrage du Fermont also obtained access to the Fermont fortification in 1976 and opened it to the public the following year.[85] In 1979, the association managing the Fermont fortification established a museum there and received an award for its work of historic restoration.[86]

The audience intended for the restored Maginot sites was clearly different from that of the official war monuments such as Oradour. Rather than the sense of national unity sought in the Resistance sites or mourning and victimization associated with Oradour, the Maginot fortresses gave an otherworldly feeling, described in 1979 by Paul Gamelin, who wrote several books about them:

On a visit one day to an abandoned fortification, alone or in the company of others, one gets the feeling of being in another world. One could imagine being a person from the year 2000, who, having escaped a cataclysm, traveled to discover the past and visited caverns where there had lived a generation that has disappeared.[87]

While private and public agencies worked to restore the Maginot forts, the town of Vichy, still struggling with its image, lost much of its tourism with a diminution in its spa clientele. Many spa visitors had been French colonial officials, given six-month vacations every ten years that they often spent at Vichy's spas. The end of the French empire produced a decline from a record 129,600 cure-seekers in 1931 to 19,009 in 1983. Meanwhile, a bookseller in Vichy noted that the mere suggestion of printing postal cards picturing the Hôtel du Parc had brought threatening phone calls. As an observer put it in 1985, *Vichyssois,* the innocent residents of the town, as much victimized as others in France by the war, were still confused with *Vichyistes,* who had served either in Pétain's government or had held ideological affinities with it.[88] By the late 1980s, however, a growing number of tourists sought out specific sites of the various 1940–44 ministries and state functions in Vichy. Facing the loss of its spa trade, the tourism office yielded to tourist curiosity, largely from Germans and Americans, and in 1987 created a "Vichy sites of the Pétain regime" (*sites vichyssois du régime de Pétain*) circuit, where twenty-five francs bought a two-hour tour, guided by a history student. The government had to gain approval for the tour from police agencies and Resistance veterans and overcome objections from the management of the Hôtel du Portugal, former seat of the Gestapo in Vichy. In 1988, Marc Ferro, a historian with no partiality to the Pétain government, invited to lecture in Vichy about a new biography of the marshal he had written, was not allowed to speak in the town because of allegations that even to speak of Pétain in Vichy was a step toward rehabilitating him.[89]

Lyon's Hôtel Terminus, where Klaus Barbie had headed the local Gestapo, was put on the tourist circuit by Barbie's trial in 1987, helped along by Marcel Ophuls's film *Hôtel Terminus,* just as his *The Sorrow and the Pity* had featured Clermont-Ferrand and spotlighted Sigmaringen. Interviewed about the making of *Hôtel Terminus,* Ophuls recalled he had endured severe criticism for his making of *The Sorrow and the Pity.* Claude Lanzmann, who had made the film *Shoah,* had asked with apparent sarcasm, "You will do for Lyon what you have done for Clermont-Ferrand?"[90] Whereas Ophuls did not work to promote nostalgic Vichy tourism, the rise to prominence of Jean-Marie Le Pen's National Front with pro-Vichy overtones was another matter. Its Joan of Arc Day pilgrimages in the 1980s, evoking those of the 1950s Pétainists, may have helped put a tourist circuit of "the other side" on the map. A guidebook for the political Right, published as the *Guide to Paris for the Man of the Right* (*Guide de l'Homme de Droite à Paris*), subtitled, in English, *Paris by Right*, written by Francis Bergeron and Philippe Vilgier in 1987, offered a small Vichyite circuit of some fifteen sites in a list of two thousand.

Recommended Vichyite sites in *Paris by Right* included the cemeteries where writers Robert Brasillach, executed for collaboration in 1945, and Pierre Drieu la Rochelle, a suicide following the liberation of France, were buried.[91] *Paris by Right* also mentioned bookstores, shops, and museums where Vichy-related objects could be viewed and some purchased. These included a book-shop on the premises of what had once been the offices of the Parti Populaire Français, a political party established in 1936 that became collaborationist after 1940, and a shop where for seven hundred francs in 1986 visitors could purchase a street marker plaque with the inscription "Place du maréchal Pétain."[92] By the late 1980s, the Association to Defend the Memory of Marshal Pétain was soliciting funds to establish a museum of Pétain memorabilia in the newly restored house in which he had been born, in Cauchy-la-Tour.[93]

The creation of the Vichy tourist circuit, renewed interest in Lyon's Hôtel Terminus, and, to a lesser extent, the publication of the *Paris by Right*, all in 1987, manifested a shift in attitudes whereby sites associated with the "other side" were losing their taboo status. Interest in the Maginot Line appeared to mount. Claude-Armand Masson's 1942 Maginot Line memoir was republished in 1985 and sold in souvenir kiosks at the sites, for example at the Fermont fortification. Tour guides were often local volunteers, some of them war veterans. The French authorities continued to consider what to do with the fortifications. Fermont remained the property of the French army, which occasionally held military maneuvers on its grounds, as in a demonstration of 150 helicopters of the Air Mobile Division on July 14, 1986, in the presence of President Mitterrand.[94] By the late 1980s, an Association des Amis du Simserhof (Association of the Friends of Simserhof) organized tours of the fortress.[95] Several of the restored fortifications had also set up museums, each claiming to be "the museum of the Maginot Line," with collections similar to that at Simserhof. The authors of the *Guide to the Maginot Line* (*Guide de la Ligne Maginot*) cautioned tourists that none of the museums had received the official imprimatur of the Ministry of Culture. According to the *Guide*, the three most important of the museums were at Simserhof, Fermont, and Hackenberg. The intended audience for the fortifications and their museums was largely veterans and war enthusiasts, and, not surprisingly, there was considerable interest in the Maginot Line among Germans, who purchased many of the small related items sold by the French military in the 1970s.[96] In 1988, the British monthly magazine *After the Battle*, which features stories about historic battlefields and what has become of them, published a map of the Maginot Line, showing some twenty-five fortifications, including four along the

Francis Bergeron   et   Philippe Vilgier

Guide de l'Homme de Droite à Paris

« Paris by Right »

EDITIONS DU TRIDENT

Title page from Bergeron Vilgier, *Guide de l'Homme de Droite à Paris* (Paris by right) (Paris: Editions de Trident, 1987).

Franco-Italian frontier. Of the twenty-five forts, ten were open to public touring, attracting some two hundred thousand visitors annually.[97]

Another kind of memorial site opened in 1988 was the Caen Memorial-Museum of Peace (Mémorial-Musée de la Paix). The Lower Normandy city of Caen, heavily damaged by fighting in 1944, was chosen to house the Memorial-Museum of Peace, an impressive structure containing exhibits, a library, a bookstore, and meeting rooms for activities related to the history of the war, as well as larger issues of war and peace.[98] During the late 1980s and early 1990s, Strasbourg also continued its iconic evolution from Franco-German recrimination to symbol of European reconciliation, echoed in a 1989 *Michelin Guide,* as "the 'capital' of Europe."[99] By 1990, the European Parliament in Strasbourg welcomed 450,000 people annually, more than the city's famous cathedral.[100] Tourist literature in Strasbourg promoted the city as a European capital, focusing on its dual French and German heritage.[101]

Controversy over war-related tourist sites continued into the 1990s, swirling around François Mitterrand, who, as recently as 1992, had followed previous presidents in having wreaths placed at Marshal Pétain's grave at Port-Joinville on the Île d'Yeu.[102] Also in 1992, the Lyon Gestapo office at the Hôtel Terminus, filmed in Marcel Ophuls's movie of the same name, was converted into a part of the Center for the History of the Resistance and Deportation. From its opening in 1992 through 1996, 230,000 visitors registered, at least half of them "young," many brought in school excursions.[103] As of 1992, the only memorial to be found in Vichy commemorating the history of 1940–44 was a plaque on the opera building in honor of the eighty parliamentarians who had voted there on July 10, 1940, against the granting of constituent powers to Marshal Pétain.[104] A 1992 Michelin republication in French and English of a 1947 map, entitled "The Battle of Alsace," contained a history of the battle, together with a list of twenty-one historic sites. The map described the liberation of Colmar, for example, as "an example of the splendid spirit of cooperation which existed between the French and American armies." In its section on the history of the battle, the map indicated that "over four years of occupation had not diminished the Alsatian spirit of resistance and their faith in France."[105] In contrast to the Resistance vision of the Michelin map, however, heightened interest in wartime French complicity in the Holocaust lent related sites enhanced visibility. In 1993, the site of the Vélodrome d'Hiver roundup of Jews was made into an official memorial on July 16, the anniversary of the 1942 roundup. Mitterrand decreed July 16 a "day of remembrance," and the site of the arena, since demolished, was declared an official memorial in a ceremony in which he, Prime Minister Édouard Balladur, and Jacques Chirac, then mayor of Paris, participated. In a gesture stimulated by the legacy of the Barbie trial, Mitterrand also participated in the inaugural in 1994 of a museum-memorial at Izieu, where forty-four Jewish pupils and their teachers had been rounded up by Barbie on April 6, 1944, for ultimate deportation to Auschwitz.[106]

A measure of the evaluation of World War II tourist sites is the *Michelin Guide,* one of the most prestigious tour guides in France. Under "Vichy," its 1994 English-language guide to France noted that the town "gave its name to the government of the French State, the regime led by Marshal Pétain which ruled the country under close German supervision from 12 July 1940 until 20

August 1944."[107] Some 1,320 sites were listed in the Michelin guidebook, of which 32 made specific mention of World War II events. Of the 32 references, 20, or 63 percent, were to battle sites, mainly from the 1940 and 1944 campaigns, and destruction, largely during the latter. There were four references to the Resistance fighting: in the town descriptions of Ajaccio, Lille, Lyon, and Paris.[108] The guidebook described the Traboules network of covered passageways in the Croix-Rousse hill above the Rhône River in Lyon that was "much used by the Resistance in the Second World War."[109] In its Paris section, the Michelin tour book referred to forty-five hundred Resistance fighters killed in the clearing on Mont Valérien, where there was now a memorial to Fighting France. It said nothing of the differences in Gaullist and Communist perspectives in creating the monument, referred to the "many victims of the Nazi racial myth" rounded up at the Vélodrome d'Hiver, and highlighted German brutality in its description of the Oradour-sur-Glane massacre.[110] General de Gaulle appeared in the historical introduction and at three specific sites: Bayeux, where he first set foot on French soil after the Liberation and where he laid out the principles for a new constitution in June 1944; Colombey-les-deux-Eglises, and Abbeville.[111] In Colombey, La Boisserie, now a museum, served as the country house of "this great Frenchman" from his purchase of it in 1933 through his death. Two additional sites of pilgrimage in Colombey were the memorial, a giant cross of Lorraine, and the general's tomb in the village churchyard.[112] The description of Abbeville focused on the role of General de Gaulle's Fourth Armored Division in the May 1940 battle of the Somme.[113]

The year 1994 was the fiftieth anniversary of the Normandy landings, with some twenty museums in the Normandy area, in addition to one in Portsmouth, focusing on the invasion. The Portsmouth museum housed the Overlord Embroidery, completed in 1968 after five years' labor, modeled after the Bayeux tapestry that depicted William the Conqueror's successful invasion of England. In addition to the twenty museums in Normandy, a *Visitor's Guide to Normandy Landing Beaches, Memorials, and Museums* identified 177 memorials, not including the many names of streets and squares commemorating the events of 1944.[114]

By requesting to participate in the fiftieth anniversary commemorations of the Normandy landings, German Chancellor Helmut Kohl called into question the iconicity of the battle sites there as a kind of family shrine shared by the French with their World War II allies. Although Kohl represented a democratic Germany, reconciled with France in the European Union, the French rejected his request. Undoubtedly, his presence at the Normandy commemoration would have diluted its unifying national symbolism, hinting at the possibility that the war had also witnessed anti-Nazi "good" Germans and pro-Axis "bad" Frenchmen. Fifty years after the Liberation, the much visited Normandy battlefields still carried a heavy emotional charge among France's leaders, for whom the last pages of the postwar period had not yet been turned and who still guarded the unified Resistance imagery. The French decision regarding one emotionally charged tourist site—Normandy—in 1994 led to another. In an effort to assuage German pique over the Normandy snub, President Mitterrand invited the seven hundred soldiers of the Eurocorps, which included two hundred Germans, to join the traditional July 14, Bastille Day military parade. This decision provoked objections in France when German soldiers of the Eurocorps paraded down the Champs-Élysées, reminding some of the victorious German parades of the Occupation years.[115]

Conclusion: French Cultural Tourism and the Vichy Problem in the Present

The years 1994 and 1995 marked a stock taking, if not a turning point, in the evolution of French views of the World War II years and, accordingly, of war-related tourism. The fiftieth anniversary of the Liberation, the first conviction of a French citizen, Paul Touvier, of crimes against humanity, and the increased publicity given to President Mitterrand's Vichy activities, culminating in a television interview, all occurred in 1994.[116] These events were followed in 1995 by the election of Jacques Chirac, followed by his formal apology for the crimes committed by Vichy. Contested memory in the construction of tourist sites was complicated in 1995 with the election of National Front candidates as mayors, with real power to affect cultural tourism, in Toulon, Orange, and Marignane. Continued attempts in 1996 by the National Front to appropriate Joan of Arc as a tourist icon were criticized by President Chirac, who stated that "the purity of the ideal" of Joan belonged to all in France and was not the property of a faction.[117] In 1997, a National Front candidate was elected mayor of Vitrolles. Although National Front electoral successes resulted from contemporary issues more than nostalgia for the Occupation, Toulon critics of the Front referred to the "Vichyization of spirits" (vichysation des esprits) of daily life in their city.[118] At the least, National Front pressure changed library book purchasing in the towns under their control, with consequences for the literature of cultural tourism regarding World War II that are yet to be determined.[119] In Vitrolles, the National Front administration renamed streets that had formerly honored President Mitterrand and Nelson Mandela among others.[120]

Far right elements in France spread "revisionist" texts on the internet, calling into question the veracity of the Oradour massacre account and challenging the historical signification given the site during the previous half century since the war. Authorities in Caen dismissed a secondary school teacher for using these materials in his teaching.[121] The preservation of the Oradour

ruins from the ravages of time and weather necessitated intervention that necessarily altered the 1944 wreckage. Such unavoidable change, a problem for all
historic preservation, called into question what Dean MacCannell termed the
touristic "authenticity" of such sites.[122]

Questions of "authenticity" have been raised with regard to the still
preserved Compiègne clearing, where annual celebrations commemorate
the 1918 armistice, often in the presence of the president of the Republic, but
with an ersatz railway car.[123] As Serge Barcellini and Annette Wieviorka note,
however, little is ever said of the other—the 1940—armistice that was signed
there.[124] Authenticity and preservation are also issues for the Maginot
fortifications, whose rise in interest since the 1970s may most reflect shifting
perspectives on the war. More than the other sites, the Maginot Line
addresses both the aging French and German veterans of the war and, as the
German plaque at La Ferté indicates, symbolizes reconciliation among
them. There is also a clientele for war-related tourism in general, as seen in
the preponderance of battlefields among the war sites listed in the 1994
Michelin Guide, the success of the magazine *After the Battle,* and the activity
of the British Holt travel agency, which offers some eighty battlefield tours
annually. In 1997, the French military continued to wrestle with the problem
of decommissioning World War II facilities, for example, the Kéroman sub-
marine base near Lorient, in Brittany, built by the Germans for their U-
boats. Scheduled for closure at the end of 1997, the Kéroman base, "mon-
strous but fascinating," is visited by fifteen thousand tourists each year, the
majority of them German. Future uses being considered included a subma-
rine museum and a pleasure park.[125]

The Kéroman base issue shows how new tourist sites related to the memory of the war continue to appear and older ones are reinterpreted. In 1997, a
new tourist circuit was created of museums in and around Paris displaying
some 987 artworks taken by the Nazis during the Occupation. After the war,
these works came into the possession of the French government, which only in
the mid-1990s made efforts to locate the original owners and their heirs.[126]
Also in 1997, the discovery in a public trash container of archival documents
pertaining to the Rivesaltes concentration camp, near Perpignan in southern
France, intensified efforts by the Association of the Sons and Daughters of
Jewish Deportees of France (Association des fils et filles des déportés juifs de
France) to have the camp declared a site of memory. The camp had been used
in 1939 for Republican Spanish refugees, in May 1940 to incarcerate German
and Austrian citizens, of whom half were Jewish refugees, and then during the
Occupation as a staging area for rounded-up Jews, many of whom were eventually deported to the extermination centers in the east. After the war, it
housed "displaced persons" and in 1963 held more than thirteen hundred
harkis, pro-French Algerian Muslims who had fled in fear of their lives after

Algerian independence. In 1997, the camp housed illegal immigrants on their way to forced repatriation.[127]

Continuing struggles over Rivesaltes, Kéroman, the Maginot fortresses, Oradour, and other sites show not only the multiplicity of voices contending for influence but also the powerful hold of World War II over the imagination in France and among visiting tourists. This hold was stimulated in 1998 by the release of Steven Spielberg's film *Saving Private Ryan*, which highlighted again the Normandy sites related to D-Day and was described in France as "the memory of the century as theme park."[128] In 2000, a satirical newspaper noted that the Caen Memorial-Museum of Peace bookstore, "for a place which speaks of peace, sells only things relating to war."[129] Following the annual June 18 ceremony at Mont Valérien, President Chirac opened a wing dedicated to General de Gaulle in the Invalides war museum, the fourth most popularly visited museum in France.[130] That post-war Franco-German reconciliation was not yet complete even at the turn of the century more than fifty years after the war was illustrated in the interaction of politics and tourism occasioned by the first visit of an official German delegation to the Oradour ruins. The group was accompanied by the Bavarian minister of European affairs and welcomed by the president of the Limousin regional government and the mayor of Oradour, who had initiated the visit but who also explained that it was still too early to invite official representatives of the Berlin government to the site. Reticence on the part of the association of the families of Oradour's victims concerning the visit, together with the continuing failure of the German government to apologize for the 1944 massacre, contributed to the unease that surrounded the visit.[131]

The present growth and anticipated expansion of cultural tourism worldwide, together with the related increase in historians' study of it, will engender better understandings of war-related tourism and the ways it both reflects sociopolitical values and helps shape them. Historians will examine the relationships between television programs, such as the 1965 series on the Maginot Line, and films, including those of Ophuls and Spielberg, with cultural tourism in France. They will explore the role of private as well as state initiative in war-related tourism and the influences of the various pressure groups on both. Finally, time will determine what impact the National Front, which split in two in 1999, and those who deny the historicity of the Holocaust, will have on the evolution of cultural tourism and the Vichy problem in France.

NOTES

1. Roger-Pol Droit, "Tous touristes," *Livres* section, *Le Monde*, May 30, 1997, vi.

2. Richard Butler and Geoffrey Wall, "Introduction: Themes in Research on the Evolution of Tourism," *Annals of Tourism Research*, 12, no. 3 (1985): 292–93.

3. For France as a tourist destination, see Valene Smith, ed., *Hosts and Guests: The Anthropology of Tourism* (Philadelphia: University of Pennsylvania Press, 1977), 2. France's "Vichy problem" is the debate over the degree to which the French collaborated with Nazi Germany during the 1940–44 occupation of France by the Germans during World War II. Following the defeat of France by Germany in June 1940, the French government moved from Paris to Vichy, where, under the leadership of Marshal Philippe Pétain, a World War I hero, it transformed the French Republic into the French State (État Français), an authoritarian government committed to some sort of accommodation with what many anticipated to be a permanent European "New Order" under Nazi leadership. A good introduction to the history of Vichy France is Robert O. Paxton, *Vichy France: Old Guard and New Order, 1940–1944* (New York: Knopf, 1972). For the continuing debate over the war years in France, see Henry Rousso, *The Vichy Syndrome: History and Memory in France since 1944,* trans. Arthur Goldhammer (Cambridge: Harvard University Press, 1991); Éric Conan and Henry Rousso, *Vichy: An Ever-Present Past,* trans. Nathan Bracher (Hanover, N.H.: University Press of New England, 1998); and Bertram M. Gordon, "The 'Vichy Syndrome' Problem in History," *French Historical Studies* 19, no. 2 (1995): 495–518. Discussion of books such as Rousso's *Vichy Syndrome,* first published in 1987 in France, and the continuing interest in World War II produced more research by historians on that period than on any other in French history except for the 1789 Revolution. See Robert Tombs, "The Dark Years," *Times Literary Supplement,* January 28, 1994, 9. In recent years, debates about Vichy have focused increasingly on French complicity in the Nazi Holocaust against the Jews. Convictions in 1987, 1994, and 1998 of wartime Lyons Gestapo chief SS Obersturmführer Klaus Barbie, Vichy *milice* (militia) officer Paul Touvier, and Vichy's secretary general of the Gironde Prefecture, Maurice Papon, respectively, of crimes against humanity highlighted retrospective controversies over Vichy in 1980s and 1990s France. Increased publicity in 1994 surrounding then President François Mitterrand's Vichy activity also intensified debate about the war years in France. In 1995, shortly after his election as president, Jacques Chirac, head of the Gaullist Rassemblement pour la République (Rally for the Republic) apologized on behalf of the French state for crimes committed by Vichy, a gesture Mitterrand had refused. For the debates about Vichy, especially in the 1980s and 1990s, see Bertram M. Gordon, "World War II France Half a Century After: In Historical Perspective," in *Fascism's Return: Scandal, Revision, and Ideology,* ed. Richard J. Golsan (Lincoln: University of Nebraska Press, 1998), 152–81. For the background leading to the Papon trial, see Bertram M. Gordon, "Afterword: Who Are the Guilty and Should They Be Tried?" in *Memory, the Holocaust, and French Justice,* ed. Richard J. Golsan (Hanover, N.H.: University Press of New England, 1996), 179–98.

4. Bertram M. Gordon, "The Morphology of the Collaborator: The French Case," *Journal of European Studies* 23, nos. 89–90 (March–June 1993): 2.

5. Chris Rojek, "Indexing, Dragging, and the Social Construction of Tourist Sites," in *Touring Cultures: Transformations of Travel and Theory,* ed. Chris Rojek and John Urry (London: Routledge, 1997), 54–55.

6. David Lowenthal, *The Heritage Crusade and the Spoils of History* (Cambridge: Cambridge University Press, 1998), xiii. See also Dean MacCannell, *The Tourist: A New Theory of the Leisure Class* (New York: Schocken, 1976), 41. In the United States, sites of memory correspond to "cultural tourism" and "heritage tourism," which to the California Council for the Humanities means "a destination with a story." See James Quay, "Cultural Tourism and the Humanities," *Humanities Network,* 19, no. 2 (1997), 1 and 6.

7. Chris Rojek and John Urry, "Transformations of Travel and Theory," in Rojek and Urry, *Touring Cultures*, 12. For the distinction between "tours" and "pilgrimages," see David W. Lloyd, *Battlefield Tourism: Pilgrimage and Commemoration of the Great War in Britain, Australia, and Canada, 1919–1939* (Oxford: Berg, 1998), 19 and 40–44.

8. Lloyd, *Battlefield Tourism*, 29.

9. Jean Leveque, "Dear Friends," *For You*, June 1945, 4. *For You* had a brief life, appearing in 1945 only.

10. Francis Ambrière, preface to *Les Guides Bleus: Normandie* (Paris: Hachette, 1965), vi. Ambrière was director of the *Guides Bleus*. Among several memorials introduced to the tourist was the American Military Cemetery at Colleville-sur-Mer (443).

11. Jean-Pierre Bady, *Que sais-je? Les monuments historiques en France* (Paris: Presses Universitaires de France, 1985), 78.

12. For a report of an unauthorized use of the term *lieux de mémoire* in Italy, see Nicolas Weill, "Démarquage sauvage des 'lieux de mémoire' en Italie," *Livres* section, *Le Monde*, January 3, 1997, viii.

13. Emmanuel de Roux, "Jacques Le Goff, historien, 'L'amour du patrimoine peut s'accomplir en respectant l'autre,'" *Le Monde*, January 7, 1997, 30.

14. See "Un Guide touristique mis à l'index," *Le Monde*, November 8, 1996, 12; also Bertram M. Gordon, "German Tourists in World War II France," *Annals of Tourism Research* 25, no. 3 (July 1998): 632. Recent debates over memorials to World War II and to President Franklin D. Roosevelt in the United States show that such controversies are by no means limited to France. For the projected American World War II memorial, see Janny Scott, "A Planned War Memorial Sets Off a Battle of Its Own," *New York Times*, March 18, 1997, B1; and for the Roosevelt memorial, Michael Wines, "Monuments Are a Risky Business," *New York Times Week in Review*, May 4, 1997, 1.

15. Bertram M. Gordon, "Collaboration, Retribution, and Crimes against Humanity: The Touvier, Bousquet, and Papon Affairs," *Contemporary French Civilization* 19, no. 2 (1995): 250.

16. These trials, focusing on "crimes against humanity" and highlighting French complicity in the Holocaust, evoked formal apologies in France that included that of President Jacques Chirac in 1995.

17. Julian Jackson, *The Popular Front in France: Defending Democracy, 1934–38* (Cambridge: Cambridge University Press, 1988), 136.

18. Christian Faure, *Le Projet culturel de Vichy: Folklore et révolution nationale, 1940–1944* (Lyon: Presses Universitaires de Lyon, 1989), 30.

19. Gordon, "German Tourists," 621–22.

20. Gaston Mortier, *Le Tourisme et l'économie nationale: Un passé encourageant ... Vers un meilleur avenir* (Paris: B. Arthaud, 1941), 31.

21. "L'Importance du tourisme dans la France de demain," *Lyon Touriste/Journal Officiel du Syndicat d'Initiative de Lyon et de ses environs*, 37:292 (1st half 1943), 1.

22. "Le Congrès des présidents des chambres départementales de la Zone Sud des 9 et 10 mars 1943, à Brive-la-Gaillarde," *L'Hôtelier Alpin. Organe de la Chambre Professionelle départementale de l'industrie hôtelière et debitants de boissons des Hautes-Alpes*, March 1943, 1.

23. Georges Mathiot, *Le Tourisme réceptif français. Sa place dans l'économie nationale et internationale. Sa position devant la nouvelle règlementation de 1942–1943* (Nancy: Société d'Impressions Typographiques, 1945), 170–71.

24. *Vichy, Vichyite*, and *Vichyssoise* in *Oxford English Dictionary*, 19:603.

25. "Les Bars parisiens dits ... Américains," *L'Hôtelier Français, La Gazette de la Vie Hôtelier et du Tourisme*, June 5, 1944, 13.

26. *Paris und Umgebung. Odé-Buch* (Paris: Odé, 1941), 36–38. For the political and military significance of the 1940 Compiègne armistice, see Bertram M. Gordon, "Compiègne," in Bertram M. Gordon, ed., *Historical Dictionary of World War II France: The Occupation, Vichy, and the Resistance, 1938–1946* (Westport, Conn.: Greenwood Press, 1998), 83–84.

27. Heinrich Hoffmann, *Mit Hitler im Westen* (Munich: Verlag Heinrich Hoffmann, 1940), 113 and 115, respectively.

28. C. de Hauteclocque, "Leclerc, Philippe," in Gordon, *Historical Dictionary*, 218.

29. Bitterly described as a "useless bastion" by one of its French defenders, the fortifications had cost an estimated five billion francs in the 1930s; see Claude-Armand Masson, *La veille inutile* (Paris: Sercap, 1985), title page.

30. Anthony Kemp, *The Maginot Line: Myth and Reality* (London: Frederick Warne, 1981), 101.

31. Vivian Rowe, *The Great Wall of France: The Triumph of the Maginot Line* (London: Putnam, 1959), 14–15. See also Francis Deron, "La Grande Muraille, du Maginot imaginaire," *Le Monde,* December 28, 1996, 10.

32. David Pryce-Jones, *Paris in the Third Reich* (New York: Holt, Rinehart, and Winston, 1981), 13.

33. Hoffmann used one of his photos showing Hitler at Trocadéro with the Eiffel Tower in the background as the cover of his photo album commemorating the 1940 victory. See Hoffmann, *Mit Hitler im Westen,* cover; also Gordon, "German Tourists," 620.

34. A CD-ROM was produced by the historian Marc Ferro featuring this, among other moments of the war, in France. See Daniel Schneidermann, "La Seconde Guerre mondiale, pour mémoire," *Le Monde Télévision Radio Multimédia,* October 20–21, 1996, 35. Emblematic of the iconic status of Paris was the photo book published within months of the Liberation, see *La Semaine héroïque, 19–25 Août 1944* (Paris: S.E.P.E., 1944).

35. Larry Collins and Dominique Lapierre, *Is Paris Burning?* (New York: Simon and Schuster, 1965), see especially 39, 53, and 89–90.

36. Ibid., 89.

37. Gérard Namer, *Batailles pour la mémoire: La commémoration en France 1944–1982* (Paris: S.P.A.G., 1983), 13.

38. Rousso, *The Vichy Syndrome,* 22.

39. Extrait du B. O. [Bulletin Officiel] du 20.6.1945, 45; in Archives Nationales (abbreviated hereafter as AN), F21/7075, folder "Seine."

40. For Parodi, see Odile Rudelle, "Parodi, Alexandre," in Gordon, *Historical Dictionary,* 275–76.

41. Alexandre Parodi, introduction to *La Libération de Paris,* English-language edition (Paris: Comité de Tourisme de Paris, 1945), n.p; emphasis added.

42. COFBA [Franco-Allied Goodwill Committee], *France* (Paris: Franco-Allied Goodwill Committee, 1947), 23.

43. Ossip Pernikoff, letter to the Minister of Education and Beaux-Arts, October, 11 1947; AN, F21/7075, folder "Seine Ossip Pernikoff." On Pernikoff, see also Edmond Labbé, preface to *La France pays du tourisme,* by Ossip Pernikoff (Paris: Plon, 1938), 15.

44. Namer, *Batailles pour la mémoire,* 7–8.

45. M.-P. de Leonard, letter to Reverend Father Regamey, September 22, 1947, and René Perchet, Director of Architecture in the Education Ministry, letter to the General Director of Arts and Letters, in AN, F21/7085D, folder "Paris/Monuments commémoratifs 'La voie douloureuse' "; also Serge Barcellini and Annette Wieviorka, *Passant, souviens-toi! Les lieux du souvenir de la Seconde Guerre mondiale en France* (Paris: Plon,

1995), 170–75. Sites related to Jewish memory of the war were also constructed almost immediately after the war, such as one in Paris, where, in 1948, the Union of Jewish 1939–45 Veterans dedicated a monument to Jews who had died in the war and in the Resistance. See Union des Engagés Volontaires Anciens Combattants Juifs 1939–1945, letter to Robert Rey, Director of Artistic Production, Ministry of Education, November 26, 1948, in AN, F21/7085C, folder "Paris/Monument des Combattants Juifs."

46. Direction de l'Architecture, Sites, Ministry of Education, letter to M. Jaujard, Director General of Arts and Letters, October 14, 1948, in AN, F21/7079, folder "Monuments Commémoratifs/Protection des Sites Classés."

47. R. Panau, *Verdun dans l'histoire/Tavannes, lieu historique sur la route du Fort de Vaux* (Verdun: Les Editions Lorraines, Frémont, n.d.), 24. This brochure appears to have been published in, or shortly after, 1948.

48. Marie-Théophile-Armand-Théodore Codevelle, *Armistice 1918 sa signature la clairière Compiègne* (Compiègne: Imprimerie du "Progrès de l'Oise," 1950), 13. For another argument that the statue of Foch was left standing "by derision," see Marc Boulanger, *Juin 1940. Trois semaines en France. Vers l'armistice de Compiègne* (Luneray: Editions Bertout "La Mémoire Normande," 1992), 132.

49. Namer, *Batailles pour la mémoire*, 172. On souvenirs and symbols of the sacred in tourism, see Nelson N. H. Graburn, "Tourism: The Sacred Journey," in Smith, *Hosts and Guests*, 28–29.

50. Sometimes referred to as "premier" or "prime minister," Pierre Laval was formally vice president of the Council of Ministers (under Pétain, the president) from July through December 1940 and again from April 1942 through the end of the Vichy government in August 1944.

51. Letter from de Barroy, secretary general, Union Française des Associations d'Anciens Combattants, to the mayor of Compiègne, April 1948; AN, F21/7085A Oise/Compiègne/Monument commémoratif.

52. Codevelle, *Armistice 1918*, 15.

53. Council of Europe/Conseil de l'Europe, "Série de fiches d'informations, Activités et Réalisations," published by the Directorate of Information, September 1992, back cover.

54. Wesley White, "Oradour-sur-Glane," in Gordon, *Historical Dictionary*, 267–68.

55. Sarah Bennett Farmer, "Oradour-sur-Glane: Memory in a Preserved Landscape," *French Historical Studies* 19, no. 1 (1995): 35 and 40.

56. Rousso, *The Vichy Syndrome*, 73.

57. Guide du Pneu Michelin 1945 (Paris: Services du Tourisme Michelin, 1945), 975–77.

58. Eric Conan, "Vichy malade de Vichy," *L'Express*, June 26, 1992, 36–37.

59. Rousso, *The Vichy Syndrome*, 42. In November 1951, an Association pour Défendre la Mémoire du Maréchal Pétain (ADMP, Association to Defend the Memory of Marshal Pétain), was created. It has worked assiduously since to sacralize the sites connected with his life. One of its early and continuing goals was the reburial of Pétain's remains at Douaumont, a fortification at Verdun, where the marshal had asked that he be allowed to rest with his World War I soldiers.

60. "Itinéraire No. 1100, le circuit de la Libération," in *Horizons de France et d'Europe* (Paris: Compagnie Française de Tourisme, 1953), 1–2.

61. "Itinéraire No. 1110, circuit 'Aux Léopards' de la Normandie," in *Horizons de France et d'Europe*, 12.

62. Barcellini and Wieviorka, *Passant, souviens-toi*, 461–62.

63. A. Cornu, secretary of state for beaux-arts, letter to the prefect of the Seine, September 17, 1953, in AN, F21/7085C, folder "Paris/Monument Gambetta."

64. Conan, "Vichy malade de Vichy," 36–37.

65. H. Dorgérès, "L'Oeuvre constructive du Maréchal pour la paysannerie," *Le Maréchal*, April 1959, 1.

66. "Une Visite à Faire," *Le Maréchal*, May 1959, 2.

67. Pierre Henry, "La Célébration de la mort du Maréchal à l'Île d'Yeu," *Le Maréchal*, June–July 1959, 4.

68. "Pèlerinage à Verdelais," *Le Maréchal*, June–July 1959, 4.

69. M.-P. de Leonard, letter to Reverend Father Regamey, September 22, 1947, and René Perchet, director of architecture in the Education Ministry, letter to the general director of arts and letters, in AN, F21/7085D, folder "Paris/Monuments commémoratifs 'La voie doulourouse,'" also Barcellini and Wieviorka, *Passant, souviens-toi*, 170–75.

70. Rousso, *The Vichy Syndrome*, 73.

71. Gilbert Fernez, secretary general, Comité du Souvenir de la Résistance du Havre et de la Région, letter to General Direction, Arts and Letters, October 16, 1961, in AN, F21/7085D, folder "Seine-Maritime/Le Havre/Monument commémoratif de la Résistance."

72. Dr. Camino, deputy mayor of Cambo, letter to Goutal, Ministry of Education, March 28, 1962, in AN, F21/7074, folder "Basse-Pyrénnées."

73. Gérard Le Marec, *Guide des maquis et hauts-lieux de la Résistance en Bretagne* (Paris: Presses de la Cité, 1987), 10.

74. Pierre Koenig, preface to *Guide des plages du débarquement*, by Patrice Boussel (Librairie Polytechnique Béranger, 1964), 5.

75. Barcellini and Wieviorka, *Passant, souviens-toi*, 7–8.

76. Jean-Paul Pallud, "The Maginot Line," *After the Battle* 60 (1988): 35.

77. Alain Hohnadel and Michel Truttmann, *Guide de la Ligne Maginot*, published as *39/45 Guerres contemporaines Magazine*, special issue, no. 6 (August–September 1988): 29–30.

78. Pallud, "The Maginot Line," 15–16. As early as in 1941, French prisoners, removing mines from the La Ferté area, discovered the remains of soldiers there who had been summarily buried by the Germans. They received German permission to identify rebury their fallen comrades in local cemeteries. See Barcellini and Wieviorka, *Passant, souviens-toi*, 42.

79. Herbert R. Lottman, *Pétain, Hero or Traitor: The Untold Story* (New York: William Morrow, 1985), 383.

80. The 1974 ceremony was attended by the author. See Bertram M. Gordon, *Collaborationism in France during the Second World War* (Ithaca, N.Y.: Cornell University Press, 1980), 353; also Barcellini and Wieviorka, *Passant, souviens-toi*, 461–62.

81. Victor H. Belot, *La France des pèlerinages* (Verviers, Belgium: Guides Marabout, 1976), 219–20.

82. H. Nonn, "Strasbourg, ville internationale: Forces, faiblesses, objectifs," *Revue Géographique de l'Est* 2 (1992): 100. The Council of Europe adopted the present European flag of twelve gold stars in a circle on a field of blue in 1955.

83. Conan, "Vichy malade de Vichy," 37.

84. Paul Gamelin, *La Ligne Maginot Hackenberg Ouvrage A 19/Die Maginot-Linie Besichtigung des Werkes Hackenberg im Bezirk Thionville* (Nantes: The Author, 1976), 14.

85. Hohnadel and Truttmann, *Guide de la Ligne Maginot,* 40.

86. Pallud, "The Maginot Line," 19. See also Hohnadel and Truttmann, *Guide de la Ligne Maginot,* 30.

87. Paul Gamelin, ed., *La Ligne Maginot. Images d'hier et d'aujourd'hui,* published as *Gazette des armes,* Hors-série, no. 9, 1979, 68.

88. Michel Braudeau, "L'Album de vacances (V) Vichy," *L'Express,* September 6, 1985, 62–67.

89. Conan, "Vichy malade de Vichy," 37.

90. "Un Cinéaste sur la piste de Klaus Barbie," *Le Point,* September 26, 1986, 77.

91. Francis Bergeron and Philippe Vilgier, *Guide de l'Homme de Droite à Paris, "Paris by Right"* (Paris: Trident, 1987), 58 and 64, respectively.

92. Ibid., 105–6 and 190–92.

93. "Un Patrimoine à sauver," *Le Maréchal,* 149 (1988): 16. For the Association to Defend the Memory of Marshal Pétain, see footnote 65 above.

94. Hohnadel and Truttmann, *Guide de la Ligne Maginot,* 40.

95. Pallud, "The Maginot Line," 35.

96. Kemp, *The Maginot Line,* 106.

97. Pallud, "The Maginot Line," inside front cover. Twelve fortifications were open to the public at the end of 1987, according to Hohnadel and Truttmann, *Guide de la Ligne Maginot,* 30.

98. Daniel J. Sherman, "Objects of Memory: History and Narrative in French War Museums," *French Historical Studies* 19, no. 1 (1995): 50.

99. Guide de Tourisme/Alsace Lorraine Vosges (Paris: Michelin, 1989), 158.

100. Thierry Gandillot and Marcelle Padovani, "Europe, la guerre des capitales," *Le Nouvel Observateur,* November 29–December 5, 1990, 104. French political leaders defending the interests of Strasbourg in the fight over the seat of the European Parliament in the period 1988 through 1990 included, in addition to Mitterrand, Jacques Delors, Édith Cresson, Roland Dumas, and Laurent Fabius. See various issues of the *Dernières Nouvelles d'Alsace,* also "Strasbourg défie Bruxelles," *Le Monde,* March 8, 1990.

101. See, for example, the brochure published by the Strasbourg Office of Tourism, *Office de Tourisme de Strasbourg et sa Région* (Strasbourg: Office de Tourisme de Strasbourg et sa Région, 1993), 25, which, in addition to the European Parliament and the Council of Europe, lists six international organizations based there.

102. Claire Andrieu, "Managing Memory: National and Personal Identity at Stake in the Mitterrand Affair," *French Politics and Society* 14, no. 2 (1996): 28.

103. Philippe-Jean Catinchi, "Un Centre pour mémoire," *Le Monde Télévision Radio Multimédia,* January 19–20, 1997, 5.

104. Conan, "Vichy malade de Vichy," 37.

105. "Battle of Alsace/Bataille d'Alsace," map no. 104 (Clermont-Ferrand: Michelin, 1992).

106. Laurent Guigon, "Le Mémorial d'Izieu sans sa 'dame,'" *Le Monde,* October 19, 1996, 34. See also Bertrand Poirot-Delpech, "Procès Barbie, dix ans déjà," *Le Monde,* May 7, 1997, 18.

107. *France* (Watford, Herts: Michelin, 1994), 272.

108. Ibid., 57 and 143.

109. Ibid., 151.

110. Ibid., 187 and 174.

111. For Bayeux, see ibid., 75.

112. Ibid., 112. General de Gaulle's tomb in the churchyard at Colombey has become a shrine for pilgrimages on the anniversary of his death by leaders of the Gaullist party, the Rassemblement pour la République, most recently headed by President Jacques Chirac. See Pascale Amaudric, "Semaine de tempêtes en Chiraquie," *Le Journal du Dimanche*, November 10, 1996, 5.

113. *France* (Michelin, 1994), 54.

114. Toni and Valmai Holt, *The Visitor's Guide to Normandy Landing Beaches, Memorials, and Museums* (Ashbourne, Derbyshire: Moorland, 1994), 263–66 and 36.

115. "M. Pasqua conteste la date choisi par M. Mitterrand pour la présence des soldats allemands," and Daniel Schneidermann, "14 Juillet, gross symbole!" *Le Monde*, July 15, 1994, 21 and 20, respectively.

116. For the television interview, see Sylvie Pierre-Brossolette, "Mitterrand rattrapé par l'histoire," *L'Express*, September 22, 1994, 8–9.

117. Régis Guyotat, "Jacques Chirac défend à Orléans la 'pureté de l'idéal' de Jeanne d'Arc," *Le Monde*, May 10, 1996, 7.

118. Danielle Rouard, "Les Toulonnais: 'Prenez garde que votre tour ne vienne...,'" *Le Monde*, April 1, 1997, 7.

119. Fl. N., "Les Bibliothèques et l'extrémisme," *Livres* section, *Le Monde*, March 28, 1997, x.

120. Street names in Vitrolles honoring François Mitterrand, Nelson Mandela, and the assassinated political leaders Olof Palme of Sweden, Salvador Allende of Chile, and Dulcie September, an antiapartheid leader in South Africa, were changed. The Avenue François Mitterrand reverted to its previous name, the Avenue de Marseille, the Place Nelson Mandela became the Place de Provence, and the Carré Dulcie September was renamed after the thirteenth century queen Marguerite de Provence. The Avenue Salvador Allende was renamed in honor of Mother Teresa, the only foreigner to retain a street name in Vitrolles. The Avenue Jean-Marie Tjiboue, named for the murdered autonomist New Caledonian, was renamed for the late second in command of the National Front, Jean-Pierre Stirbois, killed in an auto accident in 1988. See Julian Nundy, "National Front Renames Place Mandela in Purge," *Electronic Telegraph*, September 26, 1997. Other towns in France, however, not under National Front control, renamed their streets in honor of those who had lost their names in Vitrolles; see Nicole Cabret, "Les 'Débaptisées' de Vitrolles trouvent asile politique," *Le Monde*, October 13, 1998, 13. The National Front split in early 1999 raises the prospect that the party may lose control in Vitrolles and that the streets may again be renamed.

121. Sandrine Blanchard, "Première révocation pour révisionnisme dans l'enseignement secondaire," *Le Monde*, April 25, 1997, 11.

122. MacCannell, *The Tourist*, 98–99.

123. Inge von Wangenheim, *Der Goldene Turm: Eine Woche im Paris* (Rudolstadt: Greifenverlag, 1988), 120.

124. Barcellini and Wieviorka, *Passant, souviens-toi*, 78–79.

125. "Lorient, une base sous-marine surdimensionée," *Le Monde*, February 11, 1997, 24.

126. Philippe Dagen, "Les Musées français face à l'histoire, pendant l'Occupation," "Le Centre Pompidou présente 39 oeuvres volées par les nazis," and "Sous l'Occupation, le marché de l'art se portait à merveille," *Le Monde*, November 19, 1996, 27, April 4, 1997, 26, and April 12, 1997, 27, respectively. See also Alan Riding, "France to Display Art Looted by the Nazis," *New York Times*, April 3, 1997, B1.

127. Laurent Grailsamer, "Le 'Drancy de la zone libre,' selon Serge Klarsfeld," *Le*

Monde, May 10, 1997, 11. See also Jean-Claude Marre, "Des archives du camp d'internment des juifs à Rivesaltes sont retrouvées dans une décharge" and "L'Employé ayant découvert les archives du camp de Rivesaltes s'explique," *Le Monde,* May 10, 1997, 11, and May 11, 1997, 10, respectively.

128. Jean-Michel Frodon, "La Mémoire du siècle comme parc d'attractions," *Le Monde,* October 1, 1998, 27.

129. Daniel Letouzey, "Revue de presse," April 29, 2000, message on internet list, H-Français (h-français@h-net.msu.edu).

130. Raphaëlle Bacqué, "Jacques Chirac inaugure le Musée Charles-de-Gaulle," *Le Monde,* June 18–19, 2000, 7.

131. Lucas Delattre, "A Oradour, dernière étape de la réconciliation franco-allemande," *Le Monde,* May 30, 2000, 3.

Consuming the Beach

Seaside Resorts and Cultures of Tourism in
England and Spain from the 1840s to the 1930s

The seaside holiday was an English invention of the eighteenth century that
became a cultural norm as the standard vacation model for Britain and much
of western Europe. As a cultural export its influence challenges that of association football (soccer), demonstrating that the British were pioneers in dissem-
inating the play principle as well as the work ethic, probably with both greater
commitment and greater success. But the nature of the experience varied
widely within the society that nurtured it, and seaside resorts in Britain itself
come in a remarkable variety of guises, whether in terms of scenery, architecture, visiting public or entertainment provision.[1] It is therefore not surprising
to find that the seaside holiday has taken different forms in different countries,
especially as its diffusion has occurred at different stages of its own development. As such, the layers of infrastructure and tradition that are present in the
oldest settings are entirely absent from new foundations, tabula rasa, which in
their inception reflect the current state of the art before developing distinctive
trajectories and histories of their own.[2] The analysis of these developments also
needs to take account of the interaction between resort identities and holiday
practices, and the societies that nurtured and responded to them, both in terms
of visiting and other more vicarious consuming and investing publics, and of
local residents. The genuinely comparative international study of beach resorts
and the holiday practices associated with them is still in its infancy; and most
recent writing has been at a level of generalization that obscures the essential
variety of particular experiences, especially when its assumptions are based
implicitly on generalizing outward from a single European country.[3]

    This essay offers a comparative analysis of the consumption and control of
the beach as part of the development of the seaside holiday in England and
Spain from the steam revolution in transport, which opened out the natural
resources of shorelines to consumers of their attractions on a novel scale, to the
transitional years of the 1930s, when new developments were put on hold by the

Spanish Civil War and the Second World War. The focus will be on case studies of two resorts with emblematic status in their own national cultures: Blackpool, a northern resort with a strong provincial accent that became the epitome of the English popular playground, the mecca of the English (and increasingly Welsh and Scottish) working class; and San Sebastián, which became Spain's largest and most fashionable resort, a haunt of royalty, aristocracy, and diplomats. We shall see that they had more in common than these sharply contrasting images suggest. As Albert F. Calvert remarked in 1905, "San Sebastián . . . has some features in common with our own bustling, bourgeois Blackpool. There is always something doing here during the season; always some excitement . . . a continual state of racket and rockets."[4] But the cultures of seaside consumption in the two resorts differed from each other in ways that owed at least as much to national characteristics as to local experiences and identities. British seaside resorts developed in a culture that sought to minimize the role of the state, prioritizing the self-regulating liberal subject's duty to self-control and the sovereignty of market forces, while increasingly having to admit the importance of local government intervention to enable resorts themselves to compete as effectively as possible in the marketplace, within which their collective identities were effectively individual actors needing coherent guidance and control from a central nervous system. Spain (and even the Basque Country in which San Sebastián was situated, which had a distinctive regime) had more authoritarian and hierarchical assumptions, with (in theory) stronger local government powers to regulate and plan, subject to more active interference and direction from superior authorities at provincial and national levels. The practice was usually inefficient enough to subvert the theory, but San Sebastián had an unusually effective administrative regime, as contemporaries recognized. Moreover, although the seaside holiday was diffused internationally from English origins, by the time it had reached Spain it was far enough removed for the original practices to be unfamiliar at first hand, and San Sebastián's direct models were French and Belgian rather than English, although it soon imparted a flavor of its own to the seaside experience. This essay teases out the aspects of these differences that relate to the consumption of the beach, taking account also of the differences in the social structure of demand between Blackpool, where the pioneering English role in opening out the seaside to the working classes came to fruition earliest, and San Sebastián, whose dominant visiting publics were aristocrats and comfortable metropolitan bourgeois.

THE SEASIDE HOLIDAY: ORIGINS, DEVELOPMENT, AND DISTINGUISHING FEATURES

Blackpool, in the county of Lancashire on England's northwest coast and within easy reach of the Lancashire "cotton towns" and Manchester itself, grew very rapidly from the 1870s to attain an off-season population of over fifty thousand early in the new century. It was second only to Brighton (the pioneer large specialized seaside resort) in dominating a cluster of smaller nearby destinations; but other systems were emerging in (for example) North Wales and Kent, providing a variety of habitats for differing market segments while allowing visitors to one resort to sample the delights of its neighbors.[5] The first similar resort complex in Spain was that which centered on San Sebastián, whose population at a turn-of-the-year census likewise passed fifty thousand in the early twentieth century, though from larger beginnings and after a more measured process of growth than in Blackpool's case. This Basque resort system, which spanned the national boundary into southwest France and generated visitor interchange across the border from Biarritz to Zarauz, was becoming articulated as transport innovations proceeded around 1900, from roots already visible in the 1870s.[6] The chapter will focus on the large resorts at the core of these developments.

The seaside holiday as an activity capable of generating and sustaining commercial investment and entrepreneurial innovation began, in its modern guise, in eighteenth-century England.[7] Its rise was fueled by a medical fashion for sea bathing, promoted by the prescriptive writings of entrepreneurial doctors, who had appropriated notions of the prophylactic and curative powers of seawater from popular practices associated with calendar customs. This medical vogue coincided with a revaluation of the aesthetics and moral connotations of maritime environments, in which the sea and the shore became associated with pleasurable contemplation, sublimity and fecundity, and invested with associations of religion and antiquity, rather than being stigmatized as dangerous, unproductive, and savage, spawning monsters and negating civilization.[8] But the manner in which resorts developed, from an early stage, owed less to these medical and philosophical currents (though the former formed a necessary pretext) than to more banal and mundane concerns associated with fashion, consumption, and display. Seekers after health through carefully regulated medicinal sea-bathing were soon joined by pleasure-seekers and socialites of the kind who had already colonized the inland spas and created the London "season," and resorts that aspired to growth and transformation had to provide assemblies, dances, public breakfasts, circulating libraries, theaters, and the other amenities of polite society, to augment the natural assets that had lured their original visitors to decaying seaports and deserted shorelines.[9]

This did not necessarily marginalize the sea, although some places saw a trend in this direction by the later nineteenth century, as entertainments developed on a grander scale, featuring star artistes and exciting new technologies.[10] But the beaches and promenades remained focal points of resort life, even though many of their habitués were more interested in watching

C. A. y L. / 880. SAN SEBASTIAN
Balneario "Perla del Océano,,

The La Perla bathing establishment as rebuilt in 1911. (Postcard, author's collection.)

people and commenting on fashions and the presentation of self than in contemplating misty blue distances or picturesque scenery, unless the sea drew attention to itself by offering a dramatic spectacle involving wild waves and abundant foam.[11] Seaside towns came to celebrate their combinations of the urbane and the natural, and the balance of priorities tilted increasingly often toward the former. The trend toward bathing for pleasure rather than health, which was becoming visible in the late nineteenth century, and the vogue for sunbathing and the open air that gathered momentum rapidly (from earlier origins) after the First World War kept the "natural" aspects of the seaside to the fore, demanding investment in such amenities as parks and bathing pools in their support. Sporting activities such as golf were also becoming essential to a resort's success, which also involved tinkering with the environment to form an attractive synthesis of the "artificial" and the "natural."[12]

The seaside resort spread from its English origins in the middle decades of the eighteenth century to France, the Low Countries, and the German maritime states toward the end of the eighteenth century, reaching Sweden at the turn of the century, consolidating after the Napoleonic wars, and colonizing parts of the Spanish and Danish coasts soon afterward.[13] Movement further east, and transatlantic developments, came rather later. The pattern of early development owed much to medical fashion, which prescribed cold, boisterous seas and damned the Mediterranean as enervating, pestilential, and malarial. The rise of the French and Italian Rivieras as international resort systems owed more to medical perceptions of suitable winter climates for lung diseases than to scope for bathing, which only became a popular summer activity for outsiders in the interwar years.[14] But the accessibility of suitable coastlines from population centers, and the availability of disposable wealth and time, were key factors alongside the international dissemination of medical ideas. English advantages were strong on all counts. It was here that resort networks became articulated earliest, and substantial specialized seaside watering places (to use a term that remained current until the 1960s) began to grow. European developments lagged by half a century.[15]

The seaside resort was a distinctive kind of town, whose common elements shared across cultures form a valid foundation for the examination of contrasts within a well-defined genre. Their economies were based on providing access to and use of a culturally desirable environment, sustaining and embellishing preferred landscapes and natural attributes, and offering accommodation, services, entertainments, and (crucially) personal comfort and security of life and property to those who came to enjoy them during (usually) a relatively short summer season. As they grew beyond primitive simplicity and accumulated urban characteristics, conflicts between natural and built environments, purity and use, and contrasting and sometimes mutually inimical definitions of comfort and enjoyment had to be mediated through local government, which acquired a particularly broad remit in this setting. Municipalities often had to step in to supervise and even to supply amenities and entertainments that private enterprise was unwilling or unable to regulate, offer, or sustain, as well as taking a high profile in more orthodox municipal services such as lighting, sewering, waste disposal, public transport, and especially public order. Sea defenses and the promenades that often ran along them were expensive local responsibilities, and the allocation, supervision, and regulation of urban space was a strong feature of local government. Seaside resorts also became demographically and industrially distinctive, as by the turn of the century they attracted commuters and retired residents, and the role of accommodation and services in their economies generated disproportionate amounts of work for women of mature years and domestic servants, while providing fewer jobs for men. Employment tended to be casual and seasonal, and predominantly in very small businesses, often family-run and using child labor; and these consumer towns also presented problems of seasonal unemployment and winter poverty. The need to defuse poverty and keep it out of sight, preventing begging, theft, and aggressive behavior in areas frequented by visitors, was a constant preoccupation of local authorities at the seaside.[16]

Above all the seaside resort was, and is, a place that is consumed, although the variety of forms consumption takes, from gazing to ingesting, complicates this bald statement, as does the problematic status of resort place-images that are actually collectivities made up of a swirl of ever-changing offerings from smaller businesses, projects, and experiences within the greater whole, which may complement each other or compete with each other in different ways at different times. In one sense, the seaside resort as a kind of place has a strong generic identity, as I have just described; in other senses each individual resort is a kaleidoscopically complicated organism, in which the identities within the whole are forever transforming themselves and their relations with each other, but always in relation to what has gone before in the context of particular topographies, local societies, and demand flows.[17] Appreciation of this poses the challenge of trying to generalize comparatively about regional or national seaside resort cultures, and such attempts are probably best initiated through case studies. This is the object of the closer analysis of Blackpool and San Sebastián that follows.

BLACKPOOL AND SAN SEBASTIÁN: COMPARATIVE CONTEXT

In terms of their dominant place-images and modes of self-presentation, Blackpool and San Sebastián might appear to be at opposite ends of the category "seaside resort," sharing a common grammar of basic economic structure and preoccupations but little else. Blackpool's claim to be the world's first working-class seaside resort is well established. It began its career in the later eighteenth century as a bathing place for the manufacturing and professional middle classes of the industrializing county of Lancashire, and such people remained at the core of its prosperity, identity, and growth up to the 1870s. The railway, which arrived in 1846, merely made their journeys cheaper, faster, and more convenient. But even before the rise of the "polite" summer season, Blackpool had also attracted plebeian visitors, small farmers and hand-loom weavers, to bathe in the sea at the August spring tides, when it was popularly supposed to have quasi-magical prophylactic and therapeutic virtues. This was a widespread practice across Lancashire, with many counterparts elsewhere in Europe, and it continued into the railway age. This popular sea-bathing tradition was one of the roots of Blackpool's growing capacity to attract working-class visitors when its railways provided cheap trains, and the traditional summer holidays of its urbanizing hinterland were converted from local celebrations into vehicles for the development of popular seaside holidays.[18]

This transition was a product of the last quarter of the nineteenth century, a time of rising real wages and family incomes in the cotton industry whose distinctive urban economies provided the bulk of Blackpool's working-class visitors. The "cotton towns" generated a culture of savings, mutual insurance, and mutual assistance that fostered saving for deferred gratifications, such as holidays, as well as to guard against a rainy day. Their nascent popular consumerism spilled over into Blackpool, generating a three-month popular season that was sufficient to attract extensive investment. The municipally funded promenade and privately promoted piers that had catered for the middle classes in the 1860s were invaded by more boisterous crowds, and entertainment complexes and fairgrounds provided mass entertainment on a novel scale, promoted from 1879 by municipal advertising as well as by the individual companies. A feedback effect was created, and Blackpool built on its existing popularity and extended its advertising schemes across new areas of northern and midland England, taking the lion's share of rapidly increasing demand for working-class holidays and accommodating it in new districts of purpose-built lodging-houses, which offered basic amenities at prices of unparalleled cheapness. These developments in turn reduced the centrality of the beach, and especially of bathing, to Blackpool's holiday attractions, as alternatives multiplied. Additional attributes derived from a local government system that came to be dominated by the entertainment and building interests. From 1887 the corporation ran its own police force, and noisy but unthreatening fun was tolerated in the central streets as part of a culture of consensually limited excess. Blackpool lacked a dominant landowner and was effectively unplanned, making it easier for working-class visitors to take over central spaces in this way; and when proactive formal planning came further to the fore in the interwar years, it tended to be directed toward extending leisure space and providing amenities to meet changing tastes, rather than regulating or redeveloping existing working-class haunts.[19]

Under this regime Blackpool's visitors grew in (very approximate) numbers from perhaps 850,000 in 1873 to nearly 4 million in 1913 and perhaps 7 million in the mid-1930s. It achieved this transition to world leadership in its field without losing the patronage of middle-class visitors at either end of the long promenade, and from the turn of the century it also developed a residential population of commuters, commercial travelers, and retired people.[20]

San Sebastián, as a seaside resort, was a later developer with a very different emphasis, catering from the outset for the Spanish aristocracy and the comfortable middle classes of the capital. A formal sea-bathing season began in the 1830s, using the gently sloping and attractive La Concha beach, which was protected from the Atlantic rollers by the island of Santa Clara and adjoined an existing seaport, garrison town, and administrative center with a population approaching ten thousand (a figure that Blackpool did not surpass until the 1870s). The economic geography of Spain meant that visitors originally came disproportionately from Madrid, in the center of the land mass, more than two days' journey away by diligence. The existing settlement was modern, rebuilt after a great fire following the siege of 1813, but increasingly overcrowded and hemmed in by the town walls. Significant expansion in both built-up area and tourist trade was delayed until the mid-1860s, when the Paris-Madrid railway arrived. At this point the town walls were demolished, a planned *ensanche* or extension of the built-up area was set under way (Spain's third, after Madrid and Barcelona), and a local conflict over whether to pursue commercial port or tourist development was resolved in the latter's favor.[21]

At this point the town really began to develop, with a rectilinear street plan carefully supervised by the municipality. Grandiose plans for an international exhibition were scotched by the outbreak of civil war in 1873. Recovery after two years of war was swift, and San Sebastián soon became by far Spain's largest and most fashionable resort, with increasing specialization in the holiday industry. Its core clientele was Spanish rather than international, with a highly visible group of Madrid aristocrats, politicians, and comfortable middle classes setting the tone. The opening of the Gran Casino in 1887, with roulette (which was technically illegal) on offer most of the time, coincided with the adoption of San Sebastián by the queen regent, Maria Cristina, as the site of the royal summer residence. These contrasting but overlapping attractions (the queen set a high moral tone that courtiers and diplomats did not always match) gave a further boost to an already fashionable season. San Sebastián built firmly on these foundations, remaining very much a summer resort and attaining a population of just under seventy-five thousand at the 1930 census. It became, briefly, a focal point of international high society when Spain was neutral during the First World War, and then survived the abolition of casino gambling in 1924, which hit the newly opened Kursaal casino (1922) particularly hard, and the advent of the Second Republic in 1931. As at Blackpool, attractions on dry land worked to reduce the centrality of the beach itself; but it remained at the core of most fashionable (and aspiring) holiday routines and timetables. San Sebastián remained, at bottom, a resort for the Madrid and later the provincial bourgeoisie, with a growing presence from the northern provinces of Aragón and La Rioja, and could not sustain competition with neighboring Biarritz for royalty, Russian grand dukes, and millionaires.[22]

In terms of its visitors, San Sebastián was not as different from Blackpool as might appear. From the earliest railway years it attracted down-at-heel cheap trippers who came from Madrid for the week on special trains, and many of its visitors roughed it in the spare rooms of unpretentious flats. Public display was made possible by private economies. Moreover, by the First World War it was attracting day-trippers from nearby industrial towns to sporting events and to cabarets on the unfashionable eastern side of the river. There was overlap with Blackpool in the social structure of visitors, despite the differing emphases. San Sebastián shared similar problems of economic structure, poverty, seasonality, and public order, as well as needing extensive municipal intervention in its economy to enable it to compete with rivals. In both resorts, indeed, municipal rhetoric sometimes likened the town to a limited company in which the inhabitants were shareholders, pulling together in the common goal of advancing its interests against competitors. San Sebastián's combination of royalty and roulette (both unthinkable in Blackpool) and its vulnerability to war, currency fluctuations, and political change as well as to the vagaries of aristocratic fashion make it seem to inhabit a different universe; but the two towns hold enough in common to make the comparison viable.[23]

BLACKPOOL AND SAN SEBASTIÁN:
THE ORDERING OF THE BEACH

A comparison of seaside resort cultures begins most plausibly with the beach, the original raison d'être of the seaside resort and an enduring focus for enjoyment and conflict. The rise of the seaside resort coincided with a growing concern within European elites to regulate manners and morals in the interests of a restrictive definition of civilization and a repressive version of religion. The use of the beach and shore for bathing, lounging, gazing, and promenading raised precisely these issues of morality (in terms of the disrobing and exposure of bodies in a public arena) and civilization (challenges to prescribed formality of dress and behavior), in an intermediate setting between land and sea, culture and nature, mundane solidity and dangerous fluidity, in which property rights and legal jurisdictions were often in flux. By the mid–nineteenth century the pressures to control were becoming particularly strong, driven by the need for nascent resorts not to alienate potential visitors who might be offended by lapses from or challenges to the evolving codes of decorous sociability. In practice, English resorts tended to be more relaxed and accommodating toward bodily exposure in bathing than the rhetoric of by-laws and controls that was provided for the consumption of censorious outsiders. Even so, conflicts arose between contrasting value systems, which cut across class and status, about the nature and extent of regulation (though not about the need to intervene). They were exacerbated when fashions and preferences in the use of the beach changed. Such moments of tension arose when the arrival of working-class visitors with distinctive standards and expectations disrupted established regimes and conventions; when a move from health and regimentation to pleasure and playfulness in the later nineteenth century brought leisurely swimming and splashing to the fore, as opposed to medicinal bathing in brief, prescribed doses; and when the rise of sunbathing encouraged the ostentatious exposure of hitherto occult areas of the body and the spread of skimpier and more revealing fashions in beachwear. Conflicts were complicated by the emergence of vested interests in the maintenance of established regulatory systems, especially the owners and operators of bathing establishments, machines, and cabins, whose incomes depended on requiring bathers to use their facilities. These were not trivial flashpoints: they reflected deep-seated attitudes to the body and its public and private display and generated emotive rhetoric about immorality and savagery on one side, and prudery and obsessive restrictiveness on the other.[24]

Blackpool and San Sebastián can be contrasted in interesting ways in relation to the topography, spatial organization, and moral/political economy of their original prime environmental assets, the beach and the seafront. Blackpool has a long stretch of open beach, directly in front of the town as it extends along the shore, and devoid of bays or coves, with no natural divisions that might become associated with different classes, patterns of usage, or bathing practices, although its North and Central Piers came to demarcate the popular or "tripper" sector from the rest.[25] San Sebastián's La Concha beach lies at the side of the original settlement and of the main later-nineteenth-century extension, with villa development scattered across the hillside behind. This was the original, fashionable bathing beach. At the mouth of the Urumea, on the other side of the town, lay the unfashionable, more open and dangerous beaches of the Zurriola and of Gros, with unrestrained Atlantic waves and a powerful undertow; but the use of these declined in the early twentieth century.[26] Meanwhile, La Concha beach was becoming overcrowded, especially as part of it was reserved for the royal family's bathing machine, a remarkable turreted structure that ran on rails, drawn by a stationary steam-engine under the cliff.[27] The corporation drained and opened out a new beach to the west at Ondarreta, which opened in 1925, and by the later 1920s this was creaming off the Madrid elite among the visitors. This left the poorer locals without accessible, safe, or comfortable bathing arrangements: they were not formally excluded, but made to feel uncomfortable, and the price of access to what the guardians of the beach regarded as appropriate costume and necessary services was beyond their reach.[28] So San Sebastián's beach regime was more complex than Blackpool's. It was also more strictly regulated on class lines, both officially and informally.

A further contrast between Blackpool and San Sebastián lay in the predominant concerns of the regulating authorities. After the initial installation of a formal regulatory regime in 1853–54, under a locally sponsored act of Parliament, Blackpool's authorities (a local board of health from 1851 to 1876, and a municipal corporation thereafter) showed little concern about problems arising from regulating bathing, as such. What exercised them much more was generating revenue from, and controlling the content of, the stalls and entertainments that popular entrepreneurs installed on the beach to meet the rising demand from working-class visitors that became increasingly apparent during the 1870s and 1880s. This theme continued into the twentieth century.[29] San

Sebastián's municipal corporation, or *ayuntamiento,* on the other hand, remained much more concerned with regulating the bathing arrangements for the comfort of its majority of self-consciously respectable visitors, while trying not to lose the patronage of the more relaxed clientele who were drawn by casino gambling and related entertainments. The close relationship between the *ayuntamiento* and the fashionable bathing establishment on the Concha, La Perla del Océano, complicated matters further.[30] These contrasts arose not only out of the differing patterns of demand, and the ways in which "penny capitalists" strove to meet working-class expectations in Blackpool by providing the cheap fairground amusements with which they were familiar, but also from different traditions of local government. Spanish local authorities were more concerned with acting as moral preceptors to their citizens than English ones, for whom a stronger laissez-faire tradition left such matters more to charities and religious bodies.

Blackpool's bathing had been regulated by consensus in its middle-class origins in the late eighteenth century, when notions of civility and decorum were coming to the fore even in this decidedly provincial milieu.[31] There were bathing boxes and horse-drawn bathing machines to safeguard the modesty of people undressing for their therapeutic encounter with the waves at high tide (which was easier to police), and demarcated times for women's bathing were announced by the ringing of a bell, after which any gentleman remaining on the beach forfeited a bottle of wine. No penalty is mentioned for women watching men bathe, which was within the bounds of cultural possibility, although a second bell was rung to announce the changeover.[32] This relaxed attitude to the external policing of the gaze was to be challenged by the rise of Evangelical prudery among some of the visitors, but no serious problems arose until the railway began to offer cheap excursion trains at prices within the reach of (especially) unattached young working-class people from industrial Lancashire. This precipitated a regulatory crisis, as trippers bathed naked, men and women in close proximity, in front of the "best houses" at high tide without benefit of bathing machine, enjoying the experience noisily rather than enduring it as part of a strict medicinal regime; and they were joined by "ladies and gentlemen" who were happy to take advantage of this license. Donkeys were provided to amuse them, arousing complaints about cruelty to animals. Sabbatarianism was also an issue: the most popular and controversial excursions arrived on Sundays, disrupting the pristine quiet that many established visitors preferred. The flashily dressed "barbers' apprentices and shoe-blacks" set established policing at defiance, and the local authorities felt the need to strengthen the law.[33]

The clash of conflicting cultures meant that the beach could no longer be left to the "nature" that had inspired its devotees. A grid of controls began to be imposed. Two attempts at beach regulation through act of Parliament, in

Blackpool Central Beach at high tide in the 1890s. (Reprinted from *The New Album of Blackpool and St. Annes Views* [London, n.d.].)

1846 and 1849, failed because they were attached to wider measures for expensive sanitary and other improvements that threatened increased local taxation. By 1853 the threatening aspects of Blackpool's problems were more widely seen to outweigh the costs associated with dealing with them, and the Blackpool Improvement Act of that year supplied the necessary powers. By-laws forbade bathing without use of a machine. They also required the sexes to bathe at least fifty yards apart, and men were enjoined to wear drawers. Boats and bathing machines were forbidden to operate at church service times on Sundays. A spate of fines at the start of the 1854 season made these restrictions effective: the beach was made safe for subscribers to the narrower definitions of respectability that had been advancing within the mainstream middle-class visiting public for a generation.[34]

On paper, San Sebastián had a much stricter official bathing regime, as befitted an elite resort with a strong municipal commitment to public order, which needed to control the local lower orders who had been accustomed to casual unregulated bathing. The municipality, which already had established powers and a developed sense of its own importance when sea bathing became fashionable, proclaimed its power to divide the beach between the sexes for bathing purposes in its new police regulations of 1839.[35] Richard Ford, who wrote the first English travel guide to Spain, commented soon afterward that little huts made of reeds did duty for bathing machines,[36] and in 1848 Francisco Madrazo emphasized the strict separation of the sexes, with the women bathing closer to the town and the men further away. "Highly vigilant civil guards are entrusted with enforcing this law which we might call that of modesty." Ladies were dipped in the sea by "strong young women," in contrast with nearby Deva, where men did the job, and this made it less of a public spectacle.[37] In the same year Ramón de Navarrete tells us that modesty was further enforced by the standard bathing dress, which was voluminous, of dark wool, and covered the body from shoulders to feet. But Navarrete undermines the picture of unquestioning obedience to authority: his bathers have agency. The fashionable bathing hours were between seven and ten in the morning, when the regulations were strictly enforced, although the young women wore the green caps that gathered up their hair with "remarkable coquetry." In the afternoon, all was transformed: the beach was taken over by small unclad children who crossed to and fro between the male and female sectors, while the soldiers of the garrison bathed under the supervision of their officers, and a social mix of bathers, including women of the popular classes, took advantage of the relaxed regime. This was the hour of liberty, "that of grotesque sights, in a word," when the fashionable visitors' timetable took them elsewhere.[38] This is a reminder that San Sebastián's concern for the regulation of La Concha beach paid more heed to the assumed susceptibilities of its fashionable visitors than to abstract notions of propriety and morality. During the fashionable hours of the morning, discretion was imposed. After ten o'clock, and especially toward evening, liminality regained its natural territory, and the imagined boundaries became visibly permeable.

After the introduction of the municipal regulation of bathing, which took much longer to arrive in the English provincial setting of Blackpool than in "the Brighton of Madrid,"[39] where it was brought in as soon as a bathing season began, the established arrangements continued undisturbed through the middle decades of the nineteenth century. The regulation of Blackpool's beach was relaxed after its midcentury crisis: the taboo on nude bathing was far from universal among the middle classes at this time, and too strict a regulatory regime would have been as bad for business as a complete laissez-faire approach. Similar developments occurred at, for example, Margate and Brighton, as resorts tried to become "all things to all people" and accommodate themselves to a contending variety of gazes and practices.[40] As visitor numbers began to increase sharply, with a growing working-class admixture, during the 1860s, there were not enough bathing machines to accommodate all the excursionists. We should not assume that most of the new visitors came to bathe, however: taking the sea air, enjoying the beach environment, and paddling at the water's edge probably took precedence for most, and new entertainments on shore were developing to supplement and rival the natural attractions. The number of licensed bathing machines grew slowly—far outpaced by visitor numbers—to reach a peak that averaged around 110 between 1876 and 1895, falling back to less than half that number in the early twentieth century; but avoiders of the machines' tolls and enjoyers of informal encounters with the sea were not seen as a major problem. In 1868 Blackpool's local board set up a special committee to act against "promiscuous bathing," but only one prosecution ensued. Complaints had to be seen to be taken seriously, but there was no strong will to suppress the freer spirits. The extent of the local board's jurisdiction over the beach below high-water mark was disputed until its successor, the corporation, bought up the rights in 1887, and bathing at low tide along several miles of beach was physically difficult to regulate. In 1884 the corporation issued its inspector with a telescope to aid the apprehension of men bathing without drawers at low tide, but no spate of prosecutions followed. After the early crisis, when nude bathers at high tide in the center of the original settlement had been impossible to avoid, the spread of Blackpool's buildings along the coastline and the development of social zoning, together with the long retreat of the tide and the decline of sea bathing itself as a popular attraction, relegated the issue to the sidelines.[41]

Instead, controversy over the consumption of the beach reflected the growing pressure for commercial exploitation of Blackpool's growing working-class visiting public, in informal "penny capitalist" ways as well as through the town's big entertainment companies. It revolved around the rise of a fairground on the sands between Blackpool's original two piers, beginning in the late 1860s with the opening of the cheaper and more popular one, the South Jetty or "People's Pier" with its German dance bands and excursion steamers. The beach opposite Bonny's Estate, an early and down-market seafront development, was the last area to be covered by the tide and therefore attractive to profit-maximizing showmen. When a court case in 1869 confirmed that the local authority's power to regulate businesses and levy rents extended only to high-water mark, the fairground stalls and shows that had congregated on empty lots and in pub gardens nearby were quick to occupy the rent-free space, which became crowded with stalls of all kinds: vendors of everything from oysters to books, musicians, shooting galleries, cheapjack auctioneers, and Blackpool's own specialties, phrenologists and gipsy fortune-tellers. The local authority worried about disorder and loss of amenity, but further attempts to clear the area in 1873 and 1880, fueled by a lobby that sought to keep Blackpool safe for "respectable," "better-class" visitors, could not be enforced in the courts, despite additional powers from Parliament in 1879. A truce followed, during which the working-class market developed apace. The fairground became one of Blackpool's recognized popular attractions. By 1895 at least 315 people had "standings on the shore," including retailers of various kinds, exhibitors of novel technologies, and presenters of alternative medicine. Techniques involved participant observation, as sufferers had their corns cut before admiring crowds and phrenologists read their clients' characters in front of their neighbors and workmates. Palmistry was also practiced, and vendors of medical recipes entertained the crowds with florid language.[42] This was similar entertainment to that provided at the big weekend markets or at the annual fairs in industrial towns like Blackburn or Oldham.[43] It was proletarian and unpretentious, celebrating the grotesque body in carnivalesque style, and it also diverted trippers' sixpences away from the entertainment companies that had opened lavish premises in Blackpool since the 1870s, and whose representatives were now powerful on the corporation.[44] The battle lines were drawn.

By the mid-1890s the beach's legal liminality had been lost. The corporation purchased the foreshore rights in 1887, and a parliamentary Improvement Act of 1893 secured legally watertight powers to control all commercial activities up to low-water mark. Licensing was introduced in 1896, when 140 permits were issued and minimum distances between stalls were laid down. A year later, however, the corporation decided to clear the sands entirely, to the surprise and dismay of the press, whose coverage had emphasized the popularity of the fairground among amused "better-class" visitors as well as the working-class element. The *Bradford Observer* suggested that more Blackpool visitors would be annoyed than pleased at this "curious freak of exotically delicate sentiment." With this important backing, the outcry from the growing excursionist interest forced the corporation to retreat to a policy of licensing and regulating, with only the most controversial kinds of stall being outlawed: direct competitors with shopkeepers who paid property taxes, and offenders against current concepts of rationality and intellectual property that offered alternative medical approaches by "unqualified" practitioners or alternative ways of understanding the world. Thus chiropodists, phrenologists, quack doctors, and palmists were banished from a beach that was now to be consecrated to rational fun and appropriate usages. They soon reappeared on shore at South Beach, in front gardens and vacant lots, beyond the legal reach of the local authority. It was here that Blackpool's most liminal and carnivalesque spaces were henceforth to reside, along the "Golden Mile," with its exhibitions of giantesses and two-headed mermaids. The beach kept its fairground, but policed, cleaned up, brought into the market place (with pitches being formally auctioned from 1902), and generally rationalized.[45]

Municipal voting divisions on this issue pitted an unprincipled front of entertainment company interests and advocates of "respectability" and a "better-class" policy, against small shopkeepers from working-class areas and owners of cottages and stalls in the South Beach area.[46] The victory for the populist lobby was of symbolic and practical importance. It meant that Blackpool's central stretch of beach, which was crucial to definitions of its identity as a seaside resort, retained activities that identified it as a working-class haven, however permeable it might be to other social groups and however shorn it might be of the grotesque and carnivalesque. Activities that a generation previously had been regarded as prejudicial to Blackpool's future, then envisaged in terms of conciliating and encouraging a mainstream middle-class market with assumed preferences for quiet and decorum, were now recognized as indispensable to a holiday market dominated by working-class pleasure-seekers who sought familiar pleasures in unfamiliar but recognizable settings. This confirmed Blackpool's new dominant identity as a populist and popular resort, in which controlled but real concessions were made to visitors' preferences for the informal and the demotic. Subsequent developments to the south provided even more impressive endorsement of the change.[47]

Central Beach was only part of the story. Concentrating the fairground between the piers left extensive areas to north and south available as playgrounds for the middle-class families who did not desert Blackpool, but found their own enclaves within it, from which they were free to invade the popular districts when the fancy took them. Care was taken to sustain the quieter character of North Shore, which had been recognized as the "better side" of town since the 1860s.[48] Part of South Shore proved less defensible. From 1892 onward the sandhills beyond the coastal tramway terminus were colonized by gypsy fortune-tellers, exhibitions of giantesses and fat bullocks, shooting galleries and hot pea saloons. In 1897 these petty entrepreneurs were joined by exiles from South Beach, such as phrenologists. Mechanization got under way as roundabouts, bicycle railways, and other novelty rides appeared. A miniature Coney Island began to coalesce on this cheap and marginal land, which could not be built on until the promenade and sea defenses were extended; and residents in the semidetached villas of a nearby estate found that their earlier complaints about a small fairground on a nearby vacant lot paled into insignificance beside the new developments. This was land above high-water mark, where normal conventions of property ownership applied, and over the next decade these barren sandhills became concentrated in the hands of an Anglo-American syndicate, fronted by W. G. Bean, a Londoner with several years' experience of the American amusement industry. In 1905 the rapidly developing site first began to call itself the Pleasure Beach. New rides proliferated: water-chute, helter-skelter, dodgem cars, haunted cabin, oscillating staircase, "Monitor and Merrimac" battle show. The fairground was developing the characteristics of Coney Island: it was becoming a liminal pleasure zone where entertainment entailed encountering the unexpected, being moved and manipulated in disconcerting ways, and being exposed and thrown together in unaccustomed public intimacy. This was much more challenging than anything that had hitherto occurred on Blackpool's beach, and it alarmed some of the neighbors, who tried in 1906 to persuade the corporation to use its building regulation powers to suppress the fairground. The agitation was led by traders who feared that South Shore would lose its "better-class" residents and visitors; but it failed. The Pleasure Beach already attracted too many visitors to be lightly suppressed, and it generated impressive revenues for the corporation's tramways and electricity works. Moreover, South Shore itself was developing a popular party that preferred to encourage the new visitors and assumed that this seafront development could coexist with suburbia and high-class shops inland. The corporation settled for regulation and the removal of abuses (especially the despised fortune-tellers); and by 1914 Blackpool's answer to Coney Island had a summer staff of six hundred, up to one hundred thousand visitors on an ordinary summer day and two hundred thousand on a bank holiday, and a total investment of two hundred thousand pounds in its various attractions. This was the ultimate in consuming the beach, even though it was becoming a beach in name only, as concrete spread across the sandhills. There remained ample quiet space elsewhere along Blackpool's seafront for middle-class families, who took what they wanted from the lively popular side of Blackpool when they wanted it.[49]

San Sebastián's problems and opportunities were very different, with an emphasis on sustaining a comfortable, secure environment for aristocrats and middle-class families with the minimum of scandal and conflict. To further this the beaches were zoned, both formally and informally, in sophisticated ways, but the question of regulating popular commercial ventures did not arise. Sea bathing (and associated sociability) remained the dominant focus of beach use, and there was no counterpart to the Blackpool fairgrounds, even on the unfashionable eastern beaches. Fairgrounds there were, but they developed away from the shore, inland at Martutene and then as part of the development of Monte Igueldo in the west as a leisure complex, reached by a funicular, after 1912. Bathing from La Concha beach became organized increasingly on business lines, as the new town beyond the walls began to spread and visitor numbers to increase after the arrival of the railway from the mid-1860s. It was also carefully policed, as the corporation introduced a special force of beach inspectors, the *celadores de la playa*. By 1864 La Concha had eighty wheeled bathing machines, drawn by oxen, and used mainly by ladies to undress and dress in private for what was still essentially a medicinal activity.[50] But a female English visitor remarked that the proprietors were unwilling to move the machines to the water, so bathers often had to walk some distance to the sea: "They do not, however, sport buff, and the costume of the ladies is (intended to be) becoming." The same author observed "straw-hatted hirsute mermen . . . smoking cigarettes even in the water."[51] A Spaniard went further, commenting on the "grotesque" character even of the fashionable bathing period in the morning, with aristocratic ladies wearing clinging wool and displaying the outlines of their bodies to the curious observer, and lines of nervous ladies in strange costumes shrieking and leaping in the water.[52] In 1875 a

French observer enjoyed the spectacle of well-sculpted women trotting lightly to the water, displaying unclad legs and splashing their unbraided hair. This direction of the gaze at bathers, with an interest in bodies as well as behavior and a prurient emphasis on relaxation and décolletage, all of which made a mockery of the segregation of the sexes, was to be a lasting feature of La Concha, causing increasingly overt controversy after the First World War.[53]

The expansion of the bathing season encouraged investment in a wooden bathing establishment, La Perla del Océano, which brought a range of bathing-related services under its roof. The corporation took care to safeguard the threatened bathing-machine proprietors, some of whom had been in business for twenty-five or thirty years on the site: the bathing machines were said to provide employment for many necessitous families with no other means of subsistence. La Perla opened in 1869, to the west of the existing bathing area, and a similar installation has remained on the site ever since; but the continuing growth in visitor numbers was sufficient to keep the *bañeros* healthily occupied for many years.[54]

La Concha beach remained the fashionable morning gathering-point throughout San Sebastián's years of expansion between the 1870s and the 1930s, although the favored morning times moved back to begin at ten and then eleven, and late-afternoon bathing also became fashionable. Around the turn of the century, too, Spanish visitors belatedly adopted the fashion of spending time on the beach chatting and enjoying the scenery, rather than leaving immediately after a therapeutic bathe. New amenities of the later nineteenth century tended to cluster around La Concha, with the Gran Casino of 1887 at the eastern edge, close to the shady Bulevar of the late 1860s with its bandstand and evening strollers and dancers and the Alderdi-Eder park, while the Miramar Palace of Queen María Cristina, which was completed in 1893, overlooked it from the west. In 1911 the municipality, always concerned to keep control over beach amenities, completed the rebuilding of an increasingly dilapidated La Perla, which became the focal point of polite society on the beach. Photographs from the early 1920s show the beach crammed, even at low tide, with well-dressed Spanish families, the men wearing suits, ties, and straw hats, the women in cardigans, calf-length skirts, and stockings, standing around or sitting on wooden chairs while children play in the sand, supervised by servants. Essential beach furniture included the *toldos,* canvas awnings under which families sheltered from the sun's rays while enjoying the fresh air and relaxed environment. Bathing was still part of the story, but it became increasingly recreational rather than therapeutic. The *tertulias* or conversation parties were more important, and in a complex political system where allegiances and coalitions shifted rapidly, access to these alfresco political salons was essential to aspiring politicians. This aspect of the beach's appeal was lost with the coming of Primo de Rivera's dictatorship in 1923: two years later a

journalist complained of the loss of spicy opposition conspiracies to investigate. Meanwhile, more conventional pressures for change and conflict were
gathering.[55]

In the first place, congestion on La Concha increased, not only due to
growing visitor numbers, but also to the disappearance of the beaches east of
the river. The beach at Gros had a vogue in the early twentieth century, for
those who preferred quietness and informality and did not mind bathing
alongside the less-affluent locals. The ethos was symbolized by the variegated
collection of bathing vans, in contrast with the "almost complete uniformity"
of La Concha. The *Guide Diamant* of 1914 warned its readers of the dangers
here at high tide, and bathing began to decline at this time after a sequence of
accidents. The seal was set by the development of an extensive building estate
on land reclaimed from the sea, which effectively destroyed the beach in the
early 1920s. Bathing was prohibited on the remnant, although locals were still
risking their lives there in 1931. This apart, they were bereft of their bathing
facilities, and the visitors were pushed back on La Concha, where the space
available was also constricted by the presence of the royal bathing machine on
the palace side.[56]

The royal presence helped to construct the social gradations of La Concha, as described by the novelist Victor Iván in about 1913. At the eastern end
were children and nurses, the latter taking the opportunity to gossip happily;
then came the comfortable bourgeois families from Spain's interior and the
better-off locals. Here, plump ladies argued over children's misbehavior or
whether chairs had been reserved. Then, "as you advanced towards Miramar,
the elegance of the company increased by degrees . . . and the nature of the
bathers also changed." Bathers became more svelte, youthful and flirtatious,
fashionably dressed and displaying their bodies as the photographers and vendors of sweets and newspapers went to and fro. This reached a climax at La
Perla, where bathers came straight to the sea from changing-rooms under the
gaze of lounging men with aperitifs and binoculars. After this came a short
near-deserted stretch that was reserved for women who preferred to segregate
themselves, where (as it was unkindly put) "you only saw a few strange camels
and ostriches." Then came the royal bathing machine, which was sometimes
surrounded by sightseers with cameras; but the main focus of their attention
was the young King Alfonso XIII, who was less in evidence as he grew up, married, and sought distractions elsewhere.[57]

Important changes in beach organization came in the mid-1920s. In 1925
the municipality opened the new beach and gardens at Ondarreta, which was
partly reclaimed from an old military training ground, recently used for elite
sports such as tennis and show jumping. It was immediately proclaimed as
"the most attractive novelty of the summer," and it pulled the most fashionable of the visitors away from La Concha.[58] This new elite provision was the

context for José Ciganda's lament about the regular fatalities among teenagers who bathed, naked and unsupervised, at the river's mouth, having nowhere else to go. He urged formal official propaganda in schools to discourage this, but he also advised the corporation to "set aside a well-supervised area on the beach for the poor to bathe, that is, those who cannot allow themselves the luxury of paying a peseta for every session, with the municipality providing bathing costumes, towels and cabins." This would cost a little, but it would be a worthwhile combination of charity and good government.[59] The proposal fell on deaf ears, however, despite the corporation's overall commitment to providing amusements and distractions for the potentially disruptive poor. San Sebastián's more impecunious citizens remained effectively excluded from the jealously guarded municipally controlled foreshore during the season. But, only three years later, renewed complaints began about the overcrowding of La Concha.[60]

In the following year La Concha, belatedly in a wider European setting, replaced its bathing machines by cabins. This reform was extravagantly praised by a local columnist, who claimed the beach had "acquired extra space, complete comfort, and a very beautiful appearance in panorama." Potential conflict had been defused by allowing the bathing-machine proprietors to run the new cabins. But the change symbolized the more relaxed approach to the sea and to bathing that had been gathering momentum and was now developing controversial aspects.[61]

The most serious conflicts arose from the growing fashion for sunbathing and bodily display, which was already gaining ground before the First World War. In the first instance it was men rather than women who displayed themselves, in contrast with the United States, where scandals over women's scanty swimwear appeared at this time. In August 1914 a columnist who emphasized his credentials as man of the world endorsed female complaints about male exhibitionists "showing off their anatomical shapes before and after bathing," and at the start of the 1915 season the policemen allocated to the beach were instructed to intervene.[62] Complaints and occasional prosecutions were particularly directed against foreign visitors, accustomed to more relaxed regimes elsewhere; but in 1918 the local republican newspaper printed a eulogy of the male fashion for "toasted skin" in "rustic style," which young women saw as a "symbol of almost savage virility" and preferred to the waxy or rosy tints of yesteryear, associating it with a healthy outdoor lifestyle and the demise of tubercular effeteness.[63] Two years later *La Constancia*, a local newspaper of the puritanical Catholic Right, launched a campaign against sunbathing on the beach that was to continue until the Civil War resolved it in the moralists' favor for more than a generation, adding a denunciation of men who spied on women's bodies through holes in the wood while they undressed in the bathing machines, and attacking a whole catalog of immoralities.[64] In

1927 San Sebastián's more worldly *El Pueblo Vasco* admitted that there was a genuine problem, as male bathers romped around and displayed themselves in front of pious sedentary family parties: a measure of segregation was needed, as had been introduced even in the more relaxed setting of Biarritz.[65] The fashion for revealing bathing dresses then spread to women, and in 1929 a Catholic campaign for a compulsory standard, modest bathing dress (reaching from neck to ankle, and including a skirt) attracted the attention of the London *Times*. Even when part of the beach was set aside for sunbathers, the protests continued, as people began to undress in public (indicating a loss of control by the *bañeros* who rented the bathing cabins from the corporation) and displays of near-nudity became difficult to police when offenders included influential people as well as the inevitable showgirls. Complaints reached a strident crescendo in the early 1930s, when the advent of the secular regime of the Second Republic made pious Catholics feel particularly vulnerable, and by 1934 the provincial Catholic Parents' Association renewed its campaign for a standard bathing dress. The corporation tried to localize the problem, confining sun bathing to the *tostadero* (toaster) or *secadora de bacalao* (cod drier) on La Concha and to the most distant section of Ondarreta beach (between the prison and the sewer outfall). Furious debate continued right up to the outbreak of the Civil War in 1936, with Catholics beginning to cast doubt on the healthiness of sunbathing and even making links with skin cancer. The conflict between a secularizing, hedonistic, new middle-class Spain and an older set of Catholic values exemplifies some of the divisions that precipitated the war itself.[66]

Mainstream middle-class opinion was quite relaxed. Local columnist Gil Baré was optimistic in 1928, arguing that the controls were moderate, tolerant, and in tune with the expectations of the visitors, who did not want the freedom of French resorts where people came into hotels and had lunch in their bathing costumes. The regime was relatively conservative, and the threshold of complaint was perhaps low, but there was room for a variety of preferences, and few were deterred. And the beauties of the beach were still celebrated— like an impressionist painting, said one commentator, bringing out the artificiality of the conventions of seeing—alongside the artificial attractions. On blustery or stormy days, the Atlantic waves breaking over the rocks and promenades were an attraction in themselves, powerful but contained, and occasionally giving those who played with their power a good soaking. The beach as a social system might be regulated, formally and informally, and ways of enjoying it might be argued over; but the natural power of the waves remained an essential part of the attraction.[67]

In practice, San Sebastián's sea was less than pristine, despite this celebration of nature. Blackpool's beach was increasingly polluted by untreated sewage, but the town's situation was helped by the declining role of the beach in the town's inventory of attractions as commercial entertainment on land held increasing sway from the late nineteenth century. The promenade, the sea view, the sea air, and the simple pleasures of sitting on the sands in the sunshine were essential to the Blackpool holiday, and descriptions of the crowds in the 1930s emphasize this. As one travel writer (among many) commented in 1935, "The seven mile, sun-baked promenade was crowded; the three piers were black with people; and the beach was literally one heaving mass of humanity."[68] But this was no longer about bathing: as the remaining machines were gently phased out during the interwar years, no new regulatory regime was needed to replace them, because contact with the sea itself was almost confined to cautious paddling, and visitors usually remained fully clad or in consensual bathing dress, posing no problems of the sort that plagued San Sebastián. The overwhelming majority of visitors did not use the beach (although enough did to make it very crowded toward high tide) and were indifferent to the sea; and actual bathers could be numbered in dozens rather than hundreds even when the sands were crowded. This lack of interest helped the local authority to dismantle its remaining restrictions on bathing in 1932, although it continued to police trade and auction pitches on the beach.[69] All this was very different from San Sebastián. From 1923 most bathing was transferred to the open-air swimming pool at South Shore, a municipal initiative on a monumental scale with more room for spectators than swimmers, where observance of official rules on dress and comportment was a condition of enjoyment and the timetable rather than the tide governed accessibility. There was scant scope for transgression or unpredictability, although badinage between swimmers and spectators was a regular feature, especially when the carnivalesque aspects of bloated bodies were on display.[70]

It was after dark that Blackpool's beach played host to sexually transgressive activities, which became built into the town's reputation just as Brighton (whose beach was similarly invaded) became associated with the "dirty week-end."[71] Mass-Observation, the group of anthropological investigators who discovered Blackpool through their project on the "cotton town" of Bolton, were at pains to debunk this perception, surveying beach and sand dunes with relentless pertinacity and concluding that almost all of the huddled couples were cuddling and touching rather than engaging in full sexual intercourse; but even the reported behavior went beyond normal public boundaries in the context, fueling the expectations of the prurient and censorious. San Sebastián's beaches were carefully policed to prevent such behavior, in keeping with other policies, although what went on in the bathing cabins overnight was sometimes a subject for speculation. But whereas prostitutes were few and insignificant in Blackpool, they became an accepted part of San Sebastián's holiday menu for unaccompanied males, but operating from the cabarets and bars rather than alfresco. Liminality was a relative concept, at the seaside as elsewhere, and Blackpool couples usually kept to a set of norms of expected behavior that they brought with them and that limited the liberating effects of the beach and the holiday atmosphere.[72] The freedom of the beach was always subject to imposed restraint, whether official, communal, or internal. At San Sebastián the official restraints are most noticeable in this account; at Blackpool, commercial controls apart, the emphasis at working-class level is on the communal restrictions imposed by awareness of the probable proximity of neighbors and workmates and their capacity to generate gossip.

COMPARATIVE CONCLUSIONS

This thematic treatment enables us to compare and contrast the ways in which the allegedly liminal space of the beach was consumed and controlled in two European cultures and urban contexts. The seaside holiday and its practices were diffused through Europe from English origins, but took on differing forms in different national settings; and within this framework local differences also mattered, based on topography, patterns of demand, climate, prevailing attitudes to and conflicts over morality and bodily display, and the regulatory policies of local authorities. Generalizations need to take account of these contrasts, and of change over time within each culture. When we focus on the case studies, Blackpool and San Sebastián had different (but overlapping) dominant markets, contrasting (but converging) cultures of local government, differing worries about what needed to be regulated, licensed, and prohibited, and contrasting moral economies of space that arose from the wider contextual background. Their beach cultures evolved at different speeds in response to contrasting pressures and opportunities. Particularly interesting is the way in which the moral economy of the beach became consensual in Blackpool (although its political economy was capable of generating conflict over stall regulation and revenue that had moral overtones), while it generated increasing controversy in the international setting of San Sebastián and against the bitter background of Spanish cultural politics. Some of the differences arise from the contrasting influence of working-class demand, which was uniquely powerful in Blackpool; but this is an international as well as a local contrast, for the working-class presence was ubiquitous in large English resorts and enduringly limited elsewhere. A more extended study, moving beyond the beaches to the wider urban environment, would develop these themes in relation to town planning (or the lack of it) as a whole; the allocation and regulation of space for differing lifestyles, entertainments, and publics by market forces and local (not forgetting regional and national) government; and the nature of what was proscribed, tolerated, and encouraged. As between England and Lancashire on the one hand, Spain and the Basque

Country on the other, such contrasts might include attitudes and policies toward prostitution, casino and other kinds of gambling, retailing and consumption as entertainment, drink, blood sports, religious festivals, and public celebrations. The beach was one object of consumption and one locus of display among many in the developed seaside resort. As it is, this potent microcosm brings out contrasting concerns, expectations, problems, and policies that have to do with international and civic cultural differences, while demonstrating the cross-cultural potency of issues involving contested spaces and class conflicts. This array of themes worked themselves out in very different ways in Blackpool and San Sebastián, within the overarching parameters of a shared transnational bathing-resort culture; but what needs to be emphasized here is the importance and richness of the differences.

It is tempting to generalize about the social history of the beach across broad swathes of Western culture, and to let speculative theory set agendas that may become self-fulfilling. Such approaches are a necessary formative stage, enabling questions to be asked and providing hypotheses to be tested; but other priorities will become apparent from an interrogation of the evidence at the level of the individual resort, which will enable a more textured, nuanced picture to emerge, alert to differences within and between national and regional cultures. This essay is intended as an early contribution to that further stage of development.[73]

NOTES

1. J. K. Walton, *The English Seaside Resort: A Social History, 1750–1914* (Leicester, 1983), and "The Seaside Resorts of England and Wales, 1900–1950," in *The Rise and Fall of British Coastal Resorts*, ed. G. Shaw and A. Williams (London, 1997), chap. 2; J. D. Urbain, *Sur la plage: Moeurs et coutumes balnéaires* (Paris, 1994).

2. See the special issue on seaside resorts, *Built Environment* 18 (1992).

3. Comparative studies include R. Lewis, "Seaside Holiday Resorts in the United States and Britain," *Urban History Yearbook*, 1980, 44–52; J. V. N. Soane, *Fashionable Resort Regions* (Wallingford, 1993); J. K. Walton, "Leisure Towns in Wartime: The Impact of the First World War in Blackpool and San Sebastian," *Journal of Contemporary History* 31 (1996): 603–18.

4. A. F. Calvert, *Summer in San Sebastián* (London, 1905), 54.

5. Walton, *The English Seaside Resort*, chap. 2.

6. J. K. Walton and J. Smith, "The First Century of Beach Tourism in Spain: San Sebastián and the *Playas del Norte*, from the 1830s to the 1930s," in *Tourism in Spain: Critical Perspectives*, ed. M. Barke et al. (Wallingford, 1996); M. Chadefaud, *Aux origines du tourisme dans les pays de l'Adour* (Pau, 1987), 570–90, 640–50.

7. A. Corbin, *The Lure of the Sea* (Cambridge, 1994), 47; L. Lenek and G. Bosker, *The Beach: The History of Paradise on Earth* (London, 1998), chap. 2, for classical antiquity.

8. J. K. Walton, "The World's First Working-Class Seaside Resort? Blackpool

Revisited, 1840–1974," *Transactions of the Lancashire and Cheshire Antiquarian Society* 88 (1992): 1–30; Corbin, *Lure of the Sea*, 82–84.

9. Walton, *The English Seaside Resort*, 156–63; R. S. Neale, *Bath: A Social History, 1680–1850* (London, 1981); P. Borsay, *The English Urban Renaissance, 1660–1760* (Oxford, 1989).

10. L. Pearson, *The People's Palaces: The Story of the Seaside Pleasure Buildings of 1870–1914* (Buckingham, 1991); K. Peiss, *Cheap Amusements* (Philadelphia, 1986), chap. 5; M. Arsuaga and L. Sese, *Donostia–San Sebastián: Guía de arquitectura* (San Sebastián, 1996).

11. E. W. Gilbert, *Brighton, Old Ocean's Bauble*, 2d ed. (Brighton, 1976), 181; *La Voz de Guipúzcoa*, August 3, 1891 (visitors at San Sebastián choosing to sit with their backs to the sea).

12. J. Travis, "Continuity and Change in English Sea-Bathing, 1730–1900," in *Recreation and the Sea*, (Exeter, U.K.: University of Exeter Press, 1997), ed. Stephen Fisher, 23–30; Walton, "England and Wales," 41–42; Urbain, *Sur la plage*, 118–23; Chadefaud, *Aux origines;* A. J. Durie and M. J. Huggins, "Sport, Social Tone, and the Seaside Resorts of Great Britain, 1850–1914," *International Journal of the History of Sport* 15 (1998): 173–87.

13. Corbin, *Lure of the Sea*, chap. 11; J. K. Walton, "The Seaside Resorts of Western Europe, 1750–1939," in Fisher, *Recreation and the Sea*, chap. 3; Esbjerg Museum, *Strandlover og badenymfer* (Esbjerg, 1989).

14. M. Blume, *Côte d'Azur: Inventing the French Riviera* (London, 1992), chaps. 4–5.

15. Walton, "Western Europe," 24–38, 40–43; J. Towner, *An Historical Geography of Recreation and Tourism in the Western World, 1540–1940* (Chichester, 1996), chap. 7.

16. J. K. Walton, "Seaside Resorts and Maritime History," *International Journal of Maritime History* 9 (1997): 125–47.

17. J. Urry, *Consuming Places* (London, 1995).

18. J. K. Walton, *Blackpool* (Edinburgh, 1998), chap. 4, and "World's First?"

19. J. K. Walton, "The Social Development of Blackpool, 1788–1914," Ph.D. diss., University of Lancaster, 1974, chap. 8.

20. Walton, "World's First?"

21. M. J. Calvo Sánchez, *Crecimiento y estructura urbana de San Sebastián* (San Sebastián, 1983); R. de Izaguirre, *Estudios acerca de la bahía de San Sebastián* (Pasajes de San Pedro, 1933), 65–78.

22. Walton and Smith, "First Century."

23. Calvo Sánchez, *Crecimiento;* Walton and Smith, "First Century"; J. K. Walton, "Municipal Government and the Holiday Industry in Blackpool, 1876–1914," in *Leisure in Britain, 1780–1939*, ed. J. K. Walton and J. Walvin (Manchester, 1983); *El Pueblo Vasco*, November 14, 1922, August 15, 1930.

24. These issues are pursued in Travis, "English Sea-Bathing"; Lenek and Bosker, *The Beach;* J. Fiske, *Reading the Popular* (London, 1989), chap. 3; Urbain, *Sur la plage;* M. Ridha Boukraa, *Hammamet: Le paradis perdu* (Aix—en-Provence, 1993), for an interesting Islamic context; G. Désert, *La Vie quotidienne sur les plages normandes du second empire aux années folles* (Paris, 1983); Chadefaud, *Aux origines.*

25. Walton, *Blackpool*, chaps. 2–4.

26. *El Pueblo Vasco*, September 16, 1923.

27. *La Voz de Guipúzcoa*, August 16, 1887; *La Unión Vascongada*, July 17, 1892, July 10, 1894.

28. *El Pueblo Vasco*, May 15, 1927.

29. Walton, "Social Development of Blackpool," chap. 8; and compare R. Shields, *Places on the Margin,* (London: Routledge, 1991), chap. 2; and Travis, "English Sea-Bathing."

30. *El Pueblo Vasco,* July 5, 1930.

31. P. Langford, "British Politeness and the Progress of Western Manners: An Eighteenth-Century Enigma," *Transactions of the Royal Historical Society,* 6th series, 7 (1997): 53–72, both documents this and brings out paradoxes.

32. W. Hutton, *A Description of Blackpool in 1788,* 2d ed. (Preston, 1944), 23–24.

33. Walton, "Social Development of Blackpool," 382–85.

34. Ibid., 387.

35. Archivo General de Gipuzkoa, Tolosa (AGG), SM ISM SS 26.III 8/1 and 8/5. This issue was not mentioned in a previous code thirteen years earlier.

36. Richard Ford, *A Hand-book for Travellers in Spain,* 2d ed. (London, 1847), 573.

37. F. de P. Madrazo, *Una Espedicion a Guipúzcoa en el verano de 1848* (Madrid, 1849), 125–26.

38. R. de Navarrete, "El Verano en San Sebastián," *Semanario Pintoresco Español 1848,* 194–96.

39. Ford, *Hand-book,* 573.

40. Travis, "English Sea-Bathing," 19–23.

41. Walton, "Social Development of Blackpool," 387.

42. Ibid., chap. 8.

43. D. Hodson, "Civic Identity, Custom, and Commerce: Victorian Market Halls in the Manchester Region," *Manchester Region History Review* 12 (1998): 34–43, and references cited there.

44. Walton, "Municipal Government."

45. Walton, "Social Development of Blackpool," chap. 8; cf. Shields, *Places on the Margin,* chap. 2.

46. Walton, "Municipal Government."

47. Walton, "World's First?" 13–14.

48. J. K. Walton, "Residential Amenity, Respectable Morality, and the Rise of the Entertainment Industry: The Case of Blackpool, 1860–1914," *Literature and History* 1 (1975): 62–78.

49. Walton, "Social Development of Blackpool," 88–91, 326–28; P. Bennett, *A Century of Fun* (Blackpool, 1996), chap. 2; Peiss, *Cheap Amusements,* chap. 5.

50. N. de Soraluce, *Historia de la . . . provincia de Guipúzcoa* (Madrid, 1864), 25–27.

51. Mrs. William Pitt Byrne, *Cosas de España* (London, 1866), 1:67.

52. Felipe (F. Picatoste Rodriguez), *Andar y ver: Escursion a las provincias del norte* (Madrid, 1865), 146.

53. P. L. Imbert, *L'Espagne: Splendeurs et misères* (Paris, 1875), 4.

54. AGG, DM IDM SS 67, alcalde to Ministro de Fomento, June 19, 1869.

55. B. Anabitarte, *Gestion del municipio de San Sebastián (1901–1925)* (San Sebastián, 1971), 72–73; *El Pueblo Vasco,* August 9, 1915, July 19, 1925.

56. R. Izaguirre, *El Barrio de Gros en el primer cuarto del siglo XX* (San Sebastián, n.d.), n.p., Koldo Mitxelena, San Sebastián, C286–F39; L. Lheureux, *Guide diamant: Saint-Sébastien* (Paris, 1914), 9; *El Pueblo Vasco,* September 16, 1923; *La Voz de Guipúzcoa,* September 12, 1931.

57. Victor Iván, *Costa de plata* (San Sebastián, 1928), 88–92.

58. *El Pueblo Vasco,* July 11, 1925; Anabitarte, *Gestion,* 74.

59. *El Pueblo Vasco,* July 4, 1925.

60. *El Pueblo Vasco,* July 26, 1928.

61. *El Pueblo Vasco,* September 2, 1914, July 12, 1922, and Alfredo de Laffitte in idem., July 6, 1926.

62. Lenek and Bosker, *Beach,* 191–93; *El Pueblo Vasco,* August 23, 1914, July 3, 1915; *La Epoca,* August 8, 1914.

63. *La Constancia,* August 1, 1916; *La Voz de Guipúzcoa,* July 17, 1918, August 1, 1918.

64. *La Constancia,* August 5, 1920.

65. *El Pueblo Vasco,* August 11, 1927.

66. *El Pueblo Vasco,* July 13 and 18, 1929; August 18, 1934; July 5, 14, and 17, 1935; *The Times,* July 16, 1929; *La Voz de Guipúzcoa,* July 6 and August 2, 1933; *La Constancia,* July 24, 1934 and following; *La Cruz,* April 28, June 30, 1935; Koldo Mitxelena J.U. 5280, *Accion Católica de la mujer en Guipúzcoa* (1934), passim.

67. *La Voz de Guipúzcoa,* September 24, 1918, July 3, 1931; *El Pueblo Vasco,* July 15, 1925, July 22, 1928, August 7, 1930.

68. F. I. Cowles, *Not Far from the Smoke* (London, 1935), 57.

69. G. Cross, ed., *Worktowners at Blackpool* (London, 1990), 89–94.

70. Cowles, *Smoke,* 58.

71. Shields, *Places on the Margin,* chap. 2, citing Goffman.

72. Cross, *Worktowners,* 188–91.

73. See the papers by Laura Chase and by Ellen Furlough and Rosemary Wakeman in *International Journal of Maritime History* 9 (1997).

Culture for Export

Tourism and Autoethnography
in Postwar Britain

A lot of British men and women of a certain kind were traveling abroad in the
years 1947–48. Sir Alexander Maxwell, J. G. Bridges, and A. Emil Davies visited
the United States, Davies including the West Indies in his trip; Maxwell and
Bridges also took in Canada, where they were followed by W. G. Abel. Major
W. T. Blake, "well-known in South America," made a trip to Brazil and
Argentina. Sir Bracewell Smith and Sir James Milne went to South Africa, as
did Miss M. Moor.[1] Mr. A. Dunscombe Allen journeyed to Australia and New
Zealand. Sir Harry Brittain visited Belgium. Others made their way to Czechoslovakia, Denmark, France, Holland, Norway, Sweden, and Switzerland. All
these travelers were travel writers of a sort, too: they all wrote reports of their
tours, setting forth aims and recounting high and low points. Yet none of
these would be likely to appear in even the most inclusive anthology of (say)
British travel writing produced in the mid–twentieth century by men and
women of the upper and professional classes. This is so, not because these
travelers were spies or members of the diplomatic corps, but because they
were representatives or agents of the British Travel Association (BTA, sometimes called the Travel Association of the United Kingdom) which was in
those years the Tourist Division of the British Tourist and Holidays Board
(created 1947). The travels they undertook (which are recorded in the BTA's
annual report for the year ended March 31, 1948) and the writings they produced amount to something like the very defining opposites of what we tend
to understand by *travel* and *travel writing:* these people left home not to see
other parts of the world but to prepare other parts of the world to see their
home country; they wrote not of their impressions of foreign scenes but of
their progress in the effort to attract foreigners to the scenes of Britain. Insofar
as "travel writing" has tended to be construed within modern literary studies
as a special branch of the memoir—as the form in which unique individuals
represent their idiosyncratic responses to alien lands—then the writings and

representations produced by the agents and institutions of modern tourism would seem to embody that form's disavowed secret sharer or scapegoat, and in that capacity they can make a special claim upon our attention.

In this essay, I propose to consider the development of modern touristic representation in Britain, focusing upon the immediate postwar years but also looking backward and forward from there. In the process I will examine a few of the texts and images that promoted Britain as—in the words of the BTA's official historians—"a tourist area of the first importance,"[2] while also attending to the obverse side of these national representations created for tourists, namely the representation of tourism itself, and of the state that would ultimately manage it, to the nation. If, as those historians maintain, the BTA's message was "hammered home in all the varied overseas publicity," if "no effort was spared to secure tourist traffic" to Britain, the organization so energetically performing these functions also campaigned no less diligently, though perhaps less visibly, for the acceptance of tourism by Britons.[3] As a result of an administrative reshuffling shortly after the war, the BTA acquired a clearer picture of its mandate than it had yet possessed: leaving such matters as home holidays, hotels, and catering to other divisions of the new British Tourist and Holidays Board, it was to concentrate its energies on the paired concerns of overseas promotion and home advertising, the latter designed "to emphasize the economic importance of tourism to Britain, the enormous potential for the future and to encourage the public to welcome visitors to Great Britain."[4] What I shall call tourism's national "autoethnography"—the authoritative representation of "ourselves," of "our" landscape, traditions, and way of life that was presented in the millions of promotional materials disseminated each year—was shadowed by this other representation, which, in contrast to the historical associations and picturesque images employed by the tourist-luring productions, used statistics as its evidence and economic reasoning as its means of persuasion. The two must be taken together, for in their interaction, "Britain" came effectively to be defined as a territory marked out by the overlap—or the collision—of these two seemingly incommensurable modes of representation.

My use of "autoethnography" here derives from Mary Louise Pratt's influential book *Imperial Eyes: Travel Writing and Transculturation* (1992); but whereas Pratt applies the label to textual and other forms "in which colonized subjects undertake to represent themselves in ways that *engage with* the colonizer's [ethnographic representations of them],"[5] I want to use it in connection with the beginnings of the postimperial stage in the history of the leading modern colonizer. Neither the New World peoples Pratt studies nor the mid-twentieth-century Britons I consider here possess or produce their "own culture" in a spontaneous, unmediated fashion—which is to say that neither *fully* possesses "its culture," but shares it with influences from outside. In both contexts, though for obviously different reasons, cultural identity emerges as something dislocated, embroiled in, and beholden to processes not confinable to the physical or conceptual space of the nation. The autoethnographic account is in both instances made for consumption by powerful outsiders (Western colonizers, in Pratt's scheme; money-spending tourists, in mine), and what it yields is a product we might call culture-for-export.

The period with which I am concerned here was the immediate postwar one, of course. The British wayfarers I mentioned at the outset were part of a highly self-conscious and deliberate movement not only to package Europe for tourists but to reorient Europe economically and administratively in the direction of the tourist. As early as 1933, in a book entitled *The Tourist Movement: An Economic Study,* the British economist F. W. Ogilvie had noted, "In general, the international aspect of the tourist movement is now so widely recognised as important that there is hardly a country in the world which does not devote public money in one way or another to the development of tourist facilities, with the special object of attracting foreign visitors."[6] Ogilvie was an early commentator on a stage in the evolution of modern tourism that is still with us, though in highly intensified form. In the aftermath of the First World War, European governments had made the first, in retrospect rather tentative, moves toward establishing official structures for the soliciting and organizing of tourist traffic through their regions. Among the first of these were the French Office National du Tourisme, established in 1910, and the Italian Ente Nazionale per le Industrie Turistiche, set up in 1919.[7] National tourist organizations arrived on the European scene just in time to cope with what had only recently been identified as "the tourist problem," a phenomenon that appeared measurable and masterable only by the instruments of the new social sciences. (Ogilvie accorded Italy the distinction of having been "the country where the scientific study of tourist problems first began, . . . in 1899, with an article *Sul movimento dei forestieri in Italia e sul denaro ch vi spendono* . . . by L. Bodio, Director of the Italian Statistical Office.")[8] The year 1925 had seen the convening of the International Congress of Official Tourist Traffic Associations in The Hague; 1934 the founding of the International Union of Official Tourist Propaganda Organizations, later known as the International Union of Official Travel Organizations, later still the World Tourism Organization. Britain's BTA dates from 1929 and spent its first, depression-era decade (before going into wartime hibernation) eking out a living on whatever minuscule government grants-in-aid, private subscriptions, and advertising revenue it could get.

Their birth between the wars made it nearly inevitable that the new agencies of systematic tourism would revamp old ideas about the role of travel in the furtherance of international understanding, and the flattering image of the industry as a great peacemaker arose again, phoenix-like, from the ashes of the

Second World War. Tourism was vital to the British way of life, the BTA's *20th Annual Report* argued, "not only from the economic point of view, but from the more important aspect of international goodwill."⁹ In a celebratory history of the Thomas Cook company published in 1953, John Pudney voiced an "abomination of all that restricts travel" and proclaimed that travel agencies like Cook's, "implying liberty of choice and circulation, [were] the very antithesis of war."¹⁰

In 1946, the brand new Organization for European Economic Co-operation (OEEC) had sponsored a conference in London, "American Tourists in Europe," and later brought out a study entitled *Tourism and European Recovery* (1947) that laid out present circumstances and future prospects for European revitalization through American tourism. "From the very outset," this work made clear, the OEEC "ha[d] been concerned with the question of American tourism in Europe, for it was realised that [it] could make an important contribution towards solving the dollar shortage."¹¹ Britain did not make use of its Marshall Aid funds to rebuild tourist facilities, as several European nations did (and the BTA historians pointed out this distinction),¹² but it could not much more easily than they afford to ignore the means of its salvation lying so close at hand. The BTA's report for the year ended March 31, 1948, conveyed in capital letters the information that "in spite of the restricted volume of American travel in 1947, travel expenditures in Britain and on British ships and planes by Americans represented the largest single item of Britain's export trade with America, and exceeded in value the export of any single manufactured commodity to the United States."¹³ A great shift was in the making, from a conception of British ways of life in particular, and of national identities in general, as matters based on a quantity of domestically produced exportable goods, to a conception based on a certain relationship among representations, some of which were sent out into the wider world as images of the national culture for export, while others circulated in the interior as means of shoring up public opinion. This transition was plainly under way by 1938, when 720,429 foreign visitors spent almost 28 million pounds in Britain—a figure comparable to what the nation was then earning in a year on exports of wool or coal. The postmodern era it initiated, characterized by the predominance of representation and symbolic exchange, is with us still.

The effort to stimulate tourist demand had to be matched by a determined effort to ready the nation—materially, as well as imaginatively, emotionally, and intellectually—to receive its new visitors. The J. G. Bridges I have named above was director-general of the BTA, and his considerable time spent in the air and on the roads and rails in 1947–48 was devoted especially to the purpose of—as the annual report put it—"correct[ing] false impressions" brought about by the economic crisis following the war "that Britain was not a desirable place for American and Canadian tourists."¹⁴ The highlight of his tour—one feels bound to mention it—was his address to the American Society of Travel Agents Congress at French Lick Springs, Indiana. But all his labors needed to be supplemented by others aimed at "Making Britain Tourist-Conscious." The report acknowledged "the generous support of all sections of the British press in furthering [BTA] efforts" and singled out "Leader Page articles by Sir Alexander H. Maxwell [chairman of the British Tourist and Holidays Board] and Lord Hacking [founder of the BTA]" in the *Daily Telegraph* and the *Observer* as "only two outstanding examples" of the press's cooperative spirit in affording such prominent space to BTA home propaganda. The BBC was also to be thanked for the many "news bulletins, feature and television programmes, which have focussed attention on the tourist."[15]

By such means as these could tourism attempt to exercise some of its reputed calmative influence upon the *domestic* population, taming it by "bringing home to [it] the importance of the tourist" to its national prosperity and way of life. Of course, popular consensus must be approximated or fabricated around the issue of tourism development because such development is unlikely to succeed on any appreciable scale without public funds and other resources being devoted to it. People must be won over to the idea that the nation should pay, directly or indirectly, for an organization charged with the publicizing of its charms in foreign markets. The OEEC's *Tourism and European Recovery* points out that expenditure on European tourist propaganda in 1949 totaled only $2 million, the same amount that was spent during that period by "the town of Miami alone"; it uses a principle "that to be effective publicity should generally entail an expenditure of 3% of the earnings which can reasonably be expected," determining that the proper figure ought to have been $7 million.[16] In 1933, its fourth year of operation, the BTA received a government grant-in-aid of only four thousand pounds, just .02 percent of the estimated foreign tourist income during that year. (According to Enzo Paci, currently chief statistician for the World Tourism Organization, "the total amount [of money spent on tourism promotion today] is still ridiculously small . . . not nearly enough to cope with the fierce competition that destinations are facing.")[17]

In the touristic theater of postwar Europe, time, energy, and money needed to be spent on the easing of international travel restrictions, as well as on the easing of lingering British fears of invasion by foreigners—even if the foreigners in question were armed with cameras, not rifles. Also liable to provoke domestic unease, and thus to require mollifying efforts from the tourist institutions, was the implementation of "concessionary ration schemes" to provide tourists with freedom of access to petrol, confectionery, and other still-rationed goods; the same holds good for the decision, taken around this time, to exempt tourists from the purchase tax.[18] Structures damaged during wartime might have been destined for repair anyway—as the House of Commons certainly was—but their status as potential tourist attractions lent momentum to the restoration efforts. The postwar BTA pamphlet *London: A Brief Account of Its Many Beautiful and Interesting Sights* acknowledges, "The Museums and Art Galleries of London have not yet fully recovered from the damage done to their structures during the Second World War. Although great, even giant, strides have been made in the work of restoration, there remain, in some museums and galleries, rooms which have not yet been rebuilt or reconditioned"; but it assures us that, in general, "after spending the war in safety in the country, the great wealth of London's treasures—artistic, scientific, and documentary—has returned home and is once more on view."[19] On another front, the inadequacies of the British hotel industry became painfully apparent during these years, as the number of foreign tourists began to grow. To facilitate the construction of new hotels and the improvement of old, the British Tourist and Holidays Board had to clear away a tangle of restrictions on construction licenses, on imports of equipment, food, and drink, and so forth. For the Festival of Britain in 1951, the government began a program of limited grants to assist hotels in preparing for the influx of visitors. This set a precedent for the "massive increase in investment in the hotel industry in Britain" that took place under the Hotel Development Incentives Scheme, part of the watershed Development of Tourism Act of 1969, which finally nationalized the British tourist industry in establishing the statutory British Tourist Authority.[20]

All the factors cited above, and surely others as well, contributed to an environment in which, alongside its aggressive overseas advertising, the BTA found it expedient to distribute to the British public, whose cooperation it sought, a variety of materials bearing titles such as "The Travel Industry and Its Value to the British Isles."[21] Tourism's prospective hosts had to understand the industry's potential to lead the way among those forms of trade that the discourse of economics rather poetically calls "invisible exports": the OEEC referred to tourism as "this invisible export in the fullest sense of the word"— a rather vague phrase (*which* word? *invisible* in the fullest sense of the word?) by which it apparently meant to identify tourism as the *quintessential* invisible export—which it indeed can seem to be.[22] The *insubstantiality* of tourism's peculiar export trade, its reliance upon or entire constitution out of images, helped make a hyperbolic appeal for the enlistment of each and every British subject seem necessary: no longer could the material basis of the British way of life be left to this or that sector of the population (such as manufacturers or financial speculators). As the BTA historians put it, "personal contact between buyers and sellers"—and who was *not* a seller in the arena of postwar tourism?—could "overc[o]me the disadvantage that tourist products (accommodation, attractions and amenity) could not be displayed in the market place except through posters and literature, or other promotional media."[23] Tourism's hosts had to be primed to participate effectively in this one export trade above all others "in which every individual citizen can play his or her part."[24] The BTA's *20th Annual Report* emphasized the necessity for all Britons to show themselves equal to the role of host: "A friendly welcome and courteous reception may seem small things in themselves," the report confided, "but they make a lasting impression on our visitors."[25] Market research had revealed early on that "visitors would not travel long distances simply for advantages which Britain's countryside, national heritage and special attractions offered. There had to be the added satisfaction of good service and courtesy."[26] On the postwar British scene, tourism was not so much proving the antithesis of war as supplying the successor to wartime propaganda. The vast, newly perceived, and as yet untapped potential of the tourist market made the postwar years into something like Britain's finest hour come round again, another moment of national trial, which afforded a new sort of chance for every Briton to stand up and be counted. As we shall see, this rhetorical induction of all British subjects into the national service of tourism seems to be the counterpart, in the materials produced for domestic consumption, of a "saturation" motif found in the exported representations, which described a British landscape that seemed replete in every atom with touristic value or cultural significance.

It is no exaggeration to say that tourism had never before appealed to the patriotism of each and every Briton—or, more accurately, each and every subject of the United Kingdom; but it would be misleading to suggest that tourism had not appealed in some such fashion to the members of any single people of the United Kingdom. About 150 years earlier, following the 1801 Act of Union that established the United Kingdom of Great Britain and Ireland, many literary (and also musical and artistic) works presented themselves as the autoethnographic accounts of one marginal people now joined to England and under its political and economic sway. What Britain or the United Kingdom as a whole needed to do after 1945—and, that is to say, what *England* needed to do for the first time—was akin to what had seemed necessary for Ireland and Scotland in the first two decades of the nineteenth century: to speak up for itself, to represent itself to the powers beyond it. After 1945, the center now felt the need to organize itself for definitive exportable self-representation, much as the margins had earlier felt it; and the experience of the margins could illuminate that of the center.

In the early nineteenth century, when those "powers beyond" that had to be addressed were located in London, no figure loomed larger than did Walter Scott, who both produced and understood himself to be producing the most effective promotions of English tourism to Scotland during the post-1801 period. Scott first realized his powers during the furor over his narrative poem

The Lady of the Lake (1810), which flooded the hitherto little-visited region of Loch Katrine with excursionists eager to see the scenes described in the poem. Four years later, in *Waverley,* the first of his best-selling novels, Scott referred to his own text as a "humble English post-chaise" and undertook to conduct his readers by this vehicle into the "picturesque and romantic country" of the Highlands.[27] The entire novel was slanted toward the perspective of the English outsider, whose presumable prejudices toward the Scots could be, not confronted, but allayed. In the general preface to his series of Waverley novels (1829), the author aligned his whole project as a writer of fiction with Maria Edgeworth's earlier effort (in works such as *Castle Rackrent* [1800] and *The Absentee* [1812]) to "make the English familiar with the character of their gay and kind-hearted neighbours of Ireland"—an effort so successful "that she may truly be said to have done more towards completing the Union than perhaps all the legislative enactments by which it has been followed up." "Without being so presumptuous as to hope to emulate [this precursor]," Scott graciously added, "I felt that something might be attempted for my own country of the same kind with that which Miss Edgeworth so fortunately achieved for Ireland—something which might introduce her natives to those of her sister kingdom in a more favourable light than they had been placed hitherto, and tend to procure sympathy for their virtues and indulgence for their foibles."[28] In 1822, the man who in his writings had so influentially represented his own culture for English touristic consumption received the opportunity of a lifetime, the chance to organize welcome festivities for the royal visit to Scotland of George IV. The regent who had long been Scott's friend and fellow romanticizer of the Jacobites was by then king, and in an act meant to symbolize a peaceably united Britain, he rather reluctantly permitted himself to become the first Hanoverian monarch to set foot in his northern domain.

For Scott, the opportunity to render the whole of Scottish culture in Edinburgh for a fortnight, for the delectation of one man symbolizing the whole of Britain, presented the cicerone's challenge of a lifetime. "In charge of everything" related to the visit, he would choreograph all Scotland into one suave gesture of greeting: "Every trade and craft, every rank, profession, and public body, must play a part in the welcome, from Castle garrison to candlemakers, from peers to porters."[29] His country's distinctive features, "all those peculiarities which distinguished us as Scotsmen," must come to the fore in this representation: and so we find Scott writing to one of the several clan chieftains whom he would contact, urging him to bring his "tail" of followers to Edinburgh, "so as to look like an island chief, as you are . . . [for] Highlanders are what [the king] will best like to see."[30] In constructing this grand fiction of autoethnography, Scott's "mind glowed with scenes like those he had conjured up in Waverley: the triumphal appearance of bonnie Prince Charlie at Holyrood, swirling visions of serried Highlanders, 'all plaided and plumed in their tartan array,' claymores, targes, bagpipes." The resulting extravaganza delighted the sovereign, though it had a few detractors. "Sir Walter Scott," wrote one, "has ridiculously made us appear to be a nation of Highlanders, and the bagpipe and the tartan are the order of the day."[31] "A great mistake was made by the Stage Managers," Elizabeth Grant recalled, "one that offended all the southron Scots; the King wore at the Levee the Highland dress. I daresay he thought the country all highland, expected no fertile plains, did not know the difference between the Saxon and the Celt."[32]

Now, the dynamic according to which the English center follows the British or United Kingdom peripheries in learning to export its cultural self-representations was not entirely unprecedented at the dawning of the BTA. On the contrary, it is possible to regard the development of the novel in nineteenth-century Britain as obeying roughly this same pattern—as describing the English appropriation and adaptation, during the 1840s, of an early-nineteenth-century novelistic model identified with Scott and with lesser reputations like Edgeworth or Sydney Owenson (Lady Morgan, author of the celebrated *The Wild Irish Girl,* among other works). To pursue this interpretation in any detail is plainly beyond my scope here,[33] but it should be added that, as was the case a hundred years later, in the Britain of around 1850 there had emerged a consciousness of vulnerability to, or determination by, outside forces, a suspicion that seems to have provoked (in the novel) intricate and "total" visions of English or British culture in response. With the Corn Laws abolished, political economy regnant, empire expanding, Irish hordes arriving, Catholics "invading" by reestablishing their English church hierarchy, and a Jew (Rothschild) notoriously pressing for the right to sit in Parliament, midcentury England might well have seemed a place newly exposed to influences alien or indifferent to the preservation of Englishness. By the middle of the century, the *English* novel was well on its way to becoming the form recognizable for its mapping out of "a slowly built up picture with England—socially, politically, morally charted and differentiated in immensely fine detail—at the center and a series of [unrepresented] overseas territories connected to it at the peripheries"[34]—as if the literary genre then becoming preeminent were determined to push back the international or extranational scenes and entanglements that were increasingly to be felt in the English way of life.

It was just as true in Britain after the Second World War as it had been in 1820s Edinburgh that the domestic population needed to be persuaded to accept, or at least not openly to reject, the representations made of their nation by those charged with attracting foreign tourists, and even to participate in the making of those representations—which meant, in effect, accepting a kind of national split personality: the present and capitalist economic rationality on one side, the past and ancient traditions, on the other. Taken together, the two

sides of the national personality exist in a condition akin to what Homi
Bhabha calls "double-time," in which "the people" are at once "the historical
'objects' of a nationalist pedagogy [or tradition] . . . and the 'subjects' of a
process of signification that must erase any prior or originary presence of the
nation-people to demonstrate the prodigious, living principle of the people"
that continually reinvents the national life. Joseph Valente has admirably
characterized Scott's paradoxical view, which involved a "commitment to a
new order" that would "necessarily both create and dignify the old":

> The development of a modern industrial Scotland [which began after
> England crushed the 1745 rebellion described in *Waverley*] will bring her
> past into glorious view. . . . The Hanover ascendancy enshrines the Stuart
> cause; capitalism defines and aggrandizes feudalism. In brief, under this
> model, progress, and progress alone, can engender tradition, the value of
> which lies precisely in its being not-progress.[35]

The success of this model may be measured by the ease with which the line
between touristic interest and noninterest gets drawn in the promotional literature of modern tourism. A fine example—pertinent to Scott country, in
fact—may be found in a BTA booklet of the 1950s: "Surrounding Glasgow are
many important manufacturing towns . . . but the holiday visitor, it may be
presumed, will be more interested to see those parts of the country which have
escaped the juggernaut advance of industry."[36] That effortless partitioning of
domains, that untroubled erasure of the touristically irrelevant, is the gesture
I want to isolate here. Its opposite appears, among other places, in the very
first sentence of the first chapter of the OEEC's *Tourism and Economic Recovery*, which reads, "Political and cultural considerations apart, the importance
of American tourism to Europe is determined by the amount of dollars it
brings to Member countries."[37] As in a mirror-image of the Glasgow example,
here the rationality "specific to the economic domain" blithely and rather
ruthlessly slices away those aspects of tourism development with which it
refuses to concern itself.

　　In an account of how the BTA's campaigns of the late 1940s and 1950s
were received at home, the organization's official historians provide a miniature narrative about the triumph of a rationality specific to the *touristic*
domain, a tale whose main lines will be familiar to anyone who recalls Roland
Barthes's classic essay on the dehistoricizing and naturalizing ideology of the
French *Guides Bleu* (in *Mythologies*).

> Emphasis in [BTA] advertisements upon historic aspects of Britain—
> castles, half-timbered buildings, thatched cottages and Beefeaters—pro-
> voked some criticism in the United Kingdom. It was argued by the critics

that this advertising was at variance with the impression export industries were seeking to establish of Britain as a nation in the vanguard of technological progress. But, in the later 'sixties, when it became generally realized that overseas visitors were attracted by the unique characteristics of a country, rather than by bigger and better power stations, criticism was stilled by the understanding that the Association was in the right to concentrate in its promotion upon the very things which made Britain different.[38]

In this view—Scott's view as well—history, the force that made for national and cultural differences, is *finished;* those power stations, talismans of modernity, are the same the world over, and one uniform capitalist instrumental reason obtains, or ought to and soon will obtain, in societies everywhere—except on the tourist's itinerary. Like the twentieth-century ethnography of Malinowski and his followers, touristic autoethnography aims to preserve or "salvage" social forms that are passing away or passing into irrelevance. Like that ethnography, it tends to reify and stereotype the collective life it studies in the interest of creating one coherent picture of a unified "culture"—a unit that may be narrow (the village, the region) or broad (the nation), so long as it is both different from the tourist's point of origin and relatively consistent unto itself. Unlike the anthropologist's fieldwork science, of course, touristic autoethnography operates upon its "own" culture, which it grasps with canny economic logic as its potentially most valuable export. The Enlightenment end-of-history dream, in which differences will be subjected to the Hegelian magic of *Aufhebung*—negated, transcended, and retained—seems reachable through tourism, which holds fast to difference at the same time that it affixes it to the Procrustean bed of modern marketing strategies.

After the Second World War, it became virtually self-evident to European governments that in order to realize this universal reconciliation of sameness (we're all one family) and difference (otherwise why travel?), the many actors and agencies involved in tourism would have to coordinate and concentrate their efforts as never before. According to the professionals, their aim has still not been realized. Those tourism textbook authors of the 1980s are still looking forward to a time when "the industry will become more united and speak with a single voice. . . . Firms will become larger, and the weak links in tourism's chain of services will be eliminated."[39] As F. W. Ogilvie had seen back in 1933, the task of bringing this rather ominous-sounding future to pass could proceed only under the auspices of states: a globalizing tourist industry pressured states to organize themselves for tourism or be left behind. The textbook writers echo and surpass Ogilvie in noting that "practically every country in the world is now looking to tourism as an important factor in national prosperity and realizing that results cannot be achieved by 'hit or miss' methods."[40] The International Union of Official Travel Organizations declared in 1974, also in rather frightening language, that the stakes of the game were so high, the potential gains and losses so enormous, that in order to develop the industry "on a scale proportionate to its national importance and to mobilize all available resources to that end, it is necessary to centralize the policy-making powers in the hands of the state so that it can take appropriate measures."[41] Governments' collaboration with transport and travel agencies to stimulate and reward tourist demand would tighten that circle of tourist expectations and responses which, even in the nineteenth-century dawn of modern tourism, had been the subject of much wary comment—of the sort I have tried to analyze in my book *The Beaten Track: European Tourism, Literature, and the Ways to "Culture," 1800–1918*. States would now increasingly take the lead in identifying which attractions tourists could be induced to visit and in organizing the flow of tourist traffic to and around those sites. In the process, the touristic identities of various nations—that is, the rough consensus among visitors or potential visitors about what distinguished those nations from one another and made them worth visiting— identities sustained hitherto largely by anecdote and private enterprise, now approached a systematic articulation as states assumed the responsibility to represent their nations to the tourist market. (Today the most cursory tour of the World Wide Web will furnish dozens of examples, finely differentiated, of official national self-representation.) Inserting itself between the increasingly boundary-less tourist market and its own nation's touristic "product," the state implicitly depicted *itself* to the nation as the one agency capable of handling the national autoethnography.

Yet in the case of Britain, it is important not to overstate the speed or the alacrity with which the state entered into the "culture for export" business. Indeed, an important part of the distinctive self-portrait that the British state seemed bent on supplying was devoted to showing government *reluctance* to shoulder direct control of tourist promotion. This was an image in keeping with the traditional one of Britain as the home of individual liberty and minimal state interference—land of the Magna Carta and the Glorious Revolution. Those BTA travelers of the postwar years with whom I began were preceded by the truly prescient Richard Pinney, author of a memorandum submitted to government in April 1944: entitled "Britain—Destination of Tourists," and referred to reverentially in the trade as "the Pinney Memorandum," this pamphlet foresaw the coming transatlantic tourist boom and urged the nationalization of the tourist industry, the creation of an overarching tourist authority "for which the Government would accept ultimate financial responsibility."[42] Some of Pinney's recommendations were followed, but the House of Commons still preferred to keep the business of stimulating tourism at arm's length: despite some administrative changes, the prewar system of a nongovernmental travel service, only a small proportion of whose funding came from government grants-in-aid, was essentially preserved (though with higher levels of funding). The historians of the BTA catch the spirit of the British government at this time when they write, "The social climate in Britain perhaps favoured the voluntary, as opposed to statutory, or 'dirigiste,' approach sometimes preferred by foreign ministries of tourism."[43] This chimes with centuries of tendentious British distinctions that stress the decentralized, democratic vitality of Britain, in contrast to the autocratic and dully homogeneous character of other nations, particularly France.

It was not until the watershed Development of Tourism Act of 1969 that "the organization of tourism in Britain was transformed from a voluntary framework to a largely statutory one with a strong Government interest and involvement."[44] The British Tourist Authority created by that legislation now operates as a "Non-Departmental Public Body" under the auspices of the Department for Culture, Media, and Sport. Up to 1969, the affairs of British tourism were conducted in such a way as to give the impression of a state determined to show itself, not as overriding individual and local initiatives in British community self-representation, but as encouraging them. Under the terms of the 1931 Local Authorities (Publicity) Act, for example (enacted two years after the creation of the BTA), Parliament gave boroughs and urban district councils the (extremely limited) power to levy funds "for the purpose of publicising overseas the attractions of their areas."[45] The severe restrictions placed upon this power had an effect that appears to have contributed to the rhetorical effort in which the state was engaged: it stimulated local authorities to behave in ways that could be taken as signs of a characteristic British resourcefulness and cooperation. The 1948 annual report seems proud to note that, since each borough or council was not licensed to collect enough money to carry out any appreciable amount of foreign advertising, "the more enlightened municipalities [had] gladly availed themselves of the services of the Association in pooling their resources to carry out publicity abroad."[46] This was the image of British pluck and solidarity in the face of material obstacles that had been given everlasting embodiment in the months of blitzkrieg—during which, ironically enough, German bombers had seemed especially keen to demolish those tourist attractions that symbolized Britain, in a series of attacks that came to be known as the "Baedeker raids."

It was with a powerful awareness of the international competition for tourist dollars that BTA members set out upon their journeys in the years following the Second World War. Especially from 1950, when a second postwar reshuffle took place and the BTA received its clearest mandate yet (expressed in a hortatory letter to Maxwell from Board of Trade chairman Harold Wilson), the association's productions seem to have been created in the consciousness that there was no time left for delay and no room left for "weak links" in British tourism. Britain had to be presented, not just as a desirable vacation spot, but as the destination to top all challengers, "a country which by reason of its structure, position and history has, perhaps, more of beauty, interest and variety to offer the visitor than any other country in the world."[47] The work from which these words come is a characteristic product of this era, a booklet of the early 1950s entitled *Britain: A Book Which Attempts To Do More Than Its Size Permits* (probably 1952). The title is in keeping with the spirit of the volume, which darts breathlessly through each county of England, Wales, Scotland, and Northern Ireland, suggesting at every turn that Britain is the veritable home of the touristic sublime, a land so teeming with sites valuable to tourists that it beggars representation. "In writing of Great Britain, even in thinking of it," the booklet begins,

> the use of superlatives is difficult to avoid, and when used they seem inadequate for their purpose. What vocabulary could describe the thrilling, vast, and ponderous majesty of Windsor Castle, the towering, fairy-like grace of Salisbury Cathedral, or the ancient and mellow charm of a Cotswold village? Such scenes as these . . . abound in Britain, and wherever he may go the visitor will find wherewith to delight his eye and to stimulate his interest.[48]

This hyperbolic "wherever he may go" partakes of what I have elsewhere called the "saturation" motif in nineteenth-century travel writing, according to which the visited place is imagined as a totality so densely packed with significance that a step in any direction sets off historical and affective resonances.[49] It is a totality highly selective in nature, of course: one would hardly expect those power stations—which must, after all, be *somewhere* in Britain— to feature in the booklet *Britain*.

Of the dozens of images that are reproduced in the booklet, only two show structures recognizably—and actually rather stunningly—modern in design, and both of these are the sites of activities not connected to the domain of power stations or material production: the De La Warr Pavilion at Bexhill-on-Sea, Sussex (oceanside leisure), and the Shakespeare Memorial Theater at Stratford-upon-Avon ("culture"). Among the few other definitively twentieth-century images in the volume, those set in peripheral, non-English regions of the United Kingdom figure prominently, as if to suggest how materially the union with England had benefitted these hitherto backward places: we see Douglas Bay, off the Isle of Man, full of modern freighters; the Forth Bridge at Queensferry, West Lothian, "one of the engineering wonders of the world";[50] and the Parliament Buildings at Stormont, Belfast, opened in 1932 as the imposing home of the Ulster government. Of the last it is pointed out that: "During the Second World War, the Senate Chamber was used as an R.A.F.

operations room, and it was from here that the Bismarck was located and hastened to her end."⁵¹ It seems part of the booklet's ideological message to suggest that each outlying portion of the United Kingdom—perhaps especially
the bitterly contested Northern Ireland?—had its crucial role to play in safe-
guarding the British whole.

Similar effects can be discerned in two spiral-bound series of miniature
posters entitled *Come to Britain* and designed for display at BTA offices
abroad. A potential customer flipping through the first of the series would be
conducted on a couple of virtual tours with the following stops.

> Warwick—The Castle
> London—A Sergeant of the Royal Hospital
> Teignmouth, on the Devon Coast
> Wales—Snowdon, Caernarvonshire
> Scotland—A Piper in Full Dress
> Norwich—Old Merchant's House
> Cheltenham—The Devil's Chimney
> St. Albans—The Cathedral
> Scarborough, from the Castle Ramparts
> Chester Cathedral
> Northern Ireland—The Giant's Causeway
> Royal Tunbridge Wells—The Pantiles
> Carlisle—Border City and Gateway to Scotland
> Lincoln—The Cathedral and Exchequer Gate
> Stratford-upon-Avon—The Shakespeare Memorial Theatre
> Southampton—Tudor House

And in the second:

> London—Lord Mayor's Coachman
> Scotland—A Member of the Royal Company of Archers
> Northern Ireland—The Harbour at Donaghadee, County Down
> Shrewsbury—On the Borders of Wales
> A Devonshire Village, Cockington
> Gloucester—The Entrance to the Close
> Guernsey—St. Peter Port
> Peel Castle—Isle of Man
> An Old By-Way in Folkestone, Kent
> The Sea Front at Hove, Sussex
> Buxton—A Derbyshire Spa
> Aston Hall, near Birmingham
> Glastonbury Abbey, Somerset—A Norman Doorway

Droitwich Spa—The Brine Baths
The Channel Islands—La Hougue Bie, Jersey
Sheffield Cathedral—The Shrewsbury Chapel
Coniston Water, Lancashire
Colchester Castle, Essex
Paignton—On the Devonshire Coast
Winchester—The Gateway to the Close

The exercise of mapping out these itineraries will yield a mass of criss-crossing lines that does not describe any possible route to take in visiting the country—no tourist would perform the inefficient, zigzagging movements required by the lists above—but that does effectively distribute the touristic potential of the United Kingdom across its several territories. The effect of constant doubling back and recrossing of large distances (Isle of Man to Folkestone, or Devon to Scotland, or Scotland to Norwich) may suggest the situation of an ideal, gigantic supertourist who is so overwhelmed to find objects of touristic value on every side and in every corner of his chosen field that he stumbles delightedly back and forth, sampling the treasures at random. This impression of touristic plenitude is secured not only by the scattering of attractions across a wide geographic territory, but by the serial arrangement of several types of attractions: castles, natural scenes, spas, country houses, cathedrals, and so forth. To travel in the turn of a page from Ulster's famed Giant's Causeway to The Pantiles at Royal Tunbridge Wells is to cross a spectrum from natural sublimity to the height of refined civility, and to identify Britain or the United Kingdom as a land that embraces the whole span. After this, to move from Tunbridge Wells to Carlisle and the gateway to Scotland is to add a third dimension, that of history, to the two poles defined by the previous transition: the photo of the grim portcullis of Carlisle Castle and the caption referring to dungeons containing "stone carvings made by Scottish prisoners taken in the rebellion of 1745" conduct the viewer into a realm of national-historical pathos, another area of prized touristic experience specialized in by Britain. The several "local color" photographs in the collection also lend support to the saturation motif: pictures such as "An Old By-Way in Folkestone, Kent" or "Norwich—Old Merchant's House" do not show us any bona fide "attractions" that we might cross the Atlantic to see (Tower of London, Buckingham Palace, etc.), but mere details of picturesque life that seem to have been gathered haphazardly and hint to the tourist that their substitutes or counterparts might be found "wherever he may go" in that country.

There are many ways to consider the principles of selection that guided the creators of these works, and I cannot pursue all them here. Of the buildings displayed in the thirty-six images, the lone modern structure is the Shakespeare Theatre—the choice of this edifice managing to convey both reverence for the glories of Britain's cultural past and a commitment to revivify those glories for the twentieth century. Portraits of individuals—in which a single person occupies most of the image and is not a mere figure in the middle distance of a scene—are, not surprisingly, limited to decorative "types" in ritual attire: a gray-bearded sergeant of the Royal Hospital in Chelsea, wearing a tricorn hat and medal-bedecked commissionaire's coat; a Scottish piper "clad in the colourful tartan of the Royal Stuarts"; the lord mayor's coachman, "seen arrayed in his traditional finery"; a member of the Scottish Royal Company of Archers. Of the remaining pictures, seventeen are scenes of buildings or landscapes entirely unpeopled; fourteen others depict such scenes with one or more people scattered about, too far off to be distinguishable and certainly engaged in no obvious productive or commercial activity.

The English pictures are spread fairly evenly across the country and out toward the edges, from Devon to Carlisle to Scarborough to Folkestone. The exclusion of Cornwall does not seem deliberate, since that county does receive significant attention in the booklet *Britain;* but the emphasis placed on Devon—depicted three times—suggests a determined effort to counteract the impression of England as a "damp and dismal island" with images of the "English Riviera."[52] Not much stress is laid on London (two images, both portraits of "types"), possibly because a separate series of posters was devoted to it; after all, the metropolis does not figure in *Britain: A Book Which Attempts to Do More Than Its Size Permits,* but is handled in the companion volume called *London: A Brief Account of Its Many Beautiful and Interesting Sights.* On the other hand, it may have been felt that comparatively little needed to be done to stimulate visits to the capital, especially since, with the coming shift from seaborne to airborne international tourism, most foreigners would enter Britain through the London airports. Eight of the images in the two poster series derive from sites outside England (two apiece from Scotland, the Channel Islands, and Northern Ireland, one apiece from Wales and the Isle of Man), and two more come from places identified as on a border between England and one of its peripheral United Kingdom partners (Shrewsbury and Carlisle)—all of which implies the aim of promulgating a fully national portrait.

The allotment of space in that portrait to many different and widespread regions of the country, of course, could help those regions profit from the tourist's visit by putting them, so to speak, "on the map." The counterpart for that saturation motif which characterizes British tourism's culture-for-export is the tourist industry's repeated theme of the need to spread tourism in Britain as much as possible in both time and space—to saturate all Britain with tourist dollars all the time. Obviously, this was an effort that could be acknowledged solely in such domestic productions as the BTA's *20th Annual Report.* In the materials made for potential tourists, one would never find the candid strategizing and unabashed opportunism of the report, which positively boasts that "tourists are being encouraged by every available means to prolong the period of their stay in Great Britain, and to spend more on goods and services. At the same time efforts are being made to persuade overseas visitors to our country hotels as well as those in London and the big cities."[53] This kind of talk would hardly do to put the tourist in the staying and spending mood; that purpose would be served by another language, another logic altogether.

To me it seems richly ironic that works like the tourist booklet *Britain* and the *Come to Britain* posters should have been published in such vast numbers at the very time when Raymond Williams was beginning his work *Culture and Society, 1780–1950*. This was, we recall, his classic critique of the British tradition that limited the concept of "culture" to the status of one privileged portion of social life—the refuge of imagination from the brutal logic of capitalist "society," with which culture was not supposed to be concerned. Williams was attempting to articulate a total or "anthropological" concept of culture as "a *whole* way of life" at the historical moment when organized British tourism seemed to have decisively instituted the sort of national split personality I have mentioned above: on the one hand, the image of the magical land sketched out in the booklet *Britain* and in other items of British culture-for-export; on the other, the representation of tourism and the state produced for domestic consumption, which relied heavily on statistics, and, in a neat reversal of the saturation motif, made its appeal to the economic rationality of "every individual citizen."

In spite of much protestation to the contrary, we have not entirely outgrown the basic tropes of romantic nationalism, the dominant narrative of which holds that a people realizes its national potential when it asserts the ability to "tell its own story" or demands "permission to narrate" its own history. In this view, which we disingenuously disavow, national culture is the outpouring of a people demanding or enjoying its autonomy. The idea that the people capable of representing itself is free from the representations imposed upon it by others has received new life in the postcolonial era, for which collective self-representation is typically seen as a militant, positive step in the overthrowing of ascribed identities by indigenous ones. The growing role of the state in the promotion and development of tourism intersects with this tenacious notion at an illuminating angle: for this role was fashioned out of the perception, not that nations inherently longed for self-expression, but that nations could not afford *not* to represent themselves to the powers outside them. Indeed, it might be a corollary of my argument here to say that the truly dominant power, the supremely confident colonizer—if there ever was such—would seem to have little use for the autoethnographic mode: that power might well prefer to leave its way of life *un*represented, so as better to discourage a distinction between it and "the way things are" or "common sense." As Perry Anderson put it, in a fascinating (though debatable) argument about the English inaptitude for totalistic thinking, "*Omnia determinatio est negatio*—the very demarcation of a social totality places it under the sign of contingency."[54] The community that submits to the necessity of representing itself must accept its limited place in a world of other, competing "cultures" and can no longer pretend to be the home of culture itself.

NOTES

An earlier version of this chapter appeared in *Studies in Travel Writing* 2 (spring 1998). Reprinted with permission.

1. Travel Association of the United Kingdom, *20th Annual Report, for the Year Ended 31st March, 1948* (London, 1948), 16.

2. British Tourist Authority, *The British Travel Association, 1929–1969* (London: British Tourist Authority, 1970), 3.

3. Ibid., 4.

4. Ibid., 17.

5. Mary Louise Pratt, *Imperial Eyes: Travel Writing and Transculturation* (London: Routledge, 1992), 7.

6. F. W. Ogilvie, *The Tourist Movement: An Economic Study* (London: P. S. King and Son, 1933), vii.

7. I thank Ellen Furlough for her helpful correction here.

8. Ogilvie, *The Tourist Movement*, 160.

9. Travel Association of the United Kingdom, *20th Annual Report*, 32.

10. John Pudney, *The Thomas Cook Story* (London: Michael Joseph, 1953), dedication and 173. It is perhaps worth observing how resilient this idea has continued to show itself. In contemporary times, when tourism has become a global phenomenon and an academic discipline in its own right—as well as a favored target of nationalist hatred and violence—one textbook designed for "college and university courses in tourism" as well as for "chambers of commerce, tourism promotion and development corporations, tourist accommodations and other businesses, transport and carrier firms, oil companies, automobile manufacturers and dealers [et al.]" concludes with a section entitled "A Philosophy of Tourism and Peace," which marshals such authorities as Augustine, Marco Polo, and the Holiday Inn publication *Passport* in support of its claim that sensitively managed world tourism can open our minds to "the unity that exists in the family of man throughout the world" (Robert W. McIntosh and Charles R. Goeldner, *Tourism: Principles, Practices, Philosophies*, 4th ed. [New York: John Wiley, 1984], 354). In the wake of the November 1997 bloodshed at Luxor's Hatshepsut Temple, the persistence of this message on a World Wide Web page entitled "President Mubarak's Concept of Tourism" (http://touregypt.net/mubarak.htm) seems especially bizarre. The Egyptian leader is there quoted as saying, "The boom today being witnessed by the [Egyptian] tourist industry could never have been achieved without stability; and stability is the responsibility of us all, not of one person, or the other but everyone. We have to foster that stability in order to encourage investment and tourism. The national characteristics of our people is [*sic*] an important element in making Egypt a unique tourist destination, where the visitor feels warmth and security. Tourism and peace are intertwined. The former cannot flourish without the latter. Moreover, tourism fosters understanding and peace." It is yet one more voice in

the seemingly tireless chorus not satisfied with acknowledging that tourism requires the absence of violence in order to reap its profits, but bent upon pressing the increasingly dubious thesis that tourism actually helps eliminate violence.

11. Organization for European Economic Co-operation (OEEC), *Tourism and European Recovery* (N.p., n.d., probably 1947), 5.

12. British Tourist Authority, *British Travel Association,* 19.

13. Travel Association of the United Kingdom, *20th Annual Report,* 3.

14. Ibid., 24.

15. Ibid., 32–33.

16. OEEC, *Tourism and Economic Recovery,* 24.

17. World Tourism Organization, "More Money Needed for Tourism Promotion," press release dated October 2, 1997.

18. See British Tourist Authority, *British Travel Association,* 20–21.

19. British Travel and Holidays Association, *London: A Brief Account of Its Many Beautiful and Interesting Sights* (London, n.d., probably 1950–51), 61.

20. A. J. Burkart and S. Medlik, *Tourism: Past, Present, Future,* 2d ed. (London: Heinemann, 1981), 156.

21. British Tourist Authority, *British Travel Association,* 4.

22. OEEC, *Tourism and European Recovery,* 5.

23. British Tourist Authority, *British Travel Association,* 35.

24. Travel Association of the United Kingdom, *20th Annual Report,* 33.

25. Ibid., 32–33.

26. British Tourist Authority, *British Travel Association,* 17.

27. Walter Scott, *Waverley: or, 'Tis Sixty Years Since* (1814; New York: Penguin, 1972), 63.

28. Ibid., 523.

29. See Edgar Johnson, *Sir Walter Scott: The Great Unknown* (New York: Macmillan, 1970), 2:790.

30. Qtd. in Hugh Trevor-Roper, "The Invention of Tradition: The Highland Tradition of Scotland," in *The Invention of Tradition,* ed. Eric Hobsbawm and Terence Ranger (Cambridge: Cambridge University Press, 1983), 30.

31. See Johnson, *Sir Walter Scott,* 2:790, 794.

32. Elizabeth Grant of Rothiemurchus, *Memoirs of a Highland Lady,* ed. Andrew Tod (1898; Edinburgh: Canongate Classics, 1988), 2:165–66.

33. It is part of the argument of James Buzard, *Anywhere's Nowhere: Fictions of Autoethnography in the United Kingdom* (Princeton University Press, forthcoming).

34. Edward W. Said, *Culture and Imperialism* (New York: Knopf, 1993), 74.

35. Joseph Valente, "Upon the Braes: History and Hermeneutics in *Waverley,*" *Studies in Romanticism* 25, no. 2 (1986): 275.

36. British Travel and Holidays Association, *Britain: A Book Which Attempts To Do More Than Its Size Permits* (London, n.d., probably 1952), 170.

37. OEEC, *Tourism and Economic Recovery,* 11.

38. British Tourist Authority, *British Travel Association,* 44. See also Roland Barthes, "The *Blue Guide,*" in *Mythologies,* trans. Annette Lavers (New York: Hill and Wang, 1981), 74–77.

39. McIntosh and Goeldner, *Tourism,* xii.

40. Ibid., xiii.

41. International Union of Official Travel Organizations, "The Role of the State in Tourism," *Annals of Tourism Research* 1, no. 3 (1974): 71.

42. British Tourist Authority, *British Travel Association,* 4.

43. Ibid., 30.

44. Burkart and Medlik, *Tourism,* 273.

45. Travel Association of the United Kingdom, *20th Annual Report,* 12.

46. Ibid.

47. British Travel and Holidays Association, *Britain,* 7.

48. Ibid.

49. See James Buzard, *The Beaten Track: European Tourism, Literature, and the Ways to "Culture," 1800–1918* (Oxford: Clarendon Press, 1993), 185–87.

50. British Travel and Holidays Association, *Britain,* 169.

51. Ibid., 140.

52. See British Tourist Authority, *British Travel Association,* 18.

53. Travel Association of the United Kingdom, *20th Annual Report,* 14.

54. Anderson, "Components of the National Culture," in *Student Power: Problems, Diagnosis, Action,* ed. Alexander Cockburn and Robin Blackburn (Harmondsworth: Penguin, 1969), 264.

"Everybody Likes Canadians"

Canadians, Americans, and the Post–World War II Travel Boom

In the 1920s, when large numbers of American motorists began to visit Canada, they brought with them their flag, draped for all to see from their automobiles. This caused great consternation to some Canadians, who considered the flying of American flags on Canadian soil an act of disrespect. Newspapers sighed about the "ignorant and blatant" American tourist, popular tourist towns such as Niagara Falls saw this affront as another example of the mixed blessings of the tourist trade, and the Canadian Legion even tried—unsuccessfully—to have the practice outlawed.[1] After World War II—another boom period for tourism—the flag debate surfaced again. In a few short decades, however, much had changed. By the 1940s and 1950s, it seemed Canadians could not hoist enough American flags to greet American tourists, and eventually, some began to worry about all this friendliness. The concern was not, however, about wounded Canadian national pride, but rather that Canadians were overdoing it, and possibly alienating or boring American visitors. Canadian flags were one sure sign that American tourists were in a foreign country; as one journalist put it, the American visitor in Canada "looks for the symbols which tell him that he is in another country."[2] In post–World War II North America the flag was a reassuring signifier that there was a indeed a difference between the two countries and, therefore, that American visitors would find at least some measure of the novel or extraordinary in Canada. Newspaper editorialists, hotel industry spokespeople, even federal cabinet ministers worried that Canadian businesses displaying American flags would appear to be "toadying," making Americans "contemptuous of us," or worse still, laugh at us. "There is a difference between service and servility," the *Hamilton Spectator* declared in 1954, though in this era it was a difficult boundary to keep in view.[3]

Here, as well as in a longer project on the history of Niagara Falls of which this essay is a part, my interest is in connecting tourism-as-gaze with tourism-as-industry, that is, understanding the ways in which tourism produces social meaning but also exploring how that meaning is shaped (not determined, but shaped) by political economy, specifically the tourist industry. I am therefore facing one of the main challenges of studies of consumption, nicely summarized recently by Victoria de Grazia as "the complex problem of relating metaphor and meaning to social change, of linking the imaginary world around consumption with the structural changes giving rise to modern consumer society." Capitalism, as de Grazia and many other scholars have noted, "is a semiotic as well as an economic system."[4] The history of tourism illustrates how extraordinarily complicated—and profitable—it has been to commodify and market nature, emotion, and nation, but also, therefore, how necessary it is to understand the intersections of commerce and sentiment.

I am going to explore some of the larger changes in the tourist industry— both structural *and* imaginative—that occurred at the national level in Canada after World War II. My focus is on national discourses, espoused by national organizations, though I will also examine how these issues were taken up provincially (in Ontario) and locally (in Niagara Falls). While Niagara Falls had been a well-known destination since the early nineteenth century, changing discourses of tourism in this era dramatically expanded the tourist industry at the falls, as anyone who has seen the vast, by now a bit tattered, motel landscapes that remain in the area can attest to. But in the rush for tourist spoils that the entire country embarked on after the war, we can see even more visibly some of the central questions of modern Canadian political economy and cultural identity.

The manner in which tourist entrepreneurs and government officials organized Canada's participation in the postwar travel boom reveals much about the prevailing cultural climate, particularly Canada's economic and cultural reliance on the United States. It is a truism of Canadian history that after World War II, Canada became increasingly integrated into the American orbit: economy, global worldview, and culture. But for a tourist industry to prosper, Canadians had to learn how to present themselves as distinctive from Americans, especially because the holiday market was defined quite narrowly. To Canadian tourist promoters, *tourist* and *American* were virtually interchangeable terms; the sole concern of the tourist industry in this era was in attracting Americans north. In this paper I will detail the expansion of the tourist industry infrastructure in Canada after World War II, explore various strategies developed by the industry to forge an "authentic," marketable, and modern Canadian identity, and finally, review civic campaigns to turn Canadians themselves into better, more attentive hosts. Through all of these discussions, I will untangle the peculiar relationship between tourism and national identity, especially the uncanny ability of the tourist industry to conflate discourses of commerce or enterprise into those of nation or region.

THE POSTWAR TRAVEL BOOM

While a travel industry had existed for many years in North America, there was a widespread conviction that the sacrifices of World War II, combined with the expected material prosperity after the war, would result in a huge travel boom. "The most significant reflection of post-war prosperity," declared the American Automobile Association in 1946, "will be in a tremendous increase in the tourist traffic."[5] Citing American statistics that suggested that more than four-fifths of private sector employees had won paid vacation leave, Arthur Welsh, Ontario's minister of travel and publicity (a bureaucracy that itself was a product of this era), also predicted that a "pent up urge to travel" would be unleashed after the war and encouraged tourist entrepreneurs in 1946 to think of Canada "as a gigantic department store, purveying travel and recreation."[6]

The primary shoppers in the Canadian department store were, in the hopeful view of tourist promoters, Americans. Tourist promoters of this era were singleminded in their determination to make Canada more attractive to U.S. visitors, and much of this essay will explore their strategies to make this happen. I start from the premise that there was nothing natural or inevitable about this, though at the time it certainly looked as though this was somehow foreordained. Contemporaries (and some less thoughtful historians) tend to speak of the postwar "pent-up" travel urge (and its cousin, the "pent-up" urge for consumer goods) as though they were predetermined, biological needs. Yet this overlooks how the complex processes of consumption come about. Consumers, like tourists, are made, not born. There are a variety of ways consumers of travel are created, from the material—paid vacation legislation and road construction—to the imaginative—the cultural and social constructions of travel in a given historical moment. Thus the obsession with luring American tourists to Canada was not a geographical given, it was a marketing strategy. In this era, new groups of Canadians were also joining the ranks of the tourist-consumer. Most workers in Ontario—private and public sector—achieved mandatory one-week paid vacation leave in 1944, and workers from British Columbia to Quebec achieved similar legislation within the next three years. Yet this fact made far less of an impact on the travel industry than the similar pattern in the United States, where one-half of wage earners had achieved, through legislation or collective bargaining, company paid vacations by 1940.[7]

"Swarms of industrial workers who will have holidays with pay for the first time in their lives" would be hitting the highways in 1946, predicted *Canadian Business*.[8] This was correct. Sixty-two percent of Americans took a vacation trip in 1949, averaging ten and a half days long.[9] "The whole world has shrunk," declared Canada's *Saturday Night* magazine in 1959, noting also the "more democratic" nature of travel after the war, since "the wealthy few have been supplanted by the masses."[10] The portrait of the tourist that emerged in postwar discussions of improvements to tourist services was based on this populist image of the "ordinary guy, who works at an ordinary job and has to save his money for several months."[11]

This language of class inclusion and gendered exclusion obscured the fact that workers were not the only newly enfranchised consumers of travel. In this era two other new and distinct vacation markets emerged: women traveling alone and families. Traveling women, according to experts, fell into four categories: the business or single "girl," the mother with young children, the matron, and the elderly woman. The travel industry seemed unconcerned about women in the latter two categories, but the first two were the object of some attention. But even as tourism consumers were occasionally gendered, they too were always identified with one particular nation, the United States. Female commentators especially argued that Canada had to work particularly hard to attract the American "business girl," for the traditional promotion of Canada as a wilderness mecca made most women think that "Canada is a man's country [lacking in] elegance and glamour." Women were more likely to travel on what were becoming known as "package tours"—group tours— which were less expensive and offered, as one male travel writer delicately put it, "protection," and Canada lacked these innovations as well.[12] The importance of the female tourist was also underscored as family travel assumed increasing proportions of the travel market, for it was commonly held that, within families, women made the decision about where to travel. The U.S.-based *House Beautiful* magazine, for example, encouraged advertising by reminding Canadian tourist promoters that "if she says 'Canada for our honeymoon, darling!' you can count on them heading north."[13]

As vacations and travel began to embrace more and different kinds of people, a new genre of writing emerged: the travel column. Popular magazines and newspapers of the era filled their pages with helpful advice, aimed at assisting uninitiated travelers ("How to Read a Travel Folder" and "Railroad Rights—and Wrongs!"), promoting the many social benefits of travel ("Vacation's the Time to Get a Husband") and debating the benefits of travel to healthy family life ("Marital Vacations Keep Love Alive").[14] Alongside this continual flow of travel news in the popular and business press, this era also produced the first mass circulation magazine devoted exclusively to travel. The glossy, lavishly illustrated *Holiday* magazine, published by the Curtis Publishing Company of Philadelphia, was launched in March 1946. *Holiday*, dedicated "to the pursuit of happiness, for all those who see 'go' signs on the horizon," was a mass-market version of *Travel* magazine, a New York publication begun in the early twentieth century. The difference between the two was striking and provides another illustration of the enormous changes in the

postwar travel market. *Travel* combined the global exoticism of another popular early-twentieth-century magazine, *National Geographic,* with the excitement of a turn-of-the-century adventure story. Readers were invited to visit
cliff dwellers in Sicily, "wild men" in Borneo, and great restaurants in Paris,
and the advertisements—primarily from steamship companies and luxury
hotels—suggested that readers might actually, as well as imaginatively, accept
such invitations. *Holiday,* on the other hand, was oriented much more toward
North American destinations, and railroad and automobile industry advertising predominated.[15]

Thus after World War II, mass travel came to represent almost everything that was good about North American culture. Indeed, an early editorial
in *Holiday* magazine hinted that the right to vacations and travel had moti-
vated the war effort:

> In that yesterday before World War Two, vacations, with pay, for those
> who were so fortunate, usually meant a week or two away from job and
> housework. Only the minority could afford the time or the cost of going
> beyond a three or four hundred mile radius from home. But this is the
> post-war world, for which great sacrifices were made. This is the new
> world, in which vacations are the rule instead of the exception.[16]

The Cold War, too, served to highlight the place of travel, leisure, and consumption in North American fantasies of itself. Writing in *Cosmopolitan* in
1957, T. F. James declared that America had fulfilled Karl Marx's famous
dream, a society that allowed one to "hunt in the morning, fish in the evening
and criticize after dinner," but only because of the "basic ingredient" omitted
by Marx, "the dynamic inspiration behind American leisure: freedom."[17]
Leisure, as Karal Ann Marling has explained, was an important symbol of the
apparent classlessness of postwar America, "a textbook example of democracy
in action."[18] In this climate of optimism and self-congratulations, the future
seemed limitless. Grand predictions issued forth: soon North Americans
would be working a three-day week, crossing oceans in thirty minutes on
atomic-powered ocean liners, criss-crossing the continent on highways that
automatically propelled one's car, perhaps even hopping spacecrafts for vacations on the moon.[19]

Changes in the social wage of advanced capitalist societies, particularly
those that emerged from the war with burgeoning economies, certainly help
explain the postwar travel boom and the escalating commodification of travel
and leisure. Tourism was not, of course, the only beneficiary of this new
regime of commodified leisure, as the popularity of everything from television
to do-it-yourself and hobby kits in this era attests to. Paint-by-number kits,
for example, began as a Christmas gift fad in 1953 and quickly mushroomed

into a $200 million empire; "a great metaphor for life in rigid McCarthy America," as screenwriter Michael O'Donahue has observed, "you stayed inside the lines."[20] But the experience of traveling outside the lines of home and community during the war had been a profound one for millions of North Americans, and this too helped to shape the postwar enthusiasm for travel.[21]

In this context, the place of travel and tourism in the culture also changed. John Urry has argued that, by World War II, there was in Great Britain "widespread acceptance of the view that going on holiday was good for one, that it was the basis of personal replenishment. Holidays had become almost a marker of citizenship, a right to pleasure."[22] Clearly the celebratory paeans to what one travel writer called "our wonderful restlessness" suggests a similar cultural meaning for holidays in postwar North America that was not simply travel industry hyperbole.

The postwar travel boom represented the culmination of what Gary Cross calls the "work-and-spend" culture of Europe and North America, a process that began before World War I and whose full implications emerged after World War II. Charting the various defeats of movements to democratize time, Cross argues that, by the 1930s, free time ceased to mean freedom from work, but rather became the occasion for mass consumption necessary to absorb the unlimited potential of industrialism. In other words, "time became money."[23] From this perspective, the achievement of paid vacations through the Western world in the twentieth century represents not a triumph but a defeat, for the paid, weeklong holiday "could be understood as an alternative to the far more expensive concession of a shorter work week."[24]

This was a compelling argument particularly from the vantage point of the paradoxical 1990s, an era characterized by a frenzied pace of work for some, and serious long-term unemployment for others. Clearly what Cross calls the "consumerist choice" was predominant in Canada as well as the United States, and, after the war, newly monied and leisured Canadians were just as interested in consumer culture.[25] In Canada, however, consumption had a far different national meaning. The vast majority of the popular culture of the era—television, magazines, music, and film—was American, and, as J. M. Bumstead has observed, those in a position to regulate popular culture took the view that "Canadian distinctiveness resided elsewhere."[26] The postwar travel boom was understood less as a triumph of Canadian ingenuity and prosperity than an opportunity to achieve national greatness through a peculiar kind of subservience: making Canada and Canadians into whatever the "travel-hungry Americans" wanted them to be.[27]

Tourism, as Marie-Francoise Lanfant has observed, has sometimes been used by emerging states to "achieve national unification." To highlight the tourist resources of a country is to "praise the idea of the nation."[28] By identi-

fying, refurbishing, and promoting Canada's assets, tourist promoters contributed considerably to the project of defining Canada's place in the postwar
world. But the view from the tourist brochure was nothing if not paradoxical.
This narrative of national greatness was geared almost solely toward catching
the eye of Canada's richer, more powerful, and apparently more discerning
neighbor—a tourist promotion strategy that cast Canada as the permanent
poor relation. Such touristic appeals to national identity also had the effect, as
we will see, of unhinging such stable designations as citizen/employee or
nation/factory, which in turn allowed the tourist industry enormous scope to
generate enthusiasm for itself.

SPRUCING UP THE 'TOURIST PLANT'

Those who gathered in Ottawa in October 1946 to discuss the future of the
Canadian tourist industry would have agreed with Arthur Welsh's prediction
that the country was poised to become "a major tourist catering nation." But
there were significant impediments to this goal, many of them stemming from
the fact that six years of war had taken a heavy toll on what Welsh called the
"tourist plant."[29] Little money had been spent on tourist industry improvements or expansion, and there were problems everywhere.

     One problem was staffing the exploding network of tourist services. The
war had depleted the nation's labor resources, and no where was this more
evident than in the service industry, where, as government officials warned
toward the end of the war, "we are reaching further and further to the bottom
of the barrel" to attract staff to the nation's resorts.[30] During the war, hotels
and restaurants were placed in the category of "restricted industries," which
meant that men between the ages of seventeen and forty-five were not allowed
to take new positions within them without special permission. "Bell girls"
even began to replace bellboys in some Canadian hotels.[31] Alongside such government regulations, the market itself was helping to make the choice clear for
Canadian workers. When offered low-paid, seasonal service work, or relatively
healthy, year-round salaries in war industries, the alternative was clear. By
1944 Ontario hotels employed one person for every 2.5 guests, while even one
year earlier the ratio had been one for every 1.5 guests. Of these, hotel industry
officials claimed that over 40 percent were part-time, inexperienced, and "frequently too young or too old to be dependable."[32]

     This mass exodus might have prompted authorities to examine why ser-
vice industry jobs were so easy to vacate when there were other alternatives.
Instead, the issue was redefined; the problem was not with the jobs but rather
with the workers, and that could be solved with the postwar mantra of training and planning.

Training for management-level positions in the hotel industry had begun at Cornell University in Ithaca in the late 1920s, and a chef's course had begun in Toronto in 1935. Small-scale training programs for waitresses had been instituted during the 1930s, primarily as a meager depression-era bit of labor reform, and after the war a number of Canadian provinces quickly instituted short, summer training courses for service industry workers. The big push after the war, however, was not economically marginal female workers, or even elite male chefs, but rather returned war veterans.

A number of commentators noted approvingly in the mid-1940s that ex-servicemen were finding "attractive job opportunities" in the tourist industry but warned that "guidance is needed so that enterprising tourist caterers will know something before they start and won't have to learn everything by experience."[33] The training course adopted in Ontario, which ran for several years through the Department of Institutional Management at the University of Toronto and was then transferred to Toronto's Ryerson Institute of Technology, seemed like a perfect solution to two problems at once: where to put the veterans and how to expand the tourist industry. Ontario minister of travel and publicity Louis Cecile added a patriotic twist to this: "to what finer purpose could our great natural heritage of forest, river and lake be put than to provide a means for the rehabilitation in civilian life of these young people and, on the other hand, a method of bolstering the overall prosperity of our province."[34]

The University of Toronto course attracted 140 students in its first year, 1945–46, 95 percent of whom were servicemen and (five) women. Two hundred more signed up the next year. The two-year program offered a wide variety of courses, including accounting, economics, English, and law, as well as specific courses in food preparation, interior decorating, and personnel administration. It was explicitly geared toward management positions in the tourist industry; the University of Toronto was quick to point out that "it is not concerned with the training of chefs, waiters etc."[35] This attempt to professionalize the tourist industry via the academic credentials of the University of Toronto did not, however, last very long. When the course was transferred to Ryerson in 1949, it became much more focused on the day-to-day operations of the hotel and restaurant industry. As the need to relocate war veterans diminished, so too did the numbers of students; Ryerson's graduating classes through the 1950s numbered fewer than twenty. This smaller, more practical program also balanced out gender ratio. For a time women outnumbered men in the Ryerson course, and male graduates were teasingly referred to in the school yearbook in 1952 as the "brave male sector of the school."[36]

Professionalization of the tourist industry may well have addressed the political imperative of the day—what to do with the war veteran—but it did not take for the simple reason that an army of well-educated professionals expecting university graduate salaries would find few places in the industry of the 1940s and 1950s. There was a small corporate ladder to be found in the expanding government tourist promotion bureaucracies of the day, and indeed most of the inspectors hired by the Ontario government when it began to regulate the mushrooming hotel/motel and restaurant industry in this era were graduates of the University of Toronto course. But, until the hotel and motel franchises began to dominate the market in the early 1960s, the Canadian tourist industry was primarily a network of medium and small businesses. In this market, what determined success was not postsecondary education but rather, as George Martin, president of the Canadian Association of Tourist and Publicity Bureaus and the owner of a popular lodge outside Toronto, explained, two other crucial credentials: a "pleasing personality" and a wife.[37] The small size of most operations, combined with the seasonal nature of the Canadian tourist industry (most motels and resorts operated only in the summer), made for a peculiar sort of management or ownership level. Most resort or motel owners were married couples, one of whom kept another paid job, or retired couples. Commentators agreed that "the perfect motel operation is by a husband-wife team" but hinted that this arrangement might put a strain on the marriage, since such a couple "had better face the fact that they will never again see a motion picture together."[38] Female tourist home operators at Niagara Falls had been vilified by local and national hotel men in the 1920s and 1930s as unwelcome interlopers who contributed nothing but chaos to Canada's tourist industry. When redefined as "wives" in the 1940s and 1950s, however, women became welcome and important assets, so long as they were playing on the appropriate "team."

The majority of people who made their living from the tourist industry, however, were neither university-trained professionals nor mom-and-pop resort owners. They were service industry workers, whose ranks in Canada doubled between 1946 and 1960. Women workers were especially welcome in this field. By 1951 there were more women than men in the service industry, and thereafter women's participation rates increased quickly.[39] Motel owners were advised by experts to hire only married women for their cleaning staff, since they are "more conscientious and competent."[40] Only women, "smartly uniformed girls," most of them university students, were hired by the province as receptionists to greet visitors at the fourteen tourist information centers operated through Ontario by the late 1950s. Outfitted in red tunics and navy blue skirts, the receptionists were quickly dubbed "lady Mounties" and became overnight sex symbols in 1952 when a visiting Marilyn Monroe posed at Niagara Falls wearing the same uniform.[41] Some believed that service industry workers were benefiting enormously from the postwar travel boom. Not only were they, like the "lady Mounties," working in highly visible plum jobs, but many, apparently, were earning huge salaries at the same time. Canadian business journalists reported ruefully that wages and salaries at the nation's hotels had increased 175 percent since before the war, and American writers estimated that New York waiters were taking home as much as two hundred (undeclared) dollars per week in tips, in addition to their union-mandated twenty-eight-dollar-a-week salary.[42]

The young women who worked in the resorts of the Muskoka region in Ontario in this era would have been amused by this opulent portrait. Their story, which became known to the provincial government when a chapter of the Local Council of Women began a lobbing campaign on their behalf, read rather differently. They complained that they worked long hours—eight-and-one-half-hour days, seven days per week—for low pay, received miserable food, and regularly had portions of their pay withheld to compensate for "breakage." Some women, returning home from summer employment, were hospitalized for malnutrition.[43] Their story received a sympathetic ear from the Local Council of Women and the Department of Travel and Publicity, perhaps of its extreme nature—most waitresses did not succumb to malnutrition—and also perhaps because most of the young women involved were middle-class university students, working during their summer vacation. But this story was not *that* different from other complaints that were lodged with the Ministry of Labour in the 1950s, from waitresses working nine-hour days for ten dollars per week, or chambermaids working twelve-hour days with no provisions for time off.[44] However, because it drew heavily on segments of the labor force—married women, young women, and student-aged summer employees—who were less powerful, typically not unionized, and thus possessing fewer employment options, there was no shortage of people willing to staff the mushrooming service industry after the war.

Another aspect of the tourist plant, accommodation, was experiencing serious shortages. When nearly seven hundred thousand Americans drove across the border to Ontario in the first eight months of 1946—the highest number ever in the history of the province—the accommodation crisis reached epic proportions. In popular tourist towns such as Niagara Falls, accommodating tourists became almost a patriotic imperative. Before Labor Day weekend in 1949, for example, the manager of the chamber of commerce, along with the *Niagara Falls Review,* issued stirring appeals, requesting that citizens "do their community a great service" by "opening all available facilities" for weekend visitors.[45] Yet as residents obligingly turned backyard garages into tourist cabins and empty lots into campgrounds, another problem emerged: quality. One travel writer estimated that 90 percent of Canadian cabins did not have heat, running water, or private bathrooms. Such "slatternly" enterprises would find no favor with Americans, who would "do better by staying at home." Others described Canadian cabins "in settings by Svengali and decor by Dostoevski, set behind old oil drums and cars waiting to have their transmissions torn out . . . places that looked like those shacks the bad guys used to get trapped in at Saturday-afternoon movies." Even Leo Dolan, director of the Canadian Government Travel Bureau and always an enthusiastic booster of the tourist industry, admitted in 1947 that accommodation, particularly for the motor tourist, was "not good."[46]

Motels seemed the answer to the dual problems of space and appearance. Just as cabins evolved in the 1930s from private autocamps, motels evolved in the 1940s and 1950s as a more efficient, "modern" version of the tourist cabin. By 1947, commentators identified a "motor court belt" that extended from the Pacific Coast of Canada and the United States to Florida, and then north as far as Maryland.[47] Motels made more economical use of space than tourist cabins and could combine elements of the hotel—comfort, privacy, and density—with the convenience and low prices of the autocamp.[48] They were heralded by travel writers of the 1940s and 1950s as a great innovation, "economical, efficient and convenient," explained one, with rates about half that of a hotel's.[49] But price and convenience were just part of the story of the popularity of the motel; they also presented a more accessible, populist alternative to the rather more forbidding, upper-class hotel. Since the nineteenth century, hotels, even in small towns, had acted as bourgeois gentlemen's clubs. Their tastefully appointed meeting and dining rooms were home not only to the traveling elite, but also served as focal points for the communities' businessmen; that was where they met for chamber of commerce meetings and service club banquets. Changes in provincial liquor-licensing regulations in the 1920s had changed Ontario's hotel landscape somewhat; some retained their stately, upper-class aura and others became workingmen's beer parlors. Neither were particularly inviting to the newly mobile family travelers of the 1940s and 1950s. A 1948 study by the American Hotel Association revealed that 69 percent of travelers surveyed had never stayed at or even eaten at a hotel. Examining these figures by gender, they found that 72 percent of women had no hotel experience and concluded that most travelers "have the same feeling when they find themselves in a hotel lobby as would the average American suddenly thrust into a palace at some court function of a king."[50] Motels were new, just as new as the working-class family car, house, and vacation itself. As one 1950s mother recounted about her travels, they were perceived to be much more welcoming institutions:

> We made the dismal discovery: there were no vacancies in the motor courts we passed on the highway into town. "We could stay at a hotel," my husband suggested. "A *hotel!*" I said, looking wildly around at the three youngsters tussling in the back seat. "I'll bet a hotel would just love to have them! And can't you see us walking across the lobby the way *we* look?"[51]

Motels, on the other hand, were nicely landscaped "haven[s] from the highway." Motel operators paid attention to such details as swimming pools and play areas for restless children and clean bathrooms for women. Showers were a must, since "many women will not sit in strange bath tubs," and an overall air of "contemporariness" prevailed.[52]

The number of Ontario motels skyrocketed, from 150 in 1951, to almost 500 in 1954, to over two thousand in 1962, while the number of hotels in this era actually slightly dropped.[53] While many hotels underwent extensive renovations and most reported booming business and low vacancy rates through these years, they did not, and, experts speculated, would not, expand. "The large down-town hotel is a dead duck today," predicted one architect in 1954. "There won't be any more built in Canada."[54] This prophesy, of course, proved exaggerated, but only because of two new innovations that kept hotels afloat in the 1950s and 1960s: the "motor hotel" that was typically located outside of the city center and featured room-side parking and separate registration areas for lobby-wary driving guests, and the arrival of the large chain hotels in the early 1960s. Holiday Inns, for example, the world's largest hotel chain, announced plans for ten new units in the Toronto-Niagara region of Ontario alone in 1963.[55]

Yet the most fundamental problem facing the tourist industry in these years could not be rectified with training courses or construction projects. The unhappy truth of travel in this era was that, while increasing numbers of Americans visited Canada and spent considerable sums of money here, even larger numbers of Canadians traveled in the United States and spent even larger sums of money there. Tourism researchers in the 1990s have identified what they term "leakages," the amount of tourist revenue that is lost, particularly in Third World tourist destinations, because of their need to import First World goods for the convenience of First World visitors.[56] In the 1940s and 1950s, Canada experienced a peculiar kind of human "leakage." Indeed, the country was one of only two advanced capitalist nations—Italy was the other—to consistently show what experts called a "travel deficit" with the United States in these years. At one particularly low point, 1954, every dollar spent by American tourists in Canada was multiplied eleven times by Canadians in the United States.[57]

The rationale for this formulation—the pairing of Canadian and American vacation habits—was never explained by the tourist industry of the era, and it is certainly arguable that these two variables have little to do with each other. Even though travel-hungry Americans owned three-fourths of the worlds automobiles in the 1950s, when it came to vacations they were homebodies. Fewer than 7 percent of Americans actually crossed their country's borders when they traveled. Canada inherited the lion's share of these visitors, 80 percent. But compared to huge numbers of Canadian travelers who visited the United States—which ranged from 60 percent in the late 1940s to 35 percent in the mid-1950s—Canada's first-place standing seemed a bit hollow.[58] According to a confidential study prepared by the Federal Department of Resources and Development in 1952, Canada's enormous travel deficit, combined with the fact that the dollar amount of expenditures by foreign visitors to Canada had remained at the same level since 1929, indicated only one thing:

> The conclusion is inescapable that despite 20 years of effort to attract more foreign, especially American, tourists to Canada we have completely failed. Our advertising and publicity, our attempts to improve roads and accommodation, have resulted in no perceptible increase in our tourist revenue.[59]

Canadian travel boosters could have attempted to use these figures to attempt to sell Canadians on their own country. But they did not, preferring instead to attribute this lopsided pattern to what one commentator called the "natural North American 'law' that says the predominant vacation travel is north and south—vacationers just don't travel east and west in large numbers."[60] It was not until 1956 that the internal vacation patterns of Canadians were even studied by the Canadian travel industry, for, the prevailing opinion, voiced by Senator Crerar to the Senate Committee on Tourist Traffic in 1953, was that the government should not "pay five cents of taxpayers' money" to gather such information, which "is not of very much interest."[61] By the late 1950s, some in the travel industry changed their opinions about the importance of Canadian vacationers, especially when they learned that fewer than one-quarter of Canadians had ever been outside their own province. By the end of the decade, the Canadian Travel Association instituted a halfhearted "See Canada First" campaign, though 100 percent of federal, and 75 to 90 percent of provincial, travel promotion budgets continued to be spent on advertising in the United States. The dominant strategy followed by the tourist industry in Canada throughout the postwar era was to try to chip away at the American market by doing whatever they could to "make Canada more attractive to Mr. and Mrs. U.S. Tourist."[62]

"Everybody Likes Canadians": Tourism and National Identity

Commenting on the sorry state of the tourist plant in the aftermath of the war, a Canadian travel writer compared the nation to "the family that kept inviting our rich cousins to pay us a visit. We bombard them with pictures of the house, snapshots of the kids. . . . But when the cousins arrive they have to wade through mud to get into the house because the sidewalk is broken. Inside, the furniture is falling apart, the plumbing has just gone out of order."[63] Modernization was obviously part of the strategy to attract Americans, as was increasing the amount spent on advertising tourism in the United States. But the tourist infrastructure was only one part of the story; Americans also had to be convinced that Canada was worth their attention.

Some favored the subliminal route, such as the "Canadian Co-operation Project," concocted by American filmmakers and the Canadian government in 1948. In this scheme, Canadian concerns about American domination of the film industry were quelled when Hollywood agreed to publicize Canada, gently, in American movies. The goal was, according to a project staff member, to get hidden advertising, "a plug for Canada without being too obvious." The Annual Report of the Canadian Co-operation Project for 1952 proudly cited a number of such subtle interventions promoting Canadian tourism, including this excerpt from the gangster film *This Is Dynamite:*

> "I'll refresh your memory. In 1932 Peter Manzinates was a produce dealer who refused to pay the organization. He went to Canada and never came back . . ."
> "Maybe the guy liked to travel."
> "March, 1932. You took a leave of absence from the police force. Gone three weeks . . ."
> "A vacation."
> "Did you like Canada?"

There is, as Pierre Berton has noted, little evidence that the tourist trade was helped along by such stray references in films or "by the sporadic production of short subjects about snow."[64] Perhaps a more effective use of Hollywood's Canada was the 1954 contest sponsored by a committee of Canadian airlines, railroad companies, theaters, and hotels. The contest coincided with a remake of *Rose Marie,* the 1936 film about Canada's north that featured heroic, singing Mounties, scenic (if savage) Indians, and plenty of wilderness and asked American filmgoers to submit their story of why they would like to visit Canada. The seven winners, chosen by the Canadian Government Travel Bureau's Leo Dolan, were awarded a weekend at Niagara Falls (where they would be hard pressed to find anything remotely resembling the landscape of northern Quebec or rural Alberta depicted in various versions of *Rose Marie*), and the grand winner got a tour of Ontario and Quebec.[65]

The irony of using a wilderness film to promote an elaborately packaged, high-consumption urban vacation illustrates quite well one of the main problems of tourism in postwar Canada. Exactly what sort of "Canada" were Americans being encouraged to visit? International tourism, as Lanfant has noted, has a paradoxical effect on national identities. Tourism identifies and promotes particular national narratives, while at the same time the host society "comes to reflect upon its own traditions and values through the confrontation with otherness signified by the presence of tourists."[66] No less an eminent Canadian than Governor General Vincent Massey reminded Canadians in 1954 that tourism is "something more than a trade—it is evidence of our increasing importance as a national community occupying a large, valuable and attractive portion of the earth's surface."[67] Yet to many, the Canada that emerged through postwar encounters with American tourists was an embarrassment, which did not measure up to modern standards of either tourism and nationhood.

Previous national narratives did not seem particularly useful after the war. As Patricia Jasen has illustrated, the search for "wild things" brought scores of pallid, urban-dwelling American and British tourists to Canada during the nineteenth century, and a great deal of fishing and hunting promotion continued in this era.[68] But how could tourist promoters reconcile the "wilderness" with the "modern"? American standards of comfort and convenience were, apparently, ill served by what was available to most fishermen and hunters, and the tourist industry in more remote parts of the country was slow to realize that, as Leo Dolan insisted, "the day is gone . . . when the sportsman who comes to Canada wants to rough it. . . . There are no more tourists who want to sleep on a bunch of boughs." But the problem was also more profoundly one of general Canadian backwardness. Pristine lakes and rivers continued to draw tourists, to be sure, but in this high-consumption, high-comfort era, nature seemed a bit old fashioned. A 1963 study of the tourist industry commissioned by the Canadian Imperial Bank of Commerce indicated that "no very large proportion (of tourists) now is interested in hunting and fishing." And Americans, especially, were nothing if not up-to-date. Dolan feared that Canadian travelogues, which, he claimed were hopelessly antiquated, would scare Americans off. "As soon as Americans see a picture showing old-fashioned styles," he declared in 1949, referring to clothing and cars, "they say 'Phooey, that's no good.' "[69]

This chasm between natural and modern surfaced again, after *Holiday* magazine published a long and lavishly illustrated 1949 feature issue on Canada. Journalists spoke at great (if patronizing) lengths about the country's multiethnic heritage, diverse regions, and especially its natural beauty, only to be reprimanded by several Canadian readers in subsequent issues for focusing only, as a Vancouver resident put it, on "Indians and trappers, Mounties and French, oxen, sod houses and snow." "We drive 1949 automobiles, not all horses and buggies," complained another Canadian reader, "and we live in homes that are just as modern and up-to-date as those of Americans, not all log cabins hewn out of the forest primeval."[70]

The question of Canada's tourist image had been debated earlier, particularly during the deliberations of the Senate Committee on the Tourist Trade in 1934, which was the first national government inquiry into the tourist industry. At that time, T. R. Enderby, manager of the Canadian Steamship Lines, encouraged federal officials to advertise Canadian tourism more widely because of the good name borne by the country internationally. "[T]he Canadian is always popular," he claimed. "I think we ought to cash in on that, capitalize it—everybody likes Canadians." The Canadian Chamber of Commerce, perhaps less convinced of the marketability of goodwill, suggested instead that the country "should cultivate a slightly foreign, i.e. un-American atmosphere." Since travelers want "something different," and "European goods in themselves attract," Canadian businessmen should dress up their store windows with a "European flavour, to enhance the effect."[71] Throughout the lean years of the 1930s, the hotel industry encouraged its members to "modernize" by replicating the flavor of English country pubs, and even after the war some agreed that peddling Canada as a poor man's Europe was an easy route to success. In a speech to the 1944 Postwar Tourism Planning conference, entitled "What Americans Want," Mr. McNally of the Toronto Convention and Tourism Association answered his question as bluntly as he asked it. "Our American visitors," he declared, "expect us to be English, much more English than we really are. Why not dress the stage for them a little?"[72]

But in the globalized climate of the 1940s and 1950s, others began to call for a peculiar sort of Canadian distinctiveness. The *Canadian Hotel Review*, for example, editorialized in 1941 that a tourist from California was not going to "get any big kick out of stopping at a tourist hotel fashioned in the form of a Spanish mission," and neither was a citizen from the Deep South likely to be impressed by "colonial pillars, exotic flower-beds, or a radio constantly blaring negro spirituals." Americans, they declared, "come to Canada to see us as we are, not to see us trying to give an imitation of themselves."[73] Other commentators, especially Americans, gently reminded Canadian entrepreneurs that travel-savvy American postwar tourists would not be fooled into believing that Toronto was London or New York. Carl Biemiller, for example, an editor at *Holiday* magazine, encouraged delegates to the Ontario Tourist Conference, held at Niagara Falls in 1949, to "publicize your differences, not your imitations." "Cocktail rooms, hotels, camps and foods with New York or London names," he explained, does not help Canada, since "imitations of tourist attractions elsewhere are a sign of an unnecessary inferiority complex." Clare Allen, a radio broadcaster from Buffalo, was rather more blunt. His advice to motel owners in convention in 1951 was to "put some snow shoes and animal skins on the walls of your place . . . have some Indian moccasins, headdresses and totem poles for sale. The Americans will eat it up."[74]

Souvenirs and food were two other icons of national difference and identity. People had been complaining about the quality of both since the 1930s, and both had been identified as major impediments to tourism success in Canada. Niagara Falls in particular was often singled out for purveying "tawdry trash . . . [that] gives a place an air of cheap vulgarity and repels the majority," and entrepreneurs were encouraged to sell souvenirs that were "distinctively Canadian." Yet only three such artistic traditions were ever identified. According to H. E. Chisholm of the Department of Trade and Commerce, two Canadian handicrafts, French-Canadian weaving and Maritime rug hooking, were flourishing, despite the unfortunate tendency of craftspeople to buy factory wool for their looms and thus "diminish the charm of the native product." But the third, Native art, was in trouble, since "the white man has destroyed the race consciousness" of Canadian Native people, and thus the "old craftsmen" were no longer plying their trade.[75] Yet few initiatives were taken, in Ontario at least, to promote Native or other handicrafts. The Canadian Handicrafts Guild, for example, lambasted government tourism officials in 1944 for failing to coordinate the distribution of "the best in Canadian crafts," leaving the market open to the "atrocities that are exhibited as Canadian handicrafts at countless service stations, hotels and auto camps." Again Niagara Falls, along with the home of the world-famous Dionne quintuplets at Callendar, Ontario, came in for special criticism.[76]

The postwar travel boom began to reshape the cultural and financial significance of Canadian crafts. As Canadian historian Ian McKay has observed, studying the handicraft tradition in the Canadian Maritimes, mass tourism helped to create "a vocabulary in which the handicraft was a sign of true 'authenticity' . . . [which] bears witness that the tourist has indeed made the journey."[77] In the nineteenth century, travelers to Niagara Falls, for example, obsessed about the authenticity of the "Indians" who sold them beadwork, particularly when some began to suspect that the vendors were Irish people made up to look like Indians. Mid-twentieth-century commentators were disturbed about the authenticity and appearance of the items themselves, especially the "gaudy, unattractive souvenirs of Canada bearing images of Indians, Mounties, beavers and maple leaves" (sic) that predominated in most tourist destinations.[78] Yet Ontario had a problem, for the province possessed no folk hero such as the Quebec habitant or the Maritime fisherfolk around which to invent a handicraft tradition. Thus, especially compared to the initiatives in the Maritimes and Quebec, little was done, at Niagara or elsewhere in the province, to change the souvenir industry or to encourage the distribution and sale of Canadian-made crafts. The Canadian Handicrafts Guild attempted to set up shop at Niagara Falls in 1948 but were rebuffed by the Niagara Parks Commission on the grounds that they had no room for another store on their premises.[79] The Niagara Parks Commission, which was the largest single public buyer and seller of tourist souvenirs in Ontario, continued to draw fire about the inferior quality of its goods well into the 1960s.[80] It was only in the mid-1960s, in anticipation of the expected tourist boom around the world's fair, Expo '67 in Montreal, that the Ontario government began to get involved in craft promotion, sponsoring conferences, contests, and exhibits, to link craftspeople with tourist industry buyers.[81]

Complaints about Canadian, and especially Ontarian, food were vociferous and, to some, just as indicative of a lack of national pride. Tourist industry conferences of the 1940s heard regular reports that Canadian food was "flat." Some, such as Senator Crerar, blamed restaurant owners, declaring that "one imagines that probably the people who run them are people who have failed in everything else and thought they might cook meals and attract tourists." But others saw the issue in terms of nation, not skill. Radio commentator John Fisher deplored our "lack of imagination" in expressing "Canadianism" through distinctive cuisine, and journalist Gordon Sinclair was characteristically blunt: "Ontario," he complained to Thomas McCall, deputy minister of travel and publicity, in 1946, "has the worst cooking on earth."[82]

While some advocated the colonial solution—serving English beefsteak and kidney pie and passing it off as Canadian—others took the quest for a distinctive Canadian menu to heart. The Junior Chamber of Commerce, for example, launched a major campaign in 1949 to boost the Canadian tourist industry through, among other things, food. Together with chefs from the Canadian National Railways and food experts from *Chatelaine*, a prominent Canadian women's magazine, they invented ten recipes, each representing a Canadian province. Of course, when one is inventing authentic traditions for outsiders, one can take a few liberties. Some "Canadian" recipes, such as Prince Edward Island clam chowder, made a certain bioregional sense, while others, for example Manitoba popovers or British Columbia pancakes, seemed a bit of a stretch. Nevertheless, the campaign spread quickly. Journalists Kate Aitken and Jeanne Benoit were recruited to explain the recipes on a special radio program, "Food for Thought," and tourist operators were especially invited to listen to the program and learn how to improve their menus. They also distributed placemats and cookbooks featuring Canadian cooking to restaurants across the country. These efforts were so well received that the Canadian Tourist Association followed them up the next year, hiring seven women to form a Canadian Cuisine Committee, to come up with extensive recipe books and encourage restaurant owners to adopt them.[83] It is difficult to judge whether these attempts resulted in happier diners. After listening to Mrs. Montgomery of the Canadian Restaurant Association explain her attempts to train her members to use Canadian cookbooks, one senator complained that now "all the meals in restaurants taste alike."[84]

Despite all of these efforts, another survey of American travelers, conducted by the Canadian National Railway in 1956, revealed the same distressing news that earlier polls had garnered. Canadian food was considered "similar but inferior to American," Canadian roads were poor, and, aside from the presence of customs officers at the border, "there was not a great deal else to make them really feel they had left the U.S. for foreign soil." The most stinging finding, however, concerned Canadians as hosts. Most Americans surveyed acknowledged that Canadians were polite, even courteous. But they were not "particularly friendly" or even interesting. "The inhabitants," declared the report, "added nothing in particular to the attractiveness of the country."[85] Perhaps the reluctance of Americans to visit lay not with food, souvenirs or accommodation, but with another aspect of the country's rusty tourist plant: people.

"Tourism Is Everyone's Business"

As early as 1946, civil servants in the Ontario Travel and Publicity Department were of the opinion that the lopsided Canada–United States travel figures were caused by the Canadian travel industry. Complaints about "misrepresentation" and "sharp practices" abounded. In order to truly attract American tourists, the authorities ought to, in the words of a senior civil servant, "clean up the industry."[86] At Niagara Falls, among other abuses, tourist entrepreneurs established official-looking "information booths" on the outskirts of town to sell visitors particular tours or accommodation (those that had provided kickbacks), motel owners kept their No Vacancy signs lit until dark, when they could raise their prices to desperate motorists, and taxi drivers dressed as police officers and flagged down motorists to offer them tours.[87] While each of these issues was addressed, in some fashion, by authorities, far more attention was focused on the general demeanor of Canadians as hosts.

Part of what made Canadians—and hence Canada—so "likeable" was, so the story went, courtesy. Yet the rush to cash in on the postwar tourist boom threatened to change this. Joining government tourist authorities in their concern about the treatment of American visitors were travel journalists, who regularly complained that Canadian standards of courtesy were low. The country must, as one journalist put it, "get down to selling service to the public," for "a good steak," commented another, "can be ruined by an indifferent waitress."[88] "We are not a nation of shopkeepers," declared a Canadian Travel Association spokesperson ruefully, "we do not bow and scrape easily." The country needed to develop "a reputation for northern hospitality with the same meaning and force as the southern variety."[89] This call was heeded by the Junior Chamber of Commerce, which launched an ambitious campaign to do exactly that in 1948.

During World War II, particularly before America entered the war, a Canadian vacation had been pitched to Americans as a friendly, patriotic act, for Canada needed American currency to help the war effort. After the war, the same association of tourism and national development was resurrected. Attempting to "extend and improve the public understanding of Canada's need for U.S. dollars," the chamber identified American tourists as an easy and obvious source of such revenue and hence tried to convince Canadians to improve "the treatment and service tourists receive while in Canada." This campaign is noteworthy for its attempt to extend the scramble for American dollars to peacetime. But the Junior Chamber of Commerce was also audaciously proposing to extend this campaign far beyond the boundaries of the tourist industry itself. Arguing that "directly or indirectly the tourist is everybody's customer [since] his dollars help buy our comforts," the group put forward ten practical suggestions that individuals could follow to encourage American travel in Canada. Courtesy topped the list. On every possible occasion, people should say "hello for Canada to American visitors."

> If you notice a car with an American licence plate parked on a street in your community do not hesitate to speak and pass the time of day. Say to the people in the car "I see that you are from the U.S. I hope that you are enjoying your visit to Canada. Is there anything I can do to be of service?"

Other suggestions included familiarizing oneself with local attractions, writing American friends to encourage them to visit Canada, and meeting excursion steamers with a band and welcoming committee.[90]

Travel industry officials warmly welcomed these initiatives, noting that they were complementary to projects initiated by the Canadian Government Travel Bureau, such as the formation of travel schools to train tourist industry personnel in the courteous treatment of visitors. The tourist industry had been busy since the war convincing its staff of the need for courtesy. Waitresses at Fran's Restaurant in Toronto, for example, had been sent to an in-house training school in the late 1940s, where they were rechristened "food merchandisers" and taught the basic principal that their personality was what sold Fran's meals. Tourist industry personnel were also encouraged to regulate relations between visitors and locals, such as the hotel staff in Nova Scotia who were warned in their training course that one of their jobs was to "keep a close eye on local menfolk who convene in hotel lobbies and ogle at the female tourists signing the register."[91] But the Junior Chamber of Commerce campaign, along with the similar initiatives of the tourist industry through this

Canadian Travel Bureau advertisement, published in *Canadian Hotel and Restaurant,* June 15, 1946. (Reproduced with the permission of the Minister of Public Works and Government Services Canada, 1997.)

era, took the concept of "hospitality" to quite a different level. During its annual Tourist Service Week, the Canadian Travel Bureau used posters and advertisements to attempt to convince all Canadians, not just those employed in the tourist or service industry, that American tourist dollars, and hence the courteous treatment of American visitors, was a national, as opposed to commercial, concern. The John Labatt Brewing Company launched a similar ad campaign that urged "Ontario citizens" to meet their "individual responsibility" toward visiting Americans. Under the slogan "Tourist Business Is Everybody's Business," the Canadian Tourist Association also embarked on what they called a "Community Relations Program." Communities were encouraged to proclaim "tourist service week" and celebrate it with open houses at

Canadian Travel Bureau advertisement, published in *Canadian Hotel and Restaurant,* June 15, 1946. (Reproduced with the permission of the Minister of Public Works and Government Services Canada, 1997.)

hotels and "know-your-local-attractions-better" contests. Service and retail industry employees were encouraged to attend "courtesy to tourist" rallies, and school, factory, and industrial employees were informed of the importance of tourism through special public addresses, employee bulletin boards, and pay envelope stuffers.[92] At Niagara Falls, residents were encouraged to attend the Niagara School of Hospitality. In case civic pride was not sufficient incentive, it was broadly hinted that successful graduates might secure employment in the tourist industry.[93]

Thus an expanded notion of the importance of courtesy became a fundamental tenet of the postwar tourist industry, applicable to service industry personnel and "civilians" alike. Indeed, the courtesy campaign quite deliberately blurred the boundaries between "citizen" and "worker." When the nation had become a "gigantic department store" or a "tourist plant," was there a difference between employment and citizenship? When Col. James McAvity, president of the Canadian Tourist Association, argued in favor of increased federal spending on tourist promotion on the grounds that "it is only common sense in the interests of the shareholders to promote as hard as one can a product that is profitable," one must realize that the "product" here was the nation, not hotel industry stock or souvenirs. When Ontario minister of travel and publicity Arthur Thomas Welsh told Ontario residents via a special radio broadcast in 1947 that tourist spending brought in over thirty dollars annually for every man, woman, and child in the province, or when John Fisher, director of the Canadian Travel Association, told Canadian workers that "the employee in a Montreal toy factory benefits because a visitor from Kalamazoo buys a souvenir gift in Manitoba to take back to his nephew," tourism was sold as a public good, which transcended the boundaries of private industry, and the American tourist especially acquired a special kind of reverence. Tourist industry insiders recognized and applauded this sleight of hand. The *Canadian Hotel Review* editorialized happily that "there is no other business which . . . (makes) its customers feel they are in reality its guests."[94] But in this industry, in this climate, the line between insiders and outsiders was not so clear. So when the provincial government asked its employees to become "salesmen of Ontario" by sending its annual tourist promotion book to friends and family outside the province, those who complied likely thought they were doing their friends, and perhaps themselves, a favor, rather than acting as unpaid shills for the tourist industry. And when a delegate remarked at the Canadian Tourist Association conference in 1961 that the "curious and heartening truth about tourism [is] that whatever is done to make a community or a country a more pleasant place to live in makes it a more attractive place to visit," the "pent-up urge to travel" had been unleashed with such force that likely no one thought about whether the reverse formulation was also true.[95] Surely few other industries have been able to tug at the boundaries of private enterprise, national goodwill, and community spirit so successfully.

NOTES

I would like to thank Ian McKay and Cecilia Morgan for their comments on an earlier version of this paper, and Ellen Furlough for her suggestions and encouragement.

1. *Niagara Falls Evening Review* (hereafter cited as *NFR*), July 11, 1929, July 12, 1929, August 16, 1929. The Canadian Legion is a service club and lobby group for war veterans.

2. *NFR*, May 21, 1949.

3. *NFR*, January 23, 1948, May 1, 1949, July 24, 1952; "On Flying the U.S. Flag," *Canadian Hotel Review*, May 1954, 21.

4. Victoria de Grazia, introduction to *The Sex of Things: Gender and Consumption in Historical Perspective,* ed. Victoria de Grazia with Ellen Furlough (Berkeley and Los Angeles: University of California Press, 1996), 21.

5. Jay Miller, "Canadian Tourist Industry Must Send More Information to U.S.," *Saturday Night,* May 4, 1946.

6. Provincial Archives of Ontario (hereafter cited as PAO), *Report of Proceedings,* Dominion Provincial Tourist Conference, Ottawa, 1946.

7. Gary Cross, *Time and Money: The Making of Consumer Culture* (New York: Routledge, 1993), 95. See also Stephen G. Jones, "Trade-Union Policy between the Wars: The Case of Holidays with Pay in Britain," *International Review of Social History* 31 (1986): 40–67.

8. "Tourist Trade Attracts Veterans," *Canadian Business,* February 1946.

9. John A. Jakle, *The Tourist: Travel in Twentieth-Century North America* (Lincoln: University of Nebraska Press, 1988), 185.

10. John Fisher, "Travel: The Technological Revolution," *Saturday Night,* August 29, 1959, 18–19.

11. James H. Gray, "A Tourist Talks Back," *Maclean's,* June 1, 1948, 16. See also John Fisher, "Tourism Is Everybody's Business," *Canadian Labour,* November 1959.

12. Mrs. R. M. Ruhlman, "Consider the Ladies," address to Second Annual Ontario Tourist Conference, April 25–27, 1950; "Our Image Abroad," *Canadian Travel Association Conference Report,* 1961; John Fisher, "Travel in Canada: How to Build It?" *Saturday Night,* April 25, 1956.

13. PAO, RG 5, series A-1, Ministers Correspondence, *House Beautiful* to A. Welsh, January 8, 1947.

14. "How to Read a Travel Folder," *Cosmopolitan,* May 1960; "Railroad Rights—and Wrongs!" *Coronet,* June 1953; Louise Levitas, "Vacation's the Time to Get a Husband," *Coronet,* July 1951; Alberta Williams "Marital Vacations Keep Love Alive," *Coronet,* January 1953.

15. On *National Geographic* see Catherine A. Lutz and Jane Collins, *Reading National Geographic* (Chicago: University of Chicago Press, 1993).

16. Editorial, *Holiday,* April 1946, 3.

17. T. F. James, "The New Pleasures," *Cosmopolitan,* June 1957.

18. Karal Ann Marling, *As Seen on TV: The Visual Culture of Everyday Life in the 1950s* (Cambridge: Harvard University Press, 1994), 51.

19. Jay C. Calhoun, "The American Weekend," *Cosmopolitan,* June 1955; James Cerruti, "Your Travel Future," *Holiday,* August 1955; Arthur C. Clarke, "Get Ready for Space Travel," *Holiday,* June 1958; "Tomorrow's Travel: Electronic Frying and Saucer Flying," *Financial Post,* January 25, 1958.

20. Craig Wilson, "From Child's Play to Prized Possessions," *USA Today,* April 20, 1992, cited in Marling, *As Seen on TV,* 64.

21. More than 15 million American civilians moved across county lines during World War II, for jobs and defense postings, while another 12 million Americans served in the military. Beth Bailey and David Farber, *The First Strange Place: Race and Sex in World War Two Hawaii* (Baltimore: Johns Hopkins University Press, 1992), 16–17.

22. John Urry, *The Tourist Gaze: Leisure and Travel in Contemporary Societies* (London: Sage, 1990), 27.

23. Cross, *Time and Money,* 77.

24. Ibid., 95.

25. Doug Owram, *Born at the Right Time: A History of the Baby Boom Generation* (Toronto: University of Toronto Press, 1996), 84–110; Joy Parr, "Shopping for a Good Stove: A Parable about Gender, Design, and the Market," in *A Diversity of Women: Ontario, 1945–1980,* ed. Joy Parr (Toronto: University of Toronto Press, 1995), 75–97.

26. J. M. Bumstead, "Canada and American Culture in the 1950s," in *Interpreting Canada's Past,* ed. J. M. Bumstead (Toronto: Oxford University Press, 1986), 402.

27. D. B. Wallace, "Tourist Trade Expects Its Heaviest Year," *Saturday Night,* February 9, 1946.

28. Marie-Francoise Lanfant, introduction and "Tourism, Internationalization, and Identity," in *International Tourism: Identity and Change,* ed. Marie-Francoise Lanfant, John B. Allcock, and Edward M. Bruner (London: Sage, 1995), 6 and 33.

29. Report of Proceedings: Dominion/Provincial Tourist Conference, Ottawa, October 21–23 1946, address by A. Welsh.

30. W. Hetherington, assistant superintendent, National Selective Service, address to Ontario Post War Tourist Planning Conference, Toronto, 1944. See also A. W. O'Brien, "Holiday Daze," *Maclean's,* July 15, 1943.

31. *Canadian Hotel Review,* April 1942, 24, January 1943, 13.

32. Ibid., October 1944, 14.

33. D. B. Wallace, "Tourist Trade Expects," "Tourist Trade Attracts Veterans," *Canadian Business,* February 1946, "Yankee Dollah!" *Canadian Business,* October 1945.

34. PAO, RG 5 Department of Tourism and Information, series A-1, Ministers Correspondence, Speech to the Throne delivered by Hon. Louis. P. Cecile, February 21, 1951.

35. University of Toronto *Calendar,* 1947–48, 6.

36. *Ryersonia* 1952. See also Ryerson Institute of Technology *Calendar* 1949–55.

37. George Martin, "Many Opportunities in Growing Tourist Industry," *Financial Post,* April 23 1949. See also Fisher, "Travel in Canada."

38. Vince Lunny, "Retire and Run a Motel?" *Financial Post,* April 26, 1958.

39. F. H. Leacy, ed., *Historical Statistics of Canada,* 2d ed. (Ottawa: Statistics Canada, 1983), D318–28 and D355–82. These figures refer to the service industry as a whole, not just the tourist industry.

40. Raymond Moriyama, "Trends in Motel Design," *Royal Architects Institute of Canada Journal* September 1960, 375.

41. "These Girls Greet 500,000 Visitors," *Financial Post,* February 22, 1958, PAO, RG 5 Ministry of Travel and Publicity, *Annual Report,* 1950, T. Johnson, Ministry of Travel and Publicity, letter to Twentieth Century Fox, (no date).

42. Harry Bowley, "Care and Cultivation of Paying Guests," *Saturday Night,* December 26, 1953, 17; George Roberts, "How Much Does a Waiter Really Earn?" *Cosmopolitan,* March 1946, 134.

43. PAO, RG 7 Ministry of Labour Low Wages and Industrial Standards Act file, March 13, 1951, Isabel Leming, Local Council of Women, letter to Deputy Minister, Department of Travel and Publicity.

44. PAO, RG 7 Ministry of Labour Low Wages and Industrial Standards Act file, June 27, 1949, Mrs. G. Mutchison, Dryden, Ontario, to Minister of Labour; January 5, 1951, H. M. Reid, United Steelworkers of America, Sudbury, to Minister of Labour.

45. *NFR,* September 2, 1949.

46. Tom Taylor, "We Must Learn the Tourist Business," *Canadian Business,* June 1947, 45; Robert Thomas Allen, "Why U.S. Tourists Are Passing Up Canada," *Maclean's,* May 28, 1955, 64; Senate of Canada, *Proceedings of the Senate Committee on Tourist Traffic, 1947,* 14.

47. Arthur D. Ellwood, "They Are Specialists for Motorists," *Canadian Hotel Review*, August 1947, 18.

48. Warren Belasco, *Americans on the Road: From Autocamp to Motel, 1910–1945* (Cambridge: MIT Press, 1979), 140 and 171.

49. Gray, "A Tourist Talks Back," 56.

50. Madelyn Wood, "Revolution in Hotels," *Coronet*, June 1953, 110; Raymond Moriyama, "Trends in Motel Design," *Royal Architects Institute of Canada Journal*, September 1960, 374.

51. Wood, "Revolution in Hotels," 110. As another writer put it, the average motorists "doesn't like to go tramping through a hotel lobby looking like Bing Crosby after a fishing trip." Hal Tracy, "Motel Business Is Booming," *Saturday Night*, September 11, 1951, 38.

52. Moriyama, "Trends in Motel Design," 337.

53. Tracy, "Motel Business Is Booming"; "Why Tourists Like Ontario," *Financial Post*, October 9, 1954; James Montagnes, "Motel Owners Step Up Investment," *Canadian Business*, July 1959; Ontario Economic Council, *Ontario's Tourist Industry* (December 1965) 17; *Canadian Hotel Review*, May 1949, 66. The number of hotels in Canada dropped from 5,656 in 1941 to 5,157 in 1952. Elizabeth Hay Trott, "For Hotels, the Boom's Still On," *Monetary Times*, July 1954, 22.

54. Trott, "Boom's Still On," 24. See also Bowley, "Care and Cultivation."

55. Arthur D. Ellwood, "Hotels, Motels Keep Pace with Changing Patterns of Travel," *Financial Post*, April 20, 1963, 60.

56. It is estimated that the "leakage" rate in the Caribbean in the 1990s, for example, is 70 percent; for every dollar generated by tourism, seventy cents is spent on imports. See Polly Pattullo, *Last Resorts: The Cost of Tourism in the Caribbean* (London: Cassell, 1996), 38.

57. Jakle, *The Tourist*, 185; Allen, "Passing Up Canada."

58. Marling, *As Seen on TV*, 132; Kenneth White, "Is Our Visitor Industry in for Record Year?" *Financial Post*, June 16, 1951; John Maclean, "Gloom in Playland," *Financial Post*, October 20, 1956. The figures cited for U.S. travel outside the United States pertain to the year 1950. John Jakle cites a similar study done in 1954, which indicates a similar pattern: 5 percent of Americans traveled outside their country in that year, 73 percent of whom came to Canada (*The Tourist*, 185).

59. David Ivor, *A Study of the Economics of Tourism in Canada*, prepared for the Department of Resources and Development, 1952. My thanks to Alisa Apostle for passing this reference on to me.

60. White, "Our Visitor Industry."

61. Senate of Canada, *Report of the Standing Committee on Tourist Traffic*, *1953*, 11.

62. Logan Maclean, "Needed: Travel Promotion," *Saturday Night*, April 25, 1956; Woodman Lamb, "The Mysterious Traveller," *Saturday Night*, April 25, 1956; Maclean, "Gloom in Playland"; James Montagnes, "Travel Bitten Canadians Head in All Directions," *Canadian Business*, March 1956; "Delegates Ponder Problems, How to Lick Tourist Lapse," *Financial Post*, September 23, 1950. By the early 1960s, provincial promotional figures had changed somewhat; 40 to 45 percent of spending focused on the United States and 55–60 percent focused on Canada. The Canadian Government Travel Bureau, however, continued to spend all of its promotional budget outside the country, mainly in the U.S. Senate of Canada, *Report of the Senate Committee on Tourist Traffic, 1964*, 15.

63. Gray, "A Tourist Talks Back."

64. Pierre Berton, *Hollywood's Canada: The Americanization of Our National Image* (Toronto: McClelland and Stewart, 1975), 171, 189, and 190.

65. "The First Word," *Canadian Hotel Review,* April 1954. On *Rose Marie* and other Royal Canadian Mounted Police films see Michael Dawson, *The Mountie from Dime Novel to Disney* (Toronto: Between the Lines, 1998). Even the trees that symbolized the Canadian wilderness, featured in *Rose Marie* and other films depicting Canada, were a Hollywood invention. The tall, sturdy ponderosa pine grows plentifully in California, but barely at all in Canada (Berton, *Hollywood's Canada,* 32). Many thanks to Michael Dawson for arboreal assistance.

66. Lanfant, "Tourism, Internationalization, and Identity," 36.

67. "A Creed for Our Tourist Trade," *Canadian Hotel Review,* May 1954, 21.

68. Patricia Jasen, *Wild Things: Nature, Culture, and Tourism in Ontario, 1790–1914* (Toronto: University of Toronto Press, 1996).

69. *Ottawa Journal,* cited in *NFR,* July 17, 1963; Senate of Canada, *Report of the Standing Committee on Tourist Traffic, 1949,* 48 and 46.

70. Sydney W. Morrell, "Canada," *Holiday,* August 1949, and letters, *Holiday,* October and November 1949.

71. Senate of Canada, *Report and Proceedings of the Special Committee on Tourist Traffic* (Ottawa: Kings Printer, 1934), 108 and 236.

72. Report of Proceedings, Post War Tourist Planning Conference, 1944.

73. "Canadiana Should Be Tourist Theme Song," *Canadian Hotel Review,* April 1941, 9.

74. Summary of Proceedings, First Annual Ontario Tourism Conference, Niagara Falls, March 1 and 2, 1949; Robert McBeth, "Claim Motor Travellers Favour Staying at Tourist Courts," *Canadian Hotel Review,* October 1951.

75. Senate Report, 1934, 234, 246–47, and 275.

76. Alex McBain, V.P., Ontario Branch, Canadian Handicrafts Guild, address to Ontario Post War Tourist Planning Conference, Toronto, April 14 and 15, 1944. A *Canadian Homes and Gardens* special travel issue in 1959, for example, dismissed Niagara as "strictly a tourist city" in which visitors would be "bombarded by hawkers peddling plastic replicas of the Falls, gaudy ash trays and pennants (*NFR,* August 20, 1959).

77. Ian McKay, *The Quest of the Folk: Antimodernism and Cultural Selection in Twentieth Century Nova Scotia* (Kingston: McGill-Queen's Press, 1994), 154.

78. "The Travel Corner," *Canadian Geographic Journal,* December 1957.

79. PAO, Niagara Parks Commission Correspondence, Canadian Handicraft Guild to Niagara Parks Commission, February 23, 1948.

80. Ontario Economic Council, *Ontario's Tourist Industry* (December 1965), 56.

81. The promotion of Native crafts figured prominently in these initiatives. The Ontario Department of Travel and Publicity hired a Native women, Flora Tabobadung, chief of the Parry Island Indian Reserve, to preside, in full dress, over their display at the Toronto Spring Gift Show in 1966, as a means of encouraging the sale of Indian crafts from Parry Sound area reserves; PAO, RG 5, series A-3, Ontario Souvenir Industry file, 1966. Despite this flurry of interest in Ontario, and especially Native crafts, a provincial tourism report in 1965 lamented that Ontario "has not made too much of its Indian heritage" and was especially weak in the area of craft production; Ontario Economic Council, *Ontario's Tourist Industry* (1965), 41.

82. Mr. McNally, speech to Ontario Postwar Tourist Planning Conference, 1944, Senate of Canada, *Report of the Standing Committee on Tourist Traffic, 1954,* 27; John Fisher, speech to First Annual Ontario Tourist Conference, 1949, PAO, RG 5, series B-1, DMO correspondence, Gordon Sinclair to Thomas McCall, July 9, 1946.

83. Mr. McNally, "What Americans Want," Post War Tourist Planning Conference, April 1944; Wallace Gillespie, "Selling 'All-Star' Food Team," *Financial Post,* May 7, 1949. Ontario's "representative" dish was blueberry crisp pudding, since "tourists go after the wild berries in Northern Ontario." See also Wallace Gillespie, "Boosting 'Eats' Native to Each Province," *Financial Post,* March 4, 1950.

84. Senate of Canada, *Report of the Standing Committee on Tourist Traffic, 1954,* 79.

85. W. Wright, "Why the Yanks Call us 'Dull,'" *Financial Post,* October 6, 1956.

86. PAO, RG 5, series B-3, memo, July 30, 1946, T. C. McCall to A. Welsh.

87. For details see Karen Dubinsky, *The Second Greatest Disappointment: Honeymooning and Tourism at Niagara Falls* (Toronto: Between the Lines, and New Brunswick, N.J.: Rutgers University Press, 1999).

88. Gray, "A Tourist Talks Back"; Fisher, "Travel in Canada." See also Taylor, "We Must Learn."

89. This comment was made by Colonel James McAvity, president of the Canadian Tourist Association. Senate of Canada, *Report of the Standing Committee on Tourist Traffic, 1959,* 21.

90. PAO, RG 5, series A-1, Junior Chamber of Commerce of Canada, "An Assignment of National Importance," 1948; "How They're Dusting Off Welcome Mat," *Financial Post,* April 30, 1949.

91. "Personality Sells Food," *Canadian Hotel Review,* June 1949, 20; Irving Whynot, "Hotel Short Course Given to Aid Nova Scotia Tourist Trade," *Canadian Hotel Review,* August 1949, 25.

92. Wallace Gillespie, "Here's Plan to Make Tourists Love Us," *Financial Post,* January 21, 1950; PAO, RG 5, series A-1, Canadian Tourist Association, "Community Relations Program for Tourist Service Week," 1950.

93. See, for example, *NFR,* May 26, May 27 and May 29, 1952, May 11, 1961, July 9, 1961.

94. "The Pleasure Is Ours," *Canadian Hotel Review,* October 1948, 20.

95. PAO, RG 5, series A-1, Welch, "Our Welcome Guests," CBC Radio Broadcast, May 3, 1947; Fisher, "Tourism Is Everybody's Business; "You Can Be Salesmen of Ontario," *Ontario Government Services,* May 15, 1954; "Create Canadian Image," Canadian Tourist Association *Proceedings* 1961.

La Grande Motte

Regional Development, Tourism, and the State

La Grande Motte opened in the summer of 1968 as the cornerstone resort of the largest state-sponsored tourist project in Europe. This bold, innovative, and expensive (940 million francs) project involved constructing five new urban seaside resorts along the 180-kilometer expanse of the western Mediterranean coastline in the French region of Languedoc.[1] It was conceived within the French government's postwar policy of *aménagement du territoire,* the technocratic code words for modernization and regional development, and was the first attempt to use tourism as the centerpiece for a vast regional development effort.[2] For the French Fifth Republic of the 1960s, firmly under Gaullist control, regional development programs were the principal means by which the technocratic ideals of "modern civilization" were to be carried into the provinces.

And indeed, La Grande Motte seemed to literalize the sanguine promises of modern urban design and to justify the extravagant state investment that went into this new city of leisure. After turning off Highway A9 just outside Montpellier, vacationers would drive southeast along tree-lined parkways toward the ocean and the city's center, Point Zero. There on the grand plaza, the mayor's office awaited them with recreation and entertainment brochures, maps to the tennis and volleyball courts, and directions to the harbor. Soaring white ziggurat condominiums looked out over the sapphire sea. The marina bobbed with yachts and sailboats. White-sand beaches sprinkled with sun umbrellas, towels, bronzed bodies and boardwalks lined with cafes, ice cream vendors, and trinket shops beckoned to weary travelers. "Vacation villages" and campgrounds tucked among the trees offered respite from the hardships of modern life. Basking in the southern sun was a modern city of pleasure fanning out in a wide arc along the blue Mediterranean. The order and comprehensiveness of La Grande Motte's urban design was meant to attune space with the imagined pleasures of beach vacations—their difference from everyday life, the promise of leisure and tranquility, the association with desire and sensuality, and the enjoyment of "nature" along the seacoast. La Grande Motte thus linked the promised pleasures of seaside vacations with regional economic growth.

This essay interrogates the political assumptions, social goals, and cultural visions of the French policy of regional development in the 1960s as it was applied to tourism, and the extraordinary expansion of state authority that it entailed. As a case study of La Grande Motte, it examines three key assumptions within the "progress talk" of French regional development and postwar modernization. First, it depended upon a rigorously hierarchical logic favoring the national over the local. Second, it assumed the goal of a new, postwar social order in which "backward" people and places would be integrated into a modern, economically vibrant new France, one in which planned abundance would mitigate the antagonisms of regional and class particularities. Third, it promoted a new cultural order in which the commercialization of modern leisure practices would contribute to the consolidation of a capitalist consumer economy. We are particularly interested in the ways in which these premises were enacted within the production of space that regional development necessarily entailed. As the work of geographers such as David Harvey has shown, the ways in which new communities and places are represented and imagined and the ways they are actually constituted and experienced may be different.[3] How does La Grande Motte delineate the relationship between the intentions of state-sponsored development and its actual realization? Were there competing visions and practices of place involved in the creation of La Grande Motte? In what ways were the state's goals and assumptions crosshatched with the aims of other interests concerned with La Grande Motte (local and regional, for example), and what were the results of the convergence and tensions? Finally, what can this study of La Grande Motte's early history tell us about the relationship between postwar tourist-oriented capitalist development and the specificities of place?

MODERNIZING LANGUEDOC: REGIONAL DEVELOPMENT AND TOURISM

French economic modernization during the postwar boom years of the late 1950s and 1960s was characterized by intense state intervention. France embraced a "national developmentalism" in which "enlightened technocrats" within state administration shaped the course of modernization through public subsidies, nationalization, regulation, and planning.[4] The impact of this state-led consolidation ushered in an era of burgeoning production and of mass (although socially uneven) consumption that dramatically transformed

both the society and the spatial arrangements traditional to France. Essential
to the Fordist model of modernization was the cohesion of the national territory around capitalist norms and centralized government control. Territorial
planning and regional development were represented as key elements in creating a European, and even more an international, dimension for France. The
competitive pressures of both the European Economic Community (which
France joined as an original member in 1957) and the global marketplace
required mobilizing every corner of the Hexagon. Even more, rationalizing
regional space was represented as the solution to the chronic inequalities that
plagued the French provinces by offering equal access to the material fruits of
modernization, and hence attempting to create a national consensus around a
wrenching transformative process. As such, from the early 1960s, regional
development planning, or *aménagement du territoire*, became the penultimate
motif through which "the political authorities in Paris would formulate a
national policy aimed at reconciling the conflicting interests of Paris and the
provinces and advancing the projects of the Gaullist state."[5] The creation of
DATAR (Délégation à l'Aménagement du Territoire et à l'Action Régionale),
a uniquely empowered independent government agency under the aegis of the
prime minister, signaled the articulation of regional development as a broad-
ranging, centralized state strategy for aligning provincial space and economic
growth within national economic objectives.[6]

The representations of space and region within state development policy
suggest the crucial role of "place construction" in French modernization and
the need to devalue older, traditional representations of place and region to
make way for modern forms. The narrative of "improvement" within state
discourse relied upon regions "catching up" with economic and social modernity. It focused upon what traditional regions, and the people who inhabited
these places, lacked: they were not sufficiently modern, they were suspended
outside of time or in an archaic past, in "backward" space. As a barrier to the
renewal of France, these older territorial configurations and the social and
economic relations that distinguished them had simply to be denounced and
destroyed. Once cleared of the detritus, the postulate of planning space was
presented as a formalized, detached, neutral object. Capitalist development
was imagined as "even and limitless."[7] Yet space is always a social and political
product. The very logic of regional development involved the site-specific
construction of new spatial forms, the inscribing of new qualities of place, and
the massive deployment of financial and political resources, strategic design,
and architectural choices. Regional development, in short, entailed the literal
formation of new or profoundly reconfigured geographic landscapes propelled by the force of the modern state.

The Languedoc region, located in southwestern France, was, from the
mid-1950s, the site of extensive scrutiny by government planners concerned

with the twin scourges of rural poverty and out-migration that plagued this region of miniature villages, vineyards, and quiet lagoons yet undiscovered by Peter Mayle. What was so striking about the south was the intense coastal development of the east side of the Rhône River, based on the tourist industry around the Côte d'Azur, and the "underdevelopment" of the west side, where the monocultural production of inexpensive wine had long held sway. The population of Languedoc was only half that of Provence, and it was aging.[8] The region was, then, among the first to feel the hand of those charged with renovating France. In 1955, Philippe Lamour's Compagnie Nationale d'Aménagement du Bas-Rhône et du Languedoc and the Société du Canal du Provence, both state mediums for the modernization of the region's agriculture, began a sweeping redesign of rural landscape and space. Vast hydraulic operations provided irrigation and electricity to some 450,000 hectares of land, while production itself was diversified and modernized with new equipment, services, and selected "zones" slated for industrial and tourist development. Lamour's work played a decisive role in state land acquisition in Languedoc and set the tone for a comprehensive interpretation of regional development. By 1963, the newly appointed administrators at DATAR targeted the Languedoc coast as an ideal site for tourism-based regional development because it was a "solution" to a growing variety of concerns. The most obvious was that it offered an economic base upon which poverty-stricken Languedoc could recover and expand. Tourism was hailed as a "passport to development," a way to diversify the economy, generate jobs, and integrate Languedoc into the modern French nation.

Second, government planners saw the tourist development of the Languedoc coast as a way to meet demands generated by the growth of mass tourism after the war. These demands included a growing cultural preference for vacations at the beach and the need for vacation options for people of modest means. The trend in France was away from the traditional trip to the familial country home, or vacationing at hotels or spas, and toward low-cost rentals, camping facilities (a tremendous growth industry), and vacation villages at the sea—all accommodations that reflected the demands of more socially diverse vacationers.[9] The government was also eager to tap into a growing international market for mass tourism, a market that was growing with postwar prosperity and with the expanded mobility afforded by inexpensive charter flights and the rise in private car ownership. The new vacation resorts along the Languedoc coast were meant to serve these new "mass tourists," both domestic and international, and to foster a leisure and vacation environment that replicated the imagined pleasures and consumerist tableaux associated with sun-drenched vacations at the beach. A rationally planned, state-sponsored tourist project along the Mediterranean coast would thus unsnarl a variety of intertwined dilemmas. It would animate the local economy and provide modern regional infrastructure, help meet market demands for moderately priced vacations at the beach, and stem the economic loss to France of vacationers (both French and foreign) heading for the inexpensive beaches of the Italian Riviera and the Spanish Costa Blanca. As one government official put it: "Why would you leave 180 kilometers of coastline undeveloped when the vast demand for beach vacations went unfulfilled by large sections of the nation?"[10] As if to signal the shrewdness of such a clever solution, this project, along with the industrial development of neighboring Fos near Marseilles, were chosen as stellar examples of the French state's policy of regional development.

The whole notion of the Languedoc coast as a major tourist site was thus largely the product of the 1960s and the state development projects. It depended on envisioning the Languedoc coastline prior to regional development in particular ways. The Gulf of Aigues-Mortes, on which La Grande Motte is situated, was historically a coastal ecosystem of lagoons, dunes, and wetlands populated by great flocks of waterfowl. This side of the French Mediterranean was inhabited primarily by fishing communities living in reed-grass hut villages called *cabanes.* They were considered little more than savages even by the local inland population. But ceremonial practices such as the bull chase on horseback through the Petit Camargue, the coot hunts, and water tournaments are evidence to ethnographers of a coastal cabaniers microsociety, largely isolated from the inland regions and the main currents of regional society.[11] From March through the summer season, the waters were filled with single-masted sterns visible by night from the Camargue to Sète. During the winter months, fishing was concentrated on the inland lagoons while herds of bulls were turned loose onto the meadows between the lagoons and the sea. During the nineteenth century, a few of the cabanes had become more permanent settlements, such as those at Grau-du-Roi, Barcarès, Gruissan, and Palavas. This isolated world of coastal Languedoc was radically changed once road and rail links were established with the inland cities. Bourgeois investors bought up property for vineyards, colonizing the coastline with a vast flood of local capital. By the late nineteenth century, members of Montpellier's high society had divided up the sandy reaches along the Gulf of Aigues-Mortes into five estate-wineries, while the Compagnie des Salins du Midi owned most of the land at Grau-du-Roi.

Nonetheless, venturing out onto the beaches remained a risky business. Outsiders considered the area an ugly, hostile place plagued by malarial mosquitoes. Echoing traditional imperialist logic, postwar modernizers endorsed and extended these views, portraying the Languedoc coast as vacant, unhealthy, and underdeveloped, yet a land of exceptional possibilities whose dormant potential awaited "a general and coherent program of tourist equipment exploitation."[12] This formulation was not only congenial in terms of the logic of modernization, but consistent with historically validated discourses about tourism. As historian Alain Corbin has noted, coastal areas prior to the invention of seaside holidays were imagined as "cultureless places over which an unchanging nature reigned." Prior to their "discovery" by tourism, sea-coasts were considered by travelers and represented by artists and writers as essentially deserted, uninhabited except by "primitive" peoples.[13] This perspective was still evoked in the mid–twentieth century. One press report, for example, described the Languedoc coast as a "desert" comprised of nothing but "sand and mosquitoes" and noted that it was "abandoned to its savage morosity."[14] When Jean Balladur, the architect chosen to build La Grande Motte, described his first impression of the area, he emphasized its nullity, its savage and violent nature; it was "la nature nue."[15] He ignored the three working vineyards that still remained in the area. Indeed, all that was left of them after the development of the resort was the name of one of the old nineteenth-century estates—La Grande Motte.

These assessments either dismissed or marginalized as "thrown together" the tourist activity that did exist along the coast. Labeled a "modest reflection of imperial Deauville," the fishing village of Palavas, just south of Montpellier, had served as a beach haven since the early 1850s, as had Valras and Grau-du-Roi since the 1930s. Vacationers were usually from local inland areas. Savvy fishermen chartered their boats for recreational outings on the bay, while heroic swimmers rode out from shore in carts and covered traps after dark to avoid the cruel attacks by mosquitoes. With the inauguration of paid vacations in 1936, the villages transmuted into miniature seaside resorts. All manner of hastily slapped together dwellings and services grew up amid the last vestiges of older maritime life, especially after the Second World War. Do-it-yourself reed-grass cabanes and plank shanties were sprinkled along the shore oblivious to health regulations, private property rights, and questions of public domain. After 1956, the piecemeal selling off of local estates and their erstwhile conversion to tourism added to the transformation. Many of the old cabanes were turned over to the marginalized poor, most notably the settlement at what became the entrance to La Grande Motte. To state planners, these local, ad hoc structures were simply "architecturally distressing" eyesores, standing in the way of progress. Labeling them "a danger to public health . . . and contrary to tourist development," the government was determined to destroy the "ugly constructions."[16] Modernization enthusiasts also dismissed the estimated 675,000 summer vacationers traveling south to this area by 1965. Over half were campers in tents and caravans, many simply pitching a tent along the dunes or in other areas not designated as a campground (camping sauvage). These were mostly French of modest means who benefited from the government policy of paid vacations and sought a quiet family beach vacation. In a 1965 government-sponsored survey, the vast majority of these vacationers were not in favor of a new tourist project, fearing it would raise prices and attract the privileged wealthy who already soaked up the sun on the Côte d'Azur. However, technocratic elites focused on the fact that these vacation consumers who spent only ten to twenty francs per day and thus were not likely to provide much stimulation to leisure-oriented regional development.[17]

Also troubling was the arrival to the French Mediterranean in the early 1960s of young Algerians and Moroccans following the Algerian War (1954–62) and the nationalization of Algerian agriculture. Provence and Languedoc were also the first port-of-call for French settlers coming from Algeria; over one hundred thousand settled in Languedoc, twenty-five thousand in Montpellier alone, suddenly stretching the demography and social dynamics of the province beyond recognition.[18] It is of no little consequences that the French government discovered the coast of Languedoc as the set piece for its new regional development programs precisely at the moment when North African immigration was reaching its peak. In the minds of state technocrats an unwholesome and dangerous anarchy reigned on the beaches—squatter cabanes settlements mixed with immigrants, seaside vendors, and sun-seekers. An untapped and more orderly tourist market was waiting to be opened along the Languedoc coast.

La Grande Motte: Composing a Landscape

The task of creating a coherent tourist development project over one hundred miles of coastline was of imperial proportions. It involved designing a workable administrative structure, conceptualizing a design for the resorts, executing vast engineering operations, and constructing the built environment. The Mission Interministerielle pour l'Aménagement Touristique du Littoral Languedoc-Roussillon (known as the Racine Mission) was the administrative force responsible for masterminding the entire scheme. Created in June 1963 for a twenty-year duration, its head was Pierre Racine (1909–1988), a high-level administrator and founder of the Ecole Nationale d'Administration with impeccable Gaullist credentials. Racine and his mission reported directly to the prime minister, although the mission had, Racine insists, an "extraordinary liberty," essentially "carte blanche," regarding its choices and programs.[19]

The division of power and responsibility within the Racine Mission partook heavily of the dirigiste statism that typified regional development in the 1960s. DATAR had selected the Languedoc-Roussillon coastline as a development site, and the mission determined the character of the project and disbursed and monitored the public funding. More than three-quarters of the mission's membership were tapped directly from state administration. Only four local notables were permitted entry, with the excuse that "most of the local politicians are only interested in quail hunting. They don't understand mosquito eradication because they say the mosquitoes help blood circulation and protect against rheumatism."[20] The feeling of suspicion and mistrust was mutual. State technocrats were well aware that the region had historically supported the political Left and was a Socialist stronghold. In 1958, the south of France had resolutely opposed de Gaulle's Fifth Republic, and it gave the Left resounding support in the 1965 presidential and 1967 legislative elections.[21] Gaullist technocrats were thus reluctant to extend their hands to known political adversaries. The degree to which the future of Languedoc was shifted from the pernicious influence of the locals to the guiding hand of the French state is illustrated in DATAR and the Racine Mission's choice of a team of experts at the Center for Ekistic Studies in Athens to provide the framework for the region's development. Their scientific model of the global urban network, or ecumenopolis, of the twenty-first century anticipated spectacular population growth and urbanization along the long arc swinging from Bordeaux down the Mediterranean coast to Italy. Based on this model, DATAR predicted a population of 11–12 million along the French Mediterranean by the year 2000 and earmarked Languedoc-Roussillon as a propitious "open" region ripe for large-scale urbanization projects.[22]

As a bureaucratic construction, then, the Racine Mission and its offshoots had the convenience of sidestepping local political squabbles as well as democratic debate and decision making. On the other hand, it received substantial local support precisely because it bypassed small-minded communal interests and afforded relief from the frustrating regional poverty. The mission did offer a hand of reconciliation, and regional interests were involved in the development of La Grande Motte. A joint development corporation (société d'économie mixte) was put in charge of land purchases and the provision of basic infrastructure and public services for the new resort.[23] Dominated by regional political elites, it offered the prospect that the leftist proclivities of the languedociens would offset the centralizing forces of Gaullism and the state in designing the region's future. It was known as the Société d'aménGement de l'Hérault (or SADH) and was presided over by Socialist Jean Bène, the president of the departmental general council and the mayor of Pézzenas. It split the loan guarantees for La Grande Motte fifty-fifty with the Ministry of Finance. Twenty years later, a Le Monde article reported that Bène "showed the way by refusing to accept that the state would make all the important decisions regarding regional development."[24] Even the local Communists applauded its efficient orchestration and representative character.[25] Once purchased, the property for La Grande Motte would be sold or leased to private real estate promoters who were to build the resort's hotels, villas, shops, restaurants, and other properties and run them on a profit-making basis. The

Racine Mission also provided Languedoc with badly needed highways and infrastructure and advocated mass tourism with public access to the coast—themes that were supported by the political Left.

In June 1963 Racine himself asked the departmental prefect for the Hérault to invite all deputies, senators, and regional and local officials to a public meeting in Montpellier at which the tourism development project for the coast of Languedoc would be unveiled. Racine later recalled that it was "met with skepticism; they had listened many times to the promises of what the government would do for the region."[26] His admission was a persuasive sign of the rival visions involved in the resort's development. For many, particularly at the local level, the *sociétés mixtes* were ever-present symbols of the authoritarian nature of regional development. Robert LaFont, perhaps the best-known spokesperson of local Occitan interests, condemned the Racine Mission as yet another example of internal colonialism. Within the rubric of the Languedoc-Roussillon "region-machine," the policy of tourism-based regional development essentially liquidated the area's native resources, industries, and land ownership and turned the south into a quiescent tourist zone made ready for exploitation by large-scale capitalism and state interests.[27] The combination of relatively low-priced land in Languedoc (especially relative to Provence) and the promise of the resort projects made the region a ripe field for speculators. Although the SADH was meant to represent local interests, it was Parisian developers that Bène and his team courted. The land was eventually sold to large-scale promoters at a lower price than that left to local real estate investors in the older resorts. Over 90 percent of the property at La Grande Motte was swept up by speculators. The SADH was quickly tarred as a government pawn ready and willing to give away the Languedoc coast as a "royal gift to the *affairistes*."[28] In 1973, the French state legally prohibited the appropriation of public lands by private promoters for real estate and marina construction. But the development of the coastline had clearly been built through the exclusionary capacity of supply and demand in the private real estate market.

From the very beginning the development of the Mediterranean coast was conceived as a national imperative. Its hinge was state-directed economic and land use management. The Racine Mission was preoccupied with meticulously planning the built environment and finding the proper relationship between urbanism and tourism. It was precisely because the state nervously anticipated that more than 13 million people from a variety of social classes would be assaulting the beaches that the order and rules of urbanism had to be imposed. When vacations were a privilege of the rich, complete freedom could be tolerated. But now, anarchy and a squandering of the best coastal sites were a threat. State planners were also eager to avoid what they saw as the "anarchy" of the Côte d'Azur and of resorts along the Florida and California coastlines.

The Racine Mission appointed a resort design team headed by George Candilis (1913–1995), one of France's best-known modernist architects. It decided upon what were called *unités touristiques*—five resorts strung like jewels along the coastal collar of the Mediterranean. They were to comprise new resorts built from the ground up, as well as renovated older beach communities. The resorts were to be set within "green zones" of protected natural coastline that would avoid the noxious ribbon-sprawl that had poisoned many an oceanfront. The development of coastal Languedoc was to take place rationally, within the tethers of a modern, planned environment of interconnected vacation communities. The Racine Mission also assumed that the *urbanisme du tourisme* mandated a new understanding of living space. Racine's directive, in favor of "an architecture of vacation, designed to banish the commonplace and to be seductive,"[29] geared the new cities solely toward leisure and tourist pleasures: beaches, pleasure-boat ports, sports facilities, restaurants and cinemas, commercial centers. Zoos and water parks would be special attractions. Designers banished industrial facilities. At La Grande Motte, for example, only one small, hidden area was reserved for repairing boats and automobiles.

The process by which La Grande Motte was "developed" demonstrated the degree to which the state composed the landscape. Once the spatial design was set, work began on the site itself. Over a ten-year period, the government purchased forty-five hundred hectares for a price of 90 million francs (much of it secretly to prevent an instantaneous inflation of land values and an orgy of private sales).[30] The next challenge was to wipe out the notorious mosquitoes. Continuing a process begun locally in 1959, the mission fought what amounted to biochemical warfare against the Camargue marshlands, using helicopters to soak the area with DDT. The whole operation had a military tinge. The *démoustiqueurs* were often former military experts called upon, in their language, to "eradicate the shelters" of the offending insects.[31] The land was then replanted with poplar, cypress, and laurel trees. In what Pierre Racine remembered as the "heroic period," engineers went to work flattening the dunes, dredging the waterways, and constructing the basic infrastructure for the future resort. The managing engineers were often brought in from Morocco, where they had made their careers on colonial projects. A good portion of the labor was provided by North African or Portuguese immigrants.

To ensure that the resorts would be internally coherent and relatively homogeneous, each was assigned a chief architect to determine its style and design. Jean Balladur (b. 1924), a Parisian architect with an interest in literature, art, and philosophy, was not quite forty years old when he was chosen as the chief architect for La Grande Motte. The vision that Balladur literalized at La Grande Motte rested upon his belief that the space and time of vacations were radically different from those of everyday life. Vacation resorts should, he argued, be places of "ideal escape, like an Eldorado." The resort was a destination, a transformative site for rediscovering the authentic self, freed from social conventions and rooted in nature and unregulated time, and for repairing for ravages of work and the city. Yet by its scale and destiny, La Grande Motte was itself a city and required ordering and connectedness. Balladur's design was heavily influenced by the modernist dogma of Le Corbusier and Mies van der Rohe. Urban paradise, for Jean Balladur, was nature mastered and civilized as gardens, a harmonious *ville-parc*. The natural environment would have a salutary effect on individuals. Rather than dwellings that focused inward to foster privacy, the architecture of vacations should "break deliberately with habitual urban decor and assure contact with the outside and nature."[32] Urban life would be invigorated in an outdoor community of leisure. However, Balladur did not interpret "leisure" as placid tourists anesthetized by the southern sun. Seaside vacations were a modern "active tourism" in which relaxation was defined as scuba diving, waterskiing, sailing. It required a whole new scale of planning and construction that would give order and dimensionality to space. The architect's rendering of equipment and infrastructure, automobile circulation, a variety of housing options—all properly zoned—were what gave the modern seaside resort its originality and tone.[33]

It can be argued that Balladur's architecture and urban design worked within a modernist idiom of progressive order and rationality that obviated any specificity of place or vernacular culture, and indeed that it vanquished the historic and natural environment along the coast. This logic would then be neatly convergent with the ideological underpinnings of French modernization, and its goal of bringing rational progress to the hopelessly eclectic "backward" provinces. Yet the motif of La Grande Motte is not strictly geometric, modernist, and transnational. There were elements of whimsy in Balladur's designs. Albert Marchais's animal carvings stood guard along the promenade, protecting the shore from invasion. Numerous other sculptures, many by local artist Michèle Goalard, were sensuous forms that did not obey a strict modernism. Point Zero itself wound sinuously through "Sun Village" and along the dunes, mirroring the curves of the shoreline. Balladur also asserted that the resort's public buildings were meant to "address inhabitants as well as visitors." They were to be specific to place and recall Languedoc's long and complex history. St. Augustin Church, built in 1975–76, showcased a seventeenth-century bell from the local village of Montagnac within an airy, looped belfry. Inscribed with the device of Henri IV, as well as the coat of arms of Nîmes, it was, as Balladur put it "to call people to pray, and equally to remember the past."[34]

It was the white concrete ziggurat-shaped high-rises facing the Mediterranean, however, that Balladur hoped would provide the new city with a "sense of place" and its most recognizable image. While Balladur acknowledged the influence of Aztec pyramids on his condominiums, he insisted that he chose the shape to echo the distant Cevennes mountains and to suggest the rise and fall of the dunes along the Camargue.[35] His pyramids evinced a whimsical and decorative character. Their honeycomb facades, brightly colored sun blinds, and porthole windows were in keeping with the architecture of vacation, the spectacle and fantasy that defined seaside tourist resorts and recalled the fanciful designs of world fairs. The Provence and the Grand Pavois pyramids along the Georges Pompidou boardwalk (both designed by Balladur) featured the signature terrace-balconies that opened the interiors to sun, sky, and sand. The sinuous curves of the three-armed Grande Pyramide broke with modern functionalism to create a sweeping backdrop to the waterfront, while the Cochant neighborhood at La Grande Motte was designed in the shape of a seashell. Balladur's design thus incorporated local history and landscape, as well as the eclecticism and playfulness traditionally associated with leisure, tourism, and spectacle. These motifs were used as forms of "style" that differentiated the architecture of vacation from the banality of the everyday. They provided La Grande Motte with its character as a vacation destination to somewhere—to a stylized Languedoc that could be recognized through aesthetic references to a past and to a landscape. This historicism, "sense of place," and aestheticization of space as resort design were also an early manifestation of the postmodern motifs that would become commonplace to everyday urban experience by the 1980s. The design of La Grande Motte and its exceptional architecture were a conscious effort at creating a visionary urban landscape dedicated to touristic pleasures.

At the time of its appearance, Balladur's design was interpreted not for its rendering of the local within modernism, but as a symbol of the touristic urbanism orchestrated by the state. Local urbanists insisted he was far more interested in solving automobile circulation and parking puzzles than in any real public space animated by beach life and spontaneous interchanges between strolling vacationers. Many judged Balladur's modernism at La Grande Motte just plain boring compared to the frankly illogical, but gregarious boardwalk scene at Palavas just down the road.[36] The uniform modernity of the new resort's aesthetics was juxtaposed against the textual, free-form feel of its vintage seaside neighbors. Palavas's image as the down-to-earth, artless mélange of bungalows, cafes, and trinket stalls, its seaside joviality seemed far more "authentically" *languedocien*—and far more entertaining, especially to younger seaside enthusiasts. The visions and practices of place along Languedoc's shore were indeed contested ones, and the state's intrusion of its own fantasies met with serious opposition. One commentator baptized Balladur's ziggurats a "wall of concrete," HLMs-by-the-sea (after the acronym for subsidized public housing in France).[37] In early 1967, local construction companies stormed Balladur's office and insisted they would build on the new site only if there was a return to a more traditional architecture. Pierre Racine, who

admitted that Balladur's pyramids left "no one indifferent,"[38] was called on to
end the impasse. He simply intoned, "None of us are architects. We have chosen one. His ideas may bewilder us, but we are not qualified to judge. We
should have confidence in him. If he is wrong, we will cut off his head."[39] The
state had decided, and the plans would go forward.

   Nonetheless, the mayors of the venerable hamlets of Palavas, Carnon,
Valras, and Sète along the coast continued to be among the most vocal critics
of the Racine Mission. They demanded to know why the French government
plan required an imperial engineering project out on the marshland to build
an entirely new-sprung settlement—except that it offered fertile ground for
construction companies and real estate promoters. They quoted an endless
stream of statistics that exposed La Grande Motte's favored status with government officialdom. Each tree planted at La Grande Motte cost fifty francs
and required thirty to forty paid gardeners to maintain. The French state
donated 7 million francs in 1969 just to convince the Tour de France to extend
the bicycle race to La Grande Motte. Palavas, on the other hand, received only
6 million francs of public money for the entire year to cover all of its urban
renewal expenses.[40] SADH president Jean Bènes, who controlled local development funds, countered by declaring the old seacoast towns antiquated and
beyond further development.

   From its earliest planning stages, the Racine Mission worked to define its
"target market." La Grand Motte was to offer *tourisme pour tous,* providing
democratic access to social practices and spaces formerly reserved for elites.
This democratization of leisure was to serve as an element of social peace. La
Grande Motte's urban landscape was oriented toward what historians and
sociologists have recognized as a new and expansive "middle strata" that combined a "new petit bourgeoisie," made up of blue-collar office, middle-man-
agement, service, and technical workers *(cadres moyens),* and a "new bourgeoisie" comprised of highly skilled, white-collar professionals and executives
(cadres supèrieurs). The growth of this "new middle class" signaled a loosening
of tightly defined class structures after the war. With it emerged a more consumer-oriented, less politicized culture and system of shared values in which
recreation and leisure held a privileged place. To reach various segments
within this new middle class, the Racine Mission sought to provide a variety of
accommodations for different income ranges. At La Grande Motte, Balladur
planned an environment for some twenty-five thousand vacationers where no
fewer than a quarter of the accommodations were earmarked for social (low
cost) tourism, meaning camping facilities as well as vacation villages. They
were zoned for the outlying spaces around the city's central port-district. The
remaining accommodations were to be evenly divided among condominium
apartments, individual villas, and a few hotels carefully set amid the "planta-
tions of trees." The premium residences were in the high-rise ziggurats along

the oceanfront with unsurpassed views of the Mediterranean. However, residential sales at La Grande Motte were far slower than anticipated. The frenzied speculation in seaside condos produced a glut of expensive, empty buildings—far beyond the buying capacity of the "middle strata" market the Racine Mission had targeted. Short-stay accommodations in moderately priced hotels were virtually nonexistent. Among the string of resorts rising along the Mediterranean beachfront, La Grande Motte almost immediately became known as the new oasis of "rich" Parisians and Lyonnaise.[41] As the project faced financial pressures, developers found they could get higher and quicker financial returns from more exclusive lodgings than from the lower-cost social tourism. They simply reduced apartment size to make the price more palatable. Potential buyers were lured with the promise of a boat-slip at the new marina. The planning strategy switched to the construction of chain hotels in a panicked effort to win back middle-class clientele.

By the early 1970s, the social composition of vacationers at La Grande Motte was predominantly "new middle class": 74 percent of those enjoying a respite from their labors were professionals or top management *(cadres supèrieurs)*, business owners, or middle managers *(cadres moyens)*. Just under 5 percent of vacationers were workers. In the larger *unité* of La Grande Motte, which included the more populist beaches of Carnon and Palavas, 61 percent were new middle class, while 13 percent were workers.[42] The atmosphere at La Grande Motte ended by being somewhere between the chic and expensive avant-gardism of St. Tropez, with its trendy boutiques, women in string bikinis, and lines of expensive cars outside elegant restaurants, and working-class "family" beaches such as Saint-Jean-de-Monts, which was "not snobbish at all," and where women wore "sensible" one-piece swimsuits and families ate in their rental units.[43] Settled in along the gentle curve of the Gulf of Aigues-Mortes, La Grande Motte appealed to the new middle strata attracted to its glitzy modernism and with money enough to afford the relatively pricey atmosphere of neo-Languedoc. As one satisfied male vacationer from Lyon, "oiled and tanned and renter of a minuscule but functional two-room unit" at La Grande Motte, declared the summer of 1974: "We are happy *congés payés* [paid vacationers], very happy!" Another vacationer, a woman, agreed: "It's not extravagant, but wholesome. It isn't Saint-Tropez with its excesses, excitement, and hubbub. Here we are a tranquil and happy community, aspiring only to rest, and with one goal only—to do nothing." Indeed, a reporter from *Paris-Match* surveying the beach scene in 1974 noted that by eleven at night the streets of La Grande Motte were deserted and people had gone to sleep after watching a little TV. There were, however, three nightclubs, in extravagant decor, that lit up the night for pleasure-seekers with money in hand. The Hippopotamus casino featured topless dancing and was a particular favorite for the steady stream of visitors from Montpellier who came to La Grande Motte for its entertainment. The Gouzi-Gouzi, La Grande Motte's exotic village, was open twenty-four hours for parties, dancing, and dining.[44]

La Grande Motte also represented an emerging order in which the vacation was understood as a time and space of leisure and consumption, a tangible benefit of capitalist abundance. It evinced the dramatic shift in France from an economy, society, and culture preoccupied with production to one oriented around the consumption and services demanded by the new middle classes. Indeed the resort "produced" leisure according to the routines and efficiency of the tourist industry, providing ample opportunities to convert economic capital into the recreational and experimental capital that suited their tastes and lifestyle. By the 1970s, available activities had expanded to include tennis, kayaking, wind surfing, volleyball, waterskiing, horseback riding, yoga, and a host of other activities dedicated to the cultivation of the body and health. All were meant to provide a perfect vacation for La Grande Motte's stream of summer visitors. With the purchase of a "Sports Discovery" card, vacationers could try out fourteen different athletic and recreational activities of their choice. The Sailing Club offered regattas and races and operated a boat rental agency for would-be sailors to try their hand at the sea.[45] In this respect, daily life at La Grande Motte reproduced the application of design and amusement as spectacle, the thematic arrangements of rides and events, that were the traditional penchant of theme parks and world's fairs. The resort intensified the present by commodifying its experiences and heightening its entertainment.

Not only was the built environment of La Grande Motte proper geared toward leisure activities and a culture of relaxation, physical recuperation, and pleasure, but the culture and heritage of the wider region was understood in touristic terms. For example, state planners encouraged the local invention of traditions "centered on the traditional past." As one government publication put it, modern tourism in the Languedoc required a "unified image" for the region, "to be created by encouraging the invention or resurgence of the region's characteristic traits." This would "allow the tourists from elsewhere to cultivate an interest in the daily life and history of local communities." The *course camarguaise,* or traditional bull chase, became an annual event paid for by corporate sponsors. The Communist mayor of Sète vied with Palavas and Cap d'Agde over the number and splendor of traditional Sètois nautical games—seen every weekend of the tourist season by the 1970s. Traditional festivals to Saint Peter the Fisherman, or the carnival, for example, were staged for summer tourists, replete with traditional ceremonies and costumes. Planners saw the larger region as the repository of tourist attractions for day-trippers, which would in turn provide an opportunity for local communities to be "cleaned, modernized, and reanimated" while preserving their local historical sites.[46] Some two thousand monuments and sites throughout Languedoc-

Roussillon were formally classified as historic and protected.[47] Regional work and culture became spectacles in which the experience and purchase of "authenticity" defined consumption. Vacationers traveled to local vineyards to view traditional wine-making techniques and buy up local stocks, searched out restaurants for the most authentic cassoulet and lobster à la sétoise, strolled through village markets relishing the "scene." Regional modernization, then, was to be effected under the sign of tourism and contribute to what sociologists have called new "heritage industries" centered on commodifying regional nostalgia, promoting picturesque historical sites that seem stable and unchanged, and providing local color for vacationers and for the advertisers that champion the region.[48] Indeed, the vacationers themselves were considered itinerant modernizers, bringing economic vitality in their suitcases.

CONCLUSION

Assessments of La Grande Motte tend to fall into two categories—optimistic and pessimistic. For those involved with the Racine Mission, state-sponsored modernization centered around tourism was a resounding success. As Racine himself put it, "This grand enterprise launched in Languedoc-Roussillon has given the region a great shock that will be good for it. It has begun to open its closed economy to the world, and to push it boldly into the complex modern economy . . . without putting its character or its nature in danger. It has stimulated public and private initiative and encouraged the spirit of enterprise."[49] And indeed, the efforts of the Racine Mission have diversified and encouraged regional economic growth. From five hundred thousand vacationers in 1964, regional tourism grew between 10 and 12 percent each year, reaching nearly 2 million by 1977 and adding 2.5 billion dollars to the regional economy. They represented over 10 percent of French tourists, and the region's beaches and seaside resorts were the primary draw. Over 70 percent of the tourists in Languedoc-Roussillon were vacationing along the Mediterranean. Some twenty thousand sun-seekers adorned the beach at La Grande Motte by 1973.[50] According to Racine, tourism added around twenty-eight to thirty thousand permanent jobs and twenty thousand seasonal ones to the regional economy, and in fact both regional employment in tourism and the money it brought in soared throughout the 1970s and 1980s.

Pessimists remained cynical about these statistics, emphasizing instead the costs of tourist-oriented regional development. It required a concerted dismantling of traditional economic and spatial arrangements as coastal Languedoc was incorporated into the global marketplace with an assigned tourist function. Given its seasonal nature, as an industry, tourism was a fragile base for sustained economic development. Those who worked at La

Grande Motte—some twenty-five hundred students, retirees, and mobile vendors in the early 1970s, found their labor was needed only during the short summer vacation season. During this frenzied few months, La Grande Motte recreated both the social segregation and the capitalist economic networks inherent in modern consumer society. Only the well-off of the "new middle classes" could afford the views of the Mediterranean from atop the pyramid condos—everyone else was stuck with the leftover spaces, camping in RV cabanes along the marshes. There were complaints that money generated locally only filled business coffers outside the region. In general, the recreational and commercial services at the coastal resorts made their purchases from large-scale national wholesalers. They were little connected to the local economy, which they considered high priced and limited in choice. By the 1980s, 60 percent of La Grande Motte's shops and hotels were created by entrepreneurs from elsewhere.[51] The mission was also blamed for manipulating the real estate market and twisting property values beyond the reach of locals.

Tourism created a new kind of monoculture of leisure. A certain kind of vision and sociability was constructed for coastal Languedoc, not around the reality of the everyday, but around "respite and recreation," the cult of the body and physical recuperation. It was a constructed space and time that functioned as a break from the routine of work. Thus the lack of any real revival or diversification of the local economy excluded a variety of traditional social classes from participating in "modernization" and kept the rate of unemployment in Languedoc painfully high.[52] Existing maritime culture, for example, was profoundly reconfigured as the fishing industry was replaced or challenged for space by sport fishing, pleasure boats, and world cup sailors.[53] Despite the optimism of the Racine Mission and of Balladur, that La Grande Motte would become viable as a new year-round city, the permanent residential population reached only five thousand by the 1980s. The long off-season from the fall through early spring was generally months of dormancy; many of the condominiums were vacant eleven months out of the year. In its 1993 report on tourism, the Languedoc Regional Council concluded that La Grande Motte and the other resorts were "inhuman, without permanent life, without cultural authenticity, filled with tourists ninety days out of the year, with little chance of modifying the situation."[54] Perhaps the most vocal and sustained critique was of La Grande Motte's arrogant and imperialist logic. One local cynic charged the French state with "selling the Mediterranean like an unknown site in Africa." Accusations of internal colonialism were pointedly expressed by graffiti (written in Occitan) at Point Zero: "Here is the ground zero of culture, the flash point of colonization in Occitania."[55] In 1970, local poet Jean-Baptiste Séguy captured the cultural dislocations:

Ruines ruinés
Des habitants de l'ombre
Glorieuses ruines
De la misère de mon pays
De mon pays touristique
De mon pays folklorisé
De mon pays tout entier méprise
Que vous avez ruiné
Vous autres de la-haut.[56]

We argue that both of these narratives capture important aspects of the history of La Grande Motte. It is impossible not to reach the conclusion that the coast of Languedoc was essentially colonized as a capitalist project of state-directed place construction—in part through coercion, in part through co-optation. It was undertaken as part of the reordering of French society required by the accelerated capitalist modernization undertaken by the state during the "thirty glorious years" of economic growth following the war. However, the process of regional development also reflected long-standing political struggles and social grievances in France. The state tourist projects galvanized the grand narrative between the centralizing and decentralizing forces historically molding French geography. That is why for state moderniz-ers regional differences, such as those in Languedoc, were so intolerable. They represented not simply economic or social disparities, but "true differences in civilization." The *languedociens* were accused outright of the most egregious offense—failure to adapt to the modern world. The state's mission (in this case, the Racine Mission) was to convert this recalcitrant backwoods region to the doctrines of progress, growth, accelerating change, and the future. It would be done with or without the consent of its unprogressive people. "New ways of life, new ways of thinking" would transform the irascible provincial puzzle that was France into a modern nation. The resort projects shaped a "development landscape" in which nature itself, the wild coast of Languedoc, was to be civilized and ordered according to the precepts of modern urbanism and regional development. The seaside utopia of La Grande Motte fell into this debate precisely during the shift to the modern consumer world of the new middle classes. The city was reimagined as a place of freedom and social harmony, a place of consumption, entertainment, and individual fulfillment, as seen from the abstracted gaze of the tourist-vacationer and created under the sign of modernizing rational technique.

This perspective left little room for unexpected effects, for the ways in which state-sponsored modernization projects such as La Grande Motte could assume their own habits and their own futures in unanticipated ways. The logic of regional development stressed the ways southerners were different, rather than seeking or acknowledging areas of convergence. Perhaps this helps explain why the Racine Mission was so intensely hierarchical, why in the name of the nation and its economic vitality, locals tended to be seen as obstacles rather than as partners, as future workers in a service economy rather than as participants within a common economic project. Yet urban utopias were a powerful tool of both state authority and local particularism, offering a critique of the present, modeling the way in which each shaped and represented culture and place. The technocratic mapping of the local as "unmodern" masked regional interests that overlapped with those of the state, and gave little credence to local people eager to leave behind the poverty of recent history and focus on economic regeneration as well as a higher standard of living. Many recognized governments funds and infrastructure as positive benefits. Local developers at La Grande Motte and other tourist projects saw their efforts backed up by government-guaranteed loans and assumed fewer financial risks. The cultural values that made up an emergent consumer culture in France, one that valorized the vacation and made acceptable the possibility of profiting from tourist spending, were hardly absent in "unmodern" Languedoc. The Racine Mission's anticipated target market for the new resorts deemphasized local people who might have seen themselves as participants in this new social space. Because planners focused on attracting a national, and even international, tourist clientele, the Racine Mission did not fully anticipate that in 1973, close to 40 percent of vacationers at La Grande Motte were from the Languedoc region, and around 30 percent were from the nearby Rhône-Alpes, Provence, or the Midi-Pyrénées regions; only 10 percent were from outside France.[57] Locals flocked to La Grande Motte, with its free beaches, public bathing facilities, and open parks, for day outings or an evening's entertainment. Although eventually La Grande Motte proper was one of the resorts identified most with a national and international clientele, 75 percent of the condominiums in the area around it were owned by people from the region.[58] Those condominiums were generally modest and, along with opportunities for camping and the vacation villages, provided accommodation for a broader social range of vacationers. The state ended up providing a weekend and vacation site, a neo-Languedoc, for the *languedociens* themselves, rather than despite them. At least half of the commercial transactions around the Gulf of Aigues-Mortes were with the new resorts, primarily with La Grande Motte.[59] The people of Languedoc were thus helping to create the new tourist-oriented economy and culture exemplified by La Grande Motte, rather than simply being "modernized" by it.

The case study of La Grande Motte shows the breadth of action of the dirigiste French state that emerged in the postwar period and underscores the importance of tourism, particularly seaside resorts, as a vehicle for French regional development. French social and political feuds of the past were to be exchanged for a bright future of consumer-oriented abundance. The fusion of this state developmentalism with the emergent culture-industry of tourism was powerfully literalized at La Grande Motte and along the whole Languedoc coastline. Investments in consumption spectacles, the selling of images of place, competition over the definition of cultural and symbolic capital all become conflated with, part and parcel of, an ever-deepening commodity culture. Yet this did not necessarily mean a complete flattening out and homogenization of the landscape to conform to sate interests. Local space indeed took on a special currency at La Grande Motte because the site was a tourist "destination." That destination was constructed not only within a larger system of images and expectations regarding beach vacations, but also in terms of its distinctiveness and particularities as a vacation site. Especially for the new "mass tourists" of the postwar era, a vacation along the Mediterranean carried with it a special cachet. If it was not the more elite Côte d'Azur, it was close, certainly more affordable, and offered the experience of imbibing in the culture and imagery of the sun-drenched Mediterranean coast—a domain once limited to the wealthy. La Grande Motte as a tourist "product," thus required an association with a regional image, a distinct flavor and panache of coastal Languedoc that anchored it within a distinct locale.

It was at this spatial juncture that the various meanings of indigenous place and culture helped to shape the realization of La Grande Motte. The sustained local criticism of the Racine Mission, combined with the historical skepticism toward state intervention and its political undertones, was a constant factor in mediating developmentalist goals. By participating in the summer life of La Grande Motte and purchasing weekend and summer residences in the resort's condominiums, some segments of the regional population helped mold its cultural tone and economic vitality. This did not end up being a space for transient vacations segregated from the local region. Rather, it was a public space whose animation came in part from the interplay of local people and vacationers from elsewhere. Some local elites participated in, and profited from, the work of the Racine Mission. The vision of economic modernity built into the logic of development ended up, in practice, to be complex and tangled, at once more reciprocal and negotiated than unilaterally imposed. The history of La Grande Motte suggests, therefore, that places are not only, to use Sharon Zukin's felicitous phrase, "landscapes of power,"[60] they are also landscapes of creative social and cultural processes.

NOTES

1. From 1963 to 1982, the total investment by the Racine Mission was 940 million francs, or 2.8 billion in 1984 francs. If the expenses of local administration are included, the total amount spent was the equivalent of 10 billion 1984 francs. Christian Pommier, "L'Impact économique de l'aménagement littoral du Languedoc-Roussillon," *Espaces*

72 (February 1985): 24. By 1985, the number of resorts had expanded to seven. At the same time as the French were constructing the Languedoc-Roussillon project, the Bulgarian and Rumanian governments were building one along the Black Sea. That project was different in that it did not involve private capital. Members of the Racine Mission did, however, travel to Bulgaria, as well as to Spain and Italy, to see the variety of coastal tourism projects under way. Pierre Racine, *Mission impossible? L'aménagement touristique du littoral Languedoc-Roussillon* (Montpellier: Midi Libre, 1980), 116.

2. On *aménagement du territoire,* see Olivier Guichard, *Aménager la France* (Paris: Laffont-Gonthier, 1965); and Philippe Lamour, *Soixante millions de Français* (Paris: Buchet-Chastel, 1967), as well as J. F. Gravier, *L'Aménagement du territoire et l'avenir des régions françaises* (Paris: Flammarion, 1964); and Joseph Lajugie, "Aménagement du territoire et développement économique régional en France (1945–1964)," *Revue d'Économie Politique* 1 (January–February 1964): 278–336. See Allan M. Williams and Gareth Shaw, eds., *Tourism and Economic Development: West European Experiences* (London: Belhaven Press, 1988) for a useful overview and excellent bibliography on tourism and regional development.

3. David Harvey, "From Space to Place and Back Again: Reflections on the Condition of Postmodernity," in *Mapping the Futures: Local Cultures, Global Change,* ed. Jon Bird et al. (London: Routledge, 1993). See also the provocative collection of essays in Michael Keith and Steven Pile, eds., *Place and the Politics of Identity* (London: Routledge, 1993); and S. Britton, "Tourism, Capital, and Place: Towards a Critical Geography of Tourism," *Environment and Planning D: Society and Space* 9 (1991): 451–78.

4. On the characteristics of French "national developmentalism," see the excellent analysis by Alain Lipietz, "Governing the Economy in the Face of International Competition: From National Developmentalism to National Crisis," in *Searching for the New France,* ed. James F. Hollifield and George Ross (New York: Routledge, 1991), 17–42. On "enlightened technocrats" see in particular Richard Kuisel, *Capitalism and the State in Modern France* (Cambridge: Cambridge University Press, 1981), chap. 9.

5. Jack Hayward, *The State and the Market Economy: Industrial Patriotism and Economic Intervention in France* (Wheatsheaf: Harvester Press, 1986), 154.

6. DATAR was the chief administrative organism for carrying out the state's policy of *aménagement du territoire* and regional development. During the 1960s, it was headed by Olivier Guichard, an avid supporter of the Fos industrial project and of tourism along the Languedoc coast. Although it was initially set up simply to "coordinate" regional development among the plethora of state agencies, DATAR quickly became the model for the kind of streamlined bureaucratic team-efficiency so prized by the French technocratic elites. It signaled a profound change in regional planning strategy toward an all-encompassing set of social, economic, and spatial reforms carried out through the 1960s modernization plans. For an analysis of DATAR, see Marcel Roncayolo, "L'Aménagement du territoire (XVIIIe–XXe siècles)," in *L'Espace français,* ed. Louis Bergeron et al., vol. 1 of *Histoire de la France,* ed. André Burguière and Jacques Revel (Paris: Seuil, 1989).

7. See Kristin Ross, *Fast Cars, Clean Bodies: Decolonization and the Reordering of French Culture* (Cambridge: MIT Press, 1995), 7–10.

8. In 1954, the total population of the Languedoc region was less than 1.5 million, while that of the Côte d'Azur reached 2.7 million. Languedoc had the lowest rate of active employment and one of the highest rates of unemployment in France. Centre de recherche d'urbanisme, *Les Villes françaises* (Paris: CRU, 1969); and Schéma général d'aménagement de la France, "Activités et régions, dynamiques d'une transformation," *Travaux et recherches de prospective* 75 (March 1978): 46.

9. The expansion of mass tourism was the result of rising incomes, improved transportation, and the extension of paid vacations to three weeks in 1956 (a fourth week was added in 1969). The rate of departure on vacation was 44 percent in 1970 for the summer season for all of France, over 60 percent for those living in urban areas, and over 80 percent for Parisians. The lack of accommodations was a major reason given for not going on vacation, along with lack of income and occupational demands. On French tourism and vacations, see Marc Boyer, *Le Tourisme* (Paris: Seuil, 1982); Françoise Cribier, *La Grande Migraton d'été des citadins en France* (Paris: CNRS 1969); and "Les Vacances: Un rêve, un produit, un miroir," special issue of *Autrement* 111 (January 1990); André Rauch, *Vacances en France de 1830 à nos jours* (Paris: Hachette, 1996); and Ellen Furlough, "Making Mass Vacations: Tourism and Consumer Culture in France, 1930s–1970s," *Comparative Studies in Society and History* 40, no. 2 (1998): 247–86.

10. Racine, *Mission impossible?* 12.

11. See Michèlle Taurines, "La Chasse à l'eau en Bas-Languedoc: Les rythmes de vie," in *Le Languedoc, le Roussillon et la mer: Des origines à la fin du XXe siècle,* ed. Jean Rieucau and Gérard Cholvy, vol. 2 (Paris: Harmatton, 1992), 177–82; as well as Gérard Cholvy, ed. *Le Languedoc-Roussillon* (Roanne: Horvath, 1982), 362–65.

12. Philippe Lamour, "Comment on 'fabrique' une second Côte d'Azur," *La Nef* 18 (April–July 1964): 42. This logic is strikingly similar to imperialist representations of landscape in the colonies. See for example, Clifton Crais, "The Vacant Land: The Mythology of British Expansion in the Eastern Cape, South Africa," *Journal of Social History* 25, no. 2 (1991): 255–76.

13. Alain Corbin, *The Lure of the Sea: The Discovery of the Seaside in the Western World, 1750–1840* (Berkeley and Los Angeles: University of California Press, 1994).

14. Charles Vanhecke, "La Transformation du littoral" *Le Monde*, May 16, 1967.

15. Jean Balladur, *La Grande Motte: L'architecture en fête ou la naissance d'une ville* (Montpellier: Espace Sud, 1994), 17–18, 73.

16. Jean-Claude Barthèz, "Le Tourisme sur le littoral du Languedoc-Roussillon, une rente immobilière," in Rieucau and Cholvy, *Le Languedoc,* 206–7. The phrase "architecturally distressing" is from Lamour, "Comment on 'fabrique,'" 42.

17. DATAR, Mission Interministèrielle pour l'Aménagement touristique du littoral du Languedoc-Roussillon, *Le Tourisme balnéaire en Languedoc-Roussillon* (Paris: La Documetation Française, 1967); Vanhecke, "La Transformation," 7.

18. John Ardagh, *France Today* (New York: Penguin, 1987), 142.

19. Racine, *Mission impossible?* 38–40. Headquartered at 1 Ave. Charles-Floquet in the 7th Arrondissement of Paris, the Racine Mission was composed of high-level technocrats and cabinet ministers, including the Conseiller d'Etat, representatives from the Interior, Finance, Construction and Public Works, and Agriculture ministries, the *commissaire général du tourisme,* the *préfet* for the Languedoc-Roussillon department, the region's departmental prefects, and a *secrétaire-général.* Racine himself was the former director of Gaullist prime minister Michel Debré's cabinet (1959–62). For a detailed description of the Racine Mission, see DATAR, "L'Aménagement touristique du littoral du Languedoc-Roussillon," *Notes et Etudes Documentaires,* no. 3326, October 13, 1966, as well as "La Mission interministérielle pour l'aménagement touristique du littoral du Languedoc-Roussillon," in a *La Politique Française d'Aménagement du Territoire de 1950 à 1985,* ed. Jean-Paul Laborie, Jean-François Langumier and Priscilla DeRoo (Pans: La Documentation Française, 1985), 27–29.

20. A member of the Racine Mission quoted in Yves Durrieu, *L'Impossible régionalisation capitaliste* (Paris: Anthropos, 1973), 94–95.

21. Even in the 1978–1981 National Assembly, of the twelve deputies of the departments of the Gard, Hérault, and Aude, six were Communist and five Socialist. Between 1977 and 1983, every major town was run by a left-wing coalition, with Communist mayors at Nîmes, Alès, Sète, and Béziers, and Socialist ones at Montpellier, Narbonne, and Carcassonne.

22. DATAR, "La façade méditerranéenne," 1ère partie, Schéma général d'aménagement de la France, *Travaux et recherches de prospective* (November 1969): 63–65, 75.

23. *Sociétés d'économie mixte* first appeared in the interwar years and were resurrected after the Second World War as part of the state's expanding regional development efforts. They coordinated public planning with private real estate and contracting firms to facilitate land purchases and the construction of development projects. For the Languedoc-Roussillon tourist project, the *société mixte* was funded through loans from the Deposit and Consignment Bank. Profits from the sale of the developed land were used to repay the public loans. Both admiration for and criticism of the *sociétés mixtes* has been intense. For a good analysis of their role in the new France, see Marcel Roncayolo, *La Ville aujourd'hui*, vol. 5 of *Histoire de la France Urbaine*, ed. George Duby (Paris: Seuil, 1985), chap. 1.

24. Marcel Viadal, "La SADH: rassembler les virtualités de l'Hérault," *Le Monde*, June 23–24, 1985.

25. Mayor Arraut of Sète, quoted in Durrieu, *L'Impossible régionalisation capitaliste*, 96.

26. Racine, *Mission impossible?* 43.

27. Robert Lafont, *La Révolution régionaliste* (Paris: Gallimard, 1967) as well as Gérard de Sède, *700 Ans de révoltes occitanes* (Paris: Plon, 1982). The question of local dispossession, state exploitation, and the expropriation of land was also wrapped up with the use of the Languedoc "desert" for boot camps and military bases.

28. Robert Ferras, Henri Picheral, and Bernard Vielzuef, *Atlas et géographie du Languedoc et du Roussillon* (Paris: Flammarion, 1972), 210–13.

29. Racine, *Mission impossible?* 109; as well as Jean Duminy, "Espaces de loisirs," *Urbanisme* 100 (1967): 26–31, and Olivier Guichard, "Une opération d'aménagement du territoire," *Urbanisme* 86 (1965): 11–15.

30. Georges Cazes, "Réflexions sur l'aménagement touristique du littoral du Languedoc-Roussillon," *L'Espace Géographique* 3 (1972): 200.

31. Roger Ringuelet, "La démoustification du littoral," *Techniques et architecture* (November 1969): 49–51.

32. Jean Balladur, "La mer et l'estivant," *La Nef* 18 (April–July 1964): 33–40. On the design and form of La Grande Motte, see Claude Prelorenzo and Antoine Picon, *L'Aventure du balnéaire: La Grande Motte de Jean Balladur* (Marseilles: Parenthèses, 1999), especially chapters 4 and 5.

33. Balladur, *La Grande Motte*, chap. 7.

34. Balladur, *La Grande Motte*, 130–32.

35. Balladur, *La Grande Motte*, 29–32. See also Charles Vanhecke, "Vive les pyramids?" *Le Monde*, September 1–2, 1968.

36. Durrieu, *L'Impossible régionalisation capitaliste*, 124–25.

37. Cazes, "Réflexions," 203.

38. Racine, *Mission impossible?* 112.

39. Balladur, *La Grande Motte*, 89–92.

40. Durrieu, *L'Impossible régionalisation capitaliste*, 109–10.

41. Ferras, *Atlas et géographie*, 213, and Durrieu, *L'Impossible régionalisation capital-*

iste, 182–83. Real estate prices along the Languedoc coast jumped from three thousand to seven thousand francs per square meter through the 1970s. The median price was around four thousand francs; real estate at La Grande Motte tended to be in the higher ranges- with the average around four to five thousand francs.

42. Michel Nègre, "Le tourisme sur le littoral du Languedoc-Roussillon au course de l'été 1973," *Repères* 1 (March 1974): 26. On social tourism, see Robert Lanquar and Yves Raynouard, *Le Tourisme social et associatif* (Paris: Presses Universitaires de France, 1991).

43. Colette Porlier and Claude Devedeus, "St. Trop et St. Jean Priez pour la France en vacances," *Paris-Match*, August 9, 1975, 18–25.

44. Dominique Lempereur, "Etre heureux à La Grande Motte," *Paris-Match*, August 17, 1974, 35–41; and François et Jessie Mahoudeau, *Guide de Montpellier et La Grande Motte* (Paris: Editions du Temp, 1970), 88.

45. Mahoudeau, *Guide de Montpellier et La Grande Motte*, 87.

46. Mission Interministérielle pour l'Aménagement Touristique du littoral du Languedoc-Roussillon, *Le Tourisme balnéaire en Languedoc-Roussillon* (Paris, 1967), 44–45; and Lamour, "Comment on 'fabrique,'" 51.

47. Région Languedoc-Roussillon, *Languedoc-Roussillon de A à Z* (Boulogne: Regard Régional, 1992), 54.

48. John Urry, *The Tourist Gaze: Leisure and Travel in Contemporary Societies* (London: Sage, 1990), 104–12. The classic analysis of the tourist's search for "authenticity" is Dean MacCannell's *The Tourist: A New Theory of the Leisure Class* (New York: Schocken, 1989). A particularly useful critique of the notion of authenticity within tourism is Eric Cohen, "Authenticity and Commoditization in Tourism," *Annals of Tourism Research* 15 (1988): 371–86.

49. Racine, *Mission impossible?* 112.

50. Verlaque, *Le Languedoc-Roussillon*, 74–75; Office Municipal de Tourisme, *Guide touristique de La Grande Motte, 1984*, 45.

51. André Matteaccioli, *Diversité régionale et cohérence nationale* (Paris: Economica, 1981), 87; and John Ardagh, *France Today*, 142.

52. Unemployment reached 16 percent in the Languedoc region in 1993. Chambre régionale de commerce et d'industrie, *Panorama du Languedoc-Roussillon* (December 1993). Note also the comments by the Socialist mayor of Montpellier, Georges Frèche, on unemployment along the Languedoc coast, including his remark that "it isn't enough to do a marketing pitch that 'here we have the sun and a splendid environment,' we have to find real employment in real industries." In Pierre Bosc, *Les "Notables" en questions* (Montpellier: Presses du Languedoc, 1977), 184.

53. See Ellen Furlough and Rosemary Wakeman, "Composing a Landscape: Coastal Mass Tourism and Regional Development in the Languedoc, 1960s–1980s," *International Journal of Maritime History* 9, no. 1 (1997): 187–211.

54. Région Languedoc-Roussillon, Conseil régional du 30 Septembre 1993, *Projet de schéma régional de développement touristique en Languedoc-Roussillon* (September 1993), 17.

55. Cholvy and Rieucau, *Le Languedoc*, 2:17; as well as R. Baretje and J.-M. Thurot, "Réflexions sur l'aménagement touristique du Languedoc-Roussillon," *Economie et humanisme* 226 (November–December 1975): 56. The Occitan phrase is reprinted in Boyer, *Le Tourisme*, 186: "Equi lo pont zero de la cultura; lo punt caud de la colonisacion en occitania."

56. [Ruined ruins / of the inhabitants of the shadow / Glorious ruins / Of the mis-

ery of my region / Of my land touristified / Of my land folklorized; / Of my land entirely misunderstood / That you have ruined / You others from elsewhere.] From P. J. Oswald, ed., *Occitanie 1970: Les poètes de la décolonisation,* cited in Cazes, "Réflexions," 209.

57. Nègre, "Le Tourisme sur le littoral," 7, 25. Georges Cazes notes that tourism is a product of at least four convergent systems: of actors, of images, of spaces, and of tourist consumer practices. *Fondements pour une géographie du tourisme et loisirs* (Rosny: Bréal, 1992), 65, 72–73.

58. Barthèz, "Le tourisme," 209–10; Durrieu, *L'Impossible régionalisation capitaliste,* 183–85; and Conseil régional, *Projet de schéma touristique,* 17–18.

59. Christian Verlaque, *La Languedoc-Roussillon* (Paris: Presses Universitaires de France, 1987), 74–75.

60. Sharon Zukin, *Landscapes of Power: From Detroit to Disney World* (Berkeley and Los Angeles: University of California Press, 1991).

Contributors

Shelley Baranowski teaches modern European and modern German history at the University of Akron in Akron, Ohio. She is the author of *The Confessing Church, Conservative Elites, and the Nazi State* (1986) and *The Sanctity of Rural Life: Nobility, Protestantism, and Nazism in Weimar Prussia* (1995), as well as articles in the *Journal of Modern History, Social History, German History,* and the *German Studies Review.* She is currently writing a book on the Nazi tourism and leisure-time organization Strength through Joy (Kraft durch Freude).

Michael Berkowitz is a Ph.D. candidate in U.S. history at Columbia University. He is currently completing his dissertation, "Making Mass Tourism: Paid Vacations, Travel Promotion, and Leisure in American Society, 1920–1955." He is the recipient of the Mellon Dissertation Writing Fellowship and the Mellon Fellowship in the Humanities.

James Buzard teaches literature in the School of Humanities and Social Sciences at the Massachusetts Institute of Technology and is Program Director of the Initiative in the Humanities and Culture, American Academy of Arts and Sciences in Cambridge, Mass. He is the author of *The Beaten Track: European Tourism, Literature, and the Ways to Culture, 1800–1918* (1993), among other publications. He is currently working on a book entitled *Anywhere's Nowhere: Fictions of Autoethnography in the United Kingdom,* which is under contract with Princeton University Press.

Catherine Cocks is the author of *A Nice Place to Visit: The Rise of Urban Tourism in the United States, 1850–1915,* which the University of California Press will publish in 2001. She is also constructing a website based on her book and is currently working on a book on U.S. tourism in Mexico and the Caribbean from 1890 to 1940 and its role in recasting ideas about nationality, race, gender, and sexuality.

Karen Dubinsky teaches history at Queen's University in Kingston, Ontario. She is the author of *Improper Advances: Rape and Heterosexual Conflict in*

373

Ontario, 1880–1929 (1993) and numerous articles in published essay collections. Her most recent book is *The Second Greatest Disappointment: Honeymooning and Tourism at Niagara Falls* (1999).

Ellen Furlough teaches modern European and French history at the University of Kentucky in Lexington. In addition to articles that she has published in journals such as *French Historical Studies* and *Comparative Studies in Society and History,* she is the author of *Consumer Cooperation in France: The Politics of Consumption, 1834–1930* (1991). She is completing a book entitled *France on Vacation: Tourism and Consumer Culture in France, 1930s to 1970s.*

Bertram M. Gordon is Acting Provost, Dean of the Faculty, and Professor of European History at Mills College in Oakland, California. He is the author of *Collaborationism in France during the Second World War* (1980) and editor of the *Historical Dictionary of World War II France: The Occupation, Vichy, and the Resistance, 1938–1946* (1998), in addition to numerous articles, including essays in *French Historical Studies* and *Annals of Tourism Research.* He is currently a member of the editorial board of *French Historical Studies.*

Suzanne K. Kaufman teaches European and French history at Loyola University of Chicago. She is currently completing a book on French popular religion in the era of early mass culture and has a forthcoming essay in the *Journal of Urban History.*

Orvar Löfgren teaches in the Department of European Ethnology at the University of Lund in Sweden. His most recent book is *On Holiday: A History of Vacationing* (1999). Along with Jonas Frykman, he has written *Culture Builders: A Historical Anthropology of Middle-Class Life* (1987) and numerous other works. He is currently head of a multidisciplinary project, "Invoking a Transnational Region: The Making of the Oresound Region," which studies the cultural and economic effects of the bridge project between Denmark and Southern Sweden.

Douglas P. Mackaman teaches late modern European cultural and intellectual history at the University of Southern Mississippi in Hattiesburg. He is the author of *Leisure Settings: Bourgeois Culture, Medicine, and the Spa in Modern France* (1998) and editor of a forthcoming essay collection of World War I and the cultures of modernity. His current research focuses on the ways in which romanticized and nationalized notions of the European past have transformed a nation's terrain into secular sites of worship.

Marguerite S. Shaffer teaches in the Departments of History and American Studies at Miami University in Oxford, Ohio. Her first book, *See America First,* which focuses on tourism, American landscape, and national identity, will be published by the Smithsonian Institution Press in 2001. She is currently working on an essay for the Blackwell companion to western history on the American West as playground.

Jill Steward teaches in the Department of Historical and Critical Studies at the University of Northumbria in Newcastle. Her recent publications include "Grüss aus Wien: Urban Tourism in Austria-Hungary before the First World War," in *The City of Central Europe* (1999), and "The Spa Towns of the Austro-Hungarian Empire and the Growth of Tourist Culture: 1860–1914," in *New Directions in Urban History: Aspects of European Art, Health, Tourism and Leisure since the Enlightenment* (2000). She also has a forthcoming publication in *Journeys*, "The Adventures of Miss Brown, Miss Jones and Miss Robinson: Tourist Writing and Tourist Performance, or—From the Memoir to the Postcard."

Rosemary Wakeman is Associate Director of the Urban Studies Program at Fordham University in New York, teaching also in the Department of History. She is the author of *Modernizing the Provincial City: Toulouse, 1945–1975* (1997) and articles on French urban planning including "Reconstruction and the Self-Help Housing Movement" for the *Journal of Housing Studies* (1999). She is currently working on a study of the cultural politics of urban design in Paris during the 1950s and is editing a volume entitled *Themes in Modern European History, 1945 to the Present*, forthcoming from Routledge.

John K. Walton teaches social history in the Department of Historical and Critical Studies at the University of Central Lancashire in Preston. His numerous books include *The English Seaside Resort: A Social History 1750–1914* (1983), *Blackpool* (1998), and *The British Seaside: Holidays and Resorts in the Twentieth Century* (2000). He is currently completing a book on San Sebastián, Spain's first seaside resort, and beginning one on fishing communities in England from 1850 to 1970.

Index